THE COMPLETE BOOK OF THE

MARINE
AQUARIUM

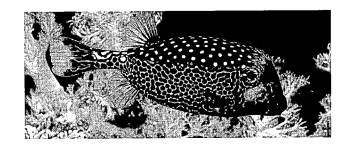

THE COMPLETE BOOK OF THE

MARINE
AQUARIUM

VINCENT HARGREAVES

THUNDER BAY
P·R·E·S·S
San Diego, California

Thunder Bay Press

An imprint of the Advantage Publishers Group

THUNDER BAY   5880 Oberlin Drive, San Diego, CA 92121-4794

P · R · E · S · S   www.thunderbaybooks.com

ISBN-13: 978-1-57145-762-2
ISBN-10: 1-57145-762-3

Library of Congress Cataloging-in-Publication Data

Hargreaves, Vincent B.
    The complete book of the marine aquarium / Vincent B. Hargreaves.
      p. cm
    Includes bibliographical references (p.).
    ISBN 1-57145-762-3
    1. Marine aquariums. 2. Marine aquarium fishes. I. Title: Marine aquarium. II. Title.

    SF457.1 .H362002
    639.34'2--dc21
                                                    2002020443

Printed in China
  5 6 7 8 09 08 07 06 05

Contents

Introduction   *8*

part four CHOOSING AQUARIUM FISHES 96

Introduction

The concept of a book that deals with both reef and marine aquariums has lived with me for several years. Research was carried out in many locations throughout the world and two years of my life were spent in Southeast Asia studying the marine life of the Indo-Pacific. Almost four decades have passed since I first set up a tropical marine aquarium and I have travelled to many countries studying aquarium technology. I have, however, only "scratched the surface".

It is more than 22 years since my first book, *The Tropical Marine Aquarium*, was published, and, having been in print for 16 years, it is now hopelessly out of date. It is time to put this right. None the less, this book is not intended as a "standard work" on tropical marine and reef aquariums, since anything purporting to be such conjures up visions of a dusty volume tucked away on the bottom shelf of some reference library. Instead, this book is intended as an insight into a truly fascinating hobby. In the past five years the number of aquarists owning a reef or marine aquariums has increased unbelievably, and it is today considered to be one of the fastest growing pastimes in the world.

I have tried to be as concise as possible so that this book remains a single volume. This simplifies the work of hobbyists, who, in the main, require easily accessible information readily to hand. But this does not mean that the accuracy of any of the information has been compromised in any way; rather, it reflects the most recent advances that have been made in this engaging hobby right up to the moment of publication.

Every time I put on a diving mask and sink below the surface of a warm tropical sea toward the myriad of life forms around a coral garden, I experience the same feeling of wonderment I did the very first time. However, I also feel frustrated that what we are attempting with reef and marine aquariums is not enough. We need to know and discover much more. This is not to say that we are not doing enough to develop the hobby: only a few short years ago, for example, it was unheard of to have red calcareous algae in an aquarium; now we treat it almost as an irritation, something to be put up with, although it is very important to the reef environment in nature and equally so in an aquarium. In earlier years it was the unsightly green and red blanket algae that covered our precious invertebrate charges, inevitably suffocating them. When you consider the earlier problems of pH control and buffering – now a thing of the past due to the advent of the calcium reactor and better synthetic sea salt mixes – you realize how far this new knowledge has brought us.

Sometimes newcomers to this hobby find that they are stepping into a forum of controversy brought about by some dealers who want to sell you just the particular range of products they happen to stock at the time – even if what they have on offer is only second rate. The novice needs to be careful. This is why I have refrained from being dogmatic in the section dealing with setting up an aquarium. The truth is that keeping coral fishes and invertebrates in an aquarium is easy, even with the minimum of equipment. Just don't rush it.

Vincent B. Hargreaves

The bizarre forms and contrasting colours of coral reef fishes, against a backdrop of corals and other tropical invertebrate animals, provides an ever-changing picture in a well designed marine aquarium.

part one
THE LIVING REEF IN NATURE

Exploring the deep

Before we concern ourselves with the main themes of this book it is a good idea to have some notion of the natural environment of coral reefs. For 2,000 years people have striven to explore the oceans, both on the surface and beneath, and it is ironic that much of the early exploration ended in disaster, of which silent and ancient remains are only now being discovered.

Hundreds of different life forms may exist in a small area of coral reef. Here, many species of invertebrates can be seen. Together they form a finely balanced ecosystem.

It is nothing less than amazing how underwater techniques have progressed since the 15th-century drawings of Leonardo da Vinci, depicting "futuristic" diving apparatus. To be fair, however, most of the effective development has been made only in the last 45 years. We are at an exciting stage in our search for full comprehension of the oceans, and new discoveries are being made almost daily. Only now are we finding out that the oceans are not, as we once so firmly believed, such stable environments. On the contrary, there is a fine balance of life, one that is easily upset by not only our physical intrusion, but also the increasing problem of pollution. Many areas of the shallow seas are being laid waste by over-fishing and the exploitation of marine resources. There is a level of life that the sea can give up without exhausting its reserves, but this is being exceeded more and more each day.

Coral reefs are places of great abundance. It is rather like driving across open country into the hustle and bustle of a large town when one swims across a sandy seabed to a large coral formation. These are the towns and cities of the sea. Each has its own population, way of life and struggle for survival. In its own way it has its hotels, restaurants, even its own barbers' shops.

Coral formations provide a haven for innumerable marine creatures and fishes. Many species abound. Swimming over a few metres of reef a diver may encounter

many of the species covered in this book: the loveable clownfish in its anemone home; the cleaner wrasse and the barbershop shrimp at their cleaning stations, ever present to attend to the removal of parasites from other fishes in the reef community; an octopus writhing deeper into its crevice as the shadow of the diver passes; a shoal of humbug-striped damselfish darting in and out of a single

*Against a backdrop of living rock a colourful damselfish (*Pomacentrus philippinus*) waits patiently as it is cleaned by a cleaner wrasse (*Labroides dimidiatus*).*

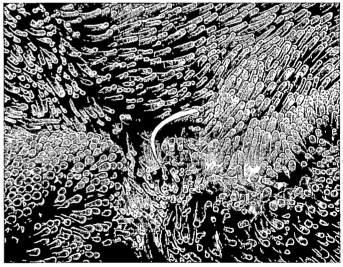

*This anemonefish (*Amphiprion sandaracinos*) seems dwarfed by comparison with its huge anemone host as it nestles with impunity among its deadly stinging tentacles.*

coral head; a flash of yellow and the diver's attention comes to rest on the delicate feeding action of the yellow long-nosed butterflyfish. The diver may also hear a loud crackling and clicking sound. This, more often than not, is caused by the feeding activities of the pistol shrimp. Colourful, dramatic, even breathtakingly beautiful, this, then, is the living coral reef in nature.

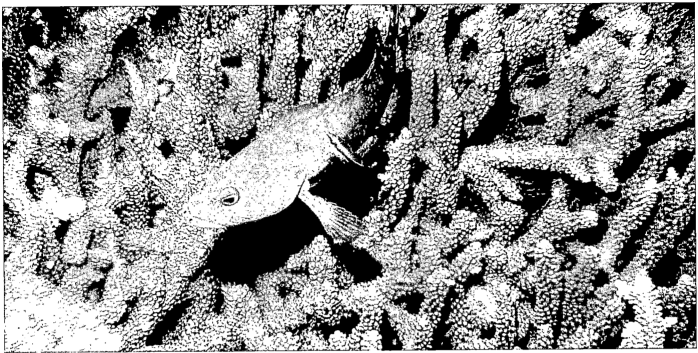

A small grouper (Cephalopholis aurantia) *receives symbiotic cleaning attention from this small wrasse* (Labroides dimidiatus).

A familiar sight on a reef, these two butterflyfish swim gracefully over a bed of coral.

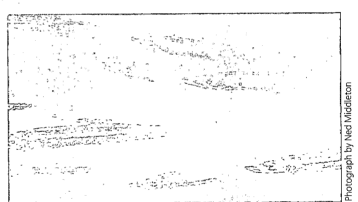

A shoal of barracuda, streamlined and fast, cruises the reef in search of food.

Soft and stony corals combine in harmony to produce this spectacular underwater garden in the Indian Ocean.

These two anemonefish (Amphiprion clarkii) *nestle with impunity among the stinging tentacles of their anemone host. This is an excellent example of symbiosis, which occurs between many reef-dwelling creatures.*

Reef communities

The oceans contain a delicate balance of life, and a reef community is a finely balanced group of interdependent living creatures. Research has shown that if this structure is upset, the living reef will quickly die. In a recent experiment, for example, divers carefully removed all the cleaner wrasse from a patch of coral reef and then monitored the results. Within a few days most of the other coral fishes had also moved in search of a reef that could provide a cleaning service. If this experiment had been left to run, it is believed that without the fishes the reef would have soon deteriorated and eventually died. This is because their eggs, fry and scraps of uneaten food provide a valuable diet for the invertebrate animals of the reef. In addition, by feeding off reef animals, fishes tend naturally to "weed out" creatures that are either unhealthy or threaten to overrun other animals by overproduction. It is easy to understand the latter case when you consider that an abundance of, say, baby prawns would soon attract a multitude of fishes to feed on them.

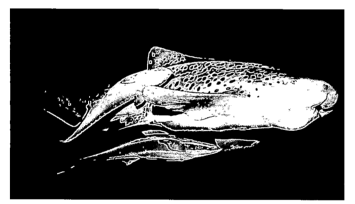

*The leopard shark (*Stegostoma fasciatum*), a frequent visitor to the reefs and harmless to people, is shown here with its ever-present followers, the remoras (*Rachycentron canadum*).*

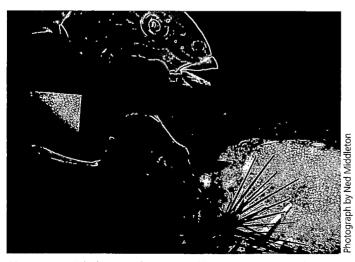

*Two wrasse (*Thalassoma lunare*), well equipped with thick, leathery lips, can be seen here eating a sea urchin, despite its needle-sharp spines.*

Pollution by man is one of the prime factors in reef destruction. The best illustration of this can be seen in the waters around Hong Kong. Although it may be true to say that there are no coral reefs in Hong Kong, there are – or were – many areas of coral platforms, particularly along the east coast of Hong Kong Island, the mainland area of Kowloon and what was formerly called the New Territories. Here, destruction of a reef community was effected in four ways, all with the help of human activity.

First, silt and pollution from the Pearl River, with its origins in mainland China and its mouth next door to Hong Kong, gradually clogged up the coral formations, killing off the delicate life forms by covering them with tons of fine muddy deposits.

Second, as Hong Kong's industry and population grew, raw sewage, factory waste and rubbish were dumped and pumped into the sea. The proximity of Hong Kong's now busy harbour and its inherent fuel oil waste were equally damaging. Added to this, organic pollution, chemical waste from dying plants and the like took a hand in destroying sea life.

Third, the population boom led to a demand for extra land. Extensive land reclamation programmes followed, resulting in large areas of coral being buried under millions of tons of rock and soil. Literally, whole mountains were moved into the sea, and this has continued to the present day. Even some of the areas that have escaped being buried directly have been killed off by a fine layer of brownish-yellow mud that, as the dumping continues, grows thicker and thicker, carried there by the ocean currents.

Finally, over-fishing by a nation striving to feed its millions has almost completed its total destruction.

There is hope, however. In a small area of the former New Territories delicate corals still flourish. Here, you can see shoals of damselfish darting in and out of healthy coral heads. Blue ring angelfish (*Pomacanthus annularis*) come here to spawn. At least three separate species of butterfly-fishes may be seen grazing on the coral polyps. Clownfishes still play among the tentacles of their anemone hosts and myriad nudibranchs, sea stars, cowries and sea urchins abound. In terms of the fish population, numbers are small in comparison with other reefs, but it's a start. This area has been made part of a larger country park and it seems, therefore, that these animals will be allowed to live and grow – at least for the time being.

In many other areas, the reef communities are healthier as brightly coloured coralfishes, darting in and out of coral branches in gin-clear water, will bear witness. In the Red Sea, for example, the diversity and colourful spectacle of underwater life contrasts sharply with the barren land that dips down to the water's edge. Here, just a metre or so from the shoreline, nature explodes in a scintillating

Photograph by Ned Middleton

cascade of colour. Around the Pacific island group that forms the Philippines you encounter perhaps the largest variety of life. From here, many of the species housed in aquariums all over the world are caught and exported.

When specimens are caught in the conventional way by reputable collectors, the ecology of the reef is not affected. In the past, however, divers looking for an easy way to make money have used unsatisfactory methods to collect specimens. Blast fishing, in which dynamite is used to stun fishes, is an effective method of collecting, but it does untold harm to the reef environment. Indiscriminate use of fish soporific, such as sodium cyanide, has also wreaked havoc in otherwise healthy reef communities.

Thankfully, these methods have now been outlawed in most regions. In general terms, I believe that the more we explore the reef and its community, the more sympathetic and conservation-minded we need to become in order to save nature's heritage for future generations.

This photograph shows the multitude of life forms that make up part of a reef community in the Philippines.

Davy Jones's Locker

Since the early days of sailing ships, storms and wars have caused vessels to flounder, sending them to the bottom to lie, for ever more peaceful, in Davy Jones's Locker. Treasure ships of the Spanish conquistadors and great warships from centuries of maritime conflict have been dispatched to the bottom by the elements or by cannonball to remain undisturbed for generations.

The advent of Self-Contained Underwater Breathing Apparatus (SCUBA) has enabled us to explore these remains of bygone eras. Untold treasures still remain to be discovered, even though much has already been recovered and is now displayed in the world's museums. But the sea does not readily give up its secrets.

When a ship finds its way to the seabed it is very quickly colonized by a host of sea creatures. In tropical regions, where corals abound, great wooden or steel hulls are soon covered over with marine life. Within months, algae and various invertebrates find their way on to the wreck. These are followed by corals, which, after a few years, begin to break up the outline of the ship until it eventually becomes part of an existing reef or the start of an entirely new one.

This Second World War freighter has begun to change its appearance due to the gradual incursion of marine growth.

Once the outline of a wreck changes it becomes difficult to find. Sometimes, where only a rough idea of its location was known, a bronze cannon or a deck outline has heralded the discovery of yet another ship.

On the seabed these artificial citadels become a haven for fishes, their monolithic lines reaching toward the surface. Apart from ships, many small items also find their way to the seabed. Often, bottles, cans or similar containers make excellent homes for sea creatures. It is not uncommon to see small fish darting in and out of a soft drink can or an octopus that has made its home in a kettle. Nothing is spared in nature's quest for harmony. Our rubbish is soon made use of by animals in search of a peaceful retreat.

Small animals called polyps, which live in colonies and secrete a skeleton of calcium carbonate, form coral reefs. Different species of polyps have their own reproductive patterns and this determines the shape of the coral head. As they reproduce and die, more of the calcareous skeletal deposits are left on which others can grow. Over thousands of years the coral builds up toward the surface. Other species grow with them. The ocean currents carry shell larvae, algae and flotsam to be deposited on the coral bed. Wave action and natural subsidence pack the coral even more tightly together until the result is a new reef.

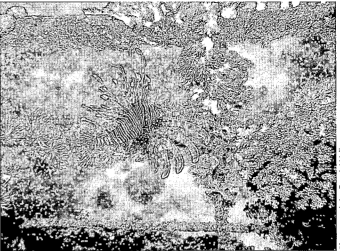

Here, a close-up of a ship's guard-rail shows heavy encrusting coral growth. It is easy to see how the outline of a sunken wreck can change in just a few short years.

Throughout the warm, shallow seas of the world, coral can be found to greater or lesser degrees. Not all coral is reef building, though. Some, such as the so-called "soft corals", do not leave hard, stony skeletons to form a solid base on which others can grow and reproduce.

Reef areas of the world

There are three main reef areas in the warm seas of the world, one of which stretches almost halfway around the globe. They are the Caribbean, the Indo-Pacific and the Red Sea. Most authors include the Red Sea area in the Indo-Pacific province. There are, however, enough diverse life forms in the Red Sea to give it a distinctive character and, accordingly, it is dealt with separately in this book.

The Caribbean Sea

The Caribbean is separated from the main part of the tropical Atlantic by a long chain of islands running more or less northwest to southeast. These islands are known collectively as the Greater and Lesser Antilles.

The area covers 1,625,000 sq miles (4,208,000 sq km) and stretches from Cuba to Brazil. The Central American

A typical Caribbean reef formation.

Continent borders it on the west side. Within this area there are examples of almost all the various types of reef formation. There are patch reefs that rise from the open sea in columns, sometimes reaching the surface; the largest barrier reef occurs off the coast of Belize and stretches for about 150 miles (240km). Although atoll formations are not common in the Caribbean, there are about 20 rings of shallow reefs, volcanic in origin, which could be classified as such. By far the most common reef formation in this area is the fringing reef, which is coastal and where almost every variety of coral can occur. There are at least 65 species of true stony coral in this sea.

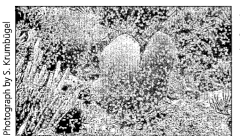

Sea whips and sea fans are a common sight in the waters of the Caribbean.

Coral reefs, such as the one shown here, are havens for a
multitude of fishes. Duplicating this in an aquarium would be
extremely difficult, but with considerably fewer species it would
not be impossible to produce a similar overall effect.

A beautifully coloured blue sea star (Linckia laevigata) along
with a feather star (Himerometra robustipinna) on a reef in
the Philippines.

Tropical Indo-Pacific

The Indo-Pacific region covers an area from the east
African coast to the relatively deep, island-free waters
of the Pacific Ocean, east of the Hawaiian Islands in the
north and the Marquesas and Gambier Islands in the
south. The southern boundary is roughly 30° south and
is determined by the water temperature at this latitude
where coral cannot grow. In the north the region stretches
from southern Japan in the east to the Red Sea in the west.

The area contains an abundance of coral reefs
supporting many forms of life. Most are widespread
throughout the Indo-Pacific, although the Hawaiian
Islands have developed certain unique species. Moreover,
because of the geographic location of this island group,
many common Indo-Pacific species are entirely absent
from the area. The reefs of the Indo-Pacific, and there are
many, are rich in life. Some of the most colourful animals
in the world are to be found here.

Much of the water in the Indo-Pacific is crystal clear
and ideally suited to SCUBA diving. One such place is the
Great Barrier Reef, the largest in the world, situated off
the coast of Queensland, Australia. It is well known and is
often the subject of underwater feature films.

The Red Sea

The northernmost part of the Red Sea splits into two deep
gulfs: in the east lies the Gulf of Eilat; in the west the Gulf
of Suez. Further south, in the Red Sea proper, the water
reaches even greater depths. This is because it is part of the
Syrian-African Rift Valley. Sea water here has a much
higher concentration of salt than is found in other tropical
seas. This density can be attributed to the low level of

rainfall in the area and the absence of rivers flowing into
it. In effect, the water is far less diluted. This is generally
believed to be the reason why this area has developed a
number of invertebrate and fish species not found in other
parts of the Indo-Pacific. There is very little current in the
area and a negligible amount of silting-up, which can
quickly destroy delicate corals. For this reason, these corals
abound in the region. As far as the diver is concerned, it is
simply a paradise. The Red Sea reaches great depths,
despite its narrow shape, and because of this the reef drop-
off is very sharp and close to the shore. Although it covers
only a relatively small area, the sea-supports more
varieties of life than any other region.

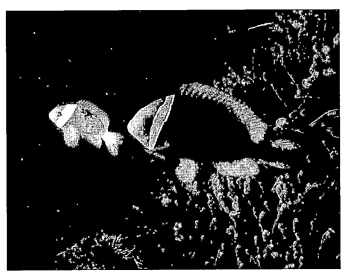

This photograph was taken on an Indo-Pacific reef and is more
in keeping with what you would try to achieve with a reef
aquarium. You should bear in mind that only a small portion of
a coral reef can be set up in this way, such as a small cave or a
valley containing all the invertebrate animals, algae and fishes
that are normally found in the natural environment.

part two

ESTABLISHING A MARINE AQUARIUM

Technical overview

Most of the technical problems that newcomers to this hobby will initially encounter originate with the system and set-up advice they receive. Most systems work to a greater or lesser degree, but beginners need only ask advice from two or more dealers, or experienced hobbyists for that matter, to discover the underlying problem – a high level of disagreement. All dealers have their preferred systems, which they will enthusiastically recommend, but these might not be the ones ideally suited to beginners. In this chapter, the information has been presented in the most unbiased way possible, pointing out

the disadvantages as well as the advantages, when dealing with systems or equipment. It is up to individuals to decide what is best suited to their particular needs or, even more important, to their pockets.

There is no getting away from the fact that a saltwater aquarium is more expensive than its freshwater counterpart, and a reef aquarium even more so. There is nothing quite so impressive, however, as a carefully planned reef aquarium, thoughtfully stocked with living rock, fish and invertebrates. These mini coral reefs can provide hours of enjoyment for beginners and enthusiasts alike.

About a reef aquarium

A reef aquarium is a closed system, and this brings with it certain problems. It is not a machine that can be switched on and off. We are dealing with living animals with their own life cycles and specific requirements. It is our task to recognize this and, with all the skills we possess, to develop a microcosm as near to nature as we possibly can. It is only in this way that we can expect any degree of success.

Unless you are a very experienced aquarist you cannot simply produce an aquarium by dumping living rocks, invertebrates, water and fish together and expect the result to be a flourishing miniature reef. This is a very

dangerous approach that could result in the total loss of all your living marine inhabitants.

A marine aquarium is one that is fish orientated – one in which all the available space is given over to the keeping of exotic and colourful coral fishes. A reef aquarium is a miniature coral reef, an environment that must have a consistently low nitrate level. With a little thought and care, high nitrate levels will not occur. All aquariums require time to mature, and efforts to shorten this period will, more often than not, result in disaster. With care, patience and forethought, aquarists will reap the benefits of an unbelievably rewarding and breathtaking aquarium.

Aquarium sizes and types

The aquarium size and type are important factors. Firstly a tank must be of sufficient size to suit the needs of the aquarist and fish alike and, secondly, it must harmonize with the environment in which it is placed. An aquarium holding less than 20 gallons (90 litres) is not suitable for either a reef aquarium or fish-only aquarium. Take this as the minimum size with which to start, but bear in mind that large aquariums are more stable from the point of changes in water quality than small ones. However, there is also a maximum size, specifically in terms of depth. For example, one that is deeper than 24in (60cm) is difficult to service. This is easy to appreciate if you measure the length of your arm from your armpit to your fingertips. Grasping something would make this distance even shorter.

For beginners, an aquarium of 55 gallons (250 litres) is ideal. It is large enough to give you the opportunity to decorate the aquarium in the form of a mini reef, but not so small that rapid changes in water quality take place. Of

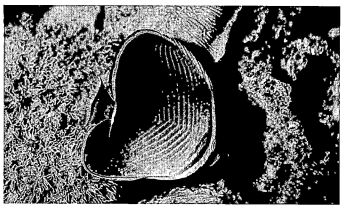

*This butterflyfish (*Chaetodon baronessa*) needs plenty of free swimming space to feel at home in a marine aquarium.*

course, for the enthusiast an aquarium of 100 gallons (455 litres) or more is not unrealistic – just more expensive. A point to bear in mind is that water depth should be at least 15in (38cm), preferably with a large surface area. This

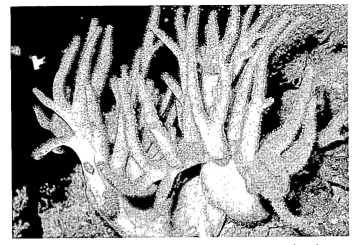

Soft corals, such as this 14-in (35-cm) Sinularia magnifica *from the Indo-Pacific, require an aquarium containing at least 100 gallons (455 litres) of water in order to develop correctly.*

brings a great deal more versatility when it comes to building and decorating a mini-reef.

Aluminium and metal-framed tanks are unsuitable as saltwater aquariums – even if specially coated they eventually corrode, releasing toxins into the water. Nor should glass top covers be used as they soon become covered in a fine film of salt. This acts as a filter and dramatically reduces the amount of light reaching the water's surface. And light, as will be covered later, is crucial to the success of a marine or reef aquarium.

The aquarium must be an all-glass construction, with the glass strong enough to support the weight of water it will contain. The drawback with all-glass tanks is that

they are heavier due to the thicker glass used to offset the lack of a frame. This is important to remember if you intend to make a tank yourself – something not recommend for beginners. It can prove more expensive, and certainly more problematic, than buying one off the shelf.

If you intend to use suspended lighting – lighting that hangs from the ceiling rather than being built into a normal aquarium hood – it may be best to use a so-called "pool aquarium". This is a little more expensive than the more conventional aquarium because it requires thicker, reinforced glass. It is, however, far more attractive, since it does away with the strengthening supports or crosspieces. Conventional designs use these horizontally placed glass-strengthening bars at right-angles to the vertical sides of all-glass tanks near the upper rim to prevent bowing (or even total collapse) when filled with water. These are not obvious when the aquarium has a close-fitting hood but can be irritating when left open to accommodate suspended lighting. One option is to use mirrored glass on the strengthening bars and crosspieces. The advantages of a pool aquarium are that it affords easy access for daily maintenance and you can view fishes and corals not only from the front and sides but also from above. For safety reasons, long aquariums must have one or more crosspieces.

One drawback with this type of open aquarium is that of water loss due to evaporation. Don't overlook this if you intend to use a trickle filter (*see pp. 30–1*), since such a system requires a constant water level and daily topping-up could eventually prove impracticable, especially if you are away on holiday for any length of time. In this case, you would need to install an automatic filling system.

Plants can be used to good effect when placed next to an aquarium. Pictured here is a semi-pool tank with support bars on the front and back, leaving the sides free.

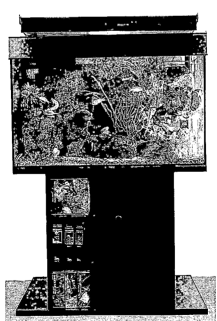

A complete marine aquarium system with built-in internal filter. Courtesy of Aqua Medic, Surry.

A seawater panorama aquarium system measuring 85 x 24 x 24in (216 x 60 x 60cm) with wooden cabinet and built-in filtration system. Courtesy of Aqua Medic, Surry.

"Panorama" aquariums, which have taken over from the old bow-fronted, easily scratched plastic types, are also a good option for hobbyists, even though they are a little more expensive. They can be made in any size, which is something that is not possible with plastic types.

The siting of the aquarium is important. Time taken over the correct siting can produce breathtaking effects. Bear in mind that once an aquarium is filled with water it will probably be too heavy to move – so try to get it right the first time.

Modern glass technology enables aquariums to be made in practically any size, shape or form – from five- or six-sided to triangular, or even L- and U-shaped. First, though, you should decide on the system to be used – whether or not you want to install a separate filter tank, for example, and if so what holes will have to be bored in the glass. Complete aquarium systems take care of all that for you and there are many available from which to choose. They are, without doubt, of the highest quality, though a little more expensive that the normal set-ups.

You need to exercise care regarding the quality of any aquarium you buy off the shelf. As a guideline choose one with expansion seams of the joints about ⅛in (2.5mm) thick. This ensures that the tension is dissipated throughout the whole framework of the aquarium. It should be sealed with silicone in such a way that the sides of the tank do not "sit" on the base – the base should be sealed between the sides. There are various coloured silicone sealants but black seams often produce the best overall appearance. Seams should be clean and well executed so that there are no areas where algae or small boring invertebrates can attack the silicon. There is absolutely no reason why a well-made aquarium should not have a life span of 50 years or more. Look for a tank with a ten-year manufacturer's guarantee.

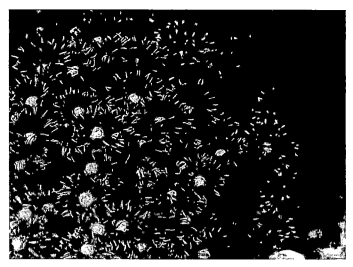

*Flower coral (*Goniopora lobata*) requires special conditions in order to do well in a tank. Correct lighting and good water circulation offer the best parameters for success.*

The background of a reef aquarium is also an important factor to consider. The best idea is a black PVC panel, cut to fit and sealed to the inside of the rear glass of the tank. After a short period, this will attract algae and small marine animals. Black tends to give an impression of shadowy depths when the panel is first installed (you can keep the panel clean, if you wish, using a scraper). If you are interested in photographing your specimens in the aquarium, then the PVC panel also does a great job of reducing reflections from your flash. For a more natural appearance, however, you may want the whole back wall of the aquarium to become colonized with red calcareous algae, sponges, clavularia and the like. You can use the same technique on the floor of the tank instead of coral sand, which will soon become covered with algae and small invertebrates.

Aquarium bases and cabinets

Before you finally decide on a suitable aquarium base, you must make sure that the siting of the whole system will not be influenced by excessive daylight from nerarby windows. With a reef aquarium it is important to be able to control the daily dosage of light the set-up receives. With a window in close proximity, that control is unfortunately lost.

Whether you use a normal, stable base or an aquarium cabinet is largely a matter of personal taste. If, however, the tank is to have an overflow weir with separate filter sump, then an aquarium cabinet is ideal. It can also be used to store any items of equipment when they are not in use. The important thing to remember is that the tank needs a stable, flat base of a suitable height. If, therefore, you intend to view the aquarium standing up, then the

height of the base or cabinet should be about 40in (1m) high. If, though, you intend to observe the tank most often from a sitting position, then the height of the base should be reduced to approximately 28in (70cm). Whatever you use to support the tank, it is crucially important that it is both flat and level. Check this with a spirit level – from side to side as well as front to back – before filling the tank with water. Check the level once more when you have placed the tank on the base and yet again once the tank is filled with water.

Remember that 1 gallon (4.5 litres) of water weighs about 10lb (4.5kg), and that about 220 gallons (1,000 litres), therefore, weighs approximately 1 ton (1,016kg), which is quite a weight to place on any flimsy structure or, more importantly, a flimsy floor.

Aquarium stands are available with special plastic-coated furnishings to help prevent corrosion.

The base should be of a suitable construction made of steel, stout wood or bricks. If wood is used or a steel frame, which is later clad on three sides with wood panelling, the wood itself should be specially coated to prevent corrosion.

If the aquarium is in a room with a wooden floor, or if the room is subject to vibration from nearby traffic, a thin sheet of foam rubber or polystyrene should be used between the stand and the tank. This ensures that the fishes and other animals in the tank are not subjected to undue stress every time somebody walks across the floor or a heavy truck passes by outside. Proximity of the tank to a power supply is obviously an important consideration when it comes to siting, unless you want to trail extension leads around the room, but keep the tank away from any heat sources, such as a radiator, since this could cause the system to overheat.

Heating and cooling

The water temperature of a natural coral reef is reasonably constant, lying between 25 and 27°C (77 and 80°F), and this is the temperature you need to duplicate in the aquarium. There are many inexpensive heaters available today capable of this. They work on mains voltage and are built into strong glass tubes, usually with adjustable, built-in thermostats. Normally they are preset more or less to the correct temperature. When buying this type of water heater, look for the appropriate seal of safety and government standard. There are also low-voltage heaters, which, though a little more expensive, have a higher safety factor.

If the tank system includes a sump, then a normal glass tube heater/thermostat is sufficient. It will not be subjected to the same wear and tear as a heater placed in the aquarium proper, where pugnacious tank inhabitants or a falling rock may damage the glass tube. It is important that you unplug the heater from the mains when setting up the aquarium. Only when the tank is full of water should it be connected. The size of the heater is usually rated in watts. The rule is: the larger the tank, the bigger the heater (*see box above right*).

Over a period of time all heaters become covered in a coat of calcium, which needs to be removed to maintain efficiency. When doing this, take great care not to damage either the seal or the glass tube. Corrosion-free stainless-steel heaters are available that take care of this problem, but they are at the moment far more expensive.

In the warm summer months it is possible for the aquarium to become too warm. There are two ways to handle this problem. The first and simplest is to fill a plastic bag with ice cubes, seal it and float it in the aquarium or, better still, in the filter sump. This is fine as a

Aquarium volume	Heater rating
25 gallons (114 litres)	50 watts
35 gallons (160 litres)	75 watts
50 gallons (227 litres)	100 watts
75 gallons (341 litres)	150 watts
100 gallons (455 litres)	250 watts
125 gallons (568 litres)	300 watts

short-term solution to an occasional problem. By far the better solution, however, if the problem occurs more frequently, is a cooling unit. The ones normally available to amateurs can handle water volumes between 50 and 1,500 gallons (227 and 6,819 litres), and utilize a heat exchanger – a plastic-coated copper tube shaped like a spiral that carries cooling fluid. Excess heat is drawn from the water and retained in the circulating cooling fluid within the copper spiral. Because the system is closed, it is environmentally friendly and safe to use. Nevertheless, it important to note that a separate recirculation pump is required for these units.

A typical cooling unit, which can also be used to set up a cold-water marine aquarium. Courtesy of Aqua Medic, Surrey.

Lighting

Light is the source of energy for all living things. It is composed of electromagnetic radiation of given wavelengths, which are measured in nanometres (nm): 1 nanometre is equivalent to one-thousand-millionth of a metre). Each wavelength of light gives rise to a different colour. The light we can see, which is only a small part of the range, starts at violet (at about 380 nm) and ends at red (at about 780 nm). All the colours we can see between these two extremes are termed the visible spectrum. Our eyes cannot distinguish all electromagnetic radiation – below 380 nm, for example, there is ultraviolet (UV) light, while at the other end of the visible spectrum there is a range of light emissions termed infrared (IR). There are also other electromagnetic waves we cannot see, such as X-rays and radio waves.

In the basic electric light bulb a substance is heated by passing an electric current through it until it starts to glow. It is not a particularly efficient way of producing light, however, since in some bulbs up to 95 per cent of the energy produced is in the form of heat. "White" light consists of all the spectral colours mixed together, and the unit of light flux is measured in lumens. This represents its efficiency. The intensity of light, that is to say its strength or brightness, is measured in lux, where 1 lux = 1 lumen over an area of 1 sq. metre. The intensity of light on the water surface of a coral reef may be 100,000 lux, but at a depth of only about 40in (1m) intensity falls by more than 50 per cent, while at a depth of about 33ft (10m) only about 1 per cent of light intensity remains.

Light is measured with a luxmeter, but for an aquarium this is not very effective and should be used only as a guide to placing those invertebrates that have different light requirements – twilight-zone animals in low light-intensity areas, for example, or invertebrates in high light-intensity zones that require a great deal of light. A luxmeter cannot, however, measure the composition of light, which is a very important factor in the health of your tank inhabitants.

Correct lighting is a prerequisite for a reef aquarium. The light in use here incorporates two 150-watt 10,000°K metal-halides, complemented by two blue "actinic" fluorescent tubes.

When, for example, a metal-halide burner nears the end of its serviceable life, the colour composition of its output alters – a fact that is obvious even to the naked eye. The effect of this colour change on invertebrates in an aquarium is drastic, yet a luxmeter will register no marked change in light intensity.

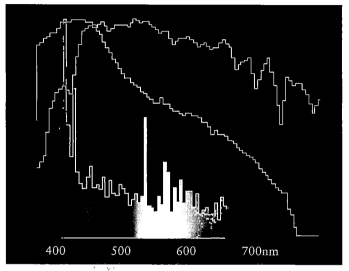

Yellow Line: This represents the spectrum of sunlight at the water's surface.
Blue Line: This represents the spectrum of sunlight at a depth of approximately 15 ft (5m) on the reef.
Block Graph: Spectrum of a 10,000 Kelvin metal-halide burner.

The composition of light – or colour temperature, to be more accurate – is probably as important to life in a reef aquarium as is the correct filtration system. The unit for colour temperature is measured in degrees kelvin (K), where the higher the temperature, the "colder" the colour of the light (for example, blue, which usually thought of as being a "cold" colour has a higher colour temperature than red, which is regarded as a "hot" colour).

Light on the surface of a tropical coral reef at midday, that is to say between about 11 am and 3 pm, will be in the region of between 5,000 and 6,000°K, depending on the weather conditions; at a depth of 15ft (around 4.5m) colour temperature will be about 8,000°K; and at an even greater depth – say, 50ft (15m) – it could be 10,000°K. This is because colour temperature is inversely proportional to the depth of the water, in which the red end of the colour spectrum is filtered out. Because of the higher energy of blue lightwaves, they are able to penetrate the water to a much greater depth than red lightwaves. That is why the deeper you dive the bluer the light becomes, until all the other colours are filtered out. Therefore, if you wish to establish a successful reef aquarium, you must try to duplicate the type of lighting effect the tank inhabitants require.

Ultraviolet (UV) light plays a significant role in the success of a reef aquarium. This portion of the spectrum is split into three wavelength groups (see box below), and many invertebrates, particularly anemones and reef-building corals, require a portion of this light (UV-A) for their growth. These are animals that have zooxanthellae living within their cell structure. These minute algae form the main part of the diet for these invertebrates and they rarely feed on anything else. Conversely, those animals without zooxanthellae have no protection against the damaging effects of UV light, because it is the zooxanthellae that act as a filter for the host animal.

Zooxanthellae are endosymbiotic unicellular algae belonging to the dinoflagellates. They are intracellular and are to be found in most anemones and stony corals. The zooxanthellae use nitrogen and carbon dioxide under the influence of light to assimilate oxygen and carbohydrate in the form of chlorophyll. This process is called "photosynthesis" and is carried out within the cell tissue of the host animal. As well as producing oxygen and carbon

---

UV wavelength groups

315–380nm = UV-A (used in solariums and important for reef growth)

280–315nm = UV-B (the type of wavelength that produces a suntan in summer)

100–280nm = UV-C (damaging to marine growth and used as a bactericide)

---

compounds, zooxanthellae are necessary for ridding the coral of certain ammoniac and phosphate wastes. They have a light requirement of between 350 and 750nm (part UV-A). Apart from zooxanthellae, there is another type of minute algae to be found living within the cell structure of corals and anemones – zoochlorellae.

A low-light aquarium (twilight zone) is intended to emulate the deep-water areas of a coral reef where certain fishes and invertebrates are adapted live in semi-darkness. The corals and other invertebrates found in this zone do not usually host zooxanthellae and, therefore, they have little protection against UV lightrays. Therefore, if you are intending to use blue tubes, such as actinic, "Blue Moon" or similar types, first determine whether or not UV rays will be emitted by them. You must take all of these factors into consideration when choosing the appropriate lighting system for your reef aquarium. Incandescent light (light bulbs), warm white, "Gro-Lux" fluorescent tubes and the like have no place in a reef aquarium.

In the final analysis, when it comes to choosing a lighting system you have only two lighting options: metal halide and fluorescent.

Blue or actinic fluorescent tubes give off long wavelengths of light, which in water have a deeper penetration determinant. But whereas blue fluorescent tubes have a lightwave range of 420 to 450nm, actinic tubes can range between 300 and 500nm. This is by no means a drawback – you should just be aware that a portion of light is dispersed in the UV-A wavelength. In fact, knowing this can prove to be an advantage, especially when specific lighting parameters are required.

Mercury-vapour (HQL) lighting, while excellent in freshwater aquariums for promoting good plant growth, is unsuitable for a reef aquarium. It gives off a light that has a high portion of red and yellow in its spectrum, and has a low kelvin index. In fact, it does not look right. During its ageing process, the light being produced can become damaging to the delicate life forms in a reef.

By far the best lighting system at present is a combination of daylight and blue lights (see box below), in which the daylight portion of the system is switched on daily for a total of eight hours – for example, between 12pm and 8pm. The blue lights should be on for 12 hours

---

Lighting for reef or marine fish aquariums

Metal halide
Type D (Daylight) – HQI TS, HQI TS/NDL, or HQI TS/D (with a colour temperature of at least 6,000°K). The Aqualine 10000 has a colour temperature of 10000°K.

or

Fluorescent (daylight)
Coralife Trichromatic (6,500°K), Osram Lumilux 11, 12 or Osram Lumilux de Lux 72.

in combination with

Fluorescent (blue)
Osram L 67, Philips TL 18, Thorn T10, Arcadia "Aqua Coral" actinic or Interpet "Blue Moon".

---

a day, overlapping the daylight period at either end – for example, from 10am until 10pm. This gives an effective dawn and dusk period and eliminates the shock of the main lighting being suddenly switched on and off. For the main lighting, fluorescent tubes are obviously cheaper to buy and for an aquarium that does not require strong light they are extremely acceptable. The effectiveness of these lights, up to 96 lumen per watt, is self-evident. In addition, they dissipate very little heat. Their drawback is that they give off very little UV light – only about 1 per cent.

Water preparation

Generally, it is impractical to use fresh sea water in a marine or reef aquarium. The problems of transporting and purifying the large volumes of water necessary for successful maintenance of aquatic life would be prohibitive. Besides, there are commercially produced salt mixes that will duplicate the composition of natural sea water with a great deal less trouble. The specific gravity (SG) of sea water lies usually between 1.023 and 1.025. What this means is that it is 1.023 to 1.025 times heavier than fresh water. It also has a high alkalinity and this can be measured using a pH meter or test kit. A pH of 8.3 would be normal for sea water while the pH of fresh water is 7.0. If you buy a commercially prepared marine salt mix, follow the instructions on the packaging. Most of them are made up to produce a pH of 8.1 to 8.3. Take care in choosing the correct marine salt mix – only those that state that they are nitrate- and phosphate-free are suitable for a reef aquarium. Fortunately there are many proprietary brands readily available.

During the preparation and mixing of sea water two factors are important. The first is that the SG must be constantly checked. This can be done with either a conductivity meter or a hydrometer. One type of hydrometer is shaped like a fishing float and is weighted internally so that it floats upright to give an SG reading along its stem, which is level with the water's surface. These are not very accurate. An improvement is the dial-type hydrometer, which is fixed to the inside glass of the aquarium. These are available from most pet stores.

The second factor is the quality of the fresh water into which the salt is mixed. This differs widely from region to region. Even treated drinking water commonly contains at least 10mg/litre nitrate contamination. The typical contaminants found in drinking water are nitrates (up to 50mg/litre), phosphates (up to 0.1mg/litre), silicates (up to 50mg/litre) and chlorine (up to 0.4mg/litre). There are other contaminants, too numerous to mention, that may also be found in drinking water but these are the main ones of concern to aquarists. So the levels of contaminants deemed fit for human consumption could prove deadly to some fishes and most invertebrates. You are advised, therefore, to ask your local water authority about the quality of the water in your area. It follows that some sort of treatment system is likely to be required if you are to have the best possible chance of success (*see Reverse osmosis units and Deionizing units, pp. 64–5*).

Using a high quality salt mix is paramount to the successful maintenance of fish and reef systems.

Bacterial and biochemical reactions

There are two main groups of bacteria found in an aquarium: aerobic and heterotrophic/anaerobic. But before we deal with the various aspects of filtration systems, we should first examine the important role that these bacterial forms play in the success of a reef or marine aquarium set-up.

Aerobic bacteria live in an oxygen-rich atmosphere and are responsible for the mineralization and nitrification processes that happen naturally when organic, or, more accurately, nitrogenous, waste is present in a reef or marine aquarium. This waste is always present because you are dealing with living animals and, whether fishes or invertebrates, they all produce their daily quota of organic waste. Most filter systems are based on the biochemical and biological conversion of organic (nitrogenous) products into relatively harmless inert solids, the basis of which is the bacterial culture within the filter. The easy

part is the conversion of these waste products through mineralization into amino acid and then, through the process of nitrification, to nitrate.

The second part of this biochemical process is much more complicated and, in some systems, almost impossible to achieve – this is the process of "dissimulation" and occurs through the second group of heterotrophic/anaerobic bacteria. In a tropical freshwater aquarium this does not present any great problem when the dissimulation process, in the form of denitrification, is not effective. Nitrate is, in itself, a plant fertilizer and the propagation of plant life is one of the prime targets for success with this type of aquarium. However, the prerequisites for a reef or marine aquarium differ greatly. A reef aquarium cannot tolerate a level of more than 10 to 20mg/litre of nitrate and this should be considered as the absolute limit. A nitrate level higher than this can prove damaging, if not deadly, to the delicate forms of invertebrate life. At a level of 20mg/litre most stony corals will not grow. In the chart shown here (*see below*) this biochemical process is seen in detail.

In an aquarium the fishes and invertebrates naturally excrete organic waste. Additionally, dead algae or scraps of uneaten food will decay to produce waste products. All these organic products have a nitrogenous content and are quickly mineralized into protein and amino acid. Once this stage is reached the amino acid serves as a foodstuff for aerobic bacteria (principally the genus *Bacterium*), which break down the amino acid to produce ammonia, ammonium and organic acid. The presence of this organic acid has a tendency to reduce the pH of the aquarium water. A by-product at this stage of the biochemical process is phenol, which gives the water a yellow cast when it is present in large quantities. Next, the ammonia/ ammonium is oxidized into nitrite by the aerobic bacteria *Nitrosomonas*. There are indications that, apart from *Bacterium* breaking down amino acid into ammonia and

ammonium, another heterotroph bacterium skips this stage completely and oxidizes it directly into nitrite. The final task in the nitrification process is the oxidization of nitrite into nitrate.

It is *Nitrobacter*, the second bacteria in the nitrification phase, that carries this out. During the mineralization and nitrification processes, various poisonous substances are present in the water. With a newly set-up aquarium this is especially the case and the bacteria must be given time to colonize the filter system in enough numbers to be able to carry out these important processes. Nevertheless, the presence of nitrite in a new aquarium can be considered a good indication that the filter system is starting to work normally. Nitrite is, however, poisonous to fish and invertebrates at levels of more than 0.05mg/litre. Ammonia, while also being damaging to fish and invertebrates, is an important source of nitrogen for the growth of algae. The end product of nitrification is nitrate, and in small amounts it is relatively harmless. It is significant as a fertilizer for the growth of algae and it is also utilized by

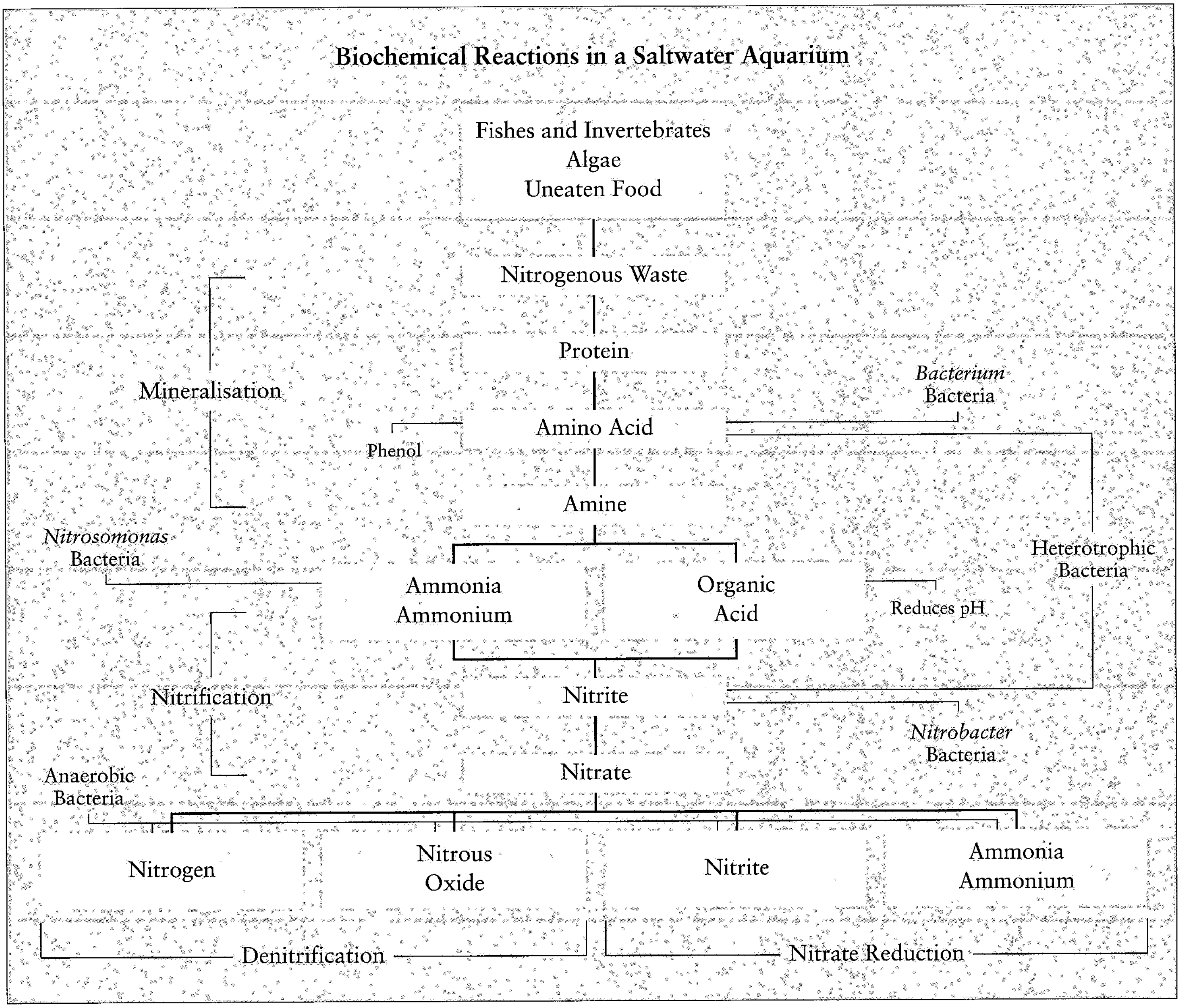

Biochemical Reactions in a Saltwater Aquarium

Fishes and Invertebrates
Algae
Uneaten Food

|
Nitrogenous Waste

|
Protein

Mineralisation   *Bacterium*
                                                        Bacteria
              Amino Acid
Phenol

Amine

Nitrosomonas   Heterotrophic
Bacteria   Bacteria

      Ammonia   Organic
      Ammonium   Acid   Reduces pH

Nitrification   Nitrite

                                          Nitrobacter
                                          Bacteria

Anaerobic   Nitrate
Bacteria

| Nitrogen | Nitrous Oxide | Nitrite | Ammonia Ammonium |

Denitrification   Nitrate Reduction

corals in minute quantities. Most coral fishes can withstand nitrate levels of up to 200mg/litre for short periods and in fish-only aquariums it is not uncommon to see levels of 50 to 80mg/litre. With a reef aquarium it is a different matter, as some of the more delicate species of invertebrates begin to show discomfort with a nitrate level of just 10mg/litre. It follows, therefore, that the nitrate content must be kept to a minimum or, where possible, eliminated. This brings us to the final stages on the chart – that of nitrate reduction and denitrification. Heterotrophic and anaerobic bacteria are responsible for these processes. Unlike the aerobic bacteria, anaerobic and heterotrophic bacteria exist in an oxygen-poor or oxygen-free environment, such as in living rock or in areas of the aquarium that remain relatively free of water circulation.

The process of nitrate reduction is out of the question since it releases poisonous chemicals into the water –

nitrite and ammonia/ammonium – and is the reverse process of nitrification. Fortunately this seldom occurs in a reef aquarium, though it may happen if large quantities of organic waste, such as quantities of uneaten food or a dead fish, lie hidden in some uncirculated corner of the tank for any length of time.

This leaves us, then, with the final and most important step in the biochemical reaction, namely denitrification. By utilizing the heterotrophic and anaerobic bacteria present in every aquarium, it is possible to achieve denitrification, but it is by no means easy. Far simpler is the addition of living rock where, within the rock, large tracts remain oxygen-free and afford a good breeding ground for this type of bacteria. There are also special denitrification filters available. In a well-balanced aquarium, with living rock and the correct form of filtration, denitrification will occur quite naturally.

Filtration

The dishcloth principle

It is possible to achieve biological filtration by simply hanging a dishcloth in the water. Aerobic bacteria will eventually colonize it and anything else that is porous and affords a good breeding ground. Good biological filtration is merely a question of surface area and water flow rate. The more surface area with water flowing through its porous structure, the more effective the filter.

Most if not all commercial filters work to a greater or lesser degree – that is, if you don't have any fish in the aquarium (or at least if you do have fish, you don't feed them). This is because the end product of protein waste that is filtered biologically is nitrate. And nitrate as we know, even in minute quantities, will kill the delicate life forms in a reef aquarium, especially living coral.

Complete system filters (CSF)

At the other end of the scale there is a wide range of complete filter and water-treatment plants from which to choose. Most are based on the trickle filter system with a prefilter, and it is as well to discuss these units at this stage before covering in detail the relative merits and drawbacks of each type.

Technically these units function perfectly, though they are quite expensive. If you are a fan of the trickle filter you will find that they fill your requirements. Nevertheless, these units must possess a nitrate reductor (denitrifying unit) in order to reduce the chance of a slow build-up of nitrate, which is often the case when such a unit is missing from the system. In addition to this, the water from the

weir in the aquarium should run into the prefilter and from there directly into the protein skimmer so that any excess organic substance is skimmed off before it reaches the main filter. CSFs are available separately or they can be incorporated in complete aquarium systems. They should not be underestimated or considered as expensive toys – a lot of technical research has gone into producing these units to obtain the best results for a reef aquarium in terms of optimal water quality.

The Aqua Medic Marin 1000 modular filter system is a 4-stage water treatment station that is mounted under the aquarium.

Photograph courtesy of Aqua Medic, Surrey

It is not only fishkeeping enthusiasts who need to consider the problems of filtration – there are many other people who have to be interested in the aesthetic value of an aquarium. Many doctors, dentists and businesses, for example, keep reef or marine aquariums in their waiting rooms or offices, and don't have the time or inclination to involve themselves in these problems. For them, the CSF is the perfect solution. Most are easily installed and it is even possible to build them into an existing system without upsetting the bacterial balance of the aquarium.

Mechanical filters

Mechanical filters still have a place in this hobby and can be relied on to clear murky water caused by large-particle impurities. They are particularly useful in a newly set-up aquarium as they will initially clear the water and then act as an effective filter for excess algae growth.

There are three main types of mechanical filter. The first is the mechanical sump filter, in which a row of three or more plates, or "baffles", are placed in the filter sump vertically to the flow of water. This type of filter has its drawbacks, however: despite regular cleaning, it has a tendency to clog up. This is particularly the case when a calcium reactor is in use, because minute particles of calcium find their way into the fine pores of the filter and within a few months they have to be replaced.

The second type of mechanical filter available is the outside filter. These may be of a similar design to a canister filter or may be open-topped. They are very effective but, as a rule, more time consuming to dismantle and clean than the third type of mechanical filter. This is the inside filter, which is a compact and effective filtering unit normally in a small canister fixed to a power-head or turbo-filter. The advantages of this type of mechanical filter are its small size (it can be hidden away quite easily in the sump or in the aquarium itself) and the ease with which it can be cleaned and serviced. The important point to remember is that the filter wadding should be cleaned at least once a week (more if the aquarium is particularly dirty). Failure to clean a mechanical filter regularly can result in it functioning as a poor biological filter and it will, eventually, cease to act as a filter at all.

Power filters

These are sometimes referred to as canister filters and they have no place in a marine or reef aquarium. They are normally closed-unit filters, mostly sealed with an O-ring and mounted on the outside of the tank. As the name implies, they are powered and have a high water-turnover rate. Nevertheless they are not recommended, except for a freshwater aquarium for which they were designed. The reason for this is that, because of their construction, which is a sealed unit, oxygen is not able to enter, except that which is in the water itself. This means that the effect of the biological process is greatly reduced because aerobic bacteria cannot colonize the filter in the same quantity as, for example, in a trickle filter: there is simply not enough oxygen in the water. Added to this, the biological filtration that does take place uses up a great deal of the available oxygen, so that the water returned to the aquarium is very poorly oxygenated.

Charcoal filters

Charcoal filtration is often used in a reef or normal marine fish aquarium for the specific purpose of removing harmful chemical elements or compounds from the water. For this "activated charcoal" is used. Carbon-based filters have been used for many years where the base element is activated charcoal. The special properties of this form of carbon have for some time been utilized by aquarium hobbyists. Through the process of nitrification by aerobic bacteria in a marine aquarium, products are created, which, in large quantities, can prove detrimental to both fishes and invertebrates. These chemicals, principally phenol-based compounds responsible for the yellow colouring in aquarium water, can be removed easily through the installation of a charcoal filter. You must take care, however, when choosing charcoal for this type of filter. Much of the charcoal available in pet stores will do more harm than good in a reef aquarium. This is because, even with some of the better-quality material, an unacceptable amount of phosphor is released into the water during use. Take great care or, if necessary, consult the dealer or manufacturer to ensure that the charcoal is phosphate-free, unless this is specifically marked on the pack.

There are differing opinions about the use of activated charcoal in reef aquariums. Some experts say that it removes important microelements from the water, thereby restricting coral growth. This has not been proved, however, and in any case it is the only tool we have at our disposal for the removal of harmful phenol or other poisonous substances from tank water. And so far there is no clear evidence that it restricts coral growth. In terms of how much charcoal to use in an aquarium, experience suggests 7 to 9oz per 22 gallons (200–250g per 100 litres) of aquarium water. The charcoal should be confined in a nylon bag and then placed in the filter compartment of the aquarium or in a canister filter. If the system has a sump aquarium it is easier to place the bags in the sump. After a period of three to six months, depending on the quality of the charcoal, it ceases to be effective and will have to be replaced. The idea that activated charcoal can be "recharged" by placing it in a hot oven for an hour or so is incorrect. In addition, the theory that old charcoal left in the filter system it will become an effective anaerobic or denitrifying filter is equally wrong.

Biological filters

The term "biological filters" is misleading, since most filters utilize bacteria to function effectively. However, what is meant here is a general term to cover a wide range of filters that have superseded the canister or power filter. (To confuse matters even more, the biological filter is also sometimes known as a "power filter"). The composition of the filter medium varies greatly, as does the filter form and size. There are inside filters and external ones and some even have a built-in trickle filter. They all have one thing in common, namely the way in which the water is treated. To amplify this point, in a biological filter the water passes through several stages of mechanical and biological filtration before being returned to the tank. The list of filter media available is endless, but includes filter wool, activated charcoal, ceramic, foam, polypropylene, and ion-exchange resins. The effectiveness of these filters for a reef or marine aquarium can also vary from example to example, and even this is dependent on which filter media are used. It is not possible, therefore, to comment in general terms with so many variables involved.

Undergravel filters

The undergravel filter, or sub-sand filter as it is sometimes known, has been around for a long time. Originally it consisted of a porous base plate covered with a thick layer of coral sand and/or crushed cockleshell. It had one or more "air-lift" tubes and was powered by a strong air pump (*see below*). Later this was modified and, instead of air, the filter was driven by a turbo-pump, thus making it more effective.

With the advent of reverse-flow undergravel filtration the whole circulation was reversed, with the filtered water

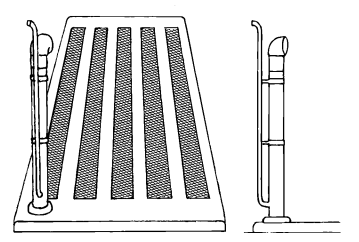

rising up through the sand instead of down through it. Although popular in the UK and USA, it never really caught on in continental Europe. Nevertheless it is still one of the most widely used filters, despite its detractors and its problems. No other filter offers the same filtration area as that of the undergravel filter. The fact that it has an excellent nitrification potential is not the only advantage: denitrification also takes place within the filter medium.

Its major drawback is that after a year or so the filter medium becomes blocked and "channelling" of the water flow occurs, thereby reducing its nitrifying capability.

Over the same period of time, however, the denitrification potential increases at an inversely proportional rate to the reduction in its nitrifying potential – and this can be considered as an advantage for a reef aquarium. But it is important not to allow the filter medium to become foul through loss of circulation. This balance between blockage and the increase in nitrification potential, which is so desirable for a reef aquarium, is best overcome by re-placing the sand in a particular way after exactly 12 months. It must be replaced – just washing it will not be effective. Over a period of time the pores and holes in the coral sand also become clogged, and if you are using a calcium reactor the sand will become "packed" almost in one piece due to the additional carbon dioxide in the water. For this reason it has to be replaced.

The best method of doing this is mentally to divide the aquarium sand into four or five strips and, with the help of a net, replace one strip per month. In this way the bacterial culture is not destroyed by a total tank strip-down, which is the greatest criticism of the system. Replacing the sand is surprisingly easy to do and takes very little time.

A further drawback of this type of filter is that instead of oxygenating the water it actually removes large amounts of oxygen during its nitrification process. Because of its high density, sea water it is not able to absorb as much oxygen from the air as fresh water, and so some form of additional aeration should be used to compensate.

Trickle filters

The trickle filter offers one of the best oxygenation possibilities of all the filter systems. Added to this, it has exceptional nitrification potential and a fully matured trickle filter produces an excellent biological "skin" over the filter medium. This skin comprises protozoa, fungus and aerobic bacteria and, when the innovative biological polypropylene balls are used, provides a greatly increased filter surface area. Furthermore, the construction of the balls enables any excess bacterial growth to be simply washed away if it gets too thick and starts to harbour anaerobic zones.

As the water trickles slowly over this skin it absorbs oxygen from the air to saturation point and through the biological filtration nitrogenous wastes present in the water are converted into inert solids. This process, carried out through several steps (some of which are poisonous to marine life) produces the relatively "harmless" nitrate, phosphate and sulphate, thereby providing a fertilizer for algal growth. In spite of these advantages it is questionable whether or not the trickle filter offers the

"Aquaballs" trickle filter medium is available from Aqua Medic, Byfleet, Surrey.

best possibilities in terms of water treatment for the marine and reef aquarium. Through the high rate of mineralization and nitrification, carbonate hardness (KH) is affected and sinks dramatically in some cases. In addition, protein-coupled trace elements are oxidized and the end products of this are minute quantities of nitric and sulphuric acids, as well as other substances. This destroys the buffering system within the aquarium water. Because of its high nitrification potential, the trickle filter mineralizes everything, and one of the end products is nitrate, which, in greater quantities, is a poisonous substance for both marine life and people. The other products mentioned – phosphate and sulphate – are equally damaging to marine life. Little denitrification can take place because of the

The Reef 500 filter system from Aqua Medic, Surrey. This is a trickle filter combined with a prefilter and a protein skimmer.

oxygen-rich environment within the filter. As has already been explained, this is not a good basis for the culture of anaerobic (in other words, denitrifying) bacteria – certainly not in enough quantity to be able to denitrify the daily dose of organic waste from a marine aquarium. And for the filter to become fully effective, it requires several weeks maturation time and generally has a high heat loss and evaporation rate. This means that the aquarium water must be constantly topped up to compensate for the loss of water through evaporation. If the trickle filter is fitted inside the tank, it is important to install an automatic top-up system, otherwise when the water level evaporates

sufficiently to become flush with the level of the weir, the filter will cease to function correctly. Nevertheless, it would be wrong to say that because of these drawbacks the trickle filter does not work. When the trickle filter is used in a system with a good denitrification potential, it is in a class of its own.

Fluidized bed filters

In the aquarium trade in the last two or three years, the fluidized bed filter has become a serious threat to the success of the trickle filter. The fluidized bed filter is a lot more compact and, volume for volume, up to 20 times more effective in its mineralization and nitrification of organic waste. Its filtration capacity is enormous when it is compared with standard biological filters, and with its optimal oxygenation capabilities it ensures that no areas within the filter harbour anaerobic zones. The water is kept moving over a thin film of bacteria to prevent any clogging or a build-up of detritus that could impair efficiency. Despite these advantages, this filter is not suitable for a reef tank.

The Merlin fluid bed filter from Red Sea provides exceptional surface area for bacteria.

Denitrification filters

Denitrification filters have never been popular due to the difficulties of getting them to function correctly and because they need constant "feeding" – more or less daily. The setting up of these filters takes time with an existing aquarium (14 to 28 days), and even longer with a newly established one. The essential item of peripheral equipment required is a control unit for redox (Reduction/Oxidization), which is measured in mV. With a denitrification filter, the water is treated anaerobically. The anaerobic bacteria must first be cultured in the filter and supplied with organic-based foods, such as lactose (milk sugar). Once this culture has developed, water from the aquarium can be trickled in very slowly at the rate of about a ½ gallon (2 to

3 litres) per hour. In the oxygen-starved environment of the filter, the bacteria are able to utilize the nitrate in the water instead of oxygen, and when the system is functioning correctly the water that is returned to the aquarium is relatively free of nitrate. This denitrification produces nitrogen gas, which, due to the construction of the filter, is "gassed off" – in other words, the excess gasses pass into the atmosphere.

Although it sounds simple in theory, it has always been difficult to control the various parameters involved. The bacteria must neither be overfed nor underfed; and the slow water flow rate in and out of the filter must be controlled so that it does not start to function aerobically. Thankfully, there is the option to control this with the redox meter (*see Water Management and Control, pp. 46–55*). On no account must the water from this type of filter be allowed to flow directly into the aquarium. It must be directed into either a trickle filter or a protein skimmer so that it is re-oxygenated before being returned to the tank. You should seriously consider the denitrification filter if you have a constantly increasing problem with the nitrate level in your aquarium.

The new generations of denitrifying filters are far easier to control than earlier types. They can be external or fitted into a filter sump. In addition, bacterial feeding has been simplified with the production of a filter medium that is itself biodegradable, thus eliminating the need to feed the anaerobic bacteria on a daily basis. In this way, there is no chance of under- or overfeeding and the balls are degraded as they are needed. In some systems, a full charge of these balls will last about a year.

During the initial start-up period of a denitrification filter it is a good idea to reduce the output of the protein skimmer, if one is in use, since this will shorten the time required for the anaerobic bacteria to colonize the filter medium by providing a nitrate-richer environment. Additionally, if a calcium rector is used the carbon dioxide supply should also be reduced in the initial phase. Furthermore, it is understandable that oxygen-rich water, such as that from a trickle filter, should not be directed into this system. Nor, for that matter, should you use ozone or UV sterilizing units, since these will seriously affect the efficiency of these filters. Recently, small electrically operated denitrifying "filters" have appeared on the market. They have proved successful for small aquariums. For larger systems, however, more than one of these units are required and, since they are quite expensive at the moment, they are not as popular as they deserve to be.

Protein skimmers

Protein, or organic waste, can be removed from an aquarium using biological filtration. But this, as has been mentioned before, causes problems. In simplified terms, the nitrification of protein by bacteria is carried out a great deal quicker than denitrification, so the nitrate level gradually rises. There is another way to remove cellulose and protein waste, however, by using what is known as a protein skimmer. Protein skimming should take place before any form of biological filtration is introduced to the tank. After all, why put stress on the biological filter system when there is a means to remove most of it at source? This device removes organic waste instead of mineralizing it by simply skimming it off. The advantages of this are obvious and, as a bonus, it does not require days or weeks of maturation time – it works immediately.

pushed up to the top of the reaction tube by normal foam in a continuous action, to dissipate in the collection cup. (In some units it is tapped off rather than collected).

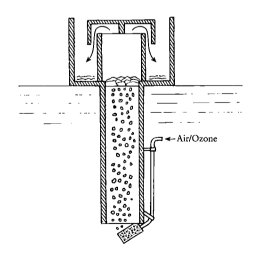

How they work

Using this simplified diagram(*see right*), you can see that the protein skimmer consists of a collecting container at the top and a reaction tube in which air, in the form of fine-pearl bubbles, is developed. Through the foaming action, the surface tension of the water is absorbed. The electrically charged protein molecules stick to the bubbles and gradually form stable foam. This foam is in turn

When the foam collapses it leaves behind a very concentrated protein-rich liquid, which is light to dark brown in colour depending on the tuning of the skimmer. Take special note: on no account should this liquid be allowed to re-enter the aquarium. The water that is returned to the aquarium from the skimmer is, however, of surprisingly high quality.

This is an ingenious way to remove organic waste and, when working effectively, can daily remove 80 to 90 per cent of all protein from the water. Unfortunately it, too, has a disadvantage – it also removes heavy metals, trace elements and iodine, all of which are important for reef growth. You must replace these on a weekly basis.

There are five basic types of protein skimmers: air driven; counter-current air driven; foam fractionation; rotation skimmer; and Venturi skimmer.

If you are thinking of buying one of these, bear in mind that a good protein skimmer is not cheap, and a cheap one is not good. Choose the largest unit you can afford. It is almost impossible to over-skim a reef or marine aquarium.

Air-driven skimmers These are technical developments of the one shown in the basic diagram. They require an air pump and an air diffuser to work. Lime-wood diffusers should be used because they have a very low pressure-resistance, allowing high airflow, and produce the finest bubbles, which are required for skimming. After four to six weeks the diffusers become blocked due to the build-up of minerals and should be replaced. Ceramic diffusers and conventional air stones should not be used because the bubbles they produce are not fine enough. Air-driven skimmers are normally attached to the inside of the aquarium with the collecting cup above the water's surface.

Counter current air-driven skimmers This type of skimmer employs a water pump to circulate the water into the reaction tube while one or more air diffusers are utilized for foam production. In this way, the turnover rate of the water treated is greatly increased. There are many versions of this type of skimmer on the market and they come in all forms and sizes. Some work quite well, others not so well. Check with your dealer if you need advice.

Foam fractionation skimmers The name "foam fractionation" is often used as a general term for conventional protein skimmers. In fact it should be applied only to those that are motor-driven and pump water and air through a special nozzle. This nozzle, or valve to be more precise, incorporates high-speed needle wheels, which chop up the bubbles to produce a very fine and effective foam. These devices are also sometimes referred to as "turbo skimmers".

Rotation skimmers In this system, water/air is injected as fine foam into a discharge system, which, despite its horizontal and compact form, has a reaction length of up to 4ft (1.2m). Because of the long reaction time – the length of time that the rotating bubbles are in contact with the water – protein is very effectively skimmed off into the discharge container.

Venturi skimmers The Venturi skimmer is an extremely effective device that utilizes the "Bernoulli effect" of the Venturi nozzle to pump a fine and profuse diffusion of air bubbles into a reaction tube. This is one of the best forms of skimming when used with a powerful water pump. To maximize the air contact time the skimmer should be at least 15in (38cm) high without the collection cup and have a diameter of a minimum of 6in (15cm). A well-designed Venturi skimmer should have the water intake directed from the water's surface and the outlet at the bottom. This is because protein waste has a tendency to accumulate at the water's surface. In a filter sump where the water is supplied from an overflow weir, this is not so important since all the water in the sump comes from the surface. However, with "hang-on" Venturi skimmers – those attached inside or outside the aquarium – it is very important. This fact applies to other skimmers as well. In

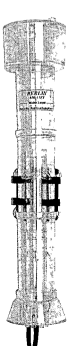

The Air 90 from Red Sea is an internal air driven skimmer with high contact time. It is suitable for aquariums up to 90 gallons (360 litres).

The Berlin skimmer from Red Sea has long been the bench-mark for venturi driven skimmers due to it's patented triple-pass system.

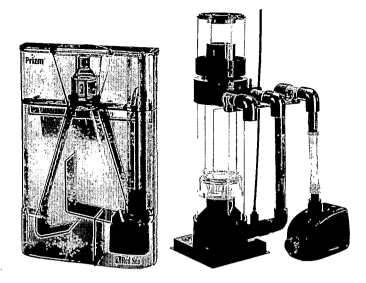

ABOVE LEFT *The Prizm skimmer from Red Sea incorporates the latest designs in foam fractionisation for optimum efficiency.*

ABOVE RIGHT *The Berlin HO skimmer from Red Sea is capable of handling aquariums up to 250 gallons (1000 litres).*

a reef aquarium using the natural system of filtration, a Venturi skimmer can be considered almost as a necessity because of its efficiency and high output in relation to other skimmers.

General comments Beginners are advised to take care in choosing the correct protein skimmer and, if necessary, to seek advice from an experienced marine aquarist or a reliable dealer. Tuning the skimmer is important in the beginning, which entails adjusting the water and air intakes to obtain the best effect. The column of bubbles in the reactor tube should be fine and milk-white in colour. The collection of foam should be slow, however, and concentrated enough to produce a liquid colour of middle to deep brown. If the colour is too light this means that normal foam is entering the collection container and so the water level must be adjusted. These tuning adjustments are tricky and can take some time to get right in order to obtain the maximum effect from the skimmer.

The skimmer should be large enough and have sufficient capacity to turn over the complete aquarium water volume in one hour. Also, in order to maintain this efficiency, the skimmer cup should be emptied and cleaned twice weekly.

Use hot water to remove the fat deposits. This is crucial, since fat seriously reduces the effectiveness of the skimmer. This can be easily demonstrated. Note that when you feed your fish and invertebrates with fresh or frozen food how the protein skimmer reacts with a drastic reduction in foam production, which can last for several hours. This is due to the fat content present in the food. Nevertheless, a protein skimmer is an important item of equipment for a marine or reef aquarium and a routine of twice-weekly cleaning will take you only a few minutes.

Ozone reactors

When oxygen is passed through an electric field its atomic structure is altered so that it becomes "trivalent", which means that each oxygen molecule takes on an extra atom to form the unstable gas ozone. This gas is poisonous and has the ability to split molecules of organic origin. When released into the air it has a pungent, almost refreshing smell, when present even in only minute amounts. Ozone is often present after a thunderstorm, giving rise to the clean clear smell in the air often experienced. In large doses, though, it is lethal – to fish and people.

For some considerable time ozone has been used by aquarists because of its excellent oxidizing capabilities with regard to organic waste. Moreover, it is able to remove phenol by splitting its molecular structure, thus making it available for treatment with a protein skimmer. Continual use of ozone in an aquarium will result in a rise in the redox potential, which is desirable, and an ozone reactor is used to generate this gas. In brief, air is passed through to an electrode in the reactor unit to be dis-charged as ozone, and the outlet from the reactor unit is usually connected to a protein skimmer. Recent advances in technology and design, have led to ozone reactors being

Combined redox controllers and ozonisers such as Red Sea's Aquazone Plus range now provides a safe method of dosing ozone.

combined with redox controllers to provide safe, accurate measuring and dosing of ozone for marine aquariums. Glass reaction tubes in modern units ensure that corrosion from salt water is not a concern. Used in conjunction with a good protein skimmer, ozone can greatly enhance water quality and fish well-being.

Even with a good protein skimmer in use it is almost impossible to control the correct dosage into the device, and there is a real danger that this poisonous gas, despite its excellent oxidizing capabilities, will find its way into the air or aquarium, where it will do untold damage to all living things it contacts. The risks of using ozone in a closed system, such as an aquarium, far outweighs any of the benefits. A much more realistic solution is to install a larger protein skimmer right from the start. This will have the same effect on the water quality.

Ultraviolet (UV) sterilizing units

Deoxyribonucleic acid, or DNA is the principal constituent of chromosomes in all higher living organisms. The chromosomes themselves are microscopic thread-like or rod-like structures, which occur in pairs within the nucleus of cells. These structures are gene-carrying bodies and it is the genes that are the biological factors or units determining the inherited characteristics of the cell itself.

Ultraviolet light with a wavelength range of 100 to 280nm (UV-C) has long been known to have damaging, sometimes lethal, effects on living cell tissue. By utilizing this knowledge it is possible to achieve a sterilizing effect. Since UV-C light splits molecules, it upsets the synthesis of the gene carrying thread-like structures and so the inherited characteristics of the cell are destroyed. When the cell splits, the genetic information is no longer there and it dies. This enables us to produce effective ultraviolet sterilizing units for use against bacterial infection.

The ultraviolet sterilizing units made for aquariums are designed to combat fish parasites, plankton, bacteria and microalgae by destroying their reproductive capabilities. Within a sterilizing unit, water is pumped around an ultraviolet (UV-C) light source. In the construction of this light source, quartz or crystal glass is used to filter out unwanted wavelengths, leaving a specific and effective wavelength of 253.7nm. Using just a 6-watt light source, it is possible to sterilize a 100-gallon (455-litre) aquarium effectively, depending on the flow of water through the sterilizing unit.

UV sterilizing units only treat the symptoms and are not a cure. In a properly set-up and well-balanced marine or reef aquarium with good water quality, an ultraviolet sterilizing unit is superfluous: fish parasites, bacterial fish infections and explosion-like growths of unwanted algae simply will not occur. This item of equipment is of use only if you didn't get it right in the first place.

The natural (Berlin) system

Although the natural system is synonymous with the trials and experiments of members of the Berlin Marine Aquarists Association, hence the name "natural" or "Berlin" system, in order to be completely fair and accurate the original idea for this method of setting up a reef aquarium stems originally from Lee Chin Eng of Jakarta, Indonesia.

So that you are certain about which system is being discussed here, it should be pointed out that the natural system has many synonyms, including the "living rock" method, the "living rock/living sand" system and, of course, the "Berlin" method. But no matter what its name, the basic concept of this system remains exactly the same: through the specific and careful use of living rock, invertebrates and fishes, the reef aquarium is allowed to reach a balance that is then maintained using a bare minimum of technology.

It is a surprisingly simple and logical way of approaching the subject and could bring this hobby within the reach of everyone's pocket, once the ground rules for it are more widely known. In Britain and the USA, thousands of marine aquarists have already converted to this system and hundreds more are doing so all the time.

What follows is a fairly detailed description of how to set up an aquarium using the natural system, but it should be stressed right from the start that if you keep it simple, the system will work. You cannot expect to have any degree of success if you mix both high and low technology together in the same tank.

The use of "live rock"

In this system we utilize one of the most effective and perfect biological filter systems ever devised – nature itself. Consider a reef in the warm waters of a coral sea, exposed at low tide, buffeted by the waves and bearing the brunt of typhoons or hurricanes, the ever-changing framework of a reef as corals or coralline algae first gain the upper hand and then, subsequently, die. These actions leave behind a heritage of dense calcium carbonate reef substrate, which is termed living rock. This is the structure of the reef itself and provides a haven for algae, fishes and invertebrates, as well as a base on which new corals and calcareous algae can grow.

Through the action of burrowing invertebrates and ocean currents, part of this substrate becomes porous and eventually crumbles down into coral sand, the rest remaining as a building block for the reef. It is these rocks on the periphery of the reef or in the shallows near the beach that are collected for the aquarium trade before they deteriorate. These rocks, if not utilized for the hobby, would be broken down naturally, dredged by the ton and used as hard core for road building in the tropics, or even used as building blocks for houses. The rocks still have an important role to play in reef aquariums and are exported all over the world. Ecologically, the export of this natural material is meaningless: it is not the living reef that is affected – that would be culpable – rather it is nature's trash can that we are making use of.

When this carbonate substrate falls away from the reef it is already porous in nature and weakened by the action of the tiny boring and burrowing invertebrates. It is this porosity and the animals themselves that are made use of in the natural system.

Live rock is a perfect breeding ground for bacteria, both on the surface and inside its many fissures. These are mostly aerobic bacterial colonies, but deep within the structure of the rock, where it is poor in oxygen, there are anaerobic zones and here important bacteria (*Heterotrophic anaerobes*) are present in quantity. These bacteria satisfy their energy requirements through the assimilation of various organic-based compounds, one of which is nitrate. In the absence of oxygen in the core of the rock, these bacteria have no choice other than to utilize the oxygen from this compound, thereby leaving nitrogen, which is simply gassed off. This rock, then, offers the perfect filter system. In sufficient quantity it can mineralize organic waste, nitrify it and then go a stage further and denitrify it, making the circle complete. It is these special properties that are used in the natural system to such good advantage.

In order to appreciate fully the concept of the natural system, the differences to that of a normal (high-tech) aquarium can be listed.
- Neither trickle filters nor any other form of biological filtration have a place in this system. When the system is set up correctly the living rock is simply the best natural filter in existence.
- The maturation time using living rock is shortened to the point that a healthy reef aquarium can be set up within a week. There is no nitrite phase to speak of.
- A large-volume, high-output protein skimmer is crucial. A skimmer is required so that as much nitrogenous waste as possible is removed before any form of bacterial filtration is introduced.
- Ozone reactors, ultraviolet sterilizing units and denitrifying filters are not necessary where the water quality requires no further prophylactic treatment.
- Mechanical filtration is necessary and filters must be cleaned at least once a week. A good water flow is also an important requirement.
- No base medium, such as coral sand, is used – not even a light sprinkling – since this will attract detritus and subsequently create a build-up of nitrate. This does not apply when a plenum is in use (*see pp. 37–9*).

These are the basic differences, but other than these aquarium size, lighting and water preparation remain the same for all systems.

The idea is based on the fact that aerobic bacterial filters produce nitrate as an end product, and for a reef aquarium a zero nitrate level is desirable. All bacterial activity must be minimized, except that which occurs in the living rock and the aquarium itself. This means that when mechanical filters are in use they must be cleaned

regularly in fresh water to prevent protein waste being converted into nitrate within the filter.

From the start, the bacterial development within the rock functions simultaneously so that there is no ammonia/ammonium, nitrite, or nitrate phase at any meaningful levels. It simply does not take place during the setting-up procedures and for this reason the maturation time of a reef aquarium is considerably shortened. The live rock itself is filter enough for this job, and when a natural equilibrium is obtained any other form of biological filter is both unnecessary and undesirable, as it introduces nitrates within the system that the living rock or protein skimmer would not of itself produce. In effect, this means that the living rock has more work to do than is necessary. It is, therefore, counterproductive to have a trickle or under-gravel filter in the system.

The living rock will, on its own, produce a more stable and diverse environment than any other filter. It must be present in sufficient amounts to do this, however, and the rule of thumb that has been well tried and tested in recent research is 2.2lb per gallon (1kg per 4.5 litres) of aquarium volume (without allowing for water displacement). Living rock needs to be "seeded" and carefully chosen for this type of reef system (*see p. 39*).

With regard to protein skimmers, these have already been discussed in detail (*see pp. 32–4*), so it is sufficient just to say that they should be as large as possible and that it really is true that you cannot over-skim an aquarium that has been set up in the natural way. Nevertheless, trace elements should be added weekly to replace those that are removed by the skimmer.

The aquarium should be set up in such a way that there is a good flow of water within the tank – having a constant circulation of water around the rock takes advantage of its inherent capillary action. Aquarists who have dived or snorkelled on a coral reef are often surprised by the water movement they encounter there and, on returning home, realize just how slow-moving their aquarium water is, and immediately introduce additional flow in an attempt to re-create a more natural environment. It doesn't really matter how much water movement there is, short of it slopping over the sides that is. The point is that with this system the flow should be sufficient to prevent any detritus build-up in quiet corners of the tank. If this does occur, however, siphon it off immediately. With sufficient water movement though, this will not be a great problem, and a good-quality mechanical filter will take care of it.

The mechanical filter should be filled with a suitable medium – filter floss or filter matting, for example. Filter sponges are not a good idea as those that have not been treated with a flame retardant, which will poison a reef aquarium in a very short period of time, become so blocked that they are difficult to rinse, even if you clean them on a twice-weekly basis. If the aquarium has a sump, it can be utilized as a water reservoir and is a good place to hide the protein skimmer. Additionally the sump can be used as an extra mechanical filter if you direct the overflow pipe into a filter box.

There is still some doubt about the continual use of activated charcoal in a reef aquarium set-up, and in this type of system it is best to be cautious and to use it for a maximum of five days per calendar month. This should reduce any of the adverse effects the charcoal appears to have on living coral. The charcoal can be placed in either the filter sump or a mechanical filter for this period of time, after which you can rinse and dry it out, ready to be reused at a later date.

When planning a reef structure using live rock, take care to ensure that it is loose and as open as possible to allow for good water circulation and to eliminate dead spots where detritus can collect. This also increases the contact area of the bacteria, allowing better biological filtration. The reef should have minimum contact with the base, again to create good water circulation.

In an aquarium using the natural system, you should not use any base medium, such as sand, except with a plenum. That is not to say that you must live with a tank with a totally bare base. After a while, calcareous red algae will colonize the base, along with various invertebrates, producing a realistic-looking reef environment, especially if you place small pieces of living rock to fill in the blank spaces. The aquarium base should be siphoned off regularly to reduce any detritus build-up.

The plenum (Jaubert) system

Most marine and reef aquarium books make the mistake of stating that anaerobic zones in the sand base of an aquarium allow the release of poisonous substances in the water and so should be avoided. They then contradict themselves and talk about anaerobic bacteria and their denitrifying capabilities. Two-zone thinking (aerobic and anaerobic) is also misleading. There are no particular zones, only areas of differing oxygen levels where colonies of differing bacteria form.

Consider a marine aquarium with no undergravel filter but with 6in (15cm) of coral sand as the base medium. Experienced hobbyists would be right in thinking this a recipe for disaster. Nevertheless, it can be used to explain what actually happens microbiologically.

With good oxygenated water and good current flow above the surface of the coral sand you can expect the top 2in (5cm) to have various levels of oxygen saturation. The level of oxygen drops the deeper into the sand you go, until only about 5 to 10 parts per million (ppm) are present. In this layer, however, you would expect to find aerobic bacteria and the success of this colonization would be helped by the action of various burrowing invertebrates and fishes that constantly disturb the sand, thereby introducing more oxygenation.

In the next 2in (between 5 and 10cm) down into the sand, oxygen saturation is likely to become even poorer – from between 5 and 1ppm, or even less. This is the level where various forms of anaerobic bacteria form to render their valuable denitrification service for the tank water. Heterotrophic bacteria are also present and appear to be facultative, which means that they have the ability to colonize and exist in aerobic and anaerobic areas, deriving their energy and oxygen requirements not only from the water but also from such organic compounds as nitrate.

The lowest 2in (between 10 and 15cm) are devoid of oxygen and so are termed anoxic. Putrefaction occurs in this anoxic environment, producing the gas hydrogen sulphide (used in stink bombs and smells like bad eggs). It is this area that you must avoid in an aquarium, since the poisonous gasses and compounds released into the water would do untold damage to the tank inhabitants.

The original idea of the plenum system came from Professor Jaubert of Monaco. If you place a piece of filter sponge in the bottom of a basin and turn the tap directly on to it, you will see that the water runs over the sponge but very little actually goes through it. The water flow is being dissipated away from the sponge. Now, by taking this same sponge and raising it off the bottom of the basin, the water flows through it rather than over its surface. Sand raised away intact from the bottom of an aquarium induces a similar effect. This is the function and one of the basic principles of the plenum.

Because it has a porous base plate, the construction of the plenum can be likened to an undergravel filter. The plate is used to raise the sand away from the bottom of the tank, thereby allowing water to flow through the sand rather than being dissipated over its surface. But here the similarity ends. The plenum is an entirely different concept. With an undergravel filter, water is powered by a turbo pump through the sand in either a forward or a reverse current flow. The emphasis is on turnover rate in term of gallons (or litres) per hour, and its prime function is as an aerobic filter. The plenum, however, uses no power whatsoever; instead, water is allowed to diffuse through the sand in a circular motion simply by virtue of the current flow that is used in the aquarium. Due to its special construction, it is similar to live rock in that it has aerobic and anaerobic areas, and so has the ability to both nitrify and denitrify at the same time.

The plenum system employs the use of what is called "live" sand as the filter medium and is sometimes referred to as a "live-sand filter" or, more often, as a "natural nitrate reduction filter". Installing a plenum in a reef aquarium using the natural system – thus combining live sand with live rock – produces one of the most effective filters known.

There are quite a few advantages when a plenum is installed in a reef aquarium, probably the main one being that the denitrifying potential of the system is greatly increased, which brings about a drastic reduction in nitrate levels. No readable nitrate is present in the water when the system is fully functional. In addition, the nitrification phase is practically non-existent, therefore little in the way of organic acids are released into the aquarium. This produces a far better buffering capacity and a more stable pH. The use of a thick base medium is considerably more natural and advantageous both to fishes and invertebrates. There is a disadvantage, though, and this is that about 6in (15cm) of space is taken up in the aquarium for the construction of the plenum. Due to this, it is not suitable for aquariums under 55 gallons (250 litres). However, there is nothing to stop you setting up a plenum in the filter sump, since the bacteria seem to work just as well in the dark. In this way, brittle and serpent stars, along with sea cucumbers and other invertebrates, can be used to disturb the sand in the filter sump.

Construction and installation

The construction of a plenum is amazingly simple. A plastic grid is used, cut to fit snugly the bottom of the aquarium. This is placed on 1-in (2.5-cm) perforated supports, placed at intervals over the bottom. The size of the perforations in the grid is not so important (an undergravel filter plate can be used), but the grid should be of a light material that is strong enough to support the weight of sand. Over this you place a fine mesh plastic, nylon or fibreglass screen, of the type used as a fly or mosquito screen. This is important, since it stops any grains of sand blocking the perforations or holes in the grid, thus reducing the effect of the filter.

Next, the whole construction is covered with a 2-in (5-cm) layer of crushed coral or coral sand. Use a ruler to measure the correct depth as this plays an important role in keeping the filter bed from becoming anoxic. The granular size of the sand should not be too coarse or it will later allow too much oxygen through to this lower layer, which is intended to be the anaerobic zone of the filter bed. A grain size of 1 to 4mm would be ideal. After this has been done, fill the aquarium with sea water exactly to the level of the surface of the sand. Then you need to check the depth of sand again, adding more sand if necessary to compensate for any that may have settled when the water was added. You then place another fine mesh screen, previously cut to fit the aquarium, over the sand. On top of this, another 2-in (5-cm) layer of finer

sand is added and the process of measuring and filling with water is repeated again. The purpose of this second screen is to stop the lower layer from becoming disturbed by fish and invertebrates burrowing through the base medium and allowing too much oxygen into this anaerobic level. Small worms and other minute marine animals are able to pass through, though, and in this way the lower layer is prevented from becoming anoxic.

The fine sand in the upper layer should have a grain size of 1mm or less. This serves as the aerobic level and the fineness of the sand ensures that an increased surface area is available for biological filtration. In addition, this fine sand stops detritus penetrating the filter bed and eventually blocking it. Fish and invertebrates, such as hermit crabs, brittle stars, burrowing snails, serpent stars and turbo snails, prefer fine sand and their constant burrowing and disturbing of the upper layer allows enough oxygen through to maintain the aerobic equilibrium. This then, is the finished plenum filter.

All that remains to do is provide enough water circulation in the aquarium to allow a constant diffusion of water through the plenum. This is not as difficult as it seems, since as long as the current flow in the aquarium is enough to produce swaying movements among the corals, anemones and other invertebrates then this filtration system will work perfectly.

Interstitial and burrowing communities

Of course, there is more to a plenum filtration system than merely allowing aerobic and anaerobic bacteria to form in differing levels of sand. In nature, these layers are known as the interstitial zone, which means that it is the zone between the sea and the compacted seabed. In the first 4in (10cm) of the seabed there exists an unbelievable variety of different life forms. These micro- and macrofauna provide a vital service to the reef community. Here nematodes, kinorhynchs, copepods, isopods, polychaete and unsegmented sea worms abound. These and other tiny invertebrates perform the cleaning service for the reef and seabed. Interstitial animals feed on organic waste as they move between the particles without displacing them, but there are also burrowing creatures that displace particles and so allow the zone to absorb the extra oxygen that is necessary for bacterial growth. The interstitial zone is their kingdom and certain burrowing sea worms can live in an environment where the oxygen level is only 1 to 5ppm. The true aim of the plenum system is to re-create this interstitial zone as closely as possible.

Having a healthy bacterial growth and, at the same time, having minute marine organisms burrowing and loosening the sand in the aquarium, thereby allowing an equally healthy base medium for the mini-reef, can only be an advantage.

The use of "live" sand

Live sand is that which comes directly from the coral seas of the world. The best quality comes from the Caribbean. It is imported with the micro- and macrofauna still alive and healthy, and this material can be used in small quantities as the seeding medium when you are setting up a reef or marine tank. Alternatively you can use it in the upper layer of a plenum to encourage healthy interstitial and burrowing communities to grow and develop. Using normal dry coral sand is an acceptable option if living rock is also used, because the animals that are present in the rock will eventually find their way into the sand and start to colonize it. However, it is far better to use live sand, since the fauna differs from that normally associated with live rock. In this way, minute marine worms present in the sand can burrow down through the dividing screen and into the lower layer of the plenum, thus enabling at least some oxygen to reach the anaerobic layer and preventing it from becoming anoxic. Wherever possible, at least some live sand should be used in the setting up of a plenum, even if it is only 10 or 11lb (about 5kg).

Living rock

There are two types of living rock available for aquarium use – "seeded" and "unseeded". *On no account should unseeded rock be introduced to an existing reef or marine aquarium.* When living rock is collected and brought to the shippers, who pack it for export all over the world, little is done to ensure that the rock is thoroughly clean. This is understandable since rigorous cleaning, perhaps even with fresh water, would destroy most of the life forms within the rock, and it is these life forms that we are painstakingly trying to keep alive. To reach its destination in good condition, living rock must be packed "wet" so that it arrives still moist. Transportation time, inevitable delays and hot weather can all take their toll on the life within the rock and most of it unfortunately reaches dealers and shops in a very sorry condition. This rock is termed "unseeded" and requires special attention before it can be used in a marine or reef aquarium.

The rock should first be placed in a container or spare tank full of sea water. Strong water flow is required and the container should be as large as possible to ensure good water circulation. Ideally, a turbo pump with a mechanical filter cartridge should be used so that the water is also filtered to a degree. After 24 hours each piece of rock is taken out and any dead animals, sponges and algae removed before returning it to the water. The next day the rock is removed again and cleaned with sea water and an all-plastic scrubbing brush. It is a good idea to rig up the turbo pump to a hose in the aquarium so that the rock can be sprayed with water. The rock is then left in the container for a further seven days, during which time both the rock and the water may start to smell unpleasant. This is not unusual. The rock should be cleaned a further two times during this period and, if necessary, a water change made until, at the end of this seeding period, the rock smells sweeter (or at least how rock that comes from the sea should smell). Any pieces that still look blackened or smell unpleasant should be returned to the container for further treatment. At the end of this period the rock is "seeded".

Two good examples of reef aquariums that have been set up with living corals on a good base of live rock. On the left, stony corals are predominant while on the right, soft corals make an equally enchanting impression.

Photographs courtesy of S. Krumbügel Coral Fish Imports, Lindenberg, Germany

---

TIPS

When choosing live rock, select only pieces that are porous and have a good surface area for bacteria to colonize. Inspect it, smell it and weigh it in your hand – if it feels relatively light then it is likely to be good. Some of the rock from the Indo-Pacific is quite dense and is unsuitable, since it does not produce a good biological reaction in the aquarium. If it feels heavier than it should, don't buy it. The best rock seems to be that from the Red Sea, East Africa and the Caribbean. Much of this material is very porous, sometimes knobbly and encourages good reef construction.

Aquarium base media

For systems that do not utilize either an undergravel filter or a plenum, the use of coral or silica sand is not recommended. If you cannot live without some form of base medium in the bottom of your aquarium then use a light sprinkling of coral or silica sand between the aquarium decoration or reef construction, but not under it. Always bear in mind that sand in a tank attracts detritus with its inherent problems of nitrate build-up and slime algae (blue algae). It is also difficult to keep the aquarium clean by siphoning away the detritus when there is a sandy base present.

With a plenum in the aquarium, crushed coral and coral sand (live sand) should be used. This should have a total depth of 4 to 5in (10 to 12cm). In an aquarium using an undergravel filter (sub-sand filter) there have been many suggestions about which is the best form of base medium to use. Various layers have been suggested comprising crushed coral, crushed cockleshell, marble chips, quartz sand, silica sand, freshwater aquarium gravel and even crushed eggshells. Certainly one of the best base media to use for an undergravel filter, determined after many years of experimentation, is a mixture of medium fine (5mm) and coarse (10 to 15mm) crushed coral. Using this medium to a depth of 4in (10cm) over the base plate of the filter affords an enormous nitrification potential where, in fish-only aquaria and when correctly set up, it will outclass any trickle filter on the market. Since the larger pieces of crushed coral, like living rock, are also capable of harbouring anaerobic bacteria, thereby increasing the denitrification potential, it is probably still the most economically effective system for a marine (fish-only) aquarium.

Decoration and form

In the past, bleached coral was used in nearly all marine aquariums. Today, thankfully, we can build reef structures in our aquariums and introduce living corals that we can then care for, propagate and even take cuttings from to pass on to fellow aquarists. Perhaps in the future we will even be able to reintroduce aquarium-raised corals into the sea where natural or man-made catastrophes have destroyed natural reef environments. The keeping of marine fishes, corals and other invertebrates is nowadays not just a simple hobby; rather, it is a science dedicated to the wellbeing of our charges.

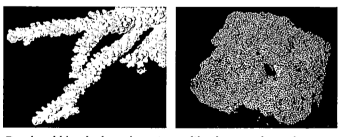

Dead and bleached coral specimens like the ones shown here should not be used as decoration in an aquarium, since their uncontrolled import only adds to the ecological damage that is being done to the coral reefs of the world.

The use of live rock as a decorative material and also as the building blocks for the construction of a reef in an aquarium is the best way to start setting up a successful system. Only when the reef structure is complete should you think about proceeding any further with the stocking of your aquarium. First, though, you must decide what sort of construction you want to build.

Valleys can be constructed with towering overhangs, under which invertebrates that require low-light conditions can be placed. Grottoes can be created and simulated "patch reefs". Even a reef bank can be built, behind which an overflow box or filter can be hidden. In this case, it is a good idea to first fit a water or turbo pump behind the intended structure before attempting to build it. This will ensure that there is a good water circulation behind the reef bank to assist in biological filtration, and it will also prevent any build up of detritus.

There are several ways to build a stable mini-reef, including the use of special cement, binding and fixings. If the rock is to be cemented together, bear in mind that it will then be difficult, if not impossible, to dismantle it again. This could be a problem if you intend to move house at some later date, for example. Cable clips work quite well but they don't produce such a stable structure: they sometimes slip and are difficult to fix precisely.

Pegging is by far the best and most versatile method of building a reef. You will need an electric drill with a 7-mm masonry bit and a 7-mm PVC doweling rod cut into 4-in (10-cm) lengths. Sort the rock through so that you have a rough idea about what you intend to do with it, and then select a suitable base rock. Drill one or more holes in it to a depth of 2in (5cm) and peg these with the precut dowel, leaving 2in (5cm) protruding. For extra stability, the dowel can be cemented into the base rock with coral cement. Then drill the second rock in a suitable place and fit it on to the peg(s) in the first rock. This should not be cemented in so that you can dismantle it later if required. Drill this rock in turn on its upper surface and cement pegs in for the third rock, and so on. If a rock is heavy, or if it is to be used for an overhang, two or more holes could be pegged to give it the extra stability it requires. It is a good idea when building high structures to try the construction out on a table or on the floor to check that it does not overbalance. If it does not seem stable enough, peg additional rocks in place to counterbalance it, or select a larger base rock. In this way it is possible to build high, stable structures, even without the use of cement, and the advantage is that the reef can be dismantled and reassembled in exactly the same position again.

Apart from live rock, which is quite expensive, there is little by way of alternatives that can seriously be recommend for a reef aquarium, although for a normal marine aquarium there are several alternatives. However, rocks that have been formed as a result of volcanic activity should not be used in a marine aquarium, despite their often attractive and bizarre appearance. This is because they almost always contain metals or metal oxides that

can contaminate the water. The exception to this is tufa rock, which, although volcanic in origin, contains little in the way of harmful substances. It is extremely porous and in an aquarium will soon be colonized by small marine animals and bacteria. After a time tufa becomes difficult to differentiate from some forms of living rock. If you cannot afford to fill your aquarium solely with living rock, it is a good idea to use tufa as a base and then place at least some living rock on top of it. You can peg tufa in the same way as live rock. You often see dolomite used as aquarium decoration. However, its composition is calcium magnesium carbonate and, because of this, it should not be used as part of a marine aquarium set-up.

There are other forms of aquarium decoration that you can use with total safety, however, including rocks and corals that are made entirely of plastic. Although inert and harmless, they are of little use biologically and of no use at all in the natural environment of a reef or marine aquarium because of their unrealistic appearance.

Current flow

Water movement is a very important aspect of both marine and reef aquariums and, as a general rule, you can never have enough of it. On the natural reef, water flow and movement is sometimes awesome and the relative stillness of an average reef aquarium is in stark contrast to the natural environment. Wherever possible, turbo pumps, surge and wavemakers should be used to rectify this situation.

With the use of turbo pumps or powerheads it is important to ensure that the current flow is not directed at any of the invertebrates placed on the reef construction, as most animals will soon succumb to this constant battering. Instead, the water flow should be directed around the tank and, with the clever use of two powerheads connected to timers, you can achieve an effect of ebb and flow by switching the pumps on and off alternately through a period of some hours. This has the added advantage of disturbing any detritus that may build up in a quiet part of the aquarium due to the fact that flow is only in a single direction. There is nothing more realistic than seeing an aquarium in which soft and hard corals, anemones and algae can be seen swaying gracefully on the reef structure in the current flow.

High-performance centrifugal pumps can also be used. These have the extra advantages of low power consumption, extreme reliability over many years and neatness, since only the impeller housing is visible below water. Like many modern powerheads, this type of pump can also be used as a wave maker with the addition of a power timer – an electronic controller designed to create pulses or surges in the pump output. These pulses can be controlled from

about one to six seconds to simulate the movement of natural wave. Multiple control modules with interval timers are also available to simulate tidal changes over a three-to-six-hour period, and these are often equipped with a food-timing facility to create a pause in current flow at feeding time. Many interesting and natural effects can be simulated with these units, and it is up to you to decide which type of current flow you want to reproduce.

Strong currents and wave or surge actions in a marine aquarium are not only for purely aesthetic reasons. Apart from stirring up detritus, which can then be more easily removed by a mechanical filter, they also increase the oxygen-absorption capabilities of the water by keeping a high turnover rate at the surface where oxygen is absorbed from the atmosphere. (Bear in mind that sea water absorbs some 250 times less oxygen from the surrounding air than fresh water.) In addition, strong water movement keeps fishes active and they appear to be healthier than those living in a still-water environment. The exception to this are seahorses (*Hippocampus* spp.), which are not really reef fishes at all, preferring sandy bottoms and dense algae beds as their natural habitat.

Strong current flow in a reef aquarium takes on an even more important role inasmuch as the delicate corals and other invertebrates are provided with a constant cleaning service, which this is crucial for their development and general wellbeing. Added to this, nutrients have a better chance of being carried to them by the currents than in an aquarium with poor current flow, where they would normally fall to the bottom to be left undisturbed and perhaps eventually be converted into nitrogenous waste.

Maturation times and processes

Having chosen the type of filtration system to use and installed it, along with pumps and decoration, your aquarium is now ready to be filled with water that has been premixed and well aerated for at least 24 hours, in order to allow all suspended salts to be thoroughly dissolved. It is a good idea to place a large bowl or dish in the bottom of the aquarium when filling it with water. You then pour the water into the dish and allow it to flow gently over the sides, and in this way you reduce the chance of the decoration being disturbed by the force of the water flowing in.

After the aquarium has been filled and you have removed the bowl, you now need to make an all-round check to make sure that everything is in order, after which you can switch on the aquarium. At this stage, however, it is important not to turn on the lighting, as the aquarium must be given time to mature.

The maturation time of an aquarium can vary a great deal and it is dependent not so much on the size of the tank but on the system being used. Each aquarium reacts differently and during this cycling phase you should monitor the water on a daily basis and test it for both nitrite and ammonia.

Any live sand and seeded live rocks that you have used in the initial setting up of the aquarium will already have their own inherent bacterial cultures, and if this material is used in sufficient quantity there will be little or no readable ammonia or nitrite phase. In a high-tech aquarium, however, where no live rock is used, the filter system must be allowed to mature, and this takes time – up to 90 days. In the initial stages of this period there will be no bacteria in the system, and these must be allowed to form, and unless ammonia is present in the water, this will not happen. Therefore, you have to introduced it manually.

There are several ammonia-based preparations on the market that you can use as a cycling accelerator or, alternatively, one or, at a maximum, two hardy fishes can be used. The advantage of using fishes is that they excrete ammonia-based products on a daily basis and, provided they are not subjected to excessive ammonia and nitrate levels, they do the job extremely well. If high levels are present, a partial water change may be necessary or you could remove the fish to another tank to ensure their wellbeing while levels are high.

During the first seven to ten days there will be a gradual and measurable build-up of nitrite in the aquarium water. This is both quite natural and a good indication that the filter system is starting to function effectively.

After the first few days the aquarium lighting can be switched on, preferably using the following timetable:
- Days 1 to 4 – no lights.
- Day 5 – blue or actinic lights for two hours.

*The neon or blue streak demoiselle (*Neoglyphidodon oxyodon*) is a hardy fish and one that is ideally suited to the aquarium maturation phase.*

- Day 6 – blue or actinic lights for four hours.
- Day 7 – blue lights for six hours and main light for two hours.
- Day 8 – blue lights for eight hours and main light for four hours.
- Day 9 – blue lights for ten hours, main light for six hours.

On day 10, the aquarium lighting can be increased to the full duration of 12 hours of blue and 8 hours of main lights. In this way, a dawn and dusk period can be utilized with the blue or actinic lights being switched on two hours before the main lights and switch off two hours after. The reason for this gradual increase in aquarium illumination is to prevent, or at least hinder, the excessive growth of unwanted algae in the initial cycling phase. This is quite important, since you are trying to achieve a natural balance within the system, which may easily be upset if large amounts of algae are present.

If everything is functioning correctly you can expect that somewhere between day 10 and day 14 a noticeable drop in the level of nitrite will occur. This means that bacteria are starting to form and already doing their job in terms of denitrification. But it does not mean that you can go ahead and add fishes and invertebrates to the system. This is where not only beginners but also many experienced aquarists make a mistake. You must be patient, for the aquarium is by no means fully cycled or matured, even if the nitrite level has dropped to zero. It merely means that the filtration system is functioning biologically. Putting stress on the system in this phase by adding fishes and invertebrates can only result in subsequent unacceptable losses. At this stage the aquarium is starting to establish an equilibrium but the growing bacterial colonies will only be able to cope with the organic waste that is already being produced and the system requires maturation time before livestock is introduced. When you finally reach that stage, stocking should be carried out with forethought and planning by adding a little at a time to allow the aquarium system to re-establish its equilibrium before you add any further livestock to the equation.

A lot has been written in the past about the maturation times for a reef and marine aquarium and much of it is misleading – in simple terms, the maturation time of a reef or marine aquarium is anything between three and a hundred days. This may sound vague and ridiculous but it is, nevertheless, true.

There are guidelines, however, that can be used to estimate the maturation time of a particular set-up and these are as follows:

- An aquarium set-up with "seeded" live rock and a "seeded" live sand filter (the natural system) – 3 to 10 days.
- An aquarium set-up with an unseeded sub-sand filter and "seeded" live rock – 14 to 28 days.
- An aquarium set-up with a trickle filter (wet/dry filter) and no live rock or live sand – 70 to 100 days.
- An aquarium set-up with a trickle filter and "unseeded" live rock – 90 to 100 days.

These are rough guidelines only and every aquarium reacts differently. A good indication of a fully matured

pH stability in the first 70 days

aquarium is the pH stability (*see chart above*). This is nothing new, of course, but it is possible to judge graphically when a tank has settled down and the system is functioning correctly. To do this, you should measure the pH on a daily basis, and at the same time each day, and plot the resultant readings on graph paper.

In the graph shown here you can see that pH stability was achieved after a period of approximately 50 days. These are actual measurements taken at 9am each morning on a 55-gallon (250-litre) aquarium using a combination of sub-sand filter and trickle filtration into a filter sump where a 155-gallon (700-litre) per hour protein skimmer was in operation. The tank contained 110lb (50kg) of seeded live rock. It is interesting to note that although there was no life in the aquarium, other

than the living rock, the protein skimmer was producing more than 2 fl oz (56ml) of dark brown protein waste daily from the living rock alone.

There are other ways to tell when a tank is fully matured, such as testing the reduction/oxidization capabilities (redox potential), which is measured in millivolts (*see pp. 53–4*).

With some systems, fishes and invertebrates can be added to the newly established aquarium after a period of only a week or so. But it does not mean that the tank has settled down and can withstand full stocking. This would not be recommended. However, once the aquarium has a bacterially functional filter system it is possible to introduce selected invertebrates, such as turbo snails and hermit crabs, for algae control. Other invertebrates may also be added to the aquarium, but take care to make sure

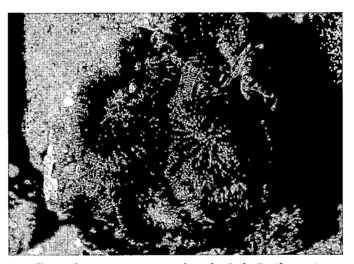

Corallimorpharian anemones, such as this Indo-Pacific species (Discosoma *sp.*), *should not be introduced until the aquarium has fully matured. Nevertheless, they are an ideal choice for the beginner to the reef aquarium hobby, since they are relatively undemanding and hardy.*

that those introduced rely solely, or at least predominantly, on their own zooxanthellae algae as a nutritional base. In this way, feeding at this critical stage of maturation will then be unnecessary.

Higher forms of algae, such as *Caulerpa* spp., *Halimenia* spp., *Galaxaura* spp. and *Halimeda* spp., may be introduced in the second or third week. In this way the undesirable blue algae (red or green slime algae) have little chance to establish themselves in the aquarium due to the natural extraction of nitrates and phosphates from the water that are so important for their development. In effect, you introduce high-order algae in order to starve the development of low-order species, such as bacterial algae, until such time as the growth of calcareous red algae takes over. Once this has taken place, it is an indication that the aquarium has, to a great extent, stabilized.

During the maturation period, where "unseeded" living rock has been used in the setting up of an aquarium, the situation is somewhat different. No high-order life forms can be added to this type of set-up for the first three months. In this way the live rock is allowed to develop its own equilibrium and much more life will ensue than if you rush the job. There will be periodic murkiness as the animals within the rocks begin to recover and expel detritus and dirt from their holes. It is an amazing thing to see, as it seems that by some concealed or secret form of marine telegraph this type of spring cleaning is undertaken by all the hidden creatures at exactly the same time. This phenomenon usually lasts for about five minutes, and the rocks in the aquarium all appear to begin to smoke. Gradually as the tank matures the rock will come to life as hitherto unseen animals begin to emerge from their hiding

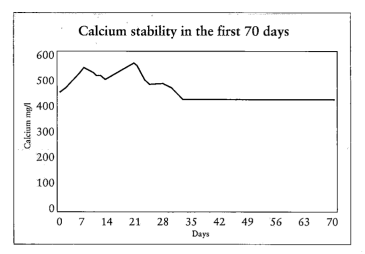

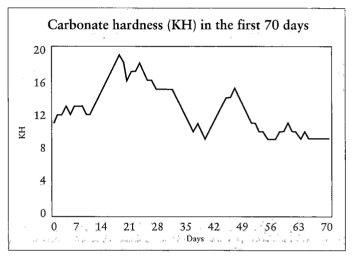

*The saddled butterflyfish (*Chaetodon falcula*) should not be introduced into a newly set-up aquarium. This fish requires mature and stable water conditions.*

places. Sponges, tunicates and tiny cirratulid and serpulid worms may be found. Various algae will also grow and appear to flourish before dying off again to be replaced by other forms with a hardier disposition.

Eventually, as the aquarium begins to establish its natural equilibrium, calcareous algae appear, usually after 50 to 60 days, and then the tank rapidly settles down. It is good practice to keep a log of all the tests that you carry out during the maturation period. Tests, not only for ammonia and nitrate, should be carried out so that you have a better picture of what is actually happening with water quality. Ask questions of any maturing aquarium, regardless of the set-up and maturation period. How much calcium is present, for example? What is the carbonate hardness (KH) of my aquarium? Have I got too much phosphate or iron? What is the nitrate level now? These questions all need to be answered and it is folly to expect that every-thing will be all right unless you test these parameters and make adjustments as necessary.

In the two graphs shown here (*above right*), the same aquarium was used as previously described with the graph concerning pH stability (*see p. 43*). Note how the calcium

level was stable by day 31, while the carbonate hardness took twice this time to settle down.

Again, these are actual measurements and reflect graphically what could happen in your aquarium during its maturation period. Of course, you may obtain an entirely different set of readings from your own aquarium, but it serves to illustrate the necessity for testing.

With a high-tech system or where "unseeded" live rock is used, the maturation period is longer. If you are impatient, use this time to note down in a diary the daily measurements and any changes in the aquarium. This can be interesting when unseeded live rock is used during the initial cycling time, since once the scrubbing and cleaning phase is over, the rock starts literally to come to life.

With regard to the so called "nitrite phase" as the aquarium matures, this can be virtually eliminated if you use sufficient quantities of "seeded" live rock, as you can see from the two graphs that follow (*see opposite*).

Algae indicators

Algae are one of the best indicators of the state of an aquarium during its maturation phase. As the water gradually moves toward a state of equilibrium, various

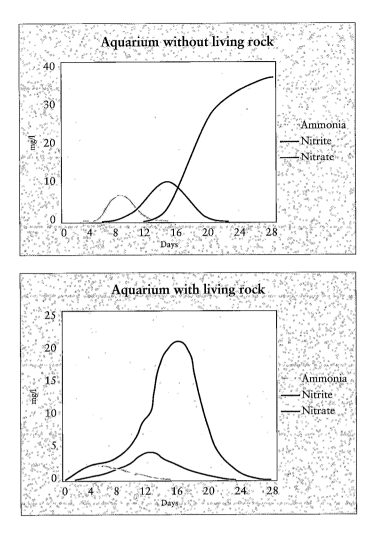

Aquarium without living rock

— Ammonia
— Nitrite
— Nitrate

Days

Aquarium with living rock

— Ammonia
— Nitrite
— Nitrate

Days

Although in a newly established aquarium it will disappear after a period of a few weeks, it can also cause problems later. High levels of nitrate, overfeeding and organic waste can cause its reappearance. This can be of plague proportions, especially in a reef aquarium, where it multiplies extremely quickly. If left uncontrolled it will rapidly spread over the whole tank, covering the precious invertebrates and the higher forms of algae in a thick red or green slime, and eventually suffocating them. It is difficult to rid an aquarium of this problem; a reduction of light duration will have no effect. The best method is to siphon it out as soon as it appears and then use a diatom filter to remove the swarmers as much as possible. This is only a prophylactic treatment, though, and its cause must be eradicated to prevent further problems.

Hair algae are the next to appear in a maturing aquarium. There are two forms to watch out for. The first is known as *Bryopsis* and when it is examined closely you can see that the individual hairs are branched, unlike the second form. The unbranched variety belongs to the genus *Derbesia*. Both of these algae occur together and can also take over the whole aquarium if they are left uncontrolled. Thankfully there are many invertebrates and fishes that graze on these and other algae. By the time *Derbesia* and *Bryopsis* appear in any quantity, the newly set-up aquarium is well on its way to reaching maturity and selected invertebrates and fishes may be introduced.

Turbo snails and hermit crabs are great algal eaters, as are surgeonfish and tangs, such as *Zebrasoma flavascens*, which is also a very decorative fish with its bright yellow colouring. Many blennies and gobies will also graze on algae and most gobies perform an additional service of sifting and filtering sand, expelling it through their gill openings in search of detritus and other morsels of food.

After about eight weeks, red and brown calcareous algae will normally become evident in the aquarium, but they will not be in any great quantity at first. If the water

forms of algae appear for a short time before dying off. Normally the first species that appears in an aquarium after it has been newly set up is diatom algae. This is seldom a problem and the algae will usually disappear after the nutrients – the silicates on which it lives – have been exhausted. It is easily recognized and will normally appear within the first few days as a middle-brown covering over the rocks and sand. It can produce problems later, however, especially if untreated tap water is used during the topping-up procedure when tank water has been lost as a result of evaporation. This practice has the effect of reintroducing silicates in the water and, consequently, induces a reappearance of diatomaceous algae.

Sporadic outbreaks of planaria (flatworms) can occur. These creatures feed on the algae and certain species of planaria can do untold damage to soft corals and anemones in an aquarium. As the aquarium matures, though, these algae gradually die off to be replaced by others. Blue algae (Cyanophyta) begin to form and while not in most cases actually blue (they are usually green or red) they will, in a short period of time, cover much of the aquarium. Again, this is normal and they will usually disperse after a further period of maturation. Blue algae, which is thought by some experts to be a bacterium and not an alga at all, belongs to the class Cyanophyceae.

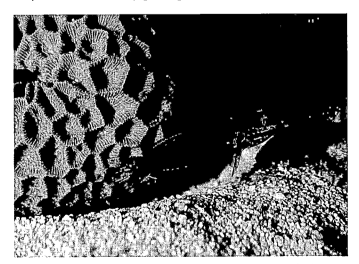

*This Indo-Pacific goby (*Amblygobius phalaena) *is an ideal choice of fish for a newly set up aquarium, providing a good housekeeping service for the tank.*

conditions are optimal, however, these algae will rapidly multiply until, by the end of three months, they will be in the majority, which is very desirable condition for your reef or marine aquarium.

The deep brown (chestnut) algae and the red calcareous algae are very important species for reef growth. On the natural reef they are known as reef-building algae because as they grow they bind together loose portions of the reef, making it a much more stable structure. In an aquarium they perform the same sort of service and in addition to this the algae will cover much of the aquarium with attractive, sometimes plate-shaped, growths. These growths do not in any way disrupt or disturb the development of the hard or soft corals that are later added to the tank, nor do they adversely affect any other invertebrates in the aquarium. Apart from being attractive, these algae perform an important service by removing nitrate from the water and in addition, when they are present in large quantities, can provide an extra haven for fishes and invertebrates. When these algae are present in the aquarium they are a good indication of the general stabilization of the environment.

In the graph here (*see below*) you can see a typical example of how the various forms of algae appear and then die off when the aquarium conditions are optimal. The timings of their appearance and disappearance, and also the quantities you are likely to encounter, may vary somewhat from aquarium to aquarium.

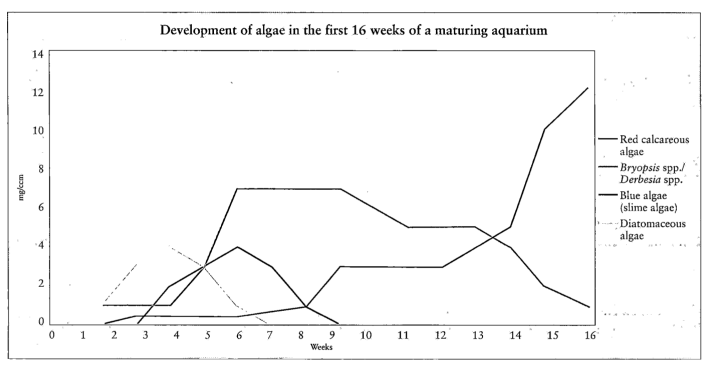

Development of algae in the first 16 weeks of a maturing aquarium

Water management and control

Good oxygenated water with plenty of movement and current flow is a prerequisite for a successful marine or reef aquarium. Along with this, water management and control should be exercised at regular intervals. Test kits are widely available to enable most water parameters to be measured. In addition, electronic control equipment can be used, and although these units are more expensive to buy they provide very accurate results and can work out cheaper in the long run.

During the maturation period, the water should be checked on a daily basis and the results recorded for later reference. With a fully matured aquarium, however, a weekly check should suffice. The main tests to carry out to ensure good water quality and provide a healthy reef environment are as follows:

• Specific gravity/conductivity
• Temperature
• pH
• Carbonate hardness (KH, sometimes referred to as dKH)
• Calcium
• Phosphate
• Ammonia/Ammonium
• Nitrite
• Nitrate
• Redox
• Strontium
• Iodine
• Iron

If you are a newcomer, it is a good idea to practise using these test kits during the initial cycling period of the aquarium. In this way you will quickly become adept in interpolating the results and be aware of the quality of the water before attempting to introduce any livestock.

It must be stressed at this stage that without carrying out these tests at regular intervals you run a very great risk

Complete laboratories are available at a relatively low cost. A kit such as this enables you to test and correct most of the important water parameters.

of a breakdown in water quality. This will inevitably result in the loss of some, if not all, of your precious charges.

Specific gravity and conductivity

Ideally SG 1.023 (Conductivity 50.1mS/cm)

The measurement of the specific gravity of sea water using a hydrometer is notoriously inaccurate. Often, totally in-explicable deaths of corals and other invertebrate animals, along with the fishes themselves, can be attributed to the inaccuracies of this instrument. Recently, conductivity

meters have become available to amateurs and in tests they have proved to be very accurate. The problem with these instruments, however, lies not in their use or even in their construction for that matter. The major problem occurs in the interpretation and conversion of the information given by the readings. Often, the maker's instructions are misleading or even inaccurate. The relationship between the conductivity of sea water at 25°C (77°F) and its specific gravity is popularly misinterpreted. The true relationship is shown in the table here (*see below*).

Specific gravity relative to conductivity in sea water at 25°C (77°F)	
SG 1.020 = 45.3mS/cm	SG 1.023 = 50.1mS/cm
SG 1.021 = 46.5mS/cm	SG 1.024 = 51.5mS/cm
SG 1.022 = 48.7mS/cm	SG 1.025 = 52.9mS/cm

As can be seen, the measurement of conductivity is calculated in milliSiemens per centimetre (mS/cm), and when it is displayed graphically it is an exponential curve that is inversely proportional to water temperature.

Marine aquarium books often refer to the salinity (salt content) of sea water, but this is arbitrary. It is difficult to test and there are far easier ways to make measurements. As an example, though, the salinity of sea water at 20°+C (68°+F) would be 34 per cent.

The graph below shows the specific gravity relative to conductivity and is an expansion of the previous table (*see above*). If you use a conductivity meter, you may find it useful for your measurements.

The ideal specific gravity of sea water for the aquarium is 1.023. This holds true for most aquariums with the

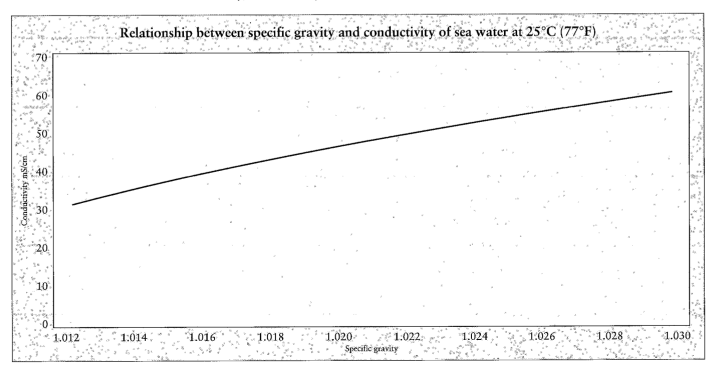

Relationship between specific gravity and conductivity of sea water at 25°C (77°F)

exception of a Red Sea aquarium. This is a set-up with animals and fishes exclusively from the Red Sea. Because of the geographic peculiarities of this sea, the density of this water is higher than in other coral seas. In an aquarium, this must be taken into consideration. In this case the specific gravity should be between 1.024 and 1.025 (conductivity 51.5 – 52.9mS/cm). At this higher density, the inhabitants in this sort of aquarium will have the best chances of success.

At the moment a specific gravity meter is available from only one source, Selzle, Germany, and it is revolutionary. It reflects state-of-the-art technology and is relatively inexpensive to buy. It is battery powered and temperature compensated, which means that whatever the aquarium temperature it will give an accurate reading. It can be switched to read the temperature or the specific gravity of the water. The push-button display saves battery life and the unit is extremely accurate, giving temperature readings to a tenth of a degree. The specific gravity readings are given to four decimal places, such as 1.0229.

Obviously this instrument eliminates any vagueness in specific gravity readings through conductivity conversions or inaccurate hydrometers, and its portability makes it ideal for testing the water in your local dealer's holding tanks. The singular drawback, if it can be called that, is that its electronic probe must be the same temperature as the water being tested to enable quick and accurate specific gravity test results. This is no great problem, though, since holding the probe in the test water for a minute or will equalize the temperature.

Temperature

Ideally 25–27°C (77–80°F)
Overheating of an aquarium can be a very real problem, as can undercooling due to a defective heater. Water control means total control and the aquarist will lose this without periodic checks. Temperature controller units, such as the one shown above right, are more than just a thermostat. First, the temperature of the water is accurately displayed in an easy-to-read LCD or LED window. More important, though, most of these units can be coupled directly to heating and/or cooling units so that at any time of the year the temperature can be compensated and brought under control. This is done by the use of a magnetic switching unit, which receives information from the temperature controller telling it to switch either the heater or cooling unit on or off.

These controllers are not cheap, but then again they can reduce the stress experienced by fishes and invertebrates due to continuous fluctuations in water temperature. The more that stress is reduced, the more chance you have of a successful aquarium. Any rapid or constant changes in basic water parameters will only serve to increase stress.

This temperature-control unit has a control range to cover both warm-space and cold-water aquariums.

pH (alkalinity)

Ideally 8.3
A dictionary gives the definition of pH as being: "the negative decimal logarithm of hydrogen-ion concentration in moles per litre, giving the measure of acidity or alkalinity of a solution." Thankfully, you don't need to become involved with the exact chemical reactions when the acidity/alkalinity of a solution is altered. When the pH rises from a value of 7 to a value of 8, for example, it means that its alkalinity has increased ten-fold. From this, it is logical to assume that abrupt or drastic alterations in the pH value in aquarium water will have a considerably adverse effect on the animals living in it. Constant control of the pH value in a marine or reef aquarium is required so that the fishes and invertebrates remain stress free. There are many inexpensive and accurate test kits available, and these usually consist of a reagent and test vial, along with some sort of colour-comparison chart to read your results against.

Meters that make the measurement of pH far easier are now widely available. They have to be calibrated periodically to maintain their accuracy, which involves placing the electrode in calibration fluid preset to a given pH value so that the necessary adjustments can be made to the meter.

If you are intending to incorporate a calcium reactor in the aquarium system for buffering purposes, it is best to use a pH control unit. These may be preset to a particular pH value, and they electronically control precise doses of calcium carbonate entering the water.

Carbonate hardness (KH or dKH)

Ideally 9 to 12dKH
The carbonate hardness of sea water in a marine aquarium can be looked on as being the pH stabilizer. Total water hardness consists of carbonate and noncarbonate

hardness. The measurement of carbonate hardness is given in degrees of German hardness (dKH) or often KH. An increase in the buffering capacity of the aquarium water means an increase in the dKH and a more stable pH. The biochemical processes that are constantly taking place within an established or maturing system affect the level of carbonate hardness. These processes produce acids. In addition, algae and other reef-building organisms, such as stony corals, utilize calcium carbonate from the water. Subsequently, the buffer system collapses.

In the sea this does not happen. Natural sea water has a carbonate hardness of between 7 and 9dKH, whereas in an aquarium you should try to maintain a buffering capacity with a reserve, at some point between 9 and 12dKH. The amount of carbon dioxide present in sea water, as carbon dioxide gas and carbonic acid, determines the amount of calcium that is dissolved from calcium carbonate. This calcium then forms a bond with the carbon dioxide to produce hydrogen carbonate. When the amount of hydrogen carbonate increases, the carbonate hardness also increases. It can be seen from this that carbon dioxide (see below) plays an important role in pH stability.

Inexpensive carbonate hardness test kits are widely available. They usually comprise a test vial and a dropper bottle of reagent. With a measured amount of aquarium water in the vial, drops of the reagent are added until a colour change takes place – say, from blue to yellow. The number of drops required for this to occur indicates the carbonate hardness – so, for example, 9 drops is 9dKH.

Carbon dioxide

This gas is the end product of photosynthesis and is important for the growth of zooxanthellae algae. Many reef-building organisms, such as corals and algae, take carbon dioxide from hydrogen carbonate. During an aquarium's maturation period there is an overproduction of carbon dioxide because of the formation of bacteria and many other microorganisms. At this stage its introduction into the tank by artificial means is not only unnecessary but also dangerous, since an over supply of carbon dioxide will serve only to reduce the pH.

Because of the base composition of sea water, carbon dioxide is quickly absorbed, and with a pH of 8.2 to 8.3 there is little free carbon dioxide in the water. As has already been discussed, there is an unbreakable bond between carbonate hardness and pH, therefore removal of carbon dioxide will result in a rise in pH. However, in the aquarium direct sunshine accelerates photosynthesis, resulting in a fall in pH, which is one reason why a tank should not be too near a window. To clarify this, when carbon dioxide is added pH falls; when removed, pH rises.

Carbon dioxide reacts with water to produce carbonic acid and increases the carbonate and hydrogen carbonate ions. Therefore, the addition of carbon dioxide results in an increase in H^+ ions and makes the water more acidic. Carbon dioxide utilized in photosynthetic processes produces the opposite effect, although many forms of algae use the carbon dioxide from the hydrogen carbonate present in the water. Obviously, then, carbon dioxide is important to the general wellbeing and stability of the aquarium. We can also use carbon dioxide as a tool to stabilize the pH and provide a buffering reserve when used in conjunction with a calcium reactor. The idea that the addition of carbon dioxide can produce sporadic outbreaks of hair algae is not true, except in the case of its addition to an aquarium that is not fully matured. Carbon dioxide is extremely important for reef growth.

Calcium

Ideally 420mg/litre
The level of calcium in natural sea water on a coral reef is about 420mg/litre, and you need to replicate this as closely as possible in your aquarium. With newly mixed sea water there is no problem because there is enough calcium reserve built in to the mixture to provide this level, at the very least. Unfortunately, in an established aquarium containing invertebrates, such as reef-building corals, the calcium level is quickly depleted – by up to 15mg/litre per day. Stony corals need calcium, in the form of calcium carbonate, in order to build their skeletons and a high percentage of their skeleton is made up of this.

But it is not only the stony corals that are responsible for a lowering of calcium levels. Crustaceans, molluscs and even leather corals have a high requirement for calcium carbonate. So you must constantly be aware of the calcium level in your aquarium. This means periodic testing and the subsequent control of levels.

Calcium test kits are now available and most seem to give quite reliable results. A typical calcium test kit comprises a titration solution, a dry reagent and a fluid reagent. A small amount of aquarium water is put into a test vial and one of the solutions is added along with the dry reagent. Then drops of the second solution are counted into the test vial until a colour change occurs, usually from pink to red. Each drop is equivalent to 20mg/litre of calcium – for example, 21 drops = 21 x 20 = 420mg/litre.

The depletion of calcium adversely affects the buffering system of the aquarium water, and although you may have enough calcium in the tank, in the form of calcium carbonate in coral sand and rock, it is of little use in this case. In water with a pH of 8.2 or more, assimilation of calcium from calcium carbonate is very slow. Therefore, with an optimal pH of 8.3 it is practically meaningless. The idea of providing enough buffering capacity in an aquarium by simply using coral sand and rock is wrong. It does not work that way. A pH of 7.5 or lower is required and a pH of 6.0 would be even more effective. But fishes and invertebrates do not like this level very much – in fact, they would not survive long. For this reason, calcium needs to be replaced on a regular basis.

Buffering

Carbonate and hydrogen carbonate ions determine the pH stability of the water in a marine aquarium. This is generally termed the "buffering capacity". When the carbonate hardness sinks, it indicates a reduction in the concentration of the negative ions, which buffer any changes. Since about 1970 efforts have been made to restore the buffering equilibrium of aquariums with the use of buffering solutions or powders, with questionable results.

Most buffering agents are only emergency solutions to the problem – a quick repair rather than a cure. The problem lies in the fact that many aquarists cannot use enough of these buffering agents and the only other alternative is a major water change, which relieves the situation only for a certain time. The underlying fault in this way of thinking is that the sums just don't add up. When you consider it, in a fully stocked reef tank with live stony corals and other invertebrates, calcium is used at an alarming rate. If you take a conservative estimate and say that the daily need is only 8mg/litre, this means that in a 100-gallon (450-litre) aquarium the daily requirement for calcium would be 3.6g. The so-called "limewater", as it is sometimes known, is a solution of calcium hydroxide. The maximum that can be dissolved in water is 1.26g/litre. Since the idea is to use buffering solutions to replace water lost through evaporation (there simply is no other way) it would mean that, in the example of our 100-gallon (450-litre) aquarium, we would require an evaporation rate of more than ½ gallon (2 to 3 litres) each day.

Many aquarists use this system and report successes. Buffering in this way is only effective if the pH of the aquarium water is lower than 8.2, which has its own dangers. In a fully dissolved solution (1.26g/litre) the "limewater" will have a pH of 12.4. This will have a seriously debilitating effect on any fishes or invertebrates that come into contact with it before the solution is fully dispersed throughout the water: it will literally burn them.

In spite of this, there are still many adherents to this way of thinking, and as long as you take care when adding it to the aquarium, and there is superfluous carbon dioxide in the water, no great harm can be done. If, however, there is a shortfall in carbon dioxide in the aquarium, then a problem does occur. Calcium carbonate is produced, and if you have used a base medium of coral sand in the aquarium then it will cement together into an almost unbreakable mass. This is particularly dangerous if an undergravel

(sub-sand) filter or a plenum is in use. Calcium chloride may also be used as a buffering agent, but it is known to cause problems with alkalinity.

Calcium reactor

This is perhaps the only item of high-tech equipment, other than a protein skimmer, to be recommended if you intend setting up a reef aquarium using the natural system. It offers a rather elegant solution to the problems of pH, carbonate hardness and calcium levels that have plagued the marine aquarium hobby since the early 1960s.

For the uninitiated, a calcium reactor consists of a diffusion chamber filled with calcium carbonate and a low-wattage circulation pump. There is an inlet to carry water from the aquarium into the diffusion chamber and a return outlet. The theory behind this system is that water is allowed to flow from the aquarium into the reactor, where it is circulated repeatedly over calcium carbonate granules (coarse crushed coral or shell works just as well since these materials are made of calcium carbonate). The

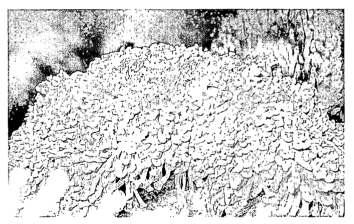

The growth-rate of stony corals, such as the hammer coral (Euphyllia ancora) shown here, have an enormous daily requirement for calcium. This 12-in (30-cm) aquarium specimen doubled its size and weight in just ten months.

idea is to retain the water for as long as possible in the diffusion chamber so that the calcium carbonate becomes soluble. But, as has already been explained, at a pH of 8.2 or more calcium carbonate will not become soluble, so it has to be given some help. This is done by injecting carbon dioxide gas from a gas bottle into the diffusion chamber at a slow rate. In effect this creates an artificial atmosphere within the reactor unit and produces a localized drop in the pH level to around about 6.0. And water at this pH can dissolve calcium carbonate, and does so quite effectively to produce calcium bicarbonate. Because calcium bicarbonate is easily soluble it can be ingested by corals and other invertebrates for conversion back to calcium carbonate, an important substance for their skeletal and shell growth. As this reverse reaction takes place, carbon dioxide is released again so that it can be utilized by zooxanthellae algae for photosynthesis.

The injection of carbon dioxide gas is carried out using an armature and reduction valve connected to a bubble counter. A bubble counter is simply a container, normally filled with distilled water, through which the gas flows producing bubbles in the liquid. It is installed in the gas line between the bottle and the calcium reactor and, by carefully adjusting the reduction valve, you can visually count the bubbles in the diffusion chamber.

The flow rate of water through the calcium reactor should be very slow and controlled exclusively from the inlet, and not the outlet. This stops any chance of a build-up of excess gasses within the reactor unit that could arrest the circulation of water through the pump housing. You can adjust the actual flow rate to allow a return to the aquarium of between 50 to 100 drops per minute. When this is coordinated with the input of gas through the bubble counter to be roughly the same rate, a maximum effect is achieved.

The results from a calcium reactor can be astonishing, and water returned to the aquarium can be expected to have values of 550 to 650mg/litre calcium and a carbonate hardness of between 20 and 30dKH. The diffusion

The photograph above shows a calcium reactor and bubble counter on the left with carbon dioxide bottle, armature and magnetic switch on the right. A pH control microprocessor is shown in the foreground.

chamber needs to be recharged periodically according to its size, as the reactor can consume up to 1lb (450g) of crushed coral per month.

These units can be controlled in several ways. For example, by increasing the water flow in and out of the reactor, greater amounts of calcium will be brought into the aquarium, but only if the flow of carbon dioxide is increased proportionally. Failure to do this will have the effect of reducing efficiency. Remember: high flow, more carbon dioxide; low flow, less carbon dioxide.

A calcium reactor does not need to be run continuously. At night, for example, aquarium requirements for carbon dioxide is not the same as during the day, and the calcium requirement also drops during at night. Because of this it is possible to connect the reactor into the light circuit, so that the unit is switched off with the aquarium lights.

But the best method of control is with a pH meter with a microprocessor. In this way, continuous monitoring of the pH is carried out automatically and, through a magnetic switch, the supply of gas to the reactor can be interrupted when the pH sinks below a given level. The calcium reactor not only makes the addition of buffering agents obsolete, it also stabilizes the pH to a great degree.

It would not be fair, however, to list these advantages without mentioning a major "disadvantage": stony corals grow very quickly, some doubling their size within a year; soft corals, such as leather coral, grow and spread and molluscs increase in size, building their shells from the freely available calcium. You may find that you have to take "cuttings" from your corals and give them to other hobbyists in order to make more room in your tank.

Phosphate

Ideally 0 to 0.01mg/litre
Phosphate is a compound of phosphorus and oxygen that all living things need in minute quantities. In natural sea water the level of phosphate is on average 0.01mg/litre, or less. But even in such small amounts it is still the major nutrient for corals. It cannot be looked on as being poisonous but if present in excess can lead to overfertilization of the water. Unfortunately this is very common in marine and reef aquaria and the cause can be traced back to its organic origins. Too much phosphate in the water leads to almost uncontrollable outbreaks of hair algae (*Bryopsis* and *Derbesia*) and slime algae (Cyanophyceae), which grow all too well under these conditions. There are many causes for an overproduction of phosphate and it may be that the root cause is a combination of many different things. The major cause is overfeeding by enthusiastic aquarists. However, when plants, plankton and other organisms die off, phosphate is produced. Detritus is another major cause and all these examples have an organic base. There are other ways that phosphate can

be inadvertently introduced into an aquarium and these could be termed inorganic. Most of the commercially produced sea-salt mixtures are phosphate free but there are still products available that are not. Make sure that the words "phosphate free" are stated clearly on the packaging. For example, a lot of activated charcoal currently available has a high phosphate content. If you are not sure if a product contains phosphate or not, place it in a bucket of water for an hour or so and then do a phosphate test.

Phosphate test kits are inexpensive and easy to use. A test vial is normally provided, which you fill with a sample of aquarium water. Reagents are then added and agitated. After a timed period, a colour reaction develops that you then compare with the colour chart supplied as part of the test kit.

When phosphate is bound to organic waste it can be removed using a protein skimmer. Biological filtration has no effect, except where oxygenated water is trickled over a bed of calcium carbonate. This method of phosphate removal is effective only when the calcium carbonate bed is periodically replaced. Iron may also be added to the aquarium to reduce phosphate to iron phosphate, which is inert. But by far the best way of reducing phosphate levels is to lower both the stocking and feeding rates of the tank.

Ammonia/ammonium

Ideally omg/litre
When the aquarium is going through its maturation or cycling phase, ammonia is often present in quantity. It is one of the intermediate stages of mineralization and nitrification. In an established tank, though, no ammonia should be detectable. Ammonia and ammonium always occur together and, depending on the temperature and pH of the water, ammonia can change into ammonium, and vice versa. Ammonia is highly toxic to fishes and invertebrates, but as the pH is lowered below 8.3 more and more of it changes to ammonium. In this form, it is relatively harmless and is used by many invertebrates and algae as a nutrient. It is important to remember the ability of ammonia/ammonium to interchange, especially with regard to the introduction of fishes to an aquarium.

Ammonia test kits measure the total ammonia present in an aquarium (ammonia + ammonium). The testing procedure is the same as that for phosphate (*see above*).

Nitrite

Ideally omg/ litre
Nitrite is normally present only in any quantity in a newly set up aquarium. Long-term exposure to levels of between 0.2 to 0.5mg/litre are damaging to fishes and invertebrates, with some species not being able to withstand levels above

0.1mg/litre Quantities higher than this are lethal. When a fish is suffering from nitrite poisoning it will swim around with folded fins clearly displaying breathing difficulties, which can be identified by the increased rate of gill movement (gill beat). The stricken fish may hang at the water surface and may occasionally give a short wild dash around the aquarium. The fish is, in fact, suffocating because the excess nitrite in the water causes its blood haemoglobin to change to methhaemoglobin.

Haemoglobin is the red oxygen-carrying substance in the blood, whereas methhaemoglobin is unable to carry oxygen. Invertebrates suffering from nitrite poisoning exhibit various symptoms. Sea anemones will expel their stomachs out through their mouths and in severe cases the basal disc will perforate. Corals remain closed and the polyps begin to die off. Other invertebrates simply expire without showing any symptoms at all.

*Angelfishes, such as this emperor angelfish (*Pomacanthus imperator)*, are unable to withstand any measurable level of nitrite.*

Nitrite test kits are available from most pet stores and with a newly established aquarium you should test the water daily. Once the tank has fully cycled, a weekly test is enough for the first half year; thereafter, only occasional checks are necessary. Nitrite can be removed by the use of ozone, which will also hinder the production of nitrate. But this is only a prophylactic treatment and in any case once the aquarium filter system is functioning bacterially, nitrite levels will fall naturally. On the rare occasion where nitrite levels rise again in an established aquarium, it is usually an indication that all is not well with the bacteria cultures in the filter. Other reasons could be a blocked filter, or it may be that a larger fish has died hidden behind the aquarium decoration. In such cases, the cause of the problem must be found and immediately rectified.

Nitrate

Ideally less than 3mg/litre

Nitrate is the end product of nitrification and some fishes can withstand levels of up to 550mg/litre for short periods of time. Nevertheless, in a reef aquarium nitrate should be kept to an absolute minimum. At levels of only 30 to 40mg/litre, algae (such as *Caulerpa* spp.) will begin to die off and invertebrates at even lower levels. Nitrate stops cell development in fishes and invertebrates and even some of the less delicate fishes are uncomfortable when the nitrate in the water rises above 30mg/litre.

Weekly checks should be made using a nitrate test kit. These are inexpensive and most pet stores stock them, but unfortunately many of them are also inaccurate. In a study recently carried out, 35 kits from various manufacturers were tested under controlled conditions, using solutions with known and calibrated levels. Only four of these test kits gave the correct readings. Two failed, even after repeated tests, to give any reading at all. All the other kits read too high; none gave a low reading.

The reason for the latter result could be that manufacturers have gone too far in their endeavours to produce a product that is safe to use. Added to this are the tight government controls that force manufacturers to re-place or reduce the amount of poisonous substances used in test kits. This has resulted in amounts being so reduced that the test kits no longer give accurate readings. You should be aware of these shortcomings when purchasing a kit and, if necessary, consult an established dealer or ask the advice of an experienced marine aquarist about which kit is the most reliable to use.

As an alternative, test strips can be used. These are small plastic strips with reaction zones on them. They have the advantage of being quick and easy to use and they are fairly accurate. The end of the strip containing the reaction zones is immersed in the aquarium for a period of about a second. After this, the colour is allowed to develop for a further 60 seconds, after which time it can be compared with the colour chart supplied with the product.

Redox

Depending on pH value, ideally 350mV

Redox measurement is used to determine the pureness of aquarium water – that is to say, the degree of freedom from contaminants. The term "redox" is an acronym derived from "reduction" and "oxidization". In any chemical reaction where an electrolyte is involved, reduction and oxidization can take place. In a saltwater aquarium, this is especially so. As a basic explanation of this, when a substance gives off electrons to another substance it can be said that it has oxidized. The receiving substance of these electrons can be considered as having

been reduced. Reduction and oxidization always take place together, since no substance can donate electrons from its atomic structure without there being a receiver for them, and vice versa.

In the study of aquarium technology, the importance of reduction and oxidization is now understood and is used as a means of testing water quality. This is carried out with a millivolt (mV) meter and a specially constructed electrode, normally platinum coated, which you immerse in the tank water. In this way, you can test its reducing and oxidizing capabilities with the result being given in millivolts. This represents the potential difference and is considered to be the "redox potential". In effect, the cleaner the water, the higher the millivolt reading.

The measurement of redox is not only dependent on the temperature of the water but also on its pH. In this respect, however, the difference in the redox potential of a given liquid at 25° and 27°C (77° and 81°F). is so small that in a tropical aquarium temperature becomes meaningless for the purpose of accurate mV measurement. The pH value of the water under test, on the other hand, significantly influences the redox potential. A rise in the pH will result in a fall in the mV reading.

Drinking water has a redox potential of between 250 and 325mV. A marine aquarium would normally be expected to have a redox potential of between 200 and 350mV, depending on water quality. A reading of 200 to 250mV would be considered a moderately functioning aquarium system, whereas a reading of 350mV or higher is excellent. Oxygen also plays an important part in the measurement, and a well-oxygenated aquarium will give a higher reading than one that is poor in oxygen. In a denitrification filter, however, negative values can be expected, due to the absence of oxygen. In this case, typical readings would be -50 to -200mV. If the redox potential falls below this level to, say, -300mV, this means that all the nitrate has been used in the filter and the bacteria are now starting to breathe sulphate. This is dangerous because by doing so the bacteria are producing hydrogen sulphide.

Redox measurement is not as easy to establish as most manufacturers and dealers make it out to be. First of all, a redox reading cannot be taken from one minute to the next. The electrode needs to be in the water and the instrument switched on for at least a week or, better still, 10 days before an accurate measurement can be taken. Because of this, it is recommended that the redox control unit is installed permanently so that day-to-day fluctuations can be monitored. Then it can be seen that at feeding time, for example, redox potential often falls by between 5 and 20mV. Even cleaning the inside of the viewing glass can produce a temporary drop of 25mV.

Note that although the instrument is meant to measure the quality of the water, where dirty or polluted water lacking in oxygen will result in a low mV reading, if the electrode is not kept clean it will give a high reading.

Because of this, if you have purchased a redox meter check that the electrode is clean at least every two weeks. The sensor tip of the electrode should be wiped with a tissue or a soft lint wad – rigorous scrubbing may damage it beyond repair.

You must bear in mind that the redox value alone is, from a scientific point of view, without foundation – you need to take into account both the pH and the redox potential. This is not only easier to understand but is also a good deal more precise. This measurement is known as the rH value and is calculated as follows:

$$rH = \frac{mV}{29} + (2 \times pH) + 6.67$$

(Baumeister 1990)

As an example, if we take a redox reading of 285mV in an aquarium with a pH of 8.3 we can calculate the rH value as 33. To illustrate this, when the actual readings are substituted in the formula we have:

$$rH = \frac{285}{29} + (2 \times 8.3) + 6.67$$

$$= 9.82 + 16.6 + 6.67$$

$$= 33.09$$

(which is then rounded to the nearest full number – 33)

To see results of these calculations in an easy-to-digest form, consider the following table:

rH Value
0 to 9 – heavy reduction
0 to 17 – light reduction
8 to 25 – neutral
26 to 34 – light oxidation
35 to 42 – heavy oxidation

(Baumeister 1990)

Strontium

Ideally 8mg/litre
Strontium is present in natural sea water in quantities up to 10mg/litre. This substance plays an important role in the formation of coral reefs in that all stony corals require it for the production of their skeletons. Strontium, along with calcium carbonate, is used in their construction.

It is obvious from this that there should be enough strontium present in a reef aquarium to permit stony corals to grow and develop and to continue to build their skeletons. Unfortunately, the strontium in synthetic

seawater mixtures is very quickly used up and has to be periodically replaced. In the past, this was always achieved by the addition of trace element solutions, but the difficulty with this method of tackling the problem is that the additives cannot be accurately controlled. In many instances, for example, the quantities or composition of these mixtures is not even listed on the packaging or bottle. This makes it a completely unsatisfactory hit-and-miss affair. If you consider that, after a period of about a month, even freshly mixed sea water in a reef aquarium will be practically devoid of strontium, then you will realize just how important it is that you add this element.

You can add strontium to the aquarium water in the form of strontium chloride. There are many commercially produced preparations on the market, but you can easily mix it yourself, and this works out a lot cheaper. For ease of calculation, metric measurements have been used here. Strontium chloride is available from pharmacies and you need to mix it with distilled water at the rate of 100g per litre. This is your basic trace solution.

From this solution, you need to add it at a rate of 1ml per week for every 100 litres of aquarium water (250 litres of aquarium water = 2.5ml per week, and so on). It is important not to exceed this dose, however, since the careless addition of strontium can do more harm than good. After a short period, the effects of the strontium solution can be seen on the corals, which will start to glow with good health.

Iodine

Ideally 0.5mg/litre
Most trace elements are introduced automatically as a by-product of the feeding regime. However, if a protein skimmer is in use it will quickly remove iodine from the water. In addition, if ozone is in use, iodine will be almost instantly oxidized. Since this substance is also important for reef growth it should be added back in to the aquarium on a regular basis. Soft and leather corals, crustaceans and fishes all benefit from its regular addition, as do stony corals. The growth of certain algae, such as the red and brown microalgae and red macroalgae, is also enhanced when iodine is added to the aquarium water. As an example to illustrate this point, consider an established aquarium containing a good growth of macroalgae, such as *Caulerpa* spp. and microalgae such as the red or brown calcareous species. Suddenly, and for no apparent reason, these algae start to die off. This is a typical indication of a serious lack of iodine.

Commercial additives are available from most aquarium dealers, and these are based on either potassium iodide or sodium iodide. Either will repair the iodine deficiency in the aquarium water, provided you follow manufacturer's instructions exactly.

CAUTION: Do not attempt to mix these chemicals yourself. Potassium iodide is extremely poisonous and should be kept out of the reach of children.

Iron

Ideally 0.05mg/litre

In natural sea water the iron content can vary between 0.02 and 0.1mg/litre. This element is important for the growth of algae, including zooxanthellae. The zooxanthellae are, in turn, required by various corals, anemones and many other invertebrates, such as bivalve molluscs of the genus *Tridacna*. It can be said, therefore, that iron in small quantities is a significant factor in reef growth. Macroalgae, such as *Caulerpa* spp., absorb iron into their cell structure, becoming deep green in colour as a result. When all the iron has been used up in the aquarium, the colours of these algae will gradually fade and then they will start to die off. To prevent this happening, and to maintain an iron level of about 0.05mg/litre in the tank, iron must be added to the aquarium water in the same way as strontium and iodine. Most aquarium stores stock seawater additives such as trace element mixtures, but once again the specific composition of these products is usually vague. It is better, therefore, to purchase a solution containing only iron.

Iron test kits are easy to use and usually contain just one reagent, which you add to a sample of aquarium water. The test vial is set aside for some minutes to allow the colour to develop, after which time you can compare it against the colour scale provided. If the iron content is under the ideal level, extra iron should be added. If, though, the iron content is too high for some reason, then a partial water change may be necessary in order to reduce this. Testing should be carried out periodically, and also before and after the use of iron additives, because too much iron in an aquarium can cause as many problems as too little.

The next step

When your set-up is fully cycled and mature and the water quality is optimal, the time is right to stock the aquarium with fishes or, in the case of a reef aquarium, with fishes and invertebrates. If you are a beginner you will no doubt have thought about this, read books and made frequent visits to dealers. You will have sought advice and will have a rough idea of the species you wish to keep. Experienced and careful aquarists are normally pragmatic in their choice, knowing that any failure at this stage can cause problems later. They know that it is no use planning and then, in the end, taking the next best thing simply because a fish or invertebrate is out of stock or temporarily unavailable. A thoughtless purchase at this stage can bring incompatibility problems later.

There are many examples of incompatibility and it is better to inform yourself of the specific needs and habits of the fishes or invertebrates that you wish to have in your aquarium. To give just a few examples, though, it is no use including a sea urchin in the set-up if you wish to have a lush growth of macroalgae or even red calcareous algae. Sea urchins are notorious "lawn mowers", which, when the macroalgae have been happily harvested, will proceed to rasp away at the living rock, expertly removing any traces of the calcareous algae as well. A fish whose main diet in nature consists of coral polyps should obviously not be purchased with the intention of including it in a reef aquarium. Many fishes are strongly territorial and will often fight to the death in order to protect their chosen terrain. Predators, such as groupers and scorpionfishes, will be pleased by the addition of small reef fishes in their tank but feeding in this way can prove to be an expensive business. Even stony corals, if placed too close to one another, will fight in their own special way until one of them succumbs.

These examples should serve to illustrate the need to plan the stocking of your marine tank and not be side-tracked by a dealer's attractive new arrival.

Stocking with fish and invertebrates

Most natural coral reefs swarm with fishes, and although they have a great deal more swimming space in their natural habitat some of the smaller species rarely use this, except perhaps when fleeing from a predator. A reef aquarium should reflect this and should have at least some fishes. Unfortunately, some experts recommend an

*The maroon clownfish (*Premnas biaculeatus*) is an ideal beginner's fish for a reef or fish-only aquarium set-up.*

*The eight-banded butterfly (*Chaetodon octofasciatus*) is a delicate fish that should not be kept with other fishes of a pugnacious nature.*

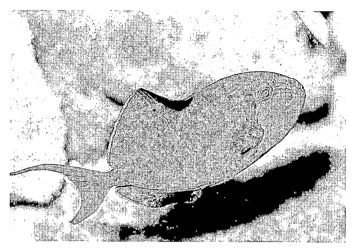

*The red-toothed triggerfish (*Odonus niger*) is an ideal specimen for a fish-only aquarium, since it is surprisingly peaceful by nature.*

aquarium comprising only invertebrates where fishes are looked upon as being merely a problem.

Fishes are an important element of a saltwater aquarium. They are attractive, colourful and bring movement and extra interest to the aquarium. They are the torch bearers for this hobby, attracting newcomers who sometime find their colours alone irresistible. Without fishes, an aquarium is not complete.

In a reef aquarium where soft and stony corals are pre-dominant along with zooanthids, the interaction between the various lifeforms is finely balanced. In this situation, the fishes play a secondary, or complimentary role. Too many fishes produce too much organic waste and the system is put under pressure, so stocking levels are smaller in order to prevent gradual build-ups of nitrate, which will only upset the water chemistry.

A marine aquarium can be completely devoid of invertebrates, but this would be as unnatural as having plastic corals, a sunken galleon or a deep-sea diver. It is a far better idea to have live rock with a few hardy invertebrates that can withstand higher nitrate levels. These, along with a mixed community of colourful fishes, can be an attractive and interesting alternative to a reef aquarium. In this type of aquarium set-up, low nitrate levels are not so important and the accent is on the fishes, whereas it is the invertebrates that take on the secondary role to complement the general effect.

In the past few years, stocking with fishes and invertebrates has been developed by some hobbyists into something of an art form, with fishes chosen for their colours to complement the living room decor. Others stock their aquariums with a mixture of what was available at the time in the dealer's tanks, and this disordered method sometimes has a certain charm. The enthusiast will try to purchase animals and fishes that are to be found together in their natural habitat, creating an aquarium that portrays a particular geographic zone, such as the Caribbean.

So, by this stage you should have decided which fishes and invertebrates you intend to keep. The stocking levels for fish are given in the accompanying table (*see below*) and have been tried and tested. If you exceed these limits you run the risk of losing stock at some later date.

Maximum fish-stocking levels

Reef aquarium
4in (10cm) of total fish length per 22 gallons (100 litres) of aquarium water.

Marine aquarium (with selected invertebrates)
6in (15cm) of total fish length per 22 gallons (100 litres) of aquarium water.

Marine aquarium (fish-only)
8in (20cm) of total fish length per 22 gallons (100 litres) of aquarium water.

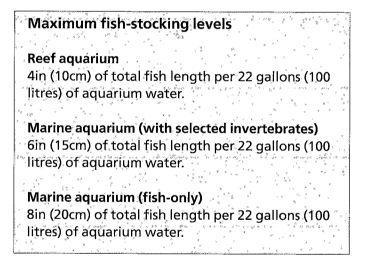

*The spotted boxfish (*Ostracion cubicus*) is suitable only for a fish-only aquarium with other peaceful tank-mates.*

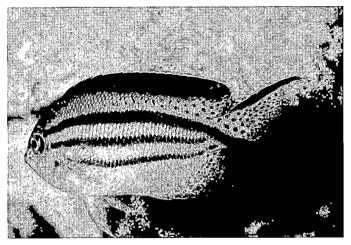

*The lyretail angelfish (*Genicanthus lamark*) is an ideal choice for a reef aquarium. It does not grow too large and it will not harm any invertebrates.*

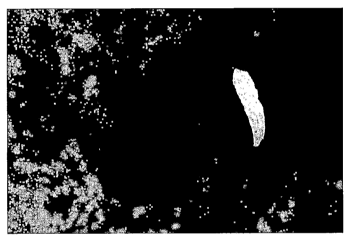

*The fire clown (*Amphiprion melanopus*) is a good choice for a reef aquarium, but it grows aggressive and territorial with age.*

Osmosis

When a semi-permeable membrane separates a low-concentration solution from a high-concentration solution, water molecules will move through the membrane, from the low to the high solution, in an attempt to equalize it. At the same time, the salt ions will move in the reverse direction, from the high to the low solution. This process is called osmosis.

A fish is composed mainly of water and it is swims in water, the two solutions being separated by the outer confines of the fish itself. Its body walls and gills function as semi-permeable membranes. In the case of a freshwater fish, its body fluids contain more minerals than the surrounding water, so energy is used to prevent the water flooding in through its body tissues. In order to retain the correct balance of body fluids, as the fish absorbs water it must excrete abundant amounts of weak urine. A saltwater fish is entirely the opposite. Its body fluids are a weaker solution than that of the surrounding water and it uses energy to stop its body fluids from flowing out into the water. To do this it must drink copious amounts of water and produce only a little but very concentrated urine. As it drinks, specially developed cells in the kidney and gills of the fish extract the salt. The way that fish control the balance of their body fluids is called osmotic regulation. It is important to understand this and to bear it in mind when introducing marine fishes into your aquarium. If the tank water has a different density to that in the transport bag containing the fish then osmotic shock will occur unless a gradual transfer is undertaken. If not, you could lose the fish or, at the very least, create undue stress and so weaken the fish and make it prone to disease.

Choosing fishes and invertebrates

Dealers' reputations are based on the quality of the items they sell and on the service they give. Novices should not be afraid to ask for advice. Fishes should be chosen with care. Any specimens with signs of disease should be left well alone. A distressed fish often loses its natural body colours and if the cause is not just a bullying tank-mate, it could be an indication of something more serious. Fishes with visible damage, such as lesions on their head or body, will often develop infections from which they may later die. You should not choose these either. The fish you select should be fat, healthy and feeding. But don't ask to see it feeding, since this could cause transportation problems – a freshly digested meal will usually be excreted into the transport bag on the way home. This will increase the ammonium content of the water and dramatically lower pH. Instead, you will need to take the dealer's word for it. Fishes that are not feeding and those that have a pinched or emaciated look should be avoided, as they will probably give you problems once you get them home. Look carefully before buying; watch the fish and take your time. Only then will you make the correct decision.

Assessing the health and quality of invertebrates is much more difficult but the following guidelines may be of some help.

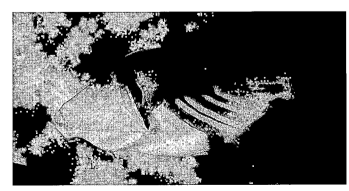

*This emaciated triggerfish (*Rhinecanthus aculeatus*) was probably the victim of cyanide poisoning during collection. It died a short time after this photograph was taken.*

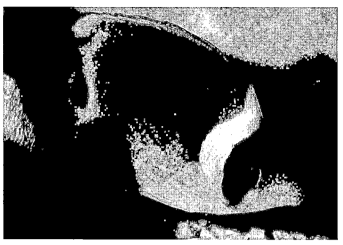

This butterflyfish (Chaetodon lunula) is in a state of shock, as can be seen from its colours. It would probably not survive the transfer to another aquarium at this stage.

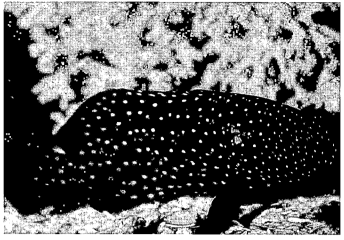

The jewel grouper (Cephalopholis argus) shown here has several lesions on its sides, presumably from its capture. These can lead to problems of disease later.

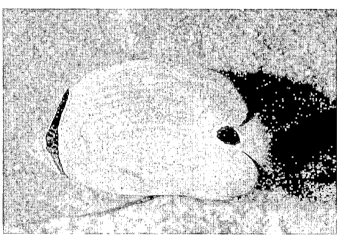

This fat and healthy coral butterflyfish (Chaetodon plebius) was photographed in a dealer's aquarium.

Sea stars, such as this Fromia sp., should be free of lesions and light patches, which could indicate infection.

- Sponges should always be kept fully immersed in water, otherwise they may lose their siphoning capabilities and subsequently die. It is important that the dealer's assistant also understands this. It is no use selecting a healthy specimen only to see it being lifted out of the holding aquarium dripping with water and then placed in a bag of water again.
- Sea anemones should have no column or basal disc damage and certainly no artificial colouring induced by dyes. They should have all their tentacles fully extended but it is not a drawback if its zooxanthellae, which are responsible for its natural coloration, have evacuated the anemone, since this often happens during transportation. This bleached look is only temporary and when the anemone has settled in to your tank under strong enough lighting it will soon return to its normal colouring once more.
- Sea urchins should not be shedding spines, although long-spined urchins often break off their brittle spines during their wanderings around the aquarium.
- Sea stars should not be patchy in appearance or have

lesions; these are signs of disease. Crinoids or feather stars should be sitting steadily on their "holdfasts" and not be hanging limply.
- Healthy leather corals periodically shed their skin and give the appearance of being unwell, or even of having expired. This is an absolutely normal process and within a day or two will appear fully normal once more.
- Stony corals should be placed in the dealer's holding tank so that there is sufficient space between them to prevent one coral stinging another, thereby starting a chain reaction from polyp to polyp that could run through the entire coral head until it eventually dies. There should be no signs of hair algae on the coral head and no missing polyps.
- Sea whips and sea fans should be purchased free of any damage and, preferably, attached to a small piece of living rock. They should have all their polyps fully extended.
- Molluscs, when they are in a healthy condition, have their mantle fully extended. This point is particularly important when purchasing clams and cowries.

As a rule, if an invertebrate looks healthy and attractive then it probably is just that. But if you are in any doubt then it is better to leave it alone. Once your choice is made the dealer will place your purchases in polythene bags and top them up with compressed air for the journey home. If you have a long way to go, the bags should be topped up with oxygen instead of air. This will give them the best chances of survival. A polystyrene transport container is handy to have and for large purchases a dealer will often offer you import boxes free of charge. The aim is to prevent undercooling at this critical stage. If there is only a short way to go, place the fish and invertebrates in a carrying bag with dark sides and keep it closed during the journey. Avoid taking your purchases out in bright sunlight, as this will only induce undue stress.

Introducing fishes to an aquarium

Before a fish can be introduced into an aquarium it has to be acclimatized. There will probably be a difference in the specific gravity of the water in the bag and that in the tank. This has to be slowly equalized. If the fish has been in the bag for more than an hour, then the pH will have dropped dramatically because of the fish's excrement and urine in the water. This will be in the form of ammonium and does no permanent harm. However, a rapid increase in pH will cause the ammonium, by this time also in the body fluids of the fish, to change to ammonia. If this happens, the fish has little chance of survival. Experienced aquarists are sometimes guilty of making this mistake. Death may not be immediate – even a week or so later it could succumb due to a lowering of its natural resistance. Even if the dealer's tank has a pH of 8.3 you can be certain that when you arrive home two hours later the water in the bag will be a great deal lower.

The accepted advice for acclimatizing a new specimen used to be to float its bag in the aquarium until the water temperature inside and outside was the same. Then the bag was opened, its top rolled down and, over a period of about 30 minutes, water from the aquarium was allowed to enter the bag until the pH and specific gravity also equalized. After this, the fish was released.

This method is fraught with problems, not only because of ammonia, but also because the bag could partially collapse and trap the fish in a small space where its stress levels would rocket. Other fishes would approach and, seeing the distressed fish through the clear sides of the bag, would often bully it before its release.

The modern way to acclimatize a fish is to use a bucket or small plastic aquarium and immediately tip the contents of the bag into this. Then, using a ¼in (6mm) tube, such as that used with an air pump, water from the aquarium is siphoned, drop by drop, into this container. A small clamp on the tube can be used to control the speed

of the process, which should be carried out over a period of about 45 minutes until the fish is swimming in 90 per cent aquarium water. At this stage, and with the aquarium light switched off for the rest of the day, the fish can be coaxed gently out of the container and into the aquarium. With any luck, the next day the fish will feed happily. The transfer to the aquarium should not be done with a net as this can cause damage. Nor should you use your hands to effect a transfer. Warm, dry hands on the skin of a fish will strip the slime coating, producing the same effect of a major burn on its body.

Another way to acclimatize a fish into new surroundings applies only if the aquarium has no other inhabitants, and involves the use of a calcium reactor and carbon dioxide. Water is allowed to flow through the calcium reactor at a fast rate and the water is then gassed with carbon dioxide at a great deal higher rate than normal. Using this method, the pH of the water in the aquarium can be quickly and temporarily dropped to the level of the water in the bag. The gas is then turned off and if the specific gravity is the same in both waters then the fish can be immediately released without any further acclimatization. The whole process is over in a matter of minutes, and this way there is a lot less stress for the fish. Through strong aeration, or a combination of protein skimmer and trickle filtration, the carbonic acid in the water will gradually disperse and pH will slowly return to normal. A variety of wholesalers using this method have reported huge decreases in the mortality rates of freshly imported fishes.

Acclimatizing invertebrates

Most invertebrates can be acclimatized using the drop-by-drop method, described above for fishes. Since invertebrates are not subjected to stress in the same way, however (a stony coral cannot be bullied), they can also be floated in the aquarium and acclimatized gradually. Often the bag is too heavy and will sink because the invertebrate is attached to a large piece of live rock. This is no problem, simply clamp the top of the bag to the aquarium glass at the water's surface using the two parts of a glass-cleaning magnet. With sponges this is the best way, and they can be clamped slightly below the surface, allowing tank water to flow in a little. Most other invertebrates require the best part of an hour to acclimatize so do not be tempted to rush this stage.

Once they have been released into the aquarium, sessile invertebrates will have to be positioned according to their need for light. Place those with high requirements on the upper half of the reef substrate, while animals that prefer semidarkness should be placed in the entrance to a cave or under a shadowy overhang. Avoid placing these sessile creatures directly in the path of a powerful water pump, as they will not survive the constant battering for long.

Foods and feeding

Once the fishes have been settled in the aquarium they need regular feeding. With some exceptions, this also applies to invertebrates. The rule of thumb is that fishes should be fed sparingly once or twice a day, so that all the food is taken within about a minute. Don't allow food to settle to the bottom of the aquarium where it will remain uneaten. If this happens, then remove it at once, and thereafter feed the fishes even more frugally. In a reef aquarium, where there are only a few fishes, another rule applies. There is usually enough natural food in this type of set-up so that feeding may be required only every second or third day. In this case, though, it is the invertebrates that should be fed and here there is no hard and fast rule.

Types of food

There are many types of food that can be given to fishes, but most of them fall into four main categories.

Flake and granulated food These are commercially prepared foods especially for marine fishes and there are many varieties available. They are an ideal supplement to the live or frozen foods that should form the staple diet of marine aquarium fish. Both flake and granulated foods normally contain up to 1 per cent phosphate, which, in the event of overfeeding, makes it a very good microalgae fertilizer. Nevertheless, they are rich in the protein, carbohydrate, fat and vitamins essential for energy and cell growth. Some medicinal flake foods contain malachite green chloride, which means that treatment for gill and skin parasites can be given orally. This has the advantage that treatment of these problems can be carried out in a reef aquarium without harm to the invertebrates. Its use, though, is very limited, especially in a saltwater aquarium.

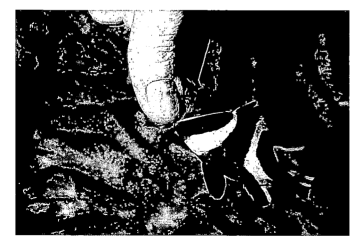

*Fishes will often take food from your hand like this small emperor snapper (*Lutjanus sebae)*, which is seen here being fed flake food.*

Frozen (frost) food The main diet of coral fishes should consist of a variety of frozen seafood and there are many from which to choose. Keep an assortment of these in your freezer to ensure that your fishes have a balanced diet. These foods are very convenient. They come in flat packs that can be easily broken up into daily sized portions. Recently, pop-out cube packs have come on to the market, and these are already separated into feeding portions. A typical assortment to keep in the freezer could consist of *mysis*, adult brine shrimp (*artemia*), krill, plankton, mussel, cockle, shrimp, squid, crabmeat and lancefish. Remember to thaw out frozen foodstuff before placing it into the aquarium. Place the food direct from the freezer in a plastic sieve and hold it under the cold-water tap for a minute or two. This method has the added advantage of washing away the phosphate-rich ice and frost coating that would normally find its way into the aquarium. You may find that as soon as your fishes see the usual plastic sieve they become agitated as you approach the tank.

Live food An occasional feeding of live food is a good idea for most carnivorous fishes, and there are some that, in the beginning at least, will accept only live food. As a rule, though, these fishes can soon be coaxed to take frozen food when live is not available.

Typical live foods that are often available from stockists are freshwater shrimp, *daphnia* (water flea), *mysis* and brine shrimp (*artemia*). Unlike frost foods, which are usually irradiated to prevent the transfer of disease organisms to an aquarium, there is always a small chance that fishes can become infected through being fed on live foods. When the food is from fresh water, wash it thoroughly before use. With seawater food, there is a greater risk of transfer, but even so the risk is so slim that it can be ignored.

Green foodstuff These consist of vegetable foods, such as lettuce, spinach and algae. Some fishes, such as surgeons and tangs, are herbivores, while many others are omnivorous, sustaining themselves on a mixed diet of algae and flesh. In order to satisfy fully the feeding requirements of these fishes, lettuce and spinach can be introduced if the aquarium alga is too sparse. The lettuce or spinach leaf should be blanched in hot water first and it is a good idea to clamp it between the two halves of a glass-cleaning magnet before placing it in the bottom of the aquarium. In this way the fishes can bite and tear at it much easier while it is anchored in one place.

The reason the leaves need to be blanched first is to eliminate the cellulose. Carbohydrate in the form of cellulose is found in the cell walls of plants and this is indigestible for fishes. Spinach is a very good substitute for algae and is high in iron and calcium.

Feeding new fishes

When you consider that most land animals are able to convert only about 10 per cent of their daily food intake into body flesh, then you may be surprised to know that fishes can convert up to 50 per cent into flesh. Because of this, they require a high-protein diet. Often a newly bought fish will refuse to feed in the first few days. It is essential in this case to understand the reasons why a fish feeds in the first place. There are six main reasons and knowing these will help in encouraging it to feed and also in understanding why it is not feeding.

The first and obvious reason is hunger. Lack of hunger can be caused by the end phase of a disease or by shock and fright. But it can also be caused by sodium cyanide, a poison used in illegal catching. In this case, the digestive enzymes in the stomach of the fish are destroyed. This means that the fish's stomach remains full and the motor function "I am hungry" in the brain is not stimulated. Thus, the fish starves to death with a full stomach.

The second reason why a fish feeds is habit. On the coral reef at a particular time of day there may be a tide or current change bringing plankton-rich water to the fish, or it may have its own particular rock on which it grazes. These are no longer there when it is in an aquarium and so it may refuse food. You can overcome this problem by making your feeding strategy as attractive as possible for the fish. In this way, the fish must, in effect, alter its behavioural characteristics and this takes time and patience on your part, and hunger on the part of the fish.

The third reason is as a reflex action. This is usually caused by something moving in close proximity to the fish that, while perhaps no longer hungry, snaps at the morsel as a reflex. The lesson to be learned here is that moving food is much more attractive for the new arrival.

Curiosity is the fourth reason that a fish will take food. In this case a fish may not be hungry, or may even be in a state of shock. But if something nearby is wriggling or swimming, and if it is attractive enough, the fish will investigate. It will briefly take it into its mouth and spit it out again as if testing it and, if it tastes good, it will proceed to eat it, even if it is a live brine shrimp that it has probably never before encountered. The solution here is to use live food in various forms for a difficult fish in the hope that it is tempted to begin to feed. Once it does, it is then much less difficult to wean it on to frost foods.

The fifth reason why a fish feeds is competition. The new arrival may be the only fish in the aquarium or there may be only one or two small tank-mates, which, at feeding time, are unobtrusive. This new fish may be accustomed to having to compete for its food in a feeding commotion with others of its kind, or even fishes of other species. In an aquarium, this may be no longer the case. The answer here is obvious – what you need to do is add a few small, but hungry, tank-mates. They will create such a

*The Moorish idol (*Zanclus canescens*) is a difficult fish to encourage to start feeding again once it has been removed from its natural environment. This fat and healthy specimen grew to almost 9in (23cm) over a period of six years, eating almost any food that was offered.*

commotion at feeding times that the new arrival will be unable to resist competing for its share.

The sixth and final reason could be termed anger. In fact, fishes are incapable of anger in the way people know the word. Rather, it is a defence mechanism where feeding is triggered as a response to a threat. Some behaviourists would term this a reflex action. It sees something as a threat but it is provocatively small, so instead of driving it off, it simply eats it. A typical case is the salmon lure that is often used by anglers. A fresh run river salmon is not hungry; it is there to spawn. The salmon lure is usually a concoction of brightly coloured tinsel and feathers and it is unlike anything the fish has ever seen before. Yet it will strike at it and swallow it if it is presented in the right way. The moral of this is to make feeding times as provocative as possible for new arrivals.

Feeding marine invertebrates

There is no single feeding strategy that will satisfy all the invertebrate lifeforms you would normally encounter in a reef aquarium. In general terms, invertebrates vary from being scavengers, such as shrimps, hermit crabs and sea stars, to filter feeders, such as sea whips, sea fans and clams. Then there are creatures that can more or less sustain themselves from their own zooxanthellae, requiring little in the way of a supplementary diet. In addition, many invertebrate animals are propitious feeders, waiting for a favourable moment to strike at their intended prey

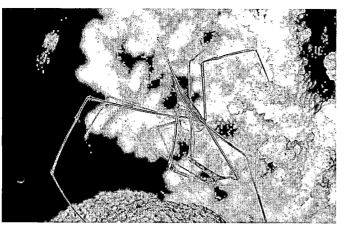

The arrow crab (Stenorhynchus seticornis) *is a typical scavenger from the Caribbean.*

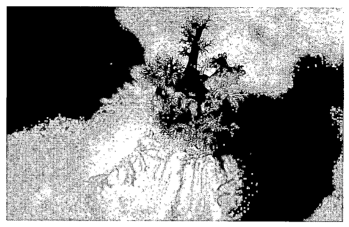

*The sea apple (*Pseudocolochirus violaceus) *is a well-known filter-feeding invertebrate.*

with the minimum of movement and effort. This group includes many sea anemones. Some invertebrates are grazers, feeding on the algal beds of the reef, and this group includes many molluscs, sea stars and sea urchins. Finally there are the active predators, such as the octopus and squid, that lie in wait for their prey or will actually hunt for it.

It can be seen from this that you need to adapt and improvise your feeding strategies depending on the types of invertebrate in your aquarium. You must utilize a wide variety of foods in several differing forms. Liquid suspension foods can be used for the filter feeders, for example, and particulate foods for the scavengers. The specific feeding methods of many invertebrates are dealt with in detail in the individual invertebrate descriptions later in the book.

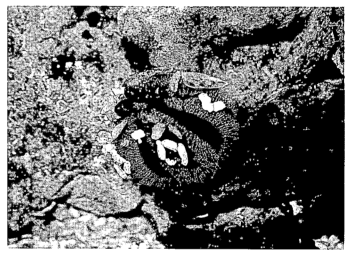

*This sea urchin (*Mespilia globulus*) spends much of its time grazing on the algae in an aquarium.*

Symbiosis

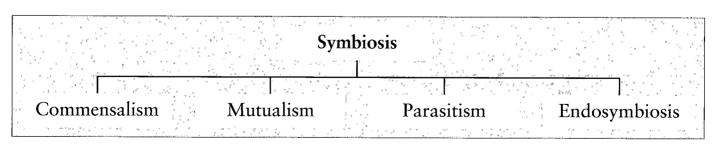

Symbiosis

| Commensalism | Mutualism | Parasitism | Endosymbiosis |

Symbiosis is a phenomenon that occurs when two unlike animal or plant species exist in close proximity to one another, and where one or both of them benefit from the association.

Most aquarists relate the word symbiosis to that special and well-known relationship that exists between the clownfishes (*Amphiprion* spp.) and their host anemones, but it is only a collective term. In fact, there are four forms of symbiosis that can be discerned on a coral reef, and all of them can occur in an aquarium. The term "symbiosis"

can thus be split into the four subforms shown in the chart here (*see above*) and explained below.

Commensalism

Basically this is a form of symbiosis that is harmless to the host animal, although the animal derives no benefit from the relationship. However, it is quite important to its symbiotic partner. A typical example of this would be a whale or shark with its remora followers. These fishes, notably *Echeneis naucrates*, follow and attach themselves to much larger fishes in the hope that morsels of food will be left for them to eat as the fish cruises through the water. Barnacles may also attach themselves to large, slow-swimming fishes for the same reason. The host derives no apparent benefit from this association but, nevertheless, it allows its followers to attach themselves to its belly, sides and back. These two examples occur in the open sea. In an aquarium, a small horseshoe worm (*Phoronis* spp.) can often be found attached to the parchment-like tube of a fireworks anemone (*Cerianthus* spp.).

Mutualism

This is by far the most common form of symbiosis on the coral reef as well as in the aquarium. Mutualism is the term used to describe the relationship between two animals where both species benefit from the association. For example, the cleaner wrasse (*Labroides dimidiatus*) performing its cleaning service to other fishes by removing the ectoparasites from them does so without any fear of being attacked or eaten. It will even swim into the mouth of a large fish to clean the gills and then exit through the gill opening. This species and many others, particularly when they are young, carry out this ritual cleaning action with impunity. That the host fish benefits from the service provided by having parasites and flukes removed from its body is unquestionable, but whether the cleaner derives nutrition from this is another matter.

It could be that the real benefit that the "cleaner" derives from this relationship is not so much to do with securing a source of food but rather a measure of protection. By performing this useful cleaning service, it protects itself from being eaten.

It is not only fishes that perform this cleaning service. Many species of crustaceans, such as crabs and shrimps, are known not only to act as cleaners for fishes, but some of them also live in a symbiotic relationship with sea anemones. Again, the benefit is that of protection, while the anemone host receives a cleaning service and often items of food supplied by its guest. Clownfishes of the genus *Amphiprion* are well known for their symbiotic relationship with anemones, but what is not so well known, and what is undoubtedly a rare occurrence in an aquarium, is the similar relationship of the domino, or three-spot, damsel (*Dascyllus trimaculatus*) with these large anemones.

The acclimatization period of this species to its anemone host is longer than that of the clownfish, and the contact time with the anemone appears to be considerably less. In addition, when a clownfish such as *Amphiprion melanopus* is given the choice between an anemone that has long tentacles, such as those of *Heteractis crispa*, for

example, and the short-tentacled *Stichodactyla haddoni*, it will always go to the long-tentacled species in preference. In contrast, however, the domino damsel will always form a symbiotic relationship with the short-tentacled *Stichodactyla* spp.

Parasitism

The name indicates exactly which form of symbiosis this is. When an animal lives to survive and multiply at the expense of another, it is said to be a parasite. Many, but not all, host animals, die as a result of parasitism. In an aquarium there are several species of parasitic dinoflagellates that can manifest themselves on fishes, often resulting in their subsequent death. Then there is a multitude of tiny animals and worms that periodically befall corals and other invertebrates, resulting in the destruction of cell tissue in the host animal.

Endosymbiosis

Endosymbiosis is the closest form of symbiotic relationship that can occur in nature. The most frequently

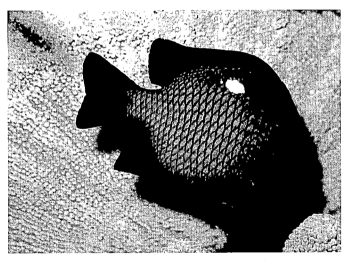

*The domino damsel (*Dascyllus trimaculatus*) can be seen here with its anemone host (*Stichodactyla haddoni*).*

encountered relationship is that which occurs between plant and animal. In this circumstance, the plant is actually intracellular within the host: in other words, it becomes part of the animal's metabolic, digestive or breathing system. Typical examples of this can be seen with *Zooxanthellae*. These, and *Zoochlorellae* are an integral part of some animals, so much so that without each other neither could survive.

General care

A certain amount of routine aquarium maintenance is required if you are to keep your fishes and invertebrates healthy. This routine includes the periodic addition of trace elements, such as strontium, iodine and iron, as well as regular topping up with water to replace that lost through evaporation. Since it is only the water that evaporates and not the salt (which becomes more concentrated), you need to use fresh water for this.

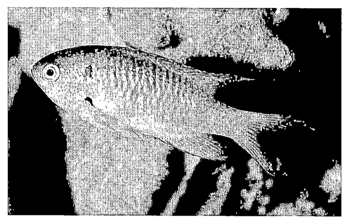

Even an aquarium containing hardy damselfishes, such as Neopomacentrus bankieri *shown here, requires a regular routine of maintenance.*

In the aquarium's first year, it is a good idea to do a daily head count of fishes and any that do not appear at feeding time should be located. In addition, carry out monthly checks on pumps and powerheads. The air pump filter wadding should be replaced if it is blocked or dirty. If limewood diffusers are being used, these will have to be replaced every six to twelve weeks. Most important of all, however, are periodic partial water changes.

Water changes

Many aquarists dispute the necessity for carrying out partial water changes on a weekly or monthly basis. The argument is usually: "My sea water is so good that I don't need to change any." This attitude is suspect simply because not enough is known about what happens to the aquarium water over a period of time, although we do know that it changes its composition. The point is that at present there is no way of measuring all the parameters and components of sea water to determine whether or not it is actually "so good". We know well enough that important elements and calcium in the form of calcium carbonate are utilized by the fishes and invertebrates, but what of the other components that make up the water? More than 70 trace elements make up natural sea water, elements such as titanium, cobalt, selenium, platinum, rhodium and gold. How much of these elements are important for reef growth? What is their level after the aquarium has been running for six months or more? We have no way of knowing. And until we do have a way to determine the total composition of the water in an aquarium, we must have a way of replacing those elements that are removed by the animals and fishes as well as those removed by protein skimming. The indiscriminate addition of a proprietary trace element mixture is not the answer.

A partial water change every month will ensure that all the valuable trace elements are regularly replaced. The amount should be restricted to 10 per cent of the actual water volume. Even better is when 2.5 per cent of the water volume is changed every week. This involves mixing the correct amount of salt and water the day before or, in some cases, the same day, depending on the salt mixture. This is then strongly aerated and, before its addition, the same amount of water is removed from the aquarium.

The water that you remove need not be thrown away immediately; it still has several uses. For example, you can use it for brine shrimp and marine rotifer cultures. Or you could also use it as cleaning water for live rock or coral sand. This material has its own bacterial culture, which, when washed in fresh water, is destroyed.

Whenever any water is mixed for an aquarium, it should not be used directly from the tap without first establishing how much the water is contaminated by nitrate and phosphate. In some areas, where lead and copper pipes are still used, there can be a lethal amount of other poisonous substances in the water. These amounts vary considerably from area to area.

Reverse osmosis units

Water can be treated effectively with a reverse osmosis unit, such as the one shown opposite. These units work by allowing water to be forced the wrong way, hence the name, through a semi-permeable membrane. The water pressure produced by the unit needs to be at least 3 bars in order to overcome the osmotic pressure. In this way, small, pure water molecules pass through the membrane, whereas larger molecules containing contaminants pass over the membrane. There are two outlets to these units, the first of which is the rejection outlet. The second outlet releases the purified water to be collected.

One of the drawbacks of using these units is that up to five times more water is rejected than is purified. Nevertheless, the rejection rates of pollution can be up to 98 per cent, depending on the type of membrane used. Rejected water is perfectly suitable to enter your household's grey water system, for use in the garden, for example.

There are two types of reverse osmosis unit differing specifically in the type of membrane they use. Units that use cellulose triacetate (CTA) membranes are usually cheaper, but they are not as efficient, having a pollution rejection rate of only 90 to 95 per cent. They also need to be run constantly to prevent the membrane from drying out and becoming brittle and porous, in which case they will then function only as a coarse sieve. In addition, these membranes will be broken down by bacteria over a period of time and have to be replaced.

The second type of membrane is far superior. It is known as the thin film composition (TFC) membrane. These units are more expensive but they have a higher pollution rejection rate (between 95 and 98 per cent). Added to this, they are a great deal more impervious to attack from bacteria and need only be replaced every three to six years, depending on whether or not prefilters are

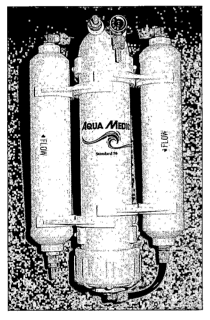

This reverse osmosis unit comes complete with sediment prefilter and carbon filter.

used. A good reverse osmosis unit will come complete with a sediment prefilter to remove large particles from the water before they can reach, and possibly block, the membrane. It will also have a carbon prefilter. This is important, since it will not only remove some of the heavy metals and larger organic molecules from the water but will also remove the chlorine. Chlorine is capable of ruining a membrane by making it porous. The use of a carbon prefilter considerably extends the life of the membrane.

Deionizing units

There are two types of deionizing units available, both of which involve the use of ion exchange resins. These resins are termed "anion", which removes the negatively charged ions from the water, and "cation", which removes the positively charged ions. These two types of resins form the basis of a deionizing unit.

In the first type, both resins are combined in one chamber and when they become saturated they have to be replaced. With the second type, two chambers are used and the resins are kept separate. The advantage of this is that the resins can be recharged using strong acid and base solutions. With mixed resins, this is not possible.

There are, however, several drawbacks with deionizing units. The first and obvious one is that the resins need to be continually replaced or recharged, which takes time and resources. Not so obvious is the fact that any contaminants, such as pesticides, that are neutrally charged, will not be removed. The units should never be used to absolute full capacity, since they could begin to release some of the contaminants they have removed back into the purified water. Their main advantage over reverse osmosis is that they are 100 per cent water efficient. Even so, they have never caught on in the aquarium world.

Some fish diseases

Practically all fish diseases that manifest themselves in an aquarium are totally unnecessary and can be avoided. They are, in the main, caused through human error and bad water quality.

In a well-matured aquarium with good water quality, no disease will break out – not unless the aquarist makes a mistake such as neglecting a fish's dietary requirements or introducing a new fish to the aquarium that is stressed. Time and time again, even experienced aquarists will accidentally introduce *Lymphocystis*, *Oodinium* or *Cryptocaryon* diseased fishes into their tanks and, within days, see that the diseases have disappeared by themselves without any treatment at all. The main cure for any fish disease is the fish's own immune system. After all, this has

been developed over many thousands of years to cope with disease organisms.

The major causes of disease in a marine aquarium are bad water quality, stress, incorrect diet, overstocking and, most common of all, stocking the aquarium before it has fully matured. The last point is obvious, since most disease problems that novices encounter occur in the first six months. After that, the tank will have settled down. The biggest mistake you can make is rushing things. Keep the water quality to a high standard and avoid obvious mistakes and you should have few disease problems.

No matter how much care you take, however, mistakes do sometimes occur, and the following diseases are the ones you are most likely to encounter.

Brooklynella hostilis, Brooklynella sp. (anemonefish disease, non-specific import disease)

DESCRIPTION: This is probably the most widespread and common disease in an aquarium. *Brooklynella* sp. are fast-swimming protozoans that can decimate a tank of fish within a few days. Very contagious, especially with newly imported anemonefishes (specifically *B. hostilis*), although similar species can attack most other newly transported fishes. Fast-swimming protozoans will attack any organic matter, including algae. In this case, *Caulerpa* sp. (such as *C. racemosa*) will turn a mottled white on the surface and subsequently collapse and die.

SYMPTOMS: Indistinct within the first 12 hours except for a slight velvety sheen on the sides of the fish. Thereafter, the victim shows signs of stress and restlessness. Fish may flick themselves against the substrate in the early stages. Later, the disease becomes obvious with the fish seeking out well-oxygenated water. At this stage, the victim releases body slime to try to get rid of the disease. This peels away in sheets and carries the disease to other parts of the tank.

CURE: Isolate the tank, nets, feeding implements and wash your hands whenever there is any contact with the disease. There are no commercially prepared cures available that effectively control this disease and it is a killer. Freshwater baths will kill a stricken fish. Remove all fish to a quarantine tank and try treating them with formaldehyde in combination with malachite green or methylene blue.

Cryptocaryon irritans (white spot disease)

DESCRIPTION: A parasitic ciliate protozoan, which goes through several stages in its lifecycle, including a free-swimming (swarming) stage. Very contagious.

SYMPTOMS: Small, white, pinhead-sized spots on the fins, head and body of the fish. Loss of appetite. In the later stages, clustering lesions appear on the fins, and there is an increased gill-beat rate and, finally, death.

CURE: Remove the affected fish to a freshwater bath and subsequently treat with a copper-based product.

Amyloodinium ocellatum (marine velvet, coral fish disease)

DESCRIPTION: A parasitic dinoflagellate protozoan, which is believed to be a type of alga. It goes through a free-swimming stage in its lifecycle. Extremely contagious.

SYMPTOMS: Dusting of peppery, minute, gold-brown-coloured spots on the sides, head and fins of the fish giving it a velvety appearance. There is an increase in gill-beat rate and the fish usually swims around with fins folded, occasionally flicking itself off the rocks in an attempt to rid itself of the irritation. Often fatal.

CURE: Remove the fish to a freshwater bath and subsequently treat with a copper-based product.

Lymphocystis (cotton wool disease)

DESCRIPTION: This is a virus infection that is seldom contagious. Although not always fatal, it is difficult to cure.

SYMPTOMS: In the early stages, small opaque lesions appear on the fins. These increase in size over a short period of time to become fluffy, almost cauliflower-like clusters on the fins and body of the fish.

CURE: This is very difficult. If the fish's own immune system cannot overcome it, the only alternative is to cut the nodule-like cysts out and subsequently treat the affected area with acriflavine.

Exophthalmus (pop eye)

DESCRIPTION: Considered not to be a disease but rather a symptom. However, it can also be caused by cyanobacteria entering the membrane of the eye or by bad "netting" of the fish.

SYMPTOMS: Very obvious swelling of one or both eyes, which become opaque. Loss of appetite and, in severe cases, it can be fatal. Recovery from this disease sometimes results in blindness in the affected eye.

CURE: Remove the affected fish to clean, mature sea water and reduce lighting to a minimum for 14 days.

Neobenedenia sp., _Benedenia mellini_ (gill and skin flukes)

DESCRIPTION: Small worm-like parasites that attach themselves to the skin and gills of a fish. In extreme cases this can prove fatal.

SYMPTOMS: Gills coloured pink instead of the usual bright red. Increase in respiratory rate, the fish will flick itself off rocks repeatedly in an attempt to displace the parasites.

CURE: Treat in a freshwater bath with the addition of methylene blue or formaldehyde-based products.

*This French angelfish (*Pomacanthus paru*) is suffering from a serious attack of marine white spot (*Cryptocaryon irritans*).*

General treatment

For disease organisms that have a free-swimming stage, such as gill and skin flukes, marine velvet or white spot disease, the use of a diatom filter can prove to be helpful, especially in a reef aquarium. This is because at the free-swimming or swarming stages the disease can be filtered out of the water.

Copper-based products

Copper-based products should always be used with extreme caution and never at all in an aquarium that contains invertebrates. Copper is lethal to most forms of invertebrates, even in minute quantities. It is a poison to fishes too, so it should only be administered as a last resort in a separate aquarium and always using a copper test kit to monitor the levels present in the water.

Freshwater bath

A freshwater bath can be prepared using a small aquarium or any other suitable container. This should be filled with 80 per cent fresh water and 20 per cent aquarium water to reduce as far as is possible undue stress. The pH is then raised to that of the aquarium by the addition of sodium bicarbonate. This will require roughly 1 teaspoonful per gallon (4.5 litres) but pH readings should be checked and carefully monitored. The temperature of the water should also be equal to that of the aquarium.

The affected fish is then gently eased into the water to induce an osmotic shock. Care must be taken at this stage to see that the fish's respiration does not become erratic. If this occurs, the fish should be immediately returned to its aquarium. It is quite normal for some fishes to respond by lying on their sides when placed in a freshwater bath, but their reactions should be closely monitored. At the least sign of difficulty the fish should be removed.

Osmotic shock has the effect of ridding the fish of the parasites, since many pathogens absorb water at such a rapid rate that they literally swell up and burst. A fish treated in this manner should never be left unattended nor should it be left in the water for longer than ten minutes. Most fishes begin to show signs of discomfort after only three to five minutes.

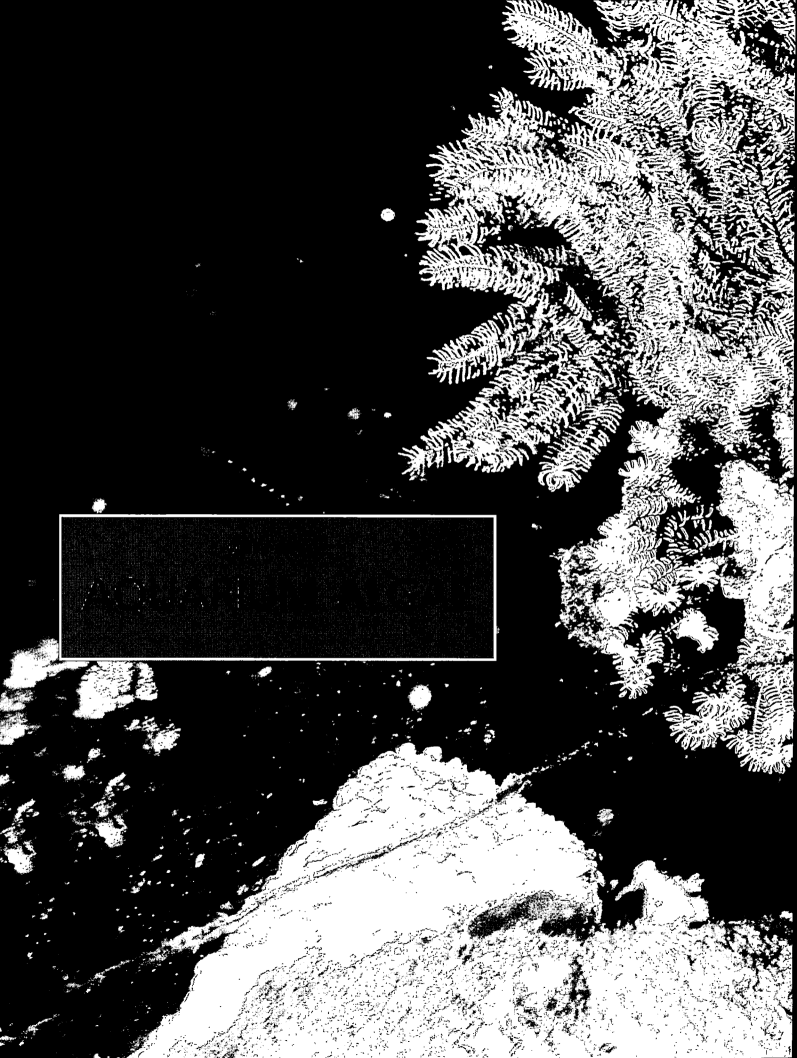

The role of algae

Through reading this part of the book you will quickly realize that algae species can be selected for enjoyment, decoration and usefulness in the aquarium, and should not be regarded as simply a nuisance that so often plagues the novice's tank. The phyla indicated in bold type in the chart here (*see below*) are of particular interest to aquarists. The chart is by no means complete, but it does list all the main phyla in the plant kingdom and the relative positions of these and the relevant classes in the phylogenetic development of the plants.

Of the higher plants, only one species is of interest to aquarists and that is covered at the end of the chapter. There are many forms of algae that are both suitable and attractive for marine and reef aquariums. The so-called "Holland" aquarium, which incorporates various algae, fishes and invertebrates, is a typical example. In this type of aquarium, the accent is on lush growths of various species of macroalgae. While this might not be everyone's idea of a reef aquarium, it does have a certain charm, even if it bears no resemblance whatsoever to the reef environment you might encounter in nature.

Various species of red algae (Rhodophyta) are highly prized by aquarists and some grow quite quickly. Light plays an important factor in the success of all algae in an aquarium, since light is a fundamental requirement for their photosynthesis. Unlike most plants, algae have no true root system. They have "holdfasts", with which they attach themselves to rocks and to the substrate, or else they have rhizoid-like appendages to anchor them to the sediment on the seabed.

Brown algae (Heterokontophyta), encompass many interesting and attractive species, such as *Sargassum* spp. Unfortunately they are not as often imported as most of the other macroalgae.

The plant kingdom

Kingdom	Phylum	Class
Plantae	Glaucophyta	Glaucophyceae
	Rhodophyta (red algae)	
	Heterokontophyta (brown algae)	
	Haptophyta	Haptophyceae
	Cryptophyta	Cryptophyceae
	Dinophyta	Dinophyceae
	Euglenophyta	Euglenophyceae
	Chlorarachniophyta	Chlorarachniophyceae
	Chlorophyta (green algae)	
	Bryophyta	Hepaticopsida
		Anthocerotopsida
		Bryopsida
	Trachiophyta	Psilotopsida
		Lycopsida
		Spenopsida
		Pteropsida
		Cycadopsida
		Ginkopsida
		Coniferopsida
		Gnetopsida
		Magnoliopsida

Higher plants

The entries in **bold** type are dealt with in detail in the following pages

By far the most popular form of algae with marine aquarists are the bright green macroalgae (Chlorophyta). Most beginners will attempt to keep *Caulerpa* spp. within the first few weeks of establishing a tank, but there are many other attractive species, some quite rare, that often turn up of their own accord when live rock is introduced. Others, such as *Halimeda* spp., are often sold attached to a small piece of rock.

Most aquarists are not content with just keeping fishes and plants. It is one of the peculiarities of fishkeepers that many have an almost irrepressible urge to know exactly which species of plant or fish they have in the aquarium and are never really content until they have positively identified all the species in question. In many cases, it is not possible even for experts to identify a particular species with any degree of accuracy. This is not because of missing information or lack of knowledge; rather, it is because the fundamental scientific research is not well enough informed or, in some examples, a particular group has not yet been fully researched. In the past, many aquarium books and other publications have fallen into the trap of doing what the aquarist does – guessing from photographs and descriptions. It is far better to admit that a species cannot be fully identified taxonomically than to simply give it the name from a species that looks similar.

In order that this book remains abreast of current scientific knowledge, in many cases a specific name and, in some instances even a generic one, have not been given. This is the accepted way at present and, although the missing information may cause you a degree of frustration, at least it does not add to the confusion and chaos that invariably results from misidentification.

Phylum: Rhodophyta (red algae)

This phylum is made up of two classes – Bangiophyceae, which encompasses five orders, and Florideophyceae, which contains 13 orders. Rhodophyta also contains some 600 genera encompassing well in excess of 5,000 known species. The algae in this group are commonly referred to as red algae.

Practically all of the members of the two classes are marine living and do not occur in fresh water. Some of the species can be found at depths of up to 900ft (274m) where little light can penetrate. The majority of these algae, however, are found at depths of up to 330ft (100m) where photosynthesis can take place.

The basic colouring of red alga is caused by the presence of beta-carotene, chlorophyll-a and phycoerythrin. The cell walls are made up of cellulose and pectin compounds along with, in some cases, calcium

Red algae

Phylum	Class	Order
Rhodophyta	Bangiophyceae	Porphyridiales
		Rhodochaetales
		Erythropeltidales
		Compsopononales
		Bangiales
	Florideophyceae	Acrochaetiales
		Palmariales
		Nemaliales
		Batrachospermiales
		Corallinales (= Cryptonemiales)
		Hildenbrandiales
		Bonnemaisoniales
		Gelidiales
		Gigartinales
		Gracilariales
		Ahnfeltiales
		Rhodymeniales
		Ceramiales

The entries in **bold** type are dealt with in detail in the following pages

carbonate. Where an alga is found to have calcium carbonate within its cell structure, it is known as a calcareous or coralline alga.

At the present time, the systematic structure of this phylum is in disarray. There are many conflicting theories and as yet too little in the way of taxonomic research. The situation is understandable to some degree, since, until recently, this type of research has played only a supporting role in our understanding of the environment. In particular, the coral reefs themselves have drawn the attention of marine biologists to the important part that some of these algae play in the formation of reef structure and reef growth. Yet it is in this particular group of red algae, the coralline and calcareous species, which play the most important part in the formation of the coral reefs, where the most confusion occurs.

The chart of red algae (*see p. 71*) is by no means complete and it deals principally with the red algae that are of concern to the aquarist interested a marine or reef aquarium. It is intended as a guide to outline the systematic organization of the various marine algae in the phylum Rhodophyta. It is also hoped that it will clarify some of the misunderstandings that popularly surround this complex group.

Class: Bangiophyceae

Of the five orders in this class, none regularly occurs in an aquarium environment – at least not so that you would notice them enough to want to know what species they in fact belonged to. For this reason, it is enough to mention species from just one particular order that may occur in a marine aquarium.

Order: Bangiales

Only one genus in this order is of interest to aquarists. This is the genus *Porphyra*, species of which may often be imported unintentionally on live rock. *Porphyra* species do not normally do well in an aquarium, although they sometimes appear to flourish for some months before eventually dying off. This is particularly the situation in a newly set-up aquarium, where algae often appear for a short time before disappearing, only to be replaced by another form of algae with a much hardier disposition. In any case, they are seasonal plants in their natural environment and usually reach their peak growth rate from September to May. Generally, the thalli are broad and compressed and similar in appearance to the green algae – *Ulva* sp. The thallus may be deep red to reddish purple and is very delicate and thin looking. While being of little interest to aquarists, *Porphyra tenera* has been an important foodstuff in Japan for more than 300 years. Nowadays *P. yezoensis* is cultured with considerable

success. Specially treated nets are spread vertically in the water to provide a surface on which the algae can settle and grow. After usually about two months, the algae can be harvested. In addition, China and Korea have also farmed *Porphyra* species as a foodstuff for many years.

Class: Florideophyceae

Red algae of this class are much more important to marine aquarists and many beautiful and decorative species are represented. The colours and forms of these algae can vary considerably, from pale yellowish-white to deep bluish-purple. They may be encrusting or branched and calcified, or they may be gelatinous and branched. Many of the species encompassed in the class are imported on living rock and will show up in an aquarium under ideal conditions, so if they do appear you need not take any particular care over them. In fact, some of the crustose coralline algae will inevitably occur in an aquarium under the correct lighting conditions. Others, however, are extremely difficult to obtain and cultivate, although they are abundant in the wild. This is usually because commercial collectors either overlook them or they simply do not travel very well in the confines of a polythene bag placed in an export box.

Of the 13 orders in this class, seven contain species that regularly occur in aquariums in one way or another. These orders are indicated in bold type in the chart already presented (*see p. 71*)

Order: Nemaliales

Members of this order have medium-to-large dichotomous branches. Some species have calcified thalli, which gives them a light-to-white toning. Others have small holes at each branching point and they may be calcified only at the tips of the branches. Some have a gelatinous feel about them and species are often multiaxial, throwing out branched thalli in the manner of small fountains. The form of the thalli can vary from cylindrical to flattened, and sometimes there are hair-like filaments covering the surfaces.

The larger species belonging to this order are attractive and are ideal for a reef aquarium set-up. They will grow well and form attractive growths that provide a colourful contrast in the aquarium when placed between corals and rocks. As a general rule, however, they require metal-halide lighting combined with blue or actinic fluorescent tubes in order to provide the ideal conditions for them to grow well and remain healthy. Special care is also required with regard to the aquarium's water conditions. Low nitrate levels and the correct water movement can often bring success with these algae.

Scinaia sp.

Family: Chaetangiaceae
Range: Tropical Indo-Pacific
Description: As far as marine aquarists are concerned this, and similar species, are well known. With this particular species, the alga forms thick, bushy growths with cylindrical thalli, which are light to dark red in colour. The branching is dichotomous and the thalli are gelatinous. The tips of the thalli are rounded and they form bushy growths in crevices on the substrata. A similar species, *Scinaia complanata*, which is light red in colour, is endemic throughout the Caribbean.
Aquarium suitability: Does well in an aquarium and when a calcium reactor is incorporated it is easy to keep and will grow quite fast. Like most, this alga requires strong light and good water circulation. *S. complanata* is one of the species ideally suitable for a Caribbean reef aquarium.

Galaxaura marginata

Family: Chaetangiaceae
Range: Circumtropical
Description: A lightly calcified alga that forms small, bushy mounds of loose compressed thalli. The dichotomous branches sometimes have faint lateral bandings with calcified tips. In the Caribbean this species can often be seen growing alongside the brown alga – *Lobophora variegata*.
Aquarium suitability: Ideally suited to aquarium conditions, this species will do well if provided with sufficient and strong enough light. When the water quality is optimal, such as in a reef aquarium, *G. marginata* will grow well and is long lasting. The calcified thallus tips are a good protection against the feeding habits of herbivorous fishes and invertebrates. Its greatest enemy is the sea urchin, which will rasp away almost any calcareous algae, including this one.

Order: Corallinales (calcareous/coralline algae)

There are so many conflicting theories, opinions and arguments concerning the systematic classification of this particular group of algae that it is not surprising that the average aquarist cannot hope to begin understand it. Furthermore, it would seem that no two experts can agree fully on the orders and how they should be presented. There appear to be three, or possibly four, different groups within this order, each with several families. In light of this, all that can done at present is to maintain the systematic status quo until the various revisions are a little more lucid.

   In general terms, it should by now be obvious that calcareous algae will not do well in an aquarium environment where there is a deficiency of calcium. Species from the order Corallinales utilize this substance for their growth and, in many cases, cannot survive for very long with out the presence of a calcium reserve in the aquarium water. This is best achieved by using a calcium reactor (*see p. 50*) in the system or by regular buffering of the aquarium water.

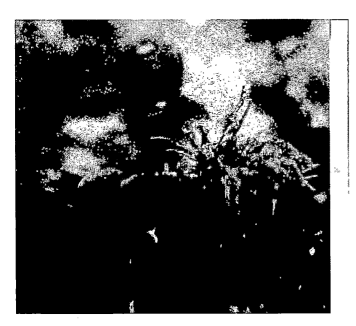

Jania sp.

Family: Corallinaceae
Range: Tropical Indo-Pacific
Description: This could be considered to be the Indo-Pacific version of a similar Caribbean species, *J. rubens*. There are, however, some differences. This particular species forms small, bushy growths that seldom exceed 1in (2.5cm) in diameter. The pink, dichotomous branches are often tipped with white due to the heavy calcification, and the joints are not as flexible.
Aquarium suitability: Grows well in an aquarium, given the correct conditions, but this is a very slow growth, which makes it an ideal alga for a reef aquarium. A combination of actinic and metal-halide lighting is required, however, along with regular pH buffering. When these parameters are fulfilled, this species will successfully adapt to tank life.

Amphiroa rigida var. *antillana*

Family: Corallinaceae
Range: Caribbean
Description: This alga forms pale, off-white clumps that are open and brittle to the touch. The heavily calcified thalli are thin, narrow and cylindrical in form. The branching is dichotomous but the joints are not so moveable as in other species in this genus.
Aquarium suitability: Because this species is found in shallow water at depths of less than 36in (91cm), metal-halide lighting is a necessity, and the alga should be placed in the upper half of the aquarium. The aquarist cannot hope to reproduce the natural light intensity found at this depth in an aquarium without the use of sophisticated lighting. Providing that there is moderate water movement and that there is enough calcium reserve available in the water, this species will do well.

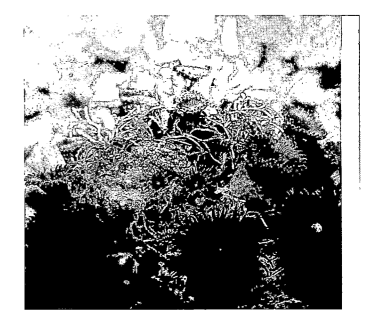

Hydrolithon boergesenii

Family: Corallinaceae
Range: Circumtropical
Description: This is an encrusting alga that can be of various colours, from pink, through red, to violet. This can be seen clearly in the accompanying photograph. It is found in most tropical seas at depths of 3 to 90ft (91sm to 27m) covering rocks and coral rubble.
Aquarium suitability: Often imported on living rock, *H. boergesenii* does extremely well in an aquarium. Even under fluorescent lighting, a good growth of this alga can be achieved once the tank is mature enough. Under metal-halide lighting it will soon encrust most of the aquarium, but it will not do any damage to delicate corals and other invertebrates. Once this alga has established itself on a rock, nuisance species of alga will not be able to grow there.

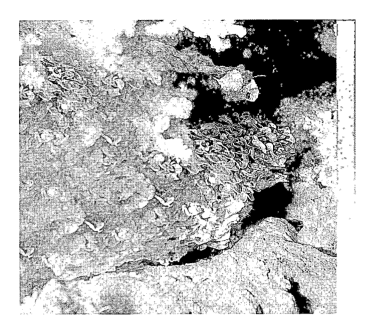

Mesophyllum mesomorphum

Family: Corallinaceae
Range: Circumtropical
Description: This is an important reef-building alga that occurs in both encrusting and conchoidal rhodolith form. The plates can be quite large and are often overlapping. They are usually pink in colour but the plate margins are fringed with white. In this form, they offer a haven to small animals and fishes by acting as breakers to the strong currents that may be present.
Aquarium suitability: Rhodolith-formed specimens are sometimes offered for sale if they are particularly attractive. This species does very well in an aquarium and will grow over much of the decoration over a period of time. Because of the lack of strong current in an aquarium, it is much more likely to develop rhodolith shapes. These are generally far smaller in size than those that occur on the natural reef.

Mesophyllum sp.

Family: Corallinaceae
Range: Central Indo-Pacific
Description: This species usually encrusts the substrata in the form of small pinkish platelets that are seldom more than ½in (1 to 1.2cm) across. Large, attractive growths can occur, particularly in reef channels and on reef crests. The best examples of this type of algae are frequently seen in Indonesia. The species is very similar to *M. mesomorphum*, but the general structure is more compact and the thalli are thinner. There is a great possibility that, although relatively common, this is an undescribed species.
Aquarium suitability: This fragile alga grows equally well under both metal-halide and fluorescent lighting. The important requirements for success with this species are supplementary actinic lighting and a strong water movement.

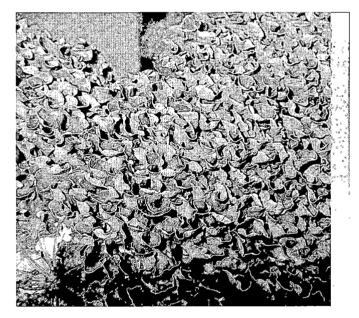

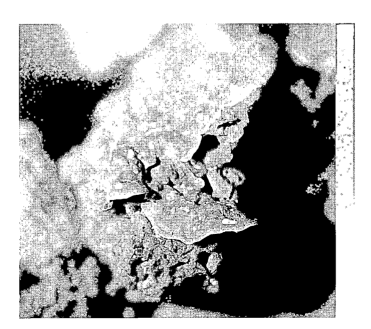

Paragoniolithon conicum

Family: Corallinaceae
Range: Indo-Pacific
Description: *P. conicum* is a typical crustose coralline algae and is heavily calcified, like the others of this group. It is known to be a reef-binder throughout the Indo-Pacific region. The colouration of this species may be purple, lilac, pink or red. This makes it an attractive species for an aquarium.
Aquarium suitability: This species is often seen on live rock and requires strong lighting in an aquarium. It should never be allowed to dry out, otherwise it will die. Crustose coralline algae are one of the most important components of the living reef, second only to the reef-building corals themselves. In an aquarium, once it is established and mature, this group of algae will grow and eventually bind the mini-reef construction together in exactly the same way as they do on a natural reef.

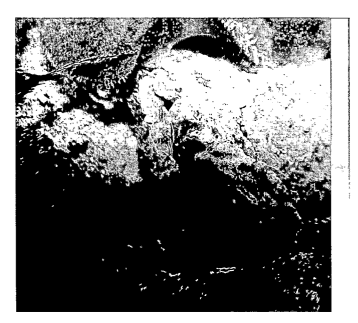

Peysonnelia sp.

Family: Squamariaceae
Range: Tropical Indo-Pacific
Description: This species is sometimes known as "chestnut algae" because of its chestnut-brown colouration. In the picture two growths can be seen between the red algae (top left and bottom right). These are typical of the form that this alga takes. It is encrusting and calcified and sometimes develops attractive leaf-like rhodoliths, which are slightly flexible to the touch. *Peysonnelia* spp. are algae that can live in deep water where very little light penetrates for photosynthesis to take place.
Aquarium suitability: This and similar species are often imported on living rock and are easy to keep in an aquarium. They usually begin to show on the underside of the aquarium decoration, or away from direct lighting, but will soon appear almost anywhere in the tank.

Titanoderma prototypum

Family: Corallinaceae
Range: Caribbean
Description: *Titanoderma* species can be identified by their colouration, which is often pinkish-violet. Areas of the encrustation develop a greyish-violet surface that is attributed to the cell structure. Part of this is expelled and changes colour to act as a barrier against epiphytes, which would otherwise grow rapidly over this species thereby suffocating it. On a natural coral reef this algae can be found in vast growths, particularly in areas where coral has died off.
Aquarium suitability: Like others, this species is occasionally imported on live rock, but this is very rare. It requires optimal water quality for it to grow. The best way of acquiring this particular alga is on rock containing the corallimorpharian *Ricordea florida* exported from the Caribbean.

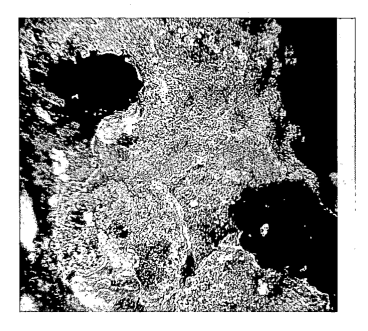

Peysonnelia sp.

Family: Squamariaceae
Range: Circumtropical
Description: This is a beautiful species that can be found at depths of up to 650ft (198m). It is an encrusting alga that is deep reddish-brown in colour. The surface of the encrustation has an unmistakable soft, velvety look. This species is not known to form rhodoliths and is moderately calcified.
Aquarium suitability: Specimens are easy to keep if the aquarist is lucky enough to get hold of a piece of live rock that has this species in evidence. Unfortunately, this is a rare occurrence. The specimen featured here has survived in a tank for several years. It is under direct lighting from two metal-halides lighting units and two blue actinic tubes. The dark brown velvety texture contrasts beautifully with the reds and mauves of other crustose corallines.

Order: Gelidiales

This is a group of algae that may be imported on living rock. Normally it is species of the genus *Gelidium*, which are usually dark red and small, forming turf-like mats between fissures in the rock. *Gelidium* spp. have dichotomous thalli that branch out from the rhizome. Species from another genus, *Gelidiella*, may also turn up on live rock. Like most other algae in this order, they are wiry and tough and in this genus the colours range from red to yellow. *Gelidiella* spp. generally have an untidy appearance. Their thalli are often fern- or feather-like, with thick stems and strong rhizomes. *Gelidiella acerosa*, from the Caribbean, is an intertidal species that can occur in a variety of colours from yellowish-green to deep reddish-brown. The sparse branches are often curved at the tips and the species forms turf-like mats, which can be up to 6in (15cm) high and several yards in diameter. It is usually found on hard substrata in the reef shallows, where the water is often turbulent.

They generally do well in aquariums, providing there are no herbivorous fishes or invertebrates. However, once they appear to have been eaten by these animals or fishes, all is not lost, since there will usually be part of the rhizome remaining on the rock. Even the scrubbing of living rock during the seeding process does not appear to have any adverse effects on many of the species. The red or yellow colouration of these algae provides an attractive contrast to the green macroalgae of the *Caulerpa* family. As with most red algae, all of these species require strong lighting and good water quality for them to survive for any length of time. The advent of metal-halide lighting for aquariums in the last few years has meant that many of the species can now be kept with relative ease.

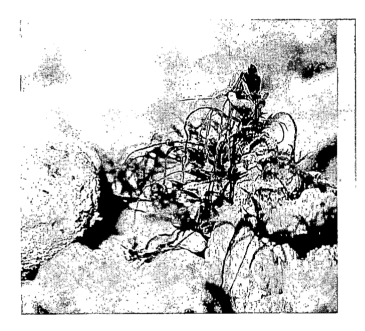

Gelidium pusillum

Family: Gelidiaceae
Range: Circumtropical
Description: This is a robust alga, deep red in colour, with pinnate (feather-like) thalli. It forms small, bushy growths, seldom more than 1in (2.5cm) in height in reef shallows and in flat water where there is a strong current.
Aquarium suitability: A strong water current should be provided for this species. This species is usually imported on live rock from Indonesia and will grow well in an aquarium, providing there are no surgeonfish or tangs present. These will quickly crop the algae and it will only reappear again once the culprits have been removed. This is one of the interesting aspects of marine algae. Many species can survive the onslaught of herbivorous fishes, seeming to die off only to reappear again months or even years later.

Gelidiella acerosa

Family: Gelidiaceae
Range: Caribbean, Tropical West Atlantic
Description: The alga has pinnate thalli, which have an untidy looking appearance. The general colouration can vary from yellow to deep reddish-brown. The thalli are curved, sometimes recurved, and are tough and wiry. They form sparse carpets on the substrata, usually in shallow water at depths of less than about 16ft (5m).
Aquarium suitability: Generally, this species does well in an aquarium but is susceptible to most herbivorous fishes, despite its tough and wiry form. In addition, it can be overgrown by crustose coralline algae, particularly under high-intensity metal-halide lighting. A combination of fluorescent and actinic tubes appears to be the answer here, and under these conditions this species tends to flourish.

Gelidiella sp.

Family: Gelidiaceae
Range: Central Indo-Pacific
Description: The individual plants are strong and wiry with slender opposite branches that are often pinnate. The tips of the thalli are extended and curved and the overall colouration is generally bright red to deep reddish-brown. This alga attaches itself to the substrate with a tough rhizomatous holdfast.
Aquarium suitability: The species is hardy and resistant to changes in water quality and light. Under metal-halide lighting it grows slowly but steadily. It will live for years in an aquarium and, because of its tough nature, can withstand all but the most persistent herbivore. Even if it is eaten, and this is normally only by sea urchins of the genus *Diadema*, there will usually be enough of the rhizome left on the rock for it to re-establish itself.

Order: Gigartinales

This order is worthy of mention since it encompasses algae with widely differing forms and thalli. They can be encrusting with rubbery blades, or they may be tall and almost arborescent (tree-like) in form. The thalli can form a loose conglomeration or they can also be strongly compacted into a single structure.

   Chondrus crispus has thalli that are flat and branched into fans. These are dark reddish-purple and rubbery and take on a multiaxial form. It is an alga that is often seen around the coasts of the northern Atlantic and has a very wide distribution. The alga is edible and well known by its popular name "Carrageen". Extracts from this and other algae in this order are often used in food production.

   Many authors attribute the genus *Gracilaria* to this group, but in fact this belongs to a separate order,

Gracilariales. Two other genera that do belong to this order may be of interest to aquarists, namely *Eucheuma* and *Hypnea*. In the Indo-Pacific there are 22 known species of *Eucheuma*, whereas in the Caribbean only five species have so far been recorded, and even some of these appear to be invalid or belong to another genus. The algae are characterized by their hard, thorny thalli with dichotomous branching. Their colouration is usually red to red-brown. Species of the genus *Hypnea* generally have smooth, somewhat serrated, dichotomous branching, and are red-brown in colour. Both genera contain some very beautiful species that are ideally suited to aquarium life when they are imported attached to a small piece of live rock. They usually grow quite fast in a tank but care should be taken when cropping back not to cut too deep into the thalli so that the base becomes damaged. If this happens the alga will usually die.

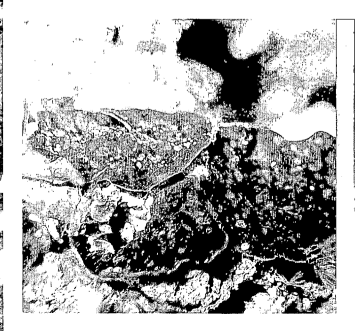

Flahaultia tegetiformis

Family: Solieriaceae
Range: Tropical West Atlantic, Caribbean
Description: There are similarities between this and some *Peysonnelia* species. But apart from being a much lighter brown, this species grows almost exclusively in rhodolith form and, like *Mesophyllum* spp., growth is indicated by whitish margins. Occasionally spherical thalli also form. These vesicles are not unlike those of *Valonia* and *Ventricaria* species. The lobed blades are quite flexible.
Aquarium suitability: This alga will grow of its own accord in an aquarium containing live rock. It will form attractive plate-like growths on rocks and also on filter pipes. In extreme cases, this alga can completely mask filter pipes within a year or so, giving them the appearance of being a natural part of the aquarium decoration.

Order: Gracilariales

There are two main genera in this order as far as the aquarist is concerned. These are *Gracilaria* and *Polycavernosa* and species from both genera are widely distributed throughout the Caribbean and Tropical West Atlantic. *Gracilaria* spp. are generally slender and graceful plants with cylindrical, sometimes flattened, branches. The name *Gracilaria* means "delicate" or "slender". *Gracilaria damaecornis* is a pinkish-red bushy alga that is strong and leathery. The cylindrical branches are dichotomous and have blunt tips. It is a shallow-water species that grows to about 6in (15cm). In contrast, *G. tikvahiae* has long, cylindrical, slightly flattened thalli that form loose growths. The branches range from deep green to bright red. *G. mammillaris*, on the other hand, is a thickly branched fleshy plant that is pinkish-red to deep brownish red. It is found in the sublittoral zone, where the water is often turbulent.

In the second genus, *Polycavernosa*, the species are usually tough and rubbery. *P. debilis* has a gnarled appearance with variable branch size up to 10in (25cm). The colour can vary from brownish-yellow, through pale pink, to pale green. *Polycavernosa crassissima*, with its creeping form, is bright metallic-gold with a silvery sheen. It grows on coral rubble in back-reef areas as well as near reef crests. It is a tough rubbery plant with tangled branches that are broad and often flattened on the margins.

Most tank species turn up in a poor state on imported live rock, but with a little care during the seeding process, the loss of these valuable additions to a reef tank can be avoided. With luck, attractive growths can be achieved in contrasting colours, especially if they are combined with the spectacular alga, *Gracilaria curtissae*, described below.

Gracilaria curtissae

Family: Gracilariaceae
Range: Circumtropical
Description: This beautiful alga is a favourite among aquarists. It grows quite large, to about 18in (45cm) and is easily confused with some of the *Halymenia* species, having similar thalli. This species is bright to brick red, sometimes with yellow at the base of the thallus. These are broad, branching out from a central rhizome, and the tips are split into uneven ruffles.
Aquarium suitability: *G. curtissae* grows quite well under strong fluorescent as well as metal-halide lighting. It is one of the most spectacular algae for the aquarium but will not tolerate high nitrate levels. The alga is easily damaged during transit and handling in the aquarium, so you should take care that the holdfast does not become separated from the thalli, otherwise the plant will die.

Order: Rhodymeniales

Taxonomically, this is quite a new order. Rhodymeniales incorporates a diverse group of algae with many beautiful species, and most of these are are ideal for a marine aquarium. Often the thalli are broad and strap-like, although they can be cylindrical or spherical. They are rubbery plants and are often slippery to the touch. Their colouration can vary from bright yellow, through bright red, to deep brown or green. Some species, such as *Halymenia floridana* from the family Grateloupiaceae, can be bright yellow or red.

Also from the family Grateloupiaceae, *Grateloupia filicina* is an attractive but untidy looking alga. It grows to 20in (50cm), forming dense bushes from a central rhizome. The colouration is red to brown generally but with dull yellow-orange toward the base of the thalli. The branching is fringed and irregularly dichotomous. If this species is bought attached to a piece of live rock it will do quite well in an aquarium with the necessary lighting. It requires a strong current and grows very fast given the right conditions. It will not tolerate high phosphate or nitrate levels, and care should be taken to remove only the tips of the thalli when it needs to be cut back.

Along with *G. filicina*, two other Indo-Pacific species, *G. livida* and *G. confervoides*, are found as far north as Hong Kong. The genus *Grateloupia* is not represented in the Caribbean or the tropical West Atlantic. In this area, apart from *Halymenia floridana*, the spectacular *H. floresia* often occurs in deeper water. Two other species from this order are frequently seen in the Caribbean. *Halymenia duchassaignii* is a fleshy plant with broad blades mottled red to cream coloured. *Kallymenia limmingii* is bright red with strap-like blades that have convoluted margins.

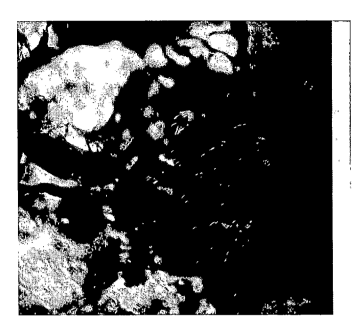

Halymenia sp.

Family: Grateloupiaceae
Range: East Africa to Central Indo-Pacific
Description: This is one of the most spectacular of all the *Halymenia* species. It has very broad, plate-like thalli that are bright to deep red in colour. It often occurs on live rocks, particularly those that are imported from Kenya. Although it may not be apparent at first, it will soon show itself and grow rapidly to about 6in (15cm).
Aquarium suitability: Requires a sheltered position with moderate water movement. Care must be taken in handling plants, as the thallus stems are brittle and easily break off from the rhizome. Without this the alga will not survive very long. Nevertheless it grows well under both fluorescent and metal-halide lighting. It is rarely offered for sale and is a very delicate species that looks extremely attractive in a reef aquarium.

Halymenia cf. *floresia*

Family: Grateloupiaceae
Range: Tropical Indo-Pacific
Description: The thalli of this species are strongly compressed and irregularly dichotomous, sometimes with an untidy look about them. They form bushy growths up to 14in (36cm) high. The normal colouration is deep brown-red and the base of the thallus may be orange, depending on its origin. As with all *Halymenia* spp. the surfaces of the thalli feel slimy to the touch.
Aquarium suitability: This species does well under both metal-halide and fluorescent lighting. It is very fast growing and is one of the species of algae from which aquarists can take cuttings. Care must be taken not to cut too deep into the basal thalli, however, or it could possibly die. The cuttings should be anchored under a rock and left undisturbed where they will eventually form a rhizome of their own.

Kallymenia sp.?

Family: Kallymeniaceae
Range: Tropical Indo-Pacific
Description: The placing of this species is uncertain. The blades are multiaxial and convoluted on the margins. They may be short and rounded or somewhat longer. The colour of the thalli is deep red to pinkish-red, but this is masked by the presence of epiphytes on the surfaces of the thalli, which give the plant an overall bluish-green appearance. This species is found in lagoons and shallow back reef areas, often growing with *Derbesia* spp.
Aquarium suitability: Grows well under fluorescent or metal-halide lighting. The alga requires moderate water movement and should be placed in a well-lit area of the sand. Specimens are usually offered attached to pebbles and sand, so care should be taken during transportation that this does not break away from the root system.

Order: Ceramiales

The algae of this order are usually small with thin-branched thalli and, more often than not, from the genera *Ceramium* or *Mortensia*. *Ceramium byssoides* can be easily identified, since the thalli have pincer-formed tips and are light to deep red in colour. This species is found throughout the Indo-Pacific, particularly in the South China Sea as far north as Hong Kong. *Mortensia pavonia* is often imported on live rock from the Caribbean. It is a small alga with dichotomous branched thalli. On one side of the branching point the thallus is stable and lightly calcified, whereas its binary partner is perforated.

Many species of this order appear on living rock and some readily establish in the aquarium. This applies to *Wranglia* spp., *Laurencia* spp. and the attractive species from the genus *Acanthophora*. Species from the family Dasyaceae, which includes the genera *Dictyurus*, *Dasya* and *Eupogon*, are more difficult to keep.

Laurencia intricata, from the family Rhodomelaceae, is a delicate and attractive Caribbean species. Its greenish-yellow branches are slender and cylindrical, with pink-coloured branchlets. It is a shallow-water species usually found in sandy areas of the reef, where it grows attached to small pieces of the substrata. Also from the Caribbean, *Dasya baillouviana* has bright red thalli that are tall and slender. They are covered in hair-thin branchlets, which feel slimy to the touch. The spiny, bright red *Wrightiella blodgettii* has a bushy form and grows in rocky areas of the sublittoral zone and in deeper water.

Most members of this order are suitable aquarium subjects, provided that there are no herbivorous fishes or invertebrates in the aquarium. They need plenty of light but the water movement should not be too strong.

Acanthophora specifera

Family: Rhodomelaceae
Range: Endemic throughout the Caribbean region
Description: This species forms compact bushy clumps, which may be up to 12in (30cm) high. The fine, dichotomous branches are spinose (spiny) and translucent and the thalli are creamy pink-white. In nature it is found near or on coral heads at varying depths of 36in to 80ft (91cm to 25m.). It is also encountered on algal beds in sandy inshore bays from Florida to Brazil.
Aquarium suitability: *A. specifera* is often imported on live rock and grows quite fast under strong enough lighting. Its delicate branches give the impression of a coral rather than an alga. Despite its spinose appearance, most herbivorous fishes and invertebrates will readily eat it, so care should be taken in stocking to ensure that no surgeonfishes or tangs are present in the set-up.

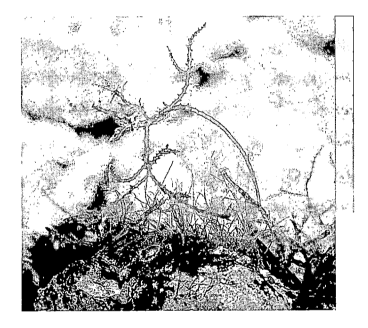

Chondria sp.

Family: Rhodomelaceae
Range: Caribbean, Tropical West Atlantic
Description: This species has cylindrical, smooth branches that are dichotomous with flexible joints at the base of each thallus. The thalli are thin and brownish-red in colour, with small branchlets. They form dense growths up to 6in (15cm) high.
Aquarium suitability: It is a relatively robust alga when it is provided with enough light and good water circulation. Although it is normally imported on live rock, dealers occasionally offer specimens on small pieces of rock when they are attractive enough. Most surgeonfishes will eat a large growth of this alga within 24 hours, so you need to take care to make sure that it remains an attractive addition to an aquarium, instead of becoming simply an expensive form of nutrition for herbivorous fishes.

Phylum: Heterokontophyta (brown algae)

This phylum contains species that are generally termed brown algae. It consists of nine classes, as shown in the table (see right). The class Chrysophyceae contains unicellular algae that build colonies of gold-brown slime and blanket algae as well as planktonic forms. These algae occur in fresh, brackish and salt water. There are about 200 recorded genera with about 1,000 species. The second and third classes, Parmophyceae and Sarcinochrysidophyceae, respectively, contain freshwater species. Xanthophyceae, the fourth class, encompasses mainly freshwater species and those that are found in swamp regions. The fifth class, Eustigmatophyceae, also contains mainly freshwater microalgae. Only one genus is truly marine. The sixth class, Bacillariophyceae, is made up of about 250 genera incorporating approximately 100,000 species, which are known as diatomaceous algae. Although these are of little interest here, since they are not what can be considered as decorative algae, they make up a greater part of the phytoplankton in the sea. The seventh class contains only 15 species of mostly freshwater microalgae. Dictyophyceae, the eighth class, contains only two planktonic species. The ninth and most important class, as far as the aquarist is concerned, is Phaeophyceae, containing more than 1,500 species of true brown algae in about 265 genera. The pigmentation of these algae consists of beta-carotene, chlorophyll-a and c and fucoxanthin, which is a xanthophyll pigment that effectively masks the colour of the chlorophylls, giving the algae a brown appearance.

These algae need to absorb an enormous amount of iodine from the sea water in order to live and grow. Well over 10,000 times more iodine is found within their structure than in the surrounding water, which is one reason why they sometimes do not live long in a tank.

Order: Dictyotales

This order contains the majority of brown algae that are suitable for an aquarium. Their forms are extremely diverse, varying from lightly calcified algae (*Padina* spp.) to the delicate, golden-brown branching of the *Dilophus* spp. These algae adapt most readily to an aquarium milieu and are by far the most important family as far as aquarists are concerned. Additionally, it appears that many species have a substance in their cell walls that makes them unappetizing to herbivorous fishes. With regular additions of trace elements, especially iodine, most species do well in a reef or marine aquarium

Generally, but not always, plants from this order have branched, strap-formed or fan-formed thalli, which are three or more cells thick. Many species occur in both tropical and temperate zones, and some are circumtropical.

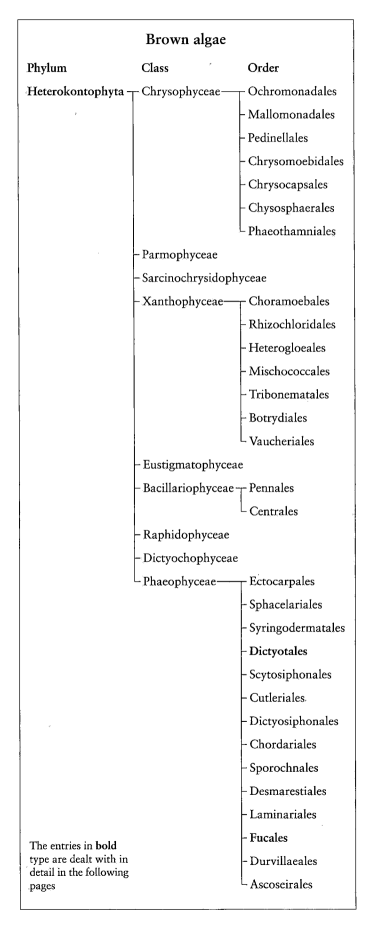

Brown algae

Phylum	Class	Order
Heterokontophyta	Chrysophyceae	Ochromonadales
		Mallomonadales
		Pedinellales
		Chrysomoebidales
		Chrysocapsales
		Chysosphaerales
		Phaeothamniales
	Parmophyceae	
	Sarcinochrysidophyceae	
	Xanthophyceae	Choramoebales
		Rhizochloridales
		Heterogloeales
		Mischococcales
		Tribonematales
		Botrydiales
		Vaucheriales
	Eustigmatophyceae	
	Bacillariophyceae	Pennales
		Centrales
	Raphidophyceae	
	Dictyochophyceae	
	Phaeophyceae	Ectocarpales
		Sphacelariales
		Syringodermatales
		Dictyotales
		Scytosiphonales
		Cutleriales
		Dictyosiphonales
		Chordariales
		Sporochnales
		Desmarestiales
		Laminariales
		Fucales
		Durvillaeales
		Ascoseirales

The entries in **bold** type are dealt with in detail in the following pages

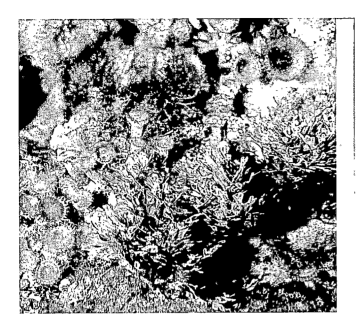

Dictyota bartayresii

Family: Dictyotaceae
Range: Tropical and subtropical Atlantic, Caribbean
Description: *D. bartayresii* is probably the most attractive of the brown algae and forms small bushy growths 4–6 in (10–15cm) high. The thalli have characteristic bifurcate branching, forming wide angles (broad Y-shapes). These branches have a blue-green iridescence that is most attractive in an aquarium. The alga is found throughout the warmer waters of the Atlantic to a depth of about 165ft (50m).
Aquarium suitability: This species adapts well to aquarium conditions but care should be taken during transportation, since it is easily damaged and in some cases can break up when handled. For the best results, it should be purchased attached to a small piece of live rock. It does equally well under strong fluorescent or metal-halide lighting.

Dictyota dichotoma

Family: Dictyotaceae
Range: Circumtropical
Description: The dichotomous branching of this species is typical of the genus. In this case, the thalli are lightly spiralled, forming wide angles, and the colouration is usually light brown. A similar alga, occurring in temperate waters, is believed to be a geographical variation of this species.
Aquarium suitability: Under strong metal-halide lighting, supplemented with blue actinic lighting, this species grows very fast and may become a problem in an aquarium. A reduction in the amount of light will, in this case, bring it under control. It is transport-fragile and should be bought attached to a piece of living rock. As with all brown algae, iodine should be added to the water at regular intervals for its continued wellbeing.

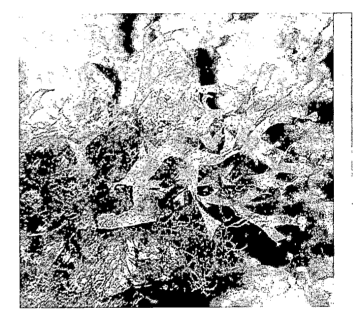

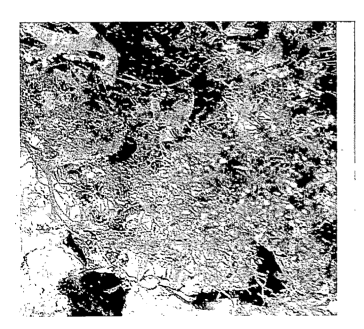

Dictyota linearis

Family: Dictyotaceae
Range: Caribbean
Description: This species has very fine dichotomous branching that is irregular and forms dense, bushy mats over rocks. The thalli are flattened and usually only about 1mm wide. The blades, however, may be up to 4in (10cm) in length and end in a pincer-form similar to that of the red algae *Ceramium byssoides*. The colouration is variable, ranging from deep olive-green to light brown.
Aquarium suitability: More often than not, this species is imported on living rock from the Caribbean. Given the correct conditions, it will grow well in an aquarium and will soon form a fine turf-like mat over the substrata. It can sometimes threaten to take over much of the tank, but a reduction in the light or, better still, periodic harvesting of its fragile thalli, will stop this.

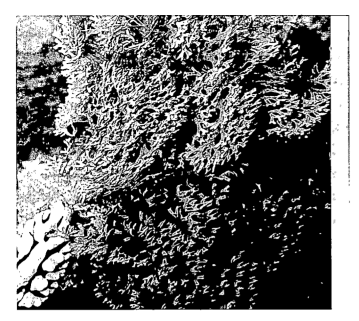

Dictyota sp.

Family: Dictyotaceae
Range: Tropical and subtropical East Atlantic
Description: The species is very similar to *D. bartayresii*, except that the thalli are generally smaller and lack the typical blue-green iridescence. In addition, whereas *D. bartayresii* has a tendency to grow as a somewhat erect bush, this species grows almost horizontally with overlapping bifurcate branches.
Aquarium suitability: Under fluorescent lighting this species tends to flourish. However, it does not seem to grow as well when cultivated under metal-halide illumination. In any event, the species requires good water quality with a light to moderate movement of water if the best results are to be achieved. The 10in (25cm) example shown here can be seen to be growing well in a small aquarium with a capacity of only 10 gallons (45 litres) of water.

Order: Fucales

Most of the algae in this order come from the temperate seas of the world and are too large for the average aquarium. The larger algae are well known, such as the bladder wrack (*Fucus vesiculosus*). The sugar wrack (*Laminaria saccharina*), or sea belt, is a familiar sight in some coastal regions, as is the channelled wrack (*Pelvetia canaliculata*) and oarweed (*Laminaria digitata*). Some of *Laminaria* spp. along the coast of North America are the largest plants on earth, attaining a length of well more than 250ft (76m). Many sea kelps (*Macrocystis* spp.) and Sea Thongs (such as *Himanthalia elongata*) belong to this order, as does the toothed or serrated wrack (*Fucus serratus*). Some can be kept in a cold-water marine aquarium but most are unsuitable even for this. Although the *Laminaria* group has been included here and and are

dealt with as a single order, some authors attribute these algae to their own order, Laminariales.

They play an important role in all seas, tropical and temperate. Within the littoral and intertidal zones, where most of these species abound, they provide a haven for small fishes and invertebrates. When the tide is out, just briefly turn over the branches of a bladder wrack to see the myriad creatures it protects within its damp thalli.

One group is of interest to marine aquarists is the family Sargassaceae. The two important genera in this family are *Sargassum* and *Turbinaria*. *Sargassum* spp. and are probably the most widespread of all the marine algae, with nine species reported from the waters around Hong Kong and more than ten separate species in the Atlantic. The Sargasso Sea is thick with island-like floating masses of these species. In terms of sheer biomass, it must be one of the most abundant of all plants.

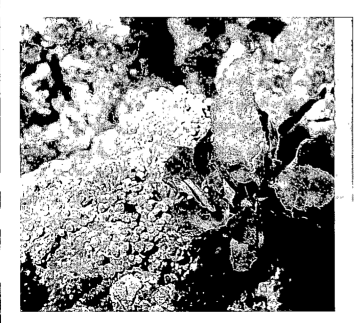

Sargassum hystrix

Family: Sargassaceae
Range: Tropical West Atlantic
Description: The stalk or stipe of this species is middle to dark brown with olive-green blades, each with a whitish midrib. The blades themselves form long ovals with bladders at their bases, which are light brownish-yellow in colour. These small gas-filled floats help to hold the alga upright and also to make it float if the stipe breaks. This often happens through wave action or storms, and the alga then becomes pelagic (free-floating).
Aquarium suitability: This is a difficult alga to keep in an aquarium and requires frequent partial water changes and a strong water movement. It grows to about 16in (40cm) and is often too large for some of the smaller types of tank. In a larger aquarium, however, this species can be an attractive and interesting alternative.

Phylum: Chlorophyta (green algae)

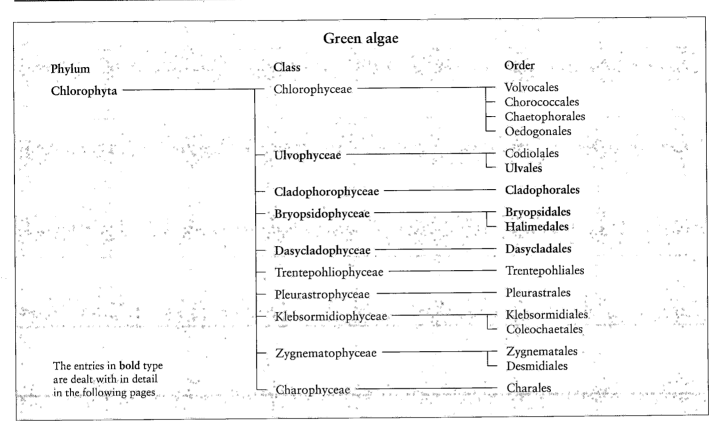

This phylum incorporates almost 8,000 individual species in about 500 genera. There are ten current classes and a total of 17 orders. These algae all have chlorophyll as their predominant pigmentation. There are about 1,100 species to be found in sea water and in these the pigmentation consists of beta-carotene and the chlorophylls a and b. The cell walls are made up of pectin compounds and cellulose.

Some species contain calcium carbonate within the cell tissue. These are generally referred to as calcareous algae. In this phylum, there are five orders that contain species that are of particular interest to the marine aquarium hobby. These are indicated in bold type in the chart here (*see above*) and are covered in more detail in the following pages. It must be pointed out at this stage that this arrangement of orders is by no means complete and it has been simplified in order that it may be more easily assimilated.

Green algae of the phylum Chlorophyta are what could be termed opportunistic plants. They are found in a variety of different habitats in both fresh water and seawater. They occur in brackish-water estuaries as well as on land. We probably all have seen old, alga-covered gravestones at one time or another, but this is not the only everyday example. The trunks of trees in damp woods and forests, for example, often have a greenish film of algae on their bark. This is usually green algae of the genera *Trentepohlia* or *Trebouxia*. In the springtime, once light

levels begin to increase, ponds sometimes have a distinct greenish cast in the water, and in the summer, wool-like growths of greenish slime appear. These are all algae belonging to the phylum Chlorophyta. Some are able to survive in extreme conditions, such as ice and snow. In the high mountains *Chlamydomonas nivalis* gives old snow a somewhat reddish appearance. A mixture of carotene based pigments (Haematochrome) causes this, because it effectively masks the chlorophyll present in the algae. The Arctic and Antarctic ice is often tinted pastel green and blue, and this phenomenon is sometimes caused by the presence of algae from this large group.

The green algae, through their special characteristics, form an almost natural phylum that differentiates it from all other algae. Despite this fact there is no getting away from their close affinity to the mosses, and the demarcation here is a great deal more difficult to establish with some species. The forms can vary a great deal. Algae can be colony-building or single-celled. They may be planktonic, many celled or microscopic, or they can occur as epiphytes on other algae. The presence of some species can indicate organic pollution, whereas the presence of others may indicate a constant influx of clean clear water.

The word "Chlorophyta" comes from the Greek (*chlorus* meaning "green" and *phyton* meaning "plant"), and means literally "green plant". Their colours range from bright apple green to leaf green, but yellow, bottle green and greenish-black may also be represented.

Order: Ulvales

The order contains about 24 genera and 175 species, of which most are marine-living organisms. These algae are found in all coastal areas of the world, including both tropical and temperate zones. One of their special abilities is that they can, in a short space of time, form thick, lush growths in otherwise barren areas of the coastline. Although algae from this order look quite delicate, they can in fact withstand the battering of surf and then periodically being covered with a layer of sand as the waves draw back.

There are three genera in this order that are of interest to reef aquarium owners. These are *Ulva*, *Ulvaria* and *Enteromorpha*. One species is well known, and it is certainly the most widespread in this group. This is *Ulva lactuca*, which is more commonly referred to as the "sea lettuce". This alga is found in both tropical and temperate waters, and in the northern part of the Atlantic around the shores of the UK it is endemic. Here, it is often found as a host to the chameleon prawn (*Hippolyte varians*), which lives within the blades of *U. lactuca* and adopts the same bright green colour. At night, however, this prawn changes its colour to translucent blue. *Ulva* is an edible alga that is much loved by the peoples of South East Asia, and it is available in dried form in delicatessens throughout the world. In Hong Kong another edible species, *Ulva pertusa*, which is cropped there in quantity, is used both in soups and also medicinally for the treatment of a high temperature or high blood pressure.

Various species from this order can be kept in aquariums with a degree of success, but they are by no means easy and many aquarists report failures. Strong lighting and a good water current are important factors for success.

Ulva fasciata

Family: Ulvaceae
Range: Circumtropical
Description: This species forms smooth, strap-shaped blades that are bright apple-green. Sometimes the central portion of the blade is light green, becoming darker toward the ruffled margins. It is a common shallow-water species found throughout the tropics, particularly in the areas of river mouths where the water is high in nutrients. The alga is edible and in some areas it is used in soups.
Aquarium suitability: The aquarium photograph shows a small colony that has appeared on the underside of a gorgonian (*Briareum* sp.), although it was not visible when the coral was initially introduced into the aquarium. Provide plenty of light and water movement and this species will grow well without any special care.

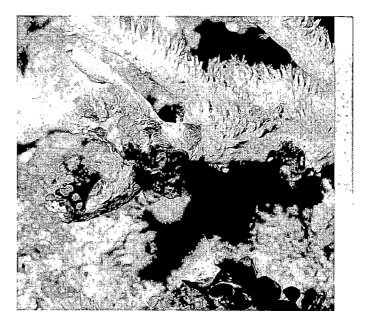

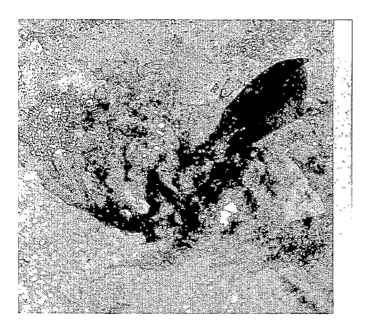

Ulva lactuca

Family: Ulvaceae
Range: All seas, both tropical and temperate
Description: Like the previous species, the thalli of *U. lactuca* are also only about a double cell-width thick. They are oval in form, sometimes almost round, with riffled margins that often appear folded. The "sea lettuce" is frequently found in the vicinity of oyster beds.
Aquarium suitability: *U. lactuca* is often imported on living rock and is usually not permanent. With care, good growths are possible in a reef aquarium and, as with all *Ulva* spp., it poses no threat to the corals or other invertebrates with which it is kept. It will not grow too fast and can easily be controlled through cropping or by a reduction in light levels. When its origin is from temperate zones it can be kept successfully in a cold-water aquarium.

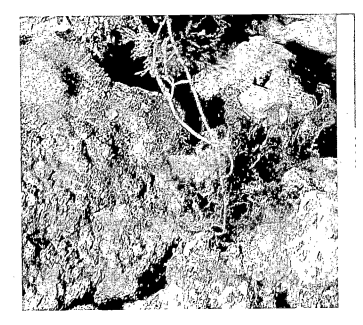

Ulva cf. linza

Family: Ulvaceae
Range: Indo-Pacific
Description: Confusion often occurs in the identity of this species compared with *Ulva fasciata*. Whereas *U. fasciata* has a circumtropical distribution with long thalli that are pleated, this species is confined to the Indo-Pacific and the thalli have wavy margins that are slightly shorter. Both species occur together throughout the Indo-Pacific on rocks, in reef shallows and in flat-water regions. The thallus colour is translucent middle-green.
Aquarium suitability: This species is often imported on live rock. With a little care it can be saved by breaking off a small piece of the "unseeded" rock containing the holdfast and placing it in a mature aquarium under strong light. A small piece will have no biological effect in the tank, but a decorative alga will be saved that would otherwise be scrubbed away during seeding.

Order: Cladophorales

This order is made up of very varied algae. In the family Cladophoraceae there are two genera containing species of interest to aquarists. In the genus *Chaetomorpha*, the growth form is often a confused tangle of small, relatively thin thalli comprising short, cylindrically formed cells. The algae occur in varying shades of green and are found in mat-formed or bushy colonies. These afford a haven for small fishes and invertebrates, which can hide within their snarled growths. The second genus, *Cladophora*, contains mostly marine species, although there are also some freshwater species. The growth is usually less tangled, with thin, tubular branches that form tufts on harbour pilings and rocks. Their colour varies from light to dark green.

The second family, Valoniaceae, encompasses algae that are spherical or oval-formed with balloon-like vesicles consisting of a single large cell. These cells, which can be anything up to 2in (5cm) in diameter, are considered to be the largest single living cell in the world. The surfaces of these vesicles are often colonized by microalgae (epiphytes). They may be attached to the substrate by hair-like rhizomes or they may be pelagic (free-floating). Some species are found in both the pelagic and benthic (attached to substrata) forms. They are to be found in all warm seas of the world to depths of at least 265ft (80m).

Species from the three genera *Valonia*, *Ventricaria* and *Dictyosphaeria* are often introduced into aquariums on living rock, where they will eventually form grape-like, very decorative colonies. They have the ability to reproduce through vegetative separation and, if left uncontrolled, can sometimes become a minor problem for aquarists. Thankfully, the vesicles can easily be removed by hand if the colony becomes too large for its environment.

Chaetomorpha aerea

Family: Cladophoraceae
Range: Caribbean, Tropical and subtropical West Atlantic
Description: The plant has stiff, filament-like thalli that are straight and unbranched. The colouration is light to deep green. It normally grows to a height of 6in (15cm) in small tufts on rocks in the sublittoral or intertidal zones, particularly where the water is relatively turbulent.
Aquarium suitability: For some strange reason, light green specimens have a tendency to become a deep, rich green under aquarium conditions. Nevertheless, this species is easy to keep and will flourish when given enough light and water movement. Despite its wiry structure, it is food for many herbivorous fishes and invertebrates, so care should be taken when choosing this alga for a reef tank that none of these fishes are present in its new surroundings.

Chaetomorpha linium

Family: Cladophoraceae
Range: Circumtropical
Description: This species looks like a tangle of thick, green fishing line and forms dense mats on rocks. These mounds may be up to 40in (1m) in diameter. The colouration is usually bright yellowish-green and the somewhat stiff thalli are tubular in form, consisting of single rows of cells, each with a diameter of about 1mm.
Aquarium suitability: Although it is no easy matter to keep this species in an aquarium, it is a very decorative addition. It needs a shadowy place in the tank, away from direct light. It also requires good water quality with low levels of nitrate and phosphate for it to grow successfully. Initial growth may be stunted, as can be seen from this aquarium photograph, but with a little care small bushes can be cultivated.

Cladophora prolifera

Family: Cladophoraceae
Range: Circumtropical
Description: The thalli of this species form stiff, filamentous dark-green balls reaching a height of 8in (20cm), but are usually shorter. Unlike the similar *Chaetomorpha aerea*, in this species the thalli are branched. Each of these growths is packed so close together that the impression is one of a dense carpet. Individual thalli are cylindrical, stiff and bristly to the touch. It is found in harbours and shallow inlets throughout its natural range.
Aquarium suitability: *Cladophora prolifera* is probably the easiest of all algae to keep in an aquarium. It seems to grow best in areas of moderate water current but it does require high levels of metal-halide illumination if it is to become well established. Once this has taken place, it will prove to be slow growing and practically indestructible.

Ventricaria ventricosa

Family: Valoniaceae
Range: Circumtropical
Description: *V. ventricosa* has dark green spherical or oval vesicles with a diameter of about ¾in (1 to 2cm). These consist of single cells, which sometimes grow to about 2in (5cm), but this is the exception rather than the rule. The alga occurs singly on the reef, attached to the substrate in crevices between coral heads or on rocks. Sometimes the vesicles may be in small groups of two or three individuals, but seldom more. The surface of the sphere can be covered in epiphytes and the species is common in shallow water throughout the Indo-Pacific and Caribbean.
Aquarium suitability: This is one of the most common algae seen in a marine aquarium. Unlike in its natural environment, however, it can form large, grape-like colonies in a tank, and it is one of the easiest species to keep.

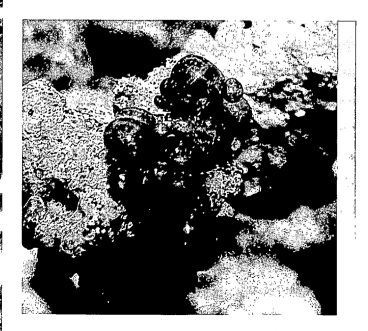

Dictyosphaeria sp.

Family: Valoniaceae
Range: Indian Ocean to East Africa
Description: The large thallus of this species is bright green and hollow. It can be anything up to 4in (10cm) across and is composed of spherical cells that grow together in an uneven, knotty group. There are several species similar in appearance throughout the Indo-Pacific from East Africa to Australia. A very similar species to this has been reported around Green Island in the Great Barrier Reef.
Aquarium suitability: This species is often imported on live rock from the coast of Kenya in East Africa. The rock is usually transported moist but not in water, and much of the algae and other life on the rock is in a sorry state by the time it reaches its final destination. However, with a little care in the seeding process, much of the life can be saved, including this species.

Order: Bryopsidales

This order contains "nuisance" algae as far as aquarists are concerned. However, it also contains a few species that can be considered ornamental. This is because they do not spread quickly, smothering valuable invertebrates.

Most often this order is combined with Halimedales. Hopefully, the following entries will clarify this confusion. The orders Bryopsidales and Halimedales should be treated as separate based on the following differences:

Plastid differences Plastids are bodies in the cytoplasm of plant cells containing food or pigments. The order Bryopsidales contains plants that only have plastids containing chlorophyll (chloroplasts), and are termed homoplastidic. The order Halimedales, however, includes plants that have both chloroplasts and amyloplasts within their cell structure. These are termed heteroplastidic.

Cell-wall differences Bryopsidales contains algae with cellulose, xylem and mannan in the cell walls, whereas the Halimedales have only xylem with little or no cellulose.

Reproductive differences In the Bryopsidales, the thalli produce reproductive cells in distinct regions (for example, sporangia). In the Halimedales the whole of the fertile thallus is given over to reproduction so that, after the gametes have been released, there is only a thallus "husk" remaining made up of empty cell walls.

Bryopsidales contains plants with fine tubular thalli that may be branched or unbranched. Two important genera belong to this group, *Bryopsis* and *Derbesia*. Many species are fast growing in nutrient-rich water.

Bryopsis plumosa

Family: Bryopsidaceae
Range: Tropical to temperate Atlantic
Description: This species is common throughout the Atlantic, from the Caribbean to the northern waters of Scandinavia. Typically it has dichotomous branching into feather-like thalli. These are fine and hair-like and can grow very quickly forming, large carpets over the rocks in the intertidal zones. The alga is light to middle green in colour and can reach a height of about 4in (10cm).
Aquarium suitability: *B. plumosa* is worthy of a mention since it turns up in almost all marine aquariums at some stage or another, usually imported on live rock. It is an attractive alga, but one that is not easy to control once it gets out of hand, so you should keep a watchful eye on it whenever it does appear.

Bryopsis sp.

Family: Bryopsidaceae
Range: Tropical Indo-Pacific
Description: There are so many similar species of *Bryopsis* in the Indo-Pacific region that not all of them have been fully identified. It is difficult to differentiate one from another, and this species is no exception. The thalli are yellowish-green and form feather-like branches up to 4in (10cm) high. The dichotomous branching forms narrow angles and the thalli are coarser than the preceding species. It is seldom found in dense mats and is more often seen in small, bushy growths on rocks.
Aquarium suitability: Isolated individuals sometime crop up on living rock imported from Indonesia. The alga is slow growing and will eventually form small, decorative clumps. It is easy to control by manually removing unwanted clumps and it requires metal-halide lighting in order to do well.

Order: Halimedales

(Syn: Bryopsidales, Siphonales, Caulerpales)
This order contains attractive macroalgae, most of which are suitable and decorative for a reef or marine aquarium. Species from the genus *Chlorodesmis* (turtle weed) are not covered here because of the difficulty in keeping them with any degree of success in an aquarium. Perhaps the best known and certainly the first algae to be kept successfully in an aquarium are the beautiful and prolific macroalgae of the genus *Caulerpa*. This genus comprises 62 different species and most of them can be kept with relative ease in an aquarium. As with all members of the *Caulerpa* genus, the thalli are liquid-filled and the cell walls are easily ruptured. Care must be taken in cropping these algae that the liquid is not allowed to leak out into the water. This will result in the death of the alga or at least part of it. The best way of cutting back *Caulerpa* sp. is to pinch the stolon between your finger and thumbnails until it becomes separated, and then pinch the ends together for a few seconds. This will have the effect of sealing the open ends together and preventing any further damage to the plant.

Some of the most exotic and interesting algae in the world come from the Caribbean and Tropical West Atlantic, in particular those of the family Halimedaceae. Algae from this family take on interesting and sometimes beautiful forms, which can be a spectacular feature in a reef aquarium. Apart from the many bizarre species that occur in the Caribbean, the genus *Halimeda* also belongs to this family. Representatives of this genus are to be found in all tropical seas. These calcareous algae are quite fast growing and in an aquarium environment they need constant cropping, which is easy to do.

Caulerpa floridana

Family: Caulerpaceae
Range: Florida and Bahamas to Brazil
Description: This alga is sometimes confused with *C. mexicana*. As can be seen from the accompanying photograph, this species has feather-like thalli that have a noticeable thickening of the individual pinnae around the margin. The thalli can grow to 8in (20cm) in height and the colouration is variable, from lime green to dark olive green.
Aquarium suitability: *C. floridana* is quite easy to keep in an aquarium and may often appear of its own accord on live rock that has been imported from the Caribbean or Florida regions. The best results are obtained when metal-halide lighting is used, but this is not essential. This species will grow reasonably well under strong fluorescent lighting when actinic tubes are used as a supplementary source of illumination.

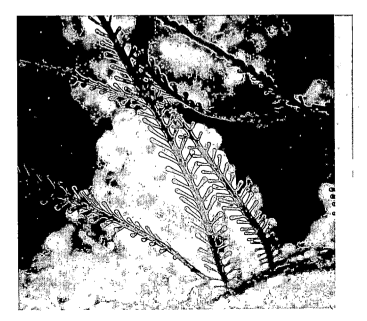

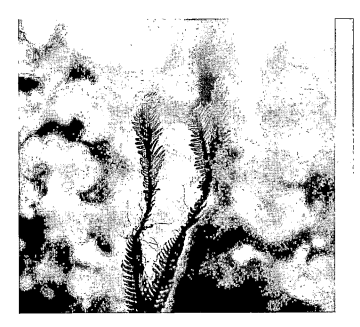

Caulerpa prolifera

Family: Caulerpaceae
Range: Mediterranean, Tropical East and West Atlantic
Description: The broad, smooth blades of this species are unmistakable. These are light to dark green in colour and grow to a height of up to 12in (30cm). They may be simple or branched and are attached to the upper surface of the stolon. The stolon can grow to a length of over 40in (1m) and attaches itself to the substrate with rhizome-like holdfasts, which often bore into the porous surfaces of rock.
Aquarium suitability: This was probably the first marine alga to be kept successfully in a tropical marine tank some 40 years ago. At first, little was known about its lighting requirements but even so hobbyists had success with C. *prolifera*. This is an indication of its hardiness. It is the ideal choice for the novice but it needs to be frequently cropped.

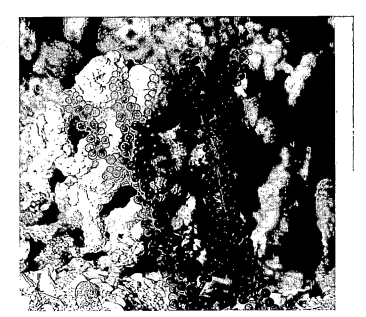

Caulerpa mexicana

Family: Caulerpaceae
Range: Caribbean, Florida to Brazil
Description: Unlike C. *floridana* the pinnae around the margins of the thalli are tapered to points and flattened in this species. This alga is also larger, the height of the thalli being about 10in (25cm). The stolon length is shorter than with most other species and rarely exceeds 12in (30cm). The thalli are seldom branched and the usual colour is light to middle green. This is a common inshore species often seen on sand sea bottoms or reef flats.
Aquarium suitability: This alga is the ideal choice for a large Caribbean reef aquarium. It is often imported and is easy to control in an aquarium because of the relatively short stolon. A good growth can be achieved with the use of metal-halide lighting and it looks spectacular in a large tank of at least 100 gallons (455 litres).

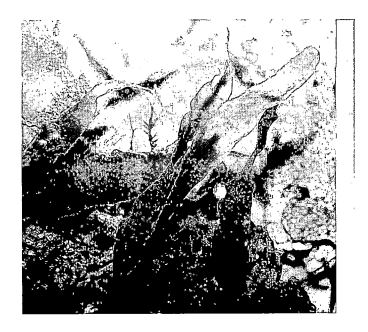

Caulerpa racemosa

Family: Caulerpaceae
Range: Caribbean, Indo-Pacific, Red Sea
Description: C. *racemosa* is an attractive species that can be found to depths of 330ft (100m) in nature. The colouration ranges from bright apple-green to deep green and the erect branches may reach a height of 12in (30cm). The thalli have clusters of spherical-formed pinnae around a central stipe, and there are many variations in form. Nevertheless, this species is unmistakable in appearance, as can readily be seen from the accompanying photograph.
Aquarium suitability: This species is often imported on live rock and is easy to keep in an aquarium. It is probably the most ubiquitous alga in European aquariums and grows well under both fluorescent and metal-halide lighting. For the best results, a strong water current should be provided.

Caulerpa serrulata

Family: Caulerpaceae
Range: South Pacific from the Great Barrier Reef to Fiji
Description: The thalli of this species are often branched dichotomously and the margins are tooth-formed with a notch at the tip of each blade. The colouration is generally bright green and the stolon reaches a length of up to 18in (45cm). This species often occurs on reef flats at depths of less than 35ft (10m) and it may also be found in sandy areas and lagoons in even shallower water.
Aquarium suitability: *C. serrulata* is seldom imported, which may be due to the strong export controls in the areas where it is endemic. It is a pity, but there are many other species of *Caulerpa* that are equally as attractive. The protection of the reef and sea environment is important and takes a greater precedence over the needs of this or any other hobby.

Caulerpa sertularoides

Family: Caulerpaceae
Range: Tropical East and West Atlantic
Description: This species is often seen in tangled growths so intertwined that it is difficult to tell where one stolon ends and the next begins. The stolons may be up to 36in (91cm) in length with descending rhizome-like holdfasts, at intervals, to attach it to the substrate. Every inch or so, erect branches arise and these are feather-like (pinnate). These thalli have margins of fine pinnae around a central stipe that can be up to 10in (25cm) high. The colouration varies between bright green and deep green, with the stolons being lighter in colour.
Aquarium suitability: *C. sertularoides* is often seen in dealers' aquariums throughout the UK and USA, but seldom in Germany. It is one of the hardiest algae for a beginner and makes an attractive addition to a marine tank.

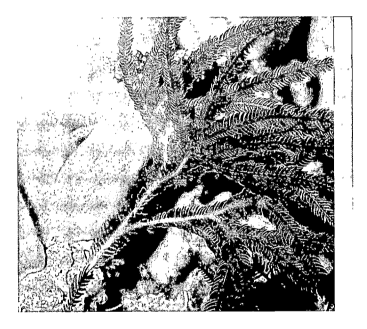

Caulerpa taxifolia

Family: Caulerpaceae
Range: Tropical East Atlantic, Indian Ocean
Description: It is easy to differentiate this alga from others by the form of the thalli and the marginal pinnae. Here, the feather-like thallus is shaped like an elongated Christmas tree, but on a single, flat plane. The radiating pinnae are long at the base of the stipe but become increasingly shorter toward the tip. The pinnae themselves are also tapered at the ends. The colour of this alga varies between deep olive green and dark green.
Aquarium suitability: This species is not quite as easy to keep as *C. sertularoides*. It requires water containing less than 20mg/litre nitrate. A strong water movement should also be provided, along with metal-halide and blue actinic lighting. Given these parameters, this alga will grow well and form lush, green growths.

Halimeda discoidea

Family: Halimedaceae
Range: Caribbean
Description: The thallus segments of this species are the largest of this genus and can be up to 1½in (4cm) in diameter. These plate-like segments are bright green in colour and heavily calcified. It is ubiquitous throughout the Caribbean region and occurs, more often than not, in deep-water regions to depths of 200ft (60m). The alga forms sparsely branched bushes that reach a maximum height of about 8in (20cm), usually on reef banks or algal plains in the West Indies.
Aquarium suitability: This alga is most often imported on live rock from the Florida and Caribbean regions. As with most algae, when this species is given enough light it will grow quite quickly and will sometimes produce extra segments on the thalli every two to three days.

Halimeda gorauii

Family: Halimedaceae
Range: Caribbean, Tropical Indo-Pacific
Description: The form that the thallus segments take and their size are good clues to the identity of this species. Three definable lobes are present on the flat plate-like segments, which are about ¼in (6mm) across. These bright green or deep green segments grow in long chains, with each new segment growing out of the middle lobe of the one before. Binary branching takes place from the side lobes about every 1in (2 to 3cm) to form densely tangled clumps attached to rocks in the reef shallows and also deeper reef areas.
Aquarium suitability: This alga is one of the most common aquarium species. Given plenty of light and a low level of nitrate in the water, it will grow well and form dense mats on rocks.

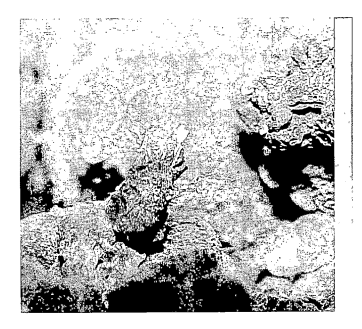

Photograph by Frank Walker

Halimeda incrassata

Family: Halimedaceae
Range: Caribbean, Indo-Pacific, Red Sea
Description: This species also has three definite lobes to each segment of the thallus, but in this case they are in the form of ribs, and the flat, fleshy segments are disc-shaped or occasionally heart-shaped, with a diameter of up to 1in (2.5cm). The bottom segment of the thallus is almost cylindrical in form, and attaches itself to the rock with a rhizoid-like holdfast. The colouration is usually bright green to middle green and it is found in all tropical seas in the reef shallows.
Aquarium suitability: *H. incrassata* is one of the most commonly imported species, usually brought in on live rock. This alga needs a lot of light, so metal-halide illumination should be used. Because of its calcareous nature, it grows best when a calcium reactor is in use in the system.

Halimeda tuna

Family: Halimedaceae
Range: Caribbean
Description: This is a shallow-water species occurring on algal beds and reef flats at depths of between 36in and 35ft (91cm and 10m). The ½- to ⅔-in (12- to 15-mm) segments are triangular, sometimes disc-shaped, and are separated by moveable joints. The colouration is deep, bright green and the alga usually forms bushy growths up to 14in (35cm) high and 16in (40cm) across.
Aquarium suitability: *H. tuna* is probably the best known but often misnamed species in the aquarium trade. It is often imported on live rock from Florida and the Caribbean region and grows well in a marine or reef aquarium when there is enough light present and good water quality is provided. This species requires a large amount of calcium for it to sustain its continual growth.

Order: Dasycladales

Small, sometimes delicate, algae make up this order. All of the species are marine living, although some species occur in brackish water. The order contains about 11 genera with 51 species and practically all are heavily encrusted with calcium carbonate and, because of this, there is a good fossil record of this group. At the moment, the oldest recorded fossil specimen is from the Cambrian period, 550 million years ago.

Many species of this order appear for a short time in new aquariums set up with live rock. However, many of them can also be cultivated. Dasycladales are represented in all tropical and subtropical seas, particularly in coastal areas and estuaries. Their forms are extremely varied and, depending on the genus, they can be cylindrical, such as *Dasycladus vermicularis* from the Caribbean, whose thalli

Halimeda opuntia

Family: Halimedaceae
Range: Caribbean, Red Sea, Indian and Pacific Oceans
Description: *H. opuntia* forms densely branched clumps and, unlike most alga in this genus, the small, about ⅓-in (5- to 10-mm) diameter segments are orientated in multiple planes so that thick, bushy mats grow with several rhizomes attaching them to the substrate. Moveable joints separate the segments, which appear to have 3 lobes – but closer inspection reveals them to be embossed ribs. This is a shallow-water species that is found in lagoons and on inshore algal plains.
Aquarium suitability: *H. opuntia* often turns up on live rock. It grows quite quickly with the thalli often producing new segments almost on a daily basis. Bright-green bushes of this alga look particularly attractive between corals in a reef tank.

grow to 3in (7.5cm) and are lightly calcified, to umbrella-formed *Polyphysa* spp., where the stipe and thallus disc are made up of a single cell and yet may be nearly ½in (1cm) high. The thallus disc is ribbed and encrusted with calcium carbonate.

Batophora spp., such as *B. oerstedii*, which is common in the Caribbean, are similar to *Dasycladus* spp., but grow to 4in (10cm). Many of the species are found in calm, sometimes brackish water, and usually appear on imports of live rock. Because of recent technological advances in lighting systems, quite a number of these algae can now be successfully kept in aquariums.

In the case of *Neomeris* spp., strong lighting is especially important, and when rock is obtained with these algae growing on it you should bear this in mind. The rock should be placed near or at the water surface, more or less directly under metal-halide lighting.

Neomeris sp.

Family: Dasycladaceae
Range: Indo-Pacific
Description: This is another species that can lie dormant on live rock for up to two years before reappearing. The single thallus is heavily calcified and cylindrical in form. It is a small alga that is slow growing, with the thallus reaching a height of 1in (2.5cm). The colouration is bright green to lime-green, with a slightly furry appearance caused by the presence of epiphytes on the thallus. It often turns up on live rock from Indonesia.
Aquarium suitability: This small alga often goes unnoticed in larger aquariums until it is almost fully grown. Its bright green colour is an attractive addition, particularly when it occurs between red and violet crustose coralline algae. The lighting should be strong and this species will not grow in water with a nitrate level of more than 20mg/litre.

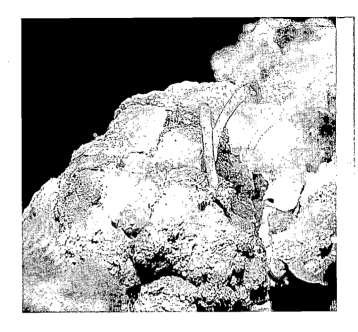

Higher plants

Rhizophora sp.

Family: Rhizophoraceae
Range: Circumtropical and subtropical
Description: This, and similar species, are well known as "mangroves". They are not algae, but belong to the higher plants. This means that they are further along than algae in evolutionary terms. Trees and flowers also belong to the higher plants. Mangroves are tropical trees or shrubs that grow in coastal mud and sand, and have many tangled roots above the ground or above the water's surface in some cases. Their underwater root system plays an important role in the development of many fish fry and invertebrate larvae. The tangled root structures that extend underwater also provide protection for many small animals. Nutrients that are harboured within the mangrove roots, both in the form of plankton and other organic debris, are vital to the ecology of some seashores, providing food for myriad animals.
Aquarium suitability: For amateur botanists, mangroves are one of the "impossible" plants in terms of propagation. For the aquarist, however, mangroves are not a problem. They require sea water, or brackish water, carrying enough nutrients to their root system to allow the plant to flourish. This may be hard for the botanist to reproduce, but for the marine aquarist these "special" requirements are already in place. In the last few years, more and more of these shrubs have appeared on offer to the marine aquarist. They are usually sold in small perforated plastic "plant pots" that you can place directly in an open-topped aquarium, amongst live rock, with the root graft above the water's surface to allow the plant to grow. Metal-halide lighting is a prerequisite, and when this is provided the mangrove will flourish. It is especially recommended for those aquarists who use a plenum-type filtration system.

part four

CHOOSING AQUARIUM FISHES

Scientific classification

The 18th-century Swedish naturalist Linnaeus devised a system of classification for the animal kingdom, the basis of which is still in use today around the world. In this system he grouped like-creatures together. These groups he called phyla, which could then be subdivided into different classes of creatures which, in turn, could be further subdivided, and so on until it was possible for scientists to place every known living creature in its correct place in the animal kingdom.

Of course this was an enormous step forward in our understanding of the natural world, and it was destined to become the universally accepted method of recognizing particular animals. Each creature was given a Latin name consisting of two parts. The first part referred to the genus (the particular branch of the family), and the second to the species (the specific animal itself). For example, in Germany, a fish may be called a "Palletten Doktorfisch"; in the USA that same fish may be referred to as a "blue surgeon" or "morpho butterfly"; while in the UK it would usually be called a "regal tang". Its systematic, or Latin, name, however, is *Paracanthus hepatus*. And it is this name that is recognized worldwide. Although common names for fishes and invertebrates have been used in this book, they are accompanied by their Latin name to prevent confusion. Taking the fish *Paracanthus hepatus* as an example, it could be systematically displayed thus:

KINGDOM: ANIMALIA
  Phylum: CHORDATA
    Subphylum: VERTEBRATA
      Superclass: GNATHOSTOMATA
        Grade: TELEOSTOMI
          Class: ACTINOPTERYGII
            Subclass: NEOPTERYGII
              Division: Teleostei
                Subdivision: Euteleostei
                  Superorder: Acanthopterygii
                    Series: Percomorpha
                      Order: Perciformes
                        Family: Acanthuridae
                          Subfamily: Acanthurinae
                            Tribe: Zebrasomini
                              Genus: *Paracanthus*
                                Species: *Paracanthus hepatus*

The modern system used for the fishes listed and described in the book, follows that of Nelson, *Fishes of the World*, John Wiley & Sons, New York, 1994. This is the most sensible system presently available and is the most often used and understood by aquarists. Identification of the fishes in the following chapter, and later of the invertebrates, should always follow these scientific names. The common names also included have little scientific meaning and are intended only to represent a cross-section of those names applied to fishes and invertebrates, and hopefully they may be of some help to beginners.

When we talk of a number of fish of the same species the plural remains the same, simply "fish". If, however, several different species are being referred to, then the plural becomes "fishes". To the uninitiated this has often caused confusion, so it is as well to know the difference at this stage. The fishes included in this book have been chosen solely for their suitability for a reef or marine fish aquarium and most are available to the aquarium trade without control. Fishes suitable only for public aquariums, because they subsequently grow too large for the average aquarist, have not been included.

The sizes of fishes given are the maximum known size that a fish will grow to in its natural habitat, as measured from the tip of its snout to the base of its caudal fin. Where the range of a fish is given, it is intended to indicate where the particular fish is found to be endemic. Isolated or un-usual occurrences have not been taken into consideration, nor have those instances where species have been artificially introduced into certain areas.

The term "difficulty" refers to the degree of expertise required to keep a particular fish in a healthy state in an aquarium. The quick glance code accompanying each fish being described indicates as follows:

O – Easy (good for beginners and experienced aquarists)
OO – Moderately easy (good for aquarists with 6 months' experience or more)
OOO – Moderately difficult (only suitable for experienced aquarists)
OOOO – Very difficult (requires optimal aquarium conditions for success)
OOOOO – Almost impossible (suitable only for the most experienced aquarist)

Notes on taxonomy

Only painstaking research, examination of the fishes themselves and a great deal of correspondence along with reference to the most up-to-date scientific literature can form a solid foundation that is reliable in terms of fish identification. The listings of the fishes given in this part of the book will, hopefully, reflect these efforts. The hundreds of species named here should at least help to clarify some of the confusion that surrounds the accurate identification of fish species. The diagram shown here (*see opposite*) is for reference purposes, since there may be certain terms used in the accompanying fish descriptions with which readers are not familiar.

Anterior or
1st dorsal fin

Posterior or
2nd dorsal fin

Caudal
peduncle

Interorbital
space

Nostril

Snout

Premaxillary

Preopercle

Gill cover
or opercle

Opercular
spine

Pelvic
fin

Pectoral
fin

Vent

Anal
fin

Caudal or
tail fin

Lateral
line

Systematics (the fishes)

In order to understand fully the way this book is laid out in terms of the descriptions of the fishes and invertebrates, it is necessary first to explain the order in which the various families appear. To some this will be unusual, since most aquarium books simply list families in alphabetical order. This is not strictly correct because it does not follow the systematic methods used by marine biologists and ichthyologists throughout the world.

The following table (*see p. 100*) shows the breakdown of the phylum Chordata. Although much of it is of no interest to the marine aquarist, it is good to know how it all fits into the animal kingdom as a whole. This is the first step to understanding the fishes and invertebrates in the aquarium. The various branches indicated in bold type are, however, of interest and this part of the book will deal with them in detail.

It is not possible in a single volume to cover and describe all of the 3,500 fishes that are found on coral reefs throughout the world; nor is it necessary, since a good 70 per cent of them are unsuitable for a home aquarium. What this book tries to do is cover a cross-section of the species that hobbyists will find at their local dealers. Some latitude is required, however, since dealers in different countries tend to stock different species.

The superclass Gnathostomata is our first step into the systematics of reef fishes. It is this class that holds the key to modern fishes. There are three grades of Gnathostomata. The first of these is the Placodermiomorphi, which consists of a single class – Placodermi – a group of primitive fishes with bony plates over much of their bodies that existed between the lower and upper Devonian Period (395 to

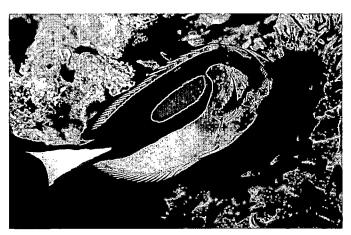

The *"Palletten Doktorfisch"* as it is known in Germany is also called a *"regal tang"* in the UK and, in the USA, as a *"morpho butterfly"* or *"blue surgeon"*. Its systematic name – Paracanthus hepatus – is, however, recognized throughout the world.

350 million years ago). All fishes of this grade are extinct and so do not appear on the chart on the previous page. Fishes of the second grade – Chondrichthiomorphi – swiftly replaced them at the end of the Devonian, although this group has existed as a taxon since the Silurian Period (430 to 395 million years ago). Chondrichthiomorphi also consists of a single class – Chondrichthyes (cartilaginous fishes) – and there is an almost complete fossil record of its development since the end of the Devonian Period with some extant genera having their origins in the Cretaceous Period (135 to 65 million years ago).

The third grade is Teleostomi, and it contains all true vertebrate animals. This not only means the tetrapods,

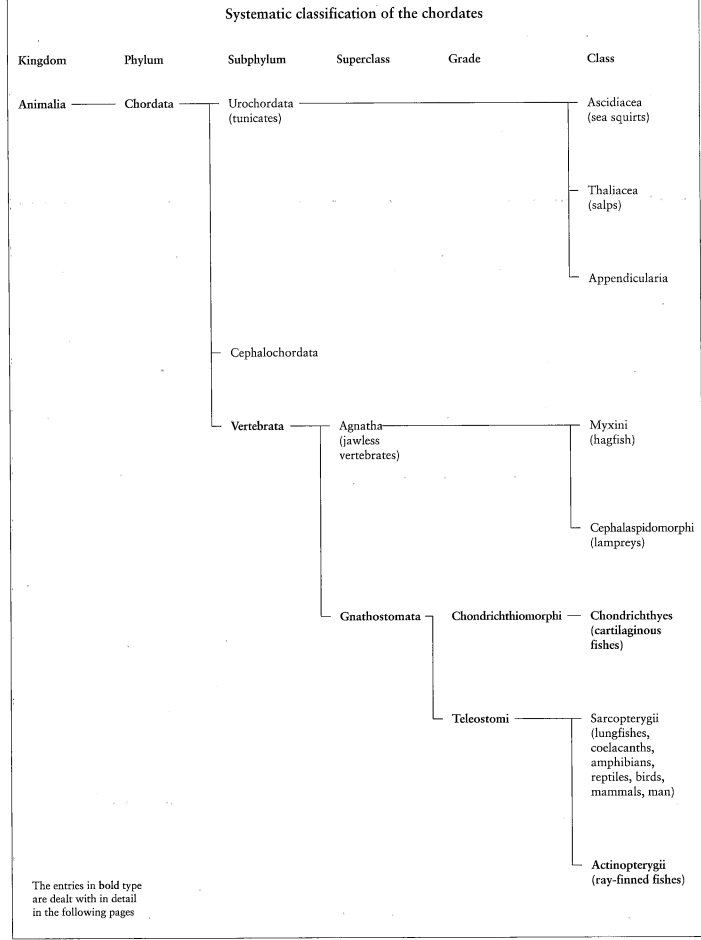

Systematic classification of the chordates

Kingdom	Phylum	Subphylum	Superclass	Grade	Class

Animalia ——— **Chordata** —— Urochordata (tunicates) —————————————————————————— Ascidiacea (sea squirts)

Thaliacea (salps)

Appendicularia

Cephalochordata

Vertebrata —— Agnatha (jawless vertebrates) ———————————————— Myxini (hagfish)

Cephalaspidomorphi (lampreys)

Gnathostomata —— Chondrichthiomorphi — **Chondrichthyes** (cartilaginous fishes)

Teleostomi ————— Sarcopterygii (lungfishes, coelacanths, amphibians, reptiles, birds, mammals, man)

Actinopterygii (ray-finned fishes)

The entries in **bold type** are dealt with in detail in the following pages

```
                    Systematic classification of the class – Chondrichthyes

Class                          Subclass                        Order

Chondrichthyes ──────────┬── Holocephali ──────────────── Chimaeriformes (chimaeras)
(cartilaginous fishes)    │
                          │
                          └── Elasmobranchii ──────────┬── Heterodontiformes (horn sharks)
                                                        ├── Orectolobiformes (carpet sharks)
                                                        ├── Carcharhiniformes (ground sharks)
                                                        ├── Lamniformes (mackerel sharks)
                                                        ├── Hexanchiformes (six-gilled sharks)
                                                        ├── Squaliformes (spiny sharks, dogfish)
                                                        ├── Squatiniformes (angel sharks)
 The entries in bold type                               ├── Pristiophoriformes (saw sharks)
 are dealt with in detail                               └── Rajiformes (sawfishes, skates & rays)
 in the following pages
```

such as mammals, man, birds, lizards and snakes, but also all modern bony fishes.

The class Chondrichthyes has two subclasses encompassing ten orders, 45 families, 170 genera and approximately 846 species. The first subclass – Holocephali – is made up of a single order and contains ancient and primitive deep-water fishes known as ghost sharks and chimaeras. Most of these are unsuitable for life in an aquarium, although they are occasionally seen on offer as an "exotic". However, they do not usually live long in captivity and so should really not be considered.

The second subclass is Elasmobranchii and consists of nine orders and contains all the true sharks, rays, skates and sawfishes. Only one order is of interest to the marine aquarist – Orectolobiformes (carpet sharks) – which also contains the world's largest living fish, the whale shark.

Generally, the characteristics of this class are well known. The skeleton is cartilaginous, sometimes calcified, but never bone. There are five to seven gill slits and the scales are not made up of overlapping plates, as is the case with most fishes. Instead, the scales are small tubercles (dermal denticles), which give rise to the sandpapery texture of the skin. The teeth are not embedded in sockets but are fused in rows to tissue that is continually growing forward. In this way, the rear teeth become erect, moving forward to replace broken or blunt teeth at the front, which are then shed. The teeth themselves are modified dermal denticles. There is no swim bladder to offset the body weight, therefore the fish must swim in order to maintain its level in midwater. In the case of sharks, the forward edges of the pectoral fins are inclined upward to produce a hydrofoil effect, thereby helping to give the fish lift.

Order: Orectolobiformes

The order Orectolobiformes is made up of seven families with a total of 14 genera and 31 species. Two dorsal fins are present without spines, and the small mouth is usually set well forward in front of the eyes. Most members of this order are bottom-dwelling, sluggish fishes whose size can vary considerably from species to species. They are mostly nocturnal and usually harmless to people, feeding on small invertebrates and fishes. Their forms are extremely diverse and they often have impressive, even striking, colour patterns.

Bamboo sharks (Hemiscylliidae)

This family has two genera – Chiloscyllium and Hemiscyllium – containing a total of 11 species. All of the

species have long bodies and the upper lobe of the tail is strongly elongated. They have short nasal barbels and are generally sluggish and slow-moving creatures. In addition, they are extremely short sighted and rely heavily on their olfactory senses to locate food. The maximum length attained by these species is about 40in (1m). Some species are quite attractively marked and are therefore often caught for the aquarium trade.

The epauletted shark (*Hemiscyllium ocellatum*) and the banded shark (*Chiloscyllium punctatum*) are perhaps the most frequently imported, with *Hemiscyllium freycineti* running a close third, since the latter is often confused with *H. ocellatum*. Both *H. ocellatum* and *H. freycineti* are brownish in colour and covered in irregular dark blotches of differing sizes. The two species both have a dark "eye spot" above the pectoral fin behind the gill slits.

However, on *H. ocellatum* it is ringed with white, whereas on *H. freycineti* it is not. A closely related species, *H. trispeculare*, also has a suprapectoral "eye spot" that is ringed with white, but in this particular example the body spots are much smaller in comparison with the other two species. Species from this family are restricted to the tropical Indo-Pacific region.

Chiloscyllium punctatum

Common name: Banded shark
Range: Central Indo-Pacific
Size: 40in (1m)
Description: The background body colouration of this species is black. There are nine broad, creamy-white bars that cross the body, giving it a striped appearance. This is a bottom-dwelling and slow-moving fish that is frequently found in areas of thick coral growth in caves and crevices.
Aquarium suitability: This peaceful species requires a large aquarium for the best chances of success. It enjoys a diet of chopped mussel and cockle, which should be given later in the evening as this fish is a nocturnal feeder. It should not be kept in an aquarium with boisterous or aggressive fishes or it will not do well in captivity.

Nurse sharks (Ginglymostomatidae)

The family Ginglymostomatidae is represented in all the tropical seas of the world and consists of three monotypic genera. These are *Ginglymostoma*, *Nebrius* and *Pseudoginglymostoma*. They are large fishes that are not really suited to life in a home aquarium. Nevertheless, young specimens often appear for sale in dealers' tanks and seem to do quite well, at least for a while. The three species have typical shark forms but are essentially bottom

Another attractive species is *Chiloscyllium plagiosum*, from the western Indo-Pacific. It is easily identified, having ten dark bands along its body and numerous small blue and white spots. This fish reaches a maximum length of 28in (71cm). The two species that are the least attractive are *C. griseum* and *C. confusum*. They are either dull-looking creatures or mottled brown in colour.

dwellers. The nostrils are short and they have middle to long barbels, which they use to search and grub the bottom for food. The two most commonly imported species are *Ginglymostoma cirratum* and its Indo-Pacific relative *Nebrius concolor*. They are not particularly brightly coloured or strikingly marked, but they can make a spectacular addition to a large show tank. A suitable tank must be very large indeed, since adults can reach a length of 10½ft (3.2m). These are definitely not fishes for the novice to undertake.

Ginglymostoma cirratum

Common name: Nurse shark
Range: Tropical West Atlantic, Eastern Pacific
Size: 10½ft (3.2m)
Description: *G. cirratum* is easily identified since it has no lower lobe to the tail, just a notch. In addition, it has two long barbels in front of its nostrils and the two dorsal fins are set well back on its body. The adult colouration is greyish-brown, whereas young fish have a suffusion of small spots. This fish is often seen basking in the reef shallows throughout its natural range.
Aquarium suitability: This is a bottom-dwelling shark. Newly born young are 14in (36cm) long and specimens slightly larger are often available to the aquarist. The minimum tank size that should be considered is 150 gallons (680 litres). It will seldom grow larger than 40in (100cm) in captivity and, since it is a scavenger, feeding is no problem. It accepts most frozen foods.

Grade: Teleostomi

The second step in this systematic breakdown is the classification of the grade Teleostomi down to the various orders. This is shown on the chart presented here (*see below*). It has been somewhat simplified for ease of

reference. From the chart, it can be seen that all the relevant orders belong to the division Teleostei, and it is an indisputable fact that most or, indeed, practically all aquarium fishes are true bony fishes, such as teleostei. This applies not only to marine fishes, but also to freshwater aquarium fishes as well.

Systematic classification of the grade – Teleostomi

Grade	Class	Subclass	Division	Order
Teleostomi	Sarcopterygii	Coelacanthimorpha		Coelacanthiformes (coelacanths)
		Dipneusti		Ceradontiformes (Australian lungfish)
				Lepidosireniformes (lungfishes)
		Tetrapoda (= Amphibia, Mammalia, Aves, Reptilia)		
	Actinopterygii	Chondrostei		Polypteriformes (bichirs)
				Acipenseriformis (sturgeons)
		Neopterygii		Semiontiformis (garfishes)
				Amiiformes (bowfins)
			Teleostei	Osteoglossiformes (featherbacks)

- Osteoglossiformes (featherbacks)
- Elopiformes (tarpons)
- Albuliformes (bonefishes, spiny eels)
- Anguilliformes (eels, moray eels)
- Saccopharyngiformes (swallowers)
- Clupeiformes (herring-like fishes)
- Gonorhynchiformes (sand fishes)
- Cypriniformes (carp-like fishes)
- Characiformes (characins)
- **Siluriformes (catfishes)**
- Gymnotiformes (knife fishes)
- Esociformes (pikes)
- Osmeriformes (smelts)
- Salmoniformes (salmon-like fishes)
- Stomiiformes (dragonfishes, lightfishes)
- Atelopodiformes (jellynose fishes)
- Aulopiformes (lizardfishes)
- Myctophiformes (lantern fishes)
- Lampridiformes (opahs, ribbonfishes)
- Polymixiiformes (beardfishes)
- Percopsiformes (trout-perch, cavefishes)
- Ophidiiformes (pearlfishes, eel pouts)
- Gadiformes (cod-like fishes)
- Batrachoidiformes (toadfishes)
- Lophiiformes (anglerfishes, monkfish)
- Mugiliiformes (mullets, grey mullets)
- Atheriniformes (silversides)
- Beloniformes (needlefishes, flyingfishes)
- Cyprinodontiformes (toothed carps)
- Stephanoberyciformes (hairyfishes)
- Beryciformes (squirrelfishes)
- Zeiformes (dories)
- **Syngnathiformes (tube-mouth fishes)**
- Synbranchiformes (swamp-eels)
- **Scorpaeniformes (scorpionfishes)**
- **Perciformes (perch-like fishes)**
- Pleuronectiformes (flat fishes)
- **Tetraodontiformes (triggers, file fishes, box fishes)**

The entries in **bold type** are dealt with in detail in the following pages

Order: Siluriformes

In the order Siluriformes you will find classified all the catfishes that you will encounter in freshwater streams, lakes and rivers throughout the world, in both tropical and subtropical regions. There are well in excess of 2,000 different known species of catfishes and these are divided up into more than 410 genera. These genera are currently subdivided into 34 families. This makes Siluriformes a very large order indeed, second only in size to the order Perciformes, which comprises 148 families.

However, although almost all members of this order are found in freshwater, there are two families – Ariidae and Plotosidae – that contain species that are truly marine living. Many species live in brackish water or there are even some that can tolerate high levels of salinity, but these are not strictly sea fishes and are, therefore, outside the scope of this book.

Quite a number of the freshwater species are well known to aquarists who specialize in tropical fishes, and you will find that all experienced fishkeepers have their own favourite species. For the tropical fish hobbyist, there is a rich selection, with many bizarre and spectacular species available.

However, for the marine aquarist the situation is very different, and for these fishkeepers the selection is extremely poor, with only one species usually being imported. This is because the few species of coral catfishes that are available tend to be drab-looking and uninteresting, and they also usually grow too large for the average-sized home aquarium.

Generally, catfishes are scavengers and bottom dwelling, and therefore it is odd that they are so poorly represented in the seas of the world. One explanation for this could be that through the process of evolution, too much competition has been developed by families of fishes from other orders, such as the blennies, gobies and goatfishes. This may have forced catfishes to seek nutrition in freshwater.

Coral catfishes (Plotosidae)

Most coral catfishes have a swarming nature when they are in the juvenile phase. It can look almost comical to see these shoals react to danger, such as threats from predators. They quickly mass into a large, whiskered ball with their tails pointing inward and their heads facing outward. The sight of this huge ball is usually sufficient to deter all but the hungriest of predators. As they grow larger, the shoals break up and they become solitary fish, often moving to deeper water.

This family is confined to the Indo-Pacific, Red Sea and West Pacific regions from Japan south to Australia. There are no representatives in the Caribbean or Tropical Atlantic waters. One of the most widespread species is *Plotosus canius*, which grows to a size of about 36in (91cm). This species is found throughout the Indian Ocean to the West Pacific, and the young lack the stripes of *P. lineatus*. *Paraplotosus albilabrus* is dark brownish-black with white around the mouth and it is endemic throughout the Indo-Australian Archipelago, eventually reaching a length of 14in (35cm).

One species, *Euristhmus nudiceps*, is restricted to the Gulf of Papua. This is a small species of fish that grows only to a maximum length of about 12in (30cm). It is mottled brown in colouration and has black margins to the fins.

Plotosus lineatus

Common names: Coral catfish, candy-striped catfish, saltwater catfish.
Range: Red Sea, Tropical Indo-Pacific
Size: 16in (40cm)
Description: The accompanying picture was taken at Guadal Canal in the Solomon Islands and shows a shoal of juvenile fish. The colouration is dark brown above the lateral line fading into pale cream at the belly. In juveniles, there are two white stripes along the body but these fade with age. At about 6in (15cm) this fish ceases to shoal and moves into deeper water. Up to this stage, they are a common sight in tide pools and reef shallows.
Aquarium suitability: These fish are equipped with venom glands that can give a very painful sting if they are incorrectly handled. They are best kept in small groups and usually grow quite quickly. Frozen foods are readily taken.

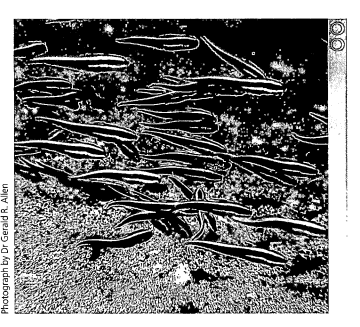

Photograph by Dr Gerald R. Allen

Order: Syngnathiformes

The order Syngnathiformes is a group of very primitive and degenerate fishes. The taxonomy is complex and the order is currently divided into 11 families containing a total of 71 genera and approximately 257 species. There are two suborders – Gasterosteoidei and Syngnathoidei. The first suborder, Gasterosteoidei, is of little interest to aquarists, since it contains sticklebacks and similar species.

The second suborder, Syngnathoidei, is split into three groups. The first of these is the infraorder Aulostomoida, which contains two superfamilies, Aulostomoidea and Centriscoidea. Aulostomidae contains the single genus *Aulostomus* comprising three species. These are the flutemouths, or trumpetfishes, which are a small family of bizarre fishes with elongated bodies and mouths. They are predatory by nature and are able to change colour with remarkable rapidity. The spinous dorsal fin is used as a defence mechanism. There is a small barbel at the tip of the lower jaw and the snout is tubular. They are often seen in shallow water on the reefs in the Caribbean and Indo-Pacific and they have very good eyesight.

These fishes have developed a peculiar method of hunting their prey. The trumpetfish will adopt a head-down position among sea whips or long growths of algae. By remaining motionless and changing colour like a chameleon, it will quickly blend in with the background. Several minutes may pass before a small fish comes near enough. When an unsuspecting fish does stray too close, the patient trumpetfish is galvanized into action. Striking quickly, it will literally suck the prey into its mouth.

The second family, Fistulariidae (cornetfishes), also has one genus, which contains four known species: *Fistularia commersonii*, whose range is circumtropical, *F. petimba* and *F. villosa*, which are found throughout the Indo-Pacific, and *F. tabacaria*, an endemic species in the Tropical West Atlantic and Caribbean. These are all predatory fishes and good swimmers. They have long snouts and the central rays of the tail are developed into whip-like extensions. The lateral line is well expanded and their scales are spine-formed. Generally, they grow larger than the trumpetfishes and their maximum size differs between species, ranging from 36in to 6ft (91cm to 1.8m).

The second of the two superfamilies is the Centriscoidea (snipefish and shrimpfish), and this is also split into two families. Macrorhamphosidae, the first of these, has three genera incorporating 12 species. These are deep-water fishes and of little interest to the aquarist. Their bodies are knife-formed and the first ray of the anterior dorsal fin is developed into a long spine. The skin of these fishes is parchment-like, often translucent, and the soft or posterior dorsal fin is set well back near the tail.

The other family in this group is of more interest. This is the family Centriscidae, which contains two genera totalling only four species. *Aeoliscus strigatus* and *A. punctulatus* make up the first genus, and *Centriscus scutatus* and *C. cristatus*, the second. All four species are restricted to the Indo-Pacific and are sometimes imported for the aquarium trade. They are small, seldom reaching a length of more than 6in (15cm), and should be kept in small groups of six to eight individuals. Generally, their bodies are laterally compressed into a knife form, with a ventral keel. The skin is almost transparent and forms a stiff carapace of bony plates that are fused together. The first ray of the dorsal fin is developed to the extreme, which shifts the soft dorsal and caudal fin into the ventral region. Fishes from this family adopt a head-down position in small shoals.

Photograph by Frank Walker

Aulostomus chinensis

Common names: Flutemouth, trumpetfish
Range: Central Indo-Pacific
Size: 40in (1m)
Description: The body of this fish may be striped and it has a yellow tail adorned with one or two black spots. Colouration is variable and may be brownish-red, orange, yellow or green. The snout is long, the scales are small and there is a visible lateral line. This is the largest of the three species. *A. maculatus* from the Caribbean reaches a length of 35in (90cm) and *A. valentini*, from the Indo-Pacific, grows only to 24in (60cm).
Aquarium suitability: Smaller specimens do well in an aquarium but it must be large enough to accommodate them. By nature this fish is a solitary predator, so it should not be trusted with small tank-mates. Most frozen shell meat will be accepted, but it is not an easy fish to keep.

Pipefishes, sea horses (Syngnathidae)

The second infraorder, Indostomoida, contains a single species, but this lies outside the scope of this book and so is not described. Syngnatha, the third infraorder, is divided into two superfamilies, Pegasoidea (seamoths) and Syngnathoidea. The latter is of interest to aquarists, however, containing as it does the two families Solenostomidae (ghost pipefishes) and Syngnathidae (pipefishes and sea horses).

The family Solenostomidae has a single genus, *Solenostomus*, encompassing four species: *Solenostomus armatus*, *S. cyanopterus*, *S. paradoxus* and *S. paegnius*. All are specialist feeders and bizarre in form. As far as is known, none has ever been kept successfully in an aquarium, therefore they are also outside the scope of this book.

There are about 190 species of pipefishes in the subfamily Syngnathinae, divided into 51 genera. The subfamily Hippocampinae, on the other hand, has only one genus containing about 25 species.

Most of the pipefishes imported come from the genus *Doryrhamphus*. Generally they are slow-swimming and easily caught by hand. They are also degenerate, their bodies comprising rings of bony armour. There is usually a ventral brood pouch and they have small, primitive gills. The pelvic fin is completely absent and the caudal fin is small or missing. All species are coastal fishes that are often seen in algae or sea-grass beds or on muddy estuary bottoms. Some species are found on coral reefs. Only 20 species have been recorded from the Caribbean region.

The sea horses are also very primitive fishes that lack the caudal and ventral fins. The tail is prehensile and they adopt an upright position when swimming. They are specialist feeders and small crustaceans form their usual diet. The males have a brood pouch into which the female deposits the eggs.

Hippocampus kuda

Common names: Spotted or yellow sea horse
Range: Indo-Pacific
Size: 10in (25cm)
Description: The colouration of this species is variable, ranging from yellow to brownish-black, sometimes with spots or irregular bands. They are found in shallow, calm water or lagoon areas, more often than not in weed beds. Their prehensile tails allow them to anchor to a convenient "hitching post", where they wait for food to be carried to them by the currents. When a morsel is close enough, it is then sucked up into their mouths with a distinctive "pipette" action.
Aquarium suitability: This is a slow-swimming species that should be kept with members of its own kind. Feeding should initially be on live brine shrimp. Later it can be weaned on to frost foods if there is enough water current in the tank to give the food movement.

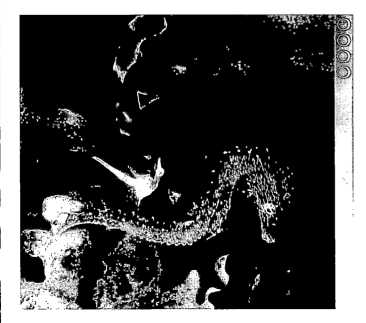

Hippocampus ramulosus

Common name: Spiny sea horse
Range: Tropical East Atlantic, Mediterranean
Size: 6in (15cm)
Description: The light, spotted areas on the head and snout and the radiating pattern around the eye are helpful in identifying this species. The bony trunk and some of the tail ring joints end in long, spiny protuberances, particularly along the back. They are smaller than most species and normally occur in sea-grass beds and inshore bays, seldom on coral reefs.
Aquarium suitability: This is a shy fish that is difficult to keep for any length of time in an aquarium. It is susceptible to shock and rapid changes in water quality. In addition, feeding presents quite a problem because of the difficulties in weaning this species on to frost foods such as frozen brine shrimp and mysis. The ideal solution is to keep them in an invertebrate aquarium.

Order: Scorpaeniformes

With 1,200 species, this is one of the largest orders of fishes. Some of them occur in freshwater, others in polar regions, but all have one special characteristic – the second suborbital bone has a comb-like extension running across the cheek to the preopercle. The order encompasses some 25 families but only one is dealt with in this book. Fishes of the subfamily Synanceiinae (family Scorpaenidae), for example, are considered to be the most poisonous fishes yet discovered. The dangerous dorsal spines contain a substance that is often fatal. Collectively they are known as stonefishes and it would be irresponsible to recommend fishes of this family to the average marine aquarist. Even so, they do sometimes appear for sale.

Practically no fishes from the other 24 families are seen for sale, since many of them are unsuitable for the home aquarium. Some fishes are pelagic by nature and cannot adapt to aquarium life. Others come from temperate zones and are, therefore, outside the scope of this book. Some are reef dwellers but the problem in keeping them alive in captivity prohibits their import.

None of the fishes from this order should be bought without careful thought, since most of them are fierce predators and will eat any fishes that fit in their gaping mouths – and this is any fish that is almost as large as the scorpionfish itself.

The group that is dealt with next – Scorpaenidae – is of considerable interest to aquarists. Although this family contains fishes that are poisonous, no known case of death can be directly attributed to a puncture wound from one of these fishes. In fact, they are shy fishes on the whole and the poisonous spines are only used in defence. Neverthe-less, if a fish feels threatened it will raise its spines and sometimes even take a short lunge forward, striking more or less like a snake.

Despite precautions and warnings aquarists are sometimes stung. In such cases, the usual first-aid advice is to immerse the wound in hot water – as hot as the victim can stand. The rationale for this is that the increase in temperature causes the neurotoxin to denature and coagulate. This advice, however, is suspect. Any increase in temperature causes the poison to become unstable, but if you follow the hot-water route, then a temperature of 46°C (115°F) is sufficient.

From practical experience, having been stung three times by these fishes, I can recommend the following procedure. First, don't cut into the wound in an attempt to extract the poison. Second, don't squeeze, suck or press the wound, as this will only exacerbate the problem. And finally, and very importantly, don't panic. The pain is similar to a bad wasp sting, nothing more. Hot water treatment should not be used, nor any form of pressure/ bandaging applied to the affected area. The difference in

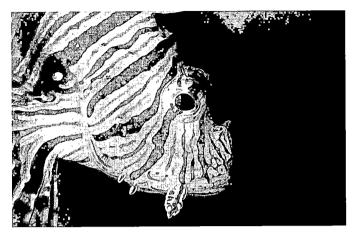

The scorpionfish (Pterois russellii) *is capable of inflicting painful wounds with its poisonous dorsal spines. It should be handled with care. Typically this species has no supraorbital antennae, as can be seen clearly here.*

the temperature of the neurotoxin and the temperature of the human body is enough to start a destabilization almost immediately. Full recovery can be expected between 48 and 72 hours. The psychological effects of suffering such a wound can be as dangerous as the injury itself. Nevertheless you should seek medical advice immediately and, where possible, give the Latin name of the fish species to the doctor. This is crucial if muscular cramp or vomiting occurs.

The family contains carnivorous fishes found in all seas in tropical and temperate climates. Their usual habitat is among rocks and reefs, where they lie, sluggish and solitary, waiting for prey. All have large heads but body form can vary between genera. Many are bizarre, such as the leaf-formed dragonfishes (*Taenianotus* spp.).

Most are extremely hardy in an aquarium. Many of the Indo-Pacific species have long, feather-like fins and make good aquarium fishes (*Pterois* spp. and *Dendrochirus* spp.). The dorsal fins of these fishes are continuous, often with a deep notch, and they are all masters of camouflage. Occasionally, species of the genus *Scorpaena* are imported for the aquarium trade, but this is infrequent and only one species is described here. The genus *Dendrochirus* contains only five species: *Dendrochirus barbari, D. bellus, D. biocellatus, D. brachypterus* and *D. zebra*. The genus *Pterois* has seven valid species. These are *Pterois antennata, P. miles, P. mombasae, P. radiata, P. russellii, P. sphex* and *P. volitans*.

> **CAUTION**
> Scorpionfishes have poisonous spines containing a powerful neurotoxin. Treat these fishes with respect and avoid hand contact. In the event of a puncture wound, seek immediate medical advice.

Photograph by Frank Walker

Scorpaena cf. picta

Common name: Red stingfish
Range: Entire Indo-Pacific
Size: 5in (13cm)
Description: This species is a camouflage expert, as can be seen from the accompanying photograph, which was taken on a reef in the Philippines. Photo-identification is difficult and since there was no specimen from which a 100 per cent identification could be made, you must compare it with the formal description in a standard work dealing with these species. The aquarium information applies to the actual species.
Aquarium suitability: *Scorpaena picta* sometimes shows up on dealer's lists, particularly from the Philippines and Indonesia. It is not a demanding fish to keep in an aquarium and it does not grow too large. It has a peaceful nature but is not to be trusted with small tank-mates.

Dendrochirus zebra

Common names: Dwarf lionfish, zebra lionfish
Range: Tropical Indo-Pacific, Red Sea
Size: 8in (20cm)
Description: The large pectoral fins with branched rays identify this species as belonging to the genus *Dendrochirus*. It is smaller in comparison with other long-finned members of this family. In the wild, it is encountered in caves and crevices, often upside down, singly or in small groups. It is usually shy and retiring but is, nevertheless, poisonous and can inflict painful stings with its hollow dorsal spines.
Aquarium suitability: This is a peaceful fish in an aquarium and it will soon learn to take frost food instead of its natural diet of live fishes. It should be provided with plenty of cover into which it can retire and feel secure. Several specimens kept together make a spectacular display.

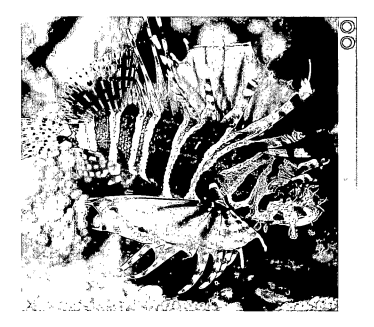

Pterois antennata

Common name: Spotfin lionfish
Range: Tropical Indo-Pacific
Size: 10in (25cm)
Description: This species is found throughout the central Indo-Pacific, but not as far as Hawaii, while a similar-looking species, *P. sphex*, is endemic in Hawaii. *P. antennata* is larger as an adult fish than the previous species. Distinguishing features include extended pectoral rays with a number of black spots on the membranes between the rays.
Aquarium suitability: Acclimatization to aquarium life seems to differ from specimen to specimen. Some adapt quite quickly, whereas others are difficult to wean on to frozen food and take a long time to settle in. This may possibly be attributed to the method of capture and/or transportation. Once they have settled down and are feeding, however, they make ideal aquarium fish.

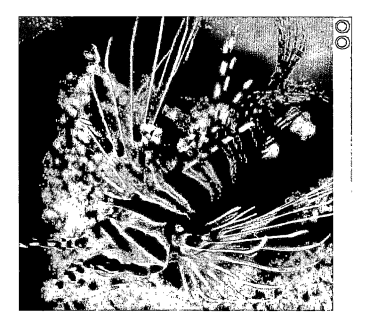

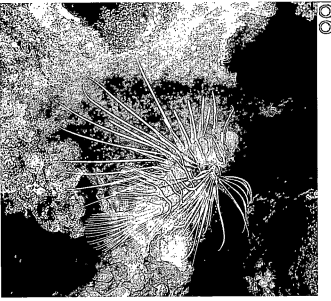

Photograph by Siegfried Krumbügel

Pterois radiata

Common names: Regal dragonfish, whitefin lionfish
Range: Indo-Pacific, Red Sea
Size: 8in (20cm)
Description: Considered by many to be the most spectacular member of this family, *P. radiata* is easily recognized by the broad horizontal bar on the caudal peduncle and the white pectoral fin rays. It is a voracious predator and is nocturnal by nature.
Aquarium suitability: *P. radiata* is usually more expensive to buy than others of this family. In the aquarium, it should be provided with a cave or hiding place when it is first introduced. Later it will forgo its nocturnal nature and soon adapt to daytime life in an aquarium.

Pterois russellii

(Syn. Pterois lunulata)
Common name: Russell's lionfish
Range: Tropical Indo-Pacific
Size: 12in (30cm)
Description: The lack of tentacles above the eyes (supraorbital) distinguishes this fish from its closest relative, *Pterois volitans*. Additionally, there are differences in the body markings, which help to separate the two species for identification purposes.
Aquarium suitability: This fish is ideally suited to life in a marine aquarium and is usually peaceful with tank-mates that are too large to eat. Due to of their huge appetites, none is suitable for a reef aquarium. Their feeding rate would ultimately put too much stress on the system, and waste products would result in a gradual rise in the nitrate level of most reef aquariums. Even in a fish-only aquarium, housing adults of this family means that frequent partial water changes are necessary.

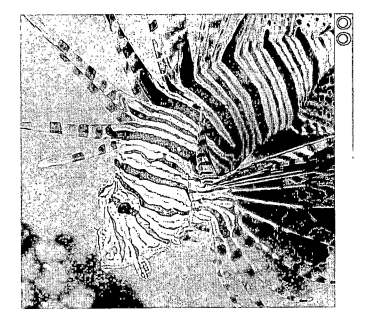

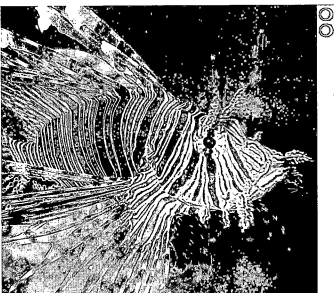

Photograph by Dr. Gerald R. Allen

Pterois volitans

Common names: Butterfly cod, scorpionfish, turkeyfish, peacock lionfish, red firefish
Range: Tropical Indo-Pacific
Size: 14in (35cm)
Description: This is the largest species in this genus and is usually slow-moving. The supraorbital tentacles are well developed and body colouration is variable. *Pterois volitans* is often confused with *P. miles*, which is almost identical.
Aquarium suitability: The tank provided should have sufficient capacity to house the fish in comfort and have plenty of hiding places. There is less chance of being stung whilst working in the aquarium if there is sufficient space for the fish to evade a carelessly placed hand or arm. If the dealer has not already weaned the fish on to frozen food, live food such as sand shrimp and small fishes must be given to the fish initially.

Order: Perciformes

This is not only the largest order within the class Actinopterygii (ray-finned fishes), it is by far the largest order in the subphylum Vertebrata (vertebrates). With almost 9,300 valid species, the order Perciformes represents almost 25 per cent of all known vertebrate animals. The order is split into 148 families, and groups together all perch-like fishes as well as modified forms of these. It includes the vast majority of the modern bony fishes. More specifically, this means important game and hobby fishes, such as tuna, mackerel and swordfish, cichlids and anabantids. A large proportion of all reef fishes is included in this order, but there are also pelagic and oceanic fishes represented, such as skipjack, bonito, marlin, billfish and albacore.

Of the 148 families included in the order Perciformes, species from only 45 of these could be considered as suitable for a reef or marine aquarium. However, many of these species are so rarely imported or so difficult to keep that they can be discounted from the outset. The families covered in the following sections contain those species that are most commonly seen for sale to hobbyists. Species from these families represent about 85 per cent of all the fishes that can be kept in a marine aquarium, therefore this order forms the central core of this part of the book.

Groupers, sea basses (Serranidae)

This is a family of fishes that is quite primitive in its development and most species lack the intermuscular bones that are present in fishes of higher orders. The family is divided into 61 genera with a total of about 450 species contained in three subfamilies. Their forms and sizes are very varied. Many of the species are circumtropical but in the Caribbean it is the combers and basslets of the genera *Serranus* and *Liopropoma* that are often seen, along with the hamlets (*Hypoplectrus* spp.). In the Indo-Pacific it is species of the genus *Pseudanthias* that are predominant.

In the first subfamily, Serraninae, 11 genera containing about 75 species are recognized. Many species are hermaphroditic although, apart from the hamlets, the two sexes do not have simultaneous development. They make ideal aquarium subjects but care should be taken in choosing the correct tank-mates, since they often prefer a diet of small fishes. This rule can be applied to most of the groupers and sea basses, and even to the small basslets, such as *Serranus* sp., have voracious appetites.

The second subfamily, Anthiinae, encompasses 21 genera with a total of 170 recorded species. Many of the fishes are ideally suited to life in an aquarium, in particular species from the genus *Pseudanthias*. Small shoals of up to eight individuals make a spectacular sight in a reef aquarium. The striking colours of these fishes range from yellow and orange to red and even violet. Because of this, they are a favourite among many marine aquarists, and fishes do not grow too large for the average aquarium. Their forms are quite varied and species from the genus *Sacura*, although seldom imported, have beautiful lyre-tails.

Some of the species have also been bred in captivity but the fry are very small and, therefore, extremely difficult to raise successfully. Often the individual species are sexually dimorphic, (the males and females can be separated by their colouration, markings or fin-form). In addition, they are hermaphroditic.

Generally, to do well, they require water of a high quality with low levels of nitrate. The tank should not be too small with plenty of free swimming space. In addition, there should be plenty of water movement since, in their natural habitat, these fishes are normally found on the outer reef slopes where the water is often turbulent.

Most of the species that are imported come from the Indo-Pacific, but there are several beautiful examples to be found in the Caribbean. Care should be taken when introducing new individuals to a tank, as they are particularly susceptible to osmotic shock. Acclimatization should be carried out over a period of about 45 minutes for the best chances of success. If you intend to keep several individuals together, which is always advisable, then the aquarium should have plenty of cover and hiding places for them to dart into if they feel threatened.

The third and final subfamily is made up of the 29 genera. There are 200 or so valid species in the group and they vary in adult size from 4in to 10ft (10cm to 3m). These large fishes are collectively known as groupers and specimens from the genus *Epinephelus* can weigh up to 1,000lb (450kg). Many of the smaller groupers from this genus can be kept in larger aquariums. The genus *Chromileptis* contains species that seldom exceed 12in (30cm), and there are even smaller species in the genera *Rainfordia* and *Liopropoma*. Quite a number of the species are brightly coloured and make good aquarium subjects. Fishes of the genus *Mycteroperca* occur both in the Indo-Pacific as well as the Caribbean, but there are others whose range is also circumtropical.

The "soapfishes", as they are sometimes known, were originally classified in the family Grammistidae. These have now been included in the subfamily Epinephelinae.

Apart from the very small species in this group, these fishes are not really suitable for a reef aquarium. Big fishes eat a lot and the amount of feeding required would put too much stress on this type of system. In a normal marine (fish-only) aquarium, however, this is less of a problem assuming that the tank is large enough.

Hypoplectrus gemma

Common name: Indigo hamlet (erroneously)
Range: Caribbean
Size: 5in (13cm)
Description: Very similar in appearance to the indigo hamlet (*H. indigo*), but this species can be identified by the dark upper and lower lobes of the caudal fin. It is also far more common on the reef than its similar counterpart. Some experts believe that most of the hamlets are merely colour variations of a single species. However, scale and ray counts reveal marked differences that discount these suppositions.
Aquarium suitability: This fish is a favourite with many aquarists. It is quite shy when it is first introduced and can sometimes prove difficult to wean on to frost food. Once settled in and feeding, however, it is an extremely hardy species.

Hypoplectrus guttavarius

Common name: Shy hamlet
Range: Caribbean
Size: 6in (15cm)
Description: A blue-edged black spot on each side of the snout typifies this attractive species. The remainder of the head and the lower portion of the body and fins are bright yellow. The upper and rear part of the fish's body may be bluish-black, as can be seen from the accompanying photograph, but this is not always the case. Sometimes the back and sides of the fish can also be bright yellow.
Aquarium suitability: This is one of the species of hamlets where success in aquarium breeding has been reported. It is a relatively peaceful and shy species, as the common name indicates. Therefore, the aquarium decoration should have plenty of hiding places into which it can retire.

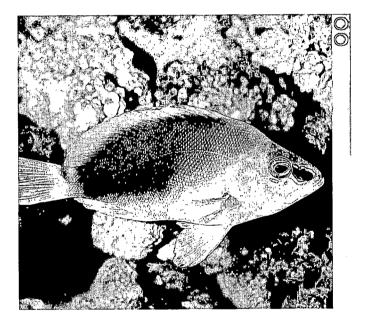

Serranus baldwini

Common name: Lantern bass
Range: Tropical West Atlantic
Size: 3in (7.5cm)
Description: The eye is rimmed with bright orange (hence the common name) and there are two parallel rows of spots on the lower half of the body. The upper of these rows is brownish-black and the lower is orange. The rest of the sides and back have a chequered brown pattern. This fish is found at various depths around rocks and coral and in sea-grass beds where it feeds on small benthic invertebrates and fishes.
Aquarium suitability: This species will eat anything once it has settled into its new home. It is a secretive little fish outside of feeding time and is a good choice for a reef aquarium because of its small size. Provide plenty of rockwork with crevices and caves and this hardy species will be in its element.

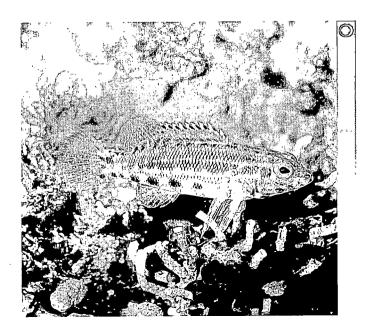

Cephalopholis argus

Common names: Jewel grouper, rock cod
Range: Red Sea, Tropical Indo-Pacific
Size: 20in (50cm)
Description: As the popular name suggests, this fish is one of the jewels of the reef. The body colouration is dark green with a suffusion of black-ringed blue spots that seem to glitter as the light plays across them. On the reef this fish is often seen lying motionless on or near the seabed waiting for prey in the form of small fishes, which form the main part of its diet.
Aquarium suitability: This fish is often imported for the aquarium trade despite its ultimately large size. Small specimens are easy to keep but they grow quite quickly on a varied diet of frozen shellfish and sand shrimps. The aquarium should have a capacity of at least 100 gallons (455 litres) and this fish is not to be trusted with smaller tank-mates.

Cephalopholis aurantia

Common name: Orange rock cod
Range: Northern and Western Indian Ocean
Size: 24in (61cm)
Description: This is one of the smaller members of this genus and it is widespread throughout its range. Occasionally it is seen among wrecks and other debris and it is readily identifiable by its bright, orange-red body and dark caudal fin and flanks.
Aquarium suitability: The orange rock cod is a voracious predator that will quickly snap up any small tank-mate in its cavernous mouth. Therefore, it cannot be classified as a beginner's fish, despite its hardy nature. This species is not often imported for the aquarium trade but in a large enough marine aquarium with other fishes, such as triggerfishes, it can prove to be a real character and provide a lot of entertainment. Small specimens are quite expensive, however.

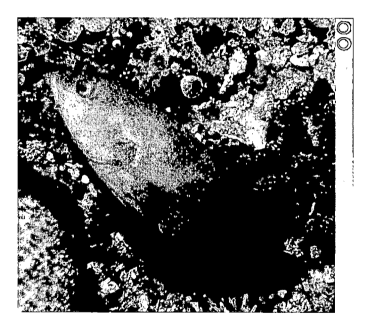

Chromileptis altivelis

Common names: Pantherfish, polka-dot grouper
Range: Tropical Indo-Pacific
Size: 26in (66cm)
Description: On the reef, *Chromileptis altivelis* does not leap anywhere, except perhaps into the fishing nets, since they are frequently served at restaurant dinner tables in the Far East and command a high price in fish markets. This is a pity as they are beautiful fish when encountered in their natural habitat, usually in their typical head-down posture among the rocks and crevices of the seabed.
Aquarium suitability: Small fishes make hardy aquarium inhabitants and the species is easy for the novice aquarist to keep. They will soon learn to accept most frozen foods and grow quite quickly. You need to provide it with a large enough aquarium, however, to ensure it thrives.

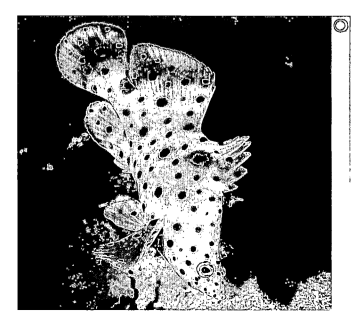

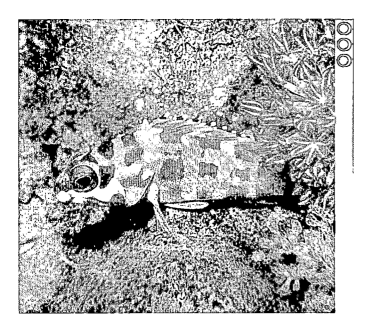

Epinephelus fasciatus

Common name: Black-tipped rock cod
Range: Western Indo-Pacific
Size: 14in (35cm)
Description: This is a very common fish throughout its natural range, as indicated above. It is often seen in the relatively shallow waters of the inshore reefs and it usually leads a solitary life on the seabed. The colouration may vary considerably, depending on its geographic location, but the dorsal fin is always tipped with black.
Aquarium suitability: Although this species is not often seen on dealer's lists, it is quite hardy. It is one of the smallest members of this genus, which contains many much larger fishes, making it a suitable specimen for a large, fish-only aquarium. Feeding is no problem as it will accept most foods offered, including frost and dried foods. It is not to be trusted with small tank-mates.

Dottybacks, pygmy basslets (Pseudochromidae)

The family Pseudochromidae contains 16 genera with almost 100 species, 60 of which belong to the subfamily Pseudochrominae and are ideally suited to marine and reef aquariums due to their small size and sometimes spectacular colouration. Fishes of the genus *Pseudochromis* are popular aquarium fishes, while the genus *Labracinus* contains colourful fishes suitable for larger tanks. Although peaceful and retiring by nature, they are not to be trusted with small tank-mates. The subfamily Congrogadinae incorporates 19 species within eight genera. New theories postulate that this family is so closely related to the families Grammatidae, Plesiopidae, Notograptidae and Opistognathidae that they may be monophyletic. So some of the most popular aquarium fishes, such as jawfishes, grammas and fairy basslets, may belong to this group.

Labracinus sp.

Common name: Flame-back basslet
Range: Northern and Western Indo-Pacific
Size: 7in (18cm)
Description: The possibility exists that this is either a previously undescribed species or a hybrid of two other *Labracinus* species (*L. cyclophthalmus* and *L. lineatus*), since neither of the formal descriptions of these fishes fits the one shown here. It was imported from Sri Lanka and the dorsal, caudal and anal fins are edged with iridescent blue, as is the underside of the snout. It has the lateral markings of *L. lineatus* but the body colouration of *L. cyclophthalmus*. This can be pinkish-red or orange-yellow and is dependent on the light intensity. .
Aquarium suitability: Easy to keep in a large aquarium and grows quite fast on a diet of frost and dried foods. A predator that will kill and eat any fish less than half its own size.

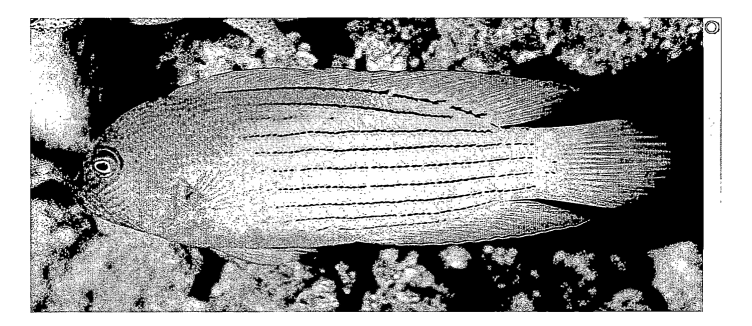

Photograph by Frank Walker

Pseudochromis porphyreus

Common name: Purple dottyback
Range: Central Indo-Pacific
Size: 2in (5cm)
Description: The colouration of this species makes it easy to identify. The bright purple stretches on to the base of the caudal fin rays but leaves the margins clear, as is the case with the dorsal and anal fins.
Aquarium suitability: This species is an ideal choice for a reef aquarium. It is far less shy than others of this genus and is often the first to appear when food is presented. Like most of its relatives, it will not tolerate others of its own kind in the same tank and can often show aggressiveness to other small fishes. Nevertheless it is a hardy species that will survive all except the most careless beginner's mistakes. This fish accepts most frost foods that will fit in its mouth.

Fairy basslets, grammas (Grammatidae)

This is a small family containing only ten species in two genera. The genus *Gramma* consists of three species: *Gramma linki*, *G. loreto* and *G. melacara*. The royal gramma (*G. loreto*) is one of the most widely and frequently imported species. It is very popular with marine aquarists because of its vivid colouration and small size.

All the species in this family come from the tropical West Atlantic and, in particular, the Caribbean. The remaining seven species belong to the genus *Lipogramma*. They are small fishes and are found only at depths of between 60 and 240ft (18 and 73m).

There are marked differences between these fishes and those of the genus *Gramma*. They have no lateral line and no spines or serration on the opercle or preopercle. Species such as *Lipogramma flavescens*, *L. evides* and *L.*

Pseudochromis paccagnellae

Common names: False gramma, dottyback, Paccagnella's dottyback
Range: Central Indo-Pacific to Australia
Size: 2in (5cm)
Description: Beginners often confuse this species with the royal gramma (*Gramma loreto*) because of the similar colouration. Closer inspection reveals a narrow but distinct white band separating the two body colours. The anterior part of the body is bright magenta, and the posterior chrome-yellow.
Aquarium suitability: This is an aquarium favourite and is ideally suited for the reef tank because of its small adult size. It is a shy species but despite this it is inclined to be a fin nipper. Often, when the water quality is less than optimal, this fish is prone to disease. Plenty of hiding places should be provided into which it can retreat if necessary.

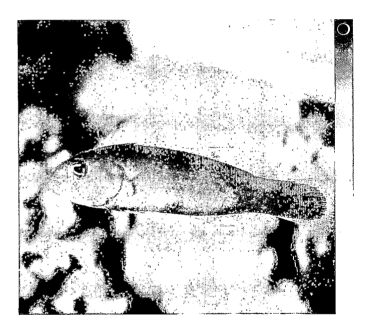

anabantoides are never seen for sale but would probably make good aquarium subjects because of their small size.

Lipogramma regia is a tiny fish that reaches a length of about 1in (2.5cm). It is attractive with an orange-red body. There are several horizontal blue bands on the head that radiate back from the snout on to the opercle. Five broad vertical stripes, pale blue in colour, adorn the sides of the body, and there is a large blue-edged black spot on the rear of the soft dorsal fin that extends on to the body.

Klay's grammid (*Lipogramma klayi*) grows to about 1½in (4cm) and its magenta colour fades into a suffusion of small spots behind and above the pectoral fins, with the rear two-thirds of the body being pale lemon-yellow.

The neon basslet (*Lipogramma trilineata*) is similar in size but is the least colourful of all, having a yellow-orange body. The head has three black-edged blue streaks that run horizontally back to the level of the preopercle.

Gramma loreto

Common names: Royal gramma, fairy basslet
Range: Tropical West Atlantic to Brazil
Size: 3in (7.5cm)
Description: The pelvic fins of the male of this species are much longer than those of the female. This is easy to establish when several individuals are seen together. The anterior half of the body is bright magenta and the posterior portion is yellow. A black spot is present on the first few rays of the dorsal fin and there is usually a black streak through the eye, although this can vary according to geographical location. In the Brazilian form this streak is missing and the head is somewhat larger.
Aquarium suitability: This is an ideal fish for the beginner who has a fully cycled aquarium. Groups of four or five do not usually fight but if so, fin damage seldom results. It is an ideal fish for a reef aquarium and one that will accept most foods, including dried preparations within the first few days.

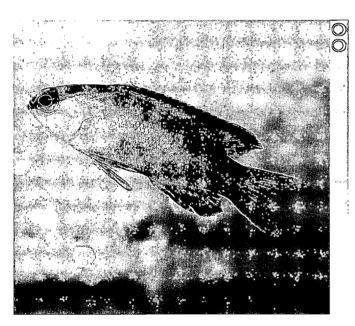

Gramma melacara

Common names: Black-cap gramma, black-cap basslet
Range: Caribbean
Size: 4in (10cm)
Description: This species is easy to identify because of the broad black cap that runs from the premaxillary through the eye, tapering on to the margin of the dorsal fin. The rest of the body is dark mauve-violet in colouration. *G. melacara* is a deep-water species that is never found at depths of less than 100ft (30m).
Aquarium suitability: A relatively shy fish at first, the black-cap gramma should be provided with plenty of niches and hiding places for it to feel at home. This species will usually accept most foods that are offered, and it will often beat its close relative, *G. loreto*, to the feeding station.

Big eyes (Priacanthidae)

These fishes are widespread throughout the tropical and subtropical Atlantic and Pacific Oceans, and they are also in the Red Sea and through the Gulf of Suez. Typically, they have large eyes and large slanted mouths. The dorsal fin is continuous and their colouration is predominantly red. All big eyes are carnivores and they are also nocturnal. They are to be found in shallow, inshore water to depths of 100ft (30m). The family consists of four genera with 18 species. Adult sizes range from 6 to 20in (15 to 50cm).

They are not easy to keep in an aquarium, since most species will accept only live food. It is often difficult for aquarists to obtain a constant and varied supply of live foods throughout the year, but this is a prerequisite if they are to have any chance of survival. Because they grow quite large they require a sizable aquarium.

Cardinalfishes (Apogonidae)

This family contains 207 species grouped into two sub-families with a total of 22 genera. It is a group of carnivorous fishes that are nocturnal by nature. The common factors here are that all species have large heads usually with a protruding lower jaw. There are two dorsal fins and all species are essentially "mouthbrooders" – the eggs and young fry are carried in the mouth of the parent until they are large enough to fend for themselves. In this case it is usually the male of the species that performs this service but with some species it can be the female, or both parents. Many of the species occur on the reef and in tide pools, with a few being found in deeper water.

The adult size of the cardinalfishes makes them ideal aquarium subjects, since they seldom exceed 8in (20cm), with most being a great deal smaller at around 4in (10cm).

In the aquarium trade it is usually species of the genus *Sphaeramia* that the aquarist is most likely to encounter, although occasional specimens of the genus *Apogon* are imported. This latter genus is by far the largest, with 110 species. Some species (*Siphamia* spp.) possess a luminous organ along the ventral plain and all members of this family are peaceful with fishes of their own size. In an aquarium they need plenty of cover and low lighting due to their nocturnal nature. A twilight aquarium would appear to be the optimal solution for the wellbeing of these fishes. Live food is preferred but they can easily be weaned on to frozen foods – some species even learn to accept dried and freeze-dried foods. Some species are ideal for beginners once the fishes have learned to accept frost foods. They make a particularly attractive sight in a reef or marine aquarium when they are kept in small groups of five or six individuals.

Apogon fasciatus

Common name: Cardinalfish
Range: Tropical Indo-Pacific to Australia
Size: 5in (13cm)
Description: There are many similarly marked species throughout the Indo-Pacific region but this one can be identified by the thicker line running through the eye to the tail, where it ends in a large black spot on the caudal peduncle. *A. fasciatus* is a common sight on the reefs and in tide pools around the Philippine Islands.
Aquarium suitability: This species is quite often imported and does well in an aquarium when given enough caves and hiding places. It is not aggressive toward other fishes and may be kept singly or in small groups of three or four. Feeding is no problem, since it will readily adapt to frozen shell meat and brine shrimp. Larger specimens should not be trusted with small tank-mates.

Sphaeramia nematoptera

Common name: Pyjama cardinalfish
Range: Widespread throughout the Central Indo-Pacific from Japan to Australia
Size: 3in (7.5cm)
Description: Typically a shoaling fish, the pyjama cardinalfish is often seen in the reef shallows of the Indo-Pacific. It is sometimes confused with *S. orbicularis*, but there are obvious differences. This species has bright orange-red eyes and orange ventral fins. The anterior dorsal fin and head are a dull orange-yellow.
Aquarium suitability: This fish is an ideal choice for a reef aquarium. In fact, no other cardinalfish is more frequently imported. Groups of six or more individuals should be kept together to make a pleasing display. They will soon overcome their nocturnal nature and will learn to accept frost and even dried foods at any time of the day.

Tilefishes (Malacanthidae)

The family Malacanthidae encompasses a total of 39 valid species divided into five genera and two subfamilies. However, it is only the first of these subfamilies, Malacanthinae, that is of interest to marine aquarists. The first of the two genera that make up this subfamily is *Malacanthus*, which comprises three species. *Malacanthus brevirostris* is a rather drab, brown fish with an elongated and torpedo-shaped body that is typical of this family. There are several vertical bars along the sides of the fish and a definite darkening of the upper and lower lobes of the caudal fin. This species is known to grow to a length of 24in (60cm).

Malacanthus latovittatus is probably the most striking of this genus, having black on the underside of the body running from the snout to the tail. The upper half of the fish is creamy-white. This, and the remaining species *M. plumieri*, which is predominantly silvery-white in colouration, reaches an adult length of approximately 18in (45cm). Occasionally, specimens belonging to this genus reach the aquarium trade.

The second genus, *Hoplolatilus*, is far more important to aquarists and at the moment contains eight valid species. These are found in shallow water at depths of around 65ft (20m). They are shy and secretive fishes that construct burrows and mounds on sandy areas of the seabed. Generally, they have blunt snouts and moderately elongated bodies and they seldom exceed a length of 8in (20cm). Species from this genus are definitely not for beginners, being shy and difficult to acclimatize to aquarium life. They are also apt to spring out of the aquarium when they are frightened, so a close-fitting hood is an essential piece of equipment. For the best survival chances, good water quality is mandatory with a strong current flow. In addition, a deep sandy bottom is required, such as you might find in an aquarium using a plenum or undergravel (sub-sand) filter system. A good depth of sand enables these fishes to construct their burrows into which they will quickly retire whenever they feel threatened. Caves and hiding places should also be provided and they should not be kept with other fishes that have a more boisterous nature. Shrimps and small prawns form part of their staple diet in the wild and these invertebrates should not be kept in the same aquarium as the fishes.

Hoplolatilus chlupatyi grows to 6in (15cm) and can change colour from yellowish-green to bluish-violet with remarkable rapidity. *Hoplolatilus cuniculus*, in contrast, has a body colouration that is a delicate pink-red with a cream belly. The eyes are blue and there is a blue line that runs from the head, along the dorsal base to the tail. This species grows to 4in (10cm). *Hoplolatilus fourmanoiri* has a purple belly and back with irregular yellow patches on the head and forebody. It grows to a length of 8in (20cm). *Hoplolatilus luteus* is a stunning fish that grows to 6in (15cm). Its colouration is bright yellow. The pale dorsal fin and the upper and lower lobes of the caudal fin have blue margins.

Another attractive species is *Hoplolatilus marcosi*, which grows to 8in (20cm). The body is pinkish-red above and pale cream below, the two colours being separated by a broad, red stripe that curves in an arc from the fish's snout to its tail. The eyes are blue and there is a large triangular-shaped mark on the tail. *Hoplolatilus starcki* is quite small, reaching a length of only 4in (10cm). This species has a deeply forked tail and the body colour may be blue or bright yellow. The head and dorsal fin are iridescent blue and there is a large, deep-blue patch on the opercle that runs on to the body behind the pectoral fin.

The second subfamily, Latilinae (=Branchiosteginae), incorporates the remaining 28 species. These are essentially deep-water fishes that are drab in colour and of little interest to the aquarist.

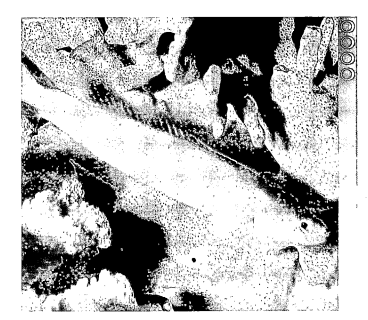

Hoplolatilus purpureus

Common name: Purple tilefish
Range: Western Pacific to central Indo-Pacific
Size: 6in (15cm)
Description: The delicate pastel colours of this fish give it an impressive appearance. The sides of the body are pinkish-violet, becoming more bluish around the dorsal fin. There is a yellow stripe extending from the tip of the snout, over the top of the head to the dorsal fin. The upper and lower lobes of the caudal fin are dull orange-red and the inner margins are blue.
Aquarium suitability: This is by no means a beginner's fish and if it is frightened or bullied by boisterous tank-mates there is a danger that it will leap out of the aquarium. A close-fitting hood and a stress-free environment are the keys to success with this shy species. Although it feeds mainly on plankton in the wild, it will snap at most chopped frozen foods and dried food granules.

Remoras (Echeneidae)

This is a small family with four genera and only eight species. They are easily identifiable by the curious sucker disc on top of the head. This is formed by a modified first dorsal fin where the rays have become flattened and are developed into lamina-like vanes contained within an oval, fleshy margin. By altering the angle of the vanes, rather like the opening and closing of a venetian blind, the fish is able to create a partial vacuum that enables it to attach itself to the belly of a large fish. They also use this sucker action on marine turtles, whales and even ships are known to play host to these species. In this way, they can feed on passing morsels of food that come their way. Their bodies are elongate, cylindrical and slightly laterally compressed. The head is depressed around the area of the suction disc and they have large mouths with protruding lower jaws. None of these species is brightly coloured.

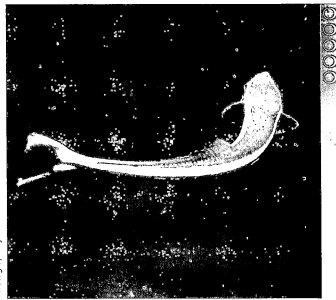

Photograph by Frank Walker

Echeneis naucrates

Common names: Remora, slender suckerfish
Range: Circumtropical
Size: 40in (1m)
Description: On the reef *Echeneis naucrates* and the brown remora (*Remora remora*) are the most commonly seen members of this family. This fish has a black mid-lateral stripe running from the snout to the tail. The tail itself is black with white outer margins. The suction disc is clearly visible in the accompanying photograph of a Philippine specimen. *E. naucrates* is probably the only member of this family that can be found free swimming without a host.
Aquarium suitability: Small specimens are occasionally seen for sale but unless a large aquarium is provided with other larger fishes, then this species will attach itself to the glass for hours at a time, seldom feeding and never acting naturally.

Snappers, fusiliers (Lutjanidae)

There are about 125 species in 21 genera in this family, incorporated into five subfamilies. The common characteristics of the first four subfamilies (snappers) are that they all have a continuous dorsal fin, sometimes with a shallow notch. They are mostly bottom dwellers that move in small to medium schools. The genus *Lutjanus* is the largest, with a total of 64 species, which represents a little over half the valid species. The maximum size of these species can be up to 40in (1m). The fifth family, Caesioninae, is collectively known as "fusiliers". They grow to a length of up to 20in (50cm) and are often brightly coloured. The dorsal fin is continuous and the tail is deeply forked. In the wild they are often encountered in huge shoals near rocks and coral reefs, particularly on the outer reef slopes. Some, however, can appear in tide-pools and lagoons, with a few species being found in brackish water, particularly near mangroves. Their bodies are laterally compressed, often streamlined and the tail is forked or truncate.

Throughout the Indo-Pacific the most common species is the Arabian, or blue-striped snapper (*Lutjanus kasmira*). Also from the Indo-Pacific, the emperor snapper (*Lutjanus sebae*) is well known by fishermen.

Quite a number of these species are imported for the aquarium trade but many of them grow far too large for the average aquarium. As a rule they require plenty of free swimming space because of their active nature and this means an aquarium with a minimum capacity of 100 gallons (455 litres). Once this is provided, members of this family can become very tame and may be hand fed.

The majestic snapper (*Symphorichthys spilurus*) is often available to the aquarist but grows quickly to reach a size of 24in (60cm). This fish is easy to identify with its dorsal and anal fins having elongated fin rays. There is a series of blue stripes along the sides of its yellow body. A black spot adorns the upper part of the caudal peduncle and there are two vertical bars on the head, one of which runs through the eye. The brown snapper (*Macolor niger*) also outgrows most aquariums and is a dull brown fish. The young fish, however, are extremely popular and attractive. At this stage the background body colour is snowy-white with a black snout and a black band around the head.

The blues and yellows of the fusiliers make them interesting for the aquarist and they do not grow as large as most snappers. *Caesio caerulaurea* and *Pterocaesio lativittata*, both from the Indo-Pacific, reach a maximum length of 7in (18cm). These and *Pterocaesio chrysozona*, a similar-sized species, are probably your best choice.

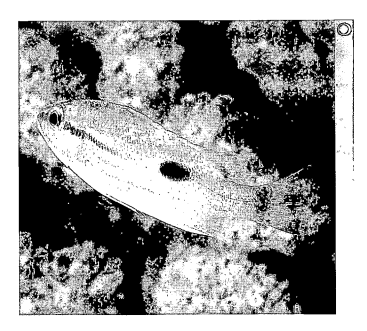

Lutjanus ehrenbergii

Common name: Snapper
Range: Central Indo-Pacific to East Africa
Size: 16in (40cm)
Description: Head olive coloured, back and dorsal fin dusky yellow. There is a large black spot above the lateral line between the spinous and soft dorsal fins. The sides are have several horizontal yellow stripes. Young specimens have a dark brown stripe running through the eye and onto the body.
Aquarium suitability: This species is not imported very often – a pity, since it is an easy species to keep and one that will survive most beginner's mistakes. Small groups need to be kept with other larger fishes or in a separate aquarium. They are inclined to nip fins on occasions but there is never any great damage done. The photograph on the left shows one of a group of six fish. Most foods are accepted.

Lutjanus kasmira

Common names: Arabian snapper, blue-striped snapper, blue-banded hussar
Range: Red Sea, entire Indo-Pacific
Size: 16in (40cm)
Description: This is a shoaling fish that is easily identified by the four, sometimes oblique, blue stripes on the sides of the body. The belly is creamy-white and the head may be bluish-white or yellow. *L. kasmira* is often seen on coral reefs and its main diet consists of small crustaceans.
Aquarium suitability: This species requires a large aquarium and several individuals should be kept together for best results. They are not easy to keep in captivity and are rather susceptible to skin parasites. Most frozen foods are accepted, especially krill, mysis and plankton. Dried, freeze-dried and granulated foods are usually refused at first.

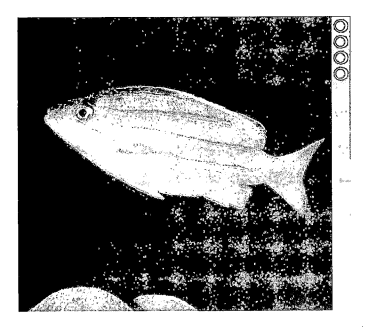

Lutjanus sebae

Common names: Emperor snapper, government bream, red snapper, red emperor
Range: Tropical Indo-Pacific to East Africa
Size: 36in (91cm)
Description: This is a handsome fish both as a juvenile, as shown in the photograph, and also as an adult, where the dark brown colouration becomes more reddish. A fully grown specimen can weigh up to 44 pounds (20 kg).
Aquarium suitability: In an aquarium, juvenile fish are hardy and easy to keep and will soon learn to accept all foods offered, including flake food. As in their natural habitat, they will quickly learn to take food from your hand, which can be a lot of fun when the fish is a young adult. Like others of this family, it needs an aquarium with a large capacity, something of the size of at least 200 gallons (908 litres).

Grunts, sweetlips (Haemulidae)

Three of the 17 genera making up this family are called "sweetlips" and the remaining 14 are termed "grunts" because of the sounds they make when they grind their upper and lower pharyngeal teeth together. In the wild, Grunts are often seen in sea-grass beds and they feed almost exclusively on benthic invertebrates. Grunts are usually aggressive with healthy, if sloppy, appetites, so a good power filter is a necessity. Most exceed 12in (30cm) as adults. They are best kept in groups of the same species so that they can happily nip each other's fins.

Sweetlips, especially those of the genus *Plectorhinchus*, are attractive as juvenile fishes. They do, however, grow very fast and very large. The young fishes are peaceful and can often be disturbed by boisterous tank-mates. This may also be the case with some adults.

✗ *Plectorhinchus chaetodonoides*

Common names: Clown sweetlips, polka-dot grunt, harlequin sweetlips
Range: Central Indo-Pacific
Size: 24in (60cm)
Description: Practically every East Indies coral reef offers this species for collectors and for observation by divers. As a young fish, *P. chaetodonoides* is quite a character. It has ridiculously large fins for its body size at this stage and paddles comically around the reef with exaggerated body and fin movements. With its white-spotted brown body it is easily identified. As an adult fish, its body colouration is yellowish-white with a suffusion of small brown speckles.
Aquarium suitability: Grows very large and overcomes its initial shyness. Most foods are accepted but frozen brine shrimp and krill are particular favourites.

✗ *Plectorhinchus albovittatus*

Common names: Sweetlips, yellow-lined sweetlips, yellow sweetlips
Range: Central Indo-Pacific to East Africa, Red Sea
Size: 8in (20cm)
Description: Background colour of young fish is a deep orange-yellow. There are two, sometimes three, chocolate-brown stripes running from the snout to the tail. As they grow these lines fade and break up, and the adults become a mottled-brown colour. This is a shy species that seldom strays far from its coral refuge. It is one of the smallest members of this genus.
Aquarium suitability: Within days of introduction, accepts most frozen and dried foods that are offered . It can be kept in an aquarium with other fishes of a peaceful nature and a few hardy invertebrates, but it is not to be recommended for a reef aquarium. Adult fish are drab and uninteresting.

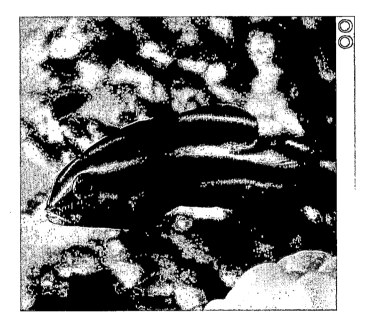

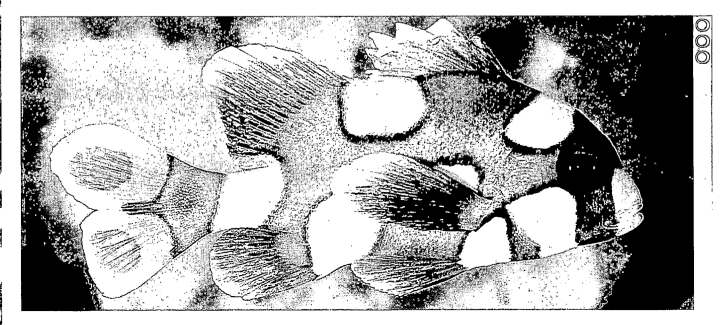

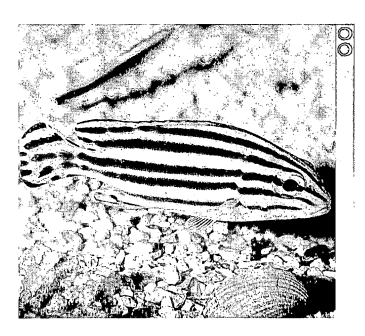

Plectorhinchus gaterinus

Common name: Yellow-finned sweetlips
Range: Indian Ocean, Red Sea
Size: 14in (35cm)
Description: This fish is common throughout its natural range and is often seen in small shoals feeding on the reef or on sandy sea bottoms. It is sometimes confused with the yellow-band sweetlips (*P. lineatus*) but in fact the pattern change is in reverse. The juvenile fish of *P. lineatus* start out spotted and subsequently develop stripes along the body, whereas the juvenile of this species, as pictured here, will eventually develop a fine sprinkling of spots on the upper half of the body and tail, and the fins will be bright yellow.
Aquarium suitability: An attractive fish that accepts most foods and is relatively hardy. But as it grows, so too do the problems of providing enough swimming space for its increasingly large size.

Plectorhinchus pictus

Common name: Painted sweetlips
Range: Red Sea, Indo-Pacific to East Africa
Size: 36in (91cm)
Description: The juvenile and adult colouration is different with this species. A young fish is shown here and is silvery-white with black stripes from snout to tail. During the transitional stage, brownish-black spots appear and increase in number between the stripes and on the fins until the entire fish is covered with yellow-brown spots. The adult fish has a yellow dorsal and caudal fins, which are also sprinkled with spots.
Aquarium suitability: Although this fish is unsuitable for a home aquarium, small specimens are often for sale and the novices may be misled into thinking it would make a suitable purchase. It grows too large for even the most ambitious aquarist and does this in a relatively short space of time.

Goatfishes (Mullidae)

The general characteristics of this family are immediately apparent: all species have two barbels underneath the jaw, which possess sensory cells (taste cells) used for detecting food. These are independently moveable and are used to probe the substrate for morsels of food. In addition the anterior and posterior dorsal fins are set wide apart and the caudal fin is more or less deeply forked. The family Mullidae contains 53 valid species and these are grouped into six genera. The first of these, *Mulloidichthys*, contains seven species, five of which are widespread throughout the Indo-Pacific. One species is restricted to the Caribbean area while the range of the seventh is the eastern Pacific region.

Mullus, the second genus, includes only three species. These are *Mullus auratus*, from the tropical West Atlantic,

and *M. barbutus* and *M. surmuletus* from the eastern Atlantic. These are two very similar species and are known commonly as red mullets. These have been important as food fishes for more than 2,000 years. It has been recorded that the Romans would pay more for a red mullet than for the fisherman's boat that brought it ashore. The third genus, *Parupeneus*, is made up of 28 species, all of which are from the Indo-Pacific. The fourth genus in this family, *Pseudopeneus*, contains only three species.

Upeneichthys is the fifth genus and the smallest, with just two valid species. Both of these are to be found in the waters of Southeast Australia and New Zealand. They are *Upeneichthys lineatus* and *U. porosus*. The last genus in this family, *Upeneus*, is also the second largest, with ten species from the Indo-Pacific, one species from the Caribbean, and the newest species, *Upeneus francisi*, from New Zealand and Norfolk Island.

Parupeneus cyclostomus

Common name: Yellow goatfish
Range: Red Sea, Tropical Indo-Pacific
Size: 20in (50cm)
Description: This is one of the most colourful of all the goatfishes. Juvenile fishes are often bright yellow in colour with a series of bluish lines radiating around the eye and on to the snout. Adult fishes are variable in colour, sometimes in the same shoal. It is possible that this is sexual dimorphism.
Aquarium suitability: Although fishes from this family are difficult to keep in a home aquarium for any length of time, this species is one of the easiest when kept in small groups. Small fish are often available to the aquarist and, as a rule, they are inexpensive to buy. They accept most frost foods and some dried foods as well. They require a large aquarium with a sandy bottom so that individuals can grub around for their food.

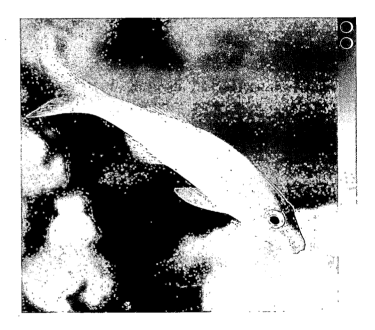

Butterflyfishes (Chaetodontidae)

The family Chaetodontidae encompasses a group of fishes whose bodies are disc-shaped and strongly compressed. Often the snout is elongated and the mouth is armed with brush-like teeth. There is a continuous dorsal fin, without a notch, between the spinous and soft parts. Butterfly-fishes are particularly colourful and many species have a black vertical line running down the head and through the eye. This, and the large black "eye spot" that many species exhibit, could mislead a predator into thinking that it is aiming for the head when, in fact, it is the tail.

The family has 114 species grouped into ten genera. Most species (97 in all) are spread through the Indo-Pacific region and Red Sea, with the remainder found in the eastern Pacific and tropical West Atlantic. The genus *Chaetodon* is split into 13 subgenera with 89 species.

All of these species are essentially shallow-water fishes, inhabiting back-reef areas, reef shallows and coral pools. Some may venture down to 100ft (30m) but this is rare. During feeding they can cover vast areas of reef and their diet is very varied. The snout is ideally developed to enable the fish to winkle out delicacies from between the corals. These fishes are often seen singly or in pairs on the reef during the day. At night they retire into any convenient crevice between the corals.

Butterflyfishes are often imported although some are protected species. They make ideal subjects for a marine aquarium, although they are not normally suitable for a reef aquarium because of their love of live corals and other invertebrates, which they will eat or damage. One species, *Chaetodon kleini*, does not usually exhibit this destructive trait. For best results, they should be kept with others of their kind in a fish-only aquarium.

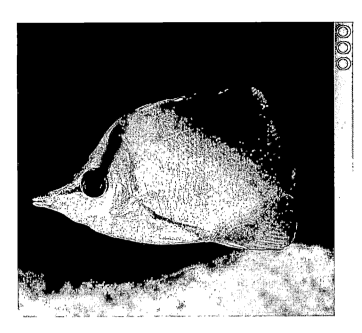

Chaetodon aculeatus

Common names: Atlantic butterflyfish, longsnout butterflyfish
Range: Caribbean, Tropical West Atlantic
Size: 5in (13cm)
Description: This is one of the few butterflyfish species that is found in the Caribbean area, usually in deeper water. It is not as attractively coloured as its Indo-Pacific relatives, being yellow to yellowish-brown in colour. The snout is only moderately elongated and young fish exhibit an orange band on the caudal peduncle.
Aquarium suitability: Young specimens are occasionally offered for sale and do quite well in a home aquarium if they are housed with other fishes of a similar placid nature. This species will soon learn to accept frozen foods, and after some weeks when it has finally settled down, it may also be induced to accept flake food supplements.

Chaetodon auriga

Common names: Threadfin butterflyfish, golden butterflyfish, threadfin, diagonal butterflyfish
Range: Entire Tropical Indo-Pacific, Red Sea
Size: 8in (20cm)
Description: The threadfin butterflyfish is common throughout its natural range and is easily befriended by divers offering morsels of food. Adult specimens have a long dorsal filament. Specimens from the Red Sea lack the ocellus on the soft dorsal fin and the dorsal filament is shorter. They are found singly or in pairs in the reef shallows to depths of up to 35ft (10m)
Aquarium suitability: This is one of the easiest of all the butterflyfishes to keep. The aquarium should be large enough and have plenty of hiding places into which it can retire at night. Provide good water quality and a varied assortment of frost foods and this fish should flourish.

Chaetodon baronessa

Common name: Triangular butterflyfish
Range: Western Pacific to central Indo-Pacific
Size: 6in (15cm)
Description: Easily confused with *Chaetodon triangulum*, this species lacks the yellow-edged triangular mark on the tail. The body has a series of chevron markings, and the margins of the dorsal, anal and ventral fins are chrome-yellow. There are three vertical bars on the head and the snout may be dull orange.
Aquarium suitability: Although this species is reported to be quite difficult to keep, the fat and healthy specimen shown here had, at the time this photograph was taken, already spent two and a half years in an aquarium, and it coped well when it was subsequently transferred to a new tank. Its diet consisted of a variety of frozen foods supplemented with flake food and it did little if any damage to the live corals in the aquarium.

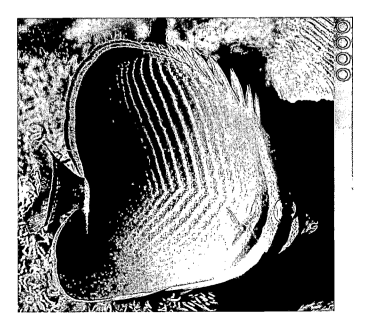

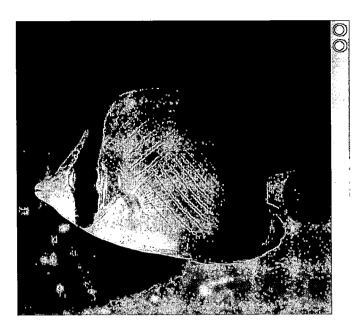

Chaetodon decussatus

Common names: Painted butterflyfish, black-finned butterflyfish
Range: Indian Ocean to East Africa
Size: 7in (18cm)
Description: *C. decussatus* is very closely related to *C. vagabundis*. Unlike the latter species, which has bright yellow on the posterior part of the dorsal and anal fins, this species is much darker with only a faint line of yellow on the anal fin. It is endemic on the reefs of Sri Lanka and India and is also represented throughout the northern part of the Indian Ocean, whereas *C. vagabundis* is normally found in the Indo-west Pacific.
Aquarium suitability: Often imported from Sri Lanka and is one of the easy species to keep in an aquarium. Provide plenty of live rock built into caves and the painted butterflyfish will feel at home. Most frost and flake foods will be accepted.

Chaetodon falcula

Common names: Double-saddle butterflyfish, black-wedge butterflyfish, saddled butterflyfish
Range: Indian Ocean to East Africa
Size: 11in (28cm)
Description: This is one of the larger members of this family and is easy to identify by its two large black wedges dorsally. The dorsal and anal fins are bright yellow, and there is a yellow bar on the caudal fin. Just in front of this is a black bar that separates the caudal fin from the yellow caudal peduncle. There is a further black bar on the head that runs through the eye.
Aquarium suitability: Although this fish is no problem to keep when young in a fully matured aquarium, older specimens require a lot of free swimming space and a larger tank is often required as the fish grows. If this is provided from the outset, then this fish will do well. Most foods are accepted.

Chaetodon fasciatus

Common names: Diagonal-lined butterflyfish
Range: Red Sea, Gulf of Aden
Size: 8in (20cm)
Description: This species was once thought to be a subspecies of *C. lunula*, with which it is confused. However, it comes from the Red Sea and adjacent areas, whereas *C. lunula* is known throughout the Indo-Pacific, though not as far as the Red Sea. Moreover, this species lacks the ocellus on the caudal peduncle and the white headband reaches only level with the top of the eye. In *C. lunula* the band ends level with the pectoral base.
Aquarium suitability: Due to import restrictions, this species is not as often imported as most members of this family. This is unfortunate, since it does well in an aquarium provided the water has a higher specific gravity than is usual for a marine tank. Most normal aquarium foods are accepted.

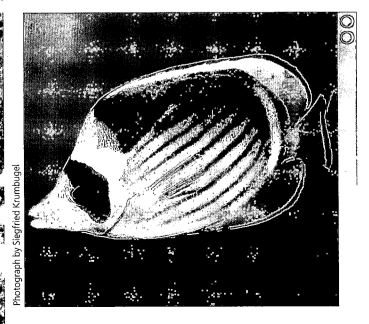

Photograph by Siegfried Krumbugel

Chaetodon fremblii

Common names: Blue-striped butterflyfish, blue-lined coralfish
Range: Hawaii
Size: 7in (18cm)
Description: Abundant in the Hawaiian Archipelago but not known elsewhere because many coral fishes have been unable to brave the Pacific in search of new reefs due to the distance involved. This fish is unmistakable because of the series of bright blue diagonal lines on the body. There is no bar through the eye and the fish has a black spot on the top of the head and a black patch on the caudal peduncle that reaches on to the dorsal fin.
Aquarium suitability: Nowadays, this fish is not so often seen on offer in aquarium shops, possibly because of export restrictions. This is a pity since it is a peaceful and attractive fish that settles down well to aquarium life. It should be given a diet of frozen shell meat and mysid shrimp.

Chaetodon kleini

Common names: Sunburst butterflyfish, Klein's coralfish, white-spotted butterflyfish.
Range: Entire Indo-Pacific, Red Sea
Size: 5in (13cm)
Description: Widespread from East Africa to Samoa. This species is relatively small and its body consists of a suffusion of white spots on a gold background. Two white bars are present, the first of which is behind the eye. The second bar is less clearly defined and occurs mid-body from the dorsal fin to the vent. The ventral fins are bluish-black, as is the bar through the eye.
Aquarium suitability: Extremely popular with some marine aquarists and a good aquarium subject that feeds well on most foods once it has overcome its initial shyness. It is ideal for a community aquarium and is probably the easiest of all the butterflyfishes to keep.

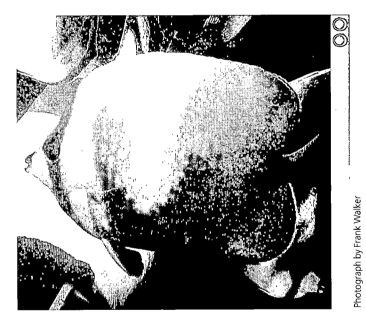

Photograph by Frank Walker

Chaetodon lineolatus

Common name: Lined butterflyfish
Range: Tropical Indo-Pacific, Red Sea
Size: Almost 12in (29cm)
Description: The snout of this species is fairly elongate and the bar through the eye quite broad. Other than this, the colouration appears to be similar to that of several other members of this genus. However, this one is not too difficult to identify if you note the direction of the body lines. In this case, they are nearly vertical. Juveniles have a dark spot on the caudal peduncle.
Aquarium suitability: C. lineolatus grows to a reasonable size so a large tank is required. It accepts a variety of food once it has settled in and, in good-quality water with plenty of current flow, it will do this almost immediately. This fish should not be kept in a reef aquarium and it is not to be trusted when soft and leather corals are present.

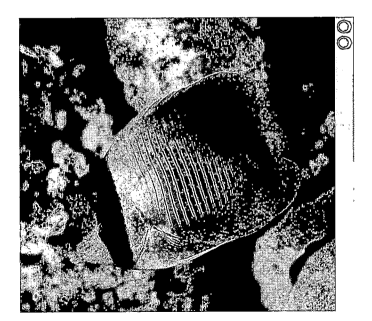

Chaetodon lunula

Common names: Racoon butterflyfish, moon butterflyfish, red-striped butterfly
Range: Tropical Indo-Pacific
Size: 8in (20cm)
Description: This is an unmistakable fish on the reef and it is common throughout its natural range. It inhabits rock-pools and reef shallows and may be observed singly or in pairs grazing on coral polyps. In back-reef areas they are sometimes encountered by professional collectors. In these zones they are usually in small groups of up to 20 individuals.
Aquarium suitability: This fish enjoys a marked popularity among aquarists because it is extremely hardy. Live rock should be included in the aquarium. This should be built up to form grottoes and crevices into which the fish can retire at night. Most commercial dried foods and frost foods are accepted with relish.

Chaetodon melannotus

Common name: Black-backed butterflyfish
Range: Tropical Indo-Pacific, Red Sea
Size: 7in (18cm)
Description: C. *melannotus* is common from East Africa to Polynesia and from Hong Kong to Australia, which makes it pretty widespread. It can be differentiated from the similar C. *lineolatus* by the narrow eye bar and the pattern of lines on the body. These lines are diagonal in this case, whereas in C. *lineolatus* the lines are vertical.
Aquarium suitability: Although the black-backed butterflyfish is not that often available, it is a superb fish, and one that is easy to keep. At night its colour becomes a shadowy black over much of its body. The startling yellow colouration of this species makes it popular with many hobbyists. Food requirements are the same as for previous species.

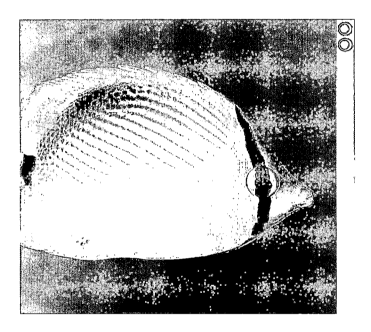

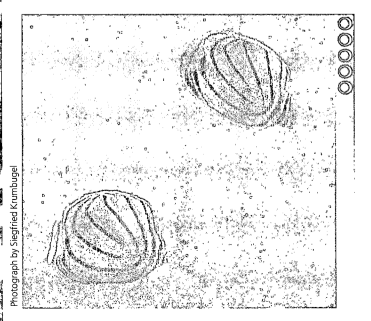

Photograph by Siegfried Krumbugel

Chaetodon meyeri

Common name: Meyer's butterflyfish
Range: Tropical Indo-Pacific
Size: 7in (18cm)
Description: Bold black lines on a bluish-white background. Dorsal, anal and pectoral fins and tail are a rich yellow with the tail being somewhat rounded in juveniles. The dorsal and anal fins have black and white margins and the caudal fin is traversed with a narrow black stripe. This species is the most striking of all the butterflyfishes and can readily be seen on the reef.
Aquarium suitability: C. *meyeri* is one of the most difficult members of this genus to keep in an aquarium. Its natural diet is almost exclusively coral polyps, and specialist feeders such as this are perhaps better left in their natural environment. They are relatively rare and an attempt to keep this species alive in an aquarium should be left only to the most experienced hobbyist.

Photograph by Dr John E. Randall

Chaetodon miliaris

Common name: Lemon butterflyfish
Range: Hawaii
Size: 7in (18cm)
Description: The photograph shows an adult specimen that came from Kaneohe Bay, Oahu. This species is restricted to Hawaii and it is one of the commonest species found around these islands. It is characterized by its yellow colouration and the series of 11 vertical rows of black spots from the base of the dorsal fin to the middle of the sides. There is a dark blotch on the caudal peduncle and the usual black bar through the eye. In the wild, this species feeds on plankton and a variety of small invertebrates.
Aquarium suitability: A good community fish that is generally peaceful and hardy when kept with others of this genus. Its diet should be frozen plankton, brine shrimp and chopped mussel.

Chaetodon multicinctus

Common names: Pebbled butterflyfish, Hawaiian striped butterflyfish
Range: Hawaii
Size: 6in (15cm)
Description: A reasonably common species around the waters of Hawaii. It is identified by the olive-yellow bars on the body and the suffusion of small orange-brown spots between them. There is a black band around the caudal peduncle and a similar bar through the eye, interrupted in the supraorbital region. The dorsal margin is fringed with yellow. This species has a diet of benthic algae, small shrimps, polychaetes and coral polyps.
Aquarium suitability: One of the more difficult species from this genus when the water quality is less than optimal. This is a fish for experienced aquarists only. Plenty of cover should be provided and a varied diet. Not a fish for a reef aquarium.

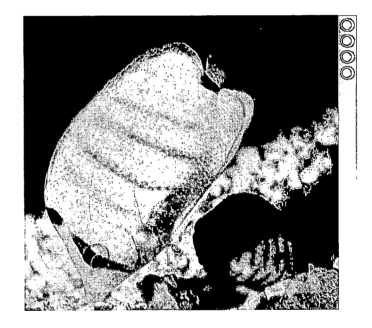

Chaetodon octofasciatus

Common name: Eight-banded butterflyfish
Range: Central Indo-Pacific to East Africa
Size: 5in (13cm)
Description: The eight-banded butterflyfish is unmistakable in appearance, having a yellowish-silver body with eight vertical bands from the head to the caudal fin. The ventral and anal fins are yellow, as is the snout. In the wild, this species is often observed in small groups around coral heads, on which they feed. They are relatively shy fish, and at the first sign of danger they will dart into the protection of the coral branches.
Aquarium suitability: A difficult species to keep in an aquarium for any length of time, although the specimen shown here lived in an aquarium for several years, where it was weaned onto frost foods and grew old and fat. This species requires good water quality.

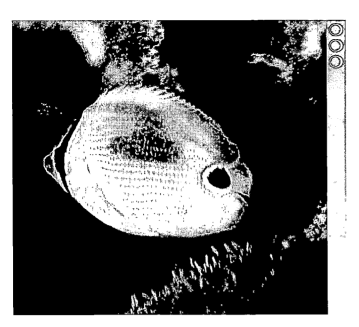

Chaetodon plebeius

Common names: Coral butterflyfish, blue-spot butterflyfish
Range: Tropical Indo-Pacific
Size: 7½in (19cm)
Description: This attractive species is often seen on the Great Barrier Reef of Australia feeding on coral heads in shallow water. The general body colouration is bright yellow with a black bar through the eye and a white-edged, black ocellus on the caudal peduncle. There is a large elongated dorsal marking, which is blue in colour.
Aquarium suitability: Although easier to keep than the preceding species, it is still not a fish for the beginner. This fish requires water that is nitrate free for it to flourish. In a good aquarium milieu, the coral butterflyfish will accept most foods that are offered, including flake food. It is not a fish to be recommended for a reef aquarium.

Chaetodon rafflesi

Common name: Latticed butterflyfish
Range: Tropical Indo-Pacific
Size: 6in (15cm)
Description: This is another butterflyfish that is predominantly yellow. Each scale on the sides is edged in black, as is the soft dorsal fin. The caudal base has a black bar through it and the snout is moderately elongated. The ocular bar is also black and fairly wide. *C. rafflesi* prefers reef shallows and coral pools, where the water is not as turbulent. They are seldom seen deeper than 35ft (11m).
Aquarium suitability: A "picky" feeder that seems to do better when kept with others of its own kind. This is no bad thing, since a small group of these fish makes a spectacular display in a marine (fish-only) aquarium. This species will eventually learn to accept frozen foods.

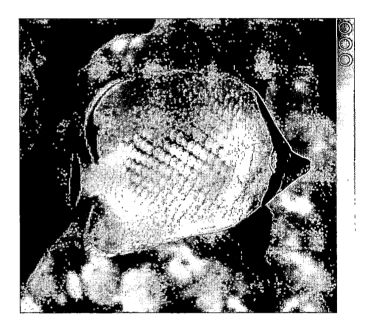

Chaetodon speculum

Common names: One-spot butterflyfish, oval-spot butterflyfish
Range: Central and west Pacific to Indonesia
Size: 6in (15cm)
Description: In their natural environment these fish are shy and secretive, and they will dive quickly into their coral refuge whenever they sense danger. This is also a shallow-water species that is often encountered at depths of less than 40in (1m). The body is bright yellow and it has a large, black dorsal spot and a narrow black band through the eye.
Aquarium suitability: An ideal choice of species to start with if you are considering setting up an aquarium containing members of this genus. Although they are shy at first, this fish is hardy and will soon learn to accept most foods that are offered. Juvenile fish under 2in (5cm) in length seem to adapt even more readily to aquarium life.

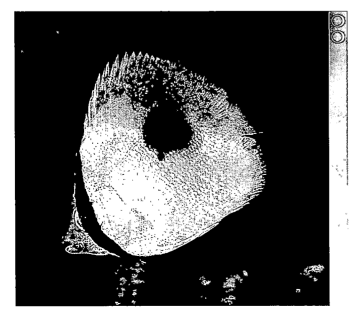

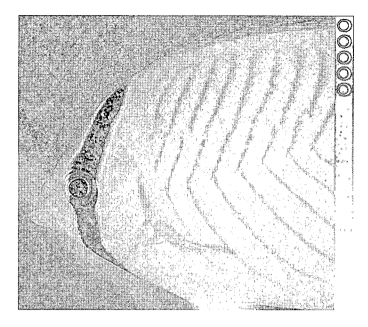

Chaetodon trifascialis

Common names: Chevroned butterflyfish, chevron butterflyfish
Range: Tropical Indo-Pacific, Red Sea
Size: 6in (15cm)
Description: On the reef this species is usually seen singly as adults and in small shoals as juveniles. Young fish have a broad posterior band from the soft dorsal to the anal fin, which disappears as it grows. The adult fish is strongly territorial and has a distinctive overall chevron pattern on the body. The soft dorsal fin is suffused with red and the margin is iridescent blue.
Aquarium suitability: This is an extremely difficult fish to keep alive and well in captivity, but despite this it is a frequently imported species. This is one of the few fishes that will refuse live brine shrimp. Occasional specimens have been encouraged to feed in captivity.

Chaetodon xanthurus

Common name: Pearl-scaled butterflyfish
Range: Central Indo-Pacific
Size: 6in (15cm)
Description: Much confusion exists over the correct name of this species. It is often referred to as *C. paucifasciatus* and sometimes as *C. mertensii*. However, *C. paucifasciatus* occurs only in the Red Sea and has an orange-red band through the eye. The dark shading on the scales assumes much more of a chevron pattern than with *C. xanthurus*. *C. mertensii* comes only from Australia and New Guinea and has a dark bar through the eye with a chevron scale pattern that is even more pronounced. To confuse matters further, *C. chrysurus* is a synonym of *C. madagascariensis*, which is probably a subspecies of this fish.
Aquarium suitability: Feeds on algae and most foods offered. It is attractive and quite hardy.

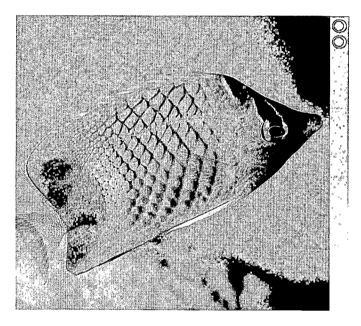

Chelmon rostratus

Common names: Copper-banded butterflyfish, beaked coralfish, banded long-snout butterflyfish, beaked butterflyfish
Range: Tropical Indo-Pacific
Size: 8in (20cm)
Description: Here is another example of nature's ability to create colour contrasts with breathtaking results. This fish is easily identified, having a long snout and bright orange bands on a silver background. There is a white-edged black ocellus at the base of the soft dorsal fin.
Aquarium suitability: This fish is susceptible to the disease lymphocystis, which can sometimes be persistent. Provide good water quality and a varied diet of frozen shellfish and brine shrimp. It is an excellent fish for ridding an aquarium of a plague of glass-roses, or rock anemones as they are sometimes called (*Aiptasia* spp.), as these are probably its favourite food.

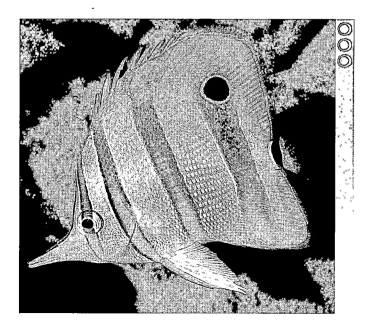

Heniochus acuminatus

Common names: Longfin bannerfish, wimplefish, pennant butterflyfish, poor man's Moorish idol, pennant coralfish
Range: Tropical Indo-Pacific, Red Sea
Size: 10in (25cm)
Description: Widespread distribution, usually in pairs or small groups. In adult fish, the fourth dorsal ray is elongated and arches high over the head. The compressed body is silvery-white in colour, with two broad black bars, and the dorsal fin and caudal fin are yellow.
Aquarium suitability: Provided the aquarium is fully mature, there is no reason why a beginner should not attempt to keep this fish from the outset. This species is robust and easy to keep and will accept most foods that are offered, even feeding from the hand. Groups of two or three look especially effective in a large tank.

Heniochus intermedius

Common names: Red Sea wimplefish, Red Sea bannerfish
Range: Red Sea, Gulf of Aden
Size: 8in (20cm)
Description: Easily confused with *H. acuminatus*. Body colouration of this species is predominantly yellow, especially the anal fin, which is more or less white in *H. acuminatus*. In addition, the second dark band runs upward almost to the middle of the dorsal ray elongation, whereas with *H. acuminatus* the band curves up behind this elongation. Finally, the general colouration of the upper part of the body of this species is much lighter with less contrast.
Aquarium suitability: Very adaptable and hardy and quickly settles in to aquarium. If anything it is easier to keep than the previous species and feeds on practically everything that it is offered. Hand feeding is fun with this fish.

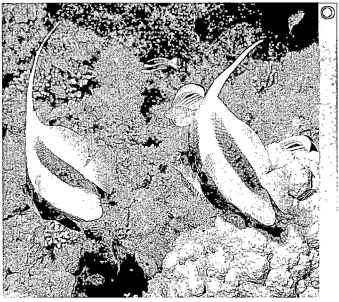

Photograph by Siegfried Krumbugel

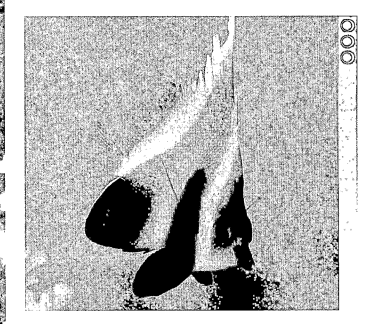

Heniochus varius

Common names: Humphead bannerfish, brown wimplefish, chocolate wimplefish
Range: Central Indo-Pacific, Western Pacific to Australia
Size: 7in (18cm)
Description: The body is more or less triangular in this species and is chocolate-brown. Two snowy-white bands adorn the sides. One runs from the first rays of the dorsal fin to the belly, and the other reaches from the caudal peduncle to the tip of the dorsal fin. In adult specimens, a large hump-like protuberance develops at the nape and two horns above the eyes.
Aquarium suitability: One of the more difficult members of this genus to keep in an aquarium because it is rather susceptible to changes in water quality. This fish will stop feeding if it is frightened or in a mild state of shock.

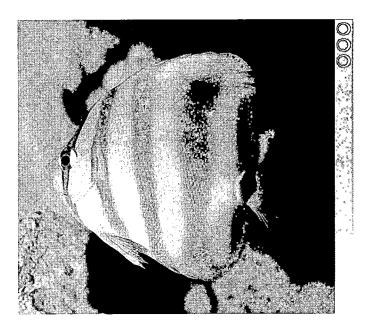

Parachaetodon ocellatus

Common names: Six-spined butterflyfish, ocellate butterflyfish
Range: Tropical Indo-Pacific
Size: 7in (18cm)
Description: This species has only six dorsal spines instead of the usual nine or so. It is an attractive fish, even though it is not particularly colourful, and is found in coastal shallows and on inshore reefs. It is easily recognizable by the four reddish-brown coloured bands on the body and a darker band running through the eye. These bands become considerably lighter with age. There is a dark spot on the caudal peduncle and a second spot on the base of the dorsal fin.
Aquarium suitability: This is not an easy fish to keep in captivity and it is not one that should be attempted by newcomers to the hobby. The tank should have plenty of hiding places into which it can retire at night.

Angelfishes, dwarf angelfishes (Pomacanthidae)

At the present time, the family Pomacanthidae contains 74 valid species incorporated into a total of nine genera. The most obvious characteristics of this family are: a large spine on the preopercle; a strongly compressed body; and elongated extensions to the posterior margins of the dorsal and anal fins.

The dorsal fin of members of the family Pomacanthidae is continuous with 9 to 15 spinous rays and 15 to 37 soft rays. The caudal fin has 15 branched rays and is rounded to lunate (crescent-shaped); in the genus *Genicanthus* this characteristic is in the extreme. The anal fin has three spinous rays and 14 to 25 soft rays. There are also numerous internal and larval differences. These have been mentioned in order to clarify the confusion that seems to exist regarding the correct systematic grouping of these fishes. It is wrong to consider the angelfishes as a subfamily of Chaetodontidae.

Fishes from this family are attractive and often highly coloured and in some cases, such as with species from the genera *Holacanthus* and *Pomacanthus*, the juveniles often display an entirely different body colouration to that of the adult fishes. The tropical Indo-Pacific contains 61 species from this family, which is the vast majority. There are only four species known from the Eastern Pacific and the remaining nine species are to be found in the tropical Atlantic region.

As a general rule, these are shallow-water fishes, and they are usually found on, or close to, reef formations at depths of up to about 65ft (20m). Species of the genus *Centropyge*, however are, often found in deeper water, to depths of more than 200ft (60m). Angelfishes occur singly, in pairs or in small groups and their diet varies between the genera.

Regarding the genus *Pomacanthus*, some of the names may seem strange to those who have read about these fishes in the past. This is understandable, since some of the previously known genera, such as *Euxiphipops*, have now been reduced to subgenera of the *Pomacanthus* group. Where this occurs in the species descriptions that follow it will be indicated within parentheses – for example (= *Euxiphipops*).

It is interesting to note that all of the species in this family can be kept, with varying degrees of success it must be said, in a home aquarium, although some of them are quite rare and are only seldom seen for sale. Fishes of the genus *Centropyge*, which are known collectively as dwarf angelfishes because of their small adult size, are ideally suited to a reef aquarium set-up.

Many of the larger species of fishes require a good-sized aquarium if you are to expect specimens to thrive, and they are best kept in a normal marine tank. With some exceptions, these fishes are generally peaceful and will accept most types of aquarium food after a period of acclimatization has taken place. In spite of this, they cannot be considered as being suitable fishes for newcomers to the hobby to keep.

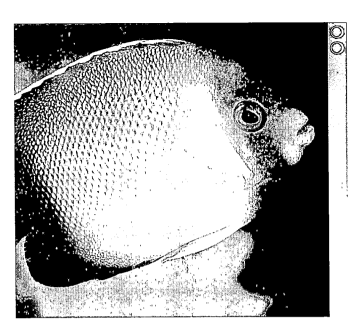

Centropyge argi

Common names: Cherubfish, pygmy angelfish
Range: Tropical West Atlantic
Size: 3in (7.5cm)
Description: The head of this species is bright yellow and the rest of the body is a deep, rich blue. The eyes are rimmed with blue and the dorsal fin and anal fin margins are light blue in adult specimens. The spine on the opercle is also blue. *Centropyge argi* is found in the reef shallows and feeds primarily on benthic algae.
Aquarium suitability: Although this is a shy species and sometimes takes three or four days to settle in, it is extremely hardy. It should be provided with plenty of hiding places and it will soon learn to supplement its natural diet with most aquarium foods, including flake varieties. It will not tolerate high nitrate levels, so the aquarium water quality must be good.

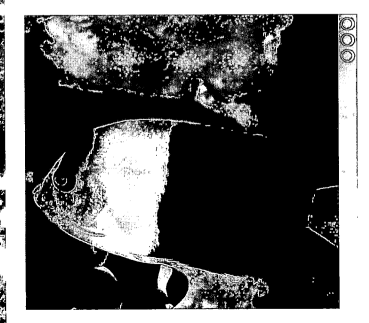

Apolemichthys xanthurus

Common names: Indian angelfish, Indian smoked-glass angelfish
Range: Indian Ocean
Size: 6in (15cm)
Description: Although this fish is similar to *A. xanthotis* from the Red Sea, the bar on the head is considerably lighter in colour. In addition, the caudal peduncle is deeper and thicker, and the eye is larger. The caudal fin is yellow and there is a brownish-black bar from the posterior part of the dorsal to the anal fin. A series of brown spots suffuse the upper two-thirds of the body. Found on the reef at depths of 15 to 65ft (4.5 to 20m).
Aquarium suitability: This is a robust fish that is relatively easy to keep. It is peaceful with other tank-mates and accepts most foods that are offered. To give it a special treat, try feeding it frozen krill and mysid shrimp.

Centropyge bicolor

Common names: Bicolor angelfish, oriole angelfish, two-coloured angelfish, bicolor cherub, blue and gold angelfish
Range: Central Indo-Pacific
Size: 6in (15cm)
Description: As the names imply, this fish has two predominant colours. These are bright yellow, to about one-third of the length of the body and the tail, and deep blue for the remainder of the body. There is also a deep blue patch from the interorbital space to the eye. These two colours are sharply defined and on the reef this fish is easily identified as it grazes the rocks and coral rubble in small groups.
Aquarium suitability: This fish is considerably less hardy than the previous species, and so is not a beginner's fish. Nevertheless, it is in great demand by aquarists. It is not as territorial as others of this genus and it will accept most aquarium foods.

Centropyge bispinosus

Common names: Coral beauty, dusky angelfish, two-spined angelfish
Range: Tropical Indo-Pacific
Size: 5in (13cm)
Description: This is a secretive species in its natural habitat and is never seen in any great numbers. The body is a deep indigo in colour, and this is interspersed with narrow vermilion bands on the sides. In adult specimens, the throat and belly are also vermilion in colour.
Aquarium suitability: It should be kept singly as it will usually fight with others of its kind. It is, however, a good community fish. Occasional specimens can be choosy about what they eat. The water quality should be good to keep the fish free of disease. This is not a beginner's fish by any means, but once the aquarist has gained enough experience it is an ideal choice.

Centropyge eibli

Common names: Eibl's angelfish, tiger angelfish
Range: Indian Ocean
Size: 6in (15cm)
Description: C. *eibli* is much rarer than the preceding species and it is only occasionally observed in its natural reef habitat. Little is known about its feeding and spawning habits in the wild, though these are thought to be no different to others of this genus. The body colouration consists of a background of reddish-gold. Over this is superimposed a series of narrow wavy lines that are bright orange in colour. The eyes are also rimmed with orange.
Aquarium suitability: This species is rarely imported but it is quite hardy in captivity. It should be fed a selection of frost foods but its particular favourite is finely chopped mussel. Provide it plenty of caves and grottoes in which it can hide.

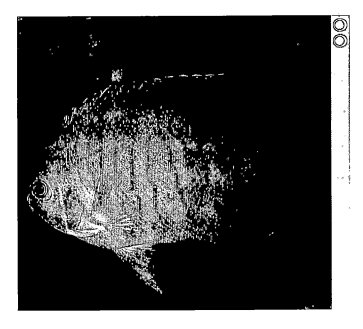

Centropyge ferrugatus

Common name: Rusty angelfish
Range: Central Indo-Pacific
Size: 4in (10cm)
Description: The body colouration of this species is brick red with numerous brownish spots covering the sides and fins. The upper half of the body is darker and the dorsal and anal fins are tipped with iridescent blue. In the wild this fish is very territorial, particularly during the breeding season. Generally it is found in deeper waters of the reef, often on the outer reef slopes, at depths of 80 to 120 feet (24 to 37 metres).
Aquarium suitability: This is a good community fish. It is generally well behaved but it can handle boisterous tank-mates when necessary. It requires good water with low levels of nitrate and if this is provided it is easy to keep and hardy. Nevertheless, this is not a beginner's fish.

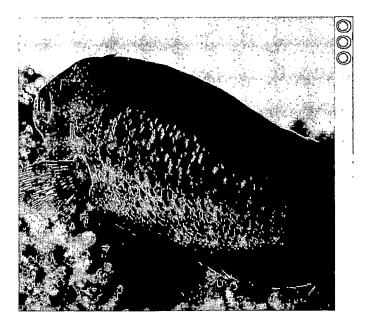

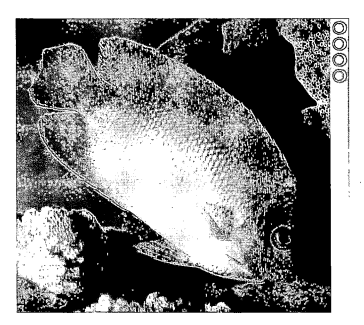

Centropyge vroliki

Common name: Pearl-scaled angelfish
Range: Central Indo-Pacific
Size: 4in (10cm)
Description: With this species, the young fish undergo a slight colour change before reaching adulthood; specifically, the eye band fades away. In juveniles, the band is quite dark and runs vertically behind the eye. The photograph shown is of a young adult specimen and only a shadow of this band can be seen. The sides are suffused with a very attractive pearly sheen. The dorsal, anal and caudal fins are dark and the eye is ringed with orange. There is also an orange streak behind the opercle. This fish inhabits reef shallows, lagoons and tide pools.
Aquarium suitability: It soon makes itself at home but it can be aggressive toward its tank-mates. It accepts most foods offered and is ideal for anyone apart from the complete beginner.

Centropyge heraldi

Common names: Golden angelfish, herald's angelfish
Range: Central Indo-Pacific
Size: 5in (13cm)
Description: This fish is easily mistaken for the lemonpeel angelfish (*Centropyge flavissimus*). Both species are bright yellow but this species lacks the blue ring surrounding its eye. Additionally, *C. heraldi* has numerous indistinct blue lines running across the dorsal, anal and caudal fins. In the wild, its bright yellow colour makes it stand out in the reef shallows where it may be observed singly or in small groups.
Aquarium suitability: A difficult fish to keep unless the water quality is 100 per cent. The experienced aquarist will supplement its natural algae diet with frozen plankton and brine shrimp, with occasional offerings of krill and mysid shrimp. It is ideal for a reef aquarium.

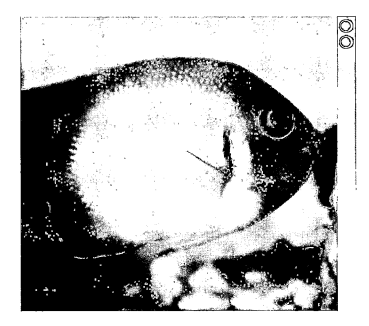

Genicanthus lamarck

Common names: Lamarck's angelfish, swallow-tailed angelfish
Range: East Africa to central Indo-Pacific
Size: 9½in (24cm)
Description: The swallow-tailed angelfish is essentially a deep-water species, preferring the outer reef slopes where it can be seen at depths of 165 feet (50 metres). It is easy to differentiate between male and female of the species, since the caudal margins and pelvic fins are darkly coloured in the female and silvery-white in the male. The males also have a yellow spot on the forehead. Their natural diet consists of bryozoans, tunicates, polychaetes and algae.
Aquarium suitability: Although this species is not often imported, it is easy to keep in an aquarium and will accept most frost foods once it has settled down to its new home. It is a hardy species that is suitable for a reef aquarium.

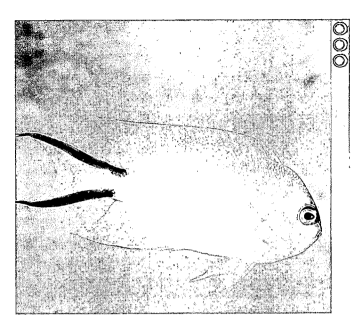

Genicanthus melanospilus

Common name: Black-spot angelfish
Range: Central Indo-Pacific
Size: 8in (20cm)
Description: This species is easy to sex: the male is adorned with 20 or so dark bands running slightly obliquely down the body; in contrast, the female of the species has no bands but the upper and lower lobes of the tail are edged in blue and black and the body is silvery-white fading into blue, dorsally. This fish also prefers deeper water and is shy and secretive.
Aquarium suitability: The black-spot angelfish turns up now and again in dealers' tanks and is quickly snapped up by aquarists because of its robust nature. It is not as easy to keep as the previous species because it can sometimes be difficult to get it to feed. Once this problem has been solved, the fish will do well. Frozen brine shrimp and plankton are good starter foods.

Holacanthus bermudensis

(Syn. = *Holacanthus isabelita*)
Common names: Blue angelfish, Bermuda angelfish
Range: Tropical West Atlantic
Size: 18in (45cm)
Description: The juvenile and adult colour phases show a marked difference in this species. In the juvenile, shown in this photograph, there are several bluish-white bars on the body and a dark band running through the eye. The anal fin is yellow with a blue margin. The adult fish has orange margins to the caudal fin and to the posterior edges of the dorsal and anal fins. The body is greenish-blue with fine black spots, particularly in the dorsal region.
Aquarium suitability: This fish accepts a variety of foods but it can be aggressive toward other tank-mates. This species requires a large tank and good water quality if it is to remain free of disease and is not a beginner's fish.

Holacanthus ciliaris

Common names: Queen angelfish, blue crown angelfish
Range: Tropical West Atlantic
Size: 18in (46cm)
Description: The juvenile phase of this species is similar to that of *H. bermudensis*, except that the body bands are more curved and the anal fin is generally bluish. The adult colouration of this fish is predominantly yellow or bluish-yellow, with a blue-edged black mark on the forehead that resembles a crown. The middle of this mark is sprinkled with blue spots. In addition, the posterior margins of the dorsal and anal fins are blue and the caudal fin is yellow.
Aquarium suitability: Similar to the previous species, this fish requires a large tank if it is to develop properly. It will not tolerate another of its own kind. Frost foods and vitamin supplements should be given for the best results.

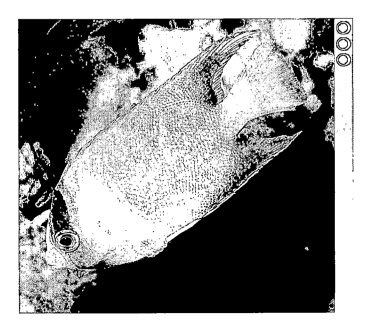

Pomacanthus annularis

Common name: Blue-ring angelfish
Range: East Africa to central Indo-Pacific
Size: 10in (25cm)
Description: The remarkable thing about this fish is its apparent
hardiness in water that is far from ideal. It has been encountered
living happily in Sri Lanka's busy Colombo harbour and in the
turbid, sometimes polluted waters of Hong Kong. It appears that
the adult fish move into shallow water to spawn in spring. By
midsummer the young fish, flashing bright blue, can be seen
darting in and out of the rocks and corals. During autumn they
retire to deeper water, returning to the same area the following
year to feed and grow. Young fish have a series of blue and white
narrow bands running down the body. As the fish grows, these
become less distinct until they disappear completely to be
replaced with diagonal wavy blue lines. The background body
colour also changes from indigo in the young fish to brownish-
orange in the adult. In addition, a blue ring appears above the
pectoral fin. The transition is illustrated in the four photographs
shown here. The first three are of the same specimen at different
stages of its life. This fish originally came from Hoi Ha Wan,
Hong Kong.
Aquarium suitability: Good water quality must be provided
and the tank should have sufficient free swimming space.
Feeding is no problem, since this fish will soon accept practically
anything that is offered. Young fish may be shy but become bolder
as they grow, but not normally aggressive toward other tank-
mates. Hand feeding is possible within a few weeks and all of the
usual frozen foods will be eagerly accepted. Young fish do not
normally damage corals. Older specimens are not suitable for a
reef aquarium: they do not tolerate others of their own kind.

RIGHT FROM TOP TO BOTTOM *Juvenile fish –1in (2.5cm);*
juvenile fish – 3in (7.5cm); subadult fish – 5in (12.5cm); and
adult fish – 8in (20cm).

Holacanthus tricolor

Common name: Rock beauty
Range: Tropical West Atlantic
Size: 10in (25cm)
Description: The rock beauty is the most widespread and
commonly seen member of this family in the Caribbean. Young
fish are bright yellow with a bluish-black spot edged with blue
on the upper part of the body. As the fish grows, this spot
enlarges to cover most of the posterior part of the body but
leaving the tail yellow. The eye is blue and the margins of the
dorsal and anal fins are bright orange-red in colour.
Aquarium suitability: Large specimens are inclined to bully
other fishes. Feeding this fish sometimes presents a problem and
it can be very choosy. Algae and frost foods form the main part
of its aquarium diet. Frozen krill, mysid and adult brine shrimp
are all usually accepted. This is not a fish for a reef aquarium.

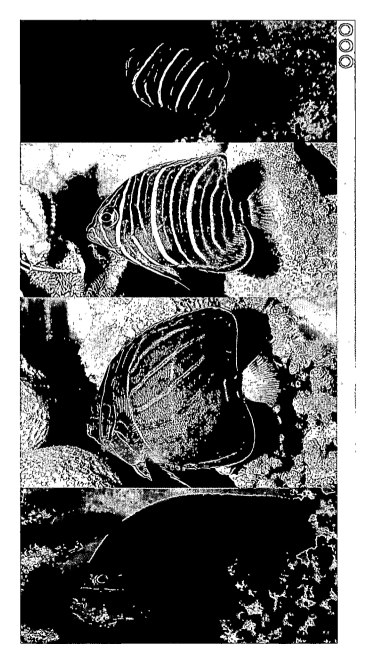

Pomacanthus arcuatus

Common names: Grey angelfish, black angelfish
Range: Tropical West Atlantic
Size: 14in (36cm)
Description: In the adult fish of this species, the first few rays of the dorsal and anal fins develop into filaments and the caudal fin is almost square. The scales on the body are edged in brownish-black to greyish-black. The young fish are attractive, with two bright yellow bars that adorn each side of the body. There are two similar bars on the head. The tail is rounded in shape and is yellow with a black rectangular spot. As the fish grows, the bars on the body become progressively lighter in colour until they finally disappear.
Aquarium suitability: Young fish are difficult to keep in an aquarium, whereas subadults, such as the one pictured here, are tough and hardy. Most frost foods will be accepted.

Pomacanthus asfur

(= *Arusetta asfur*)
Common names: Purple crescent angelfish, blue seabride, half-moon angelfish
Range: Northern Indian Ocean, Red Sea
Size: 15in (38cm)
Description: Juveniles and adult fish are somewhat similar in appearance to *P. maculosus*, but in the case of this species the tail is bright yellow more or less throughout its life. In addition, the yellow crescent on the sides of this fish is much brighter and more clearly defined.
Aquarium suitability: This is thought by many to be the most beautiful of all the angelfishes and is probably the easiest to keep in captivity, if it is given a large enough aquarium. It is very undemanding in its food requirements once the initial settling-in period has been overcome. This fish is very fond of freshly thawed-out frozen krill, mysid and adult brine shrimp.

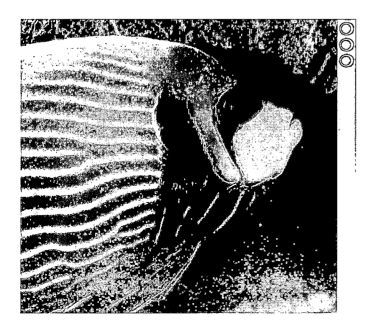

Pomacanthus imperator

Common names: Emperor angelfish, imperial angelfish
Range: Red Sea, Tropical Indo-Pacific
Size: 15in (38cm)
Description: The young of this particular species are similar in appearance to the juveniles of *P. annularis*. In the case of this species, however, the blue and white lines are curved and form a complete circle near the tail. As the fish grows, these markings are replaced by an entirely different, but equally striking, colour pattern, as shown in the photograph. It is one of the reef's most attractive inhabitants and it can be seen singly or in small groups throughout its natural range.
Aquarium suitability: This is not a beginner's fish. The tank must be large enough and it requires optimal water conditions for the fish to remain happy and healthy. If this is provided, it will usually settle down and prove to be quite hardy.

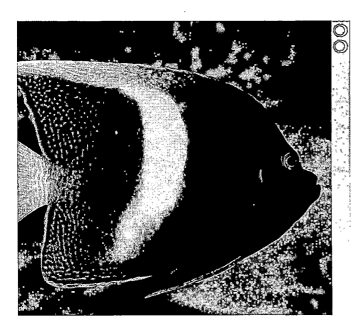

Pomacanthus navarchus

(= *Euxiphipops navarchus*)
Common names: Blue-girdled angelfish, majestic angelfish
Range: Central Indo-Pacific
Size: 10in (25cm)
Description: This spectacular-looking species is found at depths of between 10 and 100ft (3 and 30m) in areas of dense coral growth, usually in lagoons or on the outer slopes of a reef. The juveniles are blue-black in colour with a series of bluish-white vertical bars. The dorsal base is often tinged with orange. With this species of fish, the colour change comes relatively early, when they are at about 2in (5cm) in length. The colouration of adult fish is shown in the accompanying photograph.
Aquarium suitability: A hardy fish that can be quite shy at first and may be difficult to get to feed. Try offering frozen mussel and cockles as a starter food. Young fish tend to adapt better to aquarium life. This is not a beginner's fish.

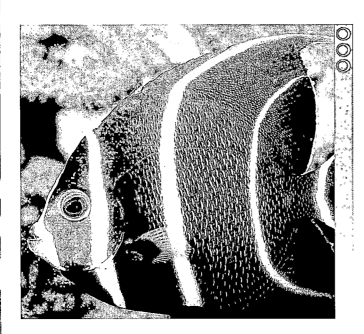

Pomacanthus maculosus

Common names: Purple moon angelfish, blue moon angelfish
Range: Red Sea, Gulf of Oman, Persian Gulf
Size: 16in (40cm)
Description: Young fish are often confused with juveniles of the species *P. annularis*. In this case, however, there are more vertical bars, and these are thinner and lighter in colour. On the reef, this is a very inquisitive fish that will allow itself to be approached by divers. Adult fish are usually solitary and are found at depths of 10 to 40ft (3 to 12m).
Aquarium suitability: A calm and peaceful fellow that requires a large tank in order to do well. *P. maculosus* is easy to acclimatize and is a good aquarium subject. Adult specimens soon learn to take food from their owner's hand. Most of the normal frost foods are suitable for this fish. Juvenile specimens may be kept in a reef aquarium.

Pomacanthus paru

Common name: French angelfish
Range: Tropical East and West Atlantic
Size: 16in (40cm)
Description: The young fish are similar in appearance to those of *P. arcuatus* except that the tail is rounded. It is also encircled with yellow and the banding on the body is more curved. In addition, this species has a darker body colour. The young fish perform a cleaning service on the reef similar to that of the cleaner wrasse (*Labroides dimidiatus*).
Aquarium suitability: A robust species that is, nevertheless, prone to disease if the water quality is anything less than excellent. Juveniles will accept most foods offered from the start, including flake food. Older specimens, however, often prove more difficult to wean on to aquarium foods and, in some cases, never make the transition. Suitable for experienced aquarists.

Pomacanthus semicirculatus

Common names: Koran angelfish, semicircle angelfish
Range: Red Sea, Tropical Indo-Pacific
Size: 18in (46cm)
Description: The photograph here shows a young adult fish. The juvenile colouration is similar to that of *P. annularis* and *P. imperator*. In this case, however, the blue and white lines form a semicircle on the body (hence its common and Latin name), which is indigo in colour. The adult fish is greenish-yellow fading into indigo on the flanks. The body is suffused with dark spots, which are green on the flanks. The preopercle, spine and opercle are all bright blue.
Aquarium suitability: This is a hardy fish that is suitable for a community tank when it is young. As it grows older, it becomes more territorial and can then cause problems. It requires a large aquarium but is not suitable for a reef set-up.

Pomacanthus sexstriatus
(= *Euxiphipops sexstriatus*)
Common names: Six-barred angelfish, six-banded angelfish
Range: Tropical Indo-Pacific
Size: 20in (51cm)
Description: The juvenile body colouration is blue-black with blue and white vertical bars. The tail is truncate at this stage. As the fish grows, the tail becomes rounded and the fish assumes the adult colouration shown in the photograph here. This shows a subadult fish measuring 12in (30cm). This species is commonly found in the southern part of the Indo-Pacific region as far as Australia.
Aquarium suitability: A young individual of the six-barred angelfish is hardy and easy to keep. It is an excellent choice for the aquarists who wants to try their hand at keeping angelfishes. Unfortunately, they grow very large very quickly, which is not a problem if the tank is large enough to accommodate them.

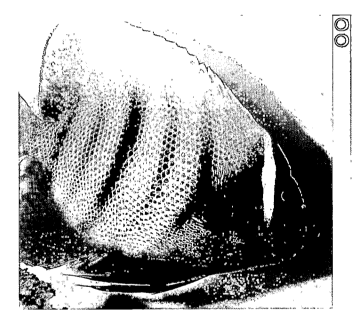

Pygoplites diacanthus

Common names: Regal angelfish, royal empress angelfish
Range: Red Sea, East Africa to Central Indo-Pacific
Size: 12in (30cm)
Description: This species is unmistakable, having an orange body and a yellow, rounded tail. The soft dorsal fin is predominantly blue and is also rounded, as is the anal fin. There is a series of black-edged blue to bluish-white lines running obliquely down the sides of the strongly compressed body.
Aquarium suitability: Acclimatization is often difficult with a fish of this species and it requires near-perfect water quality if it is to survive. A good growth of algae in the aquarium is helpful in encouraging this fish to feed, along with a good selection of frozen shellfish. A strong water current should be provided to enhance the colours and make it feel at home. Suitable only for experienced aquarists.

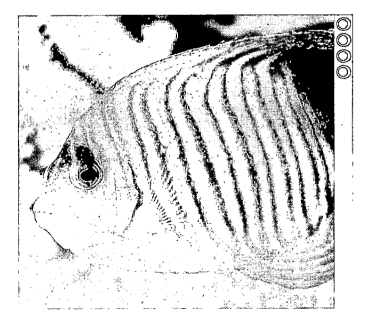

Sea chubs (Kyphosidae)

Although there is controversy regarding the organization of this family of fishes, evidence suggests that it contains a total of 42 species in 15 genera. They are shallow-water and shore fishes that occur in both the Atlantic and Pacific Oceans. With the exception of the genus *Graus*, the nibblers (Girellinae) and the rudderfishes (Kyphosinae) are herbivorous fishes that graze on algae and sea grasses. Fishes belonging to the remaining ten genera are carnivorous species.

Most of the species are drab in colour, except those known as the footballers (Microcanthinae). These are striking in appearance, particularly the eastern footballer (*Atrypichthys latus*), the western footballer (*Neatypus obliquus*), the moonlighter (*Vinculum sexfasciatus*) and the stripy (*below right*).

Microcanthus strigatus

Common names: Stripy, convict-fish, footballer
Range: Tropical Western Pacific to Hawaii
Size: 6in (15cm)
Description: The stripy is endemic in Hawaii, Japan, the Ryukyu Islands and the east coast of Australia. They are often encountered in small shoals in the surf around coral reefs. In Hawaii, the young fish appear in the shallows and tide pools from about December until May, then apparently move to deeper water. Children with dip-nets often collect them.
Aquarium suitability: In Europe, this species is not often seen, which is a pity since it is an attractive fish. It is very easy to keep in a marine aquarium and is extremely hardy. There are no problems with feeding because this fish eats anything that is offered. It is an ideal fish for the beginner and a small shoal of juvenile fishes looks spectacular in a large tank.

Photograph by Dr John E. Randall

Hawkfishes (Cirrhitidae)

These are small, shallow-water fishes, similar in many respects to scorpionfishes. Their body shape varies somewhat, but all have a continuous dorsal fin with bristles (cirri) on the interspinous membrane near the tip of the spines. The dorsal fin has ten spines and 11 to 17 soft rays. The anal fin has three pronounced spines and five to seven soft rays. Generally, the tail is not forked but may be truncate or rounded. Most species exhibit a fringe behind the first nostril.

They inhabit most warm seas, especially in the Indo-Pacific. They are poorly represented in the tropical Atlantic, with only one or two species being present. They are carnivorous fishes, whose main diet consists of small crustaceans and fishes. Sometimes they are found in large numbers where the shallow seabed is rocky, but more often they are seen singly in areas of dense coral resting on a convenient "perch". This is usually high up and is used as a vantage point from where they are able to pick out their prey (hence the name "hawkfishes").

The family comprises 32 species in nine genera. They are usually very easy to keep and some of the species are suitable for a reef aquarium because of their small adult size. In a reef or normal marine aquarium, it is a good idea to provide perches for the fish, such as flat rocks, in the upper half of the aquarium. Larger specimens are not suitable and are a danger to small tank-mates.

Hawkfishes are not often seen for sale. As a rule, they will accept most aquarium foods, such as frozen shellfish, krill, mysid shrimp and adult brine shrimp. Larger specimens will often accept frozen lancefish and sand shrimps. Very few species will settle for a diet of just dried food, and some may not accept this food at all.

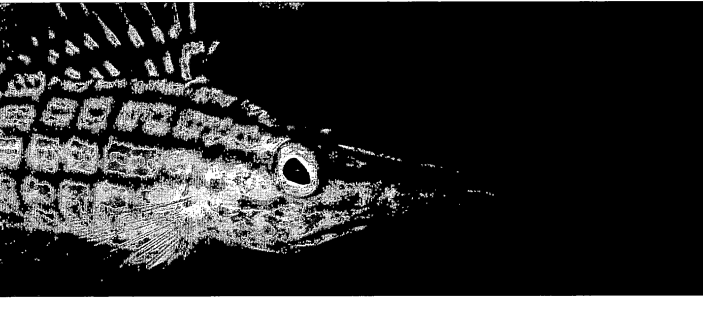

Oxycirrhites typus

Common names: Long-nosed hawkfish
Range: Tropical Indo-Pacific
Size: 5in (13cm)
Description: The fish shown here is in the characteristic pose of the hawkfishes, resting on its pelvic fins. Its bright red, chequered body colour pattern makes this species easy to identify. In addition it has a more elongated body. Most members of this family are found in the reef shallows, but the long-nosed hawkfish prefers the deeper waters of the reef. The favourite hunting ground of this fish is among gorgonian corals, and these do not grow in the reef shallows.
Aquarium suitability: Although it is not often seen for sale, this fish is very hardy. It is an ideal choice for a reef aquarium when no small shrimps or prawns are present. This species will happily accept a diet of frozen shellfish and shrimps and may even learn to take flake food.

Anemonefishes, damselfishes (Pomacentridae)

This is probably the most widespread family of all the reef fishes, having representatives in every warm sea in the world. The family contains 321 species divided into 28 genera. The six main genera are *Amphiprion* with 27 species, *Chromis* with 75 species, *Abudefduf* with 18 species, *Chrysiptera* with 25 species, *Stegastes* with 33 species and *Pomacentrus* with 53 species.

They are relatively small fishes with high and compressed bodies. All of the species have a continuous dorsal fin and one nostril on each side of the head. The mouth is small and the lateral line is incomplete. During breeding, the eggs are cared for by the males.

They prefer to live in shallow water close to the shore, where there is often an abundance of food. Accordingly, they are the fishes that are most commonly encountered by swimmers and divers. This family encompasses some of the most brightly coloured coral fishes in the sea and they are often sought by professional catchers and exported for the aquarium trade or for display tanks in zoos around the world. Generally Pomacentridae species are hardy creatures that will readily settle in to life in the close confines of an aquarium.

Although they will generally do well in an aquarium setting, they are often pugnacious and strongly territorial fishes, and on numerous occasions it has been reported that one of these fishes has bravely attack a diver who unthinkingly encroached on its territory, with seemingly little regard to the vast difference in size. They are found singly, or in large shoals above coral heads into which they will quickly disappear at the first sign of danger.

The anemonefishes, *Amphiprion* spp., are well known for their symbiotic relationship with large sea anemones. They are able to swim with impunity among the poisonous, stinging tentacles of their anemone hosts. Some species of *Dascyllus* are found in small shoals within the needle-like spines of long-spined sea urchins (*Diadema* spp.).

Many pomacentrids have been bred successfully in an aquarium, but with some species at least there are still a lot of problems that need to be overcome with regard to raising the resulting fry. Marine rotifers appear to be the solution to the problem of feeding the fry, but these are not easy to culture in themselves.

Premnas biaculeatus

Common names: Spine-cheek anemonefish, maroon clownfish, premnas
Range: Tropical Indo-Pacific
Size: 7in (18cm)
Description: As the common name implies, this fish has two spines, one under each eye. These are formed as an extension of the suborbital bone. The body colour is red to brown-red and there are three bluish-white bands, which are sometimes incomplete. Apart from the presence of the two spines, this species also differs from those of the genus *Amphiprion*, in that the scales are smaller and the bone structure is somewhat different.
Aquarium suitability: This is a fairly aggressive fish that will not tolerate another anemonefish in the same tank. It is a relatively easy fish to keep on its own, however, and it will accept most foods, including flake foods.

Amphiprion akindynos

Common name: Barrier Reef anemonefish
Range: Pacific to southern Australia
Size: 5in (12.5cm)
Description: This species is similar to A. *chrysopterus*, except that it grows larger. The colouration is somewhat different, too. The juveniles are dark brown but this lightens to orange with age. There are three white to bluish-white bands on the head and body. The adult fish usually has only two distinct bands and a pale caudal fin.
Aquarium suitability: Although this fish is seldom imported, occasional specimens do appear for sale. It is a relatively peaceful fish when it is provided with a suitable host anemone. This is not a fish for the beginner, since it is quite susceptible to disease during the acclimatization phase. It feeds well on a diet of frost and dried foods.

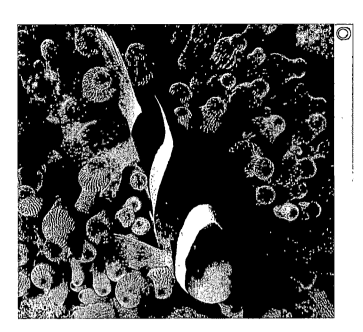

Amphiprion clarkii

Common names: Clark's anemonefish, black clownfish, brown anemonefish, two-banded anemonefish
Range: Northern Indo-Pacific from Japan to East Africa
Size: 4in (10cm)
Description: Generally, young fish have a dark brown body, an orange belly and snout, yellow fins and two broad, bluish-white bands on the body. The adult fish has a white, sometimes yellow, caudal fin. Body colour may be deep brown or brownish-black, with an orange belly and snout. There is also a black variety or phase in which the fish is mainly brownish-black and white.
Aquarium suitability: A peaceful, inquisitive fish that is easy to keep. It will accept frost and dried foods and will also eat algae. Adult fish tend to be territorial, especially when there is no host anemone. When this is the case they will use their tails to fan out a hollow in the sand, which then becomes their retreat.

Amphiprion ephippium

Common names: Saddle anemonefish, black-backed anemonefish, tomato clownfish, fire clown
Range: Indian Ocean, Central Indo-Pacific
Size: 3in (7.5cm)
Description: This is the only anemonefish species with a complete absence of white bars on its body. Instead, it has a large black saddle mid-dorsally and toward the flanks. The rest of the body is bright orange. This species is very closely related to the following species and also to *A. melanopus*.
Aquarium suitability: This species adapts to aquarium life and has been bred in captivity. It is a very attractive fish, but territorial by nature. If they are kept in small groups with a large host anemone in the aquarium, they will quickly establish a "pecking order" of dominance among themselves. It accepts most foods that are offered.

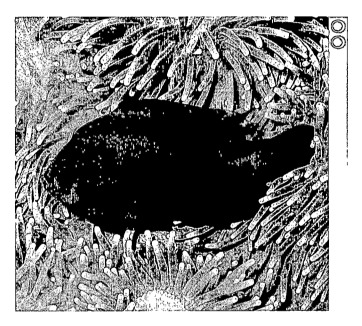

Amphiprion frenatus

Common names: Fire clown, tomato clownfish, red anemonefish
Range: Central Indo-Pacific to East Africa
Size: 4in (10cm)
Description: A white band behind the eye distinguishes this species from the previous one. The body colour is bright orange-red and the fins are orange-yellow. Juvenile fish may often have a second, mid-body band that gradually disappears as it ages.
Aquarium suitability: This is a very aggressive fish and not one to be recommended for the beginner, in spite of its hardiness. In an aquarium without an anemone, the fire clown will burrow and dig pits in the sand, move small pieces of the aquarium decoration around and generally make a nuisance of itself with its tank-mates. With an anemone, it is very territorial and belligerent. This fish eats almost any food that is offered.

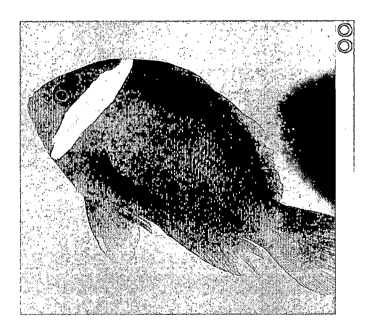

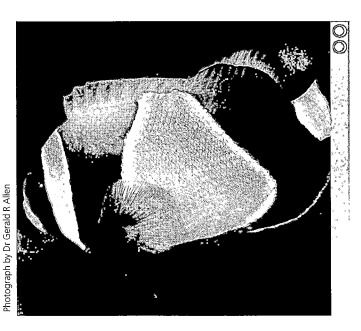

Photograph by Dr Gerald R Allen

Amphiprion latezonatus

Common name: Wide-band anemonefish
Range: Queensland, South and West Australia
Size: 4½in (12cm)
Description: This species was discovered in 1900 but up until 1971 it was known only from a single specimen. Since then, many more have turned up and the photograph here shows a specimen that was caught at Lord Howe Island. The wavy band on the caudal peduncle and the very broad mid-body band are typical of this species, as is the background body colouration. This is dark brown fading to orange-yellow dorsally.
Aquarium suitability: Up until recently, this fish was never seen on dealer's lists. However, one or two have appeared in the last few years and it would now seem that they are not as rare as first thought. The care and feeding of *A. latezonatus* is no different to others of this genus.

Amphiprion melanopus

Common names: Black anemonefish, dusky anemonefish, fire clown, teak clownfish
Range: Central Indo-Pacific to Oceania
Size: 5in (13cm)
Description: The body and flanks of this species are much darker than in *A. frenatus*. The caudal fin is rounded and the pelvic fins dark. The headband is connected dorsally but remains unconnected at the throat. This is an aggressive species that is usually found singly within a host anemone.
Aquarium suitability: Older fish and adults are very pugnacious and cause a lot of problems in a community tank. They will attack smaller fishes, leaving them shredded and injured. They are also territorial, even to the point of attacking your hand or arm if it is immersed in the water while you are working in the tank.

Photograph by Dr Gerald R Allen

Amphiprion ocellaris

Common names: Clown anemonefish, common clownfish, orange anemonefish
Range: Central Indo-Pacific to Oceania
Size: 4in (10cm)
Description: Often referred to as *A. percula*, which is a similar species. It is easy to tell the two apart, however. This species has narrow black borders around the three bluish-white bands, whereas *A. percula* has broad black margins to the bands that often extend over much of the body. This gives it an overall darker appearance. In addition, this species has 11 dorsal spines instead of the usual ten in *A. percula*.
Aquarium suitability: Tank-bred specimens are now becoming available to the hobbyist. The eggs hatch after seven to eight days and the fry are pelagic for a further 14 days. After this, they settle to the bottom and search for a suitable anemone.

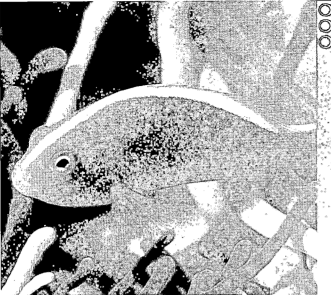

Photograph by Dr Gerald R Allen

Amphiprion sandaracinos

Common names: Orange anemonefish, yellow skunk clownfish
Range: Central Pacific to Indonesia
Size: 5in (13cm)
Description: The colouration of this species is similar to that of *A. akallopisos*, except that the white mid-dorsal stripe extends from the caudal base to the upper lip. In the case of *A. akallopisos* the stripe ends before the upper lip. In both species the body is tan to orange-yellow in colour. This is a shy species that seldom strays far from its anemone home.
Aquarium suitability: Without an anemone host in the aquarium this species does not do at all well in captivity. It is a timid creature that will be bullied by its more boisterous tank-mates. With an anemone in residence, it fares a lot better. Dried and frozen foods, such as krill and adult brine shrimp, are readily accepted. Not a beginner's fish.

Amphiprion tricinctus

Common names: Three-band anemonefish, maroon clownfish
Range: Tropical Pacific (known only from the Marshall Islands and surrounding areas)
Size: 5½in (14cm)
Description: The body colouration varies from orange to brownish-black. There are three white bands present, the first of which is behind the eye. The second band is thin and runs from the middle of the dorsal fin to the vent. The third band, on the caudal peduncle, is sometimes indistinct.
Aquarium suitability: At one time it was frequently imported, now less so. Young fish are inclined to squabble when kept in small groups, and older fish even more so. In this case, a larger tank with plenty of hiding places and caves is the solution, both for the troublesome and the troubled. So far there are no reports of breeding successes with this particular species.

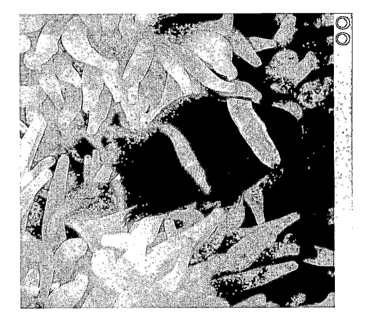

Chromis atripectoralis

Common names: Black-axil chromis, green chromis
Range: Tropical Indo-Pacific
Size: 3½in (9cm)
Description: This fish is often confused with *C. viridis*, which is understandable since they are almost identical. However, this species has a black pectoral axil while *C. viridis* does not. Additionally, the adult fish is somewhat larger than its near relative. The body colour is iridescent apple-green, which sometimes has a bluish cast to it when it is seen in sunlight. This species congregates in large shoals in open water and their basic diet is plankton.
Aquarium suitability: For the best effect, they should be kept in small groups but always in odd numbers (i.e. ones, threes, fives sevens and so on). Strangely enough these, and other damselfishes, do not seem to be so scrappy.

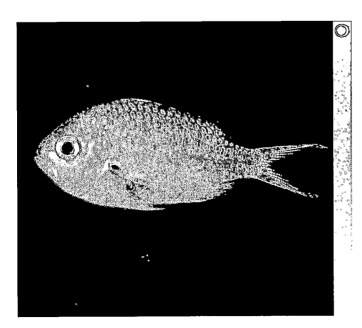

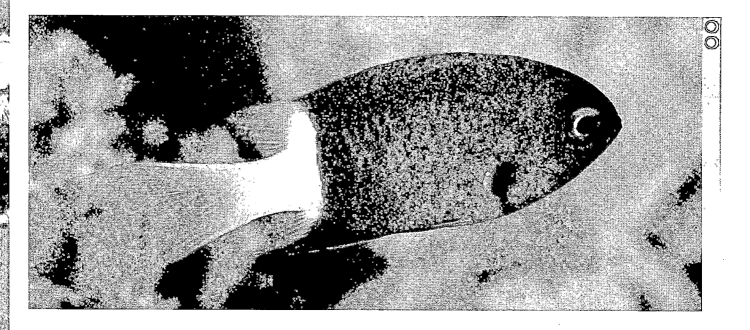

▲ *Chromis bicolor*

Common names: Bicolor chromis, two-coloured chromis
Range: Western Pacific to Java
Size: 4½in (11cm)
Description: The eye is blue-green and a large part of the body
colouration is chocolate-brown. This ends abruptly on the
flanks, and the posterior part of the body and caudal peduncle is
white. The demarcation runs vertically from the soft dorsal fin
to the anal fin.
Aquarium suitability: Like all species from this genus, this fish
is always on the move during the day and always looking for
food. Its main diet in the wild is plankton and copepods so it
needs to be fed little and often on frozen plankton and the like.
All *Chromis* spp. have an active nature and need to feed to
replace the energy lost. This means that you must offer food to
them several times a day for the best results.

▼ *Chromis cyaneus*

Common names: Blue chromis, blue reef fish, blue forked-tail
chromis
Range: Tropical West Atlantic, Caribbean
Size: 4in (10cm)
Description: The blue chromis is often seen in the reef shallows
and is easily identified by its bright blue livery. Like the
preceding species, it is a shoaling fish and large aggregations
characteristically feed above coral heads. The body colour is
metallic-blue, fading into black dorsally. The tail is deeply
forked and the upper and lower margins are dark. There is a
blue line at the dorsal base.
Aquarium suitability: Adult fish are difficult to acclimatize and
tend to be scrappy. Juveniles are easier to keep and look
attractive in small groups. They need to be fed often and their
diet should include frozen shellfish and crustaceans.

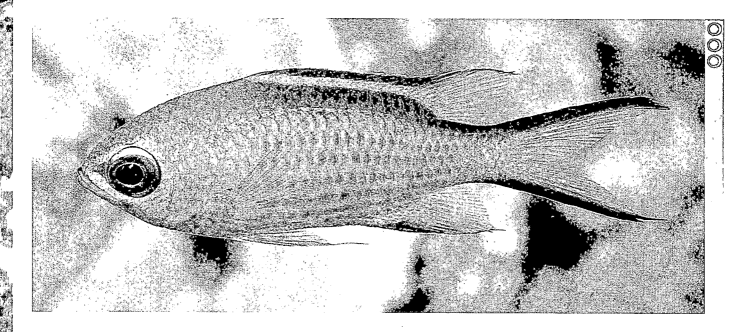

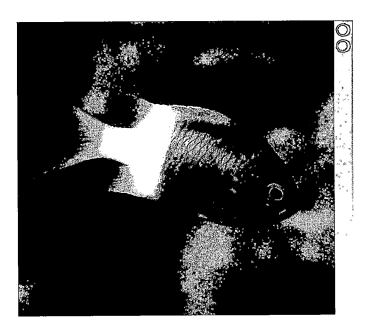

Chromis dimidiatus

Common names: Bicolor chromis (Amer.), bicolour chromis (Brit.), half and half puller
Range: Indian Ocean, Red Sea
Size: 3½in (9cm)
Description: This fish is similar to C. *bicolor* but in this case the eye is orange-brown. The demarcation of the two colours is also further forward on the body, so that the flanks and caudal peduncle are white. This ends in an abrupt line from the middle of the dorsal fin to the anterior part of the anal fin. The rest of the body is dark brown to chocolate-brown.
Aquarium suitability: Although this is not a fish for the complete beginner, it is hardy and easy to keep. As with others of this genus, it should be fed little and often. Small groups in a reef aquarium do not need to be fed so often because they derive much of their daily needs from the system itself.

Chromis scotti

Common names: Scott's chromis, blue puller
Range: Tropical West Atlantic, Caribbean
Size: 3in (7.5cm)
Description: The scales of this species are edged in deep blue and, although the body colour is black, this gives it a deep blue appearance. Several blue lines radiate from the snout around the eye and the upper and lower lobes of the caudal fin are tipped with blue. The margins of the dorsal and anal fins are also blue. This species is found in small shoals in the reef shallows and on reef drop-offs, usually around coral heads or gorgonians.
Aquarium suitability: This is a shy fish that does not travel well. They should be kept in small groups and, once they are acclimatized, they are extremely hardy. They will accept most foods that are offered. This species is ideal for a reef aquarium because of its small size.

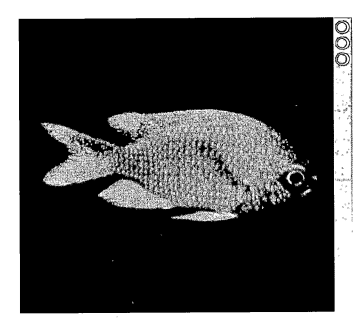

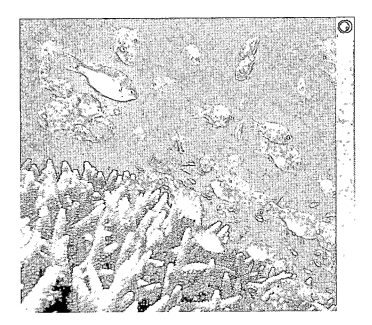

Chromis viridis

Common names: Green chromis, blue-green chromis, blue-green puller
Range: Tropical West Pacific
Size: 2½in (6.5cm)
Description: Almost identical to C. *atripectoralis* except that this species is smaller as an adult and does not have the black axil at the base of the pectoral fin. The photograph shows a typical aggregation of C. *viridis*. At the first sign of any threat or danger, the shoal will quickly dart into the protective branches of the coral head.
Aquarium suitability: A popular aquarium fish and very hardy. Single specimens tend to be bullied by other fishes. There is safety in numbers and small groups do better in a community tank. This fish is also suitable for a reef aquarium and does no harm to delicate invertebrates. A good choice for the beginner.

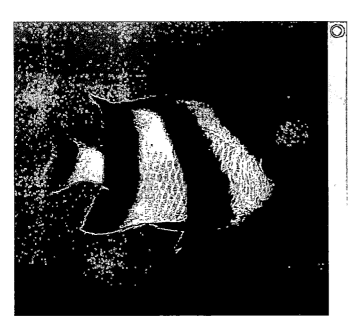

Dascyllus marginatus

Common names: Marginate damselfish, Red Sea damselfish, marginate puller
Range: Red Sea
Size: 4in (10cm)
Description: With this attractive species the soft dorsal, anal and tail fins are tinged with lilac-blue and the nape is yellow. The rest of the body is yellowish-white fading into brown on the head and chest. Older specimens tend to be less coloured, becoming darker with age. In the wild they are to be seen in large aggregations around *Acropora* coral heads into whose branches they will quickly retreat at the first threat of danger.
Aquarium suitability: This species is only occasionally imported. Older individuals are apt to be aggressive toward one another. Young individuals are hardy and bold. This is an easy fish to keep with other boisterous tank-mates.

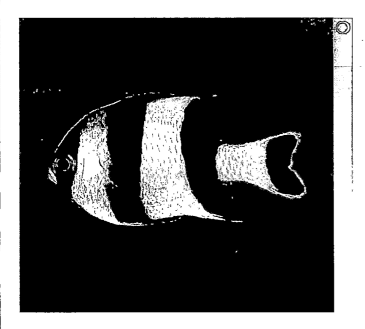

Dascyllus aruanus

Common names: Humbug dascyllus, humbug damselfish, black and white damselfish, white-tailed damselfish
Range: Western Pacific, Central Indo-Pacific
Size: 4in (10cm)
Description: A silvery-white body and tail more or less clear. It has three black bands and the pelvic fins are also black. This species is endemic throughout its natural range and is usually found in shoals around coral heads in lagoons and reef shallows.
Aquarium suitability: This is an aggressive fish that will defend its chosen territory with the utmost ferocity. In a community aquarium, the other fishes must be established and somewhat larger before this fish is introduced. Nevertheless, it is an extremely hardy fish and one that will survive most of the mistakes that a beginner is likely to make. A small shoal looks attractive in a large tank.

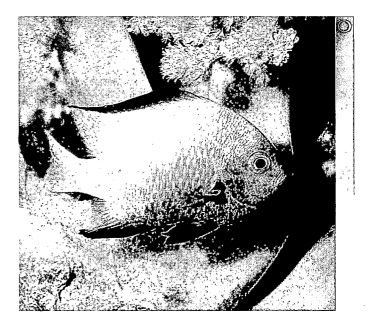

Dascyllus melanurus

Common names: Black-tail dascyllus, black-tail humbug, four-striped damselfish
Range: Central Indo-Pacific to Oceania
Size: 4in (10cm)
Description: This fish is occasionally confused with *D. aruanus*, being similarly coloured. In this case, however, there is a fourth black band because the tail is black. The margin of the caudal fin is blue. It is a shallow-water species that inhabits lagoons and bays. Its natural diet consists of algae, zooplankton and small animals picked from the rocks and coral.
Aquarium suitability: Not as often imported as *D. aruanus* because it is not as common. It is an equally bold fish, however, and more attractive. There are no problems with feeding, since this is inquisitive and perpetually hungry fish. Shoals of these fish in a reef aquarium can look spectacular.

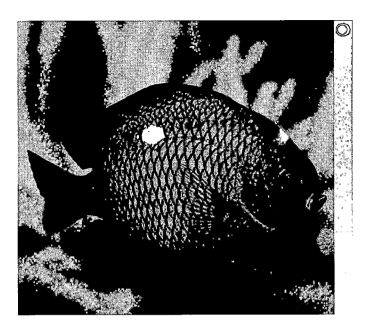

Dascyllus trimaculatus

Common names: Three-spot dascyllus, domino damselfish, three-spot damselfish
Range: Tropical Pacific and central Indo-Pacific
Size: 5in (12.5cm)
Description: In juveniles, the body and fins are black and there are three iridescent white spots. An adult fish, like the one shown here, is predominantly chocolate-brown. With a healthy fish, the spots do not become indistinct or disappear, but they do not increase in size once the fish has reached sexual maturity. The interspinous membranes of the dorsal fin are bright orange-brown to yellowish-brown and the premaxillary membrane is yellow, as is the opercular margin.
Aquarium suitability: Adult fish are not as aggressive as some members of this family. This species is ideally suited to a community aquarium, in which it will readily accept most foods.

Abudefduf bengalensis

Common names: Bengal sergeant, sergeant major, narrow-banded sergeant major
Range: East Africa to Central Indo-Pacific
Size: 6in (15cm)
Description: Most of the damselfishes that are striped in this way are referred to as "sergeant majors", irrespective of the actual species. This is another good reason for the use of Latin names, which apply only to a single species. This fish has six narrow bands on the body, often with an incomplete band behind the opercle. There is a black spot on the pectoral axil and the tail is quite deeply forked with rounded lobes.
Aquarium suitability: Occasional specimens are imported and sold under the catch-all name of *Abudefduf saxatilis*, which is covered next. This fish is much rarer, however, but it is a good fish for the beginner even though it is a little too boisterous.

Abudefduf saxatilis

Common name: Sergeant major
Range: Circumtropical
Size: 6in (15cm)
Description: Found throughout the warm seas of the world, this must be one of the most successful of all marine fishes. Recognizable by the vertical banding and the silvery-white body that fades into yellow in the dorsal region. The head is darker than the rest of the body and, in adult specimens, this may be bluish along with the fins. This fish is found in harbours, inlets, between pier pilings, in lagoons and on the reef itself.
Aquarium suitability: A robust, hardy fish suitable for the complete beginner. Eats anything and everything but is inclined to squabble with others of its own kind. Adult fish can be pugnacious and troublesome.

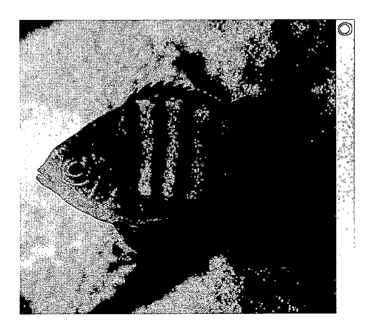

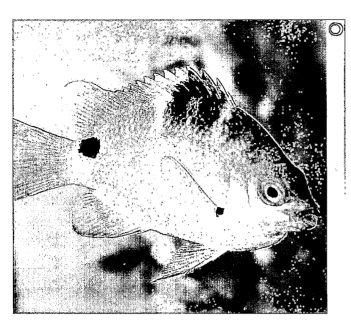

Abudefduf sordidus

Common name: Black-spot sergeant
Range: Indo-West Pacific
Size: 6in (15cm)
Description: Easily identifiable by the black spot on the upper part of the caudal peduncle and the dark patch on the first three spines of the dorsal fin, which extends on to the body. Juvenile fish are dark and the six-barred body pattern is indistinct. The older fish are greyish with six dark bars. This species occurs in tide pools and lagoons, but is also found in reef shallows and on reef crests where the water is often turbulent. In the wild, this fish feeds predominantly on benthic algae.
Aquarium suitability: A beginner's fish that is not in the least bit fussy about its food. It is hardy but quite boisterous, so care should be exercised in choosing its tank-mates.

Chrysiptera cyanea

Common names: Blue devil, blue damselfish
Range: Indo-West Pacific
Size: 3in (7.5cm)
Description: There has been much confusion concerning the correct name of this species, but the above name is correct. Confusion also exists over the correct identification of the many different colour forms. To clarify this, the female fish (shown here) has a clear tail and a black spot at the base of the soft dorsal fin. This spot is not always present in the male. The males from the central Indo-Pacific have a blue tail. Pacific and Australian males are different in that they have varying degrees of yellowish-orange on the tail, ventral fins and throat.
Aquarium suitability: An excellent fish for the beginner. It is hardy and most foods are accepted. Plenty of hiding places should be provided.

Photograph by Dr Gerald R Allen

Chrysiptera hemicyanea

Common names: Azure demoiselle, bicolor damselfish
Range: Central Indo-Pacific
Size: 4in (10cm)
Description: The amount of yellow in this species varies according to the geographic location and this often is the cause of confusion. Specimens from the Philippines display yellow only on the tail and the caudal peduncle. Examples from the Moluccas are blue with bright yellow from the middle of the ventral surface, diagonally up to the caudal peduncle and tail. Fish from New Guinea are completely blue except at Madang, where the colouration is as shown in the photograph.
Aquarium suitability: Specimens imported from the Moluccas have proved to be hardy and robust. A small group is ideal for a reef aquarium.

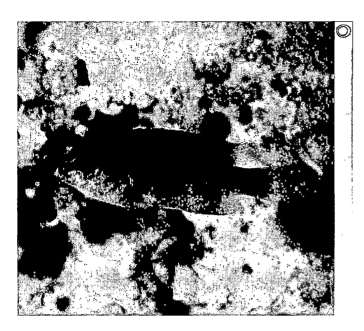

Chrysiptera leucopoma

Common name: Surge demoiselle
Range: Indo-West Pacific
Size: 5in (13cm)
Description: The colour of this fish varies as it grows, but may also vary between specimens of the same age and on the same reef. Nevertheless, the photograph here shows a subadult fish in the most frequently seen colour phase. As the fish grows older it becomes darker and less attractive. In the wild they are found in small shoals on reef crests and in surge areas.
Aquarium suitability: The surge demoiselle likes plenty of current flow and is the perfect fish for a tank that is fitted with a wavemaker. This species can be kept in small shoals without a great degree of bickering, and they are generally mild mannered with other fishes. Their diet should consist of algae, krill and mysid shrimps

Chrysiptera parasema

Common name: Yellow-tailed blue damsel
Range: Central Indo-Pacific
Size: 3in (7.5cm)
Description: This fish has a very long list of synonyms. It is strange that one of the most often seen and commonly available marine fishes is so often misnamed. The name given here is, however, correct. There is no mistaking its bright blue body and yellow tail. The yellow extends on to the caudal peduncle and the lower flanks, but not to the same degree as *C. hemicyanea*.
Aquarium suitability: This is probably the hardiest of all marine fishes and it is certainly a favourite one with aquarists. It is ideal both for a reef tank and for the complete beginner. Feeding, typical of most damselfishes, presents no problem. Flake and other dried foods should be supplemented with a selection of frost foods.

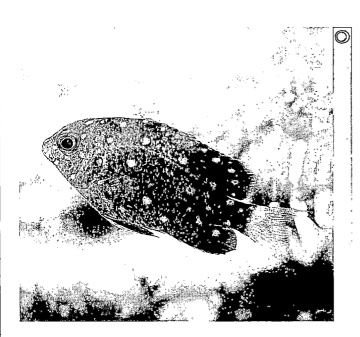

Microspathodon chrysurus

Common names: Marine jewelfish, yellowtail damselfish
Range: Tropical West Atlantic from Florida to Brazil
Size: 7½in (19cm)
Description: The young of this species have a deep blue body with iridescent blue spots and the tail is colourless. As the fish grows, the spots become smaller and the body colouration darkens to deep yellowish-brown. In adults, the tail is yellow. This is one of the largest of all the damselfishes. The attractive juvenile fishes are often seen in small shoals around coral heads in the Caribbean Sea.
Aquarium suitability: This fish is not suitable for a reef aquarium since it will occasionally feed on coral polyps when no other food is present. Its natural food is detritus and algae but in an aquarium it accepts all flake and frost foods.

Neoglyphidodon melas

Common names: Black damsel, bowtie damsel, blue fin damselfish, yellow-backed damselfish
Range: Indo-Pacific, Red Sea
Size: 5in (13cm)
Description: This is a shallow-water species that inhabits lagoons and inner reefs. The juveniles are attractively coloured with blue margins to the anterior edges of the pelvic and anal fins. The upper and lower lobes of the tail are yellow and there is a broad yellow mid-dorsal stripe that runs from the upper lip to the middle of the soft dorsal fin. Adult fish are an unattractive brown with drab yellow around the ventral and caudal region.
Aquarium suitability: Young fish are often imported but can be delicate and susceptible to disease, particularly when newly introduced. Once settled in, however, they are quite hardy and accept most foods. The adult fish are somewhat pugnacious.

Photograph by Dr Gerald R Allen

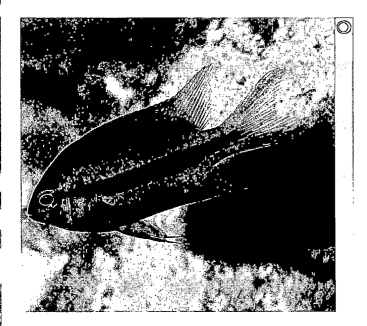

Neoglyphidodon nigroris

Common names: Royal damsel, black and gold damsel
Range: Indo-West Pacific
Size: 6in (15cm)
Description: Young fish (seen here) are yellow with two broad horizontal stripes along the sides. These are dark and often have a purplish cast. The first of these runs from the interorbital space to the end of the soft dorsal fin. The second one runs from the eye to the middle of the deeply forked tail. The upper and lower lobes of the tail and the posterior margins of the dorsal and anal fins are bright yellow. In adult fish, the stripes fade completely and the body becomes progressively darker. The yellow colour fades into greyish-black and two dark bars appear on the head.
Aquarium suitability: Juveniles are attractive and easy to keep, but older fish tend to be pugnacious and territorial. All aquarium foods are suitable.

Neoglyphidodon oxyodon

Common names: Neon damsel, blue velvet damsel, black neon damselfish, blue streak devil, neon devil
Range: Central Indo-Pacific
Size: 2in (5cm)
Description: The body colour of this fish is bluish-black. A broad white bar extends from the middle of the spinous dorsal fin to the ventral region. Two or more iridescent blue lines radiate from the snout and more are present on the flanks. The fin margins are bright blue.
Aquarium suitability: Suitable for beginners, this is a popular aquarium fish and is caught in large numbers around the Philippines. The adult fish often becomes territorial, however, ferociously guarding its particular crevice against all intruders. Juvenile specimens are suitable for a reef aquarium. Most foods are readily accepted.

Neopomacentrus azysron

Common name: Yellow-tail demoiselle
Range: Indo-West Pacific
Size: 2½in (6.5cm)
Description: The identification of fishes of this genus can be extremely difficult, particularly from photographs. This specimen, as well as the following two species, have been included to show their similarities and differences. The pectoral axil is dark and there is a dark spot at the origin of the lateral line. The body and head are brownish-blue and the tail is deeply forked and bright yellow. Yellow is also present on and below the soft dorsal fin and caudal peduncle. The eye is yellow and the anal fin is tinged with yellow.
Aquarium suitability: Occasionally this fish appears in dealers' tanks and it is very hardy. Unfortunately, professional collectors tend to overlook it and go for the more colourful species.

Photograph by Dr Gerald R Allen

Neopomacentrus bankieri

Common name: Coral demoiselle
Range: Hong Kong and surrounding areas of the South China Sea.
Size: 2in (5cm)
Description: The margin of the dorsal fin is blue and the body is pale olive with tiny blue dots on the scale edges. The eye is rimmed with yellow and there is a yellow spot at the origin of the lateral line. Tinges of yellow are present on the dorsal, anal and caudal fins. Bright yellow adorns the first few rays of the anal fin. There are no suborbital scales and the lower suborbital margin is clearly visible.
Aquarium suitability: This is a species that tends to appear in shops only by accident. This is a pity because it is an attractive well-behaved fish that is hardy and easy to keep. A small group of these fish looks very effective in a reef tank.

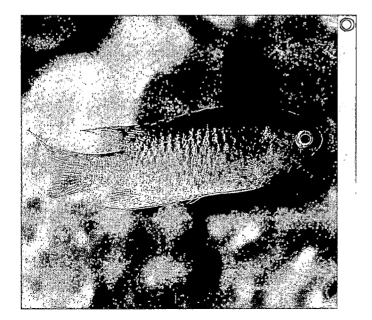

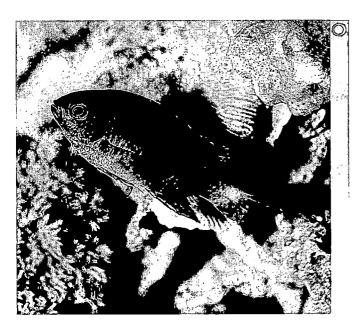

Neopomacentrus cyanomos

Common name: Regal demoiselle
Range: Indo-West Pacific, South China Sea
Size: 3in (7.5cm)
Description: There is a small black spot at the base of the pectoral fin and a second at the origin of the lateral line. The body colour is bluish-brown and the eye is yellow. The rearmost rays of the dorsal and anal fins are yellow and in adult fish these are extended. The upper and lower margins of the caudal fin are black. In some specimens, the caudal fin and the caudal peduncle are yellow. In others, only the caudal fin is yellow. This may indicate sexual dimorphism, since both variations occur together. This and the preceding species are often found on the same reef.
Aquarium suitability: The Regal Demoiselle is occasionally imported and does well in an aquarium. This fish appreciates most foods that are offered.

Pomacentrus amboinensis

Common name: Yellow damselfish
Range: Indo-West Pacific
Size: 3in (7.5cm)
Description: The colour of this species varies considerably, from drab yellow, sometimes with purplish tinges, to bright yellow. There is a small spot at the origin of the lateral line and a further one at the pectoral base. In the wild, it likes the protection of rocks and coral, into which it can retreat should there be any threat. Its natural diet consists of plankton and algae.
Aquarium suitability: This is an aggressive little fellow that is not very well suited to life in an aquarium, even though it is often imported for the hobby trade. It will dig pits in the sand and disrupt a normal peaceful community tank during the defence of its chosen territory (which is usually the entire tank). It should be kept with larger fishes.

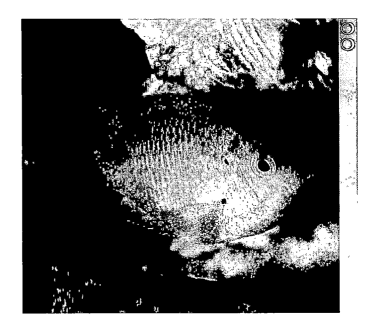

Pomacentrus philippinus

Common names: Philippine damsel, saffron blue damselfish
Range: Western Pacific, Central Indo-Pacific
Size: 5in (13cm)
Description: This fish is dark blue and the tail lemon-yellow. The demarcation between the two colours is relatively abrupt on the caudal peduncle. The pectoral and pelvic fins are also tinged with yellow. As it reaches adulthood, these colours fade and the overall body colouration is darker. On the reef, it prefers the cover of rocks and coral and occurs singly or in small shoals.
Aquarium suitability: Although this is generally a peaceful fish by nature it can become aggressive toward smaller tank-mates, particularly when it is defending its own territory in the aquarium. Plenty of hiding places and grottoes should be provided in the case of territorial squabbles. It enjoys a varied diet of frozen and dried foods.

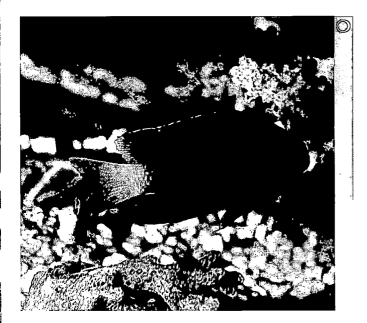

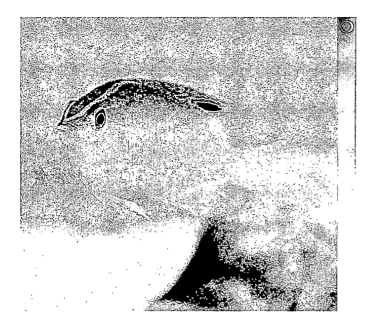

Stegastes simsiang

(Syn. *Pomacentrus simsiang, P. moluccensis*)

Common name: Molucca damsel
Range: Indo-West Pacific
Size: 3in (7.5cm)
Description: The colouration of this species is not unlike that of *Stegastes leucostictus* from the Caribbean region. In the case of this species, however, a large blue-edged black spot is present at the base of the soft dorsal fin and there are also several lines running dorsally from the snout. In addition, *Stegastes simsiang* has a much lighter yellow body colouration, which covers more of the flanks. In the wild, this species feeds predominantly on benthic algae.
Aquarium suitability: Adult specimens tend to be aggressive but cases have been recorded of them breeding successfully in captivity. Young fish are attractive and are good candidates for a reef aquarium. They soon learn to accept most foods.

Stegastes variabilis

Common name: Cocoa damselfish
Range: Tropical West Atlantic, Caribbean
Size: 5in (13cm)
Description: This species, like the previous one, is very similar in appearance to the Beau Gregory (*Stegastes leucostictus*), another Caribbean fish. In fact, many importers and collectors confuse the two species. They are easy to tell apart, however. Both species are dark blue dorsally and yellow on the belly and flanks, but this species has a pattern of fine vertical lines on the sides that separate the two colours. In *S. leucostictus*, the separation of these colours is sharper with no vertical lines.
Aquarium suitability: A very "scrappy" fish that can be a bully in a community tank. It is very territorial and much more aggressive than most damselfishes. It is hardy and easy to keep, however, and will eat everything that is offered.

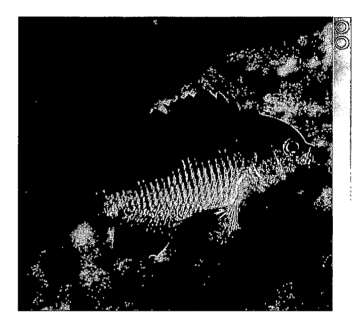

Wrasses (Labridae)

This is the second largest marine fish family and the third largest in the order Perciformes. Its 61 genera and roughly 500 species are widely represented in both tropical and temperate regions, and it is very diversified in terms of form and colour variations. Some fishes go through several colour phases and patterns before reaching adulthood. Many species are sexually dimorphic; others are not. Some females assume male characteristics when required; others start out as females and change to males as adults. The males are usually the more colourful of the two sexes. All species are characterized by a single, continuous dorsal fin and thick lips. Often they have forward projecting teeth, which gives them a "bucktooth" appearance. They are carnivorous and specialists at cracking open the shells of small invertebrates. The large teeth and thick lips enable them to bite into sea urchins without being injured.

The five species of the genus *Labroides* are known as cleaner wrasses. They perform a service by removing ectoparasites from the bodies and gills of larger fishes. For this, they set up "cleaning stations" and advertise their service by repeatedly swimming up and down in a flitting motion.

Fishes of the genus *Gomphosus* differ from other species in that they have a very elongated snout. They are much loved by marine aquarists because of their bizarre appearance. Quite a few of these fishes are brightly coloured and some are even gaudy. In an aquarium they are very hardy once they have settled down and they are quite fast growing. They soon learn to take dried foods, but this should be supplemented with fresh protein food, such as frozen cockle and mussel flesh. Some specimens develop a mean streak when they reach adulthood.

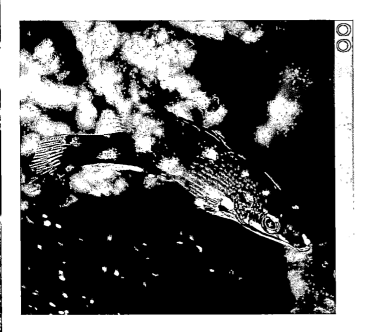

Bodianus mesothorax

Common names: Hogfish, coral hogfish
Range: Central Indo-Pacific
Size: 12in (30cm)
Description: Juvenile fish have a brownish body with yellow blotches on the sides. At this stage, the eye is also yellow. The adult fish (shown here) is purplish-brown and yellow. A dark diagonal bar running from the middle of the dorsal fin to the pectoral base separates these two colours. The eye is rimmed with red. In the wild, this fish is to be found in areas of lush coral growth and in caves in the reef.
Aquarium suitability: This is quite an easy fish to keep and one that will soon learn to recognize feeding time. It is naturally greedy and will always be where the food is, even to the point of snatching it out of the mouths of its slower tank-mates. It can be quite an entertaining character in a large aquarium.

Bodianus diana

Common names: Spotted hogfish, Diana's wrasse, red hogfish
Range: Central Indo-Pacific
Size: 10in (25cm)
Description: The adult fish have an entirely different colouration to that of the juvenile (shown here). Generally they are bright to deep red with yellowish-orange sides. The pectoral, anal and soft dorsal fins are bright red and there are four or five large yellow spots interspersed below the dorsal fin. Young fish are easily confused with those of B. *axillaris*, although in this case the eye is black, whereas B. *mesothorax* has yellow eyes and spots. This fish inhabits outer reef slopes and reef shallows in areas of dense coral growth.
Aquarium suitability: Unsuitable for a reef tank, since invertebrates form a large part of its natural diet. Feeding is not as problem, however, since most other foods will be eaten.

Bodianus pulchellus

Common names: Cuban hogfish, spotfin hogfish, scarlet hogfish
Range: Caribbean, Tropical West Atlantic
Size: 9in (23cm)
Description: Young specimens up to about 2in (5cm) in length are bright yellow. They are known to perform a cleaning service for other larger fishes by removing skin parasites from their bodies. The adult colouration is bright red with a white stripe from the lower jaw to the caudal base. The hind part of the soft dorsal fin and body to the upper portion of the tail and caudal peduncle is bright yellow.
Aquarium suitability: This is a spectacular fish that is not often seen for sale, but when it is you should expect it to be expensive. Once it has settled in it will feed well on most foods offered with the exception of green foods.

Bodianus rufus

Common name: Spanish hogfish
Range: Caribbean, Tropical West Atlantic
Size: 20in (50cm)
Description: Young fish are bright yellow with a large dorsal patch of bluish-purple. As it grows the patch spreads over most of the body, head and fins, so that adult colouration is bluish-purple with yellow tinges. Specimens found in deep water are reddish-purple. Its natural diet consists of small echinoderms, molluscs and crustaceans.
Aquarium suitability: Juvenile fish are easy to keep and should present no problems if you have just a few months' experience. Unfortunately, they grow very large very fast and can become veritable tyrants in a community tank. They will soon accept food from your hand, but with adult fish you should watch out for the four strong canine teeth on each jaw.

Clepticus parrae

Common name: Creole wrasse
Range: Tropical West Atlantic, Caribbean
Size: 12in (30cm)
Description: The young of this species have six groups of dark spots resembling short bars below the dorsal fin. The rest of the body is pale lilac in colour. As the fish reaches adulthood, the body colour deepens and the ventral region turns yellow. The tail is lunate with dark upper and lower lobes.
Aquarium suitability: Young fish are extremely attractive and, since this is a shoaling fish, they are best kept in small groups of three to seven individuals. Newly introduced specimens are often difficult to wean on to aquarium foods so you should persevere with frozen brine shrimp as a starter food. This is a good species for a reef aquarium but it cannot be recommended for beginners.

Coris aygula

Common names: Twin-spot wrasse, clown labrid, orange-spot wrasse
Range: Tropical Indo-Pacific, Red Sea
Size: 47in (119cm)
Description: Adult fish grow very large and are bottle-green to greenish-black, often with two white mid-body bars. The head is humped. Juveniles (shown here) are quite brightly coloured, having two large red blotches on the upper part of the back. The dorsal fin has two black ocelli and many smaller spots. There are also brown and black spots around the head and on the anal fin.
Aquarium suitability: This species requires a special aquarium, one that is large enough to accommodate it as an adult, otherwise it should not be considered. Young specimens are often available but they do not live long in a small aquarium. This fish should be left strictly to the experts.

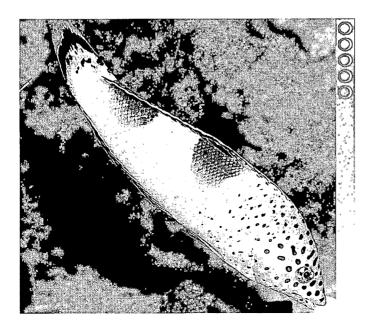

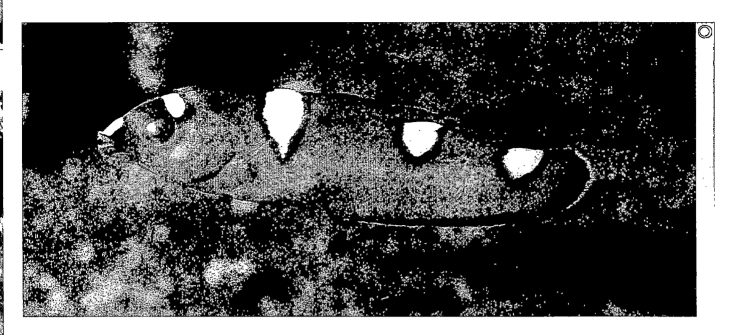

Coris gaimard africana

Common names: Clown wrasse, red labrid, yellowtail wrasse
Range: Indian Ocean
Size: 14in (36cm)
Description: This is one of two subspecies. The other is *Coris gaimard gaimard*, which can be considered to be the Pacific version of this species. As far as the two geographic variations are concerned, the colouration of the juvenile fishes is identical. They are similar in appearance to the juveniles of *C. formosa* but are bright orange-red and lack the two dorsal ocelli. In the adults, however, the difference is quite dramatic. The adult *C. g. gaimard* has an orange head and dorsal fin and the rest of the body fades into deep brownish-green colour with a suffusion of bright blue spots. There are several iridescent blue streaks on the head, and the pectoral base and pelvic fins are edged in blue. The tail has a bright yellow margin. An adult specimen of *C. g.*

africana lacks the bright body colour and the yellow tail. It is predominantly green in colour with bright green streaks around the head. The margins of the dorsal and anal fins are edged in red and then blue. Dominant males often display a light green mid-body bar.
Aquarium suitability: A good depth of sand should be provided for this fish so that it can burrow down into it at night. Although this is considered to be a fish for the beginner, it does grow quite large, so the aquarium must be of sufficient size to accommodate it as it grows in an adult. It is not a fussy eater, and most frozen and dried foods are suitable.

Gomphosus varius

Common names: Green bird wrasse, birdmouth wrasse, beakfish
Range: East Africa to central Indo-Pacific
Size: 12in (30cm)
Description: The female (shown here) has a creamy white body that fades into middle-brown on the flanks and it has a brownish-orange stripe from the snout to the eye. The males are variable in colour from pale green to deep bottle-green with a yellow daub behind the opercle.
Aquarium suitability: Strangely enough, this boisterous fish is suitable for a reef aquarium when there are no prawns or shrimps present. It leaves all other invertebrates alone. It is a hardy fish and one that can be recommended for beginners. In an open-topped aquarium, they are excellent fly-catchers. Eats all foods, including swatted flies.

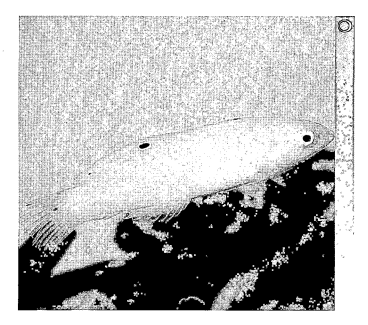

Halichoeres chrysus

Common names: Banana wrasse, golden rainbowfish
Range: Central Indo-Pacific
Size: 4in (10cm)
Description: The body of this species is completely yellow whereas a similar species, *H. trispilus* (= *H. leucoxanthus*) has a white belly. There are three ocelli on the dorsal fin and a small spot on the caudal peduncle. This fish inhabits coral outcrops and patch reef areas where the seabed is sandy enough for it to bury itself at night.
Aquarium suitability: This species is suitable for a reef aquarium provided that there is a good depth of sand for it to burrow into. Although it is a peaceful fish that will ignore other tank-mates, it does not usually tolerate others of its own kind. Most of the usual frost and dried foods are accepted and it makes a suitable beginner's fish.

Halichoeres nigrescens

Common name: None
Range: Central Indo-Pacific to Southern Australia
Size: 12in (30cm)
Description: Some members of this genus are extremely difficult to identify. One must rely heavily on the head markings for inspiration, since there are more than 40 similar species that are regularly seen in the reef shallows of the central Indo-Pacific region. This particular fish was caught at Hoi Ha, Hong Kong, at a depth of 10ft (3m). This species is encountered singly or in large groups of up to 100 individuals.
Aquarium suitability: This is one of the few species that can be kept in small groups, providing that the aquarium is large enough to accommodate them. Mysid shrimp, krill and chopped mussel should be fed at regular intervals, along with flake or granulated food.

Labroides bicolor

Common names: Bicolor Wrasse, Bicolour Cleaner Wrasse
Range: East Africa to Melanesia
Size: 5½in (14cm)
Description: Juvenile fish are attractive specimens with yellow on the snout and tail. The body is mauve-white with dark horizontal stripes. Older fish lose much of their colour and become quite drab in appearance. Adult specimens do not perform a cleaning service as frequently as the younger fish.
Aquarium suitability: Although this species is not as common as *L. dimidiatus*, the true cleaner wrasse, it is shipped fairly regularly for the aquarium hobby trade. They grow quite large in a relatively short space of time. As adults, however, they become more aggressive and so they are then of little interest to the aquarist. Young specimens are easier to acclimatize than the adults and most food is accepted.

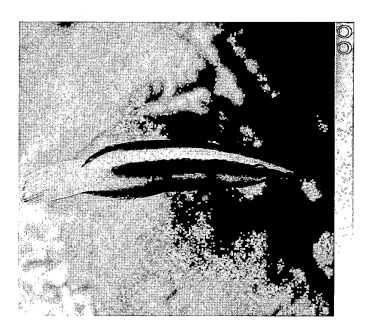

Macropharyngodon meleagris

Common name: Leopard wrasse
Range: Tropical Indo-Pacific
Size: 6in (15cm)
Description: The leopard wrasse enjoys the dubious reputation of being one of the hardest fishes to photograph. They are shy and will dive into the sand at the approach of danger. Its body is olive-green and is covered in irregular black blotches and spots. The head and fins are brownish-orange and are also spotted, particularly the dorsal, anal and caudal fins.
Aquarium suitability: This is an interesting fish for a reef aquarium, particularly one that is set up with a plenum filtration system. The constant burrowing of this fish will ensure that the top layer of sand remains oxygenated. The fish can be induced to feed with most frozen sea-foods, such as plankton and adult brine shrimp.

Labroides dimidiatus

Common names: Cleaner wrasse, bluestreak cleaner wrasse
Range: Red Sea, Tropical Indo-Pacific
Size: 5in (13cm)
Description: This fish has a brown-white head and a blue body with black stripes that thicken toward the tail. The blue colour is intense on the flanks. It is perhaps one of the best known coral fishes and it is often the subject of underwater feature films, in which it is usually shown picking parasites from other fishes. In order to encourage a large fish to open its mouth or gills to be cleaned, this little fellow will nudge the area with its snout. The host, which may be a large predator, usually obliges and the wrasse is able to swim in and out with impunity.
Aquarium suitability: It requires good water quality and newly introduced fish are prone to disease. However, once it is settled in to its new surroundings it is a hardy fish.

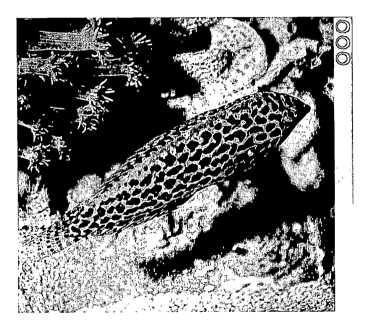

Novaculichthys taeniourus

Common names: Dragon wrasse, reindeer wrasse
Range: Indo-Pacific, Red Sea
Size: 10½in (27cm)
Description: The background colour of this fish is olive-green, with scales edged in brownish-black. The fins and body are covered with white spots and blotches and the head has several streaks that radiate from the eye, which has a cartwheel pattern around the iris. Perhaps its most important identifying feature is the two elongated rays of the dorsal fin. It is found on sandy sea beds in lagoons and inner reef zones in relatively shallow water. Its natural diet consists mainly of small echinoderms, crustaceans and molluscs.
Aquarium suitability: When it is small, this is a peaceful fish that is often intimidated by larger tank-mates. Older fish lose much of their colour and are apt to be aggressive.

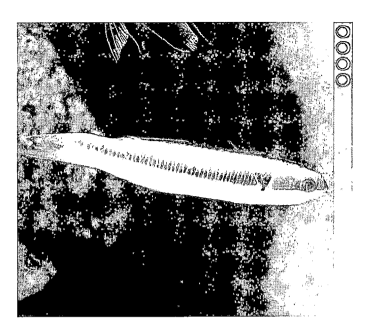

Thalassoma amblycephalum

Common name: Rainbow wrasse
Range: Tropical Indo-Pacific
Size: 6½in (16cm)
Description: Juvenile fish are silvery-white with a dark stripe from the snout to the caudal peduncle, and at this stage they are not very colourful. In contrast, adult fish have a yellow throat and white belly. The rest of the head is a greenish-blue that fades into yellow, through orange, to red along the flanks. The tail and dorsal margins are often purplish-mauve.
Aquarium suitability: The example shown here shows a fish in its juvenile colouration, since this is how it is normally imported. It is a spectacular fish when it is fully-grown but requires an extremely large aquarium with plenty of free swimming space. It is an extremely active fish and it will not do well in a small aquarium. This is a fish for the expert.

Thalassoma bifasciatum

Common names: Bluehead wrasse, bluehead
Range: Caribbean, Tropical West Atlantic
Size: 6in (15cm)
Description: Juveniles of this species are bright yellow with a black stripe running the full length of the body. They are seen on most reefs in the Caribbean and form small shoals around coral heads. Adult fish are different, having undergone a colour change during the transitional stage from juvenile to adult. In a fully grown male the head is bright blue and the remainder of the body is middle-green. Two broad black bands behind the gill plate separate these two colours.
Aquarium suitability: A large tank and plenty of hiding places and caves are required for this species. But most important, it requires a lot of swimming space. Fed on a varied diet of krill, mysid shrimp and mussel flesh, this fish stays happy for years.

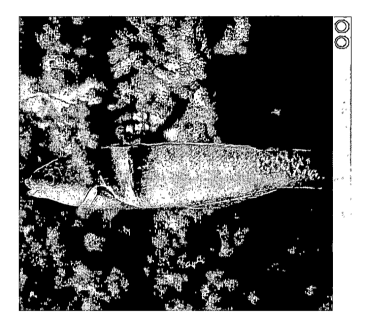

Thalassoma lucasanum

Common name: Mexican rock wrasse
Range: Tropical East Pacific
Size: 6in (15cm)
Description: Endemic in shallow, rocky areas in the Gulf of California. Juvenile fish sometimes act as cleaners and are bright yellow with a black mid-body and interdorsal stripe. The belly is white with a red stripe, which broadens toward the tail. The adult secondary male has a blue head with mauve streaks. There is a broad yellow band behind the opercle and the rest of the body is cerise to red. Tail and fin margins are violet-blue.
Aquarium suitability: Caves and grottoes and good water quality are prerequisites for this fish. All species of this genus require a large aquarium with plenty of swimming space, and this fish is no exception. This fish is easily pleased with a diet of frozen shell meat and small shrimps.

Photograph by Frank Walker

Thalassoma lunare

Common names: Moon wrasse, lyretail wrasse, green parrot wrasse
Range: Tropical Indo-Pacific, Red Sea
Size: 10in (25cm)
Description: Although there is little colour change from juveniles to adult fish, the black spots on the dorsal fin and caudal base disappear with age. Adult fish are bright green to blue-green, with blue streaks on the head. The tail is lunate with the upper and lower lobes being dark green. Its common name comes from the fact that the tail has a yellow centre, which is in contrast to the dark lobes, and gives it a lyre-tail effect.
Aquarium suitability: This is a popular, inexpensive and readily available aquarium fish. Provide a strong water flow and well-planned aquarium decoration with plenty of free swimming space. This species will eat almost any aquarium food.

Photograph by Dr John E Randall

Thalassoma lutescens

Common name: Blue fin wrasse
Range: Central Indo Pacific
Size: 6in (15cm)
Description: Juvenile fish are yellowish in colour. In adults the dominant male is not as colourful as the secondary male, which is blue with a yellow head and tail. The caudal fin has a red stripe and the head is adorned with red streaks. The upper and lower lobes of the tail are also red. In the wild, this fish feeds on small invertebrates and is found on sandy bottoms as well as in areas of dense coral growth.
Aquarium suitability: This fish requires plenty of swimming space and strong water movement. Live rock built into caves and a sandy substrate should make it feel at home. It is easily pleased with regard to water quality and food and, although it is not often imported, it is a good fish for the beginner.

Parrotfishes (Scaridae)

The family contains 83 species split into two subfamilies and nine genera. Of these, 67 species in four genera belong to the subfamily Scarinae, the largest genus being *Scarus* with 62 species. The second subfamily, Sparisomatinae, encompasses 16 species in five genera. All of these fishes have similar characteristics. The jaw teeth are coalesced (fused, parrot-like teeth), and the dorsal fin is continuous, with nine spines and 11 soft rays. They are herbivorous and rasp at algae that grow on the substrate and dead corals. They are not known to feed actively on live coral polyps or other invertebrates. Some species secrete a mucous coating at night and then lie in this until the morning. This is because the mucous covering masks their scent preventing discovery by night-time predators that rely mainly on their olfactory senses to find food.

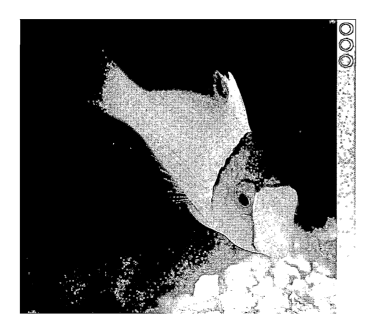

Cetoscarus bicolor

Common names: Two-colored parrotfish, red and white parrotfish
Range: Tropical Indo-Pacific, Red Sea
Size: 31in (79cm)
Description: This photograph shows a juvenile. The body is white with a black-edged orange band around the head. There is a black ocellus on the spinous dorsal fin. Adult males are green, particularly dorsally, with mauve edges to the flank scales. The head and shoulders are spotted with mauve and there is a green streak above the eye. Fins and tail are mauve and green and the throat is white. The adult female is brownish dorsally with a dark belly.
Aquarium suitability: Young fish are attractive but they grow too large for the average aquarium. Provide plenty of space and live rock on which it can "rasp". This species is particularly fond of granulated foods and frozen shellfish.

Scarus vetula

Common name: Queen parrotfish
Range: Tropical West Atlantic, Caribbean
Size: 26in (66cm)
Description: In fully grown males of this species the caudal lobes are extended, giving the tail a lunate form. The body colour is blue with green edges to the scales. There is rose and yellow on the dorsal, anal and caudal fins but the margins are blue. The pectoral fins are yellow with blue margins. The females are reddish-brown and drab by comparison.
Aquarium suitability: Small specimens of *Scarus vetula* are occasionally imported, but they grow far too large for the average-sized aquarium. Nevertheless, in a large show aquarium this fish is usually happy. The adult males are spectacular-looking fish. Provide a varied selection of aquarium foods to supplement its natural diet.

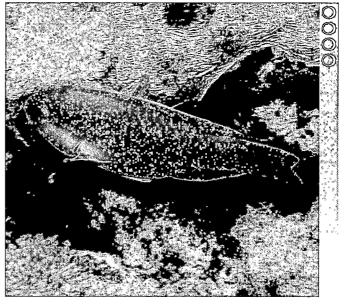

Photograph by Siegfried Krumbügel

Convict blenny (Pholidichthyidae)

Placing this fish in its own family is only a provisional measure, since there is every indication that the convict blenny belongs to the family of Triplefin Blennies (Tripterygiidae). The extraordinary presence of a septal bone (between the nostrils) would seem to indicate this probability. There is only one species in the family, *Pholidichthys leucotaenia*.

The body is eel-shaped and entirely without scales and there is one nostril on each side of the head. The dorsal, anal and caudal fins are joined together to form one long, continuous fin around the back, tail and ventral regions. The pelvic fins are set well forward of the pectoral fins. Sexual maturity in this species is reached at the age of about 14 months – at this stage, the fish is approximately 7in (18cm) long.

There are several reports of breeding activity in aquariums, with the young fry being raised to adulthood without any serious problems. The breeding pair usually retreats to a hole hollowed out under a convenient rock. After breeding has taken place the fry do not emerge until they are about ¼in (7mm) long. They are kept under control by the parent fish and swarm in groups of up to 350 individuals very close to their hatching place. For the next two to three weeks the parents are very attentive, after which time the fry must be removed to a separate tank to prevent the parent fish eating them.

Although this fish is endemic from the Philippines to the Solomon Islands, only occasional specimens are imported into Europe. However, they are a frequent sight in dealers' aquariums in the Far East and also in the USA. Most of these specimens are caught and shipped from the Philippines.

Photograph by Richard Ashby

Pholidichthys leucotaenia

Common name: Convict blenny
Range: Central Indo-Pacific
Size: 13in (33cm)
Description: Young fish are brownish-black with a neon-white
to gold stripe along the side of the body. The belly is silvery-
white. As the fish grows, this pattern begins to break up, until
zebra-like markings cover the whole of the body, as can be seen
in the subadult fish shown here. The body is stockier and the
pattern may vary between individuals.
Aquarium suitability: Live rock and a deep, sandy substrate
should be provided so that this fish can excavate a hollow under
a rock and set up home. This fish will eagerly take most frost
foods, such as frozen krill, brine shrimp, mysid shrimp and
chopped mussel. However, they usually reject the larger sand
shrimp and lancefish if they are offered.

Blennies (Blenniidae)

The family consists of 53 genera placed into 6 tribes with
345 currently recognized species. Only 45 genera contain
species of interest to the marine aquarist.

Fishes from this group are represented in all seas with
some species being found in brackish and freshwater.
Their common characteristics are that they are either
completely without scales, or that the scales are small and
primitive. The pelvic fins are set forward of the pectoral
fins and the mouth is situated low on the head. This is
neither extended forward nor is it protractile. The dorsal
fin is continuous. They are mainly bottom-dwellers and
some species have cirri on the margins of the anterior
nostrils. With the exception of the tribe Nemophini, these
fishes are often called comb-tooth blennies. Many species
are herbivorous.

Those of the tribe Nemophini are free-swimming and,
in contrast to their herbivorous cousins, they are
carnivorous. They are known collectively as the sabre-
tooth blennies. Fishes of the genus *Meiacanthus* have
poisonous flesh as a defence against predators. For this
reason other fishes often mimic their colouration. Some
species are themselves very good at mimicking other
fishes. This is particularly the case with those of the genus
Plagiotremus, which often mimic *Meiacanthus* species,
and *Aspidontus taeniatus*, which is well known for its
excellent ability to mimic the cleaner wrasse *Labroides
dimidiatus*. This particular fish not only copies the cleaner
wrasse in body colouration, but also in swimming
movements in order to entice an unsuspecting fish to its
"cleaning station" in the hope of being cleaned of the
ectoparasites on its body. Striking swiftly, the "false
cleaner wrasse" will bite a piece of flesh from its prey.

Ophioblennius atlanticus

Common names: Redlip blenny, Atlantic blenny
Range: Tropical and subtropical West Atlantic
Size: 5in (13cm)
Description: The body colouration of this species is brownish-black and, as the name implies, it has red lips, which make it easy to identify. The margin of the dorsal fin is red and the pectoral fins are often deep yellow. This fish is ubiquitous in the Caribbean. Its main diet is benthic algae.
Aquarium suitability: An excellent fish for ridding a tank of unwanted algae. It is an easy species to keep providing there are no rapid changes in water quality. It is a good choice for a reef aquarium as it will not damage any delicate invertebrates. The single drawback with this fish is its territorial nature. It will chase almost any fish, irrespective of its size, that encroaches on its territory. In a small set-up, this may include the entire tank.

Mandarinfishes, dragonets (Callionymidae)

The family Callionymidae contains 130 species incorporated into 17 genera. These interesting fishes are to be found in all warm seas but the vast majority of species occur in the Indo-West Pacific, with at least two species being known to enter brackish waters and rivers. Essentially they are inshore fishes found on the reef or in tidal pools, and in sandy or muddy areas where they may spend part of the day half-buried in the sand for protection. Occasionally they are also found in sea-grass beds. Represented by *Callionymus lyra*, they are also to be found in shallow water from Iceland to Senegal. While the female of this species is a drab brown in colouration, the male is light brown with blue stripes and spangles and the anterior dorsal fin arches high over the back.

The general characteristics of these fishes are as follows. The somewhat cylindrical body is fairly elongate and scaleless, and is often brightly coloured. The head is depressed and broad. The gill opening is reduced to a small round opening or pore, high on the shoulder. A preopercular spine is present but there are no spines on the opercle or subopercle. When threatened, it puffs out its gills, erecting the opercle and preopercle with its spines as a defence mechanism.

Sexual dimorphism is usual, with the males being somewhat more brightly coloured than the females and normally possessing longer fins. There are two dorsal fins present with small underdeveloped spines. Swimming is effected mainly by the pectoral fins and this is done in a hopping motion from one rock or resting-place to the next, where the fish will then balance on its broadly separated pelvic fins. The mouth is small with a protruding upper jaw and the eyes are relatively high on the head, sometimes pointing in an upward direction. One of the most important identifying features of this family, which is often overlooked by experts, is that the pelvic fins are set forward in front of the pectoral fins.

In reproduction, fertilization is usually external after the male and female have gone through a series of spinning motions that gradually brings them near the water's surface. Once there, the eggs are fertilized, belly to belly. The fertilized eggs are pelagic, being dispersed in the ocean's currents. At first the young lead an essentially planktonic life until they are large enough to settle to the bottom. This surface mating is not uncommon among bottom-dwelling species, and it is generally believed that by mating so high in the water the young have a far better dispersal chance than they would at the seabed, where they would quickly fall prey to any passing predators.

In the aquarium, most species are peaceful, shy and retiring, although two adult males will often fight in the close confines of a small tank. For the best chances of success with fishes from this family, live rock should be provided. This should be built up to form a good reef base. They are usually slow and careful feeders that spend much of their time picking at small, unseen animals from rocks and corals. Their staple diet in the wild comprises small worms and crustaceans. This is why, at least in the initial stages, live rock is required to provide them with enough food to pick at, since they will seldom take normal aquarium food when newly introduced to a tank. Live food, such as newly hatched brine shrimp, is usually accepted, but it can never form any sort of staple diet for these fishes.

When housing them in a tank, bear in mind that two males will usually fight among themselves, even if they are of entirely different species. All mandarinfishes and dragonets should be kept with peaceful tank-mates and provided with enough shelter and places to hide. They are not the easiest of species to keep and can never be considered as fishes for the beginner.

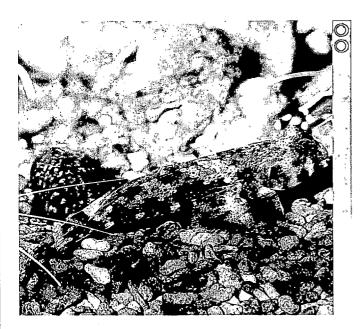

Synchiropus picturatus

Common names: Green-ringed dragonet, psychedelic fish, painted dragonet
Range: Indo-West Pacific
Size: 3in (7.5cm)
Description: The body colour is green, with orange and green spangles on top of the head. Males and females have greenish-blue spots on the body and these are ringed with orange, black and blue. The caudal fin is green. The males are more brightly coloured than the females and the dorsal fins are longer.
Aquarium suitability: *S. picturatus* is suitable for a reef aquarium, since it is small and will not harm corals or other delicate invertebrates. It is quite shy and should not be kept in a tank with pugnacious or boisterous fishes, otherwise it will allow itself to be bullied away from the food at feeding time and may eventually starve to death.

Neosynchiropus ocellatus

Common names: Peacock, eye-spot, dragonet
Range: Indo-West Pacific
Size: 3½in (9cm)
Description: *Petroscirtes* sp. (sabre-toothed blennies) are eel-formed and have 25 to 133 unbranched dorsal rays, whereas the dragonets and mandarinfishes usually have four dorsal spines and 6 to 11 soft rays. Despite confusion on the part of some authors, this photograph clearly shows the species to be *Neosynchiropus ocellatus*. The body and head are adorned with black blotches and fine blue spots. Males have a long first dorsal fin with four rays that can be raised in a fan form in order to attract females. This displays four ocelli on the membrane between the rays.
Aquarium suitability: Care and feeding is the same as for other members of this family.

Pterosynchiropus splendidus

Common names: Mandarinfish, mandarin dragonet
Range: Indo-West Pacific
Size: 3in (7.5cm)
Description: The body colouration of this fish is orange or red, which fades into deep blue around the pectoral and ventral regions. The eye is red and there is yellow below this. The body and fins are covered with a fantastic array of black-edged green streaks that are almost iridescent. There are yellow spots on the opercle and blue spots on the pectoral and ventral fins. Like the pectoral and ventral fins, the tail is rounded. The males are somewhat brighter than the females with longer rays to the first dorsal fin.
Aquarium suitability: As with the previous species this is a shy fish, but one that is ideally suited to life in a well-established reef aquarium with a good microfauna on which it can feed.

Gobies (Gobiidae)

With 212 genera and 1,875 species, this is the largest marine fish family. Generally with these fishes, the inner margins of the pelvic fins are fused together to form a sucking disc with which they attach themselves to rocks or other substrata. When present, the anterior dorsal fin is separated from the soft dorsal fin. Some species form associations with other animals such as shrimps and sponges. Others, such as the neon goby (*Gobiosoma oceanops*), perform a cleaning service for other fishes, using their sucking disc to hold on as they work.

They are small, bottom-dwellers and on the reef they, along with the blennies, form a dominant part of the benthic fish population. Many species occur in freshwater and some fishes, such as the mudskippers, are land-dwelling for at least part of their lives.

Although their taxonomy has not been fully settled, five subfamilies are recognized. The first, Oxudercinae, contains ten genera. These are predominantly land gobies and mudskippers, which inhabit mangrove foreshores and muddy swamps. The second subfamily, Amblyopinae, also contains ten genera. These are usually brackish or fresh-water species. Species of the third subfamily, Sicydiinae, are mainly freshwater fishes. There are six genera. The fourth subfamily, Gobionellinae, also contains mainly freshwater species. The two smallest freshwater fishes in the world, *Mistichthys luzonensis* and *Pandaka pygmaea*, belong to this subfamily. The final subfamily, Gobiinae, is the most important to marine aquarists. This is a very large group with 130 genera. Many of the species are marine living and some are popular aquarium fishes. The world's smallest fish, *Trimmatom nanus*, which grows to about ⅓in (9mm), belongs to this subfamily.

Amblygobius phalaena

Common name: Brown-striped goby
Range: Central Indo-Pacific
Size: 6in (15cm)
Description: Body brownish above and silver below with five dark bars along the sides. Adult fish have a pinkish-mauve tail. The top of the head is adorned with many brick-red spots and there are several blue streaks and spots below the eye from the snout to the pectoral base. In the wild, several may be seen quite close together, each peering out of its hole.
Aquarium suitability: This species is unsuitable for a reef aquarium due to its industrious way of feeding. It spends much of the day taking mouthfuls of sand, sifting it for food, expelling it out of its gills and covering corals and other delicate invertebrates in a fine layer of sand. In a marine aquarium, however, it is easy to keep and feed.

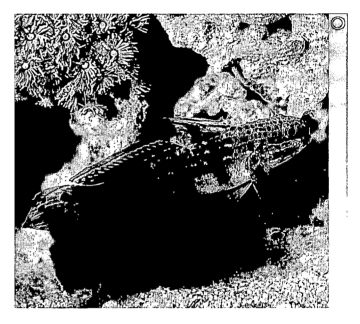

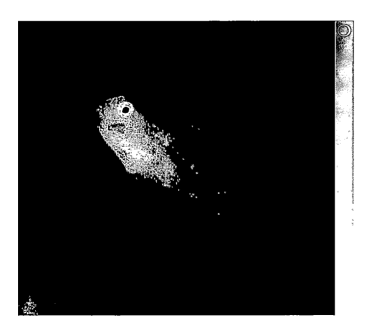

Gobiodon okinawae

Common name: Yellow goby
Range: Indo-West Pacific to Japan
Size: 1½in (4cm)
Description: The body colour is bright yellow, making it easy to confuse with *Gobiodon citrinus*. However, *G. citrinus* has blue streaks around the head and blue lines at the base of the dorsal and anal fins, whereas this species is completely yellow. It is one of the smallest fishes on the reef and is quite rare. Small aggregations of them may be seen clinging to the rocks, but never in any great numbers.
Aquarium suitability: With its own kind, this fish is strongly territorial unless you are lucky enough to obtain a pair. It is peaceful to all other tank inhabitants to the point of ignoring them. In a reef aquarium, it will not damage any of the corals or other invertebrates and it is hardy and easy to feed.

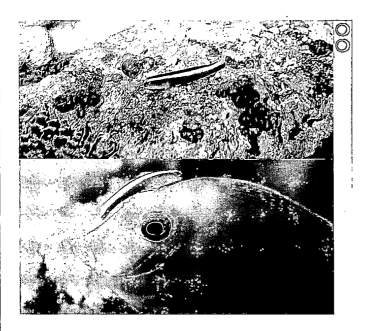

Gobiosoma evelynae

Common name: Sharknose goby
Range: Tropical West Atlantic
Size: 1½in (4cm)
Description: The body is black and the throat and belly are pale. A yellow line runs along each side of the body from the upper lobe of the caudal fin to the snout. On the snout there is a small yellow diamond-shaped spot that, along with the two lines, forms a V-shaped pattern. A similar species, *G. randalli*, has parallel lines that do not meet on the snout. This fish performs a cleaning service on the reef.
Aquarium suitability: The sharknose goby has been bred in captivity and is an easy species to keep, providing the water quality is good. It will readily perform its cleaning service in an aquarium within days of being introduced, as can be seen here (*see lower photograph on the left*).

Istigobius decoratus

Common name: Decorated goby
Range: Central Indo-Pacific
Size: 4in (10cm)
Description: The colouration and body markings of this species can vary considerably according to geographic location. It can be identified, however, by the row of double spots that run horizontally below the lateral line. These never alter. This is a burrowing fish that is often seen on sandy seabeds and in lagoons throughout its natural range. Around the shores of Hong Kong, this fish is particularly abundant.
Aquarium suitability: The decorator goby is a peaceful fish in a community aquarium and will live quite happily in water that is far from ideal. All the usual aquarium foods will be accepted but it should be provided with a good depth of base medium and a flat rock under which it can scoop out its burrow.

Lythrypnus dalli

Common names: Catalina goby, blue-banded goby
Range: Eastern Pacific, Gulf of California
Size: 2in (5cm)
Description: The Catalina goby is unmistakable, with its bright red body and brilliant blue bands. The number of these bands can vary from three to six. In adult males the first four or five rays of the dorsal fin are elongated. In the wild, it is found on rocky coasts and in surge areas, clinging to rocks in small groups.
Aquarium suitability: This fish prefers cooler water than most fishes and is not a true reef fish. Nevertheless, it can be kept at higher temperatures, but it then has a shorter lifespan. It is an active feeder that will accept all aquarium foods, including flake food. It is an ideal choice for an invertebrate aquarium if you have a few month's experience of this hobby.

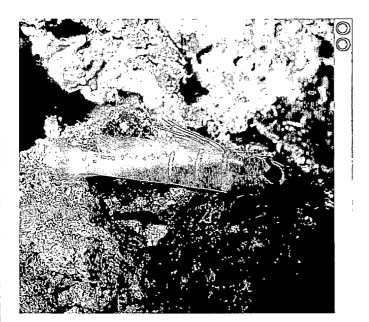

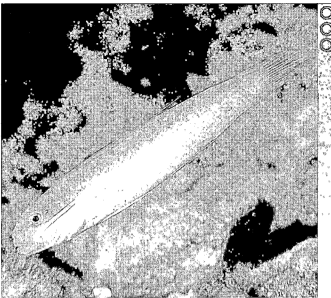

Photograph by Dr Gerald R Allen

Valenciennea strigata

Common names: Blue-cheek goby, gold-head sand goby
Range: East Africa to Central Indo-Pacific
Size: 7in (18cm)
Description: The body colour is bluish-white and the head is yellow. There are several iridescent blue streaks and spots around the lower part of the head, including a large streak that curves horizontally from the angle of the premaxillary to the pectoral axil. This fish is encountered in sandy areas in the reef shallows and lagoons, usually in pairs or small aggregations.
Aquarium suitability: This fish should be kept in pairs in an aquarium that has a good depth of sand. They will then burrow into this to build a home but they will also filter the sand constantly, always on the look out for food. For aquariums that are set up using a plenum filter system, this species will keep the sand loose and well oxygenated.

Wormfishes, dartfishes (Microdesmidae)

The bodies of this family of fishes are compressed and elongated, sometimes eel-like. At present there are two subfamilies incorporating nine genera with a total of 60 valid species, although this will probably increase.

Fishes in the first subfamily, Microdesminae, have a continuous dorsal fin that takes up most of the body length. The caudal fin is sometimes joined to the dorsal and anal fin. The body is eel-like and the lower jaw is protruding. They have small pelvic fins.

Generally, wormfishes are burrowing bottom-dwellers. They are to be found in tide pools, muddy estuaries and also on the coral reef. Often, but not always, they will utilize an existing burrow or crevice as a retreat. They may be seen swimming or hovering above their burrows, waiting to snatch at morsels of food carried past by the ocean currents. They are peaceful but shy fishes that are not often imported for the aquarium hobby. Those that do find their way to the aquarist are usually from the genus *Gunnellichthys*, which contains five species.

The second subfamily, Ptereleotrinae, contains species that are deeper bodied than the wormfishes. They possess two dorsal fins and the mouth is usually vertical. The young are shoaling fishes whereas the adults are usually seen in pairs. Many of the 30 species are brightly coloured and are often imported for the aquarium trade, where they are quickly snapped up by aquarists. They are collectively known as dartfishes, or sometimes firefishes. Again, they are shy and will quickly retreat into their burrows at the first sign of danger. Because of this, they should be kept only in an aquarium with plenty of rocks and crevices and with a good depth of sand. The tank should have a cover, since they are apt to jump out when frightened.

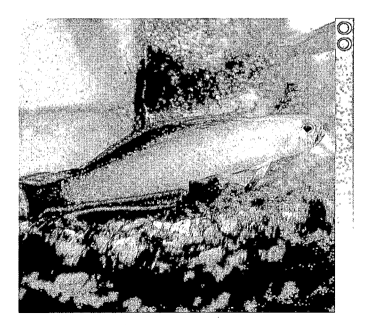

Nemateleotris decora

Common name: Purple firefish
Range: Central Indo-Pacific
Size: 3in (7.5cm)
Description: The body colour is pale tan to pinkish-tan. The central rays of the caudal fin are bluish-purple and the upper and lower lobes are red. Purple is also present from the tip of the snout to the nape. The dorsal and anal fin margins are deep blue and the extended first rays of the dorsal fin are longer in the males. They also have more red in the anal fin than the female.
Aquarium suitability: In a reef aquarium with a well established microfauna, this species is relatively easy to keep. However, it is not a fish for the complete beginner and, being quite rare, tends to be expensive. Pairs can be kept for the best chances of success, but note that two males will usually fight. Feed on live brine initially and later frozen plankton.

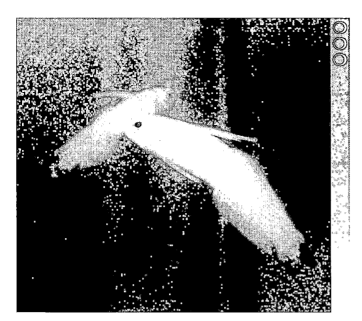

Nemateleotris magnifica

Common name: Firefish
Range: Entire Indo-Pacific
Size: 3½in (9cm)
Description: In this species the body colour is light pink, which fades into deep red or orange-red toward the tail. The upper and lower lobes of the tail are dark, almost black, and there are two dark stripes that form a V on the next innermost rays. These extend on to the soft dorsal and anal fins, respectively. The extended first dorsal rays are longer than in the preceding species and they are used as a signal in pairing rituals and as a warning to others that encroach on their territory.
Aquarium suitability: More difficult to keep than *N. decora* but not as rare, so they are less expensive. Newly purchased fish are shy and have a habit of jumping out of the tank. Keep a tight hood on the aquarium and provide hiding places and bolt-holes.

Ptereleotris zebra

(=Pogonoculius zebra)
Common name: Zebra torpedofish
Range: Entire Indo-Pacific
Size: 4in (10cm)
Description: The body of this species is torpedo-shaped and light green in colour. A row of 20 thin bars, which are violet-pink in colour, run vertically from a point behind the pectoral base to the caudal peduncle. There is a violet patch below the eye and the pectoral axil is also purplish-violet. This is one of the few members of this family whose shoaling instinct survives into adulthood. On the reef they are often encountered in small groups hovering over the substrate.
Aquarium suitability: For the best results, this fish should be kept in a group of four or five in a tank with a tight-fitting hood. When enough cover is provided they will soon settle down and snap at most foods offered.

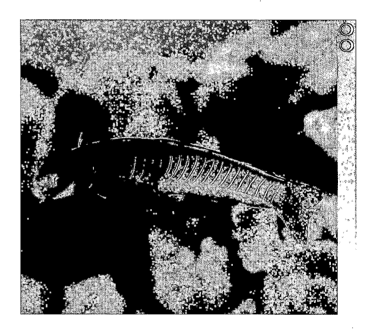

Batfishes, spadefishes (Ephippidae)

This family has undergone much taxonomic revision. The principle changes are that the genus *Drepane* has been placed in its own family, Drepanidae. This is because a closer relationship exists to the families Coracinidae and Chaetodontidae than to those of the suborder Acanthuroidei, to which this, and the next four families, belong. The genera *Platax*, *Proteracanthus* and *Rhinoprenes* have been added so that this family now has seven genera. The genus *Rhinoprenes*, which are marine and brackish-water species from the central Indo-Pacific, was previously placed in its own family, Rhinoprenidae. This is now invalid.

All are deep-bodied, laterally compressed fishes. They have small mouths and the dorsal fins are more or less separated (except in the genus *Platax*). Many grow quite large and are not suitable for the average aquarium. They are represented in all tropical seas but most species suitable for an aquarium come from the Indo-Pacific.

The Atlantic spadefish (*Chaetodipterus faber*) is often encountered on the reef, usually in small aggregations, and is sometimes imported. Unfortunately, as with most members of this family, it grows very fast and far too large for the average aquarium.

The most popular fishes belonging to this family are the long-finned batfishes from the genus *Platax*. This contains four species: *P. batavianus*, *P. orbicularis*, *P. pinnatus* and *P. teira*. Three of the species are well known and popular, but even these fishes grow quickly and become quite large. In an aquarium they accept most foods, but you should buy young specimens, since adults often refuse to feed in the initial stages. Newly introduced specimens often lie down on their sides and play dead. You should not worry, as it is a characteristic of members of this genus.

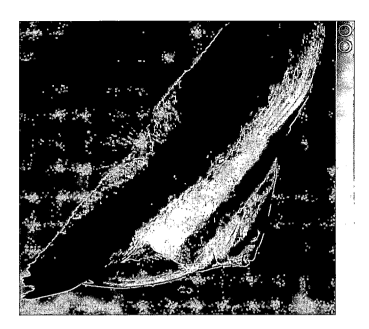

Platax orbicularis

Common name: Orbiculate batfish
Range: Indo-Pacific, Red Sea
Size: 20in (51cm)
Description: Juvenile fish have extremely long dorsal, anal and ventral fins that become progressively shorter with age. Their body colour is light brown with three broad bars of chocolate-brown. Their mimicry is well known to those who have had the opportunity to see them in the wild among mangrove roots. At the first sign of danger they will lay down on their sides, looking remarkably like a dead mangrove leaf. Adult fishes are disc-shaped with laterally compressed bodies that are silver-grey in colour with two darker grey bands.
Aquarium suitability: A large tank is required for this fish. It is happy with most aquarium foods once it is acclimatized. It grows very quickly..

Platax pinnatus

Common names: Long-finned batfish, red-finned batfish, red-faced batfish
Range: Red Sea, East Africa to Central Indo-Pacific
Size: 16in (41cm)
Description: This fish is unmistakable because of its spectacular flowing fins with the margins edged in deep red to orange-red. Although the body colour is predominantly brownish-black, it is attractive because of the red highlights to the fins and the broad red stripe that runs from the tip of the snout across the nape to the dorsal fin. Adult fish lose this red colouration almost completely. In its natural habitat, this fish may be encountered singly or in small shoals. Once again, the young fishes are masters of mimicry. Sensing danger, they will lie on their sides and wave their flowing fins to look remarkably similar to the evil tasting Platyhelminthes (flatworms), *Pseudobiceros gloriosus* and *P. hankockanus*, which also have red margins to their flowing bodies.
Aquarium suitability: *Platax pinnatus* is eagerly sought after in the aquarium trade, and when it is available it usually commands a high price. Like other batfishes it grows fast once it has learned to accept aquarium foods. This, however, is not as simple as it sounds. It is often difficult to wean this fish on to frozen or dried foods and patience is required if the aquarist is to have any chance of success. It cannot be considered as a fish suitable for beginners, but in the right hands it will reward its owner by its ability to be "petted" and hand fed. The tank should be large enough to accommodate its high, flowing fins that, unlike the previous species, do not become shorter as the fish ages. A fully grown specimen requires an aquarium with a water depth of at least 24in (60cm). Young specimens should not be housed with boisterous tank-mates or with notorious fin-nippers. In a tank with peaceful neighbours, however, it is often easier to encourage to start feeding than if it is kept on its own.

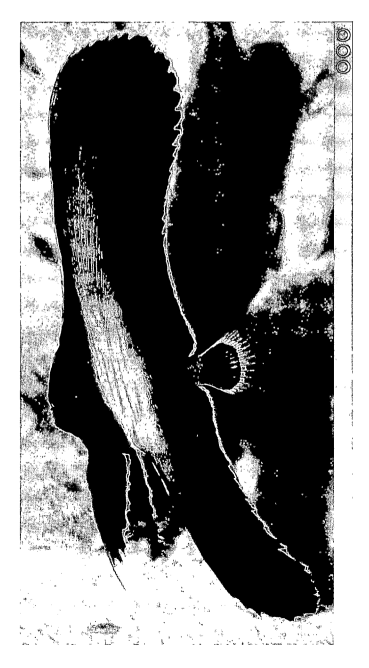

Rabbitfishes (Siganidae)

The family Siganidae consists of a single genus with two subgenera, *Lo* and *Siganus*. By tradition, *Lo* is classified at full generic level, but there is now insufficient evidence to support this conjecture any longer. There are many examples that support the view of there being only a single genus.

There are 27 species, five of which belong to the subgenus *Lo*. These are *Siganus magnificus, S. niger, S. unimaculatus, S. uspi* and *S. vulpinus*. The remaining 22 species belong to the subgenus *Siganus*. With regard to the general characteristics of these fishes, the single dorsal fin has 13 hard spines and ten soft rays. The anal fin has seven spines with nine soft rays, and the pelvic fins have two strong spines with three soft rays between. All the spines are venomous so caution should be exercised when handling these species. Most siganids are peaceful, herbivorous fishes and they are widespread throughout the Indo-Pacific region. Thirteen species are schooling fishes, while the rest are found among corals. A single species, *Siganus vermiculatus*, lives in brackish water in tidal estuaries. They are not represented in the tropical or subtropical Atlantic, although, since the opening of the Suez Canal, two species have become established in the Mediterranean Sea.

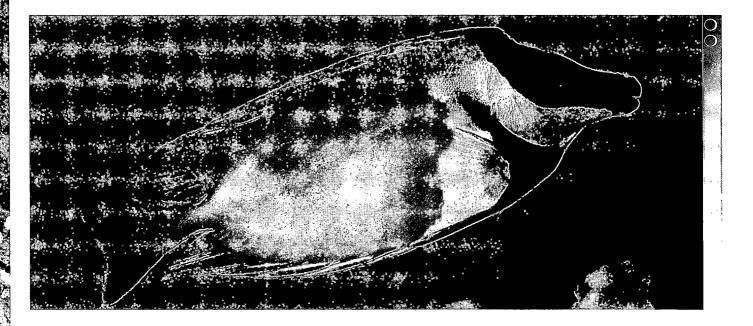

Siganus vulpinus

(= *Lo vulpinus*)

Common names: Badgerfish, lo, foxface
Range: Central Indo-Pacific, Indo-West Pacific
Size: 7in (18cm)
Description: The head and chest of this fish is white and there is a black oblique bar that runs from the snout, through the eye, to the nape. A second bar, triangular in shape, runs from the ventral region and curves upward to end behind the opercle. The rest of the body and the median fins are bright yellow.
Aquarium suitability: This fish is aggressive toward members of its own kind but is peaceful with other fishes. In the wild its main diet is algae, so vegetable matter should be provided when there are little or no algae present. This can be supplemented with flake and frozen food once the fish has settled in. Provide plenty of cover and crevices in a large tank, as this fish needs plenty of free swimming space with places to hide.

Moorish idol (Zanclidae)

The family contains a single species, *Zanclus canescens* (= *Zanclus cornutus*, a junior synonym), which resembles the butterflyfish, *Heniochus acuminatus*, in many respects. *Z. canescens* is, however, closely related to the surgeonfishes and tang family Acanthuridae. Juveniles have a small spine at the angle of the premaxillary and adult fish have protuberances in front of the eyes. Unlike members of the family Acanthuridae, this species lacks the defensive spines on the caudal peduncle. It is a true reef fish and is often encountered in small shoals around areas of dense coral growth. It has a long snout, which it uses to winkle out small invertebrates and sponges from between the coral and in crevices.

Zanclus canescens

Common name: Moorish idol
Range: Tropical Indo-Pacific, Tropical Eastern Pacific
Size: 8½in (22cm)
Description: The body colour is predominantly white, which fades into yellow on the flanks of the fish. There are three broad black bars present, the first of which runs vertically from the nape to the belly. The second bar extends from the soft dorsal fin to the anal fin and the third runs across the tail. The body is disc-shaped and strongly compressed. The dorsal fin is high and the third ray extends into a filament that arches high over the tail. There is a black-edged yellow daub across the snout and the margins of the median fins are iridescent blue. This is one of the most attractive of all the coral-reef fishes
Aquarium suitability: A Moorish idol in the aquarium is the dream that many aquarists harbour. Unfortunately, it is an extremely difficult species to keep in captivity. This is because they are feeding specialists that will seldom take to an aquarium diet. Even if you are lucky and manage to obtain a feeding specimen, the way is still paved with many difficulties. Replacement foods, for example, do not seem to provide the dietary balance that this species requires to maintain its immune system and it will often become weakened and prone to disease. Starvation is the most frequent cause of death in captivity, however. Having said that, it is by no means impossible to keep this species in captivity, but only the most experienced aquarists should attempt this. It is probably better to leave these fish happy and healthy on the reef where they can be observed in their natural environment. If success is to be expected at all, then you will need to provide a large tank, optimal water quality, plenty of live rock and a varied diet.

Surgeonfishes, tangs (Acanthuridae)

This family encompasses six genera placed into two sub-families with a total of 72 species. It is a very diverse family, comprising fishes with disc-shaped, laterally compressed bodies. Generally they are algae grazers that are found in the reef shallows and in lagoons. The family is represented in all the tropical seas. The dorsal fin is continuous, with a spinous and soft portion, and the pelvic fins have a single spine.

The first subfamily, Nasinae, consists of a single genus with 17 species. Many of them have a marked protuberance below the eyes that increases in size with age. For this reason they are known as unicornfishes. They possess two anal spines and the caudal peduncle is armed with one or sometimes two bony plate-like spines, which are sharp and used mainly for defence.

Fishes belonging to the second subfamily, Acanthurinae, have three anal spines and the caudal peduncle is armed with one or more spines. These are retractile and in the case of the genera *Acanthurus* and *Ctenochaetus*, they are set in deep grooves in the caudal peduncle. Only a sideways tail movement against the direction of the opposing spine can bring this spine erect. The spines are very sharp and scalpel-like. Careless handling often results in a painful wound. The exception to this is the genus *Prionurus*, with seven species. These lack the retractile spines. Instead they have from three to ten bony plates on the caudal peduncle. The subfamily is split into three tribes. The first, Prionurini, contains one genus, *Prionurus*. The second tribe, Zebrasomini, consists of the genera *Paracanthus* and *Zebrasoma*. These are popular aquarium fishes that are often quite hardy and easy to keep. As a rule they are colourful fishes and are useful in an aquarium since they keep excessive algae growths in check. The third tribe is formed by two genera, *Acanthurus* and *Ctenochaetus*, and although species from the genus *Acanthurus* are often brightly coloured and attractive, they are by no means easy to keep. As a rule these species are easily stressed by the rigors of transportation or by water quality that is not completely perfect. Once they are fully acclimatized, however, they can be long-lived and hardy fishes.

Zebrasoma desjardinii

Common names: Desjardin's sailfin tang, sailfin tang, western sailfin tang
Range: Indian Ocean, Red Sea
Size: 16in (41cm)
Description: This fish is often confused with its close cousin, *Zebrasoma veliferum*. Some consider it to be a geographic variation of *Z. veliferum*. However, the dorsal fin has less soft rays and, as the fish assumes its adult colouration, the dark bars change to spots in the ventral region and on the throat and head. In *Z. veliferum* these spots are restricted to the head.
Aquarium suitability: A large tank should be provided with plenty of free swimming space. This fish grows quite large and does not usually tolerate members of its own kind. Its diet should include green material, such as algae and spinach, but it will soon learn to accept other foods as a supplement.

Paracanthus hepatus

Common names: Blue surgeonfish, regal tang, morpho butterfly
Range: Tropical Indo-Pacific
Size: 9in (23cm)
Description: There is a black mark on the body that is shaped like an artist's palette. The body colouration is bright blue and the tail is bright yellow with the upper and lower lobes edged in black. In adult specimens, the membranes between the dorsal rays are dull mauve. On the reef they are often found in small shoals, usually in areas of heavy algal growth.
Aquarium suitability: Once acclimatized this fish is one of the easiest to keep in captivity, provided there are plenty of algae on which it can graze. If algae are not available, chopped lettuce and spinach should be regularly given. The aquarium needs plenty of places in which it can hide at night.

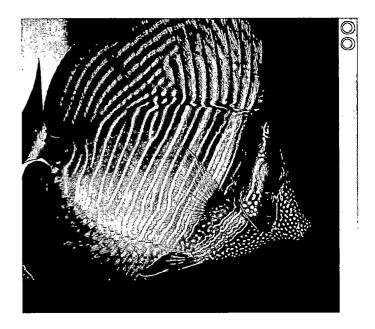

Zebrasoma flavescens

Common names: Yellow tang, yellow sailfin tang
Range: Northern Indo-West Pacific to Hawaii
Size: 6in (15cm)
Description: The body colouration of this fish is bright yellow and the caudal spine is white. The snout is moderately elongated and the eye is dark brown. It is very common in shallow waters around the Hawaiian Islands and is often encountered in small shoals throughout the region as far north as the Ryukyu Islands.
Aquarium suitability: This is the most frequently exported fish from Hawaii. It is probably the easiest of all the tangs and surgeonfishes to keep, although young specimens tend to be a little aggressive toward other fishes. A small group of them can be kept together without trouble, and in a reef aquarium they will earn their keep by controlling any nuisance algae. Most other foods are also accepted.

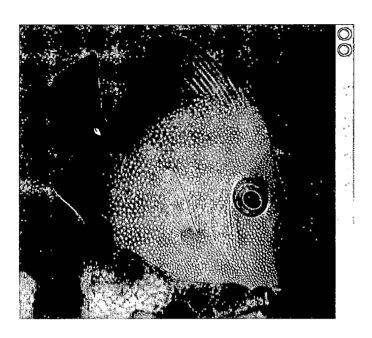

Zebrasoma scopas

Common names: Mink tang, brown tang
Range: Tropical Indo-Pacific, Red Sea
Size: 8in (20cm)
Description: The young of this species are often yellow and are very similar in appearance to Z. *flavescens*. As they grow, however, they lose much of their colour, becoming almost completely brown. The photograph here shows a subadult specimen with the intermediate colouration. The spine on the caudal peduncle remains white throughout the life of the fish.
Aquarium suitability: An often imported species, which can be very aggressive and territorial. It accepts most aquarium foods once it has settled in, but its diet should include plenty of algae or other vegetable matter. Unlike the preceding species, this fish is better kept singly in a community set-up, since it will not often tolerate members of its own kind.

Zebrasoma veliferum

Common names: Sailfin tang, striped sailfin tang
Range: Central Indo-Pacific
Size: 16in (41cm)
Description: Young fish have very high dorsal and anal fins but these tend to decrease in size with age. The barred body colouration is retained throughout the life span of the fish, with adult specimens showing a pattern of fine spots around the head and on the snout. With its fins spread, this fish looks spectacular. On the reef it is usually encountered singly or in pairs in lagoons and in back-reef areas, where the water current is not too strong.
Aquarium suitability: Ideal when kept as a single specimen in a community set-up, although a large tank is required since this fish grows quite quickly once it has settled in and is feeding. As with other members of this family, algae or green matter should be included in its diet.

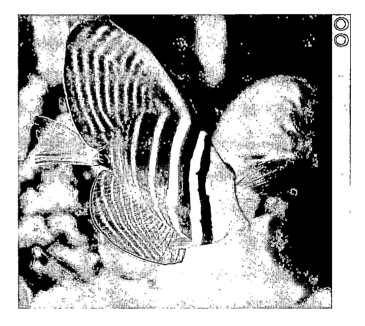

Acanthurus coeruleus

Common name: Blue tang
Range: Tropical West Atlantic, Caribbean
Size: 9in (23cm)
Description: This is a commonly seen reef fish in the Caribbean. Juveniles (*see above left*) are bright yellow with blue margins to the dorsal and anal fin. The eye is rimmed with blue. As the fish grows the colour changes to deep blue or slate blue with a series of grey longitudinal lines (*see below left*). Some specimens take on a purplish-grey colouration. Their main diet in the wild is benthic algae but small invertebrates are also taken with this.
Aquarium suitability: Unless this fish is provided with the correct diet of algae, and enough of it, it will become weak and prone to disease. Its appetite is enormous and it requires feeding several times a day when the algal growth is sparse. Young fish are apt to be a little aggressive toward their tank-mates.

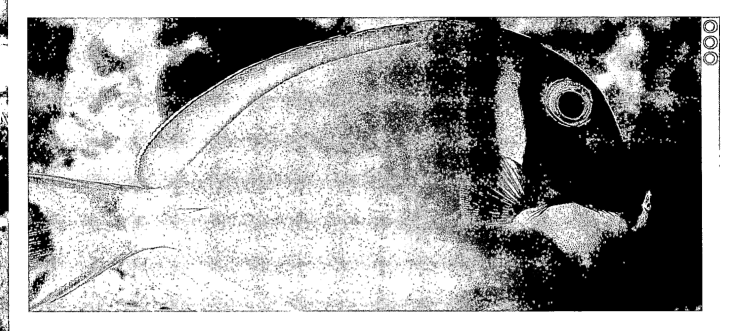

⌂ *Acanthurus leucosternon*

Common names: Powder blue tang, powder blue surgeonfish
Range: Tropical Indo-Pacific
Size: 9in (23cm)
Description: The dorsal fin and caudal peduncle are yellow and the anal and ventral fins are creamy-white, as is the throat. The upper part of the head is bluish-black and the rest of the body is a deep powder-blue. In its natural habitat, this fish is usually seen singly or in pairs. Occasionally, however, large aggregations of them can be encountered, and it is believed that mass spawning occurs at night with the individual fish shoaling and feeding prior to this taking place.
Aquarium suitability: The powder blue tang is quite an aggressive fish that requires good water quality for its continued survival. Additionally, it should be given plenty of greenstuff and algae if it is to be kept healthy and free from disease.

⌄ *Acanthurus lineatus*

Common names: Clown surgeonfish, blue-lined surgeonfish, pyjama tang
Range: Tropical Indo-Pacific
Size: 15in (38cm)
Description: The belly of this fish is white while the rest of its body has an array of bluish-white and orange lines edged in black. The dorsal and anal fin margins are edged in blue, as are the upper and lower lobes of the tail. A thin, semicircular blue line adorns the caudal fin, giving it a lyre-tail effect. The caudal peduncle spine is not highlighted by strong colouration, as is the case with most other surgeonfishes and tangs.
Aquarium suitability: The clown surgeonfish should be kept singly in a large tank. Juvenile fishes can be very pugnacious once they have settled in, but they are hardy when given a varied diet, such as greenstuff and frost foods.

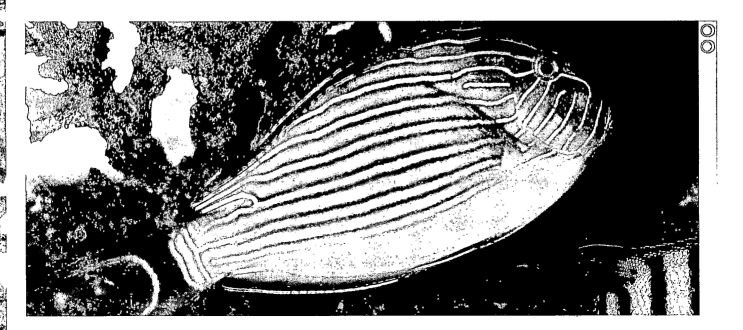

Acanthurus pyroferus

Common name: Chocolate surgeonfish, mimic surgeonfish
Range: Indian Ocean, Northern Indo-Pacific to the Ryukyu Islands
Size: 12in (30cm)
Description: Juveniles of this species adopt the colouration of various species of dwarf angelfishes. There are many reports of mimicry, with fish assuming the colouration of *Centropyge vroliki*, *C. eibli* and *C. flavissimus*, with *C. flavissimus* being the most common form. Presumably this is for defence, since dwarf angelfishes have sharp opercular spines. Adults are dark brown with a white tail margin and orange behind the gill cover.
Aquarium suitability: This is an aggressive fish when housed in a small aquarium. It should be kept singly in a large tank and fed on a variety of foods, including algae. It will accept dried foods as a supplement.

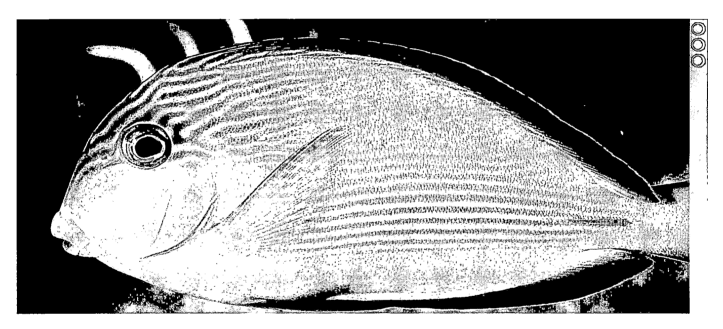

Acanthurus sohal

Common names: Zebra surgeon, majestic surgeonfish
Range: Red Sea
Size: 16in (41cm)
Description: This species has a creamy-white body with a series of uneven horizontal lines that are greyish-black in colour. The median fins are dark and edged with blue. The pectoral fins are yellow and there is an orange line near the tail, which accentuates the caudal spine.
Aquarium suitability: The zebra surgeon feeds mainly on algae and it is sometimes difficult to wean on to a diet of substitute foods. Some specimens will accept normal aquarium foods, but this is the exception rather than the rule. This fish is very aggressive, so be prepared for trouble if other surgeonfishes are present in its aquarium. A large tank should be provided and this should have pumps that produce strong water current. A newcomer to this hobby should not attempt to keep this fish.

Order: Tetraodontiformes

The preceding pages have dealt with fishes belonging to the huge order Perciformes. The last group of fishes described in this book, belonging to the order Tetraodontiformes, is considerably smaller. It contains nine families with approximately 100 genera and 339 extant species.

There is evidence to assume that the order is closely related to the preperciformes order, Zeiformes (with the exception of Caproidae, which is considered to have a closer affinity to the order Perciformes). In spite of this, the order has been retained in the postperciformes position in the classical way because the evidence at the moment is somewhat sparse and poorly researched.

Regarding the characteristics of the fishes of this order, the body is variable in form with modified scales. These may be plates, spines or shields, or they may be hidden under tissue, such as is the case with the triggerfishes. Some families have a modified stomach that enables the fish to inflate itself with a rapid intake of water when individuals become angry or frightened. These fishes are generally referred to as "puffers". A lot of species are able to produce an audible sound by grinding their pharyngeal teeth together. Most triggerfishes can enlarge their bodies in anger or in fright by extending their stomachs downward, and they have a moveable pelvic bone that enables them to do this.

The order contains two suborders, the first of which contains the spikefishes and triplespines. This is the suborder Triacanthoidei, incorporating two families. These are Triacanthodidae (with 15 species, mostly from deep-water regions) and Triacanthidae (which contains seven shallow-water benthic species). These are of little interest to the marine aquarist, however, and so will not be dealt with further in this book.

The second suborder, Tetraodontoidei, is of greater interest to aquarium hobbyists. This suborder contains the triggerfishes, filefishes, boxfishes, trunkfishes, cowfishes, pufferfishes and porcupinefishes. The suborder is split into three superfamilies, although the exact placing of the family Ostraciidae is, at the moment, very sketchy and far from certain.

Triggerfishes (Balistidae)

The triggerfish family contains ten genera and 40 species. These fishes have no pelvic fins; instead, there is a pelvic spine present. Their bodies are laterally compressed and the scales are plate-like in form. There are three dorsal spines, but in some cases the third spine is underdeveloped. All the soft fins have branched rays. The eyes are well developed and are independently moveable within their

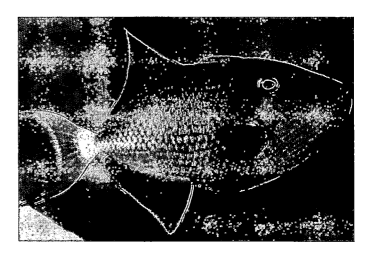

The red-toothed triggerfish (Odonus niger) is the most peaceful of all members of this normally aggressive family. It will usually be happy with a diet of frozen and dried foods.

sockets. The head is very large and in some species it can take up to one-third of the total body length.

These fishes rate among the most aggressive and territorial of all the reef fishes. They have razor-sharp teeth and powerful jaws and they have even been known to attack divers who encroach on their territory, and this is despite the fact that the trespassing diver may be several times larger and a great deal heavier. Some species attain a length of 20in (51cm), with one species reaching almost double this size.

Their common name is derived from their peculiar dorsal fin mechanism. The first spine of this fin can be raised and locked into place by the position of the second spine. This is used defensively when the fish wedges itself between rocks and coral and locks its spine. This it will do at the first sign of danger and also at night when predators may be about. Only by depressing the second spine back into its recess can the first spine be released. It would take a large predator some pretty fancy manoeuvring in order to do all this and then to get at its prey.

Many of the species are brightly coloured and they are popular aquarium fishes, despite their aggressiveness and the ultimately large size they attain. As a rule they are not to be trusted with small tank-mates and cannot be kept in a reef aquarium. Their main diet in the wild consists of small fishes and hard-shelled invertebrates, such as crustaceans and sea urchins. The latter are normally immune from attacks by predators because of their long, needle-like spines. However, triggerfishes have two solutions to this problem: either they will take in water and blow it out quickly to dislodge the urchin, bowling it over in order to reach the soft stomach with their leathery jaws, or they will patiently proceed to break off the spines one by one until the vulnerable centre is exposed.

▲ *Balistapus undulatus*

Common names: Undulate triggerfish, orange-green triggerfish
Range: Indo-Pacific, Red Sea
Size: 12in (30cm)
Description: The undulating orange lines on a dark green body make this species easy to identify. The tail is yellow and the caudal peduncle has a double row of black spines that are used for defence. There are three orange lines that run ventrally from the snout. These accentuate the small mouth, making it appear much larger than it actually is.
Aquarium suitability: This is a very aggressive fish and one that will rearrange the rockwork in the tank to suit its own particular taste. Small tank-mates will be eaten and owner's hands or arms will be bitten in defence of its chosen territory (which is the entire aquarium, irrespective of its size). Despite this, when made a fuss of, it can become a real pet.

▼ *Balistoides conspicillum*

Common name: Clown triggerfish
Range: Tropical Indo-Pacific to Australia
Size: 20in (51cm)
Description: Young specimens have large white spots over most of the body and head. The snout is yellow and the fins are pale coloured. As the fish grows, a yellow saddle begins to show around the first dorsal fin, and this becomes covered in small bluish-black spots. The yellow on the snout recedes to an area around the mouth and this is bordered with a yellowish-white line. This species is one of the most striking of all the reef fishes when it is seen in its natural element.
Aquarium suitability: It should be kept in a tank of its own or with other large fishes where it can do no harm. It is very aggressive but will accept most frozen foods, such as mussel, cockle, lancefish and so on.

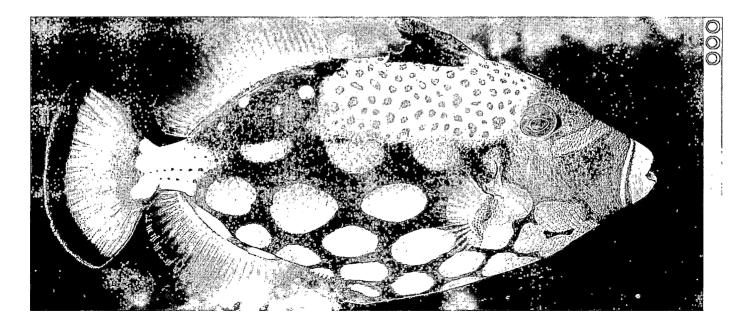

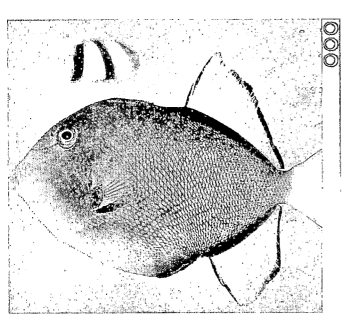

Melichthys vidua

Common name: Pink-tailed triggerfish
Range: Entire Indo-Pacific, Red Sea
Size: 15in (38cm)
Description: Adult and subadult fish have clear, soft dorsal and anal fins with black margins. The body colouration is green to brownish-green and the tail is pink with a white base. Juveniles have stripes through the soft dorsal and anal fins and the tail is almost completely pink.
Aquarium suitability: Occasional specimens can prove peaceful and they will adapt well to a community aquarium. They require a large tank with plenty of rockwork and free swimming space. Most individuals, however, become scrappy and belligerent as they get older and they are then a problem for the average aquarist. They will eat almost anything that is offered and become quite tame, even allowing their owners to pet them.

Odonus niger

Common names: Black triggerfish, red-toothed triggerfish, red-fang triggerfish
Range: East Africa to Central Indo-Pacific, Red Sea, Great Barrier Reef
Size: 20in (51cm)
Description: As the common names imply, this fish has bright red teeth, but these are apparent only in subadult or adult fish. Colour is variable, according to time of day, lighting and geographic origin. Usually though, it is blue, bluish-green or green. The lobes of the tail are extended into filaments and the head is paler than the rest of the body with blue lines and spots around the snout. Juveniles are often seen in small shoals.
Aquarium suitability: The most mild-mannered of all the triggerfishes, but it will not tolerate its own kind in a tank. It is hardy and easy to keep and will accept most aquarium foods.

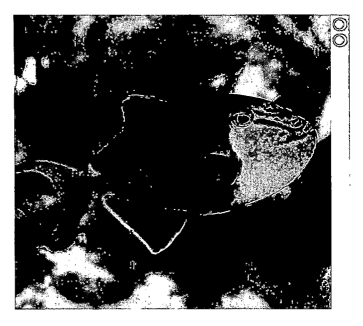

Rhinecanthus aculeatus

Common names: Picasso triggerfish, white-barred triggerfish, Hawaiian triggerfish
Range: Tropical Indo-Pacific
Size: 12in (30cm)
Description: There are three rows of spines on the caudal peduncle. The margin of the upper jaw is blue and the body pattern has a chevron arrangement of bluish-white and dark coloured bars. A yellow line extends from the mouth to below the pectoral base, giving an exaggerated impression of the overall size of the mouth. This fish is ubiquitous throughout its range, even in the reef shallows and tidal pools.
Aquarium suitability: Care should be taken when handling this species if you value your fingers. It should be kept in a large tank and fed on the usual frozen aquarium foods. It is very fond of eating smaller tank-mates as well.

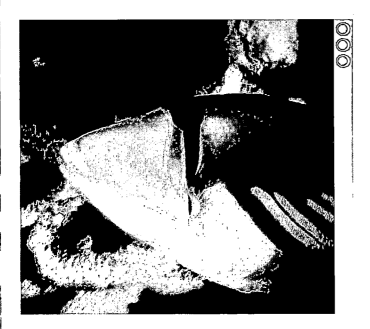

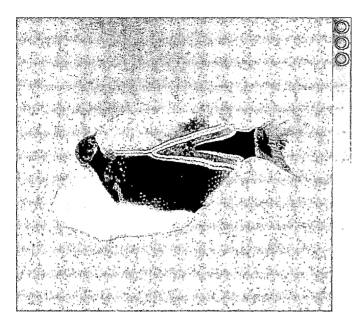

Rhinecanthus rectangulus

Common names: Black-banded triggerfish, belted triggerfish, wedge-tailed triggerfish
Range: Tropical Indo-Pacific
Size: 12in (30cm)
Description: The broad black diagonal bar that extends from the eye to the base of the anal fin differentiates this from the preceding species. In addition, there is a black wedge-shaped pattern on the caudal peduncle. This fish is endemic in the South Pacific and juveniles may often be encountered in tidal rock pools where they are easily collected.
Aquarium suitability: Although not as often imported as the Picasso triggerfish, this fish is easy to keep in captivity. Juveniles are not as attractive as the adults but they are easier to acclimatize. Most large triggerfishes become tame, even allowing their owner to stroke and pet them. This fish is no exception.

Filefishes (Monacanthidae)

This family contains small to moderate-sized bottom-dwelling fishes with strongly compressed bodies, usually disc-shaped. There are two dorsal fins present. The anterior dorsal fin consists of a single spine, sometimes with a second one that is often rudimentary. In some cases, the first spine can be erected and locked into position by the second spine. The second dorsal, anal and pectoral fins have simple, unbranched rays. There is no spine present in the anal fin. The tail is emarginate or sometimes rounded, and the ventral fins are absent.

The scales are small and sequential and usually have small spines, making their skin rough to the touch and giving rise to their name "filefishes". Some species have irregular protuberances over much of the body. Others can alter their body colouration to match their surroundings. The males of some species have a bristle-like patch of scales on the caudal peduncle.

Filefishes are represented in all tropical seas, but the largest number of species occurs in the Indo-Australian archipelago and around the coasts of Australia. They are slow-moving and may be herbivorous. Most species feed on small benthic invertebrates, however, with the diet of at least one species (*Oxymonacanthus longirostris*) consisting largely of coral polyps. One species, the scribbled filefish (*Aluterus scriptus*), the largest of this family, is found in the Tropical Atlantic and the entire Indo-Pacific region.

Altogether there are about 30 genera with 95 species. Only a few of these are imported for aquarium use and because of their invertebrate diet they are not suitable for a reef aquarium. Most species are happy in a community tank if kept with other slow-moving and peaceful fishes. They are usually quite secretive in captivity.

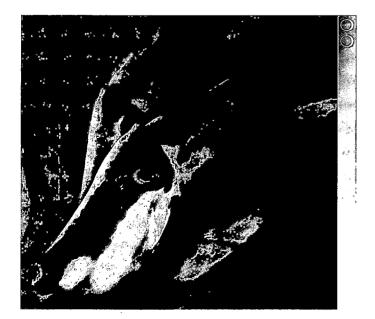

Aluterus schoepfi

Common name: Orange filefish
Range: Tropical and Subtropical West Atlantic
Size: 24in (61cm)
Description: The body colouration of this fish can range from pale grey to dark brown. Dark brown bands and stripes are often present, which give the species a marbled appearance. The head and body are covered with a suffusion of small orange spots. The lips are almost black. The body is moderately elongated and there is no pelvic terminus. The tail is rounded. This is a largely herbivorous fish that is encountered in sea-grass beds from Nova Scotia to Brazil.
Aquarium suitability: The orange filefish is not often imported but it is a mild-mannered fish that is easy to keep. It is happy when the aquarium has an ample supply of algae, but it will accept most other foods as a substitute.

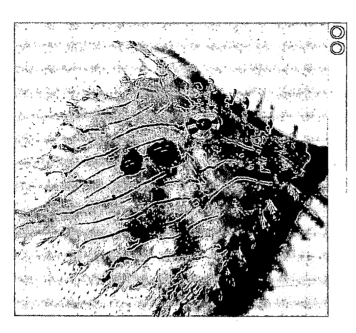

Monacanthus hispidus

Common names: None
Range: Tropical East and West Atlantic
Size: 10in (25cm)
Description: The colouration of this species can change almost as rapidly as that of a chameleon, from greenish-grey (as seen in the accompanying photograph) to a mottled brownish-green. The body is covered with small protuberances that give it a spinous appearance. This fish inhabits sea-grass beds and rocky areas in lagoons and the reef shallows. Its main diet is benthic algae although it will ingest small bethnic invertebrates along with these.
Aquarium suitability: Its natural habitat and diet should be replicated as closely as possible in captivity. This means plenty of rocks and coral with a good growth of algae and regular feedings of a variety of frozen foods.

Chaetoderma pencilligerus

Common names: Tasselled filefish, prickly leatherjacket
Range: Tropical Indo-Pacific to Japan
Size: 10in (25cm)
Description: The background body colour of this fish is greyish-white to mottled-brown. There are numerous thin and irregular black stripes that run more or less horizontally over much of its head and body. There are often two or more black blotches behind the gills, which gradually recede as the fish becomes larger. The body, head and anterior dorsal fin are all covered with fleshy tubercles.
Aquarium suitability: Although many books state the opposite, this is one of the few species that can be kept in a reef aquarium without there being any damage done to the delicate corals and other invertebrates. Given a varied diet of chopped mussel, cockle, krill, brine shrimp and mysids, this fish will stay healthy.

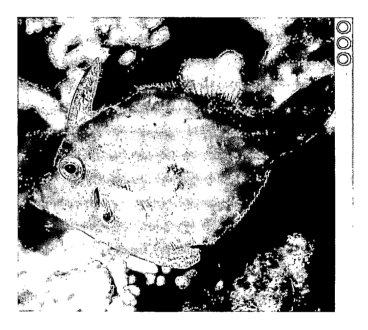

Oxymonacanthus longirostris

Common names: Long-nosed filefish, orange-green filefish, beaked leatherjacket
Range: Red Sea, Tropical Indo-Pacific
Size: 4in (10cm)
Description: This is the most colourful of all the filefishes. The snout is extended and beak-like. The elongated body is brilliant lime-green with myriad bright orange spots that extend from the snout to the tail. They make an attractive sight on the reef and are usually observed in small groups of a dozen or so, grazing among the coral heads.
Aquarium suitability: This is not an easy fish to keep in an aquarium for any length of time since its main diet is coral polyps, particularly those of the *Acropora* spp. In addition, it is a shy fish and feeding difficulties are often encountered when it is initially introduced. Plenty of hiding places should be provided.

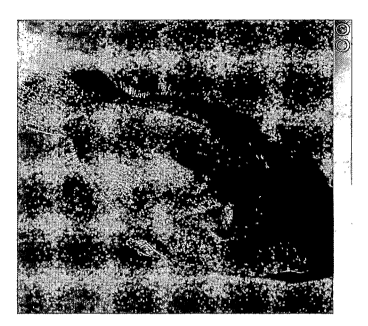

Pervagor melanocephalus

Common names: Pink-tailed filefish, red-tailed filefish
Range: Tropical Indo-Pacific
Size: 6in (15cm)
Description: The tail of this fish is pink to orange-red and the body is green. There is a dark bar that extends upward from the pectoral axil to a point behind the eye. This slow-moving fish is not a common sight on the reef and it is quite secretive by nature. Its main habitat is among weed beds and algal growths, where its body colour gives it an ideal camouflage.
Aquarium suitability: Initial difficulties may be experienced but afterward this fish usually settles in well and will accept all the usual aquarium foods. Like most filefishes, it grows quite fast, but not too large for the average aquarium. The tank should have plenty of rocks and hiding places into which it can retire at night.

Boxfishes, trunkfishes, cowfishes (Ostraciidae)

This bizarre family consists of two subfamilies with 14 genera and about 33 species. They are small fishes that can grow to a maximum length of 24in (61cm), but many are considerably smaller. Their most notable characteristic is body form, which may be square, triangular or pentagonal in cross-section. The body is covered in a carapace formed by the fusion of hexagonal or polygonal bony plates that replace the scales, producing a strong armoured box that encloses the head and body. There is no pelvic skeleton and spines are absent in the dorsal and anal fins. The jaw is not protractile, the mouth being shaped somewhat like a blunt bill. Gaps exist in the carapace for the mouth, gill openings, nostrils, fins and anus. The caudal peduncle is left free of this restriction in most species.

Many of the trunkfishes are known to exude poison when under stress. In the confines of an aquarium this poison is deadly to most, if not all, fishes, including the trunkfish itself. These species have some resistance to the poison if a partial water change is immediately undertaken.

In the first subfamily, Aracaninae, the carapace is open behind the dorsal and anal fins and the ventral keel is more defined. There are normally 11 rays in the caudal fin. These are mainly deep-water fishes that are found throughout the Indo-Pacific, from East Africa to the Central Pacific. They are seldom imported for the aquarium trade and the subfamily comprises seven genera and 13 species. In the second subfamily, Ostraciinae, the carapace is closed behind the anal fin. With these fishes there is no obvious ventral keel and the caudal fin has normally only ten rays. There are 20 species in this subfamily, also with seven genera. Many of them make ideal aquarium subjects.

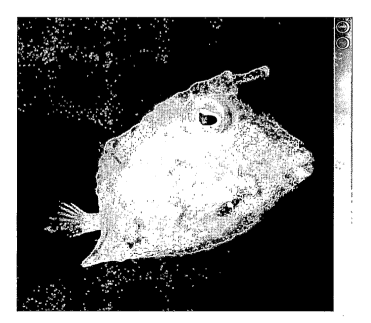

Lactoria cornuta

Common names: Cowfish, long-horned cowfish
Range: Central Indo-Pacific from Japan to Australia
Size: 19in (48cm)
Description: The basic body colour is yellow, often with black or bluish-silver speckles. Juveniles are cube-shaped but as they grow they develop long supraorbital and ventral "horns". The tail increases in length with age until it is almost as long as the body. These slow-moving and bizarre fish inhabit reef shallows and back-reef areas, as well as sandy and sea-grass beds.
Aquarium suitability: Care should be taken not to allow this fish to become damaged in transit, as the wound will become infected and it may not recover. You should also avoid housing it with boisterous tank-mates for the same reason. Despite this, it is an easy fish to keep and usually accepts most frost foods that are offered.

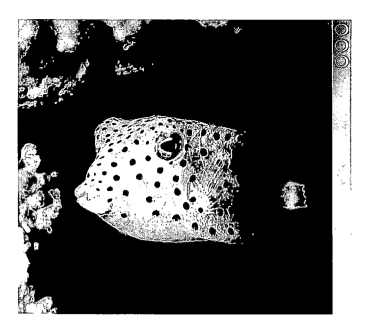

Tetrasomus gibbosus

Common names: Thornback boxfish, pyramid trunkfish, black-blotched turretfish, camel trunkfish, hovercraftfish
Range: Red Sea, Tropical Indo-Pacific
Size: 12in (30cm)
Description: Unlike the previous species, the body shape of this fish is triangular rather than cube-shaped, and it resembles a thorny pyramid. At its apex there is a sharp, triangular spine. The body is covered in bony plates and, in the case of adult fish, each plate is adorned with a delicate blue spot. The turretfish is common on inshore reefs and lagoons, particularly in the summer months when there is an abundance of food.
Aquarium suitability: This species is suitable for a reef aquarium, as it will do little or no damage to the invertebrate life. It accepts most normal aquarium foods and particularly enjoys an occasional meal of live brine shrimp.

Pufferfishes (Tetraodontidae)

The family is made up of two subfamilies with 19 genera and 121 species. These fishes are able to inflate their abdomens by taking in water (or air, when they are removed from the water). They have no ribs or pelvic fins and their skin is very tough, sometimes with short spines on the belly. There are no scales and the fins do not possess spines. The tail is often rounded or truncate.

An alkaloid poison is present in the flesh of some species, with the largest accumulation being in the viscera, particularly the liver. This can prove fatal if eaten. Some species are confined to fresh water, while quite a few are found in brackish water and mangrove swamps.

In the first subfamily, Tetraodontinae, the bodies are widely rounded when viewed from the front. The gill opening extends below the middle point of the pectoral

Ostracion cubicus

Common name: Spotted cube
Range: Red Sea, Tropical Indo-Pacific
Size: 18in (46cm)
Description: Young specimens resemble little yellow dice. Their bold black spots on a bright yellow background may serve as a warning to predators. When attacked or frightened, this fish will release poisonous ostracitoxin into the water. Adult fish lose much of their bright livery, becoming a drab brown colour.
Aquarium suitability: This fish is relatively easy to keep and will enjoy most foods that are offered. Care should be taken when introducing it into an aquarium, however, that it does not become unduly stressed. If this happens it will secrete its poison into the water, thereby causing the demise of all the tank inhabitants, including itself. For the same reason, it should not be housed with aggressive or boisterous fishes.

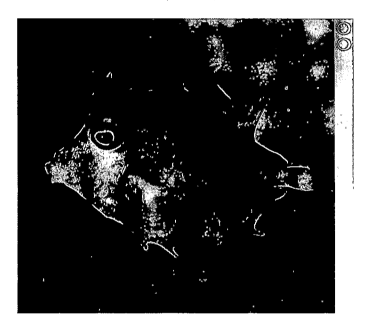

axil and there is one (sometimes two) nostril on each side of the head. The dorsal fin is set well back on the body and the anal fin is more or less below it. There are about 95 species, the largest of which grows to 36in (91cm).

Canthigastrinae, the second subfamily, comprises fishes with laterally compressed bodies when they are not inflated. The skin is scaleless and coarse, and the gill opening ends at the mid-point of the pectoral axil. There is a single nostril on each side of the head but this is not very well defined. The snout is elongated and somewhat pointed, giving rise to the popular name "sharpnosed puffers". These are shallow-water fishes that feed on benthic algae and invertebrates, and they are usually found in the vicinity of coral reefs. There are 26 species altogether and all but one is from the Indo-Pacific and Red Sea. The remaining species, *Canthigaster rostrata*, is found in the tropical Atlantic.

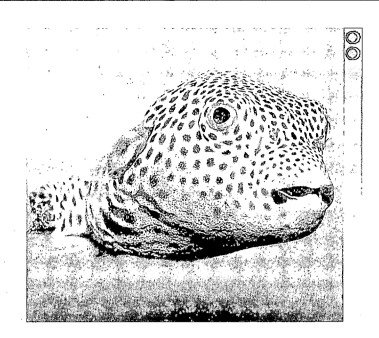

Arothron stellatus

Common names: Starry toadfish, spotted puffer
Range: Indo-Pacific, Red Sea
Size: 36in (91cm)
Description: Although there are similarities between this species and A. *hispidus*, there are no reticulated lines on the sides and belly. In addition, this fish has black spots on the body instead of white, as is the case with A. *hispidus*. This is the largest of all the pufferfishes.
Aquarium suitability: Small specimens are frequently available for sale and they soon settle in to aquarium life. Unfortunately, as with all members of this genus, they are fast growing and need plenty of food. This means that even in a large tank, the water will have a constantly increasing nitrate level if you do not undertake frequent partial water changes. This is the case with all large or fast-growing fishes, irrespective of the filter system.

Chelonodon laticeps

Common names: Pufferfish, banded puffer
Range: Indian Ocean
Size: 8in (20cm)
Description: There are four dark bands across the head and back, which help to identify this fish. The first is at the nape and is indistinct. The second is at a point level with the pectoral fins, while the third runs from the dorsal fin to the anal fin. The last bar on the caudal peduncle is often very indistinct. The body is yellowish-brown and is suffused with small white spots.
Aquarium suitability: This species is mild mannered and should never be kept with aggressive tank-mates. It accepts most of the usual aquarium foods but it should be given an occasional treat of fresh or frozen shellfish, such as sand shrimp and krill, to keep it happy and content in its captive surroundings.

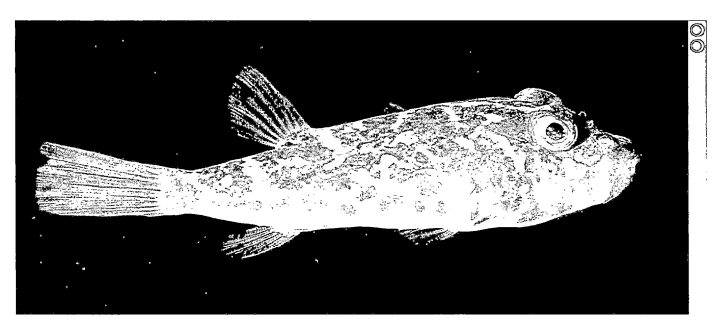

▲ *Sphoeroides marmoratus*

Common names: Bandtail puffer, Atlantic puffer
Range: Tropical and Subtropical East Atlantic
Size: 12in (30cm)
Description: Although this species is similar to its near relative, *S. spengleri*, it lacks the distinct row of spots on the lower side of the head and body. The light-coloured band on the tail is also somewhat narrower. The back and sides are covered with dark and light irregular blotches that give it a marbled effect. Short spinules adorn the body toward the tail. Their natural diet consists of small shellfish, sea stars, marine worms, polychaetes and algae.
Aquarium suitability: Because their natural diet is so varied, all dried and frozen aquarium foods may be offered. If pufferfishes are frightened they will inflate themselves, and this fish is no exception. It is unwise and cruel to terrorize these fishes so that you can see them inflate their bodies.

▼ *Canthigaster rostrata*

Common names: Sharpnose puffer
Range: Tropical East and West Atlantic
Size: 4½in (11cm)
Description: There is yellow on the sides of the head and belly and the back is brown. Blue lines radiate from the eye and there are further blue lines under the snout. The upper and lower lobes of the caudal fin are brownish-black. The lower half of the caudal peduncle has a series of short blue bands and there is a horizontal blue stripe on the upper part that separates the light and dark colours. This fish is ubiquitous throughout the Caribbean, where it is found among sea-grass beds and in areas of dense coral growth.
Aquarium suitability: Not suitable for a reef aquarium since this fish, and other sharpnosed puffers, will often do damage to delicate corals in their endless search for food. In a community aquarium, it is robust and is usually easy to keep and feed.

Canthigaster valentini

Common names: Sharpnosed puffer, black-saddled puffer, minstrel pufferfish
Range: Tropical Indo-Pacific
Size: 8in (20cm)
Description: This species is easily identifiable by the four brownish-black saddles on the light coloured head and body. Not so apparent are the myriad reddish-brown spots that cover much of the upper half of the body. The tail is chrome-yellow with dark bases to the upper and lower lobes.
Aquarium suitability: Although this fish is not as often imported as other members of this genus, it is a robust candidate for a community aquarium of relatively peaceful fishes. Nearly all the usual frozen and dried foods will be accepted with relish once it has settled in. This species, and other members of this genus, will emit grunting noises if provoked or upset.

Porcupinefishes (Diodontidae)

The last family of fishes to be described in this book contains only 19 species within six genera. This is a small group of fishes that, like the puffers, are able to inflate their bodies. In this case, though, the body is covered in sharp spines that are often only erect when the abdomen is fully inflated. These fishes normally inhabit inshore waters and lagoons but are represented in all tropical seas.

From the six genera it is usually those of the genus *Diodon* that are available for aquarists. Occasionally, though, specimens from the genus *Cyclichthys* are found. These are usually *C. orbicularis* from the Indo-Pacific and *C. schoepfi*, which is abundant throughout the tropical West Atlantic. All of these species are unsuitable for reef aquariums. They may be kept in a normal marine aquarium, though, when housed with other peaceful fishes.

Diodon holocanthus

Common names: Balloonfish, spiny puffer, porcupinefish
Range: Circumtropical
Size: 19in (48cm)
Description: The characteristic bar of dark brown behind the head differentiates this species from the similar *D. hystrix*. The body colouration is greyish-white to tan with several, dark-brown blotches and spots. The spines are erectile but are normally held flat against the body. When disturbed or frightened it will inflate its body and erect its many spines; the fish then becomes a virtual ball of spikes and this formidable object is enough to deter even the most persistent predator.
Aquarium suitability: This is one of the most commonly imported porcupinefish species. Fish do well in an aquarium on a diet of fresh or frozen protein, such as mussel, krill and squid, but flake food may also be offered as a supplement.

part five

INVERTEBRATES FOR THE REEF AQUARIUM

The five kingdoms

There are estimated to be in excess of 1.5 million different species of animal and plant life on our planet Earth. Most of them have managed, up until now, to live in some sort of harmony, at least for the last couple of million years.

In the past, scientists seriously believed that life consisted of just two kingdoms: flora, the plants; and fauna, the animals. Modern science now shows us that there are, in fact, five kingdoms, and that these complex societies have adapted themselves over a period of millions of years to live in harmony with one another. Only one species, *Homo sapiens*, is the exception. We continue, at an ever-increasing pace, to destroy our natural environment.

Through the systematic classification of invertebrates, there is an attempt in the following pages to bring about more understanding on the part of readers concerning the needs of these animals so that they can live, grow and reproduce in an aquarium. To be able not only to keep marine invertebrates in an aquarium, but also to have them flourish and reproduce, should be one of the prime aims of this hobby so that the natural world is not damaged any further.

The international laws on endangered species, such as those dealing with the export and import of stony corals, are a paradox. Many species of soft and stony corals can now be reproduced in an aquarium. In comparison, the daily damage that is being done to the natural coral reefs through land reclamation and road building, using coral rubble and coral blocks as a substrate, is unbelievable. The statistics are freely available. Consider that one or two tons of a particular species of live coral is probably sufficient to satisfy the requirements of all aquarists around the world for a year – more so if they are continually reproduced through cuttings. But then consider that literally thousands of tons of that same species are being destroyed each week through landfill programmes, road and bridge building and the like, then the situation is brought into some sort of perspective.

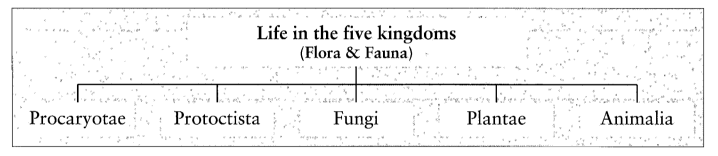

Life in the five kingdoms
(Flora & Fauna)

Procaryotae   Protoctista   Fungi   Plantae   Animalia

The first kingdom, Procaryotae, contains about 5,000 species of bacteria and blue algae (cyanobacteria). In part two of this book, the important role of bacteria in the success of a marine aquarium was discussed, as was the role of blue algae in a maturing aquarium. The procaryotes are important and essential to the balance of life as a whole.

In the second kingdom, Protoctista, there are more than 70,000 species. These are made up of one-celled organisms (protozoa), water fungi, slime fungi, ciliates, flagellates, infusoria and amoeba. These are the "good guys" and the "bad guys" as far as the aquarist is concerned. The good guys are the ciliates and infusoria, which can be utilized as microscopic food for newly born fry. The bad guys are the dinoflagellates and parasitic protozoans, such as *Amyloodinium ocellatum*, the marine velvet disease that is so common among aquarium fishes. There are the fast-swimming protozoans such as *Brooklynella hostilis*, which are probably the major cause of fish deaths in a marine or reef aquarium, especially with newly introduced specimens that supposedly die of shock.

Fungi, the third kingdom, consist of well in excess of 100,000 species of fungi, mushrooms, truffles, toadstools and various types of skin fungi. One particular group of more than 20,000 species in about 400 genera lives in symbiosis with green or blue algae. The algae provide the fungi with organic nutrition and, in return, the fungi provide the algae with essential minerals and water.

The fourth kingdom, Plantae, contains almost 400,000 species. These are the mosses and ferns, the higher plants and trees, and they are a major contributory factor to the success of life on Earth. Marine plants and algae also play an important part in the marine aquarium hobby. These were covered in some detail in part three of this book, so they will not be discussed further here.

The fifth and final kingdom, Animalia, is made up of an estimated 1 million different species. No one knows for certain, since new discoveries are continually being made. The kingdom is complex and not only includes all mammals (including ourselves), birds, fishes, lizards and amphibious creatures, but it also includes all invertebrate animals. These are the animals that do not have a backbone. They are in the vast majority on this Earth. Their forms are extremely varied and they encompass all insects, corals, sponges, worms, molluscs and crustaceans. This kingdom will be discussed next.

Kingdom: Animalia

The million or so creatures in the animal kingdom are classified into the 36 phyla, shown in the chart here (*see below*). Of these, 28 are of some interest to the marine aquarist. Only one phylum, Chordata, contains vertebrate animals – animals with backbones.

The number of vertebrate animals is currently estimated at around 50,000 species. The other 35 phyla, that is an estimated 950,000 different species, encompass the invertebrates. These are creatures that do not possess a vertebrate structure within their bodies, a lack of spinal column if you like. They are extremely diversified and occur on land and in fresh water as well as in the sea.

None of the invertebrate animals are more colourful than those encountered on the living reefs in all the warm seas of the world. In the pages that follow, some of these phyla will be dealt with in a superficial way, since they are not what would normally be thought of as species for display in an aquarium. Nevertheless, they are sometimes important to the marine aquarist who wishes to establish a good-quality, synthetic tank ecosystem. The phyla dealt with in more detail represent those colourful animals that are normally associated with life on a coral reef.

Invertebrates

Of the 36 phyla in the animal kingdom, representatives of 28 of them are to be found in marine environments. Not all of these can be seen with the naked eye, however, but all are worth mentioning. With regard to the species descriptions, once again size plays a minor role or none at all. Does you measure the size of a single coral polyp or the whole coral head or colony? How high does a sponge grow? An unanswerable question since in some areas it may be encrusting while in others the same species may be growing as tall, branched colonies. Sizes, where they are relevant, will be given within the species descriptions and not as a heading. Common names have not been included – "red sea star", for example, means nothing as there are so many different ones. The distribution of invertebrates is important to those who wish to set up, say, a Red Sea aquarium, or to those who want to know the geographic origin of a specific species, so this information has been retained as the heading "Range".

Feeding is crucial. Many invertebrate species have special requirements; others can survive on their zooxanthellae algae. Therefore, this has been introduced as a feature and comes under the heading "Feeding requirements".

The heading "Aquarium suitability" has also been retained for the species that are formally described, along with an at-a-glance indicator of the degree of difficulty for the beginner. This is, as it was for fish, as follows:

O – Easy (good for beginners and experienced aquarists)
OO – Moderately easy (good for aquarists with 6 months' experience or more)
OOO – Moderately difficult (only suitable for experienced aquarists)
OOOO – Very difficult (requires optimal aquarium conditions for success)
OOOOO – Almost impossible (suitable only for the most experienced aquarist)

The animal kingdom

Kingdom	Phylum
Animalia	Placozoa
	Porifera
	Mesozoa
	Monoblastoidea
	Cnidaria
	Ctenophora
	Gnathostomulida
	Nemertea
	Nematoda
	Nematomorpha
	Gastrotricha
	Rotifera
	Acanthocephala
	Kampozoa
	Kinorhyncha
	Priapulida
	Loricifera
	Annelida
	Echiurida
	Sipunculida
	Pogonophora
	Cycliophora
	Vestimentifera
	Arthropoda
	Onychophora
	Tardigrada
	Pentastomida
	Mollusca
	Brachiopoda
	Bryozoa
	Phoronida
	Chaetognatha
	Echinodermata
	Hemichordata
	Chordata

Phylum: Placozoa (trichoplax)

This is the simplest multicellular animal that exists and it is the single known species of this phylum. This tiny animal has been named *Trichoplax adherens*. Its body measures only 0.25 to 2mm in diameter and it looks similar to a planula larva. Nevertheless, it is important. It represents the missing link, if you like, between the single-celled forms of life on Earth and the higher orders in evolutionary development. This is because of its many celled composition.

According to Robert Brons, who rediscovered this species, it usually occurs where there is an abundant growth of algae on the aquarium glass, such as is the case when the water is rich in nutrients. Brons also stated that he was able to observe large populations of these animals feeding on the thin algal layer, presumably also ingesting other organisms such as protozoa, copepods and nematodes. Repetitive "blooms" of this species seemed to coincide with high nitrate levels in the aquarium. The body of *Trichoplax adherens* is covered with small cilia

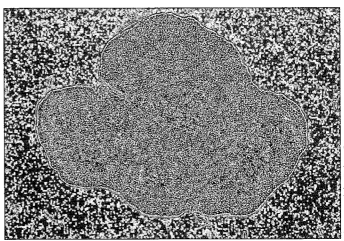
Trichoplax adherens

and is filled with fluid. Sexual reproduction is possible through the production of eggs and sperm, but asexual reproduction is also carried out.

Phylum: Porifera (sponges)

The phylum consists of three classes with seven subclasses and 21 orders. There are more than 100 families and between 8,500 and 10,000 species.

Fossilized records have shown that the history of sponges dates back to the Precambrian period, 700 million years ago. Many species of true sponges that exist today have their roots back in the Cambrian period – 540 million years ago. They existed then, before the first fish and before the first higher invertebrates.

When the planet contained only two land masses, Laurasia and Gondwanaland, the sponges reached their peak of development. This was in the Ordovician period, about 450 million years ago. For about 1 million years,

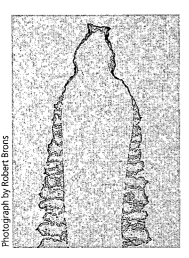

Enlarged cross-section of a calcareous sponge of the genus Sycon. *The osculum at the top is clearly visible.*

from the Ordovician period until the late Devonian, they were responsible for reef building and many fossilized examples remain. At the start of the Palaeozoic, the reef-building corals of the phylum Cnidaria overtook them.

As a group, the sponges are primitive yet complex creatures. They have run parallel to the rest of the animal kingdom, but have never become integrated into it. Until the mid 8th century they were considered to be marine plants rather than animals.

Porifera means "pore-bearer". These animals are sessile filter feeders found attached to hard substrate. Although they are multicellular, with the cells often being specialized, these are uncoordinated. This means that they do not have the ability to organize these cells into tissue and organs. They do not have a stomach, nor do they possess a nervous system or sense organs. Instead they have a water-current system that allows water to pass through channels in the body so that oxygen can be utilized from the water. In addition, food is filtered out.

The water current is developed within the sponge itself. The beating of whip-like hairs, or flagellae, located on the inner body walls, draws water through numerous pores known as ostia or sometimes porocyta. These are arranged in collar-like cells (choanocytes). The water and other waste products are expelled through one or more openings, or oscula (singular: osculum).

Organization of the three classes is based on the chemical composition of the crystalline elements (spicules) and the organic composition of the fibrous construction that forms the skeleton. Body forms within the species may be variable and are dependent on the water current, depth, amount and type of nutrition and geographic location.

Sponges show amazing regenerative abilities. A small fragment can be broken off and placed elsewhere on the reef and it will grow into a complete individual. The host sponge quickly recovers by rounding off the broken edge, which eventually grows again. The chambers and channels within the body of the sponge often become homes for small fishes and invertebrates, such as small shrimps.

They are represented in all seas, from the tropical latitudes to the polar regions, but keeping sponges in an aquarium is by no means easy and should be attempted only by experience aquarists. Deep-water species are especially difficult to keep alive, and a dying sponge often releases poisonous substances into the water that can kill most aquarium inhabitants. Loss of surface colour is often the first sign that the sponge is in trouble. Avoid brightly coloured specimens, since these are usually the difficult ones. Water current, lighting and nutrition all play an important role in the success with these animals.

In deciding which sponges to include in this book, most of the brightly coloured and exotically formed species have been avoided because of the difficulty they represent. More important for the reef aquarium are those species that turn up on live rock and take a hold in the tank without any special care.

Class: Calcarea (calcareous sponges)

The class Calcarea (= Calcispongiae) is small and contains only about 50 species. They are sponges that have skeletons composed of three- or four-rayed calcareous spicules. These consist of calcium carbonate in the form of calcite. Some species are drab in colour, others may be yellow, white, pastel coloured or almost colourless.

Calcareous sponges occur in tropical and temperate seas but never in fresh water. They often found on the underside of rocks and in small crevices and caves and most species are small. Many of them are encrusting, usually in hollows or indentations in rock; others are cushion-shaped, sometimes with branches leading away from the main body to form another cushion. Sponges of the genus *Sycon* are often vase-shaped (*see opposite*). They are seldom taller than 1in (2.5cm) and are often seen in an aquarium on live rock. Some species can be bright yellow and almost spherical in form. Several species are attach themselves to the rock with a stalk, rather like some species of algae.

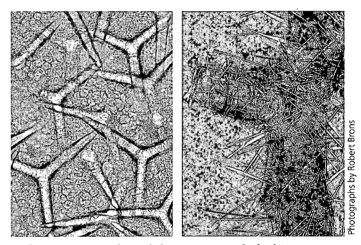

Photographs by Robert Brons

Calcareous sponges have skeletons composed of calcium carbonate spicules in the form of calcite. The photograph on the left shows the spicule form of a sponge of the genus Leucosolenia. *The one on the right is its skeleton form.*

Order: Leucosolenida

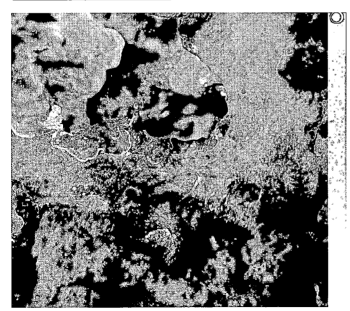

Leucosolenia sp.

Family: Leucosoleniidae
Range: Caribbean, Tropical West Atlantic
Description: The colouration of this species varies between pastel-blue and pale greyish-blue. It is encrusting to cushion-shaped depending on the water turbulence and the substrate. There is a series of visible channels that radiate from the oscula, reminiscent of many species of Demospongia (such as *Achinoe tenacior*, which comes from the Mediterranean).
Feeding requirements: In a mature aquarium, this species will flourish without any special attention to feeding.
Aquarium suitability: Small encrusting sponges such as this one often appear on rocks in a well-kept aquarium. The water should not have more than 20mg/litre nitrate present, otherwise they will very quickly die off. The species prefers a shadowy existence, particularly on porous rocks.

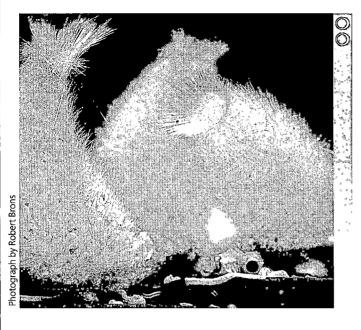

Photograph by Robert Brons

Sycon sp.

Family: Sycettidae
Range: Entire Tropical Indo-Pacific, Red Sea
Description: There are several similar species, both in the Indo-Pacific and in the tropical West Atlantic. These small urn-shaped sponges are quite fragile. The body often looks like a tiny, elongated furry ball with a hairy opening at the top. This is, in fact, the osculum. They are essentially shallow-water species found under overhangs below intertidal zones and in deeper water. They seldom exceed 1in (2.5cm).
Feeding requirements: A filter feeder that normally derives enough food from the water and needs no special care.
Aquarium suitability: This and other similar species are a common sight in mature reef aquariums. They seem to prefer strong lighting and well-oxygenated water with a strong current flow to bring food to them.

Class: Demospongiae (true sponges)

The largest and most widely distributed class of sponges. Sizes range from the microscopic to massive deep-water sponges of more than 6ft (2m) in diameter. One family, Spongillidae, is the only group that occurs in fresh water.

They are often highly coloured and take on bizarre forms. Some species are even flower- or tree-like in appearance. The body can vary from red to violet, and there are also species that are almost black or creamy-white. Some species in this class vary from reddish violet to yellow, so colour plays a secondary role in identification. Species form is also an unreliable characteristic, since some can alter their growth direction and shape.

Take into account that, on the reef, some species grow only where there is shadow, while others flourish in the reef shallows in direct sunlight. There are species that seem to do well in water that is turbulent, whereas others do not. Furthermore, it is wrong to think that because sponges are filter feeders they need well-oxygenated water with a strong current flow, since many thrive in lagoons where there is little water movement.

Many brightly coloured sponges can be kept only in nutrient-rich water. However, in these conditions most stony corals will start to die. This means that most sponges cannot be kept effectively or successfully in a reef aquarium because of the danger to other invertebrates.

The transport and transfer of sponges is also a difficult process. It must be stressed that sponges should not be removed from the water, even for a short period, otherwise they will loose their siphoning ability and part, if not all, of the cell tissue will eventually die.

Order: Hadromerida

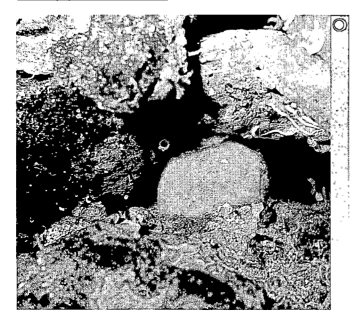

Tethya aurantium

Family: Tethyidae
Range: Circumtropical
Description: This species is often spherical in form and the surface is covered with hair-like papillae. The colouration ranges from yellowish-orange to red (often orange-red). They form small balls on the underside of rocks and in crevices in reef shallows, especially in areas where there is a high silt content. The size can vary from 1 to 3in (2.5 to 7.5cm).
Feeding requirements: A filter feeder that requires no special feeding in an aquarium.
Aquarium suitability: This is one of the easier species to keep and requires no special care. This and other similar species will often find their way into the aquarium on live rock. They prefer deep crevices and shadowy holes where detritus gathers.

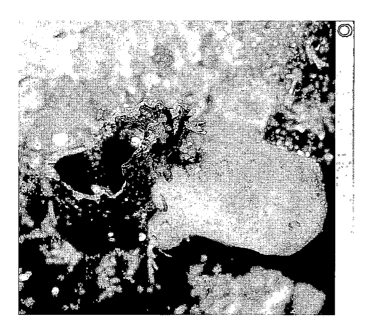

Cliona cf. *caribboea*

Family: Clionidae
Range: Tropical West Atlantic, Caribbean
Description: This and others of this genus are known as boring sponges. They have the ability to attach themselves to calcium carbonate substrata, such as live rock, shells and live coral, by giving off acidic secretions. Using these, the sponge is able to dissolve the limestone and replace it with a multiple-armed root system of sponge tissue. In many areas they are responsible for massive damage to coral reefs, which gradually become porous. This species is chrome yellow with slightly raised oscula.
Feeding requirements: A filter feeder. Needs no special care.
Aquarium suitability: Small specimens are often imported on living rock from the Caribbean region and the Florida Keys. This is a slow-growing species that is attractive and easy to keep in a reef tank.

Order: Axinellida

Axinella sp.

Family: Axinellidae
Range: Tropical and subtropical East Atlantic, Mediterranean
Description: The oscula of this species of sponges are not as clearly visible as with most other species. The sponge forms knobbly growths and dichotomous branches on hard substrate in areas of strong water currents. They are to be found under rock overhangs and in caves and grottoes, often in semidarkness. The colouration can vary from bright yellow to deep orange.
Feeding requirements: Although this, like other sponges, is a filter feeder, it requires an enormous amount of nutrients to flourish. This is best supplied in an aquarium set-up with daily doses of invertebrate food of a sort especially produced for this type of animal.
Aquarium suitability: This and similar species are difficult to keep for any length of time in an aquarium. They require strong water movement that is well oxygenated in order to survive and grow. Large specimens are best kept in a sponge-only tank. For the best success with these species, large specimens should be cut up into segments of between 1 and 2in (2.5 and 5cm) and placed under overhangs or in crevices, making sure that there is a good water flow around them. Check regularly to ensure that they do not become covered with silt or detritus. Occasionally fanning a plastic spatula around the sponge in order to dislodge any foreign matter is the best way to prevent this situation occurring. This species prefers the shadows and so should never be placed under direct aquarium lighting, such as strong fluorescent tubes or metal halides.

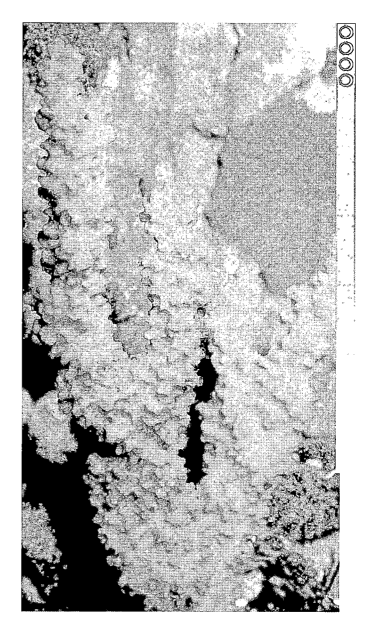

Phylum: Cnidaria (coelenterates)

Cnidarian animals are divided into four classes. There are about 10,000 known species within this phylum and their forms are extremely diverse. In all cases, the body possesses radial symmetry – ostensibly at least. The structure is very primitive and normally consists of three layers: an outer wall (epidermis), an inner wall (gastrodermis) and between these is the jelly-like body bulk of the animal (mesogloea). There is a central stomach (gastrovascular cavity) that leads to an opening surrounded by tentacles. This opening serves as both the mouth and the anus for ejecting body waste. The tentacles vary in number between species and are equipped with poisonous stinging cells (nematocysts), which are used to capture food and also as a defence.

The nematocysts, or cnidoblasts as they are sometimes known, are held encapsulated within the epidermis, gastrodermis and tentacles. On contact they are triggered, sending out hollow barbed threads armed with a powerful poison to debilitate their victim. In many cases, the cnidoblast is not strong enough to penetrate the human skin so people are not affected. This is the case with most sea anemones and corals. There are exceptions, however. The hydroid known as the Portuguese man-of-war (*Physalia physalia*) is a hazard when currents carry it into coastal waters. This and similar species can inflict serious and painful wounds. By contrast, the Australian sea wasps (*Chironex fleckeri* and *Chiropsalmus quadrigatus*), from the class Cubozoa, can kill a person within a few minutes.

There are two morphological forms: the medusa and the polyp. Many species have both a medusa and a polyp stage, others assume only one morphological form, or one in which the second form is greatly restricted. Medusae are small, often translucent, free-swimming animals that seldom exceed a an inch or so (about 2.5cm) in diameter.

They are usually bell-shaped or umbrella-formed with numerous tentacles hanging down from the bell. Often, there is a thickened margin (velum) to the bell that, through muscular action, is flexed and contracted to produce a swimming action. The mouth is situated on the underside of the bell or umbrella and leads directly to the gastrovascular cavity.

The second morphological form of these creatures is that of the polyp. In this case, the animal is sessile and stands on a pedal base, usually attached or buried in the substratum. Unlike the medusae, the tentacles and mouth are directed upward. Sea anemones have a typical polyp form. Some species, such as the scleractinids, produce hard, stony skeletons of calcium carbonate around their bodies and form large colonies. These are known as stony or reef-building corals. Many of the species live in a symbiotic relationship with zooxanthellae algae, which can produce an amazing colouration within the species concerned. Iridescent greens, yellows and pinks are usual.

Class: Hydrozoa (hydroids)

This class contains three orders but only one of these, Hydroidea, is of interest to marine aquarists, since it contains species that are often encountered on coral reefs. Many of the species are minute and often go unnoticed, both on the coral reef and in the aquarium. Others form large colonies that are difficult to overlook. *Millepora* and *Stylaster* corals are hydroid colonies that secrete a calcium carbonate skeleton. In many areas they are important reef-builders. These are the fire corals of ill repute to many swimmers and divers. Some species form beautiful but sometimes painfully dangerous feather-like plumes in

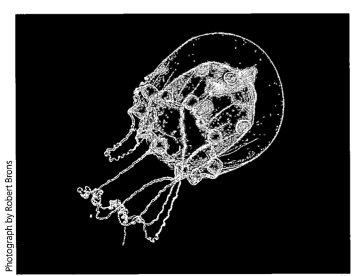

The medusa of Campanularia johnstoni *is shown here (the orange-brown spots are the gonads).*

*The attached male medusae of a hydroid (*Eudendrium sp.*) releasing sperm.*

Gonothyraea loveni.

colonies on the reef. These are normally of the genera
Aglaophenia, Lytocarpus or *Sertularia,* but there are
also many others.

There are two suborders, the Athecata and the Thecata.
The sexual reproduction of these species is complicated,
with the parent colony or individual producing asexual
budding in the form of medusae. These may become free-
swimming or remain attached to the parent colony. This
generation then reproduces sexually with the resultant
planula larvae dispersing to form new individuals or
colonies. In some instances, the colonies are formed
through asexual division or budding, but a new colony
can only occur through this medusa stage. In this way,
there are alternating sexual and asexual series of
generations. In the suborder Athecata the body of the
hydroid polyps is naked and uncovered, although many of
the species build calcareous tubes into which they can
withdraw whenever necessity dictates.

In the case of the suborder Thecata, chitinous (horn-
like) tubes are present around the central stems or bodies
of the animals. Species of both suborders are often
encountered in reef aquariums but these are usually very
minute. Nevertheless, they belong to a good ecosystem
and have their importance in a mature aquarium. Larger
hydroid colonies, such as those of the families
Stylasteridae, Milleporidae and Plumulariidae, are seldom,
if ever, available as they have small polyps and are difficult
to provide with enough food. Moreover, they do not
possess the zooxanthellae that many stony corals of the
order Scleractinia have. These take the nutrients that they
require from the algae without additional feeding. But this
should not be taken as a veto for any experienced
aquarists who want to try their hand at keeping some of
these attractive species.

*The two photographs show that, although sometimes minute,
hydroids are both impressive and beautiful.* Campanularia
johnstoni *(top) and* Obelia geniculata *(above) are both shown
with their respective medusae.*

Class: *Scyphozoa* (jellyfish)

Jellyfish are widely distributed and are found in all the seas and regions of the world. They are wholly marine-living animals and are usually free-swimming. The umbrella of the jellyfish is normally much larger than that of its hydrozoan cousins and it contains up to 94 per cent water. One species, the lion's mane jellyfish (*Cyanea capillata*), is known to have an umbrella with a diameter of well in excess of 40in (1m) with up to 800 tentacles that trail behind it for many yards.

The margin of the umbrella does not have a velum. Instead, it is often lobed with groups of tentacles hanging down. These lobes contain sensory organs in the form of light-sensitive cells. Although jellyfish are poor swimmers, and are very much at the mercy of the ocean currents, they do achieve some sort of propulsion. This is effected through a pulsing expansion and contraction of the bell margin. A primitive form of steering is achieved through the aid of the light-sensitive organs on the margin. The mouth is generally at the end of a movable stalk. This opens directly into the stomach, which has four lobes. These contain gastric filaments that produce the enzymes required for digestion.

Almost any form of prey makes a suitable meal for these carnivorous creatures. It is usually trapped and stung into immobility by a jellyfish's nematocyst-armed tentacles. Small fishes form a large part of their staple diet, although some species have a mucus coating on the upper surface of the umbrella where plankton becomes entrapped. They are then transferred to the mouth. Many species are capable of inflicting serious wounds to people. Always take care when specimens are washed up on beaches, since the nematocysts remain active long after the creature has died.

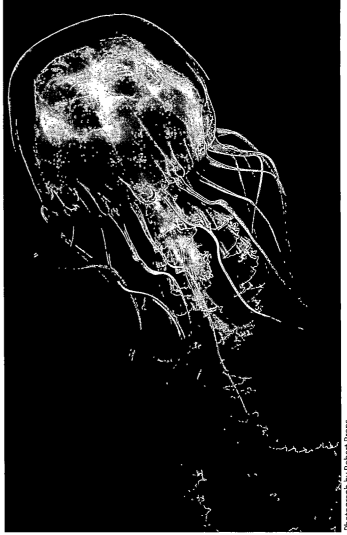

Photograph by Robert Brons

Chrysaora *sp. from the order Semaestomae is seen here in an aquarium. This and similar species of jellyfish are difficult to keep in captivity for any length of time and require special care.*

Order: *Coronatae*

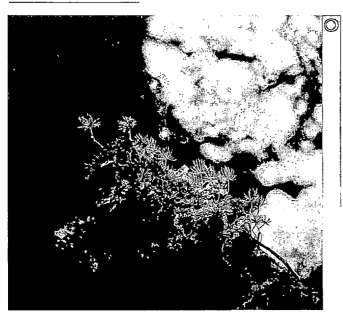

Nausithoe cf. *punctata*

Family: Nausithoidae
Range: Tropical Indo-Pacific
Description: This is the polyp stage of a jellyfish. The polyp sits in a horn-like tube, which is thin and flexible. In both the medusa and polyp stages, zooxanthellae are present and give them their colouration. The mouth of the polyp is surrounded with numerous tentacles that sway in the current. The medusa (ephyra) larvae are formed like a stack of coins, one on top of the other, while they are attached to the polyp, and they are released one by one to form small, flattened medusae.
Feeding requirements: This species lives on planktonic organisms and its own zooxanthellae.
Aquarium suitability: The polyp are usually brought into a tank on live rock. They are relatively hardy and long-lived and, under metal-halide lighting, will form attractive carpet-like growths.

Class: Anthozoa (anemones, corals)

Species from this class are by far the most important invertebrate animals as far as reef tank aquarists are concerned. Within this group are all the soft corals, gorgonian corals, stony corals, zooanthids, sea anemones and corallimorpharians. It is a large class with nine orders in two subclasses and more than 6,500 species. Because of their importance to both marine and reef aquariums, they form the central core of this part of the book. Since this is a very varied group; there is a short description at the beginning of each new order to avoid confusion

Anemones and corals differ from the previous two classes in that there is no medusa stage in their life cycle. They are predominantly sessile creatures and reproduction may be asexual or sexual. The polyps can be of two different sexes or hermaphroditic. Asexual budding, pedal laceration and longitudinal fission are common to this group. The fertilized eggs develop into larvae, which are planktonic for a short time. The larvae then develop directly into junior polyps. The polyps may have an external or internal skeleton. The external skeleton usually consists of calcium carbonate, which the polyp produces. The oral opening in the centre of the polyp leads into a gastrovascular tube or, in the case of sea anemones, through a short gullet into a gastrovascular cavity. Some species of Anthozoans feed on planktonic organisms or, in the case of larger polyps, on small invertebrates and fishes. Many other species do not feed at all, relying on zooxanthellae to provide them with their necessary nutrients.

Subclass: Octocorallia (= Alcyonaria)

Three of the nine orders belong to this subclass. One of the characteristics of this group is that the polyps do not grow as single individuals throughout their lives. Instead they live exclusively as colonies, sometimes forming large structures. The colony is developed asexually with the daughter-polyps being produced by vegetative budding (cloning). The clones and parent polyps join to make up the structure of the coral. Another important common characteristic of this group is that the polyps all have eight tentacles (hence Octocorallia).

The first order, Alcyonacea, encompasses what are commonly referred to as "soft corals". This seems to be a bad choice of name since some of them are far from soft.

Order: Alcyonacea (soft corals, leather corals)

The order encompasses five suborders. Not only is it the most diverse order within this phylum, it is also the most controversial in biological terms. The polyps form colonies on hard substrata, often without a skeleton as such. This has given rise to the terms "soft coral" or "leather coral". In fact, there is what can be termed a rudimentary skeleton in some species. The first suborder, Protoalcyonaria, contains deep-water species that are unsuitable for an aquarium and so will not be mentioned further. There is a certain amount of controversy over revisions in the classification of the second suborder, Stolonifera. This is an interesting group that has important species to contribute to aquarium life.

Alcyoniina, the third suborder, has a large number of species. These are the true soft corals, or leather corals as they are sometimes known. They are popular subjects for marine aquarists, especially those that can be kept by beginners. The fourth and fifth suborders, Scleraxonia and Holaxonia, are dealt with as a single group because for the average hobbyist there is little difference in appearance. These suborders incorporate sea whips and sea fans.

Suborder: Stolonifera In this suborder, colonies are organized along primitive lines. Instead of having a coenenchymal (mesogloea embedded with sclerites) base, the polyps are reproduced asexually from a stolon matrix or a thin crust. Gastrodermal tubes that run through this matrix interconnect the polyps. In this way, each individual polyp can provide nutrition for the whole colony. The genus *Tubipora* (red organ pipe corals) is an exception here and is somewhat unique.

These corals have a basal crust from which the polyps arise. A red calcium carbonate tube surrounds the polyps. Stolons interconnect the tubes near the upper edges and eventually become fused together to form a flat platform. From this, new polyps arise and form a second platform and so on until the colony resembles a set of organ pipes.

Suborder: Alcyoniina All soft corals have a rough, leathery look and texture due to the body mass being embedded with calcium carbonate spicules (sclerites). These tiny pieces of calcite are considered to be an important factor in the identification of the species because of their form.

The form of a soft coral can vary considerably, and even within the species to a certain extent. There are the massive forms, such as *Sarcophyton* spp., that sit on a broad pedal base, reminiscent of sea anemones. Then there are the finger or lobed forms of the genus *Sinularia* that have certain similarities with the *Acropora* group of stony corals. There are also gorgonian forms such as *Nephthyigorgia* spp. Finally there are those that are the branched tree-like forms with a tall, stem-like trunk.

Most of the massive species of this group feed from the production of their own zooxanthellae. Therefore, in an aquarium no specific feeding is necessary. They do, however, need sufficient light so that these algae can grow and replenish themselves. With light there is often the danger of algal growth over the surface of the colony. In addition, with wave action and water movement there is the question of silt settling over the surface of the polyps. This is no problem for these creatures, which have the ability to produce a shiny, skin-like secretion over the feeding surface of the colony within a few hours. Periodically this is shed, taking with it all the sediment and algae and leaving fresh feeding surfaces.

Suborders: Scleraxonia and Holaxonia These can be handled as one group, since, taxonomically,there is little difference between them. These are corals that may be tree-like or fan-shaped or even resemble a candelabra. They may form dense, bush-like colonies or, like the sea whips, form long, spindly individual shapes.

In the suborder Scleraxonia there are often sclerites present, which may or may not be fused together. Because of this, these species are often brittle and cannot live in turbulent water. Holaxonia contains extremely flexible corals that bend in strong water currents or turbulence. In both cases the central core or axis is covered by the coenenchyme, which carries the gastrovascular network of canals from whose walls the polyps develop.

Only in recent years have gorgonian corals been kept successfully in aquariums, although they have been available for a long time. Those species that derive most of their nutrition from the production of their own symbiotic zooxanthellae require strong lighting of the correct type, but they do not need to be fed very often, if at all. Those species that do not possess zooxanthellae and need to capture planktonic organisms, are more difficult to keep. They require a lighting that conforms to their natural habitat, and this can vary greatly. Thus, you must vary the light intensity according to the species. All of them, however, require constant hand feeding of plankton or plankton-like food, such as brine shrimp or Daphnia.

Briareum asbestinum

Family: Tubiporidae
Range: Caribbean, from Florida to Brazil
Description: The sclerites of this species are deep red. The open polyps are greyish-brown and the stolon matrix is often deep purplish-red when the polyps are retracted. In some examples this can also be light brown tinged with red. Originally this species was regarded as a gorgonian coral because of its frequent encrustation of dead or dying gorgonian skeletons. It was thought that this animal produced the skeleton. This theory has now been disproved. It is an encrusting species that will colonize any rock, gorgonian or coral branch.
Feeding requirements: Lives from the production of its own zooxanthellae and so does not require feeding.
Aquarium suitability: This is an easy species to keep in a reef tank, providing it is equipped with strong lighting.

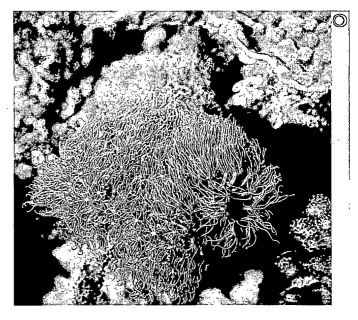

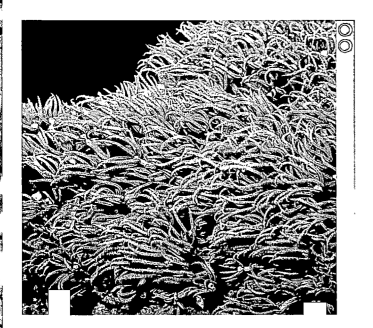

Briareum (Pachyclavularia) violacea

Family: Tubiporidae
Range: Tropical Indo-Pacific
Description: This species has often been described as *Clavularia viridis*, both in aquarium books and on dealers' lists. It has also been described as *Pachyclavularia violacea*, which is a name that has no scientific standing. Its form and habits are similar to the preceding species, with the exception that this species produces short, irregular polyp tubes that are attached to the deep-red stolon. The polyps are light brown in colour and can have a peach-coloured or green fluorescence.
Feeding requirements: Lives from the production of its own zooxanthellae.
Aquarium suitability: With strong lighting and good water quality this attractive species is easy to keep and can colonize much of the aquarium decoration within a short space of time.

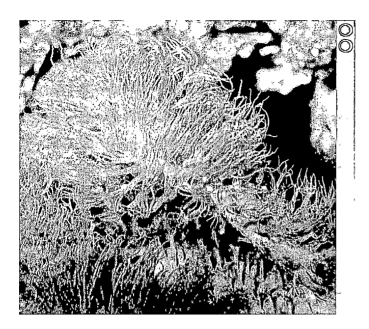

Briareum sp.

Family: Tubiporidae
Range: Caribbean, from Florida to Brazil
Description: This is an encrusting species that often colonizes dead gorgonians. The stolon matrix is compact and creamy-brown in colour. The polyps are brown and when they are extended they are long and hair-like. This species is often confused with the similar, but unrelated species *Erythropodium caribaeorum*.
Feeding requirements: Occasionally this coral will capture small planktonic organisms, but it lives mainly on the production of its own zooxanthellae.
Aquarium suitability: No feeding is required for this species. It will not tolerate high nitrate levels or low-intensity lighting. It should be kept in a tank with a strong water flow and with a combination of high-intensity metal-halide and actinic lighting.

Tubipora musica

Family: Tubiporidae
Range: Widespread throughout the Indo-Pacific
Description: The skeleton resembles organ-pipes and is bright to deep red in colour. The polyps are variable in form and colour. They may be green, white, yellow or light brown, differing between colonies. There is also a marked difference in polyp size with some "species". It is suspected that there are at least three species within this group. This genus needs a lot more work.
Feeding requirements: Feeds solely on the production of its own zooxanthellae.
Aquarium suitability: This coral is one of the more difficult to keep in an aquarium, and it is definitely not for beginners. The colony should be placed as high as possible in the aquarium, directly under high-intensity lighting. There should also be a strong water current flowing over its surface for the best results.

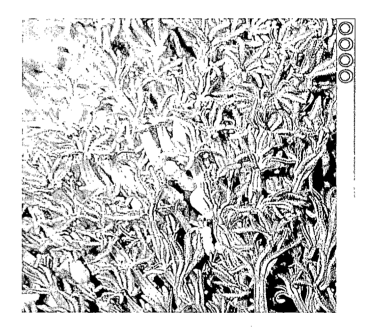

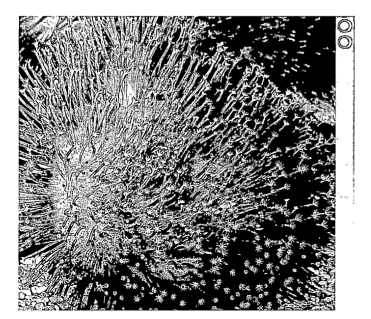

Sarcophyton ehrenbergi

Family: Alcyoniidae
Range: Tropical Indo-Pacific
Description: The species often forms dish-shaped, sometimes elongated colonies with long polyps that have eight small, white-tipped tentacles. The colouration of the polyps can be brown or green and the disc and column pale cream or white. In many areas of the Indo-Pacific this species is ubiquitous. They are to be found growing in reef channels and on reef drop-offs, as well as in shallow lagoons and on reef crests.
Feeding requirements: Obtains nourishment from its own zooxanthellae but also occasionally feeds on small planktonic organisms.
Aquarium suitability: Strong light and water movement are desirable. Can be given weekly feedings of frozen plankton when the polyps are extended, but this is not a necessity.

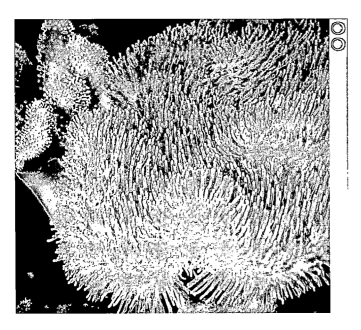

Sarcophyton glaucum

Family: Alcyoniidae
Range: Tropical Indo-Pacific, Red Sea
Description: The colony form of this species is variable but generally the disc is not as convoluted as in S. *trocheliophorum.* The pedal base is broad and the polyps fairly long when fully extended. The sclerites at the surface of the trunk are shaped like a tapering spindle. Inside the trunk they are double-tapered spindles. The body colour is light yellowish-tan, often with fluorescent-green tips to the polyps.
Feeding requirements: Lives predominantly from the production of its own zooxanthellae, but may occasionally capture other minute organisms to supplement this.
Aquarium suitability: Provide a strong water current and sufficient lighting and this species will do well without any supplementary feeding.

Sarcophyton trocheliophorum

Family: Alcyoniidae
Range: Tropical Indo-Pacific, Red Sea
Description: The name of this species is often used by laypeople for any similar looking species that are found on offer in dealers' tanks. This species is, however, not as often imported as most others of this genus. It grows quite large, up to 40in (1m) in diameter, and has a strongly convoluted pedal disc. The extended polyps are shorter and finer than the preceding species. This particular animal is often found in deeper water in large fields of several hundred individuals.
Feeding requirements: It feeds almost solely on the production of its zooxanthellae, therefore no additional feeding is necessary.
Aquarium suitability: This species can be a problem if the light composition is wrong. Provide metal-halide and actinic lighting and it will grow quite well in a reef aquarium.

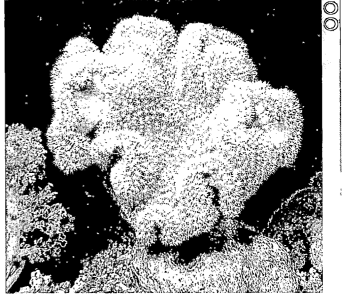

Photograph by Siegfried Krumbugel

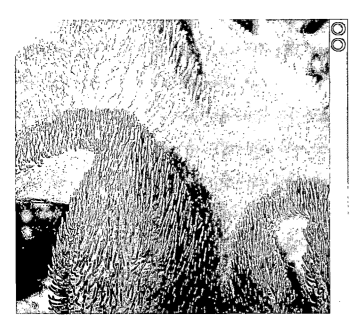

Sarcophyton sp. (tenuispiculatum?)

Family: Alcyoniidae
Range: Tropical Indo-Pacific
Description: This is one of the most attractive species in this genus. The polyps are fairly long when they are fully extended. The colony can be disc-shaped or formed into a shallow bowl, not unlike S. *ehrenbergi,* with which it shares many similarities. Species within this order often look the same, but a, close look at the sclerites within the colony often differentiates the species. Even so, this can be an unreliable way to determine the species.
Feeding requirements: Lives almost solely from its own zooxanthellae, so no additional feeding is necessary.
Aquarium suitability: This species survives equally well under fluorescent and metal-halide lighting. Colonies should be placed in an area of the aquarium that has a moderate to light degree of water movement.

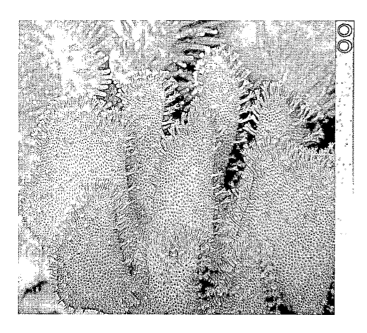

Lobophytum sp.

Family: Alcyoniidae
Range: Tropical Indo-Pacific
Description: Specimens from this genus are difficult to identify down to species level with certainty, a problem compounded by the fact that the form of the colony can vary greatly within species. The example shown here is a case in point: depending on geographical location and amount of light and water movement, it will adapt its form to suit its environment.
Feeding requirements: Its own zooxanthellae appear to be its sole source of nutrition.
Aquarium suitability: Colonies of this species are often imported. They may be finger-formed, disc-shaped or have undulating margins, such as the one here. They are all easy to keep if a moderate water movement is provided along with a combination of "daylight" and actinic fluorescent lighting.

Sinularia brassica

Family: Alcyoniidae
Range: Tropical Indo-Pacific
Description: The pedal base is broad and the branches are somewhat flattened. These may vary considerably in length and shape. They can be short and lobe-like or branched, resembling a prickly cactus. The sclerites are club-formed and stubby at the surface of the pedal base and under the branches. Within the trunk they are shaped like a double-tapered spindle.
Feeding requirements: Feeds predominantly on the production of its own zooxanthellae, but it may supplement this with organic compounds that it removes from the water.
Aquarium suitability: This is a hardy species that can withstand quite high levels of nitrate, therefore it is ideal for a marine (fish-only) aquarium. This is one of the species that can be recommended for the complete beginner.

Sinularia dura

Family: Alcyoniidae
Range: Tropical Indo-Pacific
Description: This and S. brassica, the preceding species, are considered by some to be synonymous despite outward appearances. The form of the sclerites would tend to endorse this theory. This species is looked on as being the senior synonym of the two. Its form is unmistakable and it is the easiest of the soft corals to identify. The body is lobed, like a flattened cup, and the colonies often overlap. The colouration is cream to dull orange-brown. The polyps are small and do not rise much above the level of the coenenchyme.
Feeding requirements: Feeds from its own zooxanthellae and other organic compounds.
Aquarium suitability: S. dura often turns up on live rock and will soon grow into attractive colonies requiring no special care.

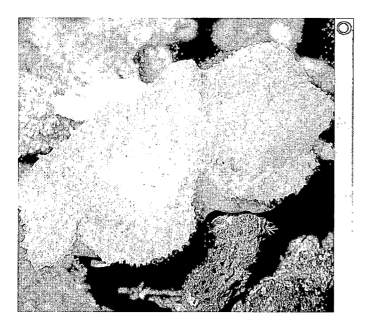

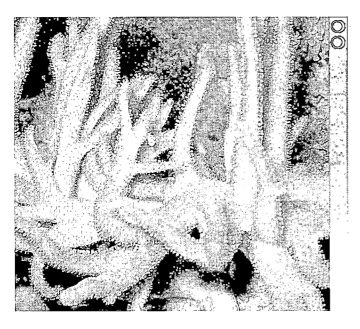

Sinularia sp.

Family: Alcyoniidae
Range: Central Indo-Pacific, Indo-West Pacific
Description: This species is frequently referred to as *Sinularia magnifica* on dealers' lists, but the name is probably invalid. The colony is similar in form to some species of *Acropora* coral and can grow to 20in (51cm) in diameter. The colouration ranges from light yellowish-brown to middle brown.
Feeding requirements: This species feeds predominantly from the production of its own zooxanthellae, but may take small planktonic organisms as well.
Aquarium suitability: This is an excellent choice for a reef or marine aquarium. It grows quite large when it is given sufficient light. No special care or feeding is necessary for this species and it can withstand nitrate levels of up to 150mg/litre without any ill effects.

Nephthea sp.

(= *Litophyton* sp.)
Family: Nephtheidae
Range: Tropical Indo-Pacific, Red Sea
Description: Although this species is often described under the name *Litophyton arboreum*, this is almost certainly an invalid synonym. In addition, the genera *Litophyton* and *Neospongodes* are probably synonymous with this genus, so that their relevant species all belong in the genus *Nephthea*. The colony has an arborescent form that is pale yellowish-brown with a lighter coloured, translucent stem and branches.
Feeding requirements: Feeds on the production of its own zooxanthellae, but will occasionally capture small planktonic organisms.
Aquarium suitability: Often imported for the aquarium trade, this species is easy to keep and very hardy. This is an ideal coral for a reef tank.

Nephthea sp.

(= *Litophyton* sp.)
Family: Nephtheidae
Range: Tropical Indo-Pacific, Red Sea
Description: Like the previous species, the stem and branches are translucent. In this case, however, the polyps are smaller and the sclerites can be seen clearly through the surface of the coenenchyme when they are inspected closely. This species is widespread in reef shallows, outer reef slopes and lagoons throughout its natural range.
Feeding requirements: Nutrition is provided by its own zooxanthellae.
Aquarium suitability: The delicate branching form of this species is an attractive addition to a reef or fish-only aquarium. The colony is quite fast growing and can withstand relatively high levels of nitrate. It is a popular species that is able to forgive most mistakes a beginner is likely to make.

Photograph by Frank Walker

Dendronephthya sp.

Family: Nephtheidae
Range: Indo-West Pacific, Central Indo-Pacific
Description: If any genus of the phylum Cnidaria is in need of revision, it is this one. Dendronephthyan coral taxonomy is in a state of confusion. This species is arborescent and translucent yellow with visible sclerites at the surface of the coenenchyme, as can be seen from the accompanying photograph. The mouths of the individual polyps are bright orange-red and the tentacles are relatively long. There are no zooxanthellae present within the tissue of this species. It is found in semidarkness under overhangs and in caves and crevices in the reef.
Feeding requirements: The polyps of this species capture plankton and other organic material.
Aquarium suitability: Difficult to keep in a reef tank. Requires low lighting and constant feeding with plankton-like foods.

Dendronephthya sp.

Family: Nephtheidae
Range: Indo-West Pacific
Description: This bright red colony resembles a cauliflower in its closed position. The extended polyps are lighter coloured than the rest of the colony and there are no zooxanthellae present in the body tissue. This species is found in relatively deep water and usually under overhangs where the water current is somewhat turbulent.
Feeding requirements: Feeds mainly on plankton and other organic material that it captures within its polyps.
Aquarium suitability: Only the specialized aquarist should attempt to keep this difficult species. Perhaps the equipment and technology that are constantly being developed could prove useful in this respect, in particular with regard to the new lighting systems that will shortly be available.

Cespitularia sp.

Family: Xeniidae
Range: Tropical Indo-Pacific
Description: This species forms small columns. The evenly to irregularly distributed polyps may be quite long and have small heads and tentacles that cannot be retracted into the coenenchyme. The polyps are fluorescent and often give off a bluish-white cast, although they may be greenish or brown as well. This species uses a pumping action with its polyp tentacles in order to create a water current around the colony.
Feeding requirements: It derives nutrients from the production of its own zooxanthellae and seems to remove certain organic-based products from the water.
Aquarium suitability: This and similar species of this genus are not easy to keep in an aquarium unless the water conditions are absolutely perfect.

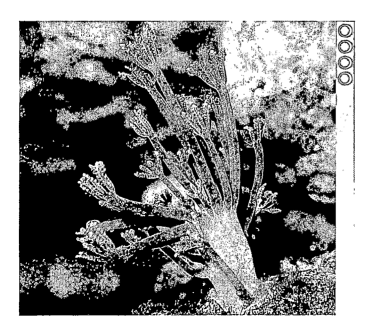

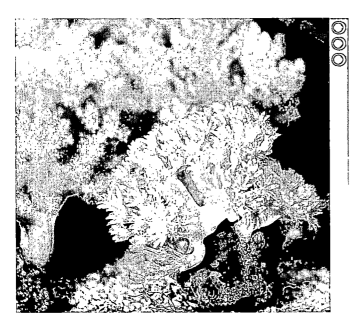

Xenia sp.

Family: Xeniidae
Range: Red Sea, Indo-Pacific
Description: All Xenia species are difficult to identify with any degree of certainty. This shallow-water species with its relatively large bluish-white polyps is often imported under the species name *Xenia umbellata*. The continuously pulsing polyps are unmistakable although species identification, from outward characteristics, is nearly impossible. The sclerites within the body are so tiny that further confusion can occur.
Feeding requirements: Mostly dependent on the production of their own zooxanthellae, but this species will absorb organic compounds as well.
Aquarium suitability: Perfect water and a pH of 8.3 are the keys to success with these species. When these conditions are not provided, they will die.

Xenia sp.

Family: Xeniidae
Range: Tropical Indo-West Pacific
Description: The polyp form is not an identifying feature of this species, for there are many similar in appearance. Nevertheless, this species from the eastern Philippines shows the grasping hand movement of the polyps in one photograph. In healthy specimens this happens continuously over the whole colony and looks like a small fireworks display.
Feeding requirements: Lives from the production of its own zooxanthellae.
Aquarium suitability: Pulse corals such as this species are difficult to keep when the water in the aquarium has traces of nitrate. Obvious signs of trouble can be seen when the colony ceases to pump continuously and closes up during the day. An increase in the amount of light can help.

Photograph by Frank Walker

Photograph by Frank Walker

Xenia sp.

Family: Xeniidae
Range: Tropical Indo-Pacific
Description: Most *Xenia* species are found in shallow water on reef crests and drop-offs. This species is no exception. They often spread like mats over a considerable area and have been called "waving hands" coral because of the continuous grasping and pumping movement of their polyps. These corals do not feed through this action, as many people believe; the movement of the polyps helps to create water currents through the colony.
Feeding requirements: Feeds on the production of its own zooxanthellae.
Aquarium suitability: For success with this and other species of *Xenia*, carbon filtration should not be used continuously. This has an adverse effect on these creatures because it removes too many of the valuable trace elements they require.

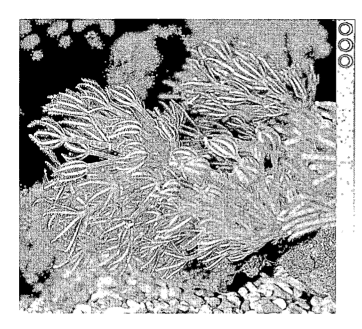

Xenia sp.

Family: Xeniidae
Range: Central Indo-Pacific
Description: The polyps of this species are similar to those of *Cespitularia* spp. but are much larger and somewhat longer. Individual colonies can form dense mats over large areas of the substrata. The pumping action is not so frequent or obvious as in others of this genus.
Feeding requirements: Lives mainly from its own zooxanthellae, but, like other *Xenia* species, it will also take organic food from the water. To do this, a mucus coating is secreted through the colony to trap minute plankton and other organic material in a type of mucus net.
Aquarium suitability: This species needs strong lighting and a high pH (8.3) to survive. If the pH drops to 8.1 or lower then the polyps will close up and begin to show obvious distress.

Erythropodium caribaeorum

Family: Anthothelidae
Range: Caribbean, Tropical West Atlantic
Description: There is a remarkable similarity between this and certain *Briareum* species. The long hair-like polyps and the café-au-lait coloured coenenchyme of this species often cause confusion. When the polyps are contracted, the surface of the coenenchyme is smooth, whereas with *Briareum* spp. it is uneven and knobbly. In addition, the polyps sway in the direction of the water current, whereas *Briareum* polyps have a tendency to open toward the light source. Both species are encrusting.
Feeding requirements: This gorgonian lives solely from its own zooxanthellae.
Aquarium suitability: Ideal for a reef aquarium, this species is hardy and easy to keep and will soon spread over much of the aquarium decoration.

Subergorgia sp.

Family: Subergorgiidae
Range: Tropical Indo-Pacific
Description: The polyps of this species are small and the coenenchyme is pale violet-blue. The colony is formed in the shape of a fan with interlocking branches that carry the gastrovascular canals. On the reef, it prefers deeper water on the outer slopes, sometimes under shadowy overhangs. The colony is flattened on a single plane and can grow to 40in (1m).
Feeding requirements: On the reef this sea fan feeds on small planktonic organisms. In an aquarium it requires almost constant feeding with frozen plankton and the like.
Aquarium suitability: Small specimens of this and similar species are occasionally imported but do not do well in a reef aquarium. They require actinic lighting and a special power-filtered "sea-fan aquarium" in order to survive.

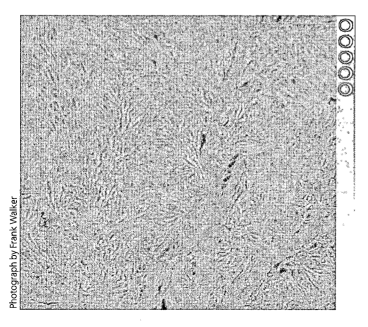

Photograph by Frank Walker

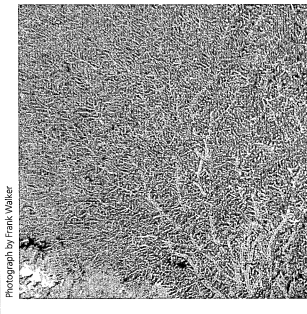

Photograph by Frank Walker

Mopsella sp.

Family: Melithaeidae
Range: Indo-West Pacific
Description: Little is known about this particular group of sea fans. They usually inhabit deeper water in lagoons and on the outer reef slopes, often growing across the direction of the current in small groups of colonies. The branches are not interlocked as in the previous species, and the polyps are white or colourless. The coenenchyme of this species is bright red and the colony is not photosynthetic.
Feeding requirements: This species feeds on plankton and other organic material that is captured by the polyps on the trailing side of the fan.
Aquarium suitability: A low-light aquarium is mandatory. Constant feeding on frozen plankton is required, along with an adequate filtration system to remove any surplus food.

Acalycigorgia sp.

Family: Acanthogorgiidae
Range: Central Indo-Pacific
Description: The coenenchyme is pale blue to bluish-white and the polyps can be pinkish or blue, usually with long tentacles. The colony is fan-formed and grows across the direction of the current on reef slopes and under reef overhangs.
Feeding requirements: This is a plankton feeder rather than a photosynthetic gorgonian that relies on its own zooxanthellae for nutrition.
Aquarium suitability: Large sea fans are often collected for the aquarium trade. They are then cut up before being sold. These "pieces" do not usually do well in an aquarium. Take care to buy only a full colony that is small and preferably attached to a piece of rock. Place it in a shadowy, well-oxygenated area of the aquarium and feed two or three times a day on frozen plankton.

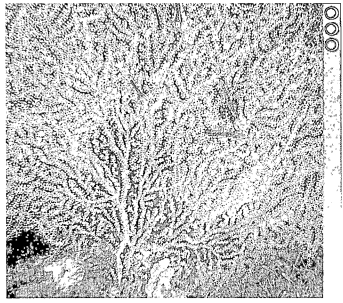

Photograph by Frank Walker

Euplexaura sp.

Family: Plexauridae
Range: East Africa to Central Indo-Pacific
Description: Colourful representatives of the genus *Euplexaura* are widespread throughout the Indo-Pacific region. This particular species has a bright red coenenchyme with small deep-yellow polyps. Colonies form loose fans, usually on a single plane. The polyps can be fully retracted into the coenenchyme.
Feeding requirements: No zooxanthellae are present in the colony. Instead, the polyps capture small planktonic organisms and other organic debris with their tentacles. In an aquarium, this species requires daily feedings of frozen plankton and like foodstuffs.
Aquarium suitability: Specimens should be purchased attached to a piece of the substrate. Provide plenty of water movement and place in a shadowy area of the tank for the best results.

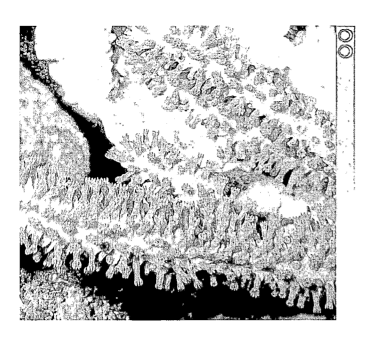

Plexaurella dichotoma

Family: Plexauridae
Range: Tropical West Atlantic, Caribbean
Description: The coenenchyme has a distinct cork-like appearance when the polyps are closed and the pores are in the form of slits rather than round, as with most *Pseudoplexaura* sp. This species forms candelabra-shaped colonies of bushy dichotomous branches on hard substrata, and may reach a height of 40in (1m).
Feeding requirements: *P. dichotoma* does not need to be fed in an aquarium, since it possesses its own zooxanthellae.
Aquarium suitability: It is an easy gorgonian to keep, providing it is given enough light. It will grow quite fast under a combination of metal-halide and actinic lighting. The base of the branches should not be buried in the sand, otherwise it will rot and the colony will die. Instead, it should be wedged between rocks or fixed with coral cement.

Pseudoplexaura flagellosa

Family: Plexauridae
Range: Tropical West Atlantic, Caribbean
Description: The polyps are longer than those of the preceding species and the coenenchyme can be light purple in colour. This is due to the presence of purple sclerites within the coenenchymal mass. *P. flagellosa* is a very large gorgonian and in the wild it can reach a height of 6½ft (2m) with vertical branches that are up to 6in (15cm) thick.
Feeding requirements: Feeding is unnecessary since this species takes all the nutrients it needs from the production of its own zooxanthellae.
Aquarium suitability: Small branches are frequently available to the aquarist. They should be fixed to a rock and placed directly under metal-halide lighting for the best growth results. The specimen shown here grew 3in (8cm) in 28 weeks.

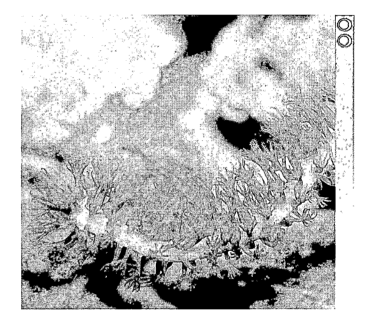

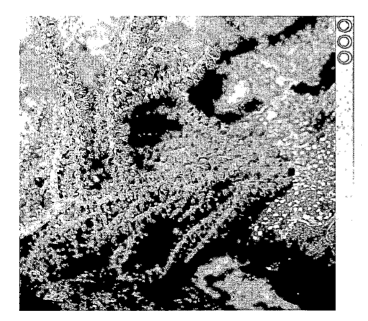

Pseudopterogorgia americana

Family: Gorgoniidae
Range: Caribbean, Florida to the Bahamas
Description: The colonies are usually bushy with slimy branches (hence the common name, "slimy sea plume"). The polyps are brown and the feather-like branches are a common characteristic of the genus, although this trait is not apparent in the accompanying photograph of a newly imported specimen. *P. americana* is the largest member of this genus and, in the wild, colonies can grow to a height of 6½ft (2m).
Feeding requirements: Feeds solely from the production of its own zooxanthellae, therefore it does not require any special feeding in an aquarium.
Aquarium suitability: This species is seldom imported but is nevertheless quite easy to keep when the water conditions are good and there is enough light and water movement.

Pterogorgia citrina

Family: Gorgoniidae
Range: Caribbean, Tropical West Atlantic
Description: The polyps are yellowish brown arranged in two rows along the sides of the somewhat flattened branches. The tips of the branches are often tinged with pale violet. This species will periodically give off a wax-like secretion in order to rid itself of foreign matter and algae from the feeding surfaces.
Feeding requirements: Nutrition is derived from the zooxanthellae production that is present within the colony.
Aquarium suitability: Despite frequent reports to the contrary, this is not an easy species to keep for any length of time in an aquarium, although it is not impossible. Provide strong lighting and place the colony in a moderately strong water current so that its periodic waxy secretions carry away the algae that are its main enemy. It will then do well.

Junceella cf. *rubra*

Family: Ellisellidae
Range: Tropical Indo-Pacific
Description: The typical whip-like colonial form of this species can be seen in the photograph here. This close-up shows the polyps with their reddish-mauve tentacles and the deep red to orange-red coenenchyme. The gastrovascular canals within the coenenchymal mass are so well developed that polyps near the tip of the whip can provide nutrition for the entire colony.
Feeding requirements: This species feeds solely on plankton and other organic material. Small colonies need to be fed several times a day in order to survive in an aquarium.
Aquarium suitability: This is a difficult species to keep. It can grow to about 40in (1m) in the wild, but in an aquarium the main problem is just keeping it alive. A special gorgonian aquarium is required.

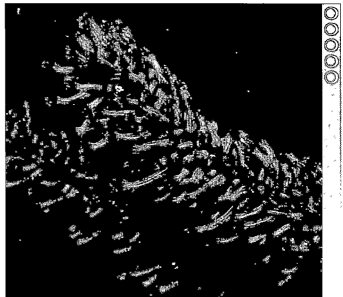

Photograph by Frank Walker

Subclass: Hexacorallia (= Zoantharia)

Unlike the octocorallians, creatures in this subclass have an internal structure that is hexamerously symmetrical (in six, approximately equal, partitions or parts). Young polyps usually have six tentacles or a multiple of this number. The skeleton, when one is produced, is made of calcium carbonate or keratin. The polyps may be solitary or in groups, each with rudimentary interconnecting stolons or gastrovascular canals. Alternatively, they may form large colonies that are variable in form. Because of the diversity of species in this subclass, these creatures are of considerable interest to marine aquarists. Stony corals, zooanthid colonies, corallimorpharians and true anemones are all familiar sights in reef aquariums. These form, along with living rock, the fundamental structure of these captive mini-reef set-ups.

The subclass encompasses six orders, the interrelationships of which are extremely complex and, as yet, not fully understood. Species of the first order in this subclass, Antipatharia, are of little interest to aquarists and are not discussed further. Tube anemones, which belong to the second order, Ceriantharia, are frequently available, however. They require special care and as a rule they are not suitable for a reef aquarium. They have powerful stinging tentacles that can do untold damage to any other invertebrates placed near them.

The third order, Scleractinia, contains creatures that build skeletons of calcium carbonate. These are often referred to as the stony corals. It is an important group, containing all the corals responsible for reef building with the exception of the two octocorallian genera, *Heliopora* and *Tubipora*. Corallimorpharia, whose form gives rise to a variety of names such as false coral, elephant ear coral, disc anemones and mushroom anemones, form the fourth order. They are outwardly similar in appearance to sea anemones but are biologically more closely related to the scleractinian corals, and can be viewed in simple terms as an intermediate stage between the anemones and the corals. They differ from the corals in that they do not build a calcareous skeleton.

Zoanthidea, the fifth order, is a poorly researched group. Until recently little was understood about these creatures and many of them have still to be given a species name. Despite this, they are common on the reef and were one of the first groups of invertebrate animals to be collected for the aquarium trade (*see right*).

Actiniaria, the last order in this subclass, groups together all the true sea anemones. Their importance to the aquarium hobby is unquestionable, especially to those aquarists who have a love of anemonefishes of the genus *Amphiprion*. But it is not only these so-called "host anemones" that are important: there are many unwanted species that may inadvertently be introduced into an aquarium. These, when left uncontrolled, can spread and reproduce so rapidly that they soon reach epidemic proportions, thereby ruining an otherwise ecologically balanced reef aquarium. Others, such as some of the Caribbean species, do not form symbiotic relationships with fishes. Instead they develop the same sort of relationships with shrimps.

Order: Ceriantharia (tube anemones)

Tube anemones of the order Ceriantharia do not have a pedal base, as do other sea anemones. They are burrowing creatures and construct cylindrical, parchment-like tubes of mucus and detritus that can be can be up to 26in (66cm) long. This is buried vertically in muddy or sandy

Two zoanthid colonies in a reef aquarium.

sediments with only the upper portion protruding. The tube often has bits of shell, sand and other debris sticking to it, as well as small invertebrates.

The order consists of three families – Cerianthidae, Arachnactidae and Botrucnidiferidae – incorporating a total of about 50 species. Representatives are known in all subtropical and tropical seas, including the Mediterranean Sea. They are found in deeper water as well as in the shallows. The natural habitats of the shallow-water species are usually mud flats and sandy bays and river mouths. They lack a hard skeleton and when they are disturbed they rapidly withdraw into their tubes.

They are predominantly nocturnal feeders and often spend much of the day retracted into their tubes. At night they extend their powerful stinging tentacles in search of prey. In an aquarium, this can prove to be a problem since a specimen with a column width of more than 1in (2.5cm) could have a tentacle length of 10in (25cm).

Pachycerianthus fimbriatus

Family: Cerianthidae
Range: Western Pacific to central Indo-Pacific
Description: The pedal column is reddish-brown to cream coloured. The outer tentacles are extremely long and violet brown, while the inner tentacles are light red. This species grows very large with a tentacle diameter of more than 40in (1m), as can be seen in the accompanying photograph, which shows a coral head (*Pocillopora* sp.) in the background.
Feeding requirements: In the wild, this species captures small fishes and free-swimming invertebrates. In an aquarium it should be fed twice weekly on fresh or frozen shellfish.
Aquarium suitability: Because of its large size, this species requires a special aquarium. On no account should it be kept with slow-moving fishes, such as mandarinfishes, sea horses. and pipefishes.

Photograph by Frank Walker

Pachycerianthus maua

(= *Pachycerianthus mana*)

Family: Cerianthidae
Range: Tropical Indo-Pacific
Description: Although *P. maua* is similar in appearance to other cerianthids, it occurs more often than not with horizontal banding on the long outer tentacles. The short inner tentacles are usually orange-brown and without bands. The column of this species seldom exceeds 8in (20cm) and it is usually yellowish in colour. In its natural habitat it is often found in muddy shallows of the inner reef or in the vicinity of sea-grass beds.
Feeding requirements: This is a predator that requires frequent feedings of fresh or frozen foodstuffs.
Aquarium suitability: Strong light and a good depth of sand are the keys to success with this frequently imported species. It should not be housed in a reef aquarium where it can sting and damage delicate corals and other invertebrates.

Order: Scleractinia (stony corals)

Reef-building corals are normally referred to as *hermatypic* and most of these possess zooxanthellae within the living tissue of the colony and polyps. Zooxanthellae are often absent from the non-reef-building corals, which are termed *ahermatypic*. The zooxanthellae play an important role in the life of a coral polyp. They provide much of the necessary daily nutrients that it requires and because of their ability to absorb pigments from the water, they also provide the polyp or colony with its colouration. In this aspect, the colouration of the cell tissue acts as a filter to block the damaging ultraviolet rays from the sun. This is particularly the case with corals from the reef shallows or on reef crests.

Hermatypic corals usually occur to depths of 150ft (46m). Below this depth, their reef building capabilities are severely limited, except in areas where the water is extremely clear. As a rule, most of them are colonial but a few species with larger polyps occur singly.

The polyps are similar to small sea anemones but in this case they construct a cup-like skeleton composed of calcium carbonate. The tentacles possess nematocysts like any other cnidarian animal. There are usually six tentacles or a multiple of this number. Each polyp has a single mouth, which lacks a ciliated groove along one edge.

In general terms, to keep hermatypic corals in an aquarium with any degree of success you need metal-halide lighting, not less than 10in (25cm) from the water's surface, in conjunction with actinic or blue tubes; the water should be as free as possible of organic substances, such as nitrate and phosphate; the water current should be strong but not directed against the coral head; and you need to provide frequent partial water changes.

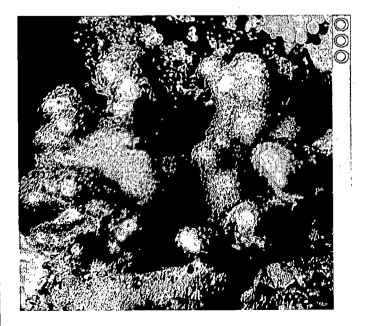

Stylophora pistillata

Family: Pocilloporidae
Range: Red Sea, East Africa to central Indo-Pacific
Description: The species *Stylophora pistillata* has thick, compact branches with blunt tips. The colony has a smooth, almost shiny surface when the polyps are retracted. The colour can vary considerably from colony to colony and the branches are often yellow or white, with green or pink tips.
Feeding requirements: The colony feeds on the production of its own zooxanthellae so no additional food needs to be introduced to the tank.
Aquarium suitability: Small colonies are often available from dealers. These should be placed very near the water's surface in order that they receive sufficient light. A strong, but indirect, water flow should be provided so that the polyps ripple over the surface of the branches.

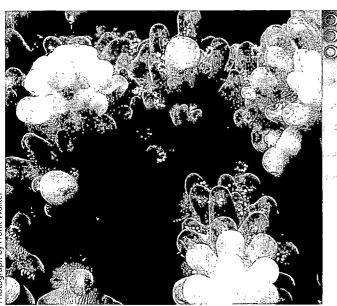

Photograph by Frank Walker

Acropora formosa

Family: Acroporidae
Range: Tropical Indo-Pacific
Description: This is a fast-growing reef-building coral that is often found in large single-species fields in the reef shallows throughout its natural range. The slender antler-like branches have pink, pinkish-violet or bluish-white tips.
Feeding requirements: Lives mainly from its own zooxanthellae, but the colony will also capture fine planktonic organisms. Frozen plankton should be given once a week.
Aquarium suitability: *A. formosa* appears to grow equally well in an aquarium with lots of water movement as it does in one where the water is comparatively calm. High-power metal-halide lighting is required and when the colony feels well it can double its size within a few months. This species will not tolerate nitrate levels of more than 10 mg/litre.

Acropora grandis

Family: Acroporidae
Range: Central Indo-Pacific
Description: The accompanying photograph shows the typical growth form of this species. The thick branches with pointed tips often grow almost parallel to the substrate. Colonies can grow quite large, up to 5ft (1.5m) from branch tip to branch tip.
Feeding requirements: This species occurs in nutrient-rich water and also in water that is relatively poor in nutrients. This would indicate that colonies are able to survive on their own zooxanthellae as well as by capturing planktonic organisms within their polyps.
Aquarium suitability: Although there is no record of this species living in an aquarium, there is no reason why the care and feeding of it should not be the same as for others of this genus. Small branches would probably be easier to keep.

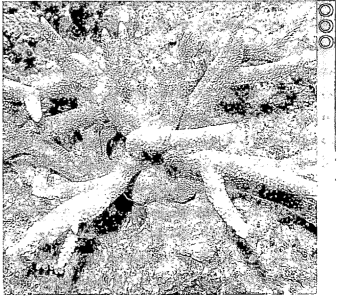

Photograph by Frank Walker

Acropora latistella

Family: Acroporidae
Range: Central Indo-Pacific
Description: The colony adopts different forms in the wild and can reach a diameter of more than 40in (1m). It may be bushy, loosely branched or shaped like a tabletop on a thick, central trunk. The overall colouration can be greenish or creamy-yellow. The tips of the finger-like branches are often yellow, but they are seldom pink.
Feeding requirements: Feeds primarily on the production of its zooxanthellae but it will also capture small plankton as a supplement. Weekly feedings of frozen plankton and organic-based liquid foods are essential to its continued wellbeing.
Aquarium suitability: Specimens are occasionally imported from the Philippines but they are not common. High-intensity lighting and good-water quality are prerequisites for this coral.

Photograph by Frank Walker

Photograph by Frank Walker

Acropora nastuta

Family: Acroporidae
Range: Tropical Indo-Pacific from East Africa to Polynesia
Description: This species is easy to identify since the cups, in which the polyps sit, are all directed upward. The growing areas of the colony are usually light pink, whereas the rest of the branch is cream or greenish-yellow. The polyp at the tip of the branch (the apical polyp) is often bright pink in colour and leads the growth direction, as is the case with most species in this particular genus.
Feeding requirements: Feeds on its own zooxanthellae but it will occasionally capture small organisms from the water.
Aquarium suitability: Colonies should be placed in the upper half of the aquarium, directly under strong metal-halide lighting, and in a strong water flow. In this way, the zooxanthellae will continue to grow and provide nourishment for the coral.

Acropora pulchra

Family: Acroporidae
Range: Central Indo-Pacific
Description: The antler-like branches have uneven radial polyps often set wide apart. The colony forms thick bushes or flat, table-like plates that are ochre yellow or brown. The branches stand out vertically or nearly so, and the tips are often pink.
Feeding requirements: Zooxanthellae provide the colony with most of the nutrients required, but frozen plankton will also be taken as a supplement.
Aquarium suitability: With sufficient light this species is hardy and fast growing. Under the right conditions a small branch cemented to a rock will soon begin to grow and will quickly become a small colony that will continue to expand, threatening to overshadow other slower-growing corals. At this stage, the branches should be pruned back and used to start other colonies.

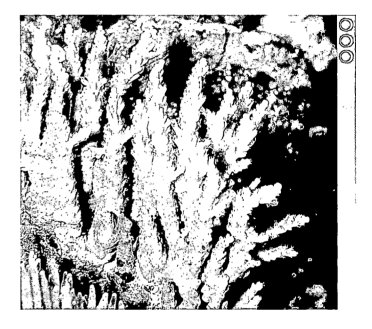

Goniopora sp.

Family: Poritidae
Range: Central Indo-Pacific
Description: The extended polyps are long and thicker at the base than toward the oral disc. The mouth is ringed with short tentacles, unlike most other corals of this genus. The polyps are usually an overall yellowish-brown.
Feeding requirements: Feeds from the production of its own zooxanthellae but will occasionally capture plankton and other small organisms. It is probable that certain organic and/or mineral products are also removed from the water that are vital to all *Goniopora* corals.
Aquarium suitability: A difficult species to keep for any length of time in an aquarium. Colonies require strong lighting and moderate to strong water movement. Try experimenting with vitamin and trace element additives to keep it healthy.

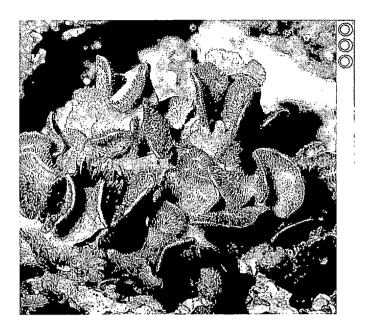

Pavona cactus

Family: Agariciidae
Range: Red Sea, Tropical Indo-Pacific
Description: The cactus coral, as this species is commonly called, is endemic throughout the Indo-Pacific. It forms colonies that, as the common name implies, are shaped like certain species of cacti. The thin and fragile blade-like growths are covered with fine brown, or sometimes green, polyps. The natural habitat of this coral is on reef crests and in reef channels where the water is often turbulent.
Feeding requirements: Feeds predominantly from its own zooxanthellae.
Aquarium suitability: A frequently imported species that does well in a reef aquarium with metal halide and actinic lighting and a moderate to strong water current. Care should be taken when handling colonies, as they are apt to break very easily.

Pavona danai

Family: Agariciidae
Range: Northern Indo-Pacific to Hong Kong
Description: Colonies form thin blades on multiple planes. The blades are creamy yellow and have a soft carpet of brown- or green-tentacled polyps. Older colonies have blades that are up to 4in (10cm) thick. They form pillars and massive growths that can be up to 10ft (3m) high and 5ft (1.5m) in diameter. The similar species, *P. cactus*, is more fragile in appearance but can form vast fields of growth.
Feeding requirements: Lives solely from the products of its own zooxanthellae.
Aquarium suitability: Although *P. cactus* is the usual species that is seen on offer in dealers' tanks, this species occasionally turns up. Perfect water is required with the usual metal-halide and actinic lighting. A moderately strong water flow is ideal.

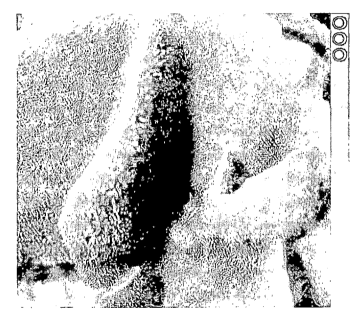

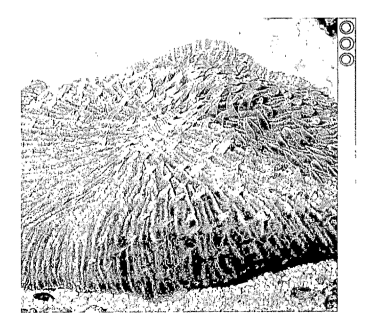

Fungia scutaria

Family: Fungiidae
Range: Tropical Indo-Pacific
Description: The colouration is variable. Specimens may be purple, green or yellowish-brown. The innermost edge of each septum is raised and rounded and the oral opening is large.
Feeding requirements: Lives primarily from the products of its own zooxanthellae but it will also capture plankton and other minute organisms to supplement this.
Aquarium suitability: This and other *Fungia* species require a well-lit tank with plenty of water movement. They should be placed on a flat piece of substratum or on a free area of sand, away from other corals that might sting them. These corals are quite fragile, so care should be taken when handling them. Newly purchased specimens should be acclimatized slowly to their new surroundings for the best chances of success.

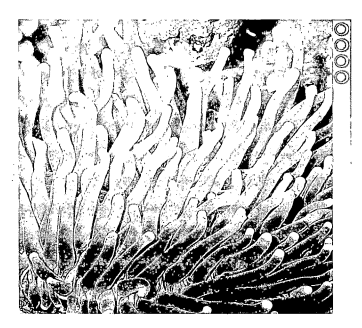

Heliofungia actiniformis

Family: Fungiidae
Range: Indo-West Pacific
Description: The septa have long tooth-like extensions when the skeleton is examined. The tentacles are long, up to 8in (20cm) in full-grown specimens. These are brown, green or white in colour and may be extended day and night. Their bulbous tips are usually white but occasionally they may be green or pink.
Feeding requirements: Feeds on its own zooxanthellae, but it will also capture other food with its tentacles. It is known that *H. actiniformis* also removes soluble organic nutrients and minerals from the water in order to survive.
Aquarium suitability: This species is often imported but does not usually live for more than a year in an aquarium because of the difficulties in providing the correct diet.

Cynarina sp.

Family: Mussidae
Range: Central Indo-Pacific
Description: The broad oral margin is usually lighter in colour than the rest of the colony, although in some specimens there can be a star-shaped pattern around the mouth. The thick polyp lobes are brick-red or orange, which can be in a radially striped pattern, as shown here, or a uniform reddish orange.
Feeding requirements: This coral is known to accept frozen plankton and similar organisms, but its main source of nutrition is derived from its own symbiotic zooxanthellae.
Aquarium suitability: Ideally, a somewhat shadowy area of the aquarium should be reserved for this particular coral. Make sure that there is enough free space around it to allow the colony to fully expand, and provide it with a moderate amount of water movement.

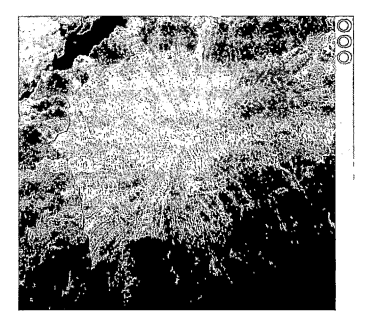

Lobophyllia hemprichii

Family: Mussidae
Range: Red Sea, Tropical Indo-Pacific from East Africa to Polynesia
Description: Very variable in colour, from deep grey-blue, through yellow and green, to brick-red. The polyps are large and fleshy and have a thick row of short feeding tentacles surrounding the outer margin of the oral opening. The colony form is usually hemispherical or cushion-shaped.
Feeding requirements: Feeds mainly on the products of its own zooxanthellae, although infrequent feedings of frozen plankton will also be accepted. Use a syringe or pipette for this.
Aquarium suitability: This decorative species is frequently imported and is relatively inexpensive. It is also one of the hardiest of the stony corals. Provide plenty of water movement and moderate to strong lighting and this species should do well.

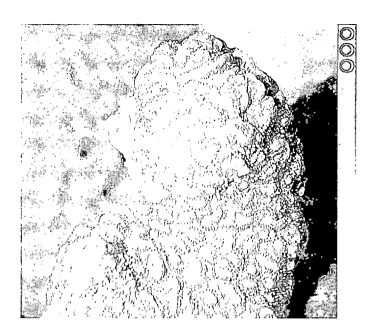

Hydnophora cf. *rigida*

Family: Merulinidae
Range: Tropical Indo-Pacific, South China Sea as far north as Hong Kong
Description: This is the typical polyp form of this genus. The colonies are light grey to brownish-grey and they take on several forms. These include encrusting growths several metres in diameter, and large, pillar-like outcrops from the reef that can be 20in (51cm) thick and 7ft (2m) high. The tentacles are short and unobtrusive in comparison to the size of the colony.
Feeding requirements: This species feeds on plankton when it is available but otherwise relies on its own zooxanthellae.
Aquarium suitability: Although this species is seldom imported, several similar species do occasionally turn up in dealers' tanks. They are quite hardy given the correct living conditions.

Favia sp.

Family: Faviidae
Range: Tropical Indo-Pacific
Description: The polyps are fairly large and green to yellowish brown, usually with lighter coloured centres. Skeletal examination shows that the polyp cups consist of laminated vanes of calcium carbonate. This species forms small-to-medium hemispherical colonies on reef crests and back-reef areas.
Feeding requirements: Lives mainly from its own zooxanthellae but will occasionally capture other food such as plankton within its tentacles. Specific feeding is unnecessary.
Aquarium suitability: The lighting should be moderately strong for this coral. It is best to place the colony mid-level in the aquarium, but not directly under the metal-halide lighting unit. This is a hardy species that will live a long time in a reef aquarium when the conditions are right.

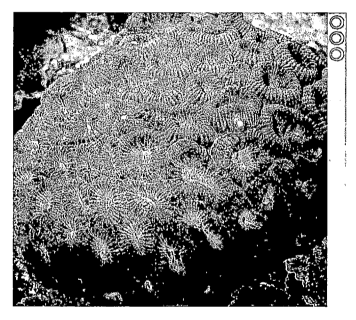

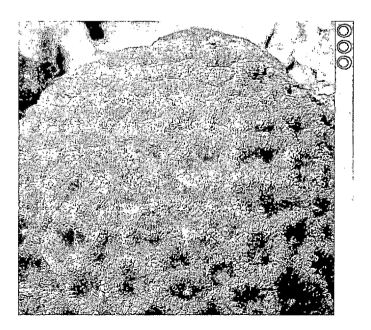

Favia sp.

Family: Faviidae
Range: Tropical Indo-Pacific
Description: The polyps can be green or brown and the colony is cushion-shaped. There is a white margin to each of the oral openings, which are elongated into small slits. It is found on reef drop-offs and reef channels as well as in lagoon areas.
Feeding requirements: Lives from the productions of its own zooxanthellae but will frequently accept frozen plankton as a supplement to this.
Aquarium suitability: This and similar species are sensitive to UV light. Care should be taken to ensure that the lighting system has the correct colour composition. Plenty of water movement should be provided and the water should have little in the way of nitrate and phosphate. The colony should be placed on a flat piece of substrate.

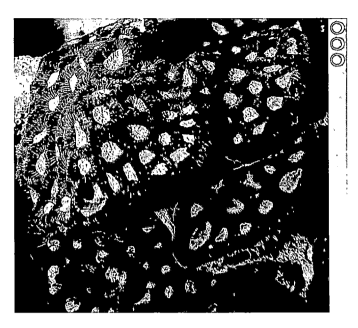

Favites sp.

Family: Faviidae
Range: Tropical Indo-Pacific
Description: The polyps are fluorescent green in colour, forming hemispherical growths. The polyp walls merge in a honeycomb effect when viewed in close-up. This polyp formation typifies the *Favites* genus.
Feeding requirements: Feeds almost exclusively on the products of its zooxanthellae. It does not need any supplementary feeding in an aquarium.
Aquarium suitability: Lighting is critical for this species. Place the colony on a flat piece of substrate at the bottom of the tank about 27in (69cm) away from a 150w metal-halide HQI lamp with a colour temperature of 10,000°K. Actinic tubes should also be used. The water should have a nitrate level of less than 10mg/litre. It requires moderate water movement.

Favites abdita

Family: Faviidae
Range: Red Sea, Tropical Indo-Pacific
Description: The skeletal walls of the polyps merge in *Favites* spp. This is not the case with *Favia* spp., where the polyps are separated. *Favites abdita* is common around the turbid shores of Hong Kong and assumes the dark brownish-black colour pictured here. The centres of the polyps are light bluish-green and this never changes, whereas in clearer water the polyp margins are light brown.
Feeding requirements: Zooxanthellae are utilized, but the colony will also capture fine zooplankton. Weekly feedings of frozen plankton are recommended.
Aquarium suitability: Requires a high-intensity light source to encourage the growth of zooxanthellae. If a moderate water movement is provided this species is very hardy.

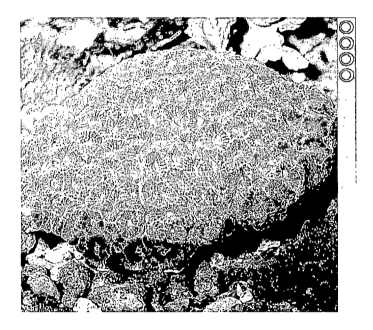

Trachyphyllia radiata
(Syn: *Wellsophyllia radiata*)
Family: Trachyphylliidae
Range: Indonesia to Northwest Australia
Description: Similarities exist between this species and the green, similarly formed colour variety of *Trachyphyllia geoffroyi*. In this case, however, the convoluted lobes of the skeleton are fused, whereas in *T. geoffroyi* they are usually unconnected. Nevertheless there is not enough genetic evidence to support a separate taxon since there are many cases of partial fusing of the skeletal lobes in larger specimens of *T. geoffroyi*.
Feeding requirements: Feeds mainly from the products of its own zooxanthellae.
Aquarium suitability: Provide strong lighting and moderate water movement for the best results. Colonies placed on the sand should have plenty of space around them to allow them to expand fully.

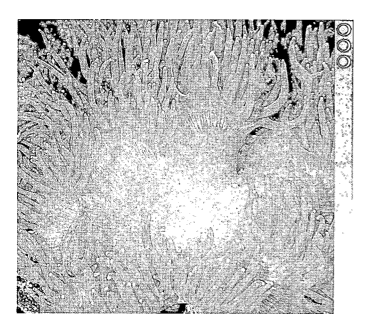

Catalaphyllia jardinei

Family: Caryophylliidae
Range: Tropical Indo-Pacific
Description: At first glance this coral resembles a long-tentacled sea anemone. The large oral surface often has more than one mouth. Colonies may be fluorescent-green or brown, usually with radiating stripes on the oral margins. Specimens can reach a diameter of 20in (51cm) and the tentacles sometimes have pink tips. These have powerful nematocysts that can penetrate the human skin and inflict irritating wounds that can last for days.
Feeding requirements: Feeds almost exclusively on the products of its own zooxanthellae.
Aquarium suitability: Requires moderately strong lighting, water movement and plenty of space in a large aquarium to spread its tentacles. This species can tolerate relatively high nitrate levels; indeed, it seems to thrive under such conditions.

Euphyllia ancora

Family: Caryophylliidae
Range: Tropical Indo-Pacific
Description: The skeleton has a typical convoluted shape and the polyp tentacles are long and slender when they are extended. Colonies are often green or brown and the tips of the tentacles are creamy-white. These are club-shaped or hammer-shaped (hence its common name, hammer coral), usually with a pale-green fluorescence under ultraviolet or actinic blue lighting. In a few specimens, this fluorescence is peach-coloured.
Feeding requirements: Utilizes the products of its own zooxanthellae but it does occasionally take other organic foods as well.
Aquarium suitability: Take care when handling this coral as the tentacles pack a powerful sting that leaves a painful rash-like wound. It needs plenty of light with a good water movement.

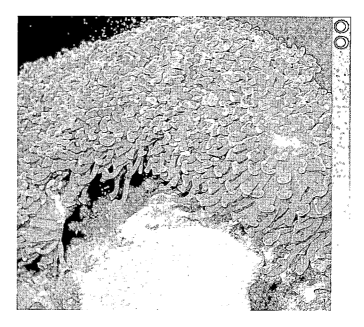

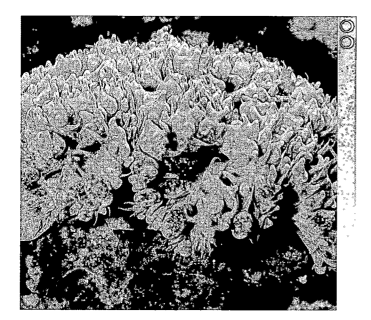

Physogyra lichtensteini

Family: Caryophylliidae
Range: Indo-West Pacific
Description: Species of the genus *Physogyra* are often confused with those of the genus *Plerogyra*. The polyps form convoluted colonies that are hemispherical in shape. These are covered with small, elongated, bladder-like vesicles. The polyp tentacles are usually withdrawn during the day and extended at night for feeding. The colony may be green, grey, white or light brown in colour.
Feeding requirements: Utilizes its own zooxanthellae but is an active plankton feeder at night. Feed frozen plankton twice a week in the evenings.
Aquarium suitability: Needs a well-lit tank with plenty of water movement. This is another species that has a painful sting when handled carelessly. It can tolerate quite high nitrate levels.

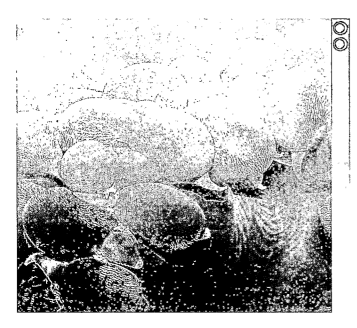

Plerogyra sinuosa

Family: Caryophylliidae
Range: Tropical Indo-Pacific, Red Sea
Description: Colonies are often light green or white in colour, and the polyp vesicles are usually oval, but sometimes round. *P. sinuosa* grows on reef drop-offs and in reef channels, usually in crevices or in entrances to caves.
Feeding requirements: Feeds on the products of its own zooxanthellae but will also capture plankton and other small marine organisms.
Aquarium suitability: This is probably the most frequently imported species of stony coral. Its sting is also painful so care should be taken when handling it. Brine shrimp and similar foods should be fed weekly. It requires moderate light and plenty of water movement for it to grow well. This is one of the easiest stony corals to keep in an aquarium.

Turbinaria peltata

Family: Dendrophyllidae
Range: Tropical Indo-Pacific
Description: The polyps form colonies that are cup-shaped, pillar-formed or plate-like. The coral is generally light brown or grey with green or yellow fluorescent polyps. The polyp cups are recessed and ⅛ to ¼in (3 to 5mm) in diameter. The colonies can reach 40in (1m) in diameter.
Feeding requirements: The colony obtains most of the nutrients it needs from the productions of its own zooxanthellae, but it will also feed on other organisms. Feed frozen plankton twice weekly for the best growth success.
Aquarium suitability: Plenty of water movement is required for this species. Colonies should not be placed too near and directly under metal-halide lights or they will die. This is because they are unable to withstand high levels of UV radiation.

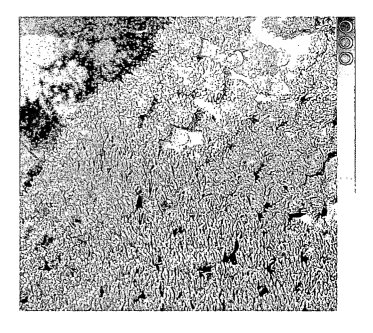

Order: Corallimorpharia (false corals, coral anemones)

The order Corallimorpharia encompasses three families incorporating ten genera with a provisionally estimated 40 to 50 species – although this number could be as high as 85 species when more information becomes available. This order is a taxonomist's nightmare because, even though quite a lot of research has been and is being carried out in this area, no workable or reliable taxon has as yet been constructed. According to Dr J C den Hartog, a leading world authority on the corallimorpharians: "We have so little to go on [with regard to the internal and external characteristics], that it is extremely difficult to differentiate these species. In addition some of the preserved specimens are in such a poor condition that this compounds the uncertainty."

The name "Actinodiscus" has often been given as a valid generic name in various aquarium publications. This name is invalid, however, and was probably coined in the first place by aquarists. The family name Actinodiscidae is also invalid. These objective synonyms usually refer to species of the genus *Discosoma* in the family Discosomatidae.

Corallimorpharians, or "false corals" as they are commonly known, occur either singly or in colonies that sometimes have interconnecting tissue between the polyps. They lack a skeleton as such, and the siphonoglyph is absent in most cases. In others the siphonoglyph is rudimentary. The basilar muscles are absent and the oral disc may be smooth or with wart-like tentacles. In a few examples, such as those of the genus *Ricordia*, the tentacles are capitate (shaped like a head). In some species they may be branched or unbranched.

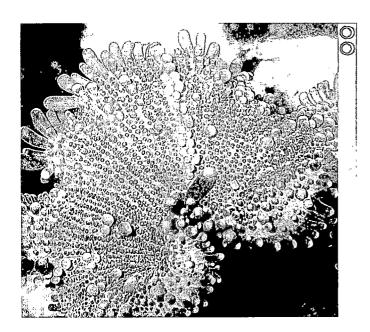

Ricordia yuma

Family: Ricordeidae
Range: Tropical Indo-Pacific
Description: The tentacles on the oral surface are small (2 to 3mm) except on the margin where they are more than twice this length. The oral disc varies from slate-purple to green. One of the important identifying features of *R. yuma* is the upraised mouth, which is surrounded by a ring of tentacles. This is one of three species in this genus. The others are *R. florida* from the Caribbean and *R. fungiforme* from the Indo-West Pacific.
Feeding requirements: Feeds almost exclusively from the products of its own zooxanthellae, therefore it does not require additional feeding in the aquarium.
Aquarium suitability: Place the colony in a well-lit place with moderate water movement. This species reproduces mainly by pedal laceration and can soon colonize large areas of the tank.

Amplexidiscus fenestrafer

Family: Discosomatidae
Range: Central Indo-Pacific
Description: The oral disc is covered with small, round tentacles but the disc margin is smooth and free of tentacles. This feature makes it easy to identify. *A. fenestrafer* is the largest of all the corallimorpharians, reaching 18in (46cm) in diameter, although 12in (30cm) is more usual.
Feeding requirements: Feeds from its own zooxanthellae but will also capture small fishes, shrimps and other organisms by very slowly contracting the margin of the oral disc to form a balloon-like purse, entrapping the unsuspecting creature inside.
Aquarium suitability: Avoid direct metal-halide lighting (fluorescent tubes are better) and do not house this species with small fishes and shrimps. Feed twice weekly with frozen shrimp and mussel and it should become enormous.

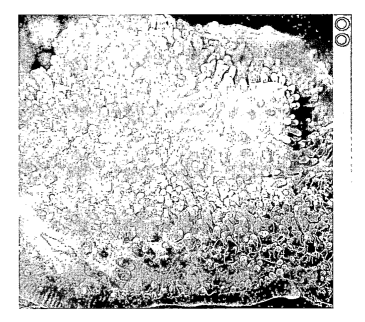

Discosoma sp. (coeruleus)

Family: Discosomatidae
Range: East Africa to Central Indo-Pacific
Description: The oral disc is deep powder-blue and the mouth is white. The tentacles are wart-like or completely absent and there are no surface or internal ribs in the mesogloea. The basilar column is short with the oral disc typically held flat against the unevenness of the substrata. This is the only species to do this.
Feeding requirements: Feeds exclusively on the products of its own zooxanthellae.
Aquarium suitability: Place this species in the shadows under fluorescent lighting or far away from metal-halide lights. The water movement should be light to moderate. This species breeds sexually in an aquarium as well as asexually through pedal laceration. It also interbreeds quite readily with other *Discosoma* spp.

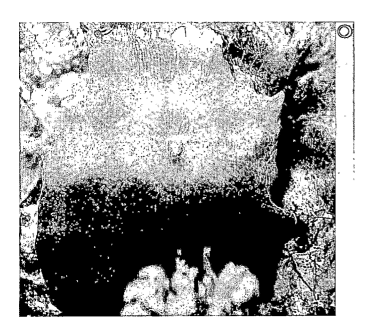

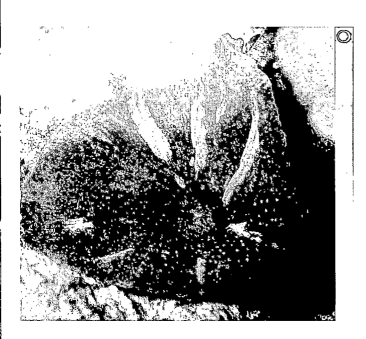

Discosoma sp. *(coeruleo-striatus)*

Family: Discosomatidae
Range: Central Indo-Pacific to South Pacific
Description: In sexually reproduced junior polyps, surface ribs are evident. As the polyp grows these become deeper embedded in the mesogloea until they are not normally visible. In asexual clones, the ribs are not in evidence. The oral disc is greenish-brown to brown and there is a series of wagon-wheel "spokes" (usually six) of greenish-blue that radiate from the mouth.
Feeding requirements: Feeds from its own zooxanthellae but it may extract other organic substances from the water.
Aquarium suitability: An ideal species under fluorescent lighting and gentle water movement. This coral anemone does not interbreed with other *Discosoma* spp. as far as I am aware. Nevertheless it is attractive and will reproduce quite readily through pedal laceration.

Discosoma sp. *(ferrugatus)*

Family: Discosomatidae
Range: Tropical Indo-Pacific
Description: This species does not vary in colour morphologically (colour morphs) – it is always brick red. There are many hybrids, however, for this species interbreeds with other *Discosoma* spp. It is easy to tell the difference between the true species and the hybrids because the mesogloea is more stable in the true species and the underside of the oral disc is brownish-grey. There are fine surface ribs and tiny round tentacles that radiate outward in linear rows from the oral opening.
Feeding requirements: Feeds solely on the products of its own zooxanthellae.
Aquarium suitability: When the colony is placed in a shaded area of the tank with moderate to light water movement, this species does well. Sexual and asexual reproduction is common.

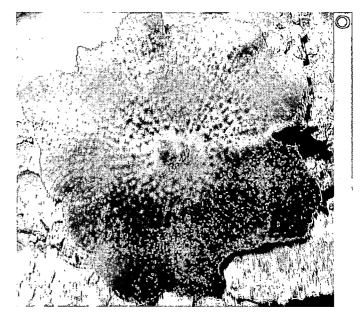

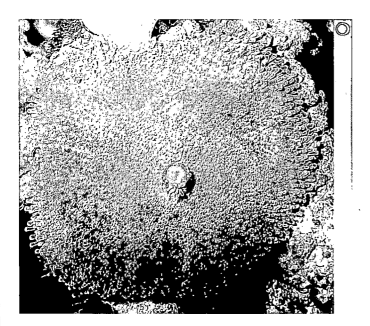

Discosoma sp.

Family: Discosomatidae
Range: Tropical Indo-Pacific
Description: The colour of the oral disc ranges from reddish-brown to green and the mouth is conical and raised up from the oral surface. The tentacles are well developed and arranged in rows radiating from the margin of the mouth. Those at the edge of the disc are elongated and tongue-like.
Feeding requirements: Feeds from the products of its own zooxanthellae but probably removes additional organic products from the water.
Aquarium suitability: Frequent partial water changes seem to encourage this species to grow and spread in the aquarium. Daylight and actinic fluorescent lighting will ensure its wellbeing. Sexual as well as asexual reproduction by pedal laceration is known. They appear not to interbreed with other species.

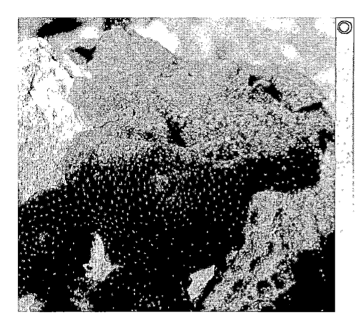

Discosoma sp. *(punctatus)*

Family: Discosomatidae
Range: Red Sea, East Africa to Indonesia
Description: The oral disc may vary from reddish-brown to green depending on geographical origin. There are fine, round tentacles, which can also vary in colour from blue or green to brown to contrast with the background colour. Occasionally a single line is present that traverses the disc and there are often short lines around the margin of the mouth. There are many hybrid variations since this species interbreeds with several other *Discosoma* species.
Feeding requirements: Feeds almost exclusively from its own zooxanthellae.
Aquarium suitability: Under actinic lighting the tentacles often fluoresce and make a spectacular display, along with other species in an aquarium devoted solely to corallimorpharians.

Discosoma sp. *(striatus)*

Family: Discosomatidae
Range: Red Sea, Tropical Indo-Pacific
Description: This is a very distinct and key species in this group of *Discosoma*. The radiating ridges on the surface of the oral disc are brown to reddish-brown and the areas between are fluorescent green to blue-green. The ridges are present throughout its life, irrespective of the thickness of the mesogloea. There are numerous tiny wart-like tentacles in some specimens; in others, they are almost completely absent. The oral disc may be oval, round or triangular as shown in the photograph.
Feeding requirements: Nutrition is derived solely from its own zooxanthellae.
Aquarium suitability: In ideal conditions, asexual reproduction through pedal laceration often occurs. This is an attractive and easy species to keep.

Notes on hybridization It is now known that hybrids are unable to reproduce sexually. Asexual reproduction is, however, possible. This is usually by pedal laceration, but longitudinal fission and budding are not unknown. The fact that there are no functional gonads in the hybrids could be nature's way of retaining the integrity of the species. It is an important indicator of the true species, the colour morphs and the hybrids.

Hybrid coral anemones are generally, but not always, about 20 per cent smaller than either of the parent species, and the mesogloea often firmer and less flexible to the touch. Sexually reproduced true species usually retain the colour of the parent. It is normal for sexual reproduction to take place within the colony. The larvae are minute and may have branched or unbranched cilia but they are not free-swimming. Junior polyps and clones of true species are identical, both in colour and form, but this can vary according to the geographical location.

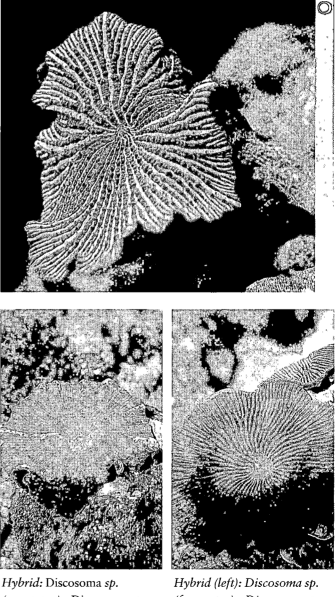

Hybrid: Discosoma *sp.* (punctatus) x Discosoma *sp.* (ferrugatus).

Hybrid (left): Discosoma sp. (ferrugatus) x Discosoma sp. (striatus).

Rhodactis mussoides

Family: Discosomatidae
Range: Central Indo-Pacific to Australia
Description: The oral opening is pinkish-white and the tentacles are short and rudimentary. The oral disc is unevenly formed and often convoluted. This species grows quite large, to at least 8in (20cm) and is usually greenish-brown to green in colour. Large species may have multiple mouths and they are often found in colonies of 10 to 15 individuals.
Feeding requirements: Captures small organisms and derives nutrients from the endosymbiotic zooxanthellae within its body. Weekly feedings of krill, mysid or brine shrimp should be given.
Aquarium suitability: This is an easy species to keep and grows well in an aquarium under strong lighting and a moderate water movement. Asexual reproduction is usually effected by longitudinal fission.

Rhodactis sp.

Family: Discosomatidae
Range: Central Indo-Pacific
Description: In some books this species is described as *Rhodactis* cf. *inchoata* but after examination of this specimen, and with reference to the formal description, its correct name is still uncertain. The column is about ⅓in (10mm) high and the oral disc is covered with a series of rosette-formed tentacles that are arranged in radially symmetrical rows around the oral opening. The oral disc is white to light blue and the tentacles may range in colour from deep blue to green.
Feeding requirements: Feeds almost solely on the products of its own zooxanthellae.
Aquarium suitability: A frequently imported species that does well in a reef or marine aquarium. It requires relatively strong lighting and a moderate water movement.

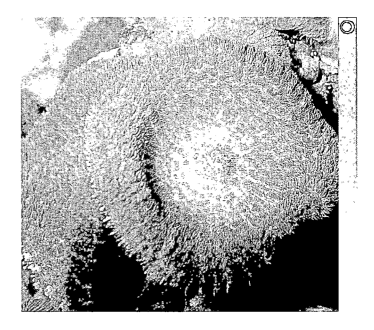

Rhodactis sp.

Family: Discosomatidae
Range: Central Indo-Pacific to Australia
Description: Identical or similar species are often described as *Rhodactis indosinensis*. The soft, branched tentacles are usually thick, sometimes with a naked margin to the oral disc. The oral disc itself is soft and flexible, and in moderate water movement will turn to show the pale underside in contrast to the green or greenish-brown disc colouration.
Feeding requirements: Feeds predominantly from the products of its own zooxanthellae but probably removes other organisms from the water as well.
Aquarium suitability: This commonly imported species is popular with aquarists because of its hardiness. Given moderate water movement and strong lighting, colonies will multiply and may have to be thinned to stop them taking over the aquarium.

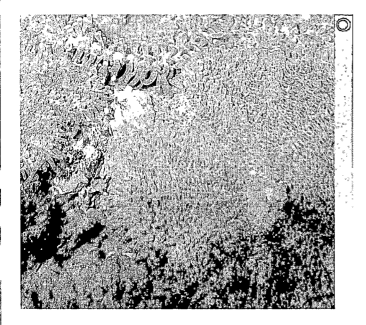

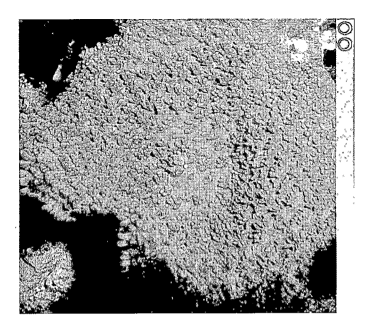

Rhodactis sp.

Family: Discosomatidae
Range: Indo-Australian Archipelago
Description: The tentacles are branched and bulbous when they are expanded. On the margin of the oral disc they are elongated and are usually a lighter brown colour than the rest. The oral disc is a brilliant metallic-green colour and is fluorescent under actinic lighting. The inner surfaces of the mouth are white. Full-grown specimens can have a disc diameter of some 12in (30cm) or more.
Feeding requirements: Feeds on the products of its own zooxanthellae but frequently takes other food, such as small fishes and shrimps. Feed weekly on chopped mussel and cockle and ensure that it closes around this.
Aquarium suitability: This is a spectacular species that is easy to keep in a well-lit tank.

Order: Zoanthidea (zoanthids, button polyps)

This order contains two suborders, each with two families, about 12 genera and about 300 currently described species. All are difficult to identify and with some it is possible to determine the species only by internal microscopic examination. Most species can be identified down to generic level, and this has been done in the following pages.

The anatomy of the individual polyps closely resembles the Tetracorallia, an extinct group of corals that had four tentacles or combinations thereof, instead of the usual six or eight in extant species. In addition, they have neither a basal disc nor skeleton.

In the family Zoanthidae, the colonies themselves can be divided into three basic groups. In the first group, the individual polyps occur singly and live partially embedded in sand (for example, the genus *Sphenopus*). In the second group, the polyps live in colonies with or without stolons or a coenenchyme between the polyps (for example, *Zoanthus*, *Isaurus* and *Protopalythoa*). The third group has polyps that are deeply embedded in the coenenchyme and can sometimes retract almost completely into this (for example, *Palythoa*).

The second group can be further divided by the presence of sand embedded in the column of the polyp. If this is the case, with or without stolons or coenenchyme, this must be a species belonging to the genus *Protopalythoa*. Where the column is without embedded sand, the colony could be from the genera *Isaurus* or *Zoanthus*. With *Isaurus* spp. the polyps are closed during the day, whereas the polyps of *Zoanthus* spp. are open during the day.

Many species are imported as *Palythoa* sp. In fact, most, if not all, of these belong either to the genera *Protopalythoa* or *Zoanthus*.

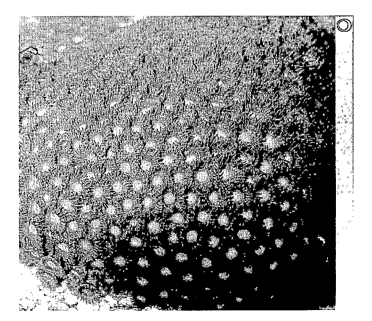

Zoanthus sp.

Family: Zoanthidae
Range: Central Indo-Pacific
Description: The polyps are small with short, almost rudimentary tentacles. The stem of the polyp is light grey and the oral disc is deep green with a pinkish-brown margin around the mouth. Stolons connect the individual polyps and there is no sand embedded in their columns.
Feeding requirements: The colony feeds solely on the products of its own zooxanthellae.
Aquarium suitability: Easy to keep when enough light is provided. Colonies should be placed in a free area of the aquarium with enough space around them. Ensure that other cnidarian animals such as corals and anemones do not sting them. If this happens, this species will usually lose the battle for space and start to die.

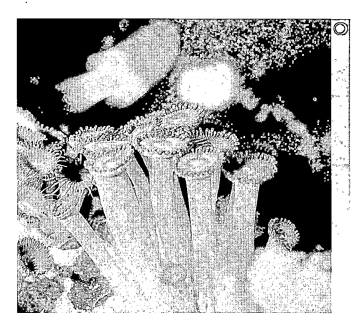

Zoanthus sp.

Family: Zoanthidae
Range: Tropical Indo-Pacific, Red Sea
Description: The polyp columns are extremely long and free of embedded sand. They are generally creamy-white to pale yellow-brown. The oral discs are not usually much wider than the diameter of the columns. There is a single ring of tentacles, brown in colour. The inner margin of the oral disc is pale rose, which fluoresces bright pink under UV or actinic lighting.
Feeding requirements: Derives all the nutrition that it requires from the products of its zooxanthellae, and so it does not need to be fed in an aquarium.
Aquarium suitability: This is an attractive species that is ideal for a reef aquarium. It is a welcome contrast to the browns and greens of other zoanthids. Colonies will survive most beginner's mistakes as long as the lighting is strong enough.

Zoanthus sp.

Family: Zoanthidae
Range: East Africa to Central Indo-Pacific
Description: At first glance, this and the next species could be mistaken for *Protopalythoa* spp. But this is not the case, since the polyp columns do not have sand particles embedded in the surface. The oral disc has a bright green margin around the mouth and the rest of the polyp is reddish-brown. The tentacles are long and the polyps are joined together by a thin coenenchyme.
Feeding requirements: Zooxanthellae provide the basic diet required but colonies will capture plankton and other small organisms. Try feeding occasionally with frozen plankton when the tentacles are fully extended.
Aquarium suitability: An ideal choice for the novice and one that is easy to keep under moderate to strong lighting.

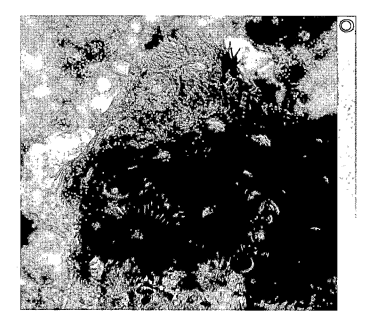

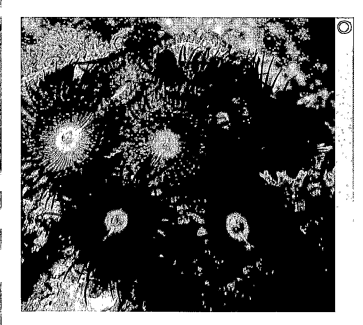

Zoanthus sp.

Family: Zoanthidae
Range: Indo-West Pacific
Description: Although this example has been included as a separate species on the basis of the thickened margin of the oral disc, it could be a geographical variation of the preceding species. Colonies are similar in colouration but the margin around the mouth is fluorescent-white and the tentacles are green. In addition, the underside of the oral disc is bluish-grey and the tentacles are not as long.
Feeding requirements: Feeds almost exclusively from the products of its zooxanthellae but it will sometimes capture food within its tentacles and partially close the oral disc.
Aquarium suitability: A light to moderate water movement seems ideal for this species. It does equally well under strong fluorescent lighting or metal-halide illumination.

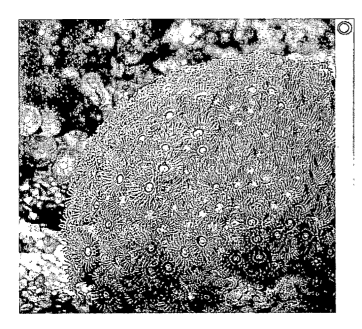

Zoanthus sp.

Family: Zoanthidae
Range: Central Indo-Pacific
Description: The polyp columns are free of embedded sand and are relatively thick and stocky. Polyps form hemispherical colonies that are connected by a quite thick coenenchyme. The tentacles are long and green, whereas the rest of the oral surface is light to middle brown in colour. The inner margin of the mouth is white.
Feeding requirements: Zooxanthellae provide the main source of food for this species, but it is believed to supplement this by feeding on small planktonic organisms.
Aquarium suitability: Colonies come in various shades of green and brown and some of them fluoresce under actinic lighting. Specimens are usually hardy and adapt well to aquarium life provided the lighting is strong enough.

Protopalythoa sp.

Family: Zoanthidae
Range: Central Indo-Pacific, especially Indonesia
Description: The name *Palythoa ignota* is often used for this species. However, the individual polyps are sometimes unconnected, as shown in the photograph, and those that are connected do not have a well developed coenenchyme. This species cannot belong to the genus *Palythoa* because of the lack of the thickened coenenchyme into which the individual polyps can retract. The polyps have sand embedded in their thick columns and the bright fluorescent-green oral disc is large, up to 1in (2.5cm) in diameter.
Feeding requirements: Feeds solely from the products of its own zooxanthellae.
Aquarium suitability: Needs plenty of light and moderate water movement but otherwise easy to keep and very attractive.

Protopalythoa sp.

Family: Zoanthidae
Range: Central Indo-Pacific
Description: The polyp columns are short and their surfaces are embedded with sand. The margin of the oral disc is thickened with short tentacles. A single white streak is often present across the oral surface and the inner margin of the mouth is white or yellow. The tentacles are brown and the oral disc may be greyish-blue or brown. A relatively thick coenenchyme connects the polyps together to form the colony.
Feeding requirements: Nutrition is provided exclusively by endosymbiotic algae, therefore it does not require any specific feeding.
Aquarium suitability: Colonies should not be placed directly under metal halides. Use moderate lighting, such as fluorescents. Plenty of water movement is vital to keep the polyps detritus free.

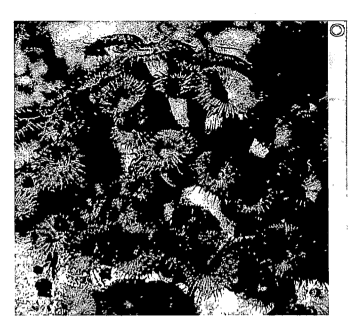

Protopalythoa sp.

Family: Zoanthidae
Range: Tropical Indo-Pacific
Description: In this species the polyp columns are quite long and the tentacles are well developed. The margin of the mouth is pale to white and the colour of the oral disc can vary from deep bright green to brown. Green specimens fluoresce under actinic or UV lighting. Sand is embedded in the basal columns and also in the stolons, which often connect the polyps.
Feeding requirements: Feeds mainly on its own zooxanthellae but will also supplement this with plankton and other small organisms. Nevertheless, no specific feeding is required.
Aquarium suitability: The colonies do well under strong illumination from metal-halide lights. Newly imported specimens tend to be brown but these will often turn green when exposed to the correct lighting.

Protopalythoa sp.

Family: Zoanthidae
Range: Red Sea, Indo-Pacific
Description: Very similar to the preceding species, but the polyps have much shorter tentacles and the basal column is more slender. The oral disc can be anything up to 1in (2.5cm) across and is deep green with a lighter green centre. Colonies of this and the previous species may often be found on the same rock, which sometimes causes confusion. Here, though, the polyps are connected by a coenenchyme rather than by creeping stolons, but again the basal columns are embedded with sand.
Feeding requirements: Lives solely from the products of its own zooxanthellae.
Aquarium suitability: Provide moderate to bright lighting and plenty of water movement. Place away from stony corals and anemones that may sting the colony. An easy species to keep.

Scientific name unknown
(Probably *Protopalythoa* sp. or *Acrozoanthus* sp.)
Family: Zoanthidae
Range: Central Indo-Pacific especially Indonesia
Description: This species is often imported as *Parazoanthus axinellae* (which it isn't), and *Parazoanthus gracilis* (which it isn't either). *Parazoanthus axinellae* is a Mediterranean species, and all *Parazoanthus* species are found encrusting gorgonians, tunicates, hydroids and sponges. This species is imported on live rock. The polyps are bright yellow with slender columns and long tentacles.
Feeding requirements: Feed on frozen plankton, brine shrimp and similar foods. Polyps utilize their own zooxanthellae but they are also active feeders.
Aquarium suitability: Do not place colonies of these corals near stony corals. This species will sting them and cause damage. Strong lighting and a moderately strong water movement produce the best results.

Order: Actiniaria (true sea anemones)

The order Actiniaria encompasses more than 1,000 species of what are commonly known as "true sea anemones". True sea anemones are solitary creatures in that they do not form colonies at all. In simple terms, they typically consist of an oral disc, a column and a pedal base or disc. The oral disc is covered with tentacles that surround the mouth. This is formed in the shape of a slit and has ciliated grooves (siphonoglyphs) at each end, which are used to direct water into the gastrovascular cavity within the column. The water carries oxygen and nutrients to the anemone and it is also used to fill the body under a form of hydrostatic pressure. This enables them to expand, contract or, with the use of muscles, to change their shape.

Light plays an important role in the life of anemones, and they require plenty of illumination to allow the correct growth of zooxanthellae algae within their body tissue. These algae provide a large part of the creatures' daily nutritional and oxygen requirements. Nevertheless, they also need to capture food to supplement this. To facilitate this function, the tentacles are armed with encapsulated nematocysts (cnidae), which are discharged when they come into contact with their prey. These spiral-like barbs release an immobilizing poison.

Large anemones, such as those belonging to the families Actiniidae and Stichodactylidae, often play host to fishes. Usually these are the anemonefishes of the genus *Amphiprion*, although the damselfish, *Dascyllus trimaculatus*, is also known to form a symbiotic relation-ship with sea anemones. The anemonefish secretes a mucous coating around itself, and will even accelerate this process during its acclimatization to its new host by biting the tips of the tentacles. This is believed to speed up the secretion of mucous. Once this is done, which can take from just a few seconds to several hours, the fish can swim into the stinging tentacles of its host anemone without any problems. During the process of acclimatization, the fish becomes, in effect, chemically and biologically invisible to its host.

The benefits of the relationship between the anemonefish and its host are complex and not as yet fully understood. Apart from the obvious reasons – the anemone extends protection to the fish and in return the fish keeps the anemone free from detritus and feeds it with unwanted scraps of food – there are other considerations. Studied closely in aquariums, fish have been observed to use anemones as holding devices so that several morsels of food can be stored temporarily until the fish has swallowed the food in its mouth. When this has taken place, the anemonefish will proceed to "rob" the anemone of its prizes, piece by piece, before they can be devoured.

Bear in mind that anemones can be incredibly long-lived, so you should do all in your power to prevent them dying while in your aquarium through lack of knowledge on your part. Note the following points:

Light A combination of metal-halide lighting with actinic fluorescent tubes seems to be the best for these creatures. The metal halides should be HQI with a colour temperature of 6,500 to 10,000°K in order to produce a full light spectrum. They need plenty of light for their zooxanthellae to grow. A good way to tell when an anemone is not receiving enough light is when it migrates to the top of the tank.

Migration When an anemone starts to move around the aquarium, there may be reasons for this behaviour apart from the quality of the lighting. Large host anemones prefer moderate to strong water movement, not only to carry food to their tentacles, but also because of their need for oxygen – for themselves and their endosymbiotic zooxanthellae. Hunger is one of the main reasons why an anemone will migrate. If it gradually starts to shrink in size and migrate, then it is slowly starving.

Feeding Large host anemones and many of the smaller species need to be fed at least once a week. This will maintain their size and stop them from migrating. The best foods to provide are whole or half pieces of freshly thawed mussel and squashed whole sand shrimps. Lancefish can also be given as an occasional treat.

Trigger response Anemones must be fed by hand and not with tweezers or plastic tongs. These instruments will not always trigger a feeding response in the creature because they are nonorganic. Anemones should always be fed in the evening or early morning, as it is at these times of day that their feeding response is at its sharpest.

Feeding strategies The piece of food should be placed on the oral disc, midway between the margin of the disc and the mouth. Never try to force feed an anemone by pushing food into the oral opening itself. This will block the siphonoglyphs necessary for hydrostatic control and water/oxygen exchange within the creature's body. As you place the food on the disc, a light pressure is required; moving your fingers from side to side (like a fish or shrimp struggling) will usually initiate a response. In addition, the tentacles should be disturbed with your finger at the same time. This will result in a discharge of some of the cnidae against your finger and trigger an effective feeding response. The cnidae are not able to penetrate human skin and so do not hurt. The sensation is nothing more than moderate or mild stickiness, like half-dried glue.

Size control If a specimen becomes too large, then the feeding rate can be reduced to every ten days or even every two weeks. This will reduce the size of the anemone.

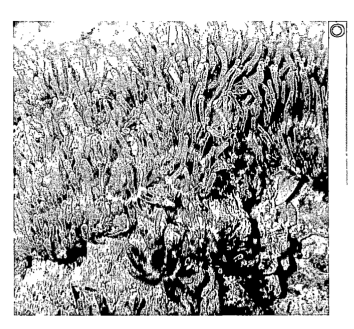

"Anemonia" manjano

Family: Actiniidae
Range: East Africa to Central Indo-Pacific
Description: Although not belonging to the genus *Anemonia*, until it has been reassigned quotation marks have been used around the name. Carlgren (1900) described this species as *Anemonia manjano*. The word *Manjano* is Swahili for "turmeric" and refers to the yellowish column of the anemone. The column is yellowish-green and the tentacles tapering are brown with fluorescent-green tips.
Feeding requirements: Feeds mainly from its own zooxanthellae but will also capture food.
Aquarium suitability: A small species that usually occurs on live rock from Indonesia. It multiplies rapidly through pedal laceration and longitudinal fission and can reach plague proportions in a tank, severely stinging soft and stony corals.

"Anemonia" sp.

Family: Actiniidae
Range: Red Sea, Tropical Indo-Pacific
Description: Fossa & Nilsen (1995) and Sprung & Delbeek (1997) describe both this and the preceding species under the names *"Anemonia"* cf. *majano* and *Anemonia* cf. *majano*, respectively. Apart from the name being misspelled, both species are included in their single descriptions. *"Anemonia"* manjano seldom has a disc diameter of more than 1in (2.5cm), whereas this species can reach almost double this in size. The column and oral disc are brown, as are the tentacles. These have fluorescent-white, club-shaped tips.
Feeding requirements: Actively captures food but relies heavily on its own zooxanthellae.
Aquarium suitability: An attractive species, particularly under actinic lighting. It does not multiply as rapidly as *"A."* manjano.

Condylactis gigantea
(Syn. *Condylactis passiflora*)
Family: Actiniidae
Range: Caribbean, Tropical West Atlantic
Description: This is the largest and most beautiful of all the Caribbean anemones. The long, flowing tentacles can reach a length of up to 6in (15cm) and have purple or green tips. The rest of the tentacles and oral disc are usually snowy-white or greenish in colouration and the column may be yellow, orange, green or white.
Feeding requirements: Feeds mainly from the products of its own zooxanthellae but will accept weekly feedings of frozen krill, cockle and chopped mussel.
Aquarium suitability: Strong lighting and good water quality are required for total success with this species. In addition, a thick, sandy bottom and plenty of crevices in living rock will ensure its wellbeing and longevity.

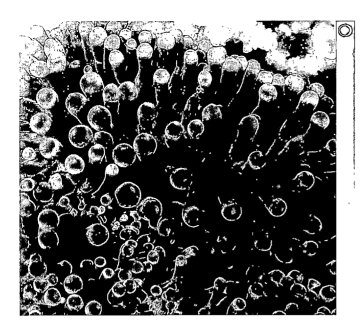

Entacmaea quadricolor

Family: Actiniidae
Range: Red Sea, Tropical Indo-Pacific
Description: An easy anemone to identify because of the bubble-like tips to its tentacles. The column does not have verrucae and may be red, violet, green or brown. The oral disc is lighter in colour, usually greenish, but some specimens can be a deep chocolate-brown. The tentacles are often tipped with violet or magenta. In the wild it grows to 20in (51cm) and is a "host" to *Amphiprion clarkii*, *A. frenatus*, *A. ephippium* and *Premnas biaculeatus*.
Feeding requirements: Feeds on its own zooxanthellae but captures small fishes and other organisms. Feed on a weekly basis with mussel and sand shrimp.
Aquarium suitability: Needs good light and a good water flow. Specimens should be slowly acclimatized to the aquarium.

Macrodactyla doreensis

Family: Actiniidae
Range: Central Indo-Pacific
Description: This is a large sand anemone that can grow to 20in (51cm) in diameter. In the wild it is normally found on sandy seabeds and in crevices between rocks and coral. The tentacles are on the periphery of the oral disc, leaving the area around the mouth free. This is often adorned with radial stripes that can extend on to the tentacles. The column, which is often buried in the sand, can be orange, red or brownish-white.
Feeding requirements: Feeds on organisms that are captured by its tentacles and supplements this with nutrients from its zooxanthellae. Feed weekly on frozen cockle or mussel flesh.
Aquarium suitability: Bright lighting, plenty of water movement and a good depth of sand are the main requirements for this easy-care species.

Phymanthus sp.

Family: Phymanthidae
Range: Tropical Indo-Pacific
Description: The column, tentacles and oral disc are reddish-brown and the branches on the tentacles are yellowish-white. The centre of the oral disc is free of tentacles and its outer margin has a series of 12 lined blotches that are pale orange-brown. These anemones are commonly called sand anemones. In their natural habitat they are to be found with their columns buried in sand or sediment in the reef shallows, with only their tentacles and oral disc visible in the sunlight.
Feeding requirements: Feeds from its own zooxanthellae but actively captures prey with its tentacles. Feed on a weekly basis.
Aquarium suitability: Most sand anemones are easy to keep and long-lived in an aquarium. They should be kept under strong lighting to encourage the growth of their zooxanthellae.

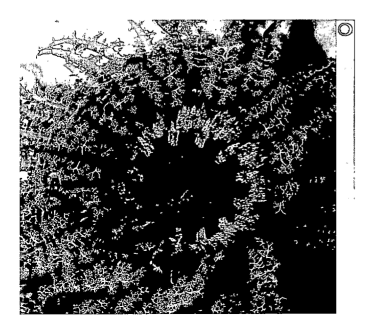

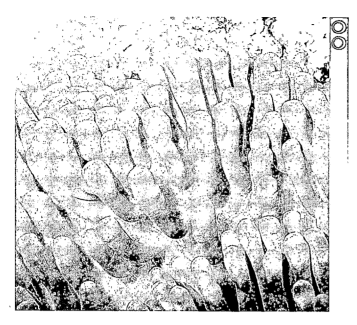

Stichodactyla haddoni

Family: Stichodactylidae
Range: Red Sea, East Africa to Polynesia
Description: Described in Friese (1972) as *Stoichactis kenti*, in Mills (1987) as *Stoichactis giganteum* and in Haywood & Wells (1989) and Dakin (1992) as *Stoichactis gigas*, this is a very sticky anemone with short, almost round tentacles. The upper half of the column is often bright pink or lilac and is covered with small verrucae. The oral disc is bluish-grey or green. Grows to 20in (51cm) or more.
Feeding requirements: Zooxanthellae are utilized but it should be fed at least once a week on shrimp, lancefish or mussel and cockle flesh.
Aquarium suitability: A good "host" anemone that can prove initially difficult to settle in to a tank. As far as lighting is concerned, metal halides are best.

Heteractis magnifica

Family: Stichodactylidae
Range: Red Sea, Tropical Indo-Pacific
Description: Known previously under the name *Radianthus ritteri*, this species often has a coloured column with contrasting tentacles and oral disc. The column is usually red or pink and the tentacles can be brown or bluish-green to green. There are rows of verrucae on the column that extend from the margin of the oral disc down the column. The tentacles have purple or green blunt tips. The oral disc can reach 40in (1m) across.
Feeding requirements: Utilizes the products of its own zooxanthellae and actively captures prey. Feed weekly on whole mussel and shrimp.
Aquarium suitability: A good host to many species of anemonefishes. It needs plenty of space and a well-lit tank with a good water flow to thrive.

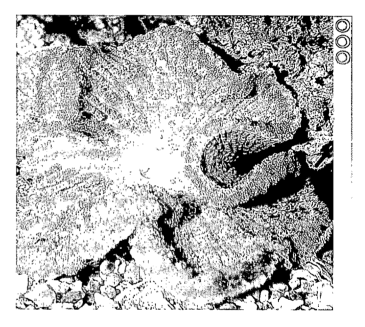

Aiptasia sp.

Family: Aiptasiidae
Range: Represented in all tropical seas.
Description: This is a small anemone with an oral disc diameter of up to 1in (2.5cm). The column is translucent brown to olive green and is trumpet-formed. It grows to a height of about 3in (7.5cm) and is found in rock crevices on the reef as well as in rocky or mangrove coastal zones.
Feeding requirements: Feeds on a variety of organisms and also utilizes its own zooxanthellae.
Aquarium suitability: Specimens enter the tank on live rock and can multiply rapidly, stinging everything in their way. They are difficult to destroy since small pieces and remains will grow into new anemones. Scraping them off rocks will only increase their numbers. The sea slug *Bergia* sp. and the butterflyfish *Chelmon rostratus* feed on and control this species.

Phylum: Platyhelminthes (flatworms)

The phylum encompasses three classes with an estimated 15,000 species. Only one of these classes, Turbellaria, with about 4,000 species, is of interest to marine aquarists. The other two classes, Trematoda and Cestoda, contain mainly parasitic worms, such as parasitic flukes and tapeworms. Many of the species are found in fresh water or in swamps and have little relevance to the content of this book. Those that are sometimes housed in aquariums are extremely attractive. These are commonly known as flatworms, and most of the colourful species belong to the order Polycladida.

Flatworms are primitive creatures that have bilateral symmetry. This means that they have a distinct head and tail area of the body. There is no anus and also no cavity surrounding the simple internal organs. Some flatworms are terrestrial and most are freshwater species, such as the planarians. Those that are marine-living are usually dull and uninteresting, but there are still many species that are brightly coloured and bizarre. The body is often shaped like a leaf and is flat and solid. The mouth is situated on the underside of the body and serves also as the anus. There are no respiratory organs as such: "breathing" is a type of gas-exchange through the skin of the animal.

You need to bear in mind that all flatworms are difficult to keep in an aquarium and this is why they are seldom available for sale.

Phylum: Gnathostomulida (jaw worms)

Surprisingly little has been written about these tiny sand- and sediment-dwelling worms. Nevertheless, they have been included here because of their importance in keeping the base medium of an aquarium well aerated, particularly when a plenum is used. Here, a good interstitial community is important and members of this phylum are often present. They are able to live equally well in an aerobic as well as an anaerobic milieu.

The phylum is small and contains only about 100 species. These animals are small, seldom exceeding 0.5 to 1mm in length, and can be overlooked very easily since they live between the grains of sand. The body is long and thread-like and its surface is covered in tiny cilia. There is no anus and waste products appear to be expelled through the walls of the body. Their nutrition comprises mainly minute marine fungi, algae and bacteria. The internal organs are simple and consist of a mouth cavity with a somewhat hardened base. This leads into a pharynx that has clutching jaws, and further into a simplified stomach. These worms are hermaphroditic and possess both ovaries and a penis and testicles. The hardened baseplate in the mouth acts as a shovel to pick up organisms, which are then transferred to the stomach by the grasping jaws.

In many aquariums they are completely absent, whereas in others they can turn up in quantity. They are important in two respects. First, they are considered to be an important phylogenetic link between the two phyla Cnidaria and Platyhelminthes, and the rest of the invertebrates. Second, they are able to live in a totally anaerobic environment, which means they derive the necessary oxygen they need from nitrite and nitrate. This would then result in a natural reduction of nitrite and nitrate into nitrogen – something that is always an advantage in an aquarium.

Phylum: Nemertea (ribbon worms)

The phylum contains about 260 genera and 1,300 species. Nemerteans are slender, unsegmented worms that range in size from tiny to several yards. Generally, they are marine-dwelling, although some are found in fresh water and a few are terrestrial. Only a comparatively small percentage of the known species are to be found on tropical coral reefs. Although they are often plentiful, they are not frequently seen because they are mainly nocturnal. Some species prefer sandy or muddy sediments and there are representatives from this phylum in all seas. Many of the species found in tropical regions are brightly coloured, sometimes with distinct body stripes. Most nemerteans

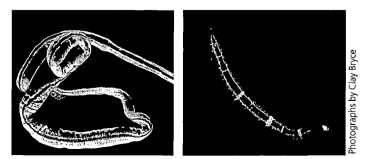

LEFT Quasilineus lucidoculatus *from Albany, Western Australia.*
RIGHT Micrura callima *taken from Rottnest Island, Western Australia.*

Photographs by Clay Bryce

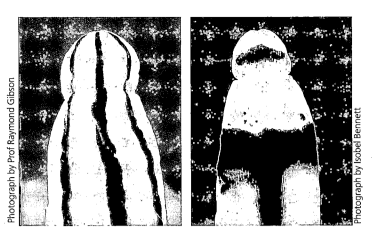

LEFT *The body of* Baseodiscus quinquelineatus *usually has five or seven stripes, three of which are shown here on the head. It is endemic throughout the Indo-Pacific to Australia.*
RIGHT Baseodiscus hemprichii *with its typical head markings, a species known throughout the Indo-Pacific.*

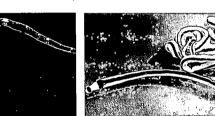

LEFT *Some nemertean worms are startlingly colourful, such as* Micrura callima *from Rottnest Island, Western Australia.*
RIGHT Baseodiscus hemprichii *(Lord Howe Island).*

have no commercial significance, nevertheless they do turn up on live rock occasionally and, although shy, seem to do quite well in aquariums.

The contractile body may be depressed or tubular and is covered with cilia. The muscular structure within the body is well developed, as is the gut, which can be almost as long as the worm itself. The mouth is situated ventrally at the anterior end of the body and the anus is usually terminal, or nearly so. In some species a long tail (cirrus) may extend beyond the anus and in pelagic species the posterior end is sometimes flattened into a rudimentary fin, which aids in swimming. Nemerteans do not possess specialized respiratory structures. In most species the head is not demarcated from the trunk, but in some the head may be developed into a distinct cephalic lobe. Eyes may be present or absent, depending on the species; when present they may number two or four, as for example in *Tetrastemma* species, while others, such as *Baseodiscus*, may possess several dozen eyes.

Perhaps the most important identifying characteristic of members of this phylum is the long tube-like proboscis that can be rapidly everted from the body; one aberrant species, *Arhynchonemertes axi*, from New Zealand, has no proboscis apparatus of any form. The proboscis is everted either through a separate anterior pore (in the Anopla) or through an aperture shared with the mouth (in

the Enopla). In most nemerteans the proboscis, which may be longer than the body, is unbranched, but a few hetero-nemerteans are known, including *Gorgonorhynchus*, which lives on coral reefs, where the proboscis is branched. In the Hoplonemertea the proboscis is armed with one or more needle-like barbs (stylets); these are used both offensively and defensively.

The Hoplonemertea is separated into two suborders. The Monostilifera include those species whose proboscis is armed with a single stylet, whereas the Polystilifera encompass species with multiple stylets in the proboscis. In all cases, the prey is captured with the proboscis being used rather like a lasso.

Most nemertean species possess separate sexes, with the eggs and sperm being released into the surrounding sea. Some species, however, show a simple form of mating, secreting a thin mucous sheath around both their bodies before releasing the eggs and sperm. In the pelagic genus *Phallonemertes*, a primitive form of copulation is found. The fertilized eggs can develop directly into juvenile worms or into larvae, depending on the species. Larvae may be free-swimming. A form of asexual reproduction is also known in some heteronemerteans, where the body fragments (or is split) into several pieces, each of which eventually develops into a complete individual.

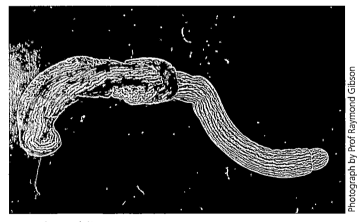

Baseodiscus delineatus.

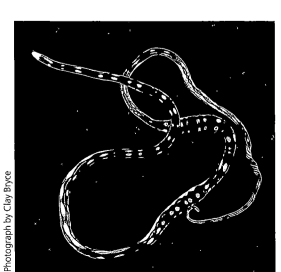

Australineus albidecus *from Albany, Western Australia.*

Phylum: Nematoda (roundworms)

This phylum contains the most abundant group of animals in existence. In the aquarium they play a significant role in the reduction of organic compounds. Just how vital this is to a successful marine aquarium was, until recently, overlooked. The coral sand in a mature reef or marine tank is full of these creatures, which act as cleaners, and there can be as many as 10,000 of these worms per 4 sq in (26 sq cm) of aquarium sand.

But not all nematodes are beneficial; many are parasitic, living on plants and animals. In general terms, "worms" when applied to house pets and to humans, usually means that parasitic nematode worms (such as *Ascaris lumbricoides*) have infested the digestive system.

Many species are minute, seldom exceeding 1mm in length, although some species can grow to 40in (1m). Most, including marine nematodes, are hardy and are able to live in extreme conditions. Because of their special body structure, which includes a very thick and strong skin, they are able to adapt to and withstand a variety of environments and circumstances.

Marine specimens are usually up to ⅛in (3mm) in length and live between the individual sand grains or in sediments where there is a high organic content. There they are able to move through and recycle the organic-rich sediments, feeding on algae, diatoms, small animals, other nematodes and detritus. They are to be found in all seas from the shallows to abyssal depths and are present in their millions on a typical coral reef.

There are two classes of nematodes, or roundworms, as they are sometimes known. These are Adenophorea and Secernentea. Adenophorea usually have bristle-like

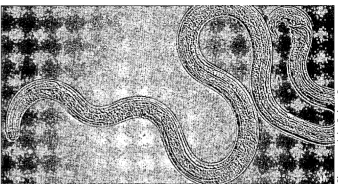

The typical body form of a marine-living nematode.

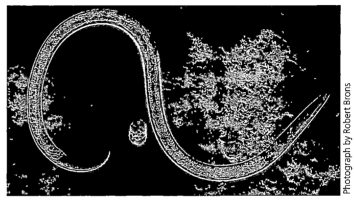

Nematodes are usually translucent. Here a specimen is seen with detritus.

cilia around the head region. Many species are marine living. In the class Secernentea the head is smooth. These are predominantly soil-dwelling and parasitic species that never occur in the sea.

Phylum: Gastrotricha (hair-bellies)

This group contains species that form a vital part of the meiofauna that makes up a mature sand bed in an aquarium. The group contains worms that are minute, with cilia present on their ventral surfaces – hence the name "hair-bellies".

The elongated body is often convex and flattened ventrally with bristle-like cilia and scales covering the surface. They have rudimentary eyes and some species have a narrowing behind the head region, which gives the

Unidentified Gastrotrich worm from the Red Sea.

impression of a neck. The posterior part of the body ends in a rounded, forked or extended tail. There are cilia on the head and in the ventral region. The ventral cilia are normally used for locomotion.

So far approximately 185 species have been described. They are mainly benthic creatures but a few species are free-swimming. Their diet consists of unicellular algae, bacteria and tiny invertebrate animals. Of the two orders, Macrodasyoida contains only marine-living species. These are found in sand and sediments in the intertidal zone and in coastal regions among alga beds. They are hermaphroditic and have adhesive tubes in the head and tail region and on the sides. The second order, Chaetonotoida, contains mainly freshwater representatives. The few marine species that do occur live near the shore in sandy bays and estuaries.

Phylum: Rotifera (rotifers)

Rotifers are an important food source, particularly for young fishes and many invertebrates. They are mostly found in fresh water and marshland, although a considerable number of the almost 1,800 species that have been described occur in the sea, where they may be free-swimming, sessile or benthic. Were it not for these creatures, the important developments in fish culture and breeding techniques within this hobby would not have taken place. They offer the ideal first-food source to fish breeders.

They are minute animals with unsegmented bodies that are often elongated. There is a small head area and a terminal foot. The main characteristic of these animals is the presence of what is often term a "wheel organ" on the head. This consists of a ring, or rings, of cilia that pulse in a beating motion to give the impression of a rotating wheel. The wheel is used to convey the animal through the water and also to carry microscopic food particles toward its mouth.

Of the three orders, Seisonidea contains only one family of parasitic rotifers that are found in the gills of some crustaceans. The ciliated wheel is very reduced and they feed mainly on organic food remains. Bdelloidea, the second order, is also a specialized group of mainly fresh-water species with elongated bodies and wheel organs that usually consist of two rings of cilia. There is, however, a marine representative that lives in the skin of sea cucumbers. The third order, Monogononta, is the important one as far as the marine aquarist is concerned. It contains animals that are found in fresh water and in the sea. The marine rotifers in this group are variable in form and can be sessile, benthic or free swimming.

There are three suborders, but only Ploima is of interest. It includes species that are sessile, each having two toe-like structures that are used to attach them to the

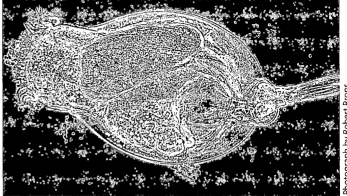

An unidentified brackish water rotifer from Holland.

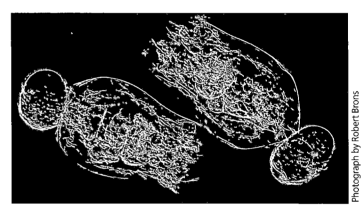

Brachionus *sp. (two females with egg sacs).*

substrata, but there are also many free-swimming forms. The suborder covers several important families – perhaps the most important for aquarists being Brachionidae. This family contains the genus *Brachionus* of which the most well known representative is the marine-living species *Brachionus plicatilis*, which is often cultured by aquarists in order to feed newly hatched fry in a marine aquarium.

Phylum: Kinorhyncha (kinorhynchs)

Currently there are less than 150 species that have so far been described, but as biologists continue to carry out research on these animals it is expected that many more will be discovered. Although they play only a supporting role in a healthy meiofauna in an aquarium, they are nevertheless important. Kinorhynchs burrow in the sand and sediment, feeding on organic debris and diatomaceous algae. They are part of the interstitial community and their constant burrowing helps to keep the base medium well oxygenated. Although these animals are not very well researched as yet, a mature reef aquarium could contain hundreds, if not thousands, of them within the substratum.

They are slightly larger than the average rotifer, with a length of up to 1mm. Kinorhynchs cannot be considered as belonging to the segmented sea worms since the surface of the body shows superficial annulation and not segmentation. The flattened ventral surface usually has a pair of adhesive tubes, which are used as holdfasts in turbulent water. The body lacks cilia but many species have well-developed tail spines that are used for steering as they burrow slowly through the substrata. Most of these creatures are a dull yellowish-brown to deep brown in colour. They are normally present in sediments and sand near the shoreline, usually within the intertidal zone, but they are also to be found at abyssal depths.

Phylum: Annelida (segmented worms)

The phylum currently contains about 11,500 species. Generally their body structure includes a straight gut, which runs from the anterior mouth to the posterior anus. There is a liquid-filled body cavity and this is surrounded by a muscular body wall. The purpose of this is to enable the worm, through hydrostatic pressure and contraction and expansion of the muscles, to lengthen or shorten its body length at will.

Each of the body segments usually has protruding bristle-like hairs. These are termed "setae", or sometimes "chaetae", and they are used primarily for locomotion, but in addition they are also used as gills for breathing. The body segments are identical in that each contains nerves, blood vessels, musculature, gonads and organs for excretion. This means that any group of segments, when separated from the rest of the animal, is normally able to regenerate and function as a complete individual.

The first class, Oligochaeta, encompasses more than 3,000 species. These are segmented worms and the group includes all the earthworms and also tubifex worms, which are well known as live food for freshwater tropical fishes. Most are terrestrial and these will not be discussed further. The second class, Polychaeta, will be dealt with next in more detail, whereas the third and final class, comprising the leeches and bloodsuckers, is also outside the scope of this book.

Class: Polychaeta (polychaetes)

The polychaetes are almost exclusively marine creatures although there are a few freshwater and land-dwelling species that have been described. The class incorporates more than 8,000 species in about 80 families. In some species, the forward part of the gut (pharynx) can be thrust out of the mouth like a proboscis. This sometimes contains jaws for seizing food. Typically, the body is cylindrical or depressed and is segmented.

There are two types of polychaete worms: those that crawl, creep or swim (errant); and those that are benthic and live in tubes (sedentary). The errant polychaetes are by far the most common, even in aquariums. In this case, they are usually introduced along with living rock or with other invertebrates. In ideal aquarium conditions they reproduce quite rapidly – sometimes reaching plague proportions. Tentacles and palps often surround the mouth, and the setae along each side of the segmented body are moveable and provide locomotion as well as being used for breathing. These chitinous bristles are sometimes long and brittle and when the worm is handled they break off in the skin, causing discomfort and sometimes sepsis. Others have fragile setae that are

poisonous and a few species also have poisonous bites. The common clamworms, bristleworms and fireworms (Amphinomidae) are all errant polychaetes.

Sedentary polychaetes are tube dwelling. They have a well-developed nervous chain through their bodies. At the threat of danger they will retract into their tubes, sometimes at the most astonishing speed. To do this they have a series of eyes on the head region that detects changes in light and shadow.

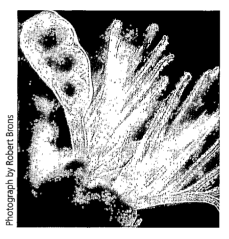

Photograph by Robert Brons

The larval sac of a serpulid worm (Spirorbis sp.) is shown clearly in this close-up photograph of the adult.

Order: Sabellida (fan worms and calcareous tube worms)

This group of marine worms is by far the most interesting for the marine aquarist. It contains those attractive creatures that live in parchment-like or calcareous tubes. Many resemble colourful feather dusters and they are sometimes referred to as "feather duster worms". The body is more or less cylindrical and is divided into two regions: the thorax and the segmented abdomen. On the segments, the parapodia and setae are greatly reduced or completely absent. The two families that are of interest here are Sabellidae (fan worms) and Serpulidae (calcareous tube worms).

Sabellid worms (Sabellidae) have flexible tubes and are often quite large. They may grow singly or in colonies, usually half buried in the sediment or sand with only the top portion of the tube and fan visible. Some species build their tubes in small holes in rock. When the worm is withdrawn into its tube there is no plug-like closure (operculum) present to cover the hole. Instead, certain species secrete mucus around the inner margin of the opening and, on withdrawing into the tube, it seals two sides of the soft opening together to form a temporary closure. This serves two purposes: it provides a certain degree of protection against predators, which are apt to winkle these worms out of their tubes; and it also prevents detritus and other debris from entering the tube.

Serpulid worms (Serpulidae) are somewhat different, although in body form they are basically the same as the sabellids. It is an interesting family that can be considered as being further developed in the evolutionary line of the invertebrates. The tubes of these worms are constructed in rings of calcium carbonate that the creatures secrete as they grow. Members of this family are usually smaller than the fan worms and often only inhabit the top part of their tubes. Calcareous tube worms are often found in large colonies but some larger species may occur singly.

If you wish to keep fan worms and tube worms in an aquarium you must bear in mind that they are filter feeders, therefore they often require specific feeding with commercially prepared foods for filter-feeding invertebrates. They should not be housed in the same tank as butterflyfishes, such as *Chelmon rostratus*, otherwise they will be eaten in a short space of time.

*The tiny cornet worm (*Spirorbis sp.*) looks like a mollusc, but is in fact a serpulid worm.*

Sabellastarte indica

Family: Sabellidae
Range: Tropical Indo-Pacific, Red Sea
Description: The tentacle crown is usually 2 to 4in (5 to 10cm) in diameter and the parchment-like tube can be up to 10in (25cm) long. The tentacles are variable in colour but are often a mottled reddish-brown and white. Until the revision of this genus is complete, all similar Indo-Pacific species should be referred to using the name given above. There are many synonyms, particularly within the aquarium hobby. Names such as *Sabellastarte japonica* and *S. sanctijosephi* have no validity.
Feeding requirements: A filter feeder that needs to be fed every other day on frozen plankton or commercial food for filter-feeding invertebrates.
Aquarium suitability: These worms are quite hardy and long-lived and are ideal for a reef tank.

Sabellastarte magnifica

Family: Sabellidae
Range: Caribbean, Tropical West Atlantic
Description: As with the previous species, until the revision of this genus is complete, the name above should be used for this and all similar species originating from the Caribbean. This species is very similar to *S. indica* from the tropical Indo-Pacific region. The tentacle crown can reach a diameter of 4in (10cm) and is usually mottled reddish-brown and white.
Feeding requirements: A filter-feeding species that needs to be fed three or four times a week to keep it flourishing.
Aquarium suitability: Provided it has sufficient food, this species will do well in the confines of an aquarium. Specimens should be placed in holes in rocks or between them. They will soon attach themselves there and begin to feed.

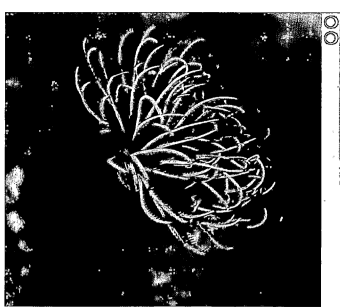

Photograph by Frank Walker

Sabellastarte sp.

Family: Sabellidae
Range: Central Indo-Pacific
Description: The tube of this species can be up to 1in (2.5cm) in diameter and the tentacle crown may be 5in (13cm) across. This makes it much larger than the the preceding species. The tentacles are creamy-white with a slight fluorescence under actinic lighting, so there is the suspicion of the presence of zooxanthellae within the tentacle structure. Typically, the tentacles are curved inward, as you can see in the accompanying photograph.
Feeding requirements: A filter feeder that requires weekly specific feeding for the best results in an aquarium.
Aquarium suitability: Needs plenty of light for it to show its full magnificence (this also points to the presence of endo-symbiotic algae), and a moderate water movement.

Salmacina sp.

Family: Serpulidae
Range: Entire Tropical Indo-Pacific, Red Sea
Description: On average, the calcareous tubes are about ⅛in (2 to 3mm) in diameter and the tentacle crown is usually less than ½in (1.5cm). The tentacles are creamy-white, as is the tube, and this is ridged on the upper third of its length. This worm forms large, intertwined colonies of brittle tubes on the substrate, usually under overhangs or in crevices and caves on the reef.
Feeding requirements: This species requires no special feeding in an aquarium, despite the fact that it is a filter feeder. It seems to derive what it needs from the water without any special care.
Aquarium suitability: Can become a real problem, but one that is easily controlled. This attractive worm multiplies very rapidly in a well-balanced system and the tubes can block filter and pump intakes unless they are periodically removed.

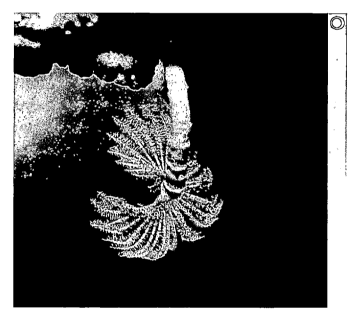

Protula bispiralis

Family: Serpulidae
Range: Tropical Indo-West Pacific
Description: This is probably the largest of the calcareous tube worms and, like the preceding species, the operculum is absent. The diameter of the tube can be almost 1in (2.5cm) and up to 8in (20cm) long. The tail of the tube is usually spiralled with the open end toward the direction of the water flow. The tentacle crown is branched into two distinct spirals that are normally orange-red and white.
Feeding requirements: Captures plankton and other organic foods with its tentacles.
Aquarium suitability: This is not an easy species to keep although it is often imported. It needs to be fed every second day on frozen plankton and the like, ideally with a pipette. It also requires a light to moderate water movement.

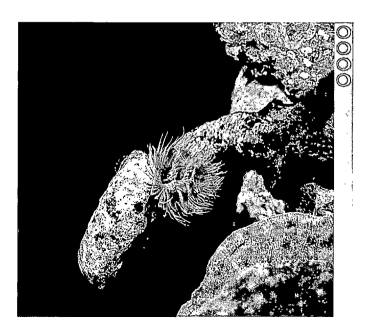

Phylum: Sipunculida (boring worms, peanut worms)

Sipunculans, or peanut worms as they are often called, are quite common in reef aquariums. They usually enter the tank along with live rock and decorative invertebrates. They are completely harmless to other tank inhabitants and belong to the natural reef environment that you are striving to replicate.

The phylum contains some 325 species that are found in all seas, from the intertidal zone to great depths. They are marine worms ranging in size from minute to more than 15in (38cm) in length. Some species burrow into sand and sediment while others bore into calcareous rock or into fissures in the substrata. The body possesses bilateral symmetry and is ostensibly divided into two parts. The main body or trunk is thick and is often covered in bristles and warts. The forward part of the body (introvert) is much thinner with a terminal mouth, usually surrounded with ciliated tentacles. These are used to capture food particles and organic debris from the water and the immediate substrata. The introvert can be withdrawn fully into the trunk but it can also be extended to a considerable length in search of food.

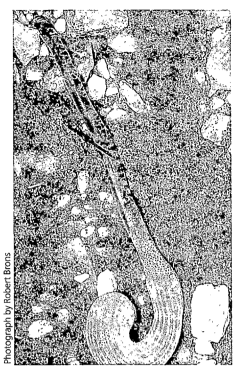

Photograph by Robert Brons

A sand-dwelling peanut worm from the Red Sea region.

Phylum: Arthropoda (joint-legged animals)

In arthropods the skin is relatively thick, often with a chitinous exoskeleton. In most species this is moulted during the larval stages or as the creature grows. The body possesses bilateral symmetry and there is a well developed nervous system with highly developed sense organs. The eyes are compound and consist of many smaller rudimentary eyes joined together to form compact and effective units. Many of the species have antennae with accompanying sensory organs, and in all species the body is segmented, usually with three pairs of walking legs attached, but there are often more. Millipedes, for example, have more than a hundred pairs of legs. All arthropods have similar blood systems and sex organs. Their eyes and muscular structures are characteristic of the phylum.

The arthropods are the only group of animals, with the exception of the vertebrates, that possess jointed legs. The phylum is very large and encompasses more than 1 million described species, but the number is probably a great deal higher if you include all those as yet unclassified. This makes up more than two-thirds of all the known species in the entire animal kingdom. It is a diverse group that contains more than 50,000 species of spiders, 32,500 species of crustaceans (although this will probably be nearer 60,000 once all the species have been described), and an incalculable number of insects. It is the insect

group that is by far the largest, and insect representatives are to be found in all climates of the world and in every milieu.

There are three subphyla that make up this group of animals. The first, Uniramia, is divided into two superclasses encompassing a total of eight classes. These are of little interest to the aquarist since they are almost exclusively land-dwelling creatures. The subphylum contains millipedes, centipedes and all the insects.

Subphylum: Chelicerata

The subphylum contains three classes, the first of which is Arachnida. This large class contains all of the land-dwelling spiders, scorpions, ticks and mites. The only truly marine representatives belong to the order Acari, which contains marine mites as well as terrestrial and parasitic animals.

The few marine species are usually from the family Halacaridae. They are tiny creatures, usually less than ⅛in (2.5mm) in length, that occur in most seas, both in the intertidal zone as well as in deeper water. They are often found crawling in algal beds on their four pairs of hairy legs. They have little meaning to the aquarist, however, although they are often present on live rock and can establish themselves quite well in an aquarium.

The second class, Pycnogonida, encompasses more than 1,200 species of sea spiders. This is an exclusively marine group of animals that are often less than 1mm in length, although some deep-sea species may grow to 20in (51cm). They are frequently introduced into an aquarium on live rock and as parasites on other invertebrates such as coral, gorgonians and sea anemones. Sea spiders are seldom good for an aquarium since their diet usually consists of the living tissue of their host. They are strange creatures with a segmented body that is long and thin. There is a head region, which bears a cylindrical proboscis that can often be as long as the body itself. The four pairs of walking legs are sometimes longer than the body and they frequently end in claw-like structures that are used to grip the substrata.

The third class, Merostomata, is small but it is of considerable interest to aquarium hobbyists and is dealt with next in more detail.

Class: Merostomata

The class contains only one order with a single family and three genera encompassing four species. Horseshoe crabs, or king crabs as they are sometimes called, are not in fact crabs at all. They are more closely related to spiders and scorpions than to the Crustacea. They are placed in the order Xiphosura, along with the long-extinct sea scorpion, which died out some 300 million years ago. This beast reached a length of 10ft (3m). The horseshoe crabs reached their peak of development toward the end of the Cretaceous period, between 60 and 80 million years ago. At that time there were many species and these had a wide distribution. There are many fossilized records and, although most of the species are now extinct, those few that do remain have retained more or less the same form up to the present day. They can be considered as being "living fossils" and they are one of the oldest groups of creatures on the planet.

The living representatives can have a body length of up to 24in (61cm) and the body itself can be divided into three distinct regions. The anterior part (prosoma) contains the eyes, mouth, five pairs of walking legs and modified appendages in front of the mouth (chelicerae), which are used for feeding. The posterior part of the body (opisthoma) bears six pairs of appendages. The first pair is developed into protective covers for the two reproductive openings, and the other five pairs are modified into gills with numerous lamellae. The third region of the body is the tail, which can make up 50 per cent of the total body length of the animal.

These creatures are bottom dwellers, preferring sandy or muddy seabeds where they can burrow and plough through its surface in search of morsels of food. They are omnivorous scavengers of considerable value because they feed on dead marine worms and molluscs, such as bivalves. They will also feed on algae and other organic matter. The heavily armoured carapace affords ample protection against predators and it appears that they have little in the way of natural enemies.

A horseshoe crab moults its shell as it grows, in order to form a larger one to accommodate its increase in body size. This is also the case with most crustaceans. The carapace splits along the forward edge and the horseshoe crab literally scrambles out of its old shell with the new one already forming around its vulnerable body. On contact with salt water a chemical reaction takes place and it starts to harden, becoming leathery at first and harder later. The empty shells are often washed up on beaches in their thousands.

Order: Xiphosura (horseshoe crabs, king crabs)

Of the four extant species in this order only one is to be found in the Atlantic. This is *Limulus polyphemus*, which is the only representative of its genus. This species is restricted to the western Atlantic seaboard from Nova Scotia to Florida and the Caribbean. The other three species are found in various regions of the Indo-Pacific.

There are two representatives of the genus *Tachypleus* and these are widespread in the northern part of the Indo-Pacific, from India to Japan and from southern China to Indonesia. They are *Tachypleus gigas*, which grows to about 20in (51cm), and *T. tridentatus*, which is slightly larger at 24in (61cm). These two species often occur together, particularly around the shores of Hong Kong. The tails of these species have a more or less triangular cross-section.

Carcinoscorpius rotundicauda has, as the Latin specific name implies, a rounded to oval tail cross-section, unlike the other three species, and this makes it easy to identify. It is the only species in its genus and is endemic from India to Brunei. This horseshoe crab is ubiquitous in the Bay of Bengal, where specimens are known to enter brackish water during the breeding season, particularly the mouths of the Ganges in Bangladesh and the Irrawaddy delta in southern Burma (Myanmar). The species is the smallest of the four and seldom reaches a size of more than 14in (36cm). It is also known from the Malaysian archipelago and as far east as the Philippine Islands.

Most, if not all, of these species are available to aquarists. However, as a general rule they require special care and a special aquarium and should usually be kept only by experienced hobbyists. Because of their often bizarre appearance they are often displayed in large public aquariums and zoos throughout the world.

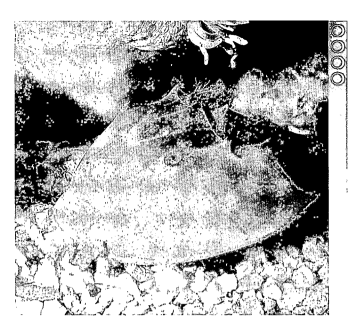

Limulus polyphemus

Family: Limulidae
Range: Tropical and sub-tropical West Atlantic
Description: The carapace colouration ranges from light tan to deep grey. There are 11 spines on the upper surface of the prosoma and these are arranged in three longitudinal rows. The centre row has three spines, the first of which is between and well below the compound eyes. The first of the four spines in the outside rows is situated near the inside margins of the eyes.
Feeding requirements: Feeds well on whole mussels or cockles. Difficult specimens can be removed from the water, inverted and fed pieces of food by hand without any adverse effects.
Aquarium suitability: A large aquarium with plenty of sandy spaces interspersed with large rocks is the best for this species. The tank should be well established, well lit and have plenty of water movement with a good power filter.

Subphylum: Crustacea

Crustaceans are predominantly marine creatures but there are some freshwater representatives and a few that have managed to venture on to land. The subphylum Crustacea encompasses seven classes with 32,500 described species and an estimated 6,000 undescribed ones. This is an extremely varied group, in both size and form. They range from the microscopic, some of which are parasitic, to the large lobsters and crabs of the Indo-Pacific. Most of the species are small, however, and these animals are of major importance to the marine food chain in that they make up a greater part of the planktonic life in the sea on which many larger animals feed.

On the reef, crustaceans are well represented and in some cases they are the dominant group. These tropical species are often highly coloured and many provide a valuable cleaning service for other invertebrates and fishes of the reef. Countless microscopic species belonging to this group inhabit the first inch or so of the seabed. They are a vital part of the interstitial community and, therefore, play an important role in the ecological stability of the seabed. They have a long fossil history and extant species are found everywhere in the sea in one form or another, from the intertidal zone to great depths.

Unlike insects, which only moult once they have reached their adult size and form, crustaceans are continually growing and so they have to moult periodically in order that the shell-like exoskeleton can accommodate the increase in their body size. To do this, the creature takes in water to make the body swell up. This causes the exoskeleton to split at a point between the thorax and the abdomen. The animal then extricates itself backward out of the old shell, leaving behind a perfect but fragile replica of its own form. Once this has been completed, a new exoskeleton begins to form and when

this has hardened the body is deflated in order to make room for more growth. At the moulting stage of its life the crustacean animal is at its most vulnerable because of its exposed soft body. This is why many of these creatures will find a cave or crevice in which to carry out the moult and most of them do this at night when the risk of being attacked by predators is at its lowest. The complete moulting process takes some time and this can vary from a few hours to several weeks, depending on the species.

Class: Branchiopoda

This is a group of animals that is almost exclusively from fresh water, or from saline seas and salt lakes. You may be wondering why a group of predominantly inland water species has been included. The reason is that they are important to marine aquarists as a source of live-food.

The class encompasses four orders with more than 900 species of mainly small crustaceans, and includes water fleas, known as *Daphnia*, and the saline crustaceans known as brine shrimp (*Artemia*). The genera *Cyclops*, *Moina* and *Diaptomus* also belong to this group. There are only a few truly marine representatives and these are planktonic animals belonging to the order Cladocera.

The order Anostraca contains a group of creatures without a carapace. They include freshwater species and also the commercially important genus *Artemia*, which is found in great numbers in inland salt lakes. There is some disagreement among the experts as to how many species of brine shrimp there are, but it is known that one species, *Artemia franciscana*, is cultured in quantity for the aquarium trade.

The order Cladocera contains two suborders, Haplopoda and Eucladocera. Haplopods are freshwater animals, whereas the few marine representatives of this group belong to the suborder Eucladocera. *Daphnia* (usually *Daphnia pulex*) belong to this order and are well known to freshwater aquarists. They can also be used as live food for marine fishes. Unfortunately *Daphnia* spp. do not live more than a few minutes in sea water so you must take care to ensure that no residual animals are left to foul the tank.

Class: Malacostraca

The diversity of the animals encompassed within this class is enormous and includes crabs, lobsters, prawns, shrimps and crayfish. There are two subclasses, the first of which is Phyllocarida. Phyllocarids are rather primitive and ancient creatures that have been in our seas for about 300 million years, most of them are now extinct. There is only one extant order, which encompasses bottom-dwelling and planktonic species.

The second subclass contains five orders, four of which are of interest to marine aquarists. The order Stomatopoda encompasses a group of creatures that are not uncommon in aquariums, although they are often undesirable. These are crustaceans that are known commonly as mantis shrimps. They are not very shrimp-like and have somewhat elongated and depressed bodies. The first five pairs of thoracic appendages are developed into shear-like claws that often have razor-sharp edges. The second pair of these is also greatly increased in size and these are used to capture food. They are predatory robbers that, in an aquarium, can do untold damage to the fish and invertebrate stock if not removed. Mantis shrimps usually enter the aquarium in live rock. Often the first indication that you have a problem is a loud clicking noise. This may be a welcome and harmless pistol shrimp from the family Alpheidae, or it could be a mantis shrimp snapping its sheared claws around some unsuspecting prey. If, at the

same time, you notice a decrease in the numbers of fishes and invertebrates in the aquarium, then it is almost certainly a mantis shrimp that is responsible. The best way to remove these animals is to find out in which rock it has set up its home and then remove that complete rock. There are also commercially available traps that can be used to the same end.

The second order of interest is Euphausiacea. For some years now, Pacific krill has been available frozen for use as marine fish food. Krill are an important part of the marine food chain for many fishes, manta rays and whales. Typically, krill seldom reach a length of much more than 1in (3cm). They are usually colourless to pink, but some deep-water species can be bright red. As food for marine aquarium fishes, they are second only to brine shrimp (*Artemia* spp.).

The third order, Decapoda, is of particular interest and will be dealt with in some detail in the following pages, since it contains many attractive and ornamental species for the aquarium.

The last order in this class is Peracarida. Apart from containing the small, bottom-dwelling isopods and amphipods, such as the sea slaters, which resemble wood lice, and sand hoppers, the order also incorporates the small opossum shrimps. These are another major food source for fishes and whales. You may be familiar with some species as aquarium food, although you may not relate them to the opossum shrimps. These have a variety of names in the hobby, such as mysid shrimps, Mysus, or sometimes just mysids.

Order: Decapoda (shrimps, prawns, lobsters, hermit crabs, true crabs)

The order contains about 68 families with a total of almost 9,000 described species. As far as marine aquarists

Artemia *sp.*

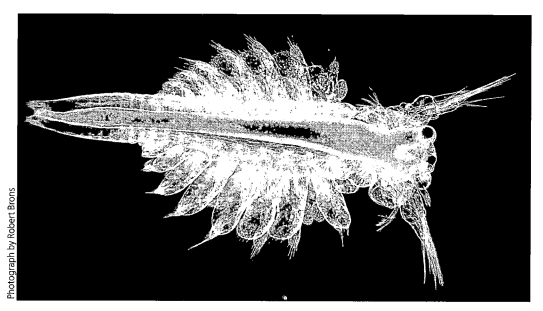

Photograph by Robert Brons

are concerned, species from this group are in constant demand. From the infraorder, Caridea, pistol shrimps and symbiotic shrimps, such as *Alpheus* spp. and *Synalpheaus* spp. from the family Alpheidae, are much sought after, as are cleaner shrimps from the genera *Thor*, *Lysmata* and *Parhippolyte*. Then there are the dancing shrimps, *Cinetorhynchus* and *Rhynchocinetes* spp. of the family Rhynchocinetidae, and the harlequin shrimps, *Gnathophyllum* and *Hymonecera* spp. from the family Gnathophyllidae. These are eagerly sought out by knowledgeable aquarists. However, there are others in this group, such as the deep-sea prawns belonging to the family Pandalidae and the freshwater shrimps of the family Atyidae. Barbershop shrimps from the genus *Stenopus* are also of great interest and some species are circumtropical in their distribution. Reef lobsters from the family Nephropidae are available as well, and those of the genus *Enoplometopus* are extremely decorative specimens for a tank. The most useful are the hermit crabs, especially those of the genera *Calcinus* and *Paguristes*. These creatures are excellent scavengers and they will happily take care of any uneaten food left in the aquarium. As well as serving this useful function, they will also keep algae growths under control. Some porcelain crabs, such as *Petrolisthes* spp., from the family Porcellanidae, are sold not only for their attractive appearance but also because they often live in symbiotic association with sea anemones. Of the true crabs, only a few are seen for sale. Most of them are too large or too aggressive toward other tank inhabitants to make them a worthwhile proposition for a reef aquarium. The arrow crab (*Stenorhynchus seticornis*) and some crabs of the genus *Camposcia* are the exceptions. These bizarre looking creatures are frequently seen in dealers' tanks for sale to the hobby trade.

Lysmata amboinensis

Family: Hippolytidae
Range: Tropical Indo-Pacific, Red Sea
Description: This species and its geographical colour morph from the tropical Atlantic are often described as *Lysmata grabhami*, although the name above has priority. To tell the two colour variations apart, look at the tail (telson). In the Atlantic colour morph, the white mid-dorsal stripe runs on to the telson, separating the two red lobes. In the Indo-Pacific form, the white stripe stops just short of the telson and the lobes are spotted.
Feeding requirements: This is a cleaner shrimp that feeds on parasites picked from the body and gills of fishes. In an aquarium it will accept most frozen and dried foods.
Aquarium suitability: It readily exhibits its cleaning behaviour in an aquarium but requires plenty of hiding places. It is best kept in groups.

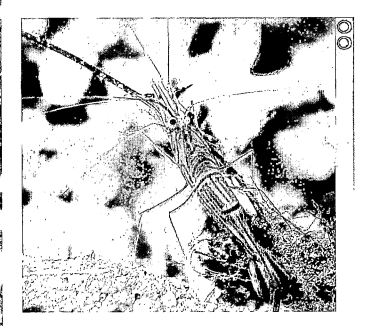

Lysmata californica

Family: Hippolytidae
Range: Eastern Pacific, Gulf of California
Description: The body colouration of this species consists of a series of red, longitudinal candy-stripes on a whitish background. There are several bars dorsally and a broad red bar is also present at the junction of the thorax and the abdomen. . The telson has red lobes with white margins. This species is often found in large groups among rocks and in caves in shallow coastal areas.
Feeding requirements: Although predominantly a scavenger, *L. californica* occasionally exhibits cleaning behaviour. It does well on a diet of frozen shellfish and plankton.
Aquarium suitability: Groups of five or six seem to fare better than solitary individuals. The aquarium should be provided with plenty of caves and overhangs to make them feel at home.

Rhynchocinetes durbanensis

Family: Rhynchocinetidae
Range: Southeast Africa to Central Indo-Pacific
Description: Often erroneously described as *Rhynchocinetes uritai* (the real *R. uritai* is restricted to an area from South Korea to Japan and is almost never exported for the aquarium trade). In addition, this species has brighter red lines on the body, between which are white lines and small spots. There is also a distinct, white Y-shaped mark in the dorsal region. *R. uritai*, on the other hand, has only spots between the somewhat duller red lines and the white lines are more or less absent.
Feeding requirements: A scavenger that soon learns to accept most frozen and dried foods.
Aquarium suitability: The dancing shrimp, as it is usually known, is often imported and has been a firm favourite with aquarists for many years.

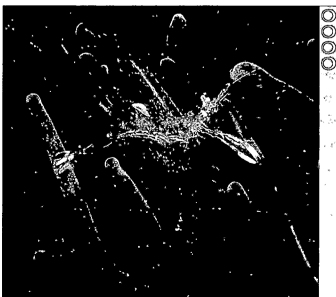

Photograph by Frank Walker

Lysmata debelius

Family: Hippolytidae
Range: Central Indo-Pacific from the Chagos Archipelago to Indonesia
Description: The body is bright scarlet with small white spots on the carapace. The lower halves of the thoracic limbs are white and the upper halves are red. In its natural habitat, this species is found in pairs or in small groups, usually in deeper water on reef drop-offs and reef channels where the water is not too turbulent.
Feeding requirements: In the wild the shrimp exhibits cleaning behaviour and feeds on the parasites that it picks from fishes. In an aquarium it will accept most foods offered.
Aquarium suitability: This species is easy to keep, although it is essentially a shy animal that needs plenty of hiding places. Single specimens do well and are an attractive addition to a reef aquarium. Groups of six or seven look spectacular.

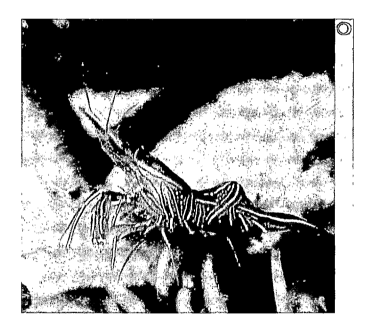

Periclimenes holthuisi

Family: Palaemonidae
Range: Red Sea to the Indo-West Pacific as far as Australia
Description: This tiny shrimp is usually less than 1in (2.5cm) in length. Its body is translucent and adorned with white spots and flecks. The tips of the claws and the telson have bluish-purple bands. This species lives in symbiotic association with various sea anemones and also several species of corals – usually those that have longer polyps, such as *Heliofungia actiniformis* and *Catalaphyllia jardinei*.
Feeding requirements: This species occasionally exhibits cleaning activities but it is a scavenger by nature. It accepts most substitute foods that are offered.
Aquarium suitability: This shrimp needs a host anemone or coral for it to do well in an aquarium. It is not an easy species to keep and should be left to the experienced aquarist.

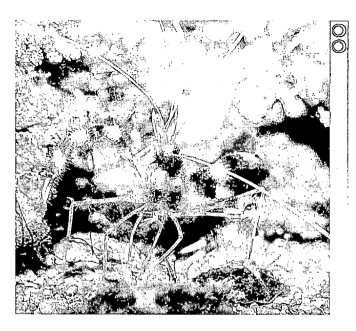

Stenopus hispidus

Family: Stenopodidae
Range: Circumtropical
Description: Known commonly as the barbershop shrimp due to its distinct colouration, this red and white banded coral shrimp performs an important service as a "cleaner" in most tropical seas. It grows to about 4in (10cm) and is easily identified by its markings. In the wild it is common in crevices and caves where it establishes a cleaning station for fishes.
Feeding requirements: Once it has settled into an aquarium, it will eagerly accept most foods that are offered within a relatively short space of time.
Aquarium suitability: Suitable for most reef and marine aquariums. This species should be kept singly or in pairs. A third specimen added later will usually be killed within a few days by those that are already established in the tank.

Enoplometopus debelius

Family: Nephropidae
Range: Indo-West Pacific from Indonesia to Hawaii
Description: The background body colour is white, fading to mauve toward the telson. The two large claws are also mauve and the entire carapace, thoracic and abdominal segments are suffused with bright reddish-mauve spots. This reef lobster is one of the most attractive of all the crustaceans. It is found in caves and crevices, or in hollows under shadowy overhangs. At night it becomes an active scavenger. Grows to 4in (10cm) in length.
Feeding requirements: Because of its scavenging nature, this species will soon learn to accept all foods that are offered.
Aquarium suitability: An ideal but somewhat shy species that will live for many years in a well-established reef aquarium. It is a good species for getting rid of any uneaten food particles that are in the tank.

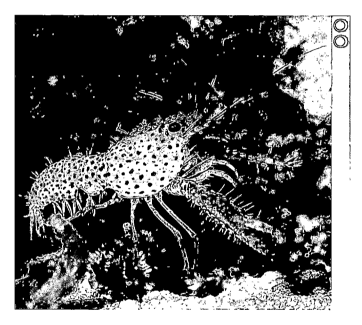

Calcinus elegans

Family: Diogenidae
Range: Southeast Indonesia to Australia
Description: The thoracic limbs of this hermit crab are black with bright blue bands. The eye-stalks are also blue and the tips of the claws are white, making this attractive species easy to identify. In addition, the moderately long antennae are bright yellowish-orange in colour.
Feeding requirements: In the wild it feeds on tiny invertebrate animals and algae. In an aquarium it will accept any food offered as well as keeping excessive growths of algae under control.
Aquarium suitability: Excellent species for a reef aquarium. Should be kept in small groups with enough spare shells available for them to be able to "move house" when they grow out of their old shells. The lifespan of this species is usually only about two years.

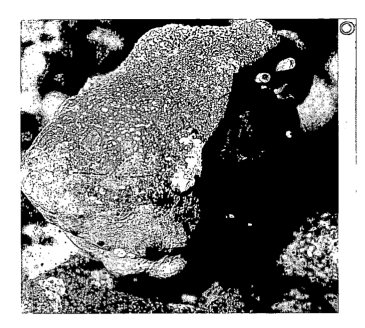

Paguristes cadenati

Family: Diogenidae
Range: Caribbean, Tropical West Atlantic
Description: The tips of the eye-stalks are yellowish-orange and the eyes green. The rest of the carapace and thoracic limbs are bright red, sometimes with white spots near the thoracic joints. On the reef this species is found singly or in small groups in deeper water. It is active at night.
Feeding requirements: In an aquarium this is a superb scavenger of food remains and an excellent algae controller. Hair algae, such as *Derbesia* spp., and various forms of microalgae will be kept to manageable proportions by this crab.
Aquarium suitability: It lives only for about two years. In a reef tank they are best kept in groups and, in sufficient numbers, will keep it clean and free of nuisance algae. Stocking levels are one crab for every 2 gallons (10 litres) of aquarium water.

Camposcia sp.

Family: Majidae
Range: East Africa to Central Indo-Pacific
Description: This, and similar crabs are often called "decorator crabs" because of the way that they adorn their carapaces. This is usually done with bits of sponges, detritus, bryozoans and algae. Often they are colourful, depending on the particular decoration that they have chosen. They can also be grotesque and, when they decorate themselves with detritus, resemble large spiders. The carapace is shaped like a pointed triangle, with the elongated point making up the head region.
Feeding requirements: This is a scavenger that accepts most of the usual aquarium foods.
Aquarium suitability: Quite good in a reef aquarium but this species has a particular affinity for eating feather duster worms (*Sabellidae* spp.).

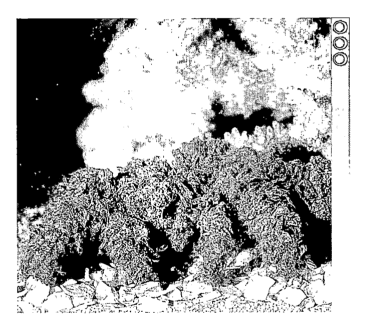

Stenorhynchus seticornis

Family: Majidae
Range: Tropical West Atlantic, Caribbean
Description: The arrow crab, as it is commonly known, has a cone-shaped body that is due to the elongated rostrum. This extends upward between the eyes into a spine. The carapace is striped with white, brown and tan. The walking legs are long and spider-like, giving this creature a bizarre appearance. The first pair of thoracic limbs is developed into thin but strong claws that are tipped in deep purple.
Feeding requirements: A scavenger that accepts most frozen shellfish. It will also feed on and destroy soft corals, such as *Xenia* spp. It will also pick at zoanthid anemones and some corals.
Aquarium suitability: Suitable for a Caribbean reef aquarium that, by definition, contains no soft corals (they are almost completely absent from this sea). An easy species to keep.

Trapezia sp.

Family: Trapeziidae
Range: Central Indo-Pacific
Description: This small coral crab has a black carapace that is covered with fine, dull orange spots. The thoracic limbs are orange and the claws are sprinkled with black spots on the upper surfaces and white spots on the underside. The underside of the trapezoid carapace is also spotted with white.
Feeding requirements: They are scavengers and will eat anything they can get their claws into. All the usual aquarium foods are accepted with relish.
Aquarium suitability: These tiny crabs, which are often less than ¾in (2cm) long, sometimes come into the aquarium as "stowaways" deep in the branches of coral, such as *Pocillopora* spp. and *Acropora* spp. They do well in an aquarium that has enough hiding places and a few branched corals.

Zoisimus aeneus

Family: Xanthidae
Range: Central Indo-Pacific to Australia
Description: This species is characterized by the deeply ridged zones on the carapace. This is often spotted with red, sometimes powder-blue, but the general colouration of the carapace is extremely varied, making species identification sometimes difficult. The claws are thick and strong and the flesh of this species contains a powerful poison (possibly saxatoxin) that, in quantities of less than 1g, is deadly to humans.
Feeding requirements: This is a scavenger that will accept most foods that are offered, but it has a preference for frozen cockle and mussel flesh.
Aquarium suitability: Although it is not to be trusted in a reef tank, it is an ideal choice for a fish-only aquarium since, because of its scavenging nature, it will keep the tank clean.

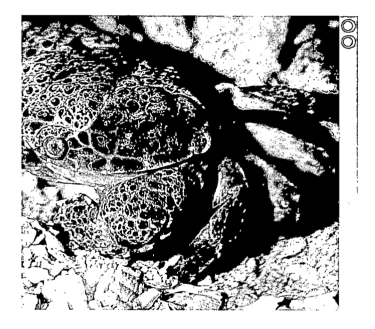

Phylum: Mollusca (molluscs)

In terms of numbers of species, the molluscs represent the largest group of marine animals and the second largest in the whole of the animal kingdom, with insects making up the largest group. Nobody knows for certain how many species there are in this group but over 120,000 have so far been described. Molluscs occur in the sea, in fresh water and on the land. Although the phylum is grouped into seven classes, only species from three of these are of interest to marine aquarists.

Molluscs evolved at the beginning of the Cambrian period, about 550 million years ago, and there are many fossilized records of their development. The shells that many of the species produce were recognized by ancient man and retained for their usefulness and for their beauty. The Romans found that a particular murex shell yielded a deep purple dye, and this was used to dye the cloth for the robes that the emperor and senators wore. Shells have a fascinating history. They have been collected and used to make buttons, ornaments and jewellery, and they have even been used as money in Africa, on many Pacific islands and in China.

Some bivalve molluscs are of great value. The oyster family produces not only the edible oyster, but some species also produce pearls. Pearls are formed from calcium carbonate in the form of aragonite and an organic substance called conchiolin. Pearls are relatively soft, but compact; it is difficult to crush them. Their size can vary from a grain of sand to a pullet's egg. In fact, the largest pearl known is in the Geological Museum in London, England. It weighs nearly 2oz (57g).

Of course, not all molluscs produce shells and in some species they are internal, such as in cuttlefish. Squid and octopus are also molluscs and, while the squid has a reduced pen-like shell, in the octopus it is completely absent. Some gastropods, such as the often brightly coloured nudibranchs, do not produce a shell at all.

Class: Gastropoda

In the gastropods, the body is asymmetrical and consists of a head with tentacles, eyes and a radula, a ventral foot, a visceral mass and a mantle. The one-piece shell is spiralled when present, and the body can be fully retracted into it. In some species the shell is internal, or completely absent. The visceral mass is large and is covered by the mantle. It contains the heart, reproductive organs, anus and a large part of the gut. A feature of the gastropods is that the visceral mass and mantle are twisted 180° to the the body, which means that the cavity containing the gills and anus is set forward, above and behind the head. This twisting (torsion) usually occurs during the free-swimming larval stage of the mollusc's life. As a result of this torsion, the gut, along with the nervous system, becomes twisted into a U-shape. The creeping ventral foot is often highly modified in swimming and burrowing forms.

Of the three subclasses of gastropods, the first is Prosobranchia. These are mostly marine-living and have shells that are thick and strong. In the few terrestrial species the shell is a great deal thinner and lighter to carry. In the subclass Opisthobranchia, the shell is often absent or completely encapsulated by the mantle. The internal gills (branchia) are smaller and regressive, but often there are more sophisticated external gills present, such as is the case with the nudibranchs, which, literally translated, means "naked gill". The radula is developed according to the specific feeding requirements of the species involved, and this feature is an important aid to taxonomists in determining the species. In most species, detorsion takes place after the larval stage and the body more or less straightens out once more.

The final subclass, Pulmonata, is of little interest to the aquarist and contains mostly land-dwelling species.

Order: Docoglossa (limpets)

Five families are usually recognized as belonging to the order Docoglossa. One family, Patellidae, is represented in all seas of the world. The common limpet (*Patella vulgata*) is a familiar sight on rocky coastlines of the northeast Atlantic. Limpets are common in the littoral and sublittoral zones, where they feed on algae, often buffeted by heavy wave action and exposed at low tide. For this reason they have a large foot with a strong suction that allows them to cling to the substrata. Throughout the northern Atlantic some species may be found attached to harbour pilings and even to algae. This is usually the sea belt or oarweed (*Laminaria* spp.).

Another family, Acmaeidae, consists mainly of small species that have a single gill structure, which can be seen on the shell margin when the animals are feeding. Most other species have no true gills. Instead they have a series of filamentous secondary gill structures.

Limpets are never imported for the aquarium trade, at least not intentionally. Nevertheless, they do show up on live rock from some areas and generally do quite well in an aquarium. Since these animals graze on algae, they are effective in combating excessive growths of nuisance algae such as *Bryopsis* and *Derbesia* spp. They require no special care and do not damage other invertebrates. Their natural enemies are the sea stars.

Photograph by Robert Brons

Cellana eucosmia

Family: Patellidae
Range: Indian Ocean, Red Sea
Description: This species is ubiquitous in the Red Sea and is a common sight in the intertidal zones among rocks and on pier pilings throughout its natural range. The shell is conical and moderately tall with reddish-brown lines radiating around the lower half. The apex is asymmetrical to the rest of the shell and is adorned with a reddish-brown blotch.
Feeding requirements: Feeds on hair algae and various species of microalgae that it rasps off the rocks with its well-developed radula. In an aquarium it requires no special feeding techniques and is ideally suited for algal control.
Aquarium suitability: *C. eucosmia* occasionally turns up on live rock. It needs plenty of light and water movement. This tropical limpet will not tolerate nitrate levels above 30 mg/ litre.

Order: Archaeogastropoda (abalones, keyhole limpets, top shells, turban shells)

The shells of these molluscs are varied in form. Many produce "mother of pearl" – a nacreous layer on the inner side of the shell that has an iridescent play of light on its smooth surface. Four families are of interest here. The abalones, from the family Haliotidae, have attractive shells. There is only one genus with about 50 described species. Occasionally abalones find their way into aquariums on live rock. They seem to do well when the water quality is good and do not usually pose a problem in a reef tank. They are never specifically imported.

Some species of keyhole limpets from the family Fissurellidae are relatively common in aquariums, although they are not readily recognizable as such. Their shells are similar in appearance to the true limpets of the order Docoglossa, but there is an anal vent present in the form of a hole near the shell apex. Additionally, a large mantle often covers the shell and effectively masks the fact that there is one present at all. This gives the creature an outward form that is similar to those of the nudibranchs.

The families Trochidae and Turbinidae contain molluscs that are termed "top shells" and "turban shells", respectively. The frequently advertised "turbo snail" (*Astraea tectum*) belongs to the latter family. Many of the species in these two families are conical in form, with spiral shaped shells. As far as aquarists are concerned they are extremely important, especially in reef aquariums. These molluscs spend most of their lives grazing on algae. These are usually microalgae, but when these are depleted they will crop any other nuisance algae from an aquarium. In a 50-gallon (227-litre) tank, five or six of these molluscs can do wonders in keeping down excessive algae growths.

Haliotis varia

Family: Haliotidae
Range: Red Sea, Tropical Indo-Pacific
Description: The species normally grows to about 2½in (6cm), which makes it one of the smaller members of this genus. It is a common mollusc with uneven ridges on the shell that are nodulose and coarse. The growth lines are readily apparent and some radial folds are present. The tentacles are prominent, as is the somewhat fleshy mantle. The five, sometimes six, holes near the shell margin are raised and the shell is oval and rounded.
Feeding requirements: Feeds predominantly on microalgae and hair algae.
Aquarium suitability: It is not unusual to see this species on imported live rock. This is why the rock must be carefully examined prior to the seeding process. This is an ideal species for a reef tank.

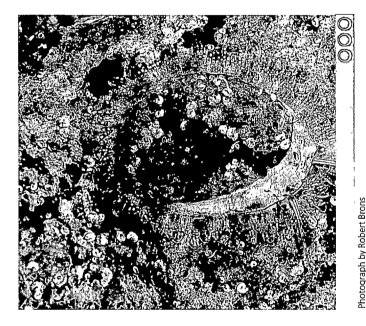

Photograph by Robert Brons

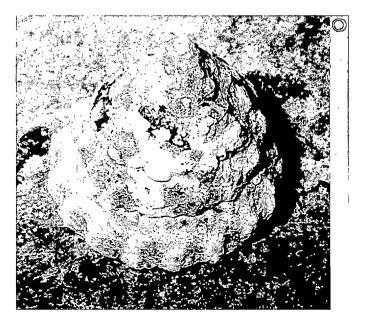

Astraea tectum

Family: Turbinidae
Range: Caribbean, Tropical West Atlantic
Description: The shell is covered with nodules along the spiral, which has a high apex. It is frequently encountered with a covering of coralline algae, small bryozoans and other growths. It seldom grows to more than 2in (5cm) and is common in sea-grass beds and in crevices among rocks throughout its natural range.
Feeding requirements: *A. tectum* feeds almost exclusively on micro- and macroalgae, but small invertebrates are often ingested along with this.
Aquarium suitability: In the aquarium trade this species is known as the 'turbo snail'. It performs an extremely useful task in an aquarium by grazing on nuisance algae. It is easy to keep and requires no special care

Order: Mesogastropoda (worm shells, conchs, cowries)

Molluscs that belong to the order Mesogastropoda have spiral shells that do not have "mother of pearl" on the inner surfaces. There is often a chitinous opercle present. This is flat and may be oval or round. It is usually on the foot and is used to block the entrance once the mollusc has withdrawn into its shell. This serves as a protection against any potential predator but it also functions as a seal to retain the body fluids within the shell should the animal become exposed at low tide. In some larger species, such as *Strombus* spp., the operculum is long and narrow and is used as a lever to right the shell if it overturns. In carnivorous species the snout is elongated, like a proboscis, and is used actively to capture food; species that graze on algae have a shorter and mobile snout.

The group encompasses not only worm shells, conchs and cowries, it also includes the edible periwinkle (Littorina littorea) and the precious wentletrap (Epitonium scalare). Many species are edible and some, such as helmet shells, are used as ornaments. One helmet shell, Cypraecassis rufa, is exploited for its beautiful shell. This is used extensively for carving shell cameos because of its layered form in differing colours. These are used by the jewellery industry but thankfully not as often as in the past. Nowadays layered agate (quartz), which has been dyed in contrasting colours, is used as a substitute. This has several advantages. It is cheaper to produce, it is harder and more resistant to wear, it is ecologically friendlier and it can be polished to a high finish.

Serpulorbis inopertus

Family: Vermetidae
Range: Indian Ocean, Red Sea
Description: *Serpulorbis* spp. do not possess an operculum and this fact makes them relatively easy to identify. The shell is more or less spiralled and often hidden within rock or coral. This and similar species are sessile creatures that feed by sending out net-formed or strand-like filaments, which are produced by a gland on the foot. These have slimy surfaces that are used to collect detritus and small organisms on which they feed.
Feeding requirements: Plenty of live rock should be present so that this species can find the food it needs.
Aquarium suitability: It is not uncommon for worm shells to be brought into the aquarium on live rock. If the tank is fully matured and has good water quality, they live quite well and pose no problems to other invertebrates.

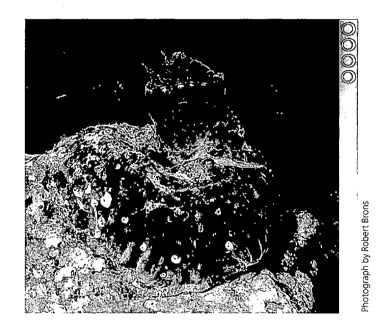

Photograph by Robert Brons

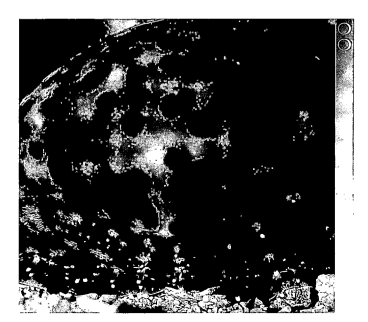

Cypraea tigris

Family: Cypraeidae
Range: Red Sea, entire Tropical Indo-Pacific from East Africa to Hawaii
Description: A common cowrie that is sometimes seen exposed in full sunlight on the reef. Most others tend to hide during daylight hours. The underside of the shell is white with a toothed aperture, and dorsally it is creamy-white with purplish-brown spots. The pattern is variable. Grows to about 6in (15cm) with the largest specimens coming from Hawaii.
Feeding requirements: Omnivorous, feeding on small invertebrates and algae. In an aquarium it will scavenge for food and keep algae in check.
Aquarium suitability: This species is frequently available and is usually referred to as the "tiger cowrie". It feeds well, grows large but is apt to disturb the aquarium decoration somewhat.

Order: Neogastropoda (whelks, murex, tulips, olives, volutes, cone shells)

The order Neogastropoda contains molluscs that are active predators. Their shells are spirally coiled and they may or may not have an operculum. The common factor of the species in this group is the presence of a siphonal canal. This is a long groove that runs from the shell aperture and carries the extended mantle siphon through which it draws water. The radula is often long and narrow, rarely carrying more than three teeth in a row.

Neogastropods are common in all tropical seas, although they may also be found in temperate regions. Depending on the particular species they feed on bivalves, other gastropods, fishes and worms. They vary in size a great deal, and some species, such as those belonging to the cone family (Conidae), are dangerous to people. Many cones are venomous, possessing a powerful neurotoxin, and so should be handled with great care. It is better to handle all cones as little as possible and for safety's sake to treat them all as being venomous. They are conical with a flattened spire and a long aperture. The operculum is also long and partially blocks the aperture when the mollusc withdraws into its shell.

Another family, the volutes (Volutidae), contains the genus *Melo* and these species, such as *Melo aethiopica*, *M. georginae*, *M. melo*, *M. miltonis* and *M. umbilicatus*, have shells with flat spires and extremely wide apertures. These are collectively called "balers" because Australian Aboriginals used them for baling out their canoes. Their distribution is restricted to the Indo-Australian archipelago. Some olives (Olividae) and margin shells (Marginellidae) lack an operculum. Almost all of the species in this order are bizarre in shape or brightly coloured.

Chicoreus palmarosae

Family: Muricidae
Range: Indian Ocean to Indo-West Pacific
Description: This well known species is sometimes called the rose-branch murex because of its rose-tipped foliate spines. The curious and bizarre form with its elaborate ornamentation is believed to be a form of camouflage to break up its outline and as a last defence against predators.
Feeding requirements: In the wild its diet consists of bivalves and other gastropods. In an aquarium it will accept fresh mussel, squid, shrimp and lancefish.
Aquarium suitability: This is not an easy species to keep for any length of time and is not ideal for a reef tank due to the danger it poses to other invertebrates. For the best chances of success, the aquarium should have plenty of deep sandy areas between columns of live rock. It is not often imported.

Fasciolaria tulipa

Family: Buccinidae
Range: Tropical West Atlantic from Florida to Brazil, Caribbean
Description: The shell is creamy white with greenish-brown spots and blotches. There is a series of minute spots in rows around the shell. The smooth operculum is deep brown, elongated and very tough. In the wild, this species is found in sea-grass beds and sandy areas.
Feeding requirements: In nature it feeds on clams and various bivalves. Provide this mollusc with squid, mussel and cockle and it will do well.
Aquarium suitability: This species is commonly referred to as the tulip snail. It is occasionally imported and lives happily in an aquarium when it is fed frequently and given enough depth of sand into which it can burrow. Because of its burrowing, predatory nature it is not suitable for a reef aquarium.

Order: Nudibranchia (nudibranchs, true sea slugs)

Nudibranchs are considered to be at a higher stage of evolutionary development than the rest of the gastropods. They have no true gill and the mantle cavity is absent. Instead they have developed other respiratory organs, such as breathing through the skin or, in the case of many species, gill tufts, which are clustered around the anus on the outside of the body. There is a wide foot that is used for gliding over the substrata or, with undulating motions of the margins, for swimming. Large, conspicuous tentacles (rhinophores) are situated on the head and in some species they can be retracted into sheaths. The mouth is ventral and set well forward and the anus is dorsal toward the tail. Some species have simple or branched outgrowths (cerata) along the back that are used for respiration or contain toxic secretions. Nudibranchs are hermaphroditic, with any individual acting as male or female. The eggs are laid in long, often brightly coloured strings or spirals, and the larvae usually have a spiral shell in the initial stages of their lives.

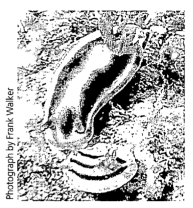

These are two commonly confused nudibranchs. Note the dorsal markings of the upper specimen (Chromodoris annae) in relationship to the lower specimen (Chromodoris quadricolor).

Casella atromarginata

Family: Chromodorididae
Range: Tropical Indo-Pacific
Description: In the accompanying photograph the egg strings can be clearly seen attached to a dead *Acropora* branch. This species is creamy-white with an undulating skirt that has a black margin. The white rhinophores also have black stripes and are retractable. The gill processes around the anus are grey with black margins. *C. atromarginata* is found on rocky reefs throughout the Indo-Pacific as far north as Hong Kong.
Feeding requirements: This is an active species that feeds mainly on spiculous sponges.
Aquarium suitability: In a newly set-up aquarium this species is impossible to keep for more than a week or so. In a mature aquarium with living rock, however, its lifespan may be extended to two years or more.

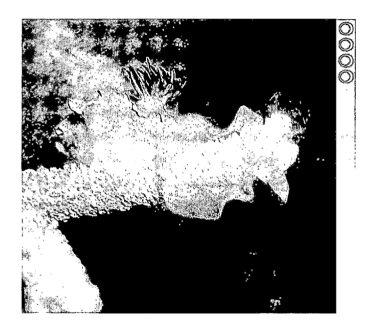

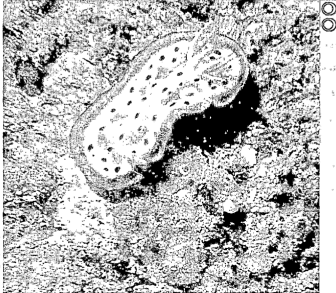

Chromodoris kuniei

Family: Chromodorididae
Range: Widespread throughout the Indo-Pacific from the Philippines to Fiji.
Description: Dorsally, this species is creamy-white with a purple-mauve margin. There is an irregular suffusion of deep red and mauve spots on the back, and in specimens from the Philippines there are also yellow streaks present. The rhinophores are yellow, as are the margins of the gill processes.
Feeding requirements: Feeds on a variety of minute benthic invertebrates, sponges and microalgae. It appears to be one of the more omnivorous and unselective nudibranchs with regard to its feeding habits.
Aquarium suitability: Very hardy and easier to keep than most nudibranches. Unfortunately they are seldom imported, which is a pity since they are ideal for a mature reef aquarium.

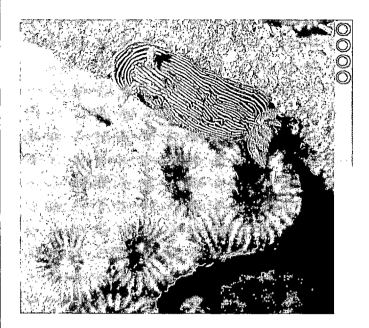

Chromodoris lineolata

Family: Chromodorididae
Range: Tropical Indo-Pacific, South China Sea
Description: The rhinophore stems are black with vertical white stripes and spots that merge into orange toward the tips. Narrow white stripes run along the length of the black mantle, which has a bright orange margin. The gill processes are spotted with black and white and the bases of the rhinophore sheaths are ringed with white. The foot is dark grey and is edged with white. This species is common on rocky shores where it inhabits inlets and coves in relatively turbulent water.
Feeding requirements: Feeds actively on sponges and ascidians (sea squirts).
Aquarium suitability: Very difficult to keep because of its specialized feeding habits. A mature tank with live rock and a good growth of sponges seem to give it the best chance.

Chromodoris marginata

Family: Chromodorididae
Range: Central Indo-Pacific
Description: The mantle is white and the rhinophores are maroon with smooth stems. The pinnate gill processes are also maroon, and parallel brown and orange lines surround the mantle margin. The white foot is tapered and there are toxic defence glands along the underside of the margin. A very similar species, *C. alba*, has a sprinkling of reddish-orange dorsal spots and the mantle margin has orange and red parallel lines.
Feeding requirements: Feeds almost exclusively on algae (*Cladophora* and *Chaetomorpha* spp.) and sponges.
Aquarium suitability: Although practically all of the species in this genus specialize in feeding on benthic sponges, this species is one of the exceptions and offers the best chances of success when its preferred algae are present in the aquarium.

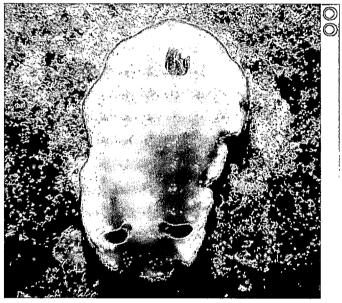

Photograph by Ned Middleton

Photograph by Frank Walker

Chromodoris pallescens

Family: Chromodorididae
Range: Entire Tropical Indo-Pacific
Description: An easy species to identify with its relatively sparse black spots and its bright orange lamellate rhinophores. The gill processes are tipped with orange and project from a sheath near the anus. The margins of the mantle and foot are edged with yellowish-orange and there are a few further spots on the foot. *C. pallescens* is found in reef channels and on reef drop-offs or on rocky coasts in deeper water.
Feeding requirements: This species feeds exclusively on spiculous sponges.
Aquarium suitability: Unless you can find some way to feed this species successfully in captivity, then it is better left on the reef. It is a feeding specialist that accepts no other food than that indicated above.

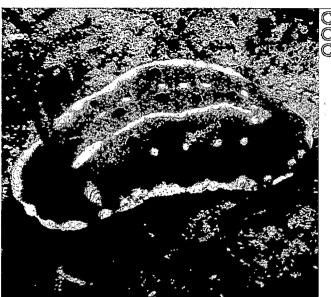

Photograph by Ned Middleton

Hypselodoris festiva

Family: Chromodorididae
Range: Central Indo-Pacific from Hong Kong to Australia
Description: The rhinophores are red with pale blue sheaths. The gill processes, which are not shown in this picture, are unipinnate and ciliated with white and red margins. These surround a mid-dorsal socket. The bright blue mantle has a yellow margin and a yellowish-white mid-dorsal stripe that is paralleled with distinct black and yellow spots and blotches.
Feeding requirements: This species feeds on ascidians and other similar benthic invertebrates.
Aquarium suitability: This species can be kept for some years in a mature aquarium with no problems, but its specialized feeding requirements make it unsuitable for beginners.

Phyllidia arabica

Family: Phyllidiidae
Range: Tropical Indo-Pacific
Description: The rhinophores are bright orange and lamellate. The white mantle is streaked with black, which may vary in pattern. The white parts of the body are covered with raised white pustular tubercles, many of which are tipped with bright orange. The anus resembles a white tubercle and is situated well back on the right of the mantle. There is an orange margin to the forward edge of the mantle skirt. The foot is pearl-grey and there are leaf-like gills between this and the underside of the mantle.
Feeding requirements: Feeds predominantly on sponges and ascidians.
Aquarium suitability: This species requires a mature aquarium with plenty of invertebrate life, live rock and a good growth of sponges. It is attractive but difficult to keep.

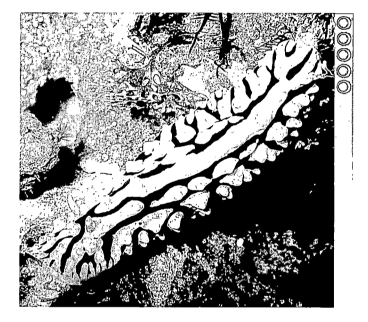

Photograph by Ned Middleton

Flabellina iodinea

Family: Flabellinidae
Range: Tropical Indo-Pacific
Description: The mantle varies in colour, depending on the geographic origin, from orange to deep mauve, and the lamellate rhinophores may also vary from orange through to mauve. The tips of these are almost always white. The dorsal cerata are long and slender and arranged in symmetrical rows. These cerata are usually orange with yellow tips irrespective of the mantle colour.
Feeding requirements: Not known but believed to feed on colonial hydroids and some ascidians.
Aquarium suitability: This is another difficult species, even for the experienced aquarist. If you are not sure that you can keep it alive and cannot provide it with the correct diet, then do not buy it. Thankfully, it is not often imported and so it is not generally available to tempt any unsuspecting novices.

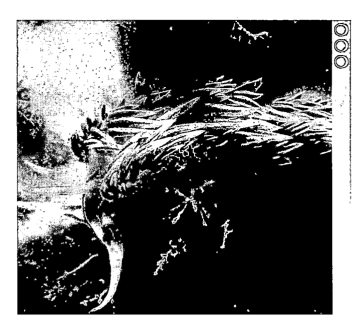

Phidiana crassicornis

Family: Phidianidae
Range: Tropical Indo-Pacific
Description: Geographical colour variations (colour morphs) are common with this species. The rhinophores are lamellate and greyish-white, often with white vertical margins, and the base is sometimes a reddish-orange. The dorsal cerata are arranged in symmetrical rows and on the back they are tipped with yellow. Those toward the margin of the mantle are usually much darker and often tinged with orange and grey.
Feeding requirements: This species of nudibranch has been observed feeding on mollusc and fish eggs. A diet of frozen fish eggs seems to be the best bet for success.
Aquarium suitability: Only very infrequently imported, which is a pity since it is probably one of the easiest of this difficult group of animals to keep alive in captivity.

Tritonia sp.

Family: Tritonidae
Range: Caribbean, Tropical West Atlantic
Description: Highly branched lamellate rhinophores with one pair retractable. The rhinophores and branched cerata are orange-brown with fine, light-grey spots. In juveniles, the anus appears as a median white spot set toward the tail. This darkens with age. The mantle is black with reticulated bright orange spots that fade to pink and purple toward the margins of the mantle skirt.
Feeding requirements: Feeds on the skin that the gorgonian corals, *Pterogorgia citrina* and *Erythropodium caribaeorum* shed periodically to rid themselves of algae and any other organic debris.
Aquarium suitability: In a tank with gorgonian corals, this is an easy species to keep and breed.

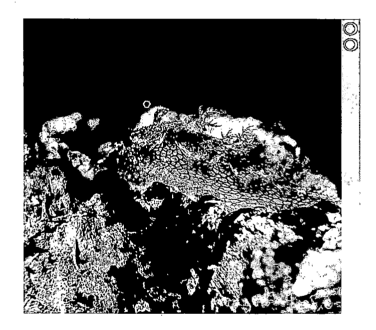

Class: Bivalvia

Clams, mussels, cockles, oysters and scallops all belong to this group. Collectively they are known as bivalve molluscs. Generally, the body is laterally compressed and enclosed between two shell halves (valves). These are hinged dorsally with a ligament of tissue that controls their opening and closing. To facilitate this, two large muscles (adductor muscles), counteracting one another, hold the two halves of the valve together. Two mantle folds are present and these are joined to enclose the mantle cavity, which contains a pair of specialized gills.

Bivalve molluscs are found intertidally as well as at depth. They are bottom dwellers found in all seas. Most of them are filter feeders but there are a few carnivorous and scavenging species. Most of the species are sessile but some scallops can swim for short distances by rhythmically clapping their valves together to create a primitive form of jet propulsion.

Order: Pterioidea (scallops, file shells, oysters)

The order encompasses familiar species of commercial interest. The common characteristics of this group are the thick irregular shell valves that may be ridged or have spinous projections. The dorsal hinge often has wing-like asymmetrical projections that in some species are developed to the extreme. Many of the species attach themselves to the substrata with byssal threads, although a few species are attached by one of the shell halves. Scallops often lie free on sandy sea beds and will retreat at the threat of danger by rapidly clapping their valves together to create propulsion.

Lima scabra

Family: Limidae
Range: Caribbean, Tropical West Atlantic
Description: You can't eat it and you can't produce pearls from it, but this is an attractive looking species, whether on the reef or in a reef aquarium. The valves are radially ridged and the mantle is deep red. The margin of this is adorned with pink to red tentacles that are long and slender. Byssal threads are produced to attach it to the substrata and this is usually in fissures between rocks at various depths.
Feeding requirements: This is a filter-feeder that requires liquid food for filter-feeding invertebrates.
Aquarium suitability: Not an easy species to keep, especially in the initial stages. It requires a shadowy area of the tank. Once it becomes permanently attached to the aquarium substrata with its byssus threads, and is fed regularly, it is surprisingly hardy.

Order: Veneroida (cockles, clams, razor shells)

This, and the closely related order Myoida, belong to the subclass Heterodonta. This is a very large group of molluscs, many of which are unsuitable for a marine or reef aquarium. In the order Myoida, only a few species may be encountered in an aquarium, usually on live rock. Most of the species in this group are burrowing molluscs. Ship worms, such as *Teredo navalis* and *Bankia setacea*, from the family Teredinidae, are not worms but molluscs. They also belong to this order and are responsible for a great deal of damage to marine timber structures and wooden boats because of their boring activities.

In contrast, the order Veneroida contains species that are beneficial to our natural world. This group incorporates clams and cockles. The clams of the genus *Tridacna* are well known to aquarists, although there are strict controls regarding their export. In spite of this they are being reproduced both as a food and for the aquarium trade, and this on a large scale. The giant clam (*Tridacna gigas*), so often the subject of Hollywood feature films, belongs to this genus. It can grow to more than 4½ feet (1.4m) and attain a weight in excess of 440lb (200kg).

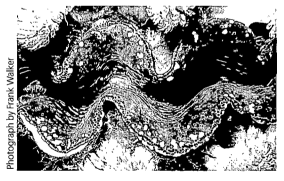

An example of Tridacna crocea.

Photograph by Frank Walker

Tridacna crocea

Family: Tridacnidae
Range: Central Indo-Pacific
Description: The valves are finely ridged with no large vanes evident. This clam is often found deeply embedded in rock or between corals. The mantle is often highly coloured and may be yellow, green or blue, or a combination of these colours, with contrasting spots and reticulated lines. In this species the byssus opening near the dorsal ligament is large. The maximum size attained is 8in (20cm).
Feeding requirements: Feeds from the production of its own zooxanthellae.
Aquarium suitability: Providing the water quality is good and a combination of metal-halide and actinic lighting is used, this species will do well in a reef aquarium. When choosing a specimen, make sure that it is attached to a small piece of rock.

Tridacna gigas

Family: Tridacnidae
Range: Entire central Indo-Pacific region from the Indo-Australian archipelago to Japan
Description: This is a large species that grows to more than 4ft (1.2m) and is often referred to as the "giant clam". The shell halves are moderately ridged and the byssus opening is small. The radial shell convolutions form sharp angles. The mantle is often yellow-ochre coloured, frequently with bright blue spots.
Feeding requirements: Its own zooxanthellae provide all the nutrition it requires.
Aquarium suitability: In a well-kept aquarium this species can live for many years, but it needs an enormous amount of light and plenty of space to grow. Most of the specimens that are imported nowadays come from commercial breeding farms. Specimens under 2in (5cm) long are difficult to acclimatize.

Tridacna maxima

Family: Tridacnidae
Range: Red Sea, Tropical Indo-Pacific
Description: The shell is asymmetrical with large vanes on the radial convolutions, particularly on the upper half toward the mantle opening. The byssus opening is large and the colour of the extended mantle is variable. It may be blue, chrome-yellow or green, often with a marbled colour pattern. The clam is often found embedded in rock but it is also found attached to the substrata by byssal threads. Grows to 14in (36cm).
Feeding requirements: Feeds exclusively from its own zooxanthellae.
Aquarium suitability: A hardy and long-lived species once it is settled in a well-kept reef tank with high-intensity lighting. Almost all of the species seen on offer today come from commercial breeding stations.

Class: Cephalopoda

The class encompasses large, highly developed invertebrates that often show a primitive form of intelligence. These are the cuttlefish, squids, octopuses, nautilus and argonauts and they are recognized by the tentacles, or arms, that surround the mouth. These arms are developed from the typical mollusc foot and often possess sucker-like processes.

Today we recognize some 700 species of cephalopods and their forms are varied. The mouth is often beaked, resembling that of a parrot. This is used to tear at prey with the use of their arms, since most of these creatures are voracious predators. The arms are equipped with powerful suckers that are used to grasp and hold their prey. The body is usually an enlarged sac that may contain a rudimentary bone, which, in the case of the squid, is transparent and pen-like. In other cases the bone may be a porous, laminated structure, such as the cuttlefish bone that is often given to cage birds. In some species, such as octopuses, the bone is completely absent.

There are two subclasses, the first being the primitive group Nautiloidea, which contains the six known species of chambered nautilus. The ancestors of the cephalopods had shells that were curved, or sometimes straight, and these were often up to 40in (1m) long. As time passed, these species became extinct, leaving only a small number, the nautilus shells, as living fossils from a once great and widely represented group.

All cephalopods have a fairly large head and a centralized mouth. Most of the species have large, well developed eyes, which are not unlike those of the vertebrates with a lens, cornea and retina. In addition, they have a large brain that is capable of memory. The vision of these animals appears to be acute, although the tentacles are also equipped with keen sensory nerves to detect danger and food.

The second subclass, Coleoidea, contains species with rudimentary shells, such as squids and cuttlefish, or octopuses, where the shell is absent. These species are equipped with a special "ink sac" that can be squirted out to effect a smoke screen into which the animal disappears.

Order: Sepioidea (cuttlefishes, bottle-tailed squids)

The giant squid of the Hollywood film mythology has nothing to do with the species belonging to this order, although there are substantiated reports of huge creatures from the order Teuthoidea being captured and brought to shore to be photographed. These have been up to 60ft (18m) long. Nevertheless this order incorporates the much smaller cuttlefish and the *Spirula* spp. from the family Spirulidae. These are cephalopods that possess either a calcareous internal shell, which may consist of spiral chambers or be straight, or the shell is absent or undeveloped and horn-like. In cuttlefish, the body is broad and stubby and there are lateral fins along the margin of the mantle to aid swimming. They are able to move quite fast through the water and do so when they are pursuing prey. These creatures are carnivorous predators with insatiable appetites. Ten tentacles, two of which are longer than the rest, surround the mouth. Only experienced aquarists should attempt to keep cuttlefish since they require special care in a large tank where there are no vulnerable tank-mates for these voracious predators to attack and eat.

Sepia pharaonis

Family: Sepiidae
Range: Red Sea, Tropical Indo-Pacific
Description: A relatively small species that grows to about 14in (36cm). The body colouration is variable depending on its surroundings but there are fine transverse lines over much of the body and tentacles that make the species relatively easy to identify. The male is larger than the female and pairing often occurs in large groups. After the mating has been completed, individuals resume their solitary living nature.
Feeding requirements: A predator that will eat anything that moves. Live food, or that which appears to be alive, will be taken with relish.
Aquarium suitability: Small specimens give the best chances of success and they sometimes appear on offer. They are quite fast-growing, so a special tank is required with a good depth of sand.

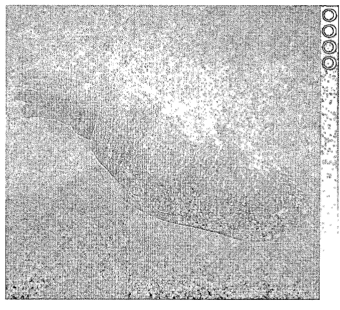

Photograph by Ned Middleton

Order: Octopoda (octopuses, paper nautilus)

Victor Hugo once described the octopus as being "A disease embodied in monstrosity", and even today they are sometimes referred to as "devil fish". All this is pretty unfair, since the octopus is a rather beautiful creature, and a real character, too.

Octopuses are shy and retiring creatures with sac-like bodies and eight tentacle-like arms that are equipped with strong suckers. Like many other cephalopods, octopuses have highly developed colour cells (chromatophores) under their skin. This enables them to blend in by adapting their colour to match that of their surroundings. The cell-like chromatophores react to the environment by expanding or contracting, which produces a colour change throughout the surface of the skin. Full retraction of the chromatophores often makes the octopus practically invisible in its surroundings, and their sustained expansion and contraction gives the effect of them literally shivering in technicolour.

They can adapt to their surroundings like a chameleon but more so: stripes and chequerboard effects will also be attempted if they are placed in such an environment. Bright red is often shown in courtship displays, or in rage. Octopuses are fascinating aquarium subjects but they are not without their problems. For example, they will climb out of the tank if a fitted aquarium hood is not securely in place, and they are very messy eaters, too. They will not harm sessile invertebrates but they will actively hunt anything else that moves in the tank.

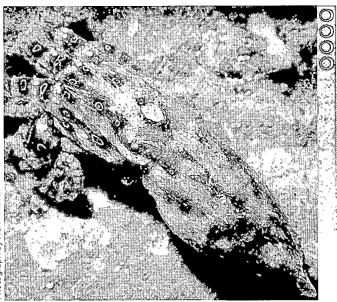

Photograph by Frank Walker

Hapalochlaena maculosa

Family: Octopodidae
Range: Tropical Indo-Pacific from Aden to Australia.
Description: This species is known commonly as the blue-ringed octopus. The body and tentacles are marbled-beige with black-edged, bright blue markings that resemble rings. It is a small species that only grows to about 4in (10cm).
Feeding requirements: This species feeds primarily on crustaceans and molluscs. In an aquarium set-up, however, it will accept most frozen foods.
Aquarium suitability: This attractive species is small and retiring, but take note that it is also extremely dangerous: even a small fraction of a gram of the poison from the bite of this octopus is deadly to people. This creature must be kept out of reach of children.

Phylum: Phoronida (horseshoe worms)

This is a small group of worms that is exclusively marine, living in both tropical and temperate areas. They are found in coastal regions in the intertidal zone and in shallow water. Horseshoe worms get their name from the shape of their lophophores. These are arranged in a horseshoe form around a central mouth. Superficially, these worms resemble some polychaete worms, but they lack the bristles and segmented body. They live in chitinous tubes attached to rocks or buried in sediment and sand. Some species burrow into rocks, shells or harbour pilings and others are found in association with tube anemones of the family Cerianthidae.

The body is cylindrical and may vary from very small up to 8in (20cm) in length. Most species have a horseshoe-shaped lophophore, although in a few specimens it is spiral-formed. The posterior end of the body is thickened to allow the animal to anchor itself firmly in its tube. The longitudinal muscles of the body are well developed and can be rapidly contracted, so that the feeding worm can quickly disappear into its tube at the threat of danger.

It is a small phylum that currently encompasses 15 recorded species in two genera. These are *Phoronis* and *Phoronopsis*. Despite the small number of known species, it is probable that there is a great many more that remain undiscovered. This is because the phylum has been subjected to little in the way of research. They are frequently present in aquariums containing tube anemones and do quite well without any special care.

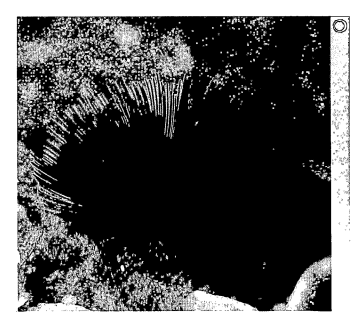

Phoronis australis

Family: Phoronidae
Range: Central Indo-Pacific to Australia
Description: The lophophore can reach a diameter of about 18mm. It is horseshoe shaped with long slender tentacles that are sooty-black in colour. At the end of its larval stage the worm burrows into the base or stem of the parchment-like tube of a cerianthid anemone. It then secretes its own tube and lives commensally with the anemone.
Feeding requirements: Feeds by filtering small organisms and organic debris from the water.
Aquarium suitability: This is an attractive species that is small and often overlooked in a large aquarium. Most specimens are brought into a tank as "stowaways" on tube anemones imported from the Philippines and Indonesia. This and similar species are easy to keep and usually need no special care.

Phylum: Echinodermata (echinoderms)

The phylum Echinodermata contains more than 6,000 species in six classes encompassing 35 orders. The class Concentricycloidea and its order Xyloplax consist of only two recorded species. These are the "deep-sea urchins", which have recently been discovered in the waters of New Zealand. They are of little interest to the aquarist but species from the other five classes are regularly available to hobbyists. The outstanding characteristic of this group is that they all possess a basic pentaradial symmetry. This means in geometrical terms that the animal has a central axis, around which the body radiates in equal sectors, much the same as in flowers such as daisies.

Echinoderms are essentially marine creatures that live in a variety of habitats. They have a long evolutionary history dating back to the Cambrian period, some 530 million years ago. There is also a good fossilized record of the sea lilies that goes back to the end of the Ordovician period, 430 million years ago. Like many of the more primitive invertebrates, they have no distinct head, but they do possess more elaborately developed organs that place them higher in the evolutionary development than most other groups. Perhaps the two most remarkable features of these animals is their five-rayed symmetry and their ability to produce skeletons. Despite their radial symmetry, their forms are diverse.

Class: Crinoidea (sea lilies, feather stars)

Two distinct types of crinoids are found in the sea: sea lilies, which are stalked; and feather stars, which are not stalked (at least not in the adult phase). As juveniles, many feather stars are attached to the substrate by a stalk but this eventually breaks away and the animal becomes free-

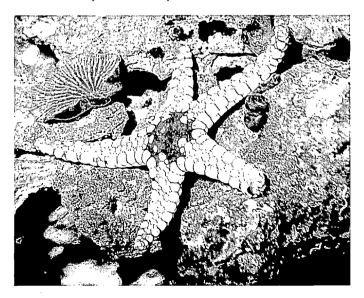

Fromia nodosa *shows the typical pentaradial symmetry of this group of creatures.*

swimming. Sea lilies are attached to the substrate their whole lives and although they are able to effect some lateral movement, they remain fairly sessile. We now know that there are at least 80 species of sea lilies, mostly from deep water, throughout the world, but none is known to have been kept successfully in a home aquarium.

Feather stars, however, are more abundant and are frequently available to aquarists. They are often found in large groups in shallow water and on coral reefs. Physiologically, feather stars and sea lilies have a lot in common. The body (cup) sits on a jointed stalk, in the case of sea lilies, or on a circle of jointed appendages (cirri) in the case of feather stars. These are attached to a plate on the underside of the cup. There are five arms, which may be branched, and these are equipped with pinnules that give them a feather-like appearance. The cup and arms are covered in calcareous plates but spines are absent, as is the madreporite.

Order: Comatulida (Crinoids, Feather Stars)

These animals are often referred to as crinoids, although this is a general term that also includes the sea lilies. In fact, the name Crinoidea means "lily-like" in Greek, referring to the stalked crinoid form. Once the stalk of the juvenile feather star has broken away, it becomes mobile and free-swimming. This is not constant, however, and these animals spend much of their time attached to part of the substrate with their claw-like jointed cirri.

The order Comatulida contains many tropical species and most of these are brightly coloured. They can be black, white, red or bright lemon-yellow. Some have arms that are laterally striped in a combination of all these colours. One species, *Oxycomanthus bennettii*, can be deep leaf-green with yellow tips to the pinnules. This and other species can vary a great deal in colour, making colouration a very unreliable characteristic on which to base an identification. The number of arms can vary a great deal, too, from five to more than 200, although most species have between 10 and 20 (always in multiples of five). The arms are jointed to allow up and down movement, but are incapable of permitting much lateral movement, and this makes them very brittle. Therefore a great deal of care must be taken when handling these creatures to ensure that they are not damaged.

Many of the species can be kept successfully in an aquarium, but it must be large enough to accommodate their ultimate size and also their swimming ability. A small tank would be out of the question here. They require a water movement that is light to moderate and will not tolerate high levels of nitrate.

Photograph by Frank Walker

Comaster sp.

Family: Comasteridae
Range: Central Indo-Pacific to Australia
Description: This species has up to 80 arms. These are black at the base and the upper half is a bluish-white. Cirri are present and the animal attaches itself to gorgonians or coral in reef shallows or at depths of up to 100ft (30m). The individual arms can grow to 9in (23cm).
Feeding requirements: Feed on liquid invertebrate food that is specially manufactured for filter-feeding invertebrates.
Aquarium suitability: This species requires a large tank. Strong water movement is inadvisable. Success with this species in a reef aquarium using the plenum system has been reported where a twice-daily feeding regime was in operation. Nevertheless, this is not to be considered as a species for the beginner. It will readily shed its arms if it is handled incorrectly.

Comanthina schlegelii

Family: Comasteridae
Range: Tropical Indo-Pacific
Description: A species that is variable in colour but usually yellow. It can have 130 arms or more. With so many arms the cirri are usually shed and the lower arms assume the function of the cirri in order to anchor the animal to the substrate. The mouth, as with all members of this family, is on the edge of the cup and the arms can be up to 8in (20cm) long. *C. schlegelii* is found in reef shallows and reef channels to a depth of 166ft (51m).
Feeding requirements: Filters plankton and other suspended organic food from the surrounding water. In an aquarium, liquid food for filter feeding invertebrates should be given daily.
Aquarium suitability: Requires top water quality, a large tank and regular feeding for it to have any chance of survival. It is a difficult species to keep.

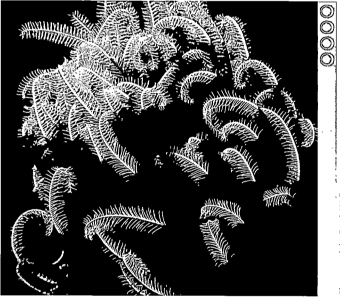

Photograph by Frank Walker

Class: Asteroidea

The class encompasses more than 1,800 species in more than 100 genera, which are placed into 30 families in six orders. Sea stars have five or more arms that should be considered as extensions of the body rather than as appendages, since they contain the reproductive and digestive organs. On the ventral (oral) side of the arms there are two, or sometimes four, rows of feet. These are set into grooves that radiate from the central mouth. The mouth lacks teeth and a jaw structure and the anus, when present, is situated dorsally (aborally).

Sea stars show an amazing ability to regenerate lost or damaged arms and in a few cases they can reproduce by splitting (fission) as well as by sexual reproduction. Most sea stars are found in rocky areas or on coral reefs, but there are some species that live on sediment and sand.

Their diet is varied and includes sponges, corals, crustaceans, bivalves, polychaetes, algae and microscopic organisms. With bivalves such as clams, the sea star uses its sensory tube feet at the tips of the arms to locate their hiding place in the sand. By sensing where the water current is flowing from the mollusc's siphon, it is able to isolate it. The sea star then grips the two shell halves with its sucker-like tube feet and slowly prizes them open, but only a fraction of an inch. This is enough to enable it to exude its thin stomach into the narrow opening and secrete its gastric juices to digest its prey from the inside out.

Order: Valvatida (cushion stars, sea stars)

Species from this order are by far the most important as far as marine aquarists are concerned, and many of the tropical and sub-tropical species are brightly coloured. The other five orders in the class Asteroidea contain only a few species that are imported as far as the aquarium trade is concerned. These are usually *Echinaster* spp. from the order Spinulosida.

With a few exceptions, sea stars belonging to the order Valvatida have five arms, each with two well developed marginal rows of plates. The suckered feet of the creatures are arranged in two rows along the arms, which can vary a great deal in length. Some species have arms that are long and slender, for example, but there are others with arms that are so short they are barely discernible. Species from this latter group are usually referred to as "cushion stars" because of their cushion-like shape. The adult size of the creatures can vary from the minuscule to individuals that are more than 30in (76cm).

In an aquarium, the most important aspect to consider is the acclimatization of newly introduced specimens. If this is not carried out correctly then many of the species within this group will die within a few days. First, the transport bag should contain enough water to ensure that the specimen cannot take in air. "Dry" conditions during transport will usually damage or destroy part of the creature's internal organs, especially the hydrovascular system of its tube feet. In addition, sea stars are extremely sensitive to changes in water quality, but not so much to changes in water temperature. The acclimatization to the aquarium water should take place over a period of 12 to 18 hours for the best chances of success. The point is that it must be done slowly enough that the internal organs do not cease to function properly. Sea stars cannot regenerate their sensitive internal organs if they become damaged.

Choriaster granulatus

Family: Oreasteridae
Range: Red Sea, Tropical Indo-Pacific
Description: The short, rounded appearance of the arms is unmistakable. It is a large sea star that grows to about 12in (30cm). The thick, smooth skin on the aboral surface is covered with warty, granular, gill structures. The colour can vary and may be creamy-white, yellow, orange or reddish-brown.
Feeding requirements: In the wild its main diet consists of coral polyps, sponges and other small benthic invertebrates. It will also scavenge for most other organic material. In an aquarium it will accept most frozen foods.
Aquarium suitability: Needs a large aquarium but not one that contains delicate invertebrates. It is hardy once acclimatized and is better kept in a fish-only aquarium, along with a few active invertebrates and plenty of rockwork and sand.

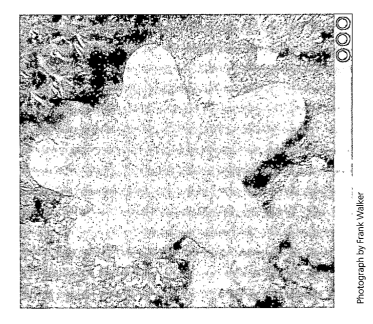

Photograph by Frank Walker

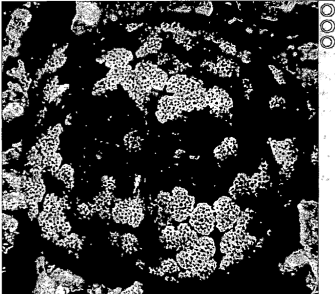

Photograph by Frank Walker

Culcita novaeguineae

Family: Oreasteridae
Range: Eastern Indian Ocean, Central Indo-Pacific as far as Hawaii
Description: Juveniles are star-shaped but as they grow they become cushion-shaped. Adults grow to about 10in (25cm) and have short spines on the dorsal surface. The colouration is extremely variable.
Feeding requirements: Its natural diet consists of coral, molluscs and other benthic invertebrates. In an aquarium it will accept frozen shellfish and even dried foods.
Aquarium suitability: Because of its natural diet of live corals and other sessile invertebrates, it is not suitable for a reef aquarium. It requires a large tank with plenty of rockwork and overhangs and there should be some deep sandy zones between the rocks.

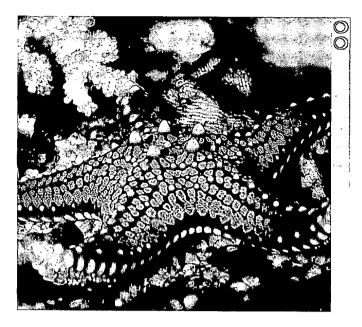

Pentaceraster tuberculatus

Family: Oreasteridae
Range: Indian Ocean, Red Sea
Description: Very variable in colour and often confused with *P. mammilatus*, which also has a variety of colours, some of which overlap. Generally, however, this species is brown and purplish-grey in colouration and the upper marginal tubercles are short. *P. mammilatus*, on the other hand, has longer marginal tubercles and the colour is usually green or greenish-yellow.
Feeding requirements: Feeds on various algae and small invertebrates, especially molluscs. In an aquarium it will eat almost anything that is offered.
Aquarium suitability: This species is not suitable for a reef aquarium because of the danger it represents to other sessile invertebrates. In a marine tank with lots of rock and sand, this sea star will do well.

Protoreaster nodosus

Family: Oreasteridae
Range: Entire Tropical Indo-Pacific, Red Sea
Description: Erhardt & Moosleitner (1995) report that this species grows to 16in (41cm), which is far in excess of those that are normally encountered. The maximum size is normally 8in (20cm). It is one of the most attractive of all the starfishes, being essentially orange and silver-grey with deep purple tubercles on the arms and central part of the aboral region. Found on rocks, sandy bottoms and lagoon areas throughout the Indo-Pacific and southern latitudes of the Red Sea.
Feeding requirements: In its natural habitat, this species is not particular about what it eats. In an aquarium it will eat anything, including your precious invertebrates!
Aquarium suitability: Provide lots of sandy areas in a large fish-only aquarium and it will prove hardy once acclimatized.

Fromia elegans

Family: Ophidiasteridae
Range: Tropical Indo-Pacific
Description: This species is almost always wrongly described by authors. This is because the formal description has not been taken into consideration. *F. elegans* has fine black pores on a brick-red body. The arms are tapered to fine, rounded points and there are no plate-like tubercles on the aboral surface.
Feeding requirements: Feeds on fine algae and micro-organisms that it rasps from the substrate. In an aquarium set-up, detritus will be eaten and also fresh shellfish.
Aquarium suitability: Once it is acclimatized this is an easy species to keep and, because it only grows to 3in (7.5cm), it is suitable for a larger reef aquarium as long as there are plenty of rocks present.

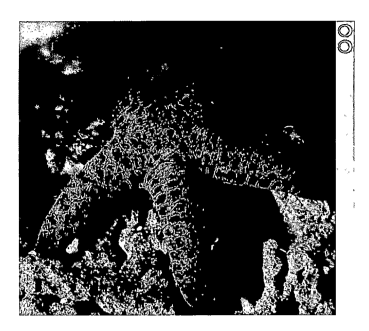

Fromia indica

Family: Ophidiasteridae
Range: Tropical Indo-Pacific from the Chagos Archipelago to Hawaii
Description: Similar to *F. elegans* species but in this case the gill pores are in the form of reticulated lines instead of spots. These surround irregularly formed flat platelets over much of the aboral surface. The tips of the arms are black in juveniles and subadults and the body is bright red to brick-red, depending on its geographic origin.
Feeding requirements: Its main diet in the wild is detritus, algae and small invertebrate organisms. In an aquarium it will accept frozen mussel and cockle to supplement that which is browsed from the aquarium decoration.
Aquarium suitability: Provide a mature tank with plenty of rocks and caves. Single specimens can be kept in a reef tank.

Fromia milliporella

Family: Ophidiasteridae
Range: Red Sea, Tropical Indo-Pacific
Description: The slightly raised tips to the arms, which are somewhat blunted in appearance, are good indicators that the species is *F. milliporella*. In addition, the margins of the arms have raised platelets and the entire aboral surface up to the arm margins is covered with pin-point-sized black spots. This species is uniform red, although specimens from the Red Sea often have powder-blue spots on the upper surface.
Feeding requirements: Feeds on algae and small organisms along with detritus. In a mature aquarium with plenty of live rock it will look after itself. Frost food will also be accepted.
Aquarium suitability: This small sea star grows to less than 3in (7.5cm). Two or three individuals can be kept in a large reef tank without any problems.

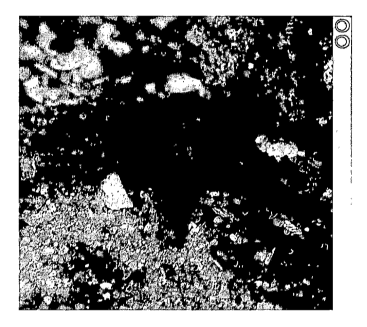

Fromia monilis

Family: Ophidiasteridae
Range: Indo-west Pacific
Description: This and the following species, *F. nodosa*, are commonly confused. In *F. monilis* the platelets on the aboral surface are not raised above the skin except on the arm margins. With *F. nodosa*, these platelets are visibly convex and protrude above the aboral surface, almost as nodules. This species is usually bright orange-red with lemon-yellow platelets and, although the body pattern can vary, these colours are retained.
Feeding requirements: Browses on microscopic algae and the minute organisms that are found within such growths. In a large aquarium it will find enough to eat on the decorative rockwork.
Aquarium suitability: The slow acclimatization is a critical factor with this species. It is best kept in a reef aquarium with plenty of live rock.

Photograph by Siegfried Krumbugel

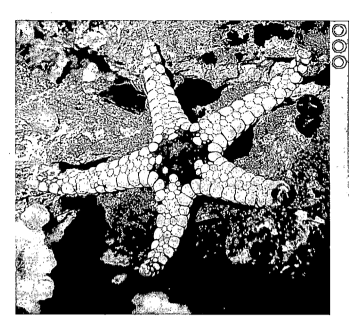

Fromia nodosa

Family: Ophidiasteridae
Range: East Africa to Central Indo-Pacific
Description: The convex, raised marginal and central platelets are more or less the same size in this species. There are rows of smaller platelets along the centre of the arms and these are somewhat irregular in shape. The body colouration is bright reddish-orange with yellow platelets. *F. nodosa* is found in lagoons and reef flats as well as back reef areas.
Feeding requirements: Its natural diet consists of microscopic organisms and microalgae. You should provide sufficient live rock in the aquarium so that this creature's natural diet is freely available.
Aquarium suitability: This sea star is quite transport sensitive, therefore great care and patience is required in the acclimatization phase. It is an ideal species for a reef aquarium.

Fromia sp.

Family: Ophidiasteridae
Range: Central Indo-Pacific
Description: The marginal platelets on the aboral surface are regular and large. Between them are irregular-shaped smaller platelets. The body is black with dull orange to bright orange platelets. This sea star is one of many belonging to this genus that can vary in colour so much it is difficult to identify.
Feeding requirements: Browses on microalgae and small invertebrates. In an aquarium, it will learn to take small pieces of shrimp, mussel and clam meat.
Aquarium suitability: A relatively easy species to keep and one that is a good scavenger in a reef tank. It is safe to keep with corals and other invertebrates but it requires plenty of holes and caves into which it can retire between feeding forays.

Fromia sp.

Family: Ophidiasteridae
Range: Tropical Indo-Pacific
Description: The body colouration is bright orange and the marginal platelets are more or less uniform in size. The platelets at the tips of the arms are lemon-yellow, while those toward the base of the arms, and on the body disc, are a greyish-purple. This species is found in reef shallows and in rocky areas where the water is not too turbulent.
Feeding requirements: A scavenger that feeds on small benthic invertebrates, algae, detritus and other organic matter. In an aquarium, most foods will be accepted to supplement that which it browses from the rocks.
Aquarium suitability: Suitable for a reef tank since it will leave the invertebrates alone when it is provided with enough food. It is an active daytime species that is extremely attractive.

Photograph by Frank Walker

Linckia guildingi

Family: Ophidiasteridae
Range: Red Sea, Tropical Indo-Pacific from East Africa to Hawaii, Tropical West Atlantic
Description: Juveniles can be spotted and are often similar in appearance to *Linckia multiflora*. At this stage of their development they are shy and spend much of their time hidden among coral rubble. Adult specimens can have five, six or seven arms and grow to 12in (30cm). The colour can vary and purple, green and deep brick-red examples are often seen, but the usual colour is a brownish-yellow.
Feeding requirements: This is a scavenger that feeds on detritus, small sand-dwelling organisms and other organic matter.
Aquarium suitability: Provide sand zones and plenty of live rock for this sea star. Despite its relatively large size, it will not damage any of your precious invertebrates.

Linckia laevigata

Family: Ophidiasteridae
Range: Entire Tropical Indo-Pacific
Description: *L. laevigata* is a relatively common species that grows to 12in (30cm) in length. It is a typical reef-dweller, preferring the shady crevices between blocks of coral. Young specimens are duller in colour than the adults, which are overall a bright blue. Although there are usually five arms, there can be up to seven of differing lengths that can be attributed to asexual reproduction.
Feeding requirements: Feeds mainly on detritus and other organic matter but it will also eat microscopic invertebrates and microalgae. In a mature aquarium feeding is no problem.
Aquarium suitability: Does very well in a reef tank once it is acclimatized. This is not so easy, because it does not travel too happily, so a great deal of care and patience is required.

Linckia multiflora

Family: Ophidiasteridae
Range: Red Sea, Tropical Indo-Pacific
Description: The body colouration may be light yellow to brownish-orange. The aboral surface is covered with irregular red, orange, yellow or brown flecks and spots. The photograph shows the "comet" stage, where the arm, half hidden under the soft coral, is considerably longer than the other four. This is because *L. multiflora* frequently reproduces asexually by shedding an arm, which after some time develops into a new individual. In this case, the arm is almost completely developed.
Feeding requirements: Feeds on detritus and microorganisms. In a mature tank it will browse the rocks and sand for its food requirements.
Aquarium suitability: Deep sandy zones should be provided along with plenty of live rock that is rich in flora and fauna.

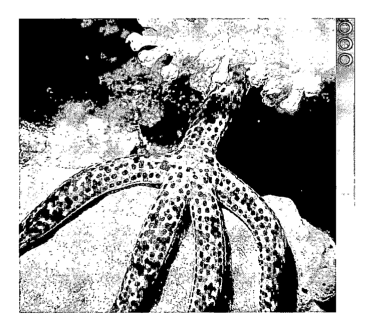

Class: Ophiuroidea

The class Ophiuroidea contains about 2,000 species, which makes it the most species-rich class in this phylum. At first glance, some of these creatures resemble sea stars, but they are not. Their bodies are organized quite differently. In the first instance, the arms are long and slender and these are, in the majority of species, covered with plates that give them a segmented-looking appearance. In addition, the arms have a distinct demarcation from the body disc, unlike the true sea stars, and there is no anus. The mouth serves not only to ingest food, but also to expel body wastes. The undersides of the arms lack the groove that is present in sea stars and the tube feet neither have suckers nor are they used for locomotion. Instead, they serve a purely sensory function. The upper surface of the body disc is covered with shield-like ossicles, or plates, and these may be spinous or covered with granules. The radial shields at the bases of the arms are usually the largest and the most dominant, and the exact arrangement of the plates is an important factor in taxonomic identification.

Ophiuroids have five or more arms and are extremely active creatures. The arms are flexible and are used for locomotion, which in some cases can be quite fast. Most of them can regenerate lost arms and, in some cases, the arm itself can develop into a completely new individual – this is the exception rather than the rule. Most species are night-time feeders, preferring to hide during the daylight hours. There are three orders in this class, two of which contain species that are often available to aquarists.

Order: Phrynophiurida (basket stars)

These animals are both spectacular and bizarre when viewed at night on the reef. During the day, the basket star curls into an unimpressive tangled ball. At night, however, it will spread its multiple-branched arms, which can be up to 40in (1m) in diameter, into a large wickerbasket-like form to capture any planktonic organisms that are carried to them by the water current. The net-like branched arms (more than 81,000 terminal branches have been counted on just one individual creature) are ideally suited for this purpose. They are flexible, and when an organism blunders into the filaments of the branches, they curl around it to ensnare it before transferring it directly to the mouth. In this way, they appear to "wilt", just like the plants that they so often resemble. They also do this at daybreak, or at night on the reef when a light is pointed directly at them. It is only in darkness that they assume their imposing, basket-like postures. To obtain their food they will seek out the best vantage point locally by "walking" on their multibranched arms to some prominent point on the reef and then spread their arms across the direction of the water current.

The order contains 12 genera, which are grouped into four families and, as far as the biological characteristics are concerned, they are entirely different from other groups within this phylum. The plates on the central body disc and arms are covered with a thick but soft skin. The branching of the arms may be simple or complex. The lateral arm plates are positioned toward the oral region and the aboral plates are greatly reduced or absent.

These creatures should not be considered suitable for beginners, They require special care under expert supervision. Although they are sometimes seen for sale, you need to be fully informed regarding their needs and have the necessary aquarium set-up to accommodate them. They need a large tank devoted to these and similar invertebrates that require constant planktonic feeding. Spectacular success is possible when they are kept with sponges and soft coral (*Dendronephthya* spp.).

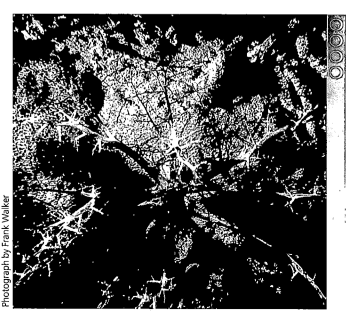

Photograph by Frank Walker

Astrophyton sp.

Family: Gorgonocephalidae
Range: Tropical Indo-Pacific, Indo-West Pacific
Description: With the arms extended an adult specimen may be 30in (76cm) in diameter. The arms are orange-brown to tan at the bases and many of the branches have white tips or patches.
Feeding requirements: Feeds on plankton and other small organisms. In an aquarium it will learn to take most foods, such as frozen plankton and brine shrimp.
Aquarium suitability: A 500-gallon (2,300-litre) aquarium should be considered as the minimum size to house this and similar species in captivity. Actinic lighting is advisable with perhaps the duration of the main lighting reduced to four hours per day. Cardinalfishes (Apogonidae) and squirrelfishes (Holocentridae) are its ideal tank-mates. This species is suitable only for the expert.

Order: Ophiurida (brittle stars, serpent stars)

In the sea, brittle stars in one form or another are everywhere, sometimes forming dense mats, and they have a variety of habitats, including mud and other sediments, sand and gravel. Some species are found twisted around finger-formed sponges or entwined in gorgonian corals. They are encountered under rocks and some species seek out a crevice or hole in the substrate. Here they position their central disc and proceed to capture food by hanging their arms out of the hole.

Brittle stars earn their name from their long, slender, extremely flexible arms that break off so easily when handled. They feed on detritus and dead organic material. Most brittle stars will also feed on microscopic organisms in the sand and surrounding water. Larger species will prey on crustaceans, bivalve molluscs and worms.

Ophiarachna incrassata

Family: Ophiodermatidae
Range: Tropical Indo-Pacific
Description: This is one of the larger brittle stars at an adult size of 18in (46cm). The body disc can be up to 2in (5cm) across and is bright olive-green, as are the arms. The upper surface of the body disc has radiating rows of fine silver-grey spots that also border the spaces between its five arms. The arms themselves have a segmented appearance and have well developed lateral spines. This is an active species that is found in the reef shallows, usually among coral rubble or in sea-grass beds.
Feeding requirements: Feeds on any organic material such as algae and detritus. In an aquarium it will accept most food substitutes.
Aquarium suitability: Hardy and easy to keep, this scavenging, active animal is an ideal choice for a reef or marine aquarium.

Class: Echinoidea

This class encompasses sea urchins, heart urchins and sand dollars. They are spiny, sometimes to the extreme. The body is enclosed in close-fitting calcium carbonate plates that are fused together. There are no arms present and although these animals have a certain amount of regenerative ability they are unable to regenerate the plates if they are badly damaged. The central mouth is ringed with five teeth, which form an elaborate chewing device known as "Aristotle's lantern". The spines are movable and can be used in a defensive role. More commonly, however, these spines are used simply as an aid to locomotion.

The pedicellariae are stalked, usually with three lobes, and are used for cleaning, feeding and for defence. The three lobes or valves allow the pedicellariae to bite and

By far the most important group for marine aquarists is the family, Ophiodermatidae. This contains many brightly coloured species suitable for both reef and marine set-ups. From this family, the bright-red brittle star (*Ophioderma squamosissimum*) from the Caribbean is occasionally available. It is one of the largest brittle stars from this region and grows to about 8in (20cm) in diameter. Also from the Caribbean, the zebra brittle star (*Ophioderma apressum*) is more often seen for sale. It is smaller than the previous species at 5in (13cm) and its body pattern is somewhat variable. Often it has yellowish-white and dark green bands along the arms and a pentagonal star on the upper surface of the body disc.

From the Indo-Pacific, *Ophiarachna incrassata* is the best known and the most often imported. Many of the brightly coloured species, such as those of the genus *Ophiozepa*, are found on the Great Barrier Reef.

grasp food before passing it down to the mouth. In some species, such as *Toxopneustes* spp., there are poison sacs at the bases of the pedicellariae. A bite from these can often prove dangerous to people. Long-spined sea urchins have hollow spines that are brittle and sharp. They can easily pierce the skin and will then break off, leaving a painful and inflamed wound. In a few burrowing species the spines are reduced to hairs. These are sand dollars, whose skeletons often pave reef shallows and lagoon areas.

Echinoids are exclusively benthic animals found on sand and sediment as well as on rocks or coral reefs. Sea urchins are usually omnivorous, feeding on animal as well as vegetable matter, and most will also eat any other organic debris and detritus.

Order: Cidaroida (lance urchins)

These strange urchins have their roots deep in history. They belong to a group that emerged some 450 million years ago, during the Ordovician period. They were widespread and successful creatures, surviving through the Silurian period when the first land plants came into existence. They lived through the Devonian and Carboniferous periods at a time when the first amphibians and winged insects emerged, and the great swamp forests existed from the which the principal coal deposits of today were later formed.

In the Permian period they outlived the emergence of the first reptiles and the mass extinction of many marine invertebrates. They survived the Triassic and Jurassic periods when the first dinosaurs, the first mammals and the first birds appeared on the planet, at a time when the north Atlantic and the early Indian Ocean came into being. These urchins lived through the time when the dinosaurs were at their peak and into the Cretaceous period when the first modern seas were formed. Then, about 65 million years ago, there was a mass extinction of much of the life on Earth. This included the dinosaurs, but also involved many other creatures. The cause of this was probably a massive meteorite strike. But even then, species from this group survived. These are the lance urchins of the order Cidaroida.

They are different from other sea urchins because they are more primitive in their development. The teeth are not keeled, as in other sea urchins, nor do their spines have a skin covering. Lance urchins are predominantly omnivorous animals. In an aquarium they will keep the algae under control, but once this is depleted they need regular feeding.

Eucidaris tribuloides

Family: Cidaridae
Range: Caribbean, Tropical West Atlantic
Description: The adult specimen here has a test diameter of 2in (5cm), which is about the maximum size for this species. The primary spines are arranged vertically in ten rows and broken spines can be regenerated. The secondary spines, also arranged in rows, are reddish-brown to tan in colouration. The primary spines can vary in colour depending on the amount of encrustation from other growths. This specimen is relatively free of this and probably shows its true colouration.
Feeding requirements: Feeds on algae, detritus and encrusting invertebrates. In an aquarium, most frozen foods are accepted to supplement its algae diet.
Aquarium suitability: A hardy, long-lived species that does well in a fish-only tank where there is live rock on which it can graze.

Order: Diadematoida (long-spined sea urchins)

This order contains only one family, with six genera, and representatives from this group occur in all tropical seas. In most cases the spines are hollow with a venomous surface skin that causes a burning sensation with a puncture wound. Take care when handling specimens. The spines are brittle and segmented, with reversed barbs. When a puncture wound is sustained, the tip of the barb stays in the skin and cannot easily be removed. Attempts to remove the spine with a needle will only result in the spine breaking up within the wound.

With the five *Diadema* species there is usually no permanent harm and the spine dissolves after a few days, leaving no lasting effects. In this case, nothing need be done, unless there is an allergic reaction. Other species, however, such as the two Indo-Pacific species from the genus *Echinothrix* (*E. calamaris* and *E. diadema*) have a lasting effect and can cause sustained pain and swelling, along with high blood pressure. The spines do not dissolve in the body and frequently cause infection accompanied by skin discoloration. You need to seek medical help.

Wounds from most of the other species are accompanied by pain in the initial stages, but this is usually short lived and will pass within a few minutes, or a few hours in some cases. The wound from one of the *Diadema* species is usually dark purple, irrespective of the colour of the spine embedded in the skin. This discoloration usually lasts for three or four days. Despite these disadvantages, they make spectacular aquarium creatures and they are excellent algal grazers. They are unsuitable for a reef tank, but are ideal for a normal marine aquarium with soft corals, anemones and fishes.

Echinothrix calamaris

Family: Diadematidae
Range: Tropical Indo-Pacific, Red Sea
Description: If there was any doubt as to which phylum this animal belongs, you need only look at this photograph. It shows the typical five-rayed radial symmetry that echinoids possess, in that the brown secondary spines are bunched together beneath the longer white-banded primary ones. Note the grey distended faecal sac in the centre of the test. This species grows to about 12in (30cm) and its spines are quite poisonous to people.
Feeding requirements: Its natural diet consists of algae, detritus and various organic matter. In an aquarium most foods are accepted, including flake.
Aquarium suitability: Unsuitable for a reef tank, as it is known to graze on stony corals. A mature, fish-only aquarium with plenty of rock is ideal.

Diadema setosum

Family: Diadematidae
Range: Tropical Indo-Pacific, Red Sea
Description: Unlike *D. savignyi*, this species lacks the bright blue star pattern on the test. Instead there are numerous tiny blue spots near the margin and five large white spots in a pentagonal arrangement around the anus. There is a bright orange ring around the anus in most specimens. The spines are banded, sometimes white, in juveniles; in adults, typically black.
Feeding requirements: Feeds on benthic algae and invertebrates that it rasps off the rocks or grazes from the sand. Provide this species with plenty of rock that has a good growth of meiofauna and algae.
Aquarium suitability: Not recommended for a reef tank since this species will strip the rocks of all the delicate life forms within a short space of time. It does well in a fish-only tank.

Photograph by Frank Walker

Order: Temnopleuroida (sea urchins, globe urchins)

If there is such a thing as a typical sea urchin, then it probably belongs in this order. Characteristically, the test, or bony plate, is spherical, rigid and radially symmetrical. The spines are generally short and used for locomotion more than defence. Unlike the long-spined sea urchins, which have poisonous spines, species from this order rely more on their pedicellariae for defence. It is usual for these species to decorate their tests on their aboral surface. This job is carried out using pieces of algae, sponges and various other debris. The pedicellariae carry these items on to the spines to serve two purposes – either as a defensive, camouflage measure or as an umbrella of debris for protection against damaging UV rays from bright sunlight in the reef shallows.

The order contains two families and representatives from both of these are regularly imported for the aquarium trade. The first family, Temnopleuridae, has many small but colourful species often seen for sale. The skin on the tests of these urchins is sometimes patterned, with or without spines, so that sharply demarcated and radially symmetrical colour contrasts occur. These urchins are essentially herbivorous but they will obviously take encrusting invertebrates, such as bryozoans and sponges, as part of their diet when these are ingested along with the benthic algae on which they are feeding. In the second family, Toxopneustidae, the pedicellariae are usually poisonous to a greater or lesser degree and many species are omnivorous. They are equipped with teeth-like structures that can be up to ⅕in (5mm) in diameter. They use their pedicellariae to grasp and immobilize prey before transferring it to the mouth.

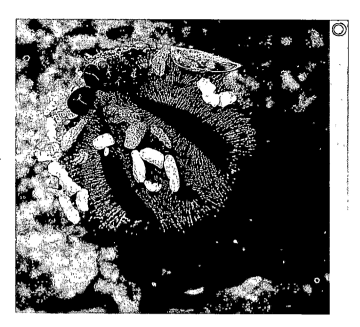

Salmacis dussemieri

Family: Temnopleuridae
Range: Red Sea, Tropical Indo-Pacific
Description: This urchin reaches a maximum diameter of about 3in (7.5cm). It has no common name, but perhaps it should be called the "salt and pepper urchin" because of the colour of its primary and secondary spines. These are important in the identification of this species.
Feeding requirements: A herbivore that will also feed on encrusting invertebrates. In a tank, most substitute foods will be accepted to supplement those that it can graze from the rocks.
Aquarium suitability: This is the "lawnmower" urchin. Any aquarists who are proud of their lush algal growth should avoid this creature at all costs, since including it in the tank will result in the total destruction of the algae. It is hardy, though, and ideal for a fish-only aquarium.

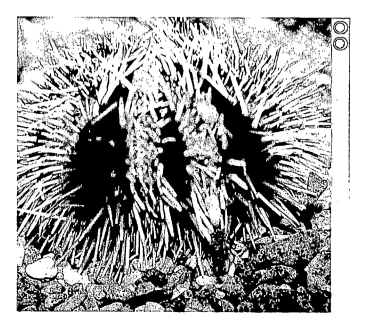

Mespilia globulus

Family: Temnopleuridae
Range: Central Indo-Pacific including the Indo-Australian Archipelago
Description: The test has five spineless, velvety-green or blue vertical zones. Between these, there are irregular rows of short spines that are reddish-brown in colour. The accompanying photograph shows the typical nature of this urchin. Pieces of broken coral, a bivalve shell and also algae (*Ventricaria* sp.) are being used as an "umbrella" for camouflage or UV protection.
Feeding requirements: Principally a herbivore that feeds mainly on algae. It will accept frozen shellfish as a supplement.
Aquarium suitability: This is one of the few sea urchins that will excuse all a beginner's mistakes. It is hardy and practically indestructible, although it is unsuitable for a reef tank because its algal diet includes calcareous algae.

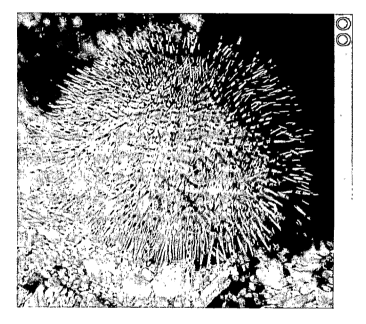

Tripneustes gratilla

Family: Toxopneustidae
Range: Red Sea, Tropical Indo-Pacific
Description: In colouration this is one of the most variable of all sea urchins. The spines can range from white to orange-red and the velvety intermediate zones are white, red or bluish-violet. Its pedicellariae are poisonous and contain a mixture of proteins and various amino acids (polypeptides), which, in this case, are painful but not usually dangerous to people.
Feeding requirements: Its main diet consists of benthic algae, but it will capture small planktonic organisms with its pedicellariae and also rasp away at encrusting invertebrates. In an aquarium, most foods are accepted to supplement this.
Aquarium suitability: Does well in a marine aquarium but is not recommended for a reef system. It is not to be trusted with soft corals but is, nevertheless, a hardy and long-lived species.

Class: Holothuroidea

This class contains about 1,250 species in six orders and 19 families. The body is usually worm-like or cucumber-formed and their collective common name, "sea cucumber", is quite apt. Holothurians lie on their sides instead of the oral side, as is the case with other echinoderms. The mouth and anus are at opposite ends of the body and there is a large body cavity present. The mouth of holothurians is ringed with 10 to 30 branched tentacles that in some species are tree-like in form. The tentacles are modified tube feet and are very flexible. The tentacles are used to capture planktonic organisms from the surrounding water or, in some cases, they are used to grub around in the sand or sediment in the search of food.

Respiratory trees are present in pairs within the body cavity. Water is drawn into the highly branched system of vesicles, where gas exchange takes place. This is then expelled and fresh water is drawn in. In this way, a type of slow breathing is carried out and, because of this, sea cucumbers are considered to have one of the most highly developed respiratory systems in the invertebrate world.

These creatures show an amazing ability to regenerate parts of their body, particularly the internal organs. If predators attack them, they will often expel their stomachs out through their mouths as an offering to their attacker. This evisceration sometimes includes the respiratory trees as well. If the animal survives the attack these organs will be regenerated later.

The main diet of most species is organic matter from the seabed. Many of the species contained in this class are relatively drab in colouration, although there are some brightly coloured and attractively marked species. Sizes range from about 1in (2.5cm) to huge specimens that have a body length of more than 6ft (2m) with a thickness of more than 12in (30cm).

In an aquarium special care must be taken with holothurians to ensure that they are not subjected to too much stress. If this happens, the creature may eviscerate and the ensuing poison will swiftly bring about the demise of all other aquarium inhabitants. Additionally, they can subject themselves to such stress if, for example, they stray too close to an anemone or attach themselves to a heater, which later switches on. They may become drawn into a filter or pump inlet, or the water quality may be poor. Each of these circumstances can cause the animal to eviscerate. For these reasons, keeping sea cucumbers should be left to experts.

Order: Dendrochirotida (sea apples)

This order contains species that are predominantly filter feeders. The mouth is surrounded by ten or more tentacles that are branched to a greater or lesser degree. The body is often almost as thick as it is long and for this reason many of the species in this order are referred to as "sea apples".

The main family of interest to aquarists is the Cucumariidae. These are small to medium sea cucumbers often inactive during daylight. At night they will creep out of hiding to feed. Others may be buried in the sand with only the ring of their feeding tentacles visible. They feed mainly on zooplankton, which are captured by the ring of tentacles and then transferred to the mouth. In a tank, the sharply contrasting colours of these animals have much to offer. Nevertheless, you need to take care. Cucumariidae are among the most frequently imported sea cucumbers and, because of this, they are responsible for the most "wipe-outs" in community aquariums because of their poison, holothurin. Novices often buy them because of their bright colours, which can be a costly mistake. Take advice from a knowledgeable dealer before buying.

Pseudocolochirus violaceus

Family: Cucumariidae
Range: Central Indo-Pacific
Description: There are two similar species and these are *Pseudocolochirus violaceus* and *P. axiologus*. There are also several invalid names for these two creatures. To put matters straight, *P. axiologus* has blue body walls with red tube feet rows that are often bordered with yellow, and the tentacles are usually pinkish-white. *P. violaceus*, however, has pale violet body walls, the tube feet are yellow and the tentacles are bright red.
Feeding requirements: A filter feeder that needs daily feedings of plankton or brine shrimp for its long-term survival.
Aquarium suitability: Specimens that are attached to the substrate or glass should not be removed by force. This will result in damage to the tube feet, from which the animal may not recover. When buying one, ensure that this does not happen.

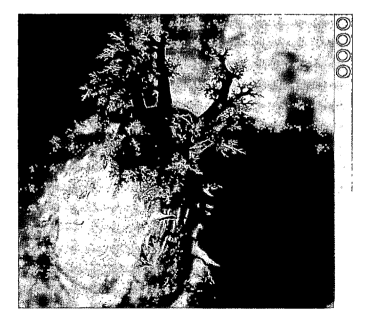

Phylum: Chordata (chordates)

The chordates are represented in most environments. The phylum is divided into three subphyla, two of which are considered to be invertebrate groupings. This is because a true backbone is lacking, although at some stage in their lives they possess a notochord. The first subphylum, Tunicata, is of some interest, since it contains the tunicates and ascidians, or sea squirts as they are sometimes called. These invertebrate animals have several chordate characteristics but these usually manifest themselves only in the larval stages. The larvae, which often resemble tadpoles, have a notochord in the tail.

The second subphylum encompasses invertebrates that are commonly referred to as "lancelets". They are fish-shaped, often translucent, and can reach a size of about 2in (5cm). The strongly compressed, elongate body, which is supported by a notochord, is tapered at each end.

In part four of this book, the fishes were dealt with in detail and these, along with all other animals that have backbones, belong to the third subphylum, Vertebrata.

Class: Ascidiacea

The class contains two orders, Enterogona and Pleurogona. These are colonial and solitary tunicates commonly known as sea squirts. They are bottom-dwelling animals often found on reef drop-offs or under overhangs and at the base of corals. They are frequently brightly coloured and can form large colonies. Solitary individuals may reach a size of 8in (20cm), although this is the exception rather than the rule.

In a typical sea squirt the body is rounded or vase-shaped and the outer wall, or tunic, may be tough and leathery or gelatinous, depending on the species. The larval stage is typically tadpole-like and at this stage there is a notochord present, along with sense organs and a limited swimming ability. Once the creature settles to the bottom, there is a gradual regression of the tail, along with the notochord, and the animal adopts its adult form, leaving a single hollow nerve cord in the dorsal region.

It is a great pity that many of these colourful creatures cannot be kept for any length of time in a reef aquarium. There are some successes but this is limited to those that are brought in by accident on live rock.

Order: Enterogona (sea squirts, ascidians)

The order contains both colonial and solitary sea squirts. As a rule, these are shallow-water species but many of them prefer shadowy areas under overhangs or on near-vertical reef walls. There are two suborders, Aplousobranchia and Phlebobranchia. Species contained in Aplousobranchia are predominantly colonial, although there are a few solitary forms. Phlebobranchia contains mainly solitary-living species. Sea squirts from this suborder often have translucent body walls and these are occasionally ornamented with sand particles.

The key to keeping these species successfully in an aquarium lies in the degree of water movement and the amount of nutrition present. In the wild, that these species are at their most successful in relatively shallow water where the wave movement and current is stronger than in deeper water, seems to reflect their needs. Additionally, at this depth the nutrition through planktonic and other microscopic organisms is at its highest.

Rhopalaea crassa

Family: Diazonidae
Range: Central Indo-Pacific to the Indo-Australian Archipelago
Description: This is one of the most attractive sea squirts. It occurs singly or in small groups and is often an intense violet or blue colour. Most specimens have a yellow margin to the inhalent and exhalent siphons, which are often different in size. The exhalent siphon is usually the smaller of the two.
Feeding requirements: Feeds on microplankton and other small organisms. In an aquarium, this species should be given liquid food suitable for filter-feeding invertebrates.
Aquarium suitability: Almost impossible to keep in captivity, but keep trying. It seems to do better under combined daylight and actinic tubes than with metal-halide lighting, irrespective of the amount of shadow. Provide plenty of water movement and feed twice daily for the best results.

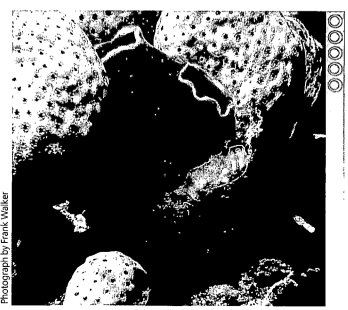

Photograph by Frank Walker

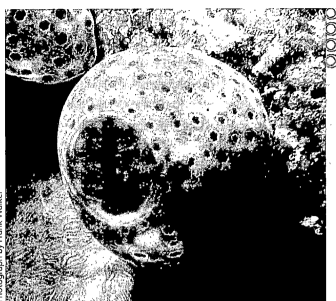

Photograph by Frank Walker

Didemnum molle

Family: Didemnidae
Range: Tropical Indo-West Pacific
Description: This sea squirt forms colonies that are rounded or barrel-shaped. Individual zooids are only about 1.5mm long. The body walls are embedded with calcium carbonate spicules, which makes the colonies very brittle. The spicules are pigmented and are responsible for the body colouration, which ranges from white to orange brown. The bright green rim of the communal exhalent siphon is caused by zooxanthellae.
Feeding requirements: A filter feeder. Feed on frozen plankton and liquid invertebrate food.
Aquarium suitability: Very transport sensitive and requires special care because of its brittle nature. Provide plenty of water movement and place it in a well-lit area of the tank, but not directly under metal-halide lights. Grows well in a reef tank.

Order: Pleurogona (sea squirts, ascidians)

This order contains four families of solitary-living or colonial sea squirts. In this case, the body is not divided into distinct zones, as is the case with the previous order. Additionally, in the enterogonan sea squirts, a single gonad is situated in or near the loop of of the gut. With species from this order, however, the gonads are present in the walls of the exhalent siphon.

Of the four families in this group, only one – Styelidae – contains species that are occasionally imported for the aquarium trade, and it contains both colonial and solitary forms. Perhaps the most well known species, as far as aquarists are concerned, are those from the genus *Polycarpa*, which are solitary, often brightly coloured animals. Their tunics are tough and leathery and these species grow quite large. One of the features of these

species is that the exhalent tubes are situated more or less in the middle of the body. These species usually belong to the genus *Botryllus*. Their colours range from violet, through red and orange, to bright yellow. There is often a contrasting colour, particularly around the inhalent siphon, and this is frequently a silver grey. *Botrylloides* and *Polyandrocarpa* species present an entirely different impression. These two genera contain species that resemble some brightly coloured encrusting sponges.

Sea squirts from this order can be kept successfully in an aquarium. In fact, there are frequent cases of living rock being imported where these animals suddenly appear and do extremely well in captivity. In such cases, where a colony or single individual establishes itself, there are usually no requirements for special care. In other cases, however, where a species is specifically imported, the picture is somewhat different and care is needed.

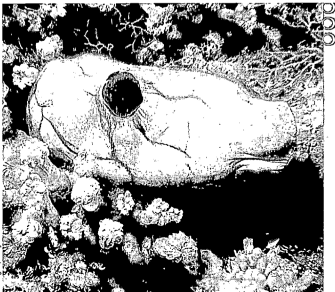

Photograph by Frank Walker

Polycarpa aurata

Family: Styelidae
Range: Tropical Indo-Pacific
Description: This solitary tunicate can grow to 6in (15cm). It has a tough, leathery tunic that has unevenly distributed swellings on the surface. The body is white, with yellow around the siphons, and there are thin, deeply embossed, lilac-coloured lines and streaks present over much of the body. This is a common species that is often found in reef shallows living in close proximity to other colonial sea squirts.
Feeding requirements: A filter feeder that requires daily feedings of liquid invertebrate food and frozen plankton.
Aquarium suitability: Surprisingly good, once it has settled in and is feeding regularly. Adult specimens do not do well in an aquarium. The aquarist should ensure that juveniles are attached to a piece of the substrate before they are purchased.

part six

BREEDING AND CULTURE OF FISHES AND INVERTEBRATES

The role of the hobbyist

Unlike professional marine biologists, aquarists are free to follow whichever aspect of the hobby that most interests them. Through a combination of interest and curiosity, it is not unusual to find that many aquarists become very expert individuals. In the short history of this hobby, aquarists have discovered more new methods of care and culture of marine fishes and invertebrates than their professional counterparts. To take an example, the successful care and reproduction of stony and soft corals in an aquarium was discovered and developed through the tenacity and hard work of amateurs.

It is astonishing, therefore, that the culture and breeding of reef fishes within the hobby has not made as much progress as has, for instance, the reproduction of stony corals. Magazine articles about the successful breeding of a particular species of coral fish are rare and sporadic, and it would appear that no new developments are being made in this area.

Some time ago, a new species of cardinalfish (*Pterapogon kauderni*) was introduced into the aquarium hobby arena. This fish is unlike most other reef fishes in that it is a mouthbrooder and the young fish do not have a larval stage. This means that they are tiny replicas of their parents and larger than most other coral fish larvae. Almost immediately, articles started to appear about the successful breeding and raising results with this fish, which shows that the interest is out there. Unfortunately, *Pterapogon kauderni* is not a typical reef fish and the successful breeding and culture of the species is in no way comparable with the successful raising of anemonefish larvae (*Amphiprion* spp.). It is true to say that the longer the larval development stage of a fish is, the more difficult it is to raise it to adulthood.

The sudden worldwide increase in articles about breeding successes with *P. kauderni* shows that the interest is there, and that aquarists are willing to attempt to breed marine fishes. Yet it also raises the question concerning why there are not more successes with other species of coral fishes. There are obviously other reasons. The answer is surprisingly simple. Coral fish breeding can be characterized as follows:
- Time consuming
- Expensive
- Requires patience and energy
- The correct equipment plays an important and decisive role
- Sufficient knowledge of breeding and care techniques

Whereas the first three points apply to individual aquarists, in that they must be prepared to invest time, patience and money, the final two points indicate that there is an overall lack of knowledge in this area.

Hopefully, this part of the book can help to point a correct way forward. However, due to the complicated nature of marine fish culture, only a small part of the subject can be dealt with here. Nevertheless, it is a significant part and probably the most important elements are covered. After all, experience can be won only by practice.

Mariculture

Coral fish culture is only a small part of the much wider aspect of mariculture, which is the reproduction of marine organisms under artificial conditions. Mariculture is a science, and those who undertake it usually become specialists in the culture of food fishes or in water-quality management. However, many of the methods used can also be adapted and applied to the culture of coral fishes. But since each reef fish species has its own requirements, each of these adapted methods is different. Despite this, it is unquestionable that the successful culture of reef fish larvae can be effected only with mariculture methods.

The subjects dealt with here are those that count for the most mistakes by aquarists – those who have taken the time and trouble, and invested a great deal of money, but were unsuccessful. There are two main types of mistake. The first involves the type of container used to raise the larvae and the second is to do with feeding and nutrition.

Tanks and containers

Most raising tanks employed in mariculture are entirely different to those used by aquarists. They are usually 6 to 10ft (2 to 3m) high, cylindrical and moderately cone-shaped with the narrower end at the top. Fresh sea water enters from the bottom of the tank and exits at the top through a filter screen. At the beginning of the larval development, the water flow is very slow, but is gradually increased, step by step, with the growth of the larvae. Because in this type of system the water surface area is relatively small, it is constantly being skimmed off into the overflow system, where protein skimmers can remove the waste products. This is important for fish larvae because they need to fill their swim bladders by taking a gulp of air at the water's surface. If the water surface is covered with an oily film caused by waste products, many larvae cannot break through, and this results in an ineffective swim

A ¼-in (6-mm) long, 35-day-old juvenile Chrysiptera parasema *is shown here for comparison against the ⅖-in (1-cm) outside diameter of these ceramic filter tubes.*

bladder. Of course they can live for some time in this state, but it costs a lot of energy for the larvae to maintain their position in the water column. As a result, they tend to sink where they die through a loss of energy and hunger.

This outcome is common with coral fishes as well, particularly damselfishes (*Pomacentridae*). When a normally shaped aquarium is used, the problem can be overcome with the use of a simple surface skimmer to remove the oily film. This is a floating frame made from PVC piping. An air diffuser directs the water into this frame and, along with it, the proteinous waste products. The concentrated oily film inside the frame is then removed simply by laying a paper tissue over it. This method has been used successfully in the raising of larvae of the yellow-tailed blue damsel (*Chrysiptera parasema*).

With a cylindrical and conical container that has an overflow at the top, the problem is less critical. If you are serious about breeding and raising reef fishes you should consider building a container to this design. The depth of the water in the container, which should be a minimum of 30in (80cm), is also important for the continued wellbeing of the larvae. Bear in mind, however, that the overflow at the top of the container is crucial.

Most commercial fish farms use natural sea water to pump through their containers. Natural sea water is used because it is cheap, but in many cases special filters and UV sterilizing units must be installed to prevent disease entering the tanks. With synthetic sea water, this problem does not occur, and nowadays you can expect excellent results from using this product for fish culture.

By far the most important theme in the successful culture of coral fishes lies in the field of feeding and nutrition at the larval stage. This is where most of the major mistakes by amateurs are made, and will continue to be made, unless and until aquarists understand the prerequisites. Not only is the type of food used reflected in the success of a fish brood, but also the nutritional quality of the food itself plays a hugely important role. The food should be of a standard that allows the larvae to develop healthily and naturally within the synthetic environment and confines of a marine hobby system.

In order to establish organisms on which the marine fish larvae can be fed, you first of all have to set up a food chain. This is not as difficult as it initially sounds, and it is certainly not the problem that it is sometimes made out to be – so don't panic! The food chain begins with a very simple organism – a single-celled algae of the type that are produced to feed marine rotifers (*Brachionus* spp.). These are then used as food for the fish larvae. It is essentially as simple as that.

Of course, there are problems you could encounter, but generally these will have nothing to do with the culture of algae and marine rotifers, since this is relatively easy when you know how (*see below*). The main problems lie in the ability of the fish breeder to produce a food that is nutritional enough to keep the larvae healthy and provide a good rate of growth.

Culture of marine rotifers (*Brachionus* spp.)

The mass culture of marine rotifers, such as *Brachionus* spp, takes a great deal of time. You must also be aware of the fact that they have little in the way of nutrition to offer fish larvae. And this fact, that *Brachionus* are especially poor in nutritional content, is most commonly misunderstood. *Brachionus* are used only because of their ability to reproduce rapidly and reach a size that is attractive to the fish larvae. It is because of their swimming movements that they are especially tempting, but as a food they are very poor.

It is the responsibility of the fish breeder to ensure that these organisms are changed into high-quality food with excellent nutritional value. This process is called "enrichment". It is based on the fact that these organisms will take in any particles that are of an appropriate size. So the possibility exists, through the targeted feeding of nutritional elements that are important for fish larvae, to change *Brachionus* into "living nutritional capsules".

A simple form of enrichment would be to feed *Brachionus* cultures on single-celled algae. But this is not as easy as it sounds. Many of the single-celled algae that are responsible for "green water" are totally unsuitable as a food source for these organisms. Even if the correct algae are used, there is always the danger that other, stronger and more robust algae might take over the culture and thereby destroy them as a food source for the rotifers. For

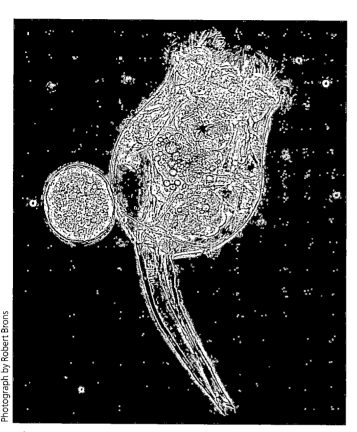

The marine rotifer, Brachionus *sp., is important for success in reef fish culture.*

Nanochloropsis culture (an extremely high-quality microalgae) for six hours before feeding begins. This form of enrichment is attractive because it is a relatively simple technique, but is often not enough for many fish larvae. In such cases, an additional enrichment is required. For this, there is a number of products available based on sea fish and invertebrate oils. These mixtures were specifically developed to provide fish larvae with all the important nutritional elements they require in the form of enriched *Brachionus*. Some time ago, a new product consisting of spray-dried alga (*Schizochytrium*) became available. The advantage for the fish larvae here is that, since it is not oil-based, the raising tank does not become as dirty as it does when other substances are used.

Enrichment techniques can sometimes represent a problem for fish breeders. Enrichment means packing the *Brachionus* with as many nutrients as possible, so the rotifers must be incubated in a thick suspension of enrichment medium. It is recommended that this is done at a temperature of 28 to 30°C (82 to 86°F). Bacteria tend to form quickly under these circumstances and they use up a lot of oxygen, which must be replenished by being pumped back in.

Generally speaking, Brachionus should be left in this suspension for about three to four hours, followed by a further three to four hours in a newly prepared suspension. After this procedure, wash them carefully in fresh sea water before feeding them to the fish larvae.

The procedure for enriching rotifers must be well organized. When the lights over the larvae container are turned on at 8am, the larvae must be fed immediately. This means that the enrichment of the *Brachionus* must take place at about 2am and again at 5am. A good idea is to connect a dosing unit to a timer so that, at a pre-determined time, the enriching medium could be added to the culture. After the *Brachionus* have been enriched, they will maintain their quality for about six hours. So, if a 12-hour feeding regime is being used, you must use a new, enriched culture after the first six hours.

this reason, many experienced fish breeders utilize the correct algae from a test tube in order to establish a culture and prevent contamination.

Unfortunately, hobbyists cannot check whether or not their algae remain uncontaminated, and there is always the danger of contamination by low-grade algae. As a safeguard, the best approach is periodically to throw away the algae and start afresh with another batch from a calibrated starter culture.

After removing enough *Brachionus* from the plankton culture to satisfy the feeding requirements of the fish larvae, the *Brachionus* should first be placed in a fresh

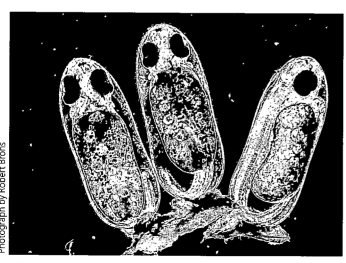

*Three eggs of an anemonefish (*Amphiprion frenatus*).*

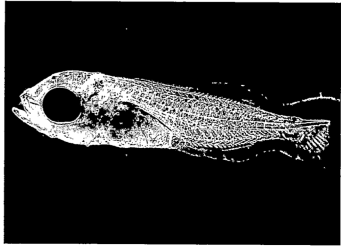

A one-day-old larva of Amphiprion frenatus.

A *four-week old* Calloplesiops altivelis *near the roots of* Caulerpa racemosa.

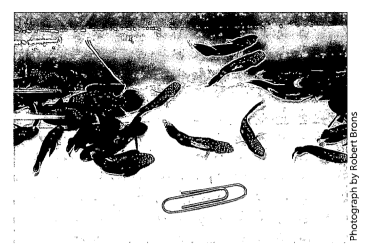

Juvenile Calloplesiops altivelis *at the age of eight weeks.*

Another view of juvenile Calloplesiops altivelis, *again at the age of eight weeks.*

An adult C. altivelis, which is often referred to as the marine betta or comet grouper.

Introducing breeding pairs

Many reef fishes are not sexually dimorphic, which means that you cannot differentiate between the male and female of the species. If you are new to this hobby and intend to breed, say, anemonefishes, then you should take advice from a knowledgeable aquarist or dealer. However, even this does not always work, for not only can experienced breeders fail to sex fish of the same species accurately, bit it is also not unknown for them to try to pair fishes of different species, such as *Amphiprion clarkii* and *A. chrysopterus*. Some anemonefishes can be sexed, but there are others that are very difficult to differentiate by anyone other than an expert. The form of the fins is often a good indicator of the sex of a fish. Other species, such as some angelfishes of the genus *Genicanthus*, are easy to tell apart, but they belong to a group of fishes that is especially difficult to breed. Wrasses are often sexually dimorphic, but again they are difficult to breed successfully in tank conditions.

There are many species that outwardly appear to be arch-enemies when two are kept in an aquarium together, although they could be a breeding pair. A typical example of this is the hermaphroditic pygmy basslets of the genus

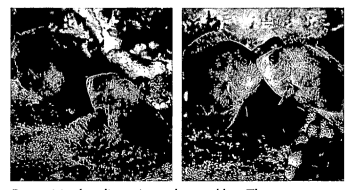

Recognizing breeding pairs can be a problem. These two photographs show the typical pairing postures of Amphiprion ephippium *in an aquarium, just before the eggs are laid.*

Pseudochromis. Fairy basslets, such as *Gramma loreto*, can be sexed quite easily. In this case the first two rays of the ventral fins are longer and more extended in the male than in those of the female.

Demoiselles (Pomacentridae) often show no outward differences between the males and females of the species, but breeding pairs will usually separate themselves from a group and then defend their chosen territory tenaciously against all comers. Again, this is not always the case. A dominant male fish will often pursue his partner and bite her fins, or it may be the other way around with the female pursuing the male.

In general, it is reasonable to say that in order to obtain a pair of fish for breeding, a certain amount of experience is required, as well as a great deal of understanding of fish behaviour.

Breeding behaviour

It is not possible in a book of this nature to describe the separate breeding behaviour of each species of reef fish, even if these facts were known. But since this is a chapter about breeding successes, rather than breeding failures, it is possible to give a few examples in order that you have some form of reference material regarding the species concerned.

The pairing postures and motions of some species are a good indication that a breeding pair is present in the tank. This is particularly the case with most anemonefishes. The photographs on page 281 show two of the typical postures, but this is preceded by one or both partners "pecking" at a suitable section of the substrate in order to clean it prior to egg-laying.

With the mandarinfish (*Pterosynchiropus splendidus*) and similar species, the pairing takes on a different form. These species scatter the fertilized eggs at random after a series of pairing motions. The pair will swim side by side or belly to belly toward the water surface. This usually takes place in the evening. Once they are at the water's

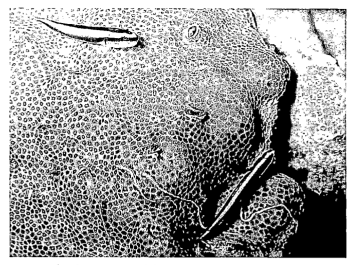

A pair of Gobiosoma randalli . *These and similar species will readily lay eggs in an aquarium when narrow PVC tubes are provided for the purpose. These should be embedded in the sand at an angle to the substrate and when the eggs are laid they can easily be removed to a separate hatching facility.*

surface they allow themselves to sink back to the bottom again, and during this time the eggs and sperm are released. The process is repeated again and again, until the female has expelled all her eggs. This can take some considerable time and the number of eggs varies between 250 and 500. The eggs are pelagic and less than 1mm in diameter. After this they should be transferred to a separate hatching tank where there is continuous, but moderate, water movement. After only about 20 hours, the larvae will hatch and need to be fed almost immediately.

Breeding and raising *Pseudochromis* spp.

Two fishes of this genus have been selected in order to illustrate the complexities of modern aquarium fish-breeding techniques. Reef fish breeding is difficult at the moment, there is no way of getting away from this. Despite this, unbelievable successes can be achieved. The genus *Pseudochromis* contains fishes that are especially interesting for the aquarist. They are very colourful and are suitable for both reef and marine aquariums.

Pseudochromis fridmani and *Pseudochromis flavivertex* do not show the dramatic loss of colour that is common with *P. diadema* and *P. paccagnellae* when they are kept in the confines of a reef aquarium. Nevertheless, they should be provided with a varied diet that includes krill and planktonic copepods, which play an important role in the deep colouration of these fishes. Failure to provide this will still result in some loss of colour, particularly in the case of *P. flavivertex*, where adult fish assume a drab, greyish colour. These are only two of the seven or eight Indo-Pacific species that are known, but they are good examples.

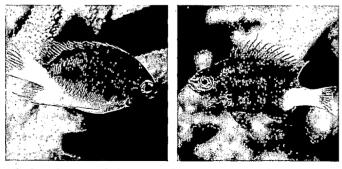

The larval stages of Chrysiptera hemicyanea (see left) *and C.* parasema (see right) *are similar. They are both blackish-silver and they both go through the metamorphosis phase, developing into young fishes, within three or four days of hatching. At this stage they already show their adult blue and yellow colouration.*

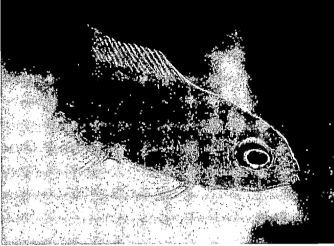

An aquarium-bred Pseudochromis flavivertex – *only 35 days old – after the larval metamorphosis stage. The true colours of the adult fish are already beginning to show.*

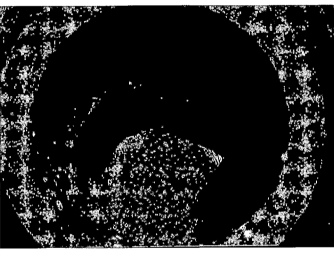

A *male* Pseudochromis fridmani *is seen here on duty caring for an egg-ball.*

To get these two species to lay eggs in an aquarium they require a varied diet of mysid shrimp, chopped mussel, brine shrimp, chopped squid, krill and a good quality flake food to provide a balanced diet. Between the egg-laying periods the female can eat an enormous amount of food, and at this stage food should not be rationed at all. This carefully formulated diet plays an important role in the success of the subsequent egg-laying process and possibly also in the initial survival chances of the newly hatched larvae.

The water quality also plays a vital role in the hatching rate of these species. In addition, good water circulation is required in order to minimize still areas of the tank and maximize the amount of oxygen in the water.

Choosing and bringing together breeding pairs of *Pseudochromis* is no easy task, but it is by no means impossible. They are hermaphroditic and the sex change usually occurs from female to male. Pairs develop from a large, dominant male and a smaller female. If the male is

removed from the tank, the female may well change to a male. For this reason, the fish breeder can attempt to bring together a large fish with a significantly smaller or juvenile one in order to establish a breeding pair.

Most *Pseudochromis* species are extremely territorial and in an aquarium one fish may attack another so strongly that the victim dies. Pairs should be carefully observed in order to prevent this happening. *Pseudochromis fridmani* is the least aggressive species of this genus and, when enough space is provided in the tank, it can be kept in small groups. Even so, this should be limited to only four fish per 100 gallons (455 litres) of water. The sexing of *P. fridmani* is not simple. As a rule, the females are smaller and have a more rounded appearance. The males are slender and larger. It would seem that the sexes of this species are determined from birth.

With *Pseudochromis flavivertex* the aggressiveness is moderately strong and only one pair can be kept in a normal-sized breeding tank. Even with breeding pairs that lay eggs regularly, it is common for the female to be chased and bitten, therefore enough hiding places must be provided. In addition, it is important to ensure that the degree of aggression does not increase. At the end of the breeding period, for example, attacks on the female will definitely increase in intensity until a point is reached where there is a real danger of losing the female. If this situation does occur, she should be given a convalescent period by inserting a separating glass in the tank.

As with *Pseudochromis fridmani*, the sex differences of *P. flavivertex* are almost nil. The male is somewhat larger and more robust than the female, which has a rounded belly region. It could be that *P. flavivertex* is a protean hermaphrodite, in that the fastest growing and most dominant of a group develops into a male. Therefore, the combination of a dominant fish with a younger fish usually results in the formation a breeding pair.

Egg-laying processes

The egg-laying processes of these two species are more or less the same. The belly of the gravid female sometimes assumes grotesque proportions, which is especially the case with *P. flavivertex*. The eggs are usually laid during the morning, at which time the male chases the female and shows his dominance. He will swim toward the female and stop. Then he will turn and swim with exaggerated undulating motions toward his hole or cave. This is repeated frequently over the period of about an hour until the female finally follows to lay her eggs.

Over the next hour the female produces a ball-like egg mass. During this time the male of *P. flavivertex* remains with the female in the hole. With *P. fridmani*, on the other hand, the male remains at the entrance to the hole as if to guard her during the egg-laying process. In the case of an allied species, *Pseudochromis diadema*, the male often leaves the hole to make excursions around the tank. When the egg-ball finally falls to the bottom of the nest, the male chases the female away and assumes an egg-caring role.

Adult females of *P. fridmani* are capable of producing an egg-ball that is 1in (2.5cm) in diameter, containing up to 500 eggs. With *P. flavivertex* the egg-balls are elliptical and are 1½in (about 3.5cm) long, containing up to 1,000 eggs. With young parents, or at the beginning of the breeding period, the number of eggs laid is usually less and the egg-balls are correspondingly smaller.

Pseudochromis fridmani lays eggs in small holes, such as those that can be provided by cutting up sections of PVC piping. *P. flavivertex*, on the other hand, needs more space. Rocks should be placed together to form a suitable cave in which they can spawn.

Male egg guarding

The role of guarding the eggs is undertaken by the male with considerable intensity and during this time he will take little or no food. The care of the eggs by *P. fridmani* is remarkable. Every few minutes the male visits the nest and stays there for up to ten minutes. During this time he will swim around the egg-ball, frequently lifting it with his snout or tail. At night it appears that the male remains permanently on duty in the nest. If a light is directed at the nest, the male fish will often press himself against the roof of the hole with the egg-ball held in the U-shaped form of his body. This behaviour is meant, presumably, to protect the eggs from the light.

With *Pseudochromis flavivertex*, the egg care is somewhat less stringent. The male visits the eggs with less frequency and the egg care itself is rougher so that the egg-ball sometimes breaks apart. In extreme cases, a portion of the egg-ball may be catapulted from the nest. Some reef-caught pairs of *P. fridmani* are capable of laying eggs continuously for a period of more than 18 months at the rate of three or four times a month.

Marine rotifers as first food

With both species, *Pseudochromis flavivertex* and *P. fridmani*, the hatching begins on the evening of the fifth day, which means a development time of four and a half days at 25°C (77°F). The larvae hatch within about an hour of each other, and within the first hour of darkness. During the hatching process, the male fish is there to provide support, inasmuch as the eggs are continually nudged and turned. In some cases, they may even be removed from the egg-ball so that they can hatch "synthetically", outside the nest. In such cases, however, the hatching rate of the eggs is much lower.

As with most reef fish larvae, the larvae of *Pseudochromis flavivertex* and *P. fridmani* react to light. They can be caught easily and transferred to the larval tank by using a concentrated light source. Directly after hatching, the larvae are 3.9 and 3.7mm long, respectively. Apart from a few pigment cells, the bodies of the larvae are transparent. The eyes show good pigmentation and the jaws are well developed, but there are only the remains of an egg sac to be seen. By first light of the next day, the larvae begin to feed on enriched *Brachionus*. They are active swimmers that can maintain their position in the water column, unlike many other larvae that accumulate at the water's surface. With enriched *Brachionus* (see p. 279), the larvae grow very quickly. Although a marked increase in size can be seen on the second and third days, their size is doubled between the seventh and tenth days. From the ninth day on, the larvae show a reddish colouration and after three weeks you cannot really refer to them as being "larvae" any longer. They are now free-swimming young fish.

With both species, no aggressive behaviour is shown until the young fish adopt a bottom-living habit. This normally occurs on the 25th day (*P. fridmani*) or on the 29th or 30th day (*P. flavivertex*). At this stage, the young of both species are about ½in (1.25cm) long and during this time their swimming movements change to the typical undulating *Pseudochromis* style.

Metamorphosis

The young fish require hiding places and cover in order to complete their metamorphosis. Use cut-up PVC tubing to provide this, because at this stage they show a territorial nature. "Tube cells" should be provided to stop the fish from actively chasing one another.

Fully coloured fish that are 35 to 40 days old have a total length of about ½in (1.25cm) and actively hunt for food. At this point they should be transferred to raising tanks. Thankfully, the young fish are not as aggressive as the adults, so that even *P. flavivertex*, the most aggressive species, can be kept in relatively large groups until they reach a size of about 2in (5cm). After this, the population must be transferred to other tanks in stages so that there are only 20 fish for every 10 gallons (45 litres). Plenty of cover and hiding places are required and the raising tanks should be fitted with covers, since the young fish tend to jump out when they are chasing one another.

Juveniles of *P. fridmani* are fully developed in five months and can then be regarded as adults. In contrast, the juveniles of *P. fridmani* require 10 to 12 months to reach this stage of development. Only when the second generation has been raised successfully can the aquarist truly say that the aquarium hobby is independent of the capture of wild coral fishes.

Reproduction of reef invertebrates

This section covers animals from only five of the many invertebrate phyla. These five groups contain creatures that can be termed ornamental reef invertebrates rather than the microscopic forms. The table below shows the various groups and their normal methods of reproduction.

Although within this part of the book so far information has often been given regarding reproductive cycles, it is appropriate here to list the ways in which you can breed and propagate most of these animals in a home aquarium.

Surprisingly enough, the list contains many endangered species and those that regulated by CITES (Convention on International Trade in Endangered Species). Corals, such as the stony corals, are now easy to propagate in a reef aquarium, assuming that the water quality is excellent. In contrast, many of the species that are ubiquitous on coral reefs in the wild are difficult to breed in a tank. These include the arthropods, such as crabs and shrimps, and the echinoderms, such as sea stars and sea urchins.

Before an analysis is made about which invertebrates offer the best chances for propagation in an aquarium, we must first consider the ways that these creatures reproduce. Unlike fishes, which may be live bearers, mouthbrooders or egg layers with the eggs being laid on the substrata or dispersed in the water, invertebrate animals are somewhat different. There are many species belonging to countless groups of creatures and each of these has its own special way, or sometimes various ways, of reproducing. Nevertheless the basic rules are simple enough, especially since these reproductive methods can be categorized, and any potential reef invertebrate breeders can react when they are equipped with this basic knowledge. However, it would be folly to attempt to list the reproductive habits of all the invertebrates encompassed in the accompanying table, nor is it even necessary. At this stage you need to know only the ways that they can reproduce.

Invertebrate reproduction

Phylum	Methods of reproduction
Porifera (sponges)	Sexual with larval development Asexual fragmentation
Cnidaria (soft corals)	Sexual (by various means) Asexual within the colony (by various means)
(stony corals)	Sexual (often mass spawning) Asexual within the colony
(coral anemones)	Sexual (usually within the colony) Asexual (by various means)
(zoanthids)	Sexual (broadcast spawning) Asexual (lateral budding or fragmentation)
(sea anemones)	Sexual (by various means) Asexual (usually vegetative propagation)
Arthropoda (crustaceans)	Sexual (eggs often carried by thoracic legs)
Mollusca (molluscs)	Sexual (by various means) Hermaphroditic reproduction
Echinodermata (sea stars)	Sexual (usually mass spawning) Regenerative fragmentation
(sea urchins)	Sexual (mass spawning)

Sexual reproduction

As a general rule, sexual reproduction occurs in three forms: internally, externally and random. Internal reproduction is when fertilization of eggs occurs within the body or colony of one of the parent creatures. External reproduction takes place with eggs being laid or ejected within a colony or on the substrata. These are subsequently fertilized by the male, or by the same animal if it is a hermaphrodite. With random sexual reproduction, eggs and sperm are scattered into the ocean currents at random, often in massed aggregations of a particular species at a certain time of the day or year.

Asexual reproduction

This takes many forms and is the key to success with invertebrate propagation at present. Each of these ways will be described below. By using this knowledge, you will be able to propagate various sponges, most soft corals and gorgonians, some stony corals, coral anemones, zoanthids and several sea anemones. Many of these are expensive to import and some are classified as endangered species. It is up to aquarists to try to reproduce these successfully to alleviate the pressure on natural resources.

Fragmentation The word "fragmentation", or "fragging", is used by aquarists to mean the mechanical separation of colonies or larger pieces of coral and sponges into smaller sections for culture. But there are many species that do this naturally. Asexual reproduction, in all its various forms, takes place by fragmentation. In addition, if a creature becomes damaged through wave action or storms, then the smaller pieces that have become separated from the main body of the animal may

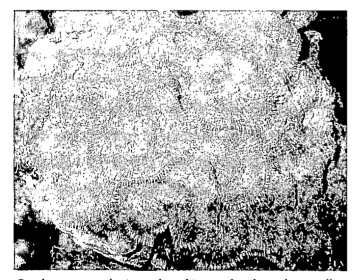

Coral anemone colonies such as this are often formed asexually through pedal laceration. It is the usual form of reproduction within this group.

Small anemones such as these can reach plague proportions in an aquarium. Often the only way to control them is to remove the colonized rocks.

regenerate, each forming a new creature. This often happens with sponges, corals, zoanthids and sea stars.

Pedal or basal laceration This form of asexual reproduction is common with some soft corals, coral anemones and true sea anemones. Usually the movement of the animal across the substratum causes small fragments to be left behind and these eventually grow into identical clones of the parent colony. Asexual budding in the form of basal budding is also a form of pedal laceration. This occurs when an anemone buds new polyps from the basal muscle.

Asexual budding This is normally restricted to coral anemones and true sea anemones. Here, a cloned polyp usually buds from the margin of the oral disc and eventually breaks away to settle on the substrate.

Transverse fission In rare cases a coral anemone will extend its basal column upward into the current, adopting a long and slender form. Eventually part of the animal will twist and break away to be carried by the current to a new site, where it will continue to grow.

Longitudinal fission This is a common form of asexual cloning. Sea anemones and coral anemones will often divide into two or more daughter polyps by splitting through the oral disc down to the pedal base. A form of longitudinal fission frequently occurs with soft corals.

Manual fragmentation

With care, many ornamental invertebrates can be propagated by taking cuttings from them and placing them elsewhere in the tank, or even in another aquarium.

To do this you will need some tools of the trade:
* Coral cement or underwater epoxy resin
* A sharp craft knife
* Sharp scissors
* Selection of cable clips
* Rocks on which to fix the fragmented invertebrate

Before you start chopping up precious invertebrates, give a little thought as to what is going to be fragmented or from what animal you intend to take a cutting. Many species will not survive this procedure. Some soft corals, such as *Sinularia* and *Dendronephthya* spp., will die if an attempt is made to take a cutting. Manual fragmentation of sea anemones, coral anemones, sea stars, crustaceans and sea urchins is also not possible. What is really wanted is the fragmentation of large invertebrates by manual intervention to produce offspring, and this can only be done with sponges, soft corals, gorgonians and stony corals.

Some species will fragment quite well by themselves. *"Anemonia" manjano* and *Aiptasia* spp., for example, are small sea anemones that reproduce by pedal laceration at an alarming rate and are difficult to control. You cannot kill them even by removing them from the rock, since enough of the basal disc will stay behind to produce several new individuals. Breaking them up manually will only result in spreading their remains over the rest of the aquarium and producing an outbreak of plague proportions. One solution is to introduce certain butterflyfish species, such as *Forcipiger flavissimus, Chaetodon mertensii, C. pelewensis,* or *C. vagabundis.*

Sponges

In the sea, most sponges reproduce sexually, although most are hermaphroditic. They have both male and female sex cells, which produce the eggs and sperm at different times. Subsequently the fertilized eggs develop into ciliated larvae, which the sponge releases into the surrounding water. After a short free-swimming stage the larvae settle to the seabed and form new sponges. Asexual reproduction is also known through the budding of gemmules within the body of the sponge. These are thick-walled bundles of cells and spicules that are, like the larvae, ejected out of the osculum.

For aquarists, the most important feature of sponges is their amazing ability to regenerate tissue if they are damaged. This can be used to advantage in reproduction. Many species can be broken into smaller fragments and each will grow into a new sponge if the water conditions are good. Most encrusting sponges will grow horizontally or vertically over small rocks that have been deliberately placed in the path of their growth direction. Once the sponge has encrusted these rocks, they can be moved elsewhere, or to another aquarium altogether.

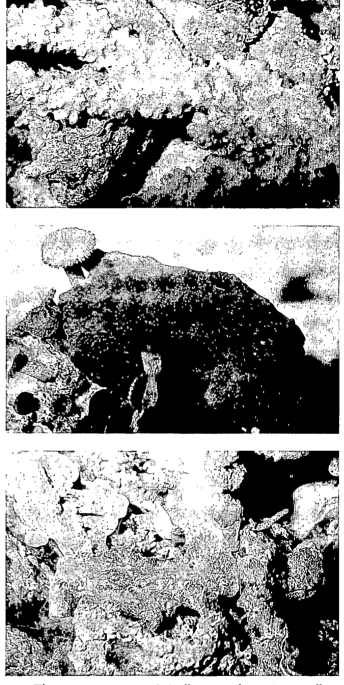

TOP *The orange tree sponge* Axinella *sp. can be cut into smaller fragments and these will grow into new sponges.*
MIDDLE *An unidentified demosponge formed by breaking a piece from a larger specimen.*
BOTTOM *This attractive blue* Leucosolenia *sp. is easily reproduced from fragments. It grows quite rapidly in shadowy areas of a tank.*

Large sponges can be cut using a sharp knife, but in all cases this must be done underwater. Removing a sponge from the water, for even the shortest time, should never happen because the surrounding air interrupts its siphoning ability. If this happens, the sponge will die.

Sexual and asexual reproduction is known to have occurred in aquariums, but this is not a common event.

Soft corals

Soft corals reproduce sexually and asexually, but only the latter is encountered in aquariums. This may be through fission or by asexual budding from the base of the colony or from the tips of the branches. In many cases, cuttings can be taken, particularly from *Lobophytum* spp., *Nephthea* spp., *Paralemnalia* spp., *Capnella* spp. and *Lemnalia* spp. Use a sharp knife or scissors and sever one of the branches at its base. Fix this to live rock using a plastic cable clip, or bind it with nylon monofilament.

In the case of *Sinularia* spp. fission often occurs but they do not do well when cuttings are taken from too deep into the stem of the colony. Branch tips can be cut and these will grow well, but keep an eye on the parent colony afterwards. Fission is longitudinal, with the colony splitting vertically down to the base over a period of a weeks.

Many of the arborescent forms will swell at the tips of the branches and pinch off by themselves. This form of asexual budding often occurs in aquariums, and the small branchlets will grow well if attached to the substrate.

With pulse or pumping corals, such as *Xenia* spp., *Anthelia* spp., *Cespitularia* spp. and *Heteroxenia* spp., rapid colonization can take place. The usual way is by budding or fission, but in some cases, such as with *Heteroxenia* spp., new colonies are also formed through pedal laceration. *Cespitularia* colonies can be propagated using sharp scissors. Branches are cut off and then attached to a piece of rock with cyanoacrylate glue.

For the propagation of *Xenia* spp., limit the use of activated charcoal to a few days a month. In addition, water quality must be good and nitrate levels low.

Leather corals

These are soft corals, but the term "leather corals"is used to distinguish branched or arborescent forms from the plate- or cup-like forms normally associated with species of the genus *Sarcophyton*.

Cuttings can be taken from these species and also the various *Lobophytum* spp. Cut into the tentacle crown or lobed plate with a sharp knife and remove a piece. Fix this to a suitable rock with a cable clip or monofilament line. The alternative is to sever the basal column and attach the whole head with a portion of the column to another rock. This will grow into a new colony and the remains of the old column will soon sprout new polyp heads

Asexual reproduction is also common. New colonies will often bud from the base of a colony and grow away from the main column. These can be easily severed and attached elsewhere. In one particular species, colony-buds form under the tentacle crown and again, these can be easily removed and fixed to other rocks. In all cases, good aquarium water quality is mandatory for success.

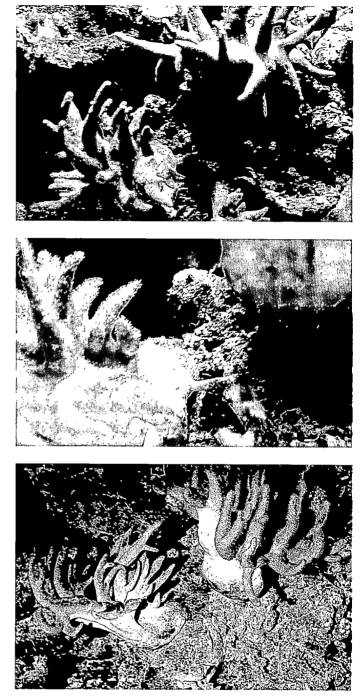

TOP *Longitudinal fission has produced these colonies from the original one.*

MIDDLE *A close-up shows that two of the three colonies are still attached.*

BOTTOM *The final bonds are severed and the colonies begin to move away from one another.*

Gorgonians

Many photosynthetic gorgonians can be cultivated and reproduced by taking cuttings in much the same way as with soft corals. Cuttings of *Pseudoplexaura* spp., *Pseudopterogorgia* spp, and *Plexaurella* spp. can be taken using sharp scissors to sever the branches. The cut area will heal within a few days. The coenenchyme must be cut

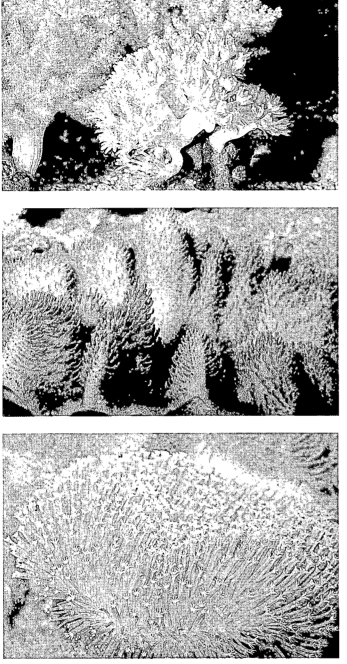

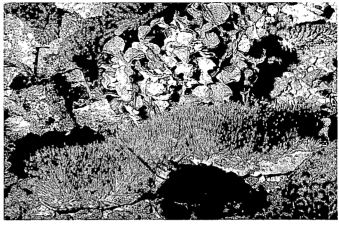

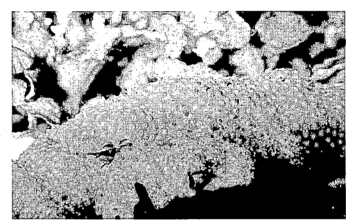

TOP Xenia *sp. reproduces quite rapidly under optimal water conditions and can spread over much of the aquarium decoration.*
MIDDLE *Cuttings can be taken from the thick, convoluted lobes of* Lobophytum *sp.*
BOTTOM *It is better to cut through the column of* Sarcophyton ehrenbergi *than to spoil the beautiful form of the tentacle crown.*

TOP *An algae-covered rock is placed in close proximity to the encrusting gorgonian coral* Erythropodium caribaeorum.
MIDDLE *After a few weeks the encroachment has started and a new colony is being formed.*
BOTTOM *The encrustation is complete and the rock can now be severed from the main colony and moved elsewhere in the tank or to a new aquarium.*

back from the severed end to reveal about ⅓in (1cm) of the central core. Choose a rock that has a hole about the same diameter as the core (or drill one). Using coral cement or an underwater epoxy resin, cement the core into the hole, leaving about a 2mm space between the coenenchyme and the rock. Within a few days the end will have healed over and will continue to grow.

In the case of *Pterogorgia citrina* and similar species the coenenchyme is so thin that there is no chance of necrosis taking place. Therefore the severed end of the coenenchyme must be cemented directly into a suitable hole in a piece of rock.

Stony corals

Perhaps the most important of all the ornamental invertebrates for the reef aquarium breeder are the scleractinian stony corals. Many of these can be successfully propagated in a reef tank set-up and they are mostly fast-growing creatures. The water conditions should be optimal in the aquarium, and levels of nitrate need to be very low. Light is an important factor, too, and metal-halide units in combination with actinic lighting are more or less mandatory for success with stony corals.

Cuttings can be taken from any branched species, such as *Acropora*, but the word "cuttings" is perhaps misleading in this context. These are, in fact, broken-off branches from a larger coral head and they are frequently seen for sale. Beginners are advised to start with one or more small coral branchlets in a reef tank and to care for them until they become established and start to grow away. Once this has been achieved, and a good growth of coral exists, it is possible to start taking cuttings or to obtain them from other aquarists.

As a rule, a freshly severed branch or lobe should be placed carefully on a rock, where there is a strong water movement, for a period of about 72 hours. This will seal the area where the coral was broken and ensure that necrosis does not occur. After this it can be cemented

LEFT *This 12in (30cm) coral head of* Acropora pulchra *was grown from a 2in (5cm) branchlet within 16 months.*

BELOW *The fragile lobes of* Lobophyllia hemprichii *are easily broken off and can be propagated separately in a reef tank set-up.*

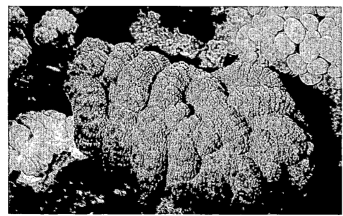

firmly to a piece of live rock using coral cement or a good-quality underwater epoxy resin. Growth rates can be remarkable, especially if the tank is equipped with a calcium reactor, and it is not particularly unusual to see a coral branchlet triple in size within the space of a few short months. *Pocillopora*, *Stylophora*, *Acropora*, *Pavona*, *Blastomussa*, *Lobophyllia* and *Caulastrea* spp. are some of the easier corals to propagate.

Coral anemones

The asexual reproduction of coral anemones is common in aquariums, and most corallimorpharian anemones reproduce by pedal laceration. Many species utilize more than one form of asexual reproduction, and longitudinal fission is the second most common way after pedal laceration. Large colonies are easy to raise from a single polyp and clones from this can take over large areas of a tank. Sexual reproduction may also occur in an aquarium, particularly in the case of *Discosoma* spp. and *Ricordia yuma*. In particular, *R. yuma* has been observed with larvae crawling among the tentacles, which may suggest that they brood their young.

With *Discosoma* and *Rhodactis* spp. the larvae crawl away from the colony, presumably to effect a wider dispersion of the colonies. The minute eggs are expelled in bundles of 20 or so between May and September. In an aquarium with a constant temperature of 28°C (82°F) and actinic lighting, they can be induced into sexual repro-duction during most of the year. The sexes of the polyps are separate and in large colonies there are usually both male and female present, although there are exceptions. It would appear that they are hermaphroditic, in that young or smaller polyps are usually male and often on the margin of the colony, with the larger female polyps situated toward the centre.

In the case of the large *Amplexidiscus fenestrafer*, it seems that they can reproduce only asexually, with longitudinal fission being the most common form. Pedal laceration has also been observed with this species and transverse fission is not rare either. Some specimens utilize asexual budding from the basal column to produce daughter polyps that later move away from the parent polyp. *Ricordia* spp. usually reproduce by longitudinal fission, but pedal laceration is not uncommon.

Many of the *Discosoma* species are able to interbreed to produce hybrids, which can cause taxonomic confus-ion. The two Caribbean representatives, *D. sanctithomae* and *D. neglecta*, produce a hybrid known as *Discosoma carlgreni*, although this name is invalid.

The Indo-Pacific red *Discosoma* species, which has been described as a colour morph of *Discosoma nummiforme* (Rueppell & Leuckart, 1828), is in fact a valid species and the name *Discosoma ferrugatus* might be

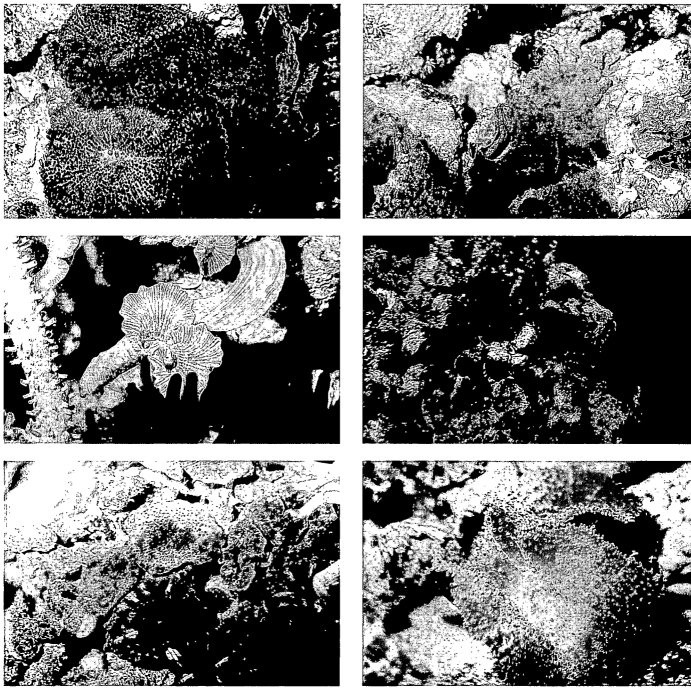

TOP Ricordia yuma *breeds in an aquarium, as well as producing asexual clones.*
MIDDLE Discosoma *sp. is shown here undergoing asexual reproduction by longitudinal fission.*
BOTTOM *These, and many other* Discosoma *species, can produce an array of hybrids.*

TOP *Aquarium bred hybrids of* Discosoma ferrugatus *and* Discosoma sp.
MIDDLE *A 14-week-old sexually reproduced polyp of* Rhodactis sp. *Note the radiating ridges. Colour is translucent bluish violet.*
BOTTOM *The same specimen at 26 months, now with a diameter of 8in (20cm). No ridges are present.*

appropriate. The ridges in the mesogloea differ in number from the rest of the group and it is the only species where columnar asexual budding occurs. Despite this, *Discosoma ferrugatus* will hybridize with most other species in this genus, and a wide variety of colour variations can result.

Many *Rhodactis* species reproduce asexually through longitudinal fission, with pedal laceration being extremely

rare. They are also capable of sexual reproduction in an aquarium, often without you ever being aware of it.

Most of the corallimorpharians that are capable of asexual reproduction, and that is practically all of them, will do so readily in an aquarium. You can help them along a bit by turning the rocks away from the light, or by partially blocking it for a week or so with another rock, to induce pedal laceration.

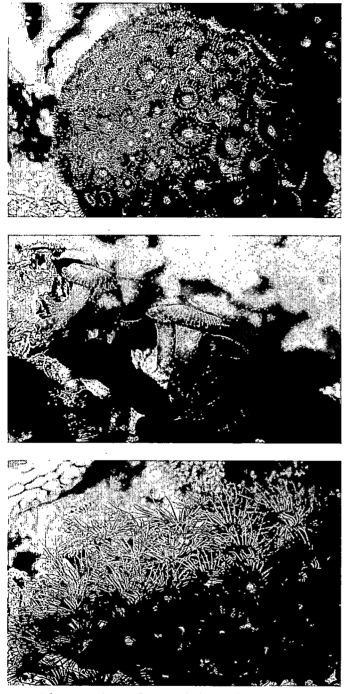

TOP *Often* Zoanthus *and* Protopalythoa *will grow together to form a large, mixed colony.*

MIDDLE Protopalythoa *sp. spreads quickly in a reef aquarium, forming attractive carpets.*

BOTTOM *"Yellow polyps" (*Protopalythoa *sp.?) reproduce readily to form large colonies.*

TOP *Shrimps such as* Lysmata amboinensis *are often imported carrying egg masses.*

MIDDLE *The larvae of* Lysmata debelius *can now be successfully raised in captivity.*

BOTTOM *Nudibranchs, like this tank-raised* Tritonia *species, are shell-less molluscs.*

Zoanthids

There is little scientific knowledge concerning the sexual reproduction of the zoanthids. It is thought that there may be separate sexes within a colony in some species. Others, however, may be simultaneous hermaphrodites, in that they develop both male and female sex cells at the same time. There are also some indications that at least one zoanthid is a sequential hermaphrodite, in which the sex cells develop at different times in order to facilitate sexual reproduction.

Asexual reproduction is very common, both on the reef and in an aquarium, and the aquarist can take advantage of this. *Palythoa* colonies are formed by asexual budding of the polyps as the creeping growth gradually extends over the substratum.

In *Protopalythoa* species, the gradual spreading of the coenenchyme and the constant asexual budding of new polyps means that large colonies can form in a relatively short time. These can then be split into smaller colonies and placed in other aquariums once they become too large. *Protopalythoa* spp. are the most commonly seen zoanthids in aquariums. The asexual budding of *Zoanthus* colonies follow similar lines with the spreading of a coenenchyme or in some cases with creeping stolons.

Zoanthid colonies offer the aquarist the opportunity to experiment with polyp propagation. A combination of different-coloured colonies in a large aquarium is an attractive sight. No special care is required to grow these species, provided that they are given enough light and good water quality.

Sea anemones

At the moment there are few successes with the propagation of true sea anemones apart from the nuisance examples, such as *"Anemonia"* and *Aiptasia* spp. In the wild, *Entacmaea quadricolor* frequently reproduces by longitudinal fission and this has on occasions been observed in aquariums.

Shrimps

Several species of shrimps have been bred successfully in aquariums, both by professional breeding stations and by amateur aquarists. One of the first species to be bred in captivity was the circumtropical barbershop shrimp (*Stenopus hispidus*). The greenish egg mass is carried under the thorax by the female. The planktonic larvae hatch after about 15 days and should then be removed to a separate rearing tank. At this stage, they are about ⅛in (3mm) long and can be fed on *Brachionus* or marine copepods. *Hymenocera picta*, the harlequin shrimp, has also been successfully raised in aquariums and, although the larvae are less than half this size, they will accept marine rotifers and copepods after the first moult. Until that stage, they do not require feeding.

Like the two preceding species, those of the genus *Lysmata* also carry their eggs ventrally until they hatch. These shrimps are simultaneous hermaphrodites and several species have been successfully raised in captivity. These include *Lysmata amboinensis*, *L. debelius* and *L. wurdemanni*, which have also been raised commercially. Generally, the planktonic larvae are small, about 2mm, and should be raised in a separate tank with the same water quality as that from which they were removed. Copepods, marine rotifers and newly hatched brine shrimp will all be accepted after the first moult, which occurs after about two days.

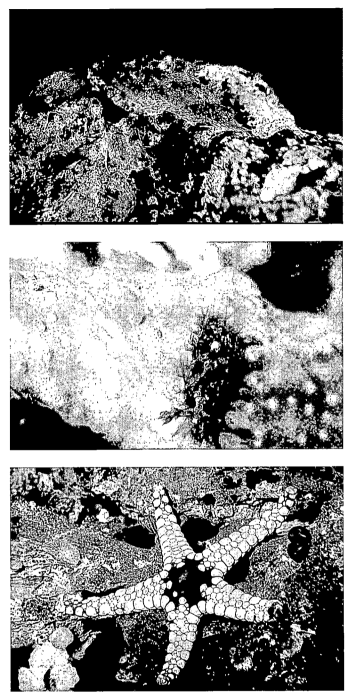

TOP *An adult* Tritonia *sp. lays strings of up to 500 eggs, which* hatch after 21 days.

MIDDLE *An 8-week juvenile* Tritonia *sp. is already feeding in the same way as the adult.*

BOTTOM *Sea stars such as* Fromia nodosa *do not have a well developed regenerative ability.*

Molluscs

Although bivalve molluscs, such as clams, are raised commercially, they are outside the scope of resources of the average aquarist. Marine gastropods occasionally lay eggs in aquariums without any intervention, but it is seldom that any of the larger specimens can be raised.

Small marine snails frequently lay eggs in aquariums and these usually hatch without any special care on the part of the aquarist. They may also reproduce so freely that large populations form and sometimes this is an unwanted addition to a reef tank. You should not worry – most of these species do no harm and they are easily controlled. One of the advantages of these small molluscs is that they help to keep unwanted algae under control.

Most of the higher-order gastropods are difficult to breed in captivity. They may be of separate sexes or hermaphroditic. The eggs of larger molluscs are fertilized within the mantle cavity, and are often brooded there until the larvae have hatched.

Nudibranchs offer the best chances of breeding success within this group, but although these shell-less gastropods will frequently lay eggs in a tank, they seldom hatch success-fully. One exception is *Tritonia* sp. (*see p. 293*). This species appears to breed readily in a reef tank, provided there is a sufficient supply of food. This comprises mainly the skin that gorgonian corals shed periodically as part of their cleaning routine. Although it is a Caribbean species, where alcyonarian soft corals are not usually represented, it has also been observed feeding on the "spring-cleaning" skin of these corals as well. In addition, it shows a positive tendency to eat, or at least to attempt to eat, the nuisance anemones *Aiptasia* spp.

Sea stars

Despite their amazing regenerative ability it is not advisable to take cuttings from sea stars such as *Linckia* spp. A reef aquarium is not the same as the open sea and there is too high a risk that infection may set in around the severed area. Most other sea stars are slow to regenerate and may die.

Sea urchins

In the echinoderm group, the majority of sea stars and sea urchins are broadcast egg layers, inasmuch as the eggs and sperm are released into ocean currents for random fertilization. It follows, then, that breeding these species in an aquarium is very difficult, but probably not impossible.

The Indo-Pacific long-spined sea urchin (*Diadema setosum*) offers perhaps the best possibilities if you want to raise young from this group. Prior to the release of eggs and sperm, the male sea urchin approaches the female and their spines touch and sometimes interlock. Following this, the male performs a series of "jumping" movements, in which it appears that he extends his tube feet or ventral spines and then retracts them in several sharp vertical bumps of the test. This happens at least 30 times within the first hour of darkness. The spines of the two animals

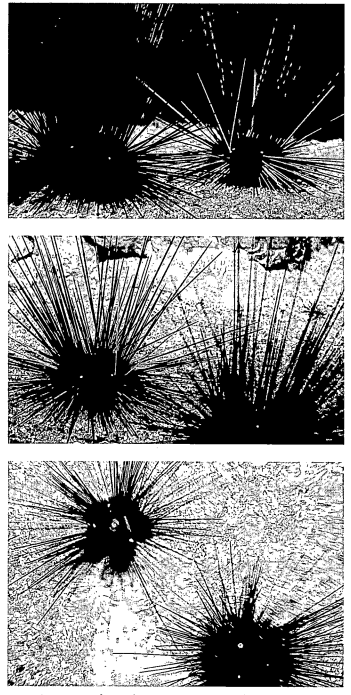

TOP *A young male* Diadema setosum *(striped spines) approaches the dark-coloured mature female.*
MIDDLE *The spines interlock and the male bumps its test sharply up and down.*
BOTTOM *The rapid release of eggs and sperm is shown here as a blurring of the water.*

then come together again and the eggs and sperm are released (*see above*).

The strange thing is that, contrary to the popular belief that sexual reproduction of this species and most other echinoderms occurs in accordance with the phases of the moon, this is not so. Recorded spawnings of this species every 10 to 22 days between the months of March and August have been reliably observed.

Glossary

Acclimatization: The gradual introduction of a newly acquired fish or invertebrate to its aquarium. Normally done by allowing the water in the aquarium to mix slowly with the water containing the animal, thus ensuring that any change in water quality does not induce shock.

Activated charcoal: A filter medium used in both internal and external filters to remove toxic substances, such as phenol, from the water.

Adductor muscle: The muscle that closes the shell halves in bivalve molluscs.

Aerobic bacteria: Bacteria that thrive in an oxygen-rich environment and break down organic waste into nitrate.

Alga: a photosynthetic plant that reproduces by spores and lacks true vascular tissue, flowers and seeds.

Anaerobic bacteria: Bacteria that live in an oxygen-poor environment and utilize the oxygen from nitrate to produce nitrogen.

Anterior: Pertaining to the front, the forward region.

Anus: The external opening of a digestive tract from which wastes are voided.

Aperture: In gastropods, the opening through which the animal emerges.

Apex: The first-formed part of a shell; the tip of the spire, usually pointed.

Aragonite: Also called tufa; calcium carbonate in the form of needle-shaped orthorhombic crystals.

Arborescent: Tree-like in form with a definite stem.

Aristotle's lantern: The five-part complex rasping and chewing apparatus of a sea urchin.

Autozooid: A polyp with eight fully developed tentacles that are used for food gathering and defence.

Axil: The acute angular region between the underside of the pectoral fin and the body of a fish. It is equivalent to the armpit of a person.

Bar: An elongated colour marking that is vertical in orientation with more or less straight sides.

Barbel: Slender sensory tentacle, usually in pairs, on the chin of certain fishes.

Barrier reef: A reef that is separated from a landmass by a deep lagoon.

Basal: Toward the base or area of attachment.

Base medium: Material, such as coral sand, silica sand or crushed shell, that is used to cover the floor of an aquarium or the base of a subsand filter.

Benthic: Bottom-dwelling.

Bilateral symmetry: Where the body is divided along a single longitudinal and vertical plane into two identical halves.

Bioluminescence: Active light that is created by living organisms.

Biomass: the amount of living matter in a given area.

Bio-system: The term used to describe an aquarium that employs bacterial filtration.

Bivalve: A group of molluscs with two shell halves or valves.

Blade: The leaf-like structure of an alga, sometimes called frond.

Brackish: A mixture of sea water and fresh water found in estuaries and the like.

Brood pouch: The pouch of an animal with an external opening in which eggs are laid. Often the young will remain in the pouch after hatching in order to be protected by one of the parents (usually the male).

Byssal threads: Flexible chitinous threads that a bivalve mollusc produces to attach itself to the substrate.

Calcareous: Composed of calcium carbonate.

Calcified: Containing deposits of calcium carbonate within its structure.

Carapace: The chitinous or calcareous skin or shell that encloses part or all of the body of crustaceans.

Carnivore: A flesh-eating animal.

Caudal fin: The tail fin (the term "tail" may indicate any portion of an organism that is posterior to the anus).

Caudal peduncle: In fish, the part of the body between the posterior bases of the dorsal and anal fins. This is usually the narrowest part of the fish.

Cerata: Finger-like processes that have a respiratory function and which are deployed dorsally along the bodies of many shell-less molluscs, such as nudibranchs. They contain the divided lobes of the stomach.

cf.: An abbreviation of the Latin word *conferre*, meaning "to compare" with the formal description. Used in tentative species identifications.

Chloroplast: Plastid containing chlorophyll.

Cilia: Hair-like processes that are often used for food gathering or for locomotion.

Cirrus: A small, fleshy appendage that is often jointed or flexible. Plural: cirri.

Cladistic analysis: The phylogenetic approach to classification where the method seeks to resolve which two taxa of a group of three or more have the closest genealogical relationship.

Class: A group of related organisms in a category ranking below phylum and above order.

Classification: The practice of arranging items into categories or groups. There are two main approaches to the systematic classification of organisms. These are the cladistic and the synthetic approaches. A third approach, phenetics, is of little use above generic level.

Cnidae: Coelenterate stinging cells used to capture and immobilize prey; also called nematocysts.

Cnidoblast: Part of the stinging cell of a cnidarian animal.

Coenenchyme: The tissue of an octocoral that supports the polyps and contains the mesogloea that is embedded with calcareous spicules.

Colony: An organism composed of connected individuals.

Column: The cylindrical central stem of an anemone.

Comb rows: Transverse rows of fused cilia that are found in ctenophores.

Commensalism: A form of symbiosis where only one of the animals benefits from the relationship, but where the host animal is not harmed.

Community tank: An aquarium containing several different species of fishes living in peaceful coexistence.

Compound eye: In arthropods, an eye that is composed of many facets, or light sensitive cells, joined together to form a larger organ.

Compressed: Laterally flattened.

Coral sand: Sand originating from coral rubble that has been broken down by burrowing animals and wave action to form fine, sandy particles.

Crustose: A hard surface layer that forms a covering or crust.

Cytoplasm: Protoplasmic content of a cell other than the nucleus.

Dendritic organ: An organ composed of cells similar to the chloride cells in the gills of fishes and the salt cells of birds.

Denticles: Small teeth.

Depressed: Vertically flattened.

Dichotomously branched: In algae, having each division of a branch or fork divided into two equal parts.

Dimorphic: Where there is a marked difference in the appearance of the two sexes of a species.

Dominant: Having the greatest influence or abundant and conspicuous.

Dorsal: The upper surface or back of an animal.

Ecology: The study of the distribution and abundance of organisms relative to their respective environments.

Ectoparasite: An external parasite. One that lives on the outside of the body.

Emaciated: Having a starved appearance.

Emarginate: Concave, used to describe the inward-curving border of the caudal fin in fishes.

Endosymbiosis: A close form of symbiosis, where one of the organisms involved lives within the cells or tissue of its symbiotic partner.

Environment: The total chemical, physical and biological surroundings.

Epiphyte: A plant that lives and grows on the surface of another organism, but does not derive any nourishment from it.

Evert: To turn outward or inside out.

Evolution: The origination of the species by development from earlier forms.

Evolutionary analysis: See *Synthetic analysis*.

Family: A collective term used to incorporate all similar genera into one group of like-creatures.

Filter bed: The filtering medium that removes debris from the water.

Filtration: The removal of unwanted matter from the water of an aquarium.

Forked: Branching into two parts.

Fringing reef: A reef running parallel to and attached to a landmass or island, but not separated by a lagoon.

Fry: Young fish, normally free-swimming.

Gastrovascular cavity: The stomach area in some invertebrate animals.

Gastrovascular tubes: In a cnidarian colony, that part of the polyp that extends into the coenenchyme.

Genus: A collective term used to incorporate like species into one group. Plural: genera.

Genealogy: The account of descent from ancestors, the line of development of an organism from earlier forms.

Gonad: The organ that produces eggs or sperm.

Gorgonin: A black or brown horn-like and protein-based substance, forming the vitreous core of many gorgonian corals.

Herbivore: A plant-eating animal.

Hermaphrodite: A creature that possesses both male and female reproductive organs.

Holdfast: A root-like structure or plate that attaches an alga or gorgonians to the substrate.

Hydrometer: A calibrated instrument used for measuring the specific gravity of a liquid, in this case sea water.

Ichthyology: The science and study of fishes.

Interorbital space: The space at the top of the head, between the eyes.

Intertidal zone: The area of shoreline between the highest and lowest tidal levels.

Introvert: The anterior region of sipunculan worms.

Invertebrates: Animals without backbones.

Iridescence: Displaying or reflecting an interplay of rainbow or metallic colours, glowing or shining.

Lamella: Thin plate or scale.

Larva: A preadult form that hatches from an egg and often leads a different life to that of the adult organism.

Lateral: Referring to the sides of an animal.

Lateral line: A sensory canal running along the sides of a fish.

Life-support system: A system where the conditions to support life are produced artificially.

Living (live) rock: Calcium carbonate rock from reef areas that has living animals within its structure. Beach-washed coral rubble or land-based rock that has been "planted" in the sea for 18 months or more and then harvested for the aquarium trade.

Lophophore: Respiratory or food-collecting organ with filaments or tentacles.
Lunate: Sickle-shaped; normally used to describe the form of the tail of a fish.

Madreporite: A sieve-like plate that connects the hydro-vascular system of some echinoderms with the exterior.
Mantle: In molluscs, the part of the body wall that produces the shell and encloses the visceral mass within its cavity, known as the mantle cavity.
Median fins: The dorsal, anal and caudal fins.
Medusa: The bell-shaped swimming stage of hydrozoans and jellyfish.
Megasclere: The large supporting spicule of a sponge.
Mesogloea: The jelly-like layer between the body walls of coelenterates.
Mesenterial filaments: Partitions or vanes arranged around the gastrovascular cavity in cnidarians.
Metamorphosis: Broadly speaking, the transformation of a larva to the adult form.
Monophyly: Sharing a common ancestor.
Monotypic: A genus containing a single species.
Mutualism: A form of symbiosis in which both of the species involved benefit from the relationship.

Nape: The dorsal part of the head.
Nematocyst: In cnidarians, a microscopic stinging cell comprising a capsule and an ejectable harpoon-like structure that is not recoverable.
Neuropodium: The lower lobe of a polychaete parapodium.
Notochord: The skeletal supporting structure, present in all chordates at some stage of their development.
Notopodium: The upper lobe of a polychaete parapodium.

Ocellus: An eye-like marking in one colour, bordered by a ring of another colour.
Octocoral: A cnidarian animal having eight pinnate tentacles.
Omnivore: An animal that is both flesh- and plant-eating.
Operculum: A calcareous or chitinous plug that closes the aperture of a tube or shell in invertebrates. In fish, it refers to the gill cover, which consists of four bones: the opercle, preopercle, interopercle and subopercle.
Opisthosoma: In chelicerates, the posterior part of the body.
Oral disc: The feeding surface of a cnidarian animal; usually includes the mouth.
Order: The category of taxonomic classification ranking above family.
Osculum: The large opening in a sponge, through which water and body wastes are ejected.
Ossicles: Small calcareous plates that form the internal skeletons or tests of echinoderms.
Oviparous: Egg-laying.

Ozone: An unstable, poisonous gas that may be utilized for killing bacteria.
Ozone reactor: An appliance used to diffuse ozone into aquarium water.
Orbital: The orbit or eye.

Palp: Sensory appendage near the mouth.
Parapodium: The lateral appendage on the body segment of a polychaete worm.
Parasite: An organism that lives on or in the body of a host animal or plant and from which it obtains nourishment, often detrimental to the host.
Pectoral fin: Situated on each side of the body in fishes, behind the operculum.
Pedal disc or foot: The foot or base of some cnidarian animals, such as sea anemones.
Pedipalp: Second appendage of an arthropod.
Pedicellariae: Small, often pincer-like, appendages on the body surface of many echinoderms. Used for cleaning the body and for food collection.
Pelagic: Free-floating or swimming; ocean going.
Permeable: Porous, through which molecules may pass.
pH: The negative decimal logarithm of a hydrogen ion concentration, giving the measure of acidity or alkalinity of a particular solution. In other words, a unitless index from 0 to 14 used to describe the degree of acidity or alkalinity of a substance, where 0 is the highest degree of acidity and 14 is the highest degree of alkalinity. A pH of 7 is thus the neutral point, related by formula to a standard solution of potassium hydrogen phthalate, which has a value of 4 at 15°C (59°F).
Pharyngeal teeth: A groups of teeth on the gill arches of certain fishes.
Pharynx: The forward part of the gut.
Photosynthesis: The process by which plants convert carbon dioxide and water into carbohydrates and chlorophyll under the influence of energy derived from light.
Phylogeny: Evolutionary history.
Phylum: The basic subdivision of a kingdom. Plural: phyla.
Phytoplankton: Microscopic plants that form part of the plankton.
Pinnate: Having branches on opposite sides of a main axis in a feather-like form.
Pinnule: The sub-branch of a feather-like branch or arm, particularly in the case of algae and crinoid echinoderms.
Plankton: Microorganisms that live in the sea and which provide a rich source of nourishment for many species of marine life.
Plastids: Small bodies in the cytoplasm of a plant cell containing pigment or food.
Posterior: Pertaining to the rear; the tail region in some species.
Predator: An animal that hunts to catch its food.

Premaxillary: The forward-most bone forming the upper jaw in fishes.

Proboscis: A protrusion or projection, often tubular, from the head region of some animals.

Prosoma: The anterior section of the body in chelicerates.

Prostomium: The forward part of the head region in polychaete worms. It may have eyes, palps and antennae.

Protein skimmer: A device designed to remove proteinous matter from a seawater aquarium.

Protoplasm: Viscous, translucent, colourless substance forming the main constituent of cells in organisms. The basis of life in animals and plants.

Pyriform: Pear-shaped.

Radial symmetry: Symmetry, where the body parts are arranged around a central axis.

Radula: A rasp-like organ, unique to molluscs, that is armed with chitinous teeth.

Ray: The bony or spinous elements of the fins that function as a support for the membranes.

Reagent: A substance that has a known reaction to a given chemical or given water conditions.

Reef crest: That part of the reef that receives the highest wave shock, usually an intertidal area.

Reef flat: The shallow protected area behind the shoreward side of a reef crest.

Respiratory trees: The respiratory processes that open into the gut of sea cucumbers.

Rhizoid: The root-like part of an alga.

Rhizome: The stolon of an alga; a horizontal stem.

Rostrum: The forward extension of the carapace in crustaceans.

Rudiment: Primitive or undeveloped and unable to carry out its normal function.

Seta: A small chitinous bristle. Plural: setae.

Sclerites: Calcium carbonate spicules embedded in the tissue of most soft corals.

Serrate: Saw-like, or notched along a margin.

Siliceous: Composed of silicon dioxide.

Siphon: In gastropods, the tube-like part of the mantle that allows the passage of water.

Siphonal canal: The channel at the anterior end of a shell through which the animal can extend its siphon.

Siphonoglyph: A ciliated longitudinal furrow at one or both ends of the slit-formed mouth of a sea anemone or corallimorpharian. Serves to provide water circulation into the gastrovascular cavity.

Siphonozooid: The rudimentary polyp in some octocoral colonies. Functions to provide water circulation through the colony.

Snout: In fishes, the region of the head in front of the eyes.

sp.: Abbreviation for species.

Specific gravity: The weight of a substance when compared to that of pure water at standard pressure and temperature (4°C/39.2°F). For example, SG 1.022 = 1.022 times heavier than pure water at 4°C/39.2°F.

Spicule: A hard slender crystalline rod of calcium carbonate; forms rudimentary skeletons in some invertebrates. In sponges these elements may consist of silicon dioxide.

Spinule: A small spine.

Spongin: The fibrous skeletal material in some sponges.

spp.: The plural form of sp., used when more than one particular species is involved.

Stipe: The stem-like part of an alga.

Stolon: In algae, the horizontal rhizome, or runner, of the plant, which connects upright fronds. In soft corals, the ribbon or tube-like extensions that are attached to the substrate and link the individual polyps together.

Stylet: A small pointed tooth or bristle.

Supraorbital: The area bordering the upper edge of the eye.

Substrate: The surfaces or substances on which organisms are growing.

Symbiosis: Two unlike creatures living and associating with one another for the benefit of one or both partners.

Synonym: An invalid scientific name of a creature that has been put forward, or proposed, after the accepted name.

Synthetic analysis: Evolutionary analysis in which the classification is based on a synthesis of knowledge concerning both the genealogical relationships and the perceived degree of evolutionary or genetic similarity or divergence from other groups.

Telson: The chitinous or calcareous tail-piece of crustaceans.

Terminal: The end, or posterior-most part, of the body.

Test: The rigid internal shell of sea urchins.

Thorax: The area of the body behind the head in crustaceans.

Thoracic: Referring to the thorax or chest region.

Truncate: Square-margined; refers to the caudal fin of some fishes that have tails with vertical terminal borders and slightly rounded corners.

Tube feet: Small sucker-like projections occurring in echinoderms, often controlled by hydrostatic pressure and used for locomotion or food gathering.

Ventral: The underside of the body. The opposite of dorsal.

Yolk sac: The yolk-containing sac, which is attached to the embryo. Common in newly born fry.

Zoochlorellae: Unicellular endosymbiotic green algae in an animal.

Zooplankton: Microscopic animals that form the basis of plankton.

Zooxanthellae: Unicellular endosymbiotic dinophyceae in an animal.

Bibliography

Allen, G. R., *Damselfishes of the South Seas*, TFH Publications Inc., Neptune City, New Jersey, 1975

Allen, G. R., *Falter- und Kaiserfische Band 2*, Mergus-Verlag Hans A Baensch, Melle, 1979

Allen, G. R. & Steene, R., *Indo-Pacific Reef Guide*, Tropical Reef Research, Singapore, 1994

Axelrod, H. R. & Emmens, C. W., *Exotic Marine Fishes*, TFH Publications Inc., Neptune City, New Jersey, 1971

Baensch, H. A., *Neue Meerwasser-Praxis*, Tetra-Verlag, Melle, 1986

Baensch, H. A. & Debelius, H., *Meerwasser Atlas*, Mergus Verlag GmbH, Melle, 1992

Baensch, H. A. & Patzner, R. A., *Meerwasser Atlas (Band 7)*, Mergus-Verlag GmbH, Melle, 1998

Baumeister, W., *Meeresaquaristik*, Verlag Eugen Ulmer. Stuttgart, 1998

Burgess, W. E., *Dr. Burgess's Atlas of Marine Aquarium Fishes*, TFH Publications Inc., Neptune City, New Jersey, 1988

Carcasson, R. H., *A Field Guide to the Coral Reef Fishes of the Indian and West Pacific Oceans*, William Collins Sons & Co Ltd, London, 1977

Clark, A. M., *Starfishes and Related Echinoderms*, TFH Publications Inc., Neptune City, New Jersey, 1977

Colin, P. L., *Caribbean Reef Invertebrates and Plants*, TFH Publications Inc., Neptune City, New Jersey, 1973

Colin, P. L. & Arneson, C., *Tropical Marine Invertebrates: A Field Guide to the Marine Invertebrates Occurring on Tropical Pacific Reefs, Seagrass Beds and Mangroves*, Coral Reef Press, Beverly Hills, 1995

Cox, G. F., *Tropical Marine Aquaria*, Hamlyn Publishing Group Ltd., London, 1976

Dakin, N., *The Book of the Marine Aquarium*, Salamander Books Ltd, London, 1992

Dring, M. J., *The Biology of Marine Plants*, Edward Arnold, London, 1982

Emmens, C. W., *Marine Aquaria and Miniature Reefs*, TFH Publications Inc., Neptune City, New Jersey, 1995

Erhardt, H. & Baensch, H. A., *Meerwasser Atlas (Band 4)*, Mergus-Verlag GmbH, Melle, 1998

Erhardt, H & Moosleitner, H., *Meerwasser Atlas (Bands 2 and 3)*, Mergus-Verlag GmbH, Melle, 1995

Fosså, S. A. & Nilsen, A. J., *Korallenriff-Aquarium (Bands 1 and 2)*, Birgit Schmettkamp Verlag, Bornheim, 1992

Fosså, S. A. & Nilsen, A. J., *Korallenriff-Aquarium (Band 3)*, Birgit Schmettkamp Verlag, Bornheim, 1993

Fosså, S. A. & Nilsen, A. J., *Korallenriff-Aquarium (Band 4)*, Birgit Schmettkamp Verlag, Bornheim, 1995

Fosså, S. A. & Nilsen, A. J., *Korallenriff-Aquarium (Band 5)*, Birgit Schmettkamp Verlag, Bornheim, 1996

Fosså, S. A. & Nilsen, A. J., *Korallenriff-Aquarium (Band 6)*, Birgit Schmettkamp Verlag, Bornheim, 1998

Friese, U. E., *Sea Anemones*, TFH Publications Inc., Neptune City, New Jersey, 1972

George, J. D. & George, J. J., *Marine Life*, George C. Harrap & Co. Ltd, London, 1979

Hargreaves, V. B., *The Tropical Marine Aquarium*, McGraw-Hill Book Company, New York, 1978

Hargreaves, V. B., *The Tropical Marine Aquarium* (revised edn), David & Charles Ltd, Newton Abbot, 1989

Haywood, M. & Wells, S., *The Interpet Manual of Marine Invertebrates*, Salamander Books Ltd., London, 1989

Hoek, C. van den, et al, *Algen (3 Auflage)*, Georg Thieme Verlag, Stuttgart, 1993

Kay, G., *The Tropical Marine Fish Survival Manual*, Ringpress Books Ltd, Lydney, Gloucestershire, 1995

Littler, D. S. et al, *Marine Plants of the Caribbean – A Field Guide from Florida to Brazil*, Smithsonian Institution Press, Washington, DC, 1989

Luther, R. & Nee, C., *Cowries and Cones of Hong Kong*, Sing Cheong Printing Company Ltd., Hong Kong, 1975

Lythgoe, J. & Lythgoe, G., *Fishes of the Sea*, Blandford Press Ltd, London, 1971

Manton, S. M., *The Arthropoda: Habits, Functional Morphology and Evolution*, Oxford University Press, London, 1977

Melvin, A. G., *Sea Shells of the World*, Charles E. Tuttle Company Inc., Rutland, Vermont, 1977

Mills, D., *The Interpet Encyclopedia of the Marine Aquarium*, Salamander Books Ltd, London, 1987

Mills, D. et al, *F. B. A. S. Dictionary of Common & Scientific Names of Marine Fishes*, Federation of British Aquatic Societies, Twickenham, 1978

Morton, B. S. et al, *The Future of the Hong Kong Seashore*, Oxford University Press, London, 1979

Nelson, J. S., *Fishes Of The World* (3rd edn), John Wiley & Sons, New York, 1994

Oliver, A. P. H., *The Hamlyn Guide to Shells of the World*, The Hamlyn Publishing Group Ltd, London, 1975

Orr, J., *Hong Kong Nudibranchs*, The Urban Council, Hong Kong, 1981

Round, F. E., *The Biology of Algae*, Edward Arnold Ltd, London, 1973

Scase, R. & Storey, E., *The World of Shells*, Osprey Publishing Ltd, Reading, 1975

Sprung, J. & Delbeek, J. C., *The Reef Aquarium* (vol. 2), Ricordia Publishing, Inc., Coconut Grove, Florida, 1997

Steen, R. C., *Butterfly and Angelfishes of the World* (vol. 1), Mergus-Verlag Hans A. Baensch, Melle, 1977

Taylor, W. R., *Marine Algae of the Eastern Tropical and Subtropical Coasts of the Americas*, University of Michigan Press, 1960

Walls, J. G., *Starting with Marine Invertebrates*, TFH Publications Inc., Neptune City, New Jersey, 1974

Index

Acknowledgements

Throughout the research and production of this book I have been amazed at the willingness of people to offer assistance. I feel it only right that I should acknowledge them from the start. Notably they are Frank Walker of Hong Kong and Ned Middleton of Portadown, Northern Ireland, for the marvellous underwater photographs they took for or with me. Additionally, Mr Richard Wong and Mr Y. K. Luk of the Fish Marketing Organization, Dept of Agriculture and Fisheries, Hong Kong were very helpful, as was my friend Colin Nash. For the field trips I thank Frank Hall for ferrying my diving equipment and me around in his car on many occasions, and for his help in collecting marine specimens; thanks also to Sam Farrell. Dr Margaret Cope should also have a mention for the loan of the diving gear on one occasion, and Pete Hardy for the use of his boat – despite the fact that it once broke down in the middle of the South China Sea and we had to paddle it for several hours. Luckily the Hong Kong Police came by and took us in tow; I thank them for saving us.

A special thank you goes to Dr John E. Randall of the Bernice P. Bishop Museum, Hawaii, and Dr Gerald R. Allen of the Western Australian Museum, Perth for their assistance in my field research and also for the wonderful photographs they made available for this book – Thanks Jack! Thanks Jerry! Also to Dr Alwynne Wheeler from the British Museum of Natural History for help with species from the Maldives.

Regarding the film research for this book, my appreciation is extended to Jenny Watts of HIT Wildlife (HIT Entertainment plc), London, who pulled out all the stops for me, and to Stephan Reinders of Westdeutscher Rundfunk, Cologne, Germany.

On the original research and general technical side I am grateful for the assistance of many people, although I hope that the feedback was, for the most part, mutual.

In the USA, I thank Dave Gauss of Bagdad, Kentucky, Dr Martin R. Brittan, Department of Biological Sciences, California State University, Sacramento, and his friend Richard Ashby.

In Germany, I am particularly grateful to Dr Manfred Schlüter and Hans E. Baensch of Melle, Dr R. Keppler of Neuhofen, Werner Baumeister of Stuttgart, Benedikt Klaes of Gimmigen, Axel Tunze of Penzberg, Gregor Beckmann of Rodgau, Siegfried and Uschi Krumbügel and Ludwig Kaiser of Lindenberg.

In Switzerland, I am grateful to Karl-Friedrich Körner of Luzern, who has supported me for some time by providing the material to enable me to give an accurate account of the water parameters in a seawater aquarium.

In Holland, I am especially indebted to Dr J. C. den Hartog of the Nationaal Natuurhistorisch Museum, Leiden, for his generous help and advice regarding sea anemones in general and the Corallimorpharians in particular. I thank Arie De Jong and Richard Dangerman, of De Jong Marinelife B V, Spijk, for their help and advice. To Robert Brons of Spijk for his unending help and his excellent photomicrographs – there is nothing that is "too much trouble" for this man – and to Joyce Malawauw of Leerdam, who has a heart of gold.

In Norway, thanks go to Alf Nilsen and Svein Fosså for their information about breeding techniques in the UK, Europe and Israel, and their helpfulness in general.

In the UK, Professor Raymond Gibson of John Moores University, Liverpool, for his help and advice with the phylum Nemertea. From one Yorkshireman to another, thanks Ray! I also thank Adrian Excell from Dorking, Surrey, and Andrew Werendel from Bury St Edmonds, Suffolk. Danny Sheehan from the Watford Aquarium should be mentioned for his kind help and advice about the plenum and natural method, and George Walpole, also of the Watford Aquarium. My old friend Adrian Jefferys of Leeds was also very helpful, as was Michael Browne of Coral Reef, Leeds.

On the production side I thank my sister, Mrs Pauline Nash, for her help and advice regarding computers. My brother, Tony Hargreaves, an award-winning koi carp breeder, helped me with many aspects, including the problems concerning the management of large volumes of water. He also read the proofs as a "complete beginner", raising some interesting questions to problems that I had overlooked. Dörthe Eschmann-Hoffmann was a great help to me with the sections on water chemistry, as was Gary Hodgson for his photographic help and advice. Most of all I would like to thank Mrs Anna Prinz, who, with unending patience, encouraged me finally to finish this book. And in conclusion I thank Dr Warren E. Burgess who helped me tremendously with this work by being so objective when he proofread my last book.

All images are copyright Vincent B. Hargreaves except for the following:

Photomax Picture Library: pages 1, 2, 3, 5, 9, 10–11, 18–19, 68–69, 96–97, 166 (centre and bottom), 188–89